TURBULENT PASSAGE

A GLOBAL HISTORY OF THE TWENTIETH CENTURY

THIRD EDITION

MICHAEL ADAS

Rutgers University

PETER N. STEARNS

George Mason University

STUART B. SCHWARTZ

Yale University

PEARSON
Longman

New York Boston San Francisco
London Toronto Sydney Tokyo Singapore Madrid
Mexico City Munich Paris Cape Town Hong Kong Montreal

Senior Acquisitions Editor: Janet Lanphier

Executive Marketing Manager: Sue Westmoreland

Production Manager: Donna DeBenedictis

Project Coordination, Text Design and Electronic Page Makeup: Nesbitt Graphics, Inc.

Cover Design Manager: John Callahan

Cover Designer: Maria Ilardi

Cover Art: Franz Kline, American (1910–1962), *Corinthian II,* 1961, oil on canvas. The Museum of Fine Arts, Houston; bequest of Caroline Wiess Law. © 2005 The Franz Kline Estate/Artists Rights Society (ARS), New York.

Photo Researcher: Vivette Porges

Manufacturing Manager: Mary Fischer

Printer and Binder: Hamilton Printing Company

Cover Printer: The Lehigh Press, Inc.

For permission to use copyrighted material, grateful acknowledgment is made to the copyright holders on page C-1, which is hereby made part of this copyright page.

Library of Congress Cataloging-in-Publication Data

Adas. Michael, 1943–
    Turbulent passage : a global history of the twentieth century / Michael Adas, Peter N.
Stearns, Stuart B. Schwartz—3rd ed.
        p. cm.
    Includes bibliographical references and index.
    ISBN 0-321-33890-1
    1. History, Modern–20th century. 2. Twentieth century. I. Stearns, Peter N. II. Schwartz,
Stuart B. III. Title.
    D421.A33 2005
    909.82—dc22   2005014287

Please visit us at http://www.ablongman.com

ISBN 0–321–33890-1

2 3 4 5 6 7 8 9 10—HT—08 07 06 05

Brief Contents

Detailed Contents

Note: Each chapter ends with Further Reading and On the Web sections.

List of Maps

Preface

The twentieth century, which has recently reached its chronological end, has in the past decade or so become a subject of historical inquiry in its own right. With the breakup of the Soviet Union and the collapse of the Communist economies there and in the rest of Eastern Europe in the 1990s, the human community around the globe clearly moved into a new phase of history, a new century in the most meaningful sense of the term. Viewed from the opening years of the next era, the twentieth century was a period of change and social upheaval; of political turmoil, war, and violence; of material advancement and environmental peril without precedent in the epoch in which the human species has dominated the earth.

In many ways it has been an era of painful transitions, a working out of the profound transformations set in motion by the industrial revolutions of the eighteenth and nineteenth centuries. By the start of the twentieth century, scientific and technological advances had given one cultural area, Europe and its settlement outliers in North America, a degree of hegemony over the rest of the peoples and societies of the globe that had no parallel in previous history. Much of the century had been dominated by the responses of non-Western peoples and cultures to this hegemony and by struggles for liberation from the colonial order that the industrial West imposed on most of the rest of the globe. As the viability of early patterns of industrialization came under scrutiny in the crowded, steadily computerized, ecologically stressed decades at century's end, it became increasingly clear that the history of the twenty-first century will differ in fundamental ways from the twentieth.

PART OVERVIEW AND NEW FEATURES IN THE THIRD EDITION

The concept of turbulent passage, which forms the title of this book, provides perhaps the most apt metaphor for global history in the twentieth century. We decided to write this book to fill what we perceived as a gap in the literature on this critical era in human history. Though texts that aim to cover the history of the world in the twentieth century exist, none gives adequate attention to both the pre-1914 decades that led up to and vitally shaped the era of World War I and the post-1945 period in which the upheavals that were precipitated by World War II were played out across the globe. The first, third, and fourth parts of this book are devoted to the pre-1914 and post-1945 eras. The second part covers the decades between 1914 and 1945 that are the focus of existing histories of the twentieth century.

By happy accident, this text was first written during one of those periods in world history (the 1990s) when all sorts of established patterns were clearly changing in major ways. In Parts III and IV of this third edition, we extend accounts of the post-cold war upheavals in Russia, Eastern Europe, the Middle East, post-Maoist China, and the Pacific Rim to the present to take into account recent developments as well as the suggestions of colleagues, students, and readers. In addition, we have added or significantly expanded discussions of the causes and impact of the three wars in the Persian Gulf region between the early 1980s and 2003 and religious fundamentalism and ethnic conflict in southeast Europe, the Middle East, South Asia, and sub-Saharan Africa. We approach these events and the broader process of globalization as a whole, not as radically new departures, and we see them as key dimensions of the transition from patterns of world history established in earlier decades. This edition also includes expanded coverage of both World Wars I and II, the Great Depression, the rise of fascism and national socialism, and the Holocaust, all of which were key features of the second edition. In addition, it includes coverage of such key themes in recent world history as the establishment of and controversies generated by international organizations for trade and development assistance, especially the World Bank and the International Monetary Fund, the reemergence of terrorism as a global threat, and the rise of the United States as a global "hyperpower." Part IV also underscores the growing importance of environmental change and movements for ecological preservation and the control of international epidemics in the last half of the twentieth century.

In dealing with each of the four phases we have identified and the twentieth century as a whole, we seek to maintain a genuinely global perspective. Developments in Europe and North America are treated in depth, but in contrast to the approach in many existing texts, the West does not become the focal point in ways that would blur the distinction between a history of Western civilization and a real *world* history text. States and societies often slighted in world history texts—such as those of Latin America, Africa, and the Pacific Rim—are discussed quite extensively. Decisions about coverage have been made in terms of global criteria, thus giving the West its respectful due but not pride of place.

Unlike a number of the recent global histories of the twentieth century that strive for comprehensive coverage and end up being little more than compendiums of facts and dates, we have taken a more selective approach. Building on comparisons between a number of key states and societies that have shaped the twentieth-century experience in critical ways, we have striven to identify patterns and pivotal themes both within each region and in cross-cultural encounters at various points in the century. We have also sought to tie these patterns and themes to larger global issues that have dominated twentieth-century history to a greater extent than in any previous epoch of the human experience. Our goal throughout has been to relate fact to interpretation while still allowing ample room for classroom exploration of key issues. Analytical emphasis is evident in the attention to periodization, which is closely tied to key shifts in global trends and cross-cultural interaction. Comparative issues are foregrounded, both as a means of raising the level of discussion above that of mere memorization and as a way to bridge the gaps between sections devoted to individual states and societies.

A review of available twentieth-century global history texts has convinced us that most of those that do make some attempt to discern larger patterns and global trends are almost exclusively focused on political and diplomatic, and to a lesser extent military, history. Though these aspects of twentieth-century history are vital and are treated in depth in this study, we have also given the social, cultural, and economic dimensions of the global experience their full due. We have placed particular emphasis on changes in gender roles and relationships at the level of the family, local community, and state that have been such a prominent feature of the twentieth century. Gender shifts have in turn been set in the larger context of social upheaval that has been played out in terms of widely varying mixes of class, ethnic, racial, and national identities. We have devoted considerable attention to ideas and intellectual currents that shaped social movements and political agendas in the twentieth century. We

have also sought, where appropriate, to go beyond broad patterns and global structures to show the ways in which remarkable individuals—from Lenin to Indira Gandhi and Martin Luther King—have helped shape the course of twentieth-century history and to give some sense of the impact of global processes on the ordinary lives of peasants in China or Russia, of workers in Pittsburgh or Singapore, and of the ascendant middle classes from Russia to Japan and India.

In this edition of *Turbulent Passage*, we have added new documents, including memories of the struggles for democracy in China, the challenges faced by the Western educated elites of Africa at independence, and the disruptive effects of revolutionary movements in China on the traditional family structure and male-dominated hierarchy. Photos included in the analytical essay sections are a new feature of this edition, and like the documents, the essay sections are highlighted more vividly than in previous editions. A number of new essays have been written for this edition, including an extended discussion of the ever more intense mechanization of warfare and the ways in which dissident movements sought to counter advances in industrial weaponry over the course of the century.

PEDAGOGICAL AIDS

Teachers (and students) of world history come from a wide range of personal and academic backgrounds. To support the thematic and analytical features of *Turbulent Passage* and to make all facets of world history as accessible as possible, a number of pedagogical features have been integrated into the book.

In addition to narrative part openers that set forth key themes in each unit, parts begin with an extensive but manageable timeline that establishes the period under consideration. The timeline includes events in all the societies involved.

Chapters open with an outline for a quick overview of major topics and with a detailed timeline specific to the topics to be discussed. Chapter introductions highlight key themes and analytical issues to consider in reading.

Each chapter contains one or more documents in a discrete section. The documents are preceded by a brief scene-setting narration and followed by probing questions. Each chapter also contains an analytical essay on a topic of broad application; the essay is followed by questions intended both to probe student appreciation of the topic and to suggest questions or interpretive issues for further thought.

The text is accompanied by photographs, line drawings, and a series of maps specially developed to enhance the global orientation. Maps in part introductions and in the chapters highlight major developments during each period and familiarize students with many non-Western arenas.

Each chapter ends with a conclusion that goes beyond a mere summary of events. Conclusions reiterate the key themes and issues raised in the chapter and again suggest areas for reflection and anticipation. Each chapter also includes several paragraphs of annotated suggested readings so that readers can pursue additional topics on their own, and a section on URLs of relevance to the material covered.

ACKNOWLEDGMENTS

Grateful acknowledgment is made to the following colleagues and reviewers, who made many useful suggestions during the development of this edition:

Christine A. Colin-Burns, *Indiana University South Bend*
David Kenley, *Elizabethtown College*
Stephen M. Leahy, *University of Wisconsin–Fox Valley*
Constance M. McGovern, *Frostburg State University*
J. Gilbert Sansing, *Drexel University*

MICHAEL ADAS
PETER N. STEARNS
STUART B. SCHWARTZ

Prologue

It is difficult to determine the extent to which the 20th century represents the last phase of an era of global history, with its origins as far back as the 15th century. Although the 20th century is over in strictly chronological terms, we are still caught up in many of the historical developments that were set in motion decades ago and that have fundamentally shaped world history throughout our lifetimes. We are so close to the patterns involved that detached judgment is impossible and it is difficult to place them in a longer term perspective. In contrast to the history of previous periods, which continues to generate debate, we do not know how many of the key processes of the 20th century will end or what their outcomes will be.

Given the challenge of assessing the meanings of events in the 20th century, it is perhaps wise to strike a balance between continuity and change in trying to place the 20th century in the larger scheme of global history. From this perspective, we can see the 20th century not as an epoch in itself, but as a time of accelerated transition, as a turbulent era of passage from one epoch to the next. On the one hand, this time of transition represents the culmination of a broader watershed in global history that resulted from an extraordinary convergence of political, socioeconomic, and intellectual changes in western Europe from the 15th century onward. From another perspective, the 20th century marks a significant break from patterns characteristic of the 19th century and earlier epochs.

Building on earlier technological innovations and social shifts, the Europeans expanded overseas with ever increasing scale and intensity in the four centuries after the voyages of exploration in the 15th century. Despite much resistance and counterthrusts that slowed their advance, the great trading and military powers of Europe gradually forged a new world order oriented to the capitalist economies of the West and dominated politically by their colonial empires. Efforts to forge this global order were greatly advanced by two further processes that fundamentally transformed first western European and eventually all human history: the Scientific Revolution that spread across much of Europe in the 17th century and the Industrial Revolution that was clearly underway by the late 1700s. Taken together these transformations represented one of the pivotal watersheds in human history, comparable to that associated with the rise of agriculture and town life in the Neolithic era over nine thousand years earlier.

Most of the other great civilizations and the multitude of local cultures spread over the rest of the globe were at first affected little by the great changes that were occurring in Europe and increasingly in its settlement outliers, particularly the United States. Excepting peoples, such as the Amerindians, whose long isolation made them disastrously vulnerable to the tactics, technology, and especially the diseases that the Europeans carried overseas, European domination was not pronounced in much of the world until well into the 18th century. By the end of the 18th century, however, and throughout the 19th, the expansive great powers of industrial Europe and North America divided most of the known world into rival colonial empires, pulled all but the most isolated of peoples into the Europe-centered world market system, and linked the diverse cultures of the globe with industrial communications and transport systems.

Seen in the context of these global transformations, the 20th century was an era in which the processes set in motion by Europe's scientific and industrial revolutions were accelerated, intensified, and diffused to much of the rest of the globe. But despite continuities, the pace and scale of innovation and diffusion increased to levels without precedent in human history. In addition, advances in communications and transportation associated with the scientific and industrial revolutions meant that contacts between civilizations and local cultures were vastly more numerous and more extensive in the 20th century than in perhaps all of the earlier periods of human history combined. In fact, cross-cultural interaction between the diverse peoples and societies that populate much of the earth became so intense in the late 20th century that a genuinely global culture and community began to emerge for the first time. Earlier empires and trading networks linked large portions of the globe. But never before has such a large portion of humanity been represented in a single political organization (the United Nations), been so dependent on international commercial exchanges, and shared so many aspects of culture—from skyscrapers to rock music—that are central to their everyday lives.

Because of the magnitude and accelerating pace of these global transformations, societal responses and adaptations were often untested and flawed. One key consequence of the upheavals and turmoil that ensued was an unprecedented level of human warfare and civil strife throughout much of the globe. As numerous writers have observed, the 20th century was truly an era of violence. And accumulating scientific discoveries and technical advances made this violence vastly more destructive than that of any period in history. But these losses need to be balanced against the key roles played by science and technology in the impressive increases in standards of living that were achieved, particularly by citizens of industrialized societies. Whether one stresses the destruction and violence or improvements in material living conditions, in this view the 20th century was an extension, possibly the culmination, of developments begun in earlier centuries.

While acknowledging these continuities, a rather different view of 20th-century history emerges if one stresses the ways in which this period marked a significant break from past trends and the extent to which it represented the early stages of a new era in the human experience. Perhaps more than any other attribute, this transitional or bridging quality of the history of the past hundred years or so permits us to conceive of the 20th century as a separate era in the greater human experience.

In the chapters that follow, we seek to strike a balance between an examination of the ways in which the history of the 20th century represented a culmination of key transformations from preceding centuries and the ways in which it marked radical departures from earlier developments. Some of the key, common links to the past have been suggested above, but these connections have also varied widely from one civilization and culture to the next. Special attention will be given to these variations in terms of the historical and cultural legacies that tempered the differing responses of Asian, African, and Latin American peoples to European expansion and the concomitant spread of aspects of the scientific and industrial revolutions.

In identifying both broad global patterns and regional variations, we will also place great emphasis on they ways in which 20th-century history represented significant breaks from the past and pointed to a new era taking shape for the global community. These shifts can be grouped under three basic processes: fundamental alterations in the balance among civilizations that occurred over the course of the 20th century; the intensification and multiplication of cross-cultural contacts; and major transformations in politics and culture that spread throughout much of the world.

A TRANSCULTURAL AND GLOBAL AGE

No period of human history is better suited to a world or global perspective than the 20th century. The extent and intensity of cross-cultural interaction in this era was without precedent and continued to accelerate as the century drew to a close. Industrial communication technologies facilitated the multiplication of political, economic, and cultural links between peoples and societies in virtually every area of the globe. These linkages meant that in the 20th century, more than in any previous period in history, innovations, natural disasters, or social upheavals in one region were likely to have major repercussions throughout the world. Never before had political disruptions, even in formerly isolated regions such as Ethiopia or Bosnia-Herzegovina, had such immediate and profound global ramifications. In earlier centuries, calamities, such as civil war and famine in Somalia or floods in Bangladesh, would have been localized concerns. In the 20th century they quickly developed into crises with international ramifications. The heads of multinational corporations make decisions about plant locations and commodity development aimed at enhancing the international standing of their firms rather than strengthening the nation-state in which they are headquartered. The decisions of ranchers or developers to burn the rain forest in the Amazon or on the island of Borneo contribute to the process of global warming.

Two additional trends suggest ways in which the 20th century marked a decisive break from earlier historical epochs. The first is the staggering increase in human population as well as in the numbers of domesticated animals that humans breed for a variety of uses. It had taken humankind tens of thousands of years to reach a population of around a billion and a half by the middle of the 19th century. By the year 2000, 150 years later, world population had increased over four times to well over six billion—and it will continue to increase, even with the most ambitious application of family planning measures, well into the 21st century. This massive increase of humans, and domesticated animals dependent upon them, has obviously placed an ever increasing strain on the resources of the planet. It has also contributed greatly to a second trend that set the 20th century off from all previous eras: an unprecedented level of human intervention in and exploitation of the natural environment. New technologies have been developed—in part to offset accelerating population increases—to permit ever more intensive farming, ever greater depletion of fresh water reservoirs, and ever higher yields of forest and mineral products. Both runaway population growth and the application of new technologies have combined to raise local and global pollution and ecological degradation to levels that pose, for the first time in human history, fundamental threats to the planetary environment on which all life depends.

STAGES IN A TURBULENT PASSAGE TO A NEW AGE

As with most centuries, the rather arbitrary chronological beginning and ending dates of the 20th century, 1900 and 2000, have little historical meaning. The year 1900 was by no stretch of the imagination a watershed year, and, as we shall argue in the final chapters, events of the late 1980s brought the third and last phase of the 20th century to a close a decade before its official stopping point in the year 2000. Some historians have argued that 1914, the year World War I began, is the most meaningful place to start the 20th century. But beginning with the dramatic breaks with previous history that the 1914–1918 war set in motion distorts history by obscuring important continuities with earlier centuries. Not only can we not understand the origins of the war if we start in 1914, we miss key episodes in the history of the decades leading up to the war that permit us to assess the impact of that global conflagration on the period of turmoil that followed in the 1920s and 1930s.

In terms of the underlying themes and historical trends that make the 20th century a distinctive and coherent era, strong arguments can be made for beginning the century in the 1860s and 1870s. In the decades before World War I, which are treated in Part I, new global powers, most notably Germany, Japan, and the United States, emerged to challenge Britain, France, China, and Russia, which had long dominated international politics. At the same time, a number of important works were published that brought to the forefront ideologies such as Marxism, Darwinism, and Liberalism that would vitally shape social thinking and political movements through much of the 20th century. These decades also saw the culminating phase of centuries of European overseas expansion and the colonization of much of the world by the industrial powers, including the United States and Japan. In important ways this outburst of imperialism

was prompted by major social and economic shifts that were also occurring in Europe, the United States, and Japan in this era, and these changes were diffused by the forces of colonialism to much of the rest of the globe.

From this perspective then, 1914 marks the end of the first phase of 20th-century history and the beginning of the second, which is dominated by a succession of global crises. Between 1914 and 1945, which ends the second phase of 20th-century history, the world was shaken by a series of catastrophic events, most of which were directly linked to the two world wars and the massive global depression that define this period. As we shall see in Part II, focusing on the 1914–1945 years, state power and, in many countries, repression reached unprecedented levels. War, between industrial and scientifically advanced powers, was vastly more devastating than anything in the past. And all pretense at distinguishing between military and civilian sectors was discarded in the face of massive aerial bombardments and a number of state-organized campaigns of genocide. The 1914–1945 period also witnessed the emergence of a new international order that featured the relative decline of western Europe and the establishment of new power centers, particularly those in the Soviet Union, the United States, and Japan. Several major political revolutions occurred in this era of crisis, which ushered in new regimes in Mexico, Germany, Italy, China, Russia, Turkey, and throughout eastern Europe. Struggles for independence—some of them, like that in Vietnam, revolutionary; others gradualist—also gained force in much of the colonized world.

The decades between 1945 and the late 1980s, which form the third phase of the 20th century and are covered in Part III, are dominated by the Cold War struggles between the United States and Soviet Union superpowers and their allies; the decolonization of Africa, Asia, and parts of Latin America; and the remarkable efforts of Europe and Japan to recover from wartime devastation and to adjust to the postcolonial world order. This period also saw a new wave of revolutions, most notably those in Vietnam, Cuba, and Iran, which had powerful global ramifications. It was a time when new patterns of social organization and mobility, changes in gender relations, and redefinitions of the roles of governments were vital features of global history, although some of these developments had begun in the crisis decades between 1914 and 1945.

In our treatment of each of the main phases of the 20th century we have attempted to combine analysis of general global processes with accounts of specific events and divergent patterns of development in different geographic regions and culture areas. In assessing the meaning of the history made and experienced at both levels, it is difficult to know which events and transformations will be the most critical in shaping the new epoch of history into which we are moving. These forces and current processes of transition are the subject of Part IV, which concludes this volume. The history of the 20th century allows us to comprehend the forces overturning the global order that had developed between the 15th and the 19th centuries, but it permits only glimpses of what the new world order might be. We know, for example, that the new period will not be dominated by the West to the same extent the previous age was. But we cannot be sure whether a successor will emerge, or what that successor will be. In addition, in the long term other kinds of shifts may prove to be far more important than the relative decline of the West that has so fascinated 20th-century observers or the breakup of the Soviet superpower and its satellite empire, which has seemed so central to the history made since 1989.

A far more influential factor in shaping the lives of future generations may be the radically new technological framework that has been built around computers in the last half century. This framework has increasingly supplanted the steam-driven machinery and production techniques of the industrial age. It opens the possibility of a postindustrial age, at least for the more economically advanced portions of the globe. For less developed areas, the new computer technology may make it possible to bypass the industrial stage of development with its high levels of pollution and resource depletion. These outcomes, which represent only a small portion of possible alternatives, suggest the difficulty of predicting future trends on the basis of our recent past or present experience. But grasping what has already occurred in the most recent phase of world history and what is now happening is the best basis for understanding what is yet to come.

PART I

THE BIRTH OF THE 20TH CENTURY

*With the Eiffel Tower as its centerpiece, the Paris exposition of
1889 not only celebrated the scientific and technological triumphs
of the industrial West but also underscored the fact that France
had joined the exclusive club of advanced, industrial societies.*

Chronology

1850–1864	Taiping rebellion in China
1853	Perry expedition to Edo Bay in Japan
1854–1856	Crimean War
1857–1858	Great Mutiny in India
1858	British Parliament assumes control over India
1859	Publication of *On Liberty* by John Stuart Mill and *Origin of Species* by Charles Darwin
1860–1868	Civil strife in Japan
1861	Emancipation of serfs in Russia; reform era begins
1861–1865	American Civil War
1863	Emancipation of slaves in U.S.
1864–1871	German unification
1867	Union of central and eastern Canada
1867	Publication of Volume I of *Das Kapital* by Karl Marx
1868–1912	Meiji (reform) era in Japan
1870	Establishment of Japanese Ministry of Industry
1870–1910	Expansion of commercial export economy in Latin America
1870–1910	Acceleration of "demographic transition" in western Europe and the United States
1871–1912	High point of European imperialism
1882	British takeover of Egypt
1885	Formation of National Congress Party in India
1886–1888	Slavery abolished in Cuba and Brazil
1894–1895	Sino-Japanese War
1895	First public motion picture show
1895	Cuban revolt against Spain
1898	Spanish-American War
1900	Sigmund Freud's *On Dreams*
1901	Commonwealth of Australia
1903	Construction of Panama Canal begins
1904–1905	Russo-Japanese War
1905	Einstein's paper on relativity
1908	Young Turk rising
1911–1912	Revolution in China; fall of Qing Empire
1913	Stravinsky's *Rite of Spring*; Ford begins assembly-line production of Model-Ts; New York Armory Show solidifies the abstract art movement worldwide
1914	World War I begins

ACCELERATING CHANGE AND THE TRANSITION TO THE 20TH CENTURY

Finding a specific date or precise starting point for the 20th century would prove a frustrating and fruitless exercise. Though chronologically correct, 1900 was not a point of significant transition in world history. It came only at the end of decades of transformations that had thoroughly remade the 19th-century world that was dominated by the French Revolution and Napoleonic Wars as well as the first phase of industrialization and the vast expansion of a world economic system oriented to western Europe. Alternatively, the outbreak of World War I in August of 1914 is frequently cited as the "real" beginning of the new century. Though the coming of the war was clearly a key point of transition, beginning in

1914 leaves us ignorant not only of the causes of the "Great War," but also with little sense of the larger forces that had been building up throughout the world in the decades before the war. These forces gave rise to a global order that differed fundamentally from that characteristic of the 19th century, and they proved to be the seedbed for the processes, struggles, and dilemmas that set the 20th century off as a distinct era in world history.

Though specific years are of little value in demarcating the transition from the 19th to the 20th century, the decades of the 1860s and 1870s were clearly a watershed period in which many of the dominant political, socioeconomic, and intellectual currents of the 20th century emerged. Thus, the last three or four decades of the 1800s, combined with the years between 1900 and 1914, can be seen as the first phase of 20th-century world history.

REDRAWING THE GLOBAL MAP

The most apparent shifts in the global order that came in the first phase of the 20th century, roughly from the 1860s to 1914, involved the emergence of several new powers and the decline of some that had been dominant through most of the 19th century. These shifts also included the partition of an already partly colonized world, with the lion's share going to the industrialized nations of western Europe and the United States. Thus, though long-established powers like France, Great Britain, Austria-Hungary, and Russia still played major roles in international politics in the pre–World War I era, there was clearly a slippage in their relative strength and ability to shape global history. The emergence of Germany, the United States, and Japan as first economic and later major military and political actors in the international arena was central to the decline of the older powers that was in turn a major factor in the coming of World War I. The collapse of the Qing Dynasty in China, combined with the simultaneous expansion of the European colonial empires and the beginnings of major challenges to them, also marked the last decades of the 1800s as a phase of critical transitions.

In western Europe, which overseas expansion and industrialization had established as the core of the global economy and paramount center of military and political power, the unification of Germany and Italy utterly transformed the geopolitical map. By the late 1860s, the traditional buffer zones (and battlegrounds, if the Napoleonic wars are any guide) of Europe had been filled in by highly chauvinistic new states. In addition, two new

competitors had entered into the incessant contests for land and influence that had been characteristic of the European state system for centuries. For both Italy and Germany the process of unification had taken decades, and it had involved both wars against external enemies and considerable, often very violent, internal strife. German unification in particular had disrupted the established power alignment. Not only was the German nation built on victorious wars against its neighbors, but the populous and highly industrialized new state appeared destined to translate its economic and military might into the political domination of continental Europe.

The wars that brought about German unification rather graphically illustrated the decline of the old order and the rise of the new. In the first in 1864, which pitted Prussia (the core kingdom of the German nation in the making) against tiny Denmark, the British, who wished to assist the Danes, found that they could do little to affect the outcome of a land war in Europe. The rout of the Austrians in 1866 left the Prussians the paramount power in central Europe. In the third and final war of unification in 1870, the wily Prussian Chancellor, Otto von Bismarck, drew the French into a conflict that sealed German ascendancy on the continent as a whole. The Franco-Prussian War not only led in 1871 to formal unification of Germany, but it made obvious what many observers had suspected for decades: France's post-Napoleonic decline was irretrievable. The actual conduct of the war also demonstrated the awesome killing power of the new, mass-produced weapons, including machine guns and rifled artillery, that were among the more dubious products of industrialization. Continuing French resistance, after most of their armies had been defeated in regular battle, also provided a preview of the guerrilla warfare and draconian reprisals that would become a prominent feature of many 20th-century military conflicts.

Although Bismarck cleverly sought to disguise the fact by renouncing further territorial claims and maintaining alliances with threatened older powers like Russia and Austria-Hungary, the German victory in the Franco-Prussian War irrevocably shattered the 19th-century balance of power. The growing strength of Germany, which the emperor Wilhelm II (who dismissed Bismarck in 1890) did little to conceal, sent its neighbors scurrying for protective alliances. In the decades before 1914, war scares and unprecedented levels of military buildup hardened the divisions between the allied camps and engendered an atmosphere of paranoia that had much to do with the outbreak of World War I.

Tensions between the powers in this period were also fed by intensified economic competition and related quarrels over territorial expansion, both within Europe (especially the Balkans) and overseas. In the late 1800s, a Western nation outside of Europe, the United States, emerged for the first time as a significant player in these contests for global dominance. Forcibly reunited by the North's victory over the South in the Civil War of the early 1860s, the industrializing and expansive American republic sought increasingly to project its growing economic capacity and newfound political power across the Atlantic and the Pacific oceans. Beginning in the 1870s, competition, inevitably spawned by the spread of the industrial revolution within western Europe and to areas like the United States and Russia, was exacerbated by the onset of a cycle of agricultural and industrial depressions that extended into the 1890s. The alternating phases of economic boom and bust in these decades fed social unrest among the working classes and prompted political leaders to seek economic outlets and political distractions in "little wars" overseas.

Thus, tensions and rivalries in Europe and the United States were projected outward through a stunning burst of imperialist expansion that led to the formal colonization of most of Africa, Southeast Asia, and the South Pacific. Ironically, in the very decades when Western global hegemony was at its zenith, movements were developing in colonized areas, especially India and the Philippines, that would provide major challenges to the colonial order by the early 1900s and eventually lead to its overthrow later in the 20th century.

In areas like Latin America, China, and Persia, the European powers—and increasingly the United States and Japan—vied for economic advantage and political influence without direct colonial control. In Latin America, divisions within the political elites and an already established economic dependence on Europe left ample openings for manipulation by the industrial powers. The accelerating collapse of the Qing dynasty in China reduced the oldest continuous and largest of humankind's civilizations to a massive black hole sucking in missionaries, merchants, and the squabbling diplomats of the great powers. The leaders of other noncolonized states, most notably Siam and Persia, proved more adept at warding off European advances, mainly by playing off the rival European powers against each other. But only Japan was able to preserve its independence in the face of the Western intrusions, to borrow heavily from the West without violating its own social and cultural integrity, and to industrialize and become an expansive power in its own right in the first half of the 20th century.

Because of the unprecedented centrality of western Europe's position in world history by the late 19th century, it is easy for us, more than a century later, to have a distorted view of the global order in the decades before World War I. Many Europeans mistakenly divided the world between the West and the rest, assuming that only Europe had achieved civilization and that all other groups, despite variations, could be lumped into an "uncivilized" category. Contrary to this highly ethnocentric conceit, a host of societies in Asia, Africa, and Latin America had, in some cases for millennia, supported complex social structures, sophisticated thought systems, and advanced material cultures—all of which Westerners equated with their vague notions of civilization. In virtually all areas of the globe where European and North American colonizers strove to assert their dominance, non-Western peoples retained much of their preexisting social and cultural systems and drew heavily upon them to build states and societies able to withstand the rapid changes of the 20th century.

These continuities should caution us against the erroneous assumption that in the 20th century, Europe—and more recently the United States—set the historical agenda for much of the rest of the world. In fact, despite the global power and influence exercised by the Western industrial nations, the world was clearly not becoming homogenized. And although human societies have changed profoundly everywhere, the direction and nature of change have varied significantly from place to place, depending on previous historical experiences and preexisting social and cultural systems. The impact of the West also varied widely in different regions, and—partly because of internal divisions—its position as global hegemon was in many ways uncertain and constantly challenged. The unprecedented levels of power that Western nations had achieved throughout the globe set the stage for the reassertion of other areas. The greatly increased and intensified cross-cultural interactions of the 20th century, and the process of globalization that was such a pronounced feature of both its first and third phases, should not cause us to lose sight of the underlying diversity that persisted on the basis of the legacy of earlier epochs of human development.

SOCIAL TRANSFORMATIONS AND THE COMING OF THE 20TH CENTURY

The dramatic political changes that signaled the beginning of the 20th century were paralleled by social transformations that departed less decisively from 19th-century patterns but nonetheless suggested transition to a new era. In the industrialized West, the numbers of the middle classes continued to grow and their longstanding dominance in invention, commerce, and manufacturing was steadily extended to politics, diplomacy, education, and the arts. Throughout Europe, the aristocracy remained a potent force in the military, government, and especially diplomacy, trends that would be decisively reversed only as a result of the failed leadership that came to be associated with World War I.

In both Europe and the United States, the proportion of the population living in cities continued to increase, as it had from the onset of the Industrial Revolution. The numbers of the urban working classes also continued to rise, but workers' organizations, particularly unions and socialist-leaning political parties, became major economic and social forces in the industrial nations for the first time. The increased voice of the working classes owed much to the introduction of compulsory education and the spread of mass literacy, which are hallmarks of the first phase of 20th-century social history. Also critical was the rise of the mass press, which heightened working-class consciousness, while raising the aspirations of the lower middle class, and drew larger and larger segments of both social strata into the political struggles of their respective nation-states. The burgeoning mass press also gave a major boost to the culture of consumption that became a key attribute of increasingly affluent industrial societies in the 20th century. Department stores, carefully organized leisure activities—especially sporting events, popular entertainments, and family vacations—and a proliferation of mass-produced commodities for the home and personal use all served to set off the late 1800s from the earlier industrial era, to indicate the beginning of a new century.

Of all the social movements in the West, perhaps none signaled the onset of a new era as dramatically as the campaigns for women's rights that emerged in most of the industrialized West, and its settler offshoots in Canada and Australia, in the decades before World War I. Though feminist organizations focused on winning the vote for women, they were also engaged in causes that ranged from efforts to improve women's legal standing and educational opportunities to opposition to draconian measures to regulate prostitution. The struggle for women's rights and the host of gender issues it subsequently raised for public debate have persisted as dominant themes, first in the West and then over much of the globe, throughout the 20th century.

Outside of the West, the decades that laid the foundations for the 20th century were marked more by continuity than change in terms of the social trends they exhibited. In directly colonized areas, indigenous elite groups perished resisting European conquest, or—more often—vied with each other to win positions of influence under the new rulers. In Latin America and other areas that came under European or American influence but not direct control, leaders and merchants collaborated with the agents of imperialism in the pursuit of greater wealth and political control within their own societies. The working classes in most of the formally and indirectly colonized world remained minuscule or nonexistent. The fate of the peasant classes was as varied and complex as these social groupings themselves. But the great majority were drawn more fully into the Western-dominated world market, and thus rendered more dependent on fluctuations in the global economic system. As markets expanded, indigenous commercial groups—both long established and newly emerging—increased in numbers and wealth. As subsistence production declined and specialized production became more pronounced throughout much of the globe, the market became the arbiter of human livelihood to a degree that was unimaginable in earlier eras.

Although Africans and Asians had begun to acquire Western education and adopt aspects of Western culture as early as the first decades of the 19th century, the late 1800s saw the emergence of substantial, Western-educated "middle" classes in colonized areas such as India, Senegal, and the Philippines. In fact, the great increase in the numbers and influence of those belonging to this social stratum can be seen as a key distinction between the 19th- and 20th-century social history of colonized peoples. The increasing politicization of these classes in the decades before World War I also marks a major difference between the two eras. At this elite level, women among the colonized peoples sometimes shared in the educational opportunities enjoyed by far larger numbers of their male counterparts. In some instances women were also the beneficiaries of major campaigns for social reform undertaken by the colonizers, often in alliance with members of the Western-educated, indigenous middle classes. But for the vast majority of women in nonindustrial societies, political rights and social emancipation would come, if at all, only in the wake of the great revolutions that sought to remake the global order in the last half of the 20th century.

INTELLECTUAL FOUNDATIONS FOR A NEW CENTURY

The political and social transitions that began in the 1860s and 1870s were in most cases closely linked to the ascendancy in roughly the same time period of ideologies, such as Marxism and Liberalism, that originated in the 19th century. In fact, with the exception of the formulation of Freudian theory and the revolution in scientific thinking that occurred just before and after 1900, the intellectual currents that were to dominate much of the 20th century were disseminated in the decades after 1860.

In his tract *On Liberty*, which was first published in 1859, John Stuart Mill enunciated the principles of Liberalism, which in its 19th-century European variant stressed individual rights, the sanctity of private property, laissez-faire economics, and minimal state intervention in the lives of its citizens. In his *Self-Help* published in the same year and his numerous biographies of enterprising Englishmen that followed, Samuel Smiles extolled the virtues of hard work, competition, self-reliance, and inventiveness. Readers of Charles Darwin's *Origin of Species*, also published in 1859, and his *Descent of Man*, which followed in 1870, were apt to see in his theory of evolution by natural selection historical confirmation of the centrality of competitiveness and the necessity for inventiveness stressed by Smiles and other popular writers.

Though Darwin's vision of the evolutionary process was decidedly not progressive and much of his thinking was crudely and mistakenly appropriated by contemporary writers, his ideas deeply influenced the theories of prominent social thinkers in his day. The Social Darwinists, for example, who wrongly claimed that Darwin's findings supported their views, stressed the centrality of the "struggle for survival" within the human species (in contrast to Darwin, who emphasized interspecies competition). In the early decades of the 20th century, the writings of those of this persuasion had a major impact on public opinion and government policy formation in areas as varied as decisions for imperialist expansion; the treatment of "primitive" or aboriginal peoples, such as the Amerindians, whom Social Darwinists concluded were doomed to extinction; and the eugenics movement, which advocated measures to improve the breeding stock of the dominant races and limit population increase among "inferior" peoples.

Counterposed to these celebrations of the virtues and aspirations of the capitalist middle and skilled working classes were the writings of Karl Marx and Frederick Engels. Though numerous works, including the *Communist Manifesto*, had appeared in the decades before, the successive volumes of Marx's master work *On Capital* (*Das Kapital*) were published in the 1860s and 1870s. In these he mounted an extensive critique of industrial capitalism and set forth a vision of history grounded in shifts in technology and production techniques that periodi-

cally resulted in revolutionary social upheavals. On the basis of what he considered a thoroughly scientific analysis of capitalist, industrial societies, Marx predicted that exploited and alienated working classes would rise up and overthrow the capitalist system and its middle-class managers and rulers. The fall of the middle classes would open the way for the creation of socialist societies that would eventually bring an end to class divisions and social strife.

Marx's ideas proved to be among the most influential of the 20th century. Leaders as disparate as Lenin, Mao Zedong, and Fidel Castro launched major revolutions aimed at fulfilling Marx's analysis of the past and prognosis for the future of humanity. Revisionist socialists struggled to provide convincing, reformist alternatives to Marx's path to utopia. Much energy was also expended by the thinkers and politicians of the capitalist West to refute Marxist doctrines and frustrate Marxist-inspired social movements in both the industrial and developing nations.

Although the ideas of European thinkers have dominated international discourse in the 20th century, important intellectual transitions were also occurring in the colonized world in the decades before World War I. The collapse of the Confucian political and social systems in China in this period left a quarter of humanity without ideological bearings. For much of the 20th century Chinese intellectuals debated alternatives drawn from both indigenous and Western precedents or a blending of the two. In neighboring Japan, a small ruling clique drawn mainly from the military classes was the first in the non-Western world to tackle the challenge of remaking their political system and social order in ways that would allow them to withstand the intrusions of the West. Across the colonized world in the late 1800s and early 1900s, leaders of resistance movements sought to rework the teachings of world religions like Islam and Buddhism or local animist creeds to rally supporters in their struggle against the dominance of the West. In addition, the rising, Western-educated elites in these areas produced both critics of industrial capitalism and colonialism and nationalist ideologues who formulated visions of national independence and development free of imperialist constraints.

PART OVERVIEW

In the four chapters that follow, we will explore in greater detail these key developments that defined the first phase of the 20th century in different areas of the globe. Chapter 1 is devoted to the impact of industrialization on the nations of western Europe and the United States, while the next chapter looks at the diffusion of this process to Russia and Japan. Chapter 3 is focused on the tensions in the industrial order that contributed to the great outburst of imperialist expansion by the European powers and the United States in the decades before the outbreak of World War I and the effects of colonization on the peo-ples of Africa, Asia, and the South Pacific. The last chapter in this section is devoted to key themes in the history of areas such as Latin America, the Middle East, and China, which were dominated economically and po-litically but not formally colonized by the industrial pow-ers in the first decades of the 20th century.

Chapter 1

Western Industrialization and the Foundations of the 20th Century

*By the first decades of the 20th century industrial towns such
as this were spread across Europe and North America and
elementary education was increasing to the working class.*

Chronology

1846–1848	Mexican-American War
1848 ff.	Writings of Karl Marx; rise of socialism
1852	New constitution in New Zealand; elected councils
1859–1870	Unification of Italy
1859	Darwin's *Origin of Species*
1861–1865	American Civil War
1863	Emancipation of slaves
1864–1871	German unification
1867	British North America Act, unites eastern and central Canada
1870s ff.	Rapid birth rate decline
1870–1879	Institution of French Third Republic
1871–1914	High point of European imperialism
1881–1889	German social insurance laws enacted
1882	U.S. excludes Chinese immigrants
1893	U.S. annexes Hawaii
1893	Women's suffrage in New Zealand
1898	Spanish-American War, U.S. acquires Puerto Rico, Guam, Philippines
1901	Commonwealth of Australia, creates national federation
1907	New Zealand dominion status in British Empire
1912–1913	Balkan Wars
1914	Beginning of World War I
1917	U.S. enters World War I

INTRODUCTION

The most dynamic force in 19th-century world history, and the most urgent backdrop to the history of the 20th-century world, was the process of industrialization. The Industrial Revolution, centered first in western Europe and the new United States, transformed the societies involved. It forced major political changes, including widespread voting rights and new government functions such as mass education. It revolutionized the activities of families by moving work outside the family context.

The industrialization process of the 19th century had almost immediate repercussions in the world at large, enhancing the power of industrializing areas at the expense of other regions. The West, already a dynamic civilization before 1800, now became the international trendsetter in many respects. Western technology, applied to weaponry, provided a massive military advantage over most other societies. Steamboats could sail the rivers of Africa or China; repeating rifles and machine guns could make a mockery of valiant but traditional fighting forces in the Middle East or Japan. Growing industrial economics sought new international markets and resources.

This chapter focuses on the nature of Western industrial society and related developments in Western diplomacy, culture, and society that were strongly influenced by industrialization. The creation of an industrial society was by no means an accomplished process by 1900, even in Great Britain, where the new economic and technological forms had first taken root. The West's 20th-century history would continue to show how the massive range of innovation compelled ongoing adjustments in institutional policies and personal lives. The later 1800s did, however, see something of an apogee in the world power position that the Industrial Revolution had created for the West.

THE INDUSTRIAL REVOLUTION IN EUROPE

The process of industrialization began to emerge more than a century before 1900, initially in Great Britain. Beginning about 1820, industrialization spread to parts of

15

continental western Europe and to the United States. The essence of this industrial revolution was technological change, particularly the application of coal-powered engines (or, later, engines powered by other fossil fuels) to the production process. The new engines replaced people and animals as the key sources of energy in many aspects of production. They were joined by new production equipment that could apply power to manufacturing through more automatic processes. Thus spindles now wrapped fiber automatically into thread, and looms automatically wove thread into cloth without direct human intervention. Hammering and rolling devices allowed application of power machinery to metals. Although textile and metallurgical production received primary attention in early industrialization, engines were also used in sugar refining, printing, and other processes.

Technological change was quickly applied to transportation and communication, essential areas now that there were more goods to be moved to ever more distant markets. The development of the telegraph, steam shipping, and the railway, all early in the 19th century, provided new speed in the movement of information and goods. These inventions were vital in facilitating a new stage in Western penetration of world affairs; they also kept the Industrial Revolution going in the West by promoting mass-marketing techniques and providing direct orders for rails and other industrial goods.

Although technology lay at the heart of industrialization, other fundamental innovations were inherent in the process as well. The Industrial Revolution depended on improvements in agriculture. Industrialization concentrated increasing amounts of manufacturing in cities, where power sources could be brought together with labor. City growth, dizzying during the first decades of industrialization, relied on better agricultural production, accomplished through improved equipment and seeds and increasing use of fertilizers.

Industrialization also meant a factory system. Steam engines had to be concentrated, for their power could not be widely diffused until the later application of electricity. Factory labor separated work from the home—one of the basic human changes inherent in the Industrial Revolution. It also allowed manufacturers to introduce greater specialization of labor and more explicit rules and discipline, which along with the incessant demands of the noisy machines permanently changed the nature of human labor.

Once Britain launched industrialization, other Western nations quickly saw the need to imitate. Belgium and France began to industrialize in the 1820s; the United States and Germany followed soon thereafter. Industrialization did not immediately sweep all before it, even in Britain; artisan production expanded for a time as cities grew and rural labor remained vital. But the forms of the Industrial Revolution gained ground steadily once implanted in the West, and factory workers and their managers became increasingly important minorities in the general labor force.

The Disruptions of Industrial Life

The Industrial Revolution opened new social divisions, as middle-class families sought to move away from the center-city poor, beginning a pattern of suburbanization that continued into the later 20th century.

Work became more unpleasant for many people. Not only was it largely separated from family, but also the new machines and factory rules compelled a rapid pace and coordination that pulverized traditional values of leisurely, quality production. Many traditional business and farm families were also appalled by the noise, dirt, and sheer novelty involved in the Industrial Revolution.

The Industrial Revolution also forced new constraints on traditions of popular leisure. Factory owners, bent on getting as much work as possible from their labor force to help pay for expensive machines, deliberately reduced recreational aspects of work; they tried to ban singing, napping, drinking, and other customary frivolities on the job.

Changes in family life revealed some of the wider stresses of the industrialization process. Middle-class people quickly moved to enhance a redefinition of the family, seeing it as a center of affection and purity. "Respectable" children and women were to be sheltered from the storms of the new work world. Women, traditionally active partners to merchants, now withdrew from formal jobs. They gained new roles in caring for children and the home, and their moral stature in many ways improved, but their sphere was more radically separate from that of men than had been true before. Children, too, were redefined. The middle class led in seeing education, not work and apprenticeship, as the logical role for children to prepare them for a complex future and, it was hoped, to maintain their innocence until they were prepared to cope with business or professional life.

The working-class family changed as well, though it could not afford all these indulgences. Young children, increasingly unnecessary on the job, were often sent to school. Women worked from adolescence until marriage, when they were often pulled away because of the demands of shopping, home care, and motherhood. Even when on the job, working-class women were more likely to be sent into domestic service in middle-class households than to factories, though there was an important minority of female factory hands. Family life became more important than ever before, to provide homemaking services and to offer some hope of emotional satisfaction in a confusing world.

Revolutionary Politics

The Industrial Revolution was paralleled by a far-reaching political upheaval in the West. Challenges to existing political regimes initially arose at the end of the 18th century, stemming from early stages of economic change, together with new ideas about liberty and democracy. By the mid-19th century, political shifts began to combine with the forces of the Industrial Revolution to produce new constitutional structures and a realignment of the functions of the European state. The era of political revolution began in 1775 with the rebellion of the American colonies against Britain. The new United States that emerged in the 1780s was remote from Europe but provided a model of a republican regime, instead of a monarchy, with a strong congressional system and constitutional guarantees of many citizen rights. This precedent played some role in inspiring the great French Revolution of 1789, which swept away France's monarchy and the principles of an aristocratic social structure, establishing religious freedom, equality under the law, and a variety of commercial liberties in place of the institutions of the old regime. The French Revolution, as it fought the armies of Europe's monarchies, also promoted a new form of nationalism, with French citizens called upon to rally their loyalties and abandon traditional allegiances to church or locality. A new citizens' army established a related principle of mass military conscription. The French Revolution and its conquests spread new political movements to other parts of western Europe.

In the wake of the great revolution, new political movements spread throughout western Europe by the 1820s. Liberals advocated limits on state interference in individual life, along with constitutional, parliamentary rule. Radicals accepted most liberal premises but also sought wider voting rights, even full adult male suffrage. Nationalists argued for the importance of national unity and glory, winning particular audience amid the divided states of Italy and Germany. A host of revolutions followed from the clash among these various movements and the established monarchies supported by church leaders. Even aside from revolution, major reform measures brought expanded voting rights in Britain (where the middle class gained the vote in 1832) and many northern states in the United States.

Railway bridges, such as this spectacular trestle at Frankenstein in Germany, were among the engineering wonders of the industrial age.

Feminism

The emergence of feminism as a major movement was one of the most striking developments in Western society around 1900. It would ultimately have global implications. Feminism resulted from broader changes in women's conditions—both new opportunities and new liabilities—and it would cause additional change in turn. Focusing on political and legal issues, feminism represented a huge challenge to the partriarchal systems that had dominated most of the world's societies for centuries.

The following passage comes from a speech delivered in 1908 by Emmeline Pankhurst, a leader of the British women's suffrage movement. Pankhurst became known for radical tactics, including blocking streets and other obstructive action, to call attention to the women's cause. Feminist protest added greatly to an atmosphere of social unrest in pre-World War I Britain. Their cause would prevail, but only after the war.

In the first place it is important that women should have the vote in order that in the government of the country the women's point of view should be put forward. It is important for women that in any legislation that affects women equally with men, those who make the laws should be responsible to women in order that they may be forced to consult women and learn women's views when they are contemplating the making or the altering of laws. Very little has been done by legislation for women for many years—for obvious reasons. More and more of the time of Members of Parliament is occupied by the claims which are made on behalf of the people who are organised in various ways in order to promote the interests of their industrial organisations or their political or social organisations. So the Member of Parliament, if he does dimly realise that women have needs, has no time to attend to them, no time to give to the consideration of those needs. His time is fully taken up by attending to the needs of the people who have sent him to Parliament. While a great deal has been done, and a great deal more has been talked about for the benefit of the workers who have votes, yet so far as women are concerned, legislation relating to them has been practically at a standstill. Yet it is not because women have no need, or because their need is not very urgent. There are many laws on the Statute-book today which are admittedly out of date, and call for reformation; laws which inflict very grave injustices on women. I want to call the attention of women who are here to-night to a few Acts on the Statute-book which press very hardly and very injuriously on women. . . .

Take what happens to the woman if her husband dies and leaves her a widow, sometimes with little children. If a man is so insensible to his duties as a husband and father when he makes his will, as to leave all his property away from his wife and children, the law allows him to do it. That will is a valid one. So you see that the married woman's position is not a very secure one. It depends entirely on her getting a good ticket in the lottery. If she has a good husband, well and good: if she has a bad one, she has to suffer, and she has no remedy. That is her position as a wife, and it is far from satisfactory.

Now let us look at her position if she has been very unfortunate in marriage, so unfortunate as to get a bad husband, an immoral husband, a vicious husband, a husband unfit to be the father of little children. We turn to the Divorce Court. How is she to get rid of such a man? If a man has got married to a bad wife, and he wants to get rid of her, he has but to prove against her one act of infidelity. But if a woman who is married to a vicious husband wants to get rid of him, not one act nor a thousand acts of infidelity entitle her to a divorce; she must prove either bigamy, desertion, or gross cruelty, in addition to immorality before she can get rid of that man.

Let us consider her position as a mother. We have repeated this so often at our meetings that I think the echo of what we have said must have reached many. By English law no married woman exists as the mother of the child she brings into the world. In the eyes of the law she is not the parent of her child. The child, according to our marriage laws, has only one parent, who can decide the future of the child, who can decide where it shall live, how it shall live, how much shall be spent upon it, how it shall be educated, and what religion it shall profess. That parent is the father. . . .

I know the cotton workers of Lancashire. Not long ago, we were in the Rosendale Valley . . . In that constituency more women earn wages than men. You find daughters earning more money than their fathers. You find wives earning more money than their husbands. They do piece work, and they often earn better wages than the men. I was talking one day to one—a married woman worker whom I met in the train. She was going home from the mill. She had a child three or four years of age, well dressed, very blithe, and looking well fed. I asked her if she worked in the mill. She said, "Yes." I asked her what wages she earned. She said, "Thirty shillings a week." She told me she had other children.

"Who looks after the children while you are at work?" I have a housekeeper," she answered. I said to her, "You are not going to be allowed to work much longer. Mr. John Burns is going to make you stay at home and look after the children." And she said, "I don't know what we shall do then. I suppose we shall have to clem." I don't know whether you all know our Lancashire word "clem." When we say clem, we mean starve. In thousands of homes in Lancashire, if we get Mr. John Burns' proposal carried into law, little children, now well clothed and well fed and well cared for, will have clemmed before many months are over. These women say a shilling that they earn themselves is worth two shillings of their husbands' money, for it is their own. They know far better than their husbands how much money is needed for food, how much is needed to be spent on the home. I do not think there is a woman in Lancashire who does not realise that it is better to earn an income of her own than to be dependent on her husband. They realise it better than women of the upper classes who provide nurses and governesses for their children. I put it to you whether the woman of the working class, so long as she sees that her children are well fed and are well enough cared for, has not as much right as her well-off sister to provide a nurse for her children. When women get the vote, they will take very much better care of babies than men have been able to do. . . .

Now let me say something on another point. Among those here are some professional women. You know what a long and a weary struggle it has been for women to get into the professions, some of which are now open to women. But you all know that the position of women in those professions is not what it ought to be, and is certainly not what it will be when women get the franchise. How difficult it is for women to get posts after they have qualified for them. I know this from practical experience on a public body. Every time we had applications from women for posts open to them, we had applications also from men. Usually the standing of the women was very might higher than that of the men. And yet the women did not get those appointments. The men got them. That would all be altered if we got political equality. It is the political key that is needed to unlock the door.

Again, in all grades of education, certainly in elementary education, women are better qualified for the work than the men. You get a better type of woman. Yet for work equal to that of men, she cannot get equal pay. If women teachers had the Parliamentary vote, those men who go to the House of Commons to represent the interests of teachers would have to represent the interests of women teachers as well as the interests of the men. I think that the gentleman who made the teachers the stepping-stone to office, and who talks at bye-elections about manhood suffrage would have taken up the interests of the women who have paid his wages if he felt that he was responsible to women voters. . . .

I hope that there may be a few men and women here who will go away determined at least to give this question more consideration than they have in the past. They will see that we women who are doing so much to get the vote, want it because we realise how much good we can do with it when we have got it. We do not want it in order to boast of how much we got. We do not want it because we want to imitate men or to be like men. We want it because without it we cannot do that work which it is necessary and right and proper that every man and woman should be ready and willing to undertake in the interests of the community of which they form a part. It has always been the business of women to care for these things, to think of these home questions. I assure you that no woman who enters into this agitation need feel that she has got to give up a single one of her woman's duties in the home. She learns to feel that she is attaching a larger meaning to those duties which have been woman's duties since the race began, and will be till the race has ceased to be. After all, home is a very very big thing indeed. It is not just your own little home, with its four walls, and your own little private and personal interest that are looked after there. The home is the home of everybody of the nation. No nation can have a proper home unless women as well as men give their best to its building up and to making it what a home ought to be, a place where every single child born into it shall have a fair chance of growing up to be a fit, and a happy, and a useful member of the community.

Questions: How radical are Pankhurst's basic arguments? How much is she trying to change women's conditions, beyond asking for the vote? Were there other kinds of arguments available? How does Pankhurst attempt to represent women across class lines? Why, despite great resistance from many men and not a few women, did feminists ultimately win out, and obtain the vote for women? How does Pankhurst's brand of feminism compare with more contemporary feminism in places like Britain or the United States?

Source: From Cheryl Jorgensen Earp, ed., *Speeches and Trials of the Militant Suffragettes* (Madison, NJ: Fairleigh Dickinson University Press, 1997), pp. 32–41.

Partly in response to agitation, partly in an effort to promote economic growth, most western European governments began some accommodation to the process of industrialization. Laws were changed to facilitate the movement of labor and the introduction of new technologies; traditional craft groups were weakened or outlawed in favor of freer commercial expansion. By the 1830s most governments began promoting railroad development; they also sponsored technical exhibits and scientific training.

In 1848 and 1849 a final round of European-wide revolutions occurred, beginning in Paris. Revolution spread throughout central Europe, where nationalist demands joined democratic pressure and intense unrest from urban workers, particularly artisans. These revolutions failed in a formal sense, as conservative monarchies regained their hold in the states of Germany and Italy and as an authoritarian empire replaced the short-lived republic that had emerged in France. Yet the new or restored regimes quickly began to introduce some political and social changes and to give new elements of the middle class a limited political voice.

THE CONSOLIDATION OF THE INDUSTRIAL ORDER, 1850–1914

In most respects the 65 years after 1850 seemed calmer than the frenzied period of political upheaval and initial industrialization. Many people became accustomed to change. City growth continued in the West, and indeed several countries, starting with Britain, neared the 50 percent mark in urbanization, the first time in human history that more than a minority of a population had lived in cities. But the rate of city growth slowed. Furthermore, city governments began to gain ground on the pressing problems growth had created. Sanitation improved, and death rates fell below birth rates for the first time in urban history. Parks, museums, effective regulation of food and housing facilities, and more efficient police forces all added to the safety and the physical and cultural amenities of urban life. Hosts of problems remained, but the horror stories of early industrialization began to abate. Revealingly, crime rates began to stabilize or even drop in several industrial areas, a sign of more effective social control and also of a more disciplined population.

Adjustments to Industrial Life

The theme of adjustment and stabilization applied to family life. Illegitimacy rates stopped rising—until 1960—which suggested that some earlier disruption in personal habits was easing. Within families, birth rates began to drop as Western society initiated a substantial demographic transition to a new system that promoted fairly stable population levels through a new combination of relatively low birth rates and death rates. Led initially by the middle classes, the low birth rate involved a reassessment of the purposes of children. Children were now seen as a source of emotional satisfaction and considerable parental responsibility, not as contributors to a family economy. This meant that individual children would be highly valued but the total number would be reduced.

Material conditions generally improved after 1850. There were important fluctuations; the industrial economy was unstable, and frequent depressions caused falling wages and unemployment. Huge income gaps also continued to divide various social groups. Nevertheless, the general trend was upward. By 1900 probably two-thirds of the Western population enjoyed conditions above the subsistence level; people could afford a few amenities, such as newspapers or family outings, and their diet and housing improved. Health got better. The decades from 1880 to 1920 saw a revolution in children's health, thanks in part to better hygiene during childbirth and better parental care. Infancy and death separated for the first time in human history. Instead of one-third or more of all children dying by age 10, rates fell to under 10 percent and continued to plummet. Adult health also benefited from better nutrition and improved work safety. By the 1880s French researcher Louis Pasteur's discovery of germs led to more conscientious sanitary regulations and procedures by doctors and other health-care specialists; this in turn reduced the deaths of women in childbirth. Women now began to outlive men by a noticeable margin, but men's health also improved. Workplace life remained tense. New machines in textiles and metallurgy sped up work while reducing skill levels. The typical industrial worker was now semiskilled, trained in very limited areas that involved little sense of pride or creativity. New methods of supervision, often pioneered in the United States, involved detailed calculations by efficiency engineers designed to spur output and limit wasted motion. From this base, managers in such industries as automobile production introduced assembly-line procedures early in the 20th century, with workers deliberately reduced to machinelike repetitions.

Yet as workers suffered under these new conditions there were new ways to compensate. By the 1890s important labor movements took shape among industrial

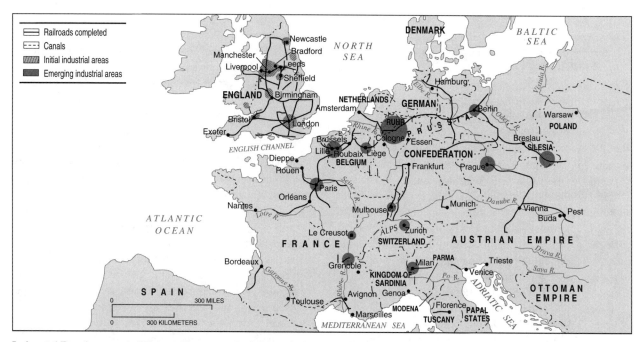

Industrial Development in Western Europe in the Mid-19th Century

workers with massive strike movements by miners, metalworkers, and others in places like the United States and Germany. The new trade union movement stressed the massive power of workers, and although often defeated by management-government coalitions, it won some important gains and gave workers some sense of voice and dignity. Furthermore, both within the labor movement and as individuals, many workers learned to react to the new systems of work instrumentally. The instrumentalist action urged workers to regard their jobs not as ends in themselves but as vehicles for other goals. Many workers, as instrumentalists, learned to bargain for better pay and shorter hours so that less of their lives would be invested in the work process. Mass consumerism developed, and the spread of glittering department stores both reflected and encouraged a new zeal for acquisition.

Political Trends

Many Western leaders worked to reduce the need for political revolution after 1850. Liberals decided that revolution was too risky and became more willing to compromise. Key conservatives strove to develop a new political consensus that would save elements of the old regime, including power for the landed aristocracy and the monarchy, but with enough reforms to reduce resistance.

Conservatives realized that they could allow parliaments with limited powers, appeal to workers through limited social reforms, and even extend the vote without necessarily losing power. Thus in 1867 a British conservative leader, Benjamin Disraeli, took the initiative of granting the vote to working-class males. In the Italian state of Piedmont, Count Camillo di Cavour began even earlier to support industrial development and extend the powers of parliament in order to please liberal forces. In Prussia a new prime minister, Otto von Bismarck, similarly began to work with a parliament and extended the vote to all adult males (though grouping them in wealth categories that protected the country from full democracy). These developments fell short of full liberal demands; parliaments did not have basic control over the appointment of ministries, but many groups gained some effective political voice. Other Prussian reforms granted freedom to Jews, extended (without guaranteeing) rights to the press, and promoted mass education. The gap between liberal and conservative regimes narrowed in the West, though it remained significant.

The new conservatives also began to use the force of nationalism to win support for the existing social order. Previously nationalism had been a radical force, challenging established arrangements in the name of new loyalties. Many liberals continued to defend nationalist causes. Now, however, conservative politicians learned how to wrap themselves in the flag, often assuring an active foreign policy in the interests of promoting domestic calm. Thus British conservatives became champions of expanding the empire, and in the United States by the 1890s the Republican party became increasingly identified with imperialist causes.

The most important new uses of nationalism within the West occurred in Italy and Germany. Cavour, after wooing liberal support, formed an alliance with France that enabled him to attack Austrian control of northern Italian provinces in 1858. The nationalist rebellion set in motion in other parts of the peninsula allowed Cavour to unite most of Italy under the Piedmontese king. This led to a reduction of the political power of the Catholic pope, already an opponent of liberal and nationalist ideas—an important part of the general reduction of Church power in Western politics.

Following Cavour's example, Bismarck staged a series of wars in Prussia in the 1860s that expanded Prussian power in Germany. A final war, against France, led to outright German unity in 1871. The new German Empire boasted a national parliament with a lower house based on universal male suffrage and an upper house that favored conservative state governments. This kind of compromise, combined with the dizzying joy of nationalist success, won support for the new regime from most liberals and many conservatives.

France, after its defeat by Germany in 1870, overthrew its short-lived echo of the Napoleonic Empire and established a conservative republic—with votes for all adult men, a reduction of Church power, and expansion of education, but no major social reform or tampering with existing property relationships. Just as a conservative Bismarck could be selectively radical, so France proved that liberals could be very cautious.

The Social Question and New Government Functions

The decline of basic constitutional disputes by the 1870s opened the way for a new set of political issues in the West and promoted the fuller development of an industrial-style state. Government functions and personnel expanded rapidly throughout the Western world after 1870. All Western governments introduced civil service examinations to test applicants on the basis of talent rather than on connections of birth alone—thus imitating Chinese innovations over a thousand years before. With a growing bureaucracy and improved recruitment,

governments began to extend their regulatory apparatus—inspecting factory safety, the health of prostitutes, hospital conditions, and even (through the introduction of passports and border controls) personal travel.

Schooling expanded, becoming generally compulsory up to age 12. By 1900 many U.S. states also began to require high school education, and most Western nations expanded their public secondary school systems. Here was a huge addition to the ways governments and individuals interacted. The new school systems promoted literacy, long gaining ground in the West and now becoming virtually universal; by 1900, 90 to 95 percent of all adults in western Europe and the United States could read. The school systems promoted numerical skills and other job-related aptitudes. They also encouraged certain social agendas. Girls were carefully taught about the importance of home and women's moral mission; domestic science programs were designed to promote better nutrition and hygiene. Boys and girls alike were taught the advantages of medical science over other health measures, and in general governments played a major role in promoting the use of doctors. Schools also carefully propounded nationalism, teaching the superiority of the nation's language and history, as well as attacking minority or immigrant cultures.

Governments also began to introduce wider welfare measures, again replacing or supplementing such traditional groups as churches and families. Bismarck was a pioneer in this area, too, in the 1880s, as he sought to wean German workers from the attraction to socialism. His tactic failed as socialism steadily advanced, but his measures had lasting importance. German social insurance began to provide assistance in cases of accident, illness, and old age. Soon some measures to aid the unemployed were also added, initially in Britain. These early welfare programs were small and their utility limited, but they sketched a major extension of government power.

Accompanying the quiet revolution in government functions during the later 19th century in the Western world was a realignment of the political spectrum that involved the replacement of constitutional issues by social issues—what people of the time called "the social question"—as the key criteria for political partisanship. Socialist and feminist movements surged to the political fore, placing liberals as well as conservatives in a new, though by no means unsuccessful, defensive posture.

The rise of socialism depended above all on the power of grievance of the working class, with allies from other groups. It also reflected a major redefinition of political theory accomplished, from 1848 through the 1860s, by one of the leading intellectuals of the century in the

West, Karl Marx. Marx's socialism was tough-minded, and he blasted earlier theorists as giddy utopians. Marx saw socialism as the final phase of an inexorable march of history, which could be studied dispassionately and scientifically. History for Marx was shaped by the available means of production and who controlled those means—an obvious reflection of the looming role of technology in the industrial world forming at that time. Class struggle always pitted a group out of power with the group controlling the means of production; hence, in the era just passed, the middle class had battled the feudal aristocracy. Now the middle class had won; it dominated production and, through this, the state and culture as well. But it had created a new class enemy, the property-less worker proletariat, that would grow until revolution became inevitable. Then, after a transitional period in which proletarian dictatorship would clean up the remnants of the bourgeois social order, full freedom would be achieved. People would benefit justly from their work, as essential equality would prevail, and the state would wither away; the historic class struggle would at last end because classes themselves would be eliminated.

Marx's vision was a powerful one. It clearly identified capitalist evil. It told workers that their low wages were exploitive and unjust. It urged the need for violent action but also assured workers that revolution was part of the inexorable tides of history. Victory was certain, and the result would be heaven on earth—ultimately, an Enlightenment-like vision of progress.

Germany led the way in the surge of socialism. As Bismarck extended the vote, socialist leaders in the 1860s and 1870s were the first to understand the implications of mass electioneering. Socialist movements were always strong in the provision of grassroots organization; available to constituents not only in election periods, they also provided fiery speakers who courted popular support instead of appealing, as many liberals and conservatives did, on the basis of their elevated social station and the respect it deserved. By the 1880s socialists in Germany were cutting into liberal support, and by 1900 the party was the largest single political force in the nation. Socialist parties in Austria, France, and elsewhere followed a roughly similar course, everywhere emerging as a strong minority force. Only in Britain and particularly the United States did socialism lag somewhat, in part because workers already had the habit of looking to liberal movements as their political expression. In Britain, too, socialism became a significant third force by 1914.

The rise of socialism terrified many people in Western society, who took the revolutionary message literally. In combination with major industrial strikes and unionization, it was possible to see social issues portending outright social war. But socialism itself was not unchanging. As socialist parties gained strength, they often allied with other groups to achieve more moderate reforms, and they became firm supporters of parliamentary democracy. A movement called *revisionism* arose, which argued that Marx's revolutionary vision was wrong—it needed revising—because industrial workers were not becoming a full majority and because success could be achieved by peaceful, gradual means. Many socialist leaders denounced revisionism, but in fact most behaved in revisionist fashion, putting their energies into building electoral victories rather than plotting violent revolution. Western socialism, in other words, although it reflected bitter grievances and class divisions as against a mood of consolidation and adjustment, worked to a great extent within the democratic political system.

Socialism was not the only challenge to the existing order. Powerful feminist movements arose by 1900 seeking various legal and economic gains for women, such as equal access to professions and higher education, as well as the right to vote. Feminism won support particularly from middle-class women, who argued that the very moral superiority granted to women in the home should be translated into political voice. Many middle-class women also chafed against the confines of their domestic roles, particularly as family size declined. A small but important group of women entered the professions directly, challenging ideas of inherent male superiority; a larger number became teachers and nurses, increasingly dominating semiprofessions that gave women both a new work role, at least before marriage, and a new sense that their opportunities were unjustly limited. In several countries feminism combined with socialism, but in Britain, the United States, Australia, and Scandinavia a separate feminist current arose that petitioned widely and even conducted acts of violence in order to win the vote. Here, too, was a major threat to political adjustment, but it was one that might be managed. Several U.S. states and Scandinavian countries extended the vote to women by 1914, in a pattern that would spread to Britain, Germany, and the whole United States after 1918.

The politics of Western society remained lively, with new forces jostling older interests and assumptions. Outside of formal policy—for example, in some new cultural currents—tensions were even more pronounced, as against the mood of complacency. These tensions challenged confidence in industrial and political progress—that remained widespread around 1900.

Popular Culture and High Culture

In the decades before 1900, key developments in popular culture reflected the maturation of industrial society in the West. Mass leisure culture began to emerge, emphasizing more secular interest over religious goals. Popular newspapers, with bold headlines and compelling human-interest stories, won millions of subscribers in the industrial West. Rather than appeals to reason or political principle, they featured shock and entertainment. Crime, imperialist exploits, sports, and even comics became the items of the day. Popular theater soared. Comedy routines and musical reviews drew thousands of patrons to music halls; after 1900 some of these entertainment themes dominated the new medium of motion pictures. Vacation trips became increasingly common, and seaside resorts grew to the level of big business.

Leisure outlets of these sorts were designed for fun. They appealed to impulse and escapism. Leisure was now a consumer commodity to be enjoyed regularly, perhaps daily, rather than through periodic festivals as in traditional society. With work increasingly disciplined, many saw leisure not as a chance for restraint and self-improvement, as the middle class still sometimes tried to insist, but as recreation.

The rise of team sports readily expressed the complexities of the late-19th-century leisure revolution. Here was another Western-wide development, though one that soon had international impact. Soccer, football, and baseball all surged into new prominence, at both amateur and professional levels. These new sports reflected industrial life. Though based on traditional games, they were organized with rules and referees. They taught the virtues of coordination and discipline and could be viewed as useful preparation for work or military life. They were suitably commercial; sports equipment, based on the ability to mass-produce rubber balls, and professional teams and their stadiums quickly became major businesses. But sports also expressed impulse and violence. They furthered irrational community loyalties and even, as Olympic Games were reintroduced in 1896, nationalist passions.

Science and Art

The size of the intellectual and artistic community in the West expanded steadily, with rising prosperity and advancing educational levels. Secularism also dominated intellectual life. Though new churches were built as cities grew, and missionary activity reached new heights outside the Western world, the churches no longer served as centers for the most creative intellectual life.

A major portion of Western cultural activity built on the traditions of rationalism that had been firmed up by the 18th-century Enlightenment. Continuing advances

Middle-class and working-class families made trips to the seaside popular before appropriate clothing had been designed, as can be seen in this scene from Yarmouth, England.

In the decades leading up to 1900 men and women at every class level were enthusiastic about spectator sports, as this 1887 engraving of a baseball game in progress at the Polo Grounds in New York illustrates.

in science kept alive the rationalist tradition. University and other research establishments increasingly applied science to practical affairs, linking science and technology in the popular mind under a general aura of progress. Improvements in medical pathology and the germ theory joined science and medicine, though no breakthrough therapies as yet resulted. Science was applied to agriculture, with Germany and then the United States in the lead, through studies of seed yields and chemical fertilizers.

The great advance in theoretical science came in biology, with publication of Charles Darwin's theory of evolution in 1859. On the basis of careful observation, Darwin argued that all living species had evolved into their present form through the ability to adapt in a struggle for survival. Biological development could be scientifically understood as a process taking place over time, with some animal and plant species disappearing and others evolving from earlier forms. Darwin's ideas clashed with traditional beliefs that God had fashioned humankind as part of initial creation, and the resultant debate further weakened the intellectual hold of religion. Darwin's advance also created a more complex picture of nature than Newton's simple physical laws had suggested. Nature now worked through random struggle, and people were seen as animals with large brains, not as supremely rational. The theory of evolution confirmed the link between science and advancement of knowledge, and Darwin's theory was in fact compatible with a continued belief in progress.

Developments in physics continued as well, with work on electromagnetic behavior and then, around 1900, increasing knowledge of the behavior of the atom and its major components. New theories arose, based on complex mathematics, to explain the behavior of planetary motion and the movement of electrical particles, where Newtonian laws seemed too simple. After 1900 Albert Einstein's theory of relativity formalized this new work by adding time as a factor in physical measurement. Again, science seemed to be steadily advancing in its grasp of the physical universe, though it was also important to note that its complexity now surpassed the grasp even of educated laypeople.

The social sciences also continued to advance, on the basis of observation, experiment, and rationalist theorizing. Great efforts went into compilations of statistical data concerning population, economic patterns, and health conditions. Sheer empirical knowledge about human affairs had never been more extensive. At the level of theory, leading economists tried to explain business cycles and the causes of poverty and social psychologists studied the behavior of crowds.

The emergence of modern artistic styles brought continual innovation into literature and art. This linked art to other facets of Western society where change and novelty were the name of the game, but it distressed many people who hoped that art would confirm traditional values. Artists were also attracted to the styles of societies outside the West. They sought to portray passions and alternative versions of reality rather than to confirm established styles. Poetry did not have to rhyme; drama did not necessarily need plot; painting could be evocative, even abstract (for literal portrayals, painters could now argue, use a camera). Each generation of artists proved more defiant than the last. After 1900 the new styles began to have an international influence, but they also pulled into the Western experience stylistic lessons from African sculpture and design and East Asian painting, newly accessible as a result of growing cultural links.

Industrialization and the Rise of the United States to Global Power

Along with Germany, U.S. industrialization formed the great economic success story in world history in the last half of the 19th century. Industrial growth began in the 1820s in the United States, with the imports of technological systems from Britain. American inventors contributed significantly to the industrialization process through such achievements as the mechanical gin for removing seeds from cotton fiber and the major strides in devising the system of interchangeable parts. But the United States remained dependent on European technological advances throughout the 19th century—British and French at first, then German and Swedish in such industries as chemicals. U.S. business was quick to imitate; locomotive construction began just a year after the first British model reached the United States. Although only local lines were laid before 1830, in the following decade 3000 miles of track were set out, mainly in the Northeast, and major interregional lines were launched by the 1840s, with the usual result of directly increasing demand in heavy industry while facilitating other industrial operations. Extensive canal building also contributed to the burgeoning process.

Textile factories formed the core of initial U.S. factory industry, as factory towns spread out in New England,

using both water and steam power. But there were also advances in machine building, printing, and other manufacturing sectors. The invention of the sewing machine in the 1840s began a transformation of clothing manufacture from handwork to faster-paced mechanized output, not only in New England but also in Midwestern factory centers such as Cincinnati, which by 1840 was the nation's third largest industrial city.

The first phase of U.S. industrialization increased the amount of manufactured goods in circulation and encouraged the further development of market specialization in other areas, such as agriculture, even as the bulk of the nations' economy remained nonindustrial. The process was also marked by relatively favorable labor conditions. Workers were in short supply, and recruitment required paying relatively high wages. Many women were drawn into the factories, expecting to put in a few years of work before returning, with a nest egg, to a farm family. Skilled male workers were also relatively well treated. Unlike their counterparts in Europe, they had the vote, which encouraged their sense of connection to the larger society. Conditions began to worsen in the 1830s, provoking a number of labor strikes; then in the 1840s growing numbers of immigrants, particularly Irish, fed the urban labor force, and standards of living deteriorated in many factory centers.

The second phase of U.S. industrialization took off with the expansion of war industries during the Civil War. American arms manufacturers extended their operations, beginning a tradition of extensive arms sales abroad, when the domestic market shrank after 1865. Development of intercontinental rail links spurred industrial growth on another front. Railroad companies were in private hands and pioneered in a number of aspects of big business in the American context: huge capital investments, a large labor force, and attempts to ensure regional monopolies over service.

Industrialization in the United States obviously displayed much the same big-business surge that characterized Germany during the same decades. Investment banks helped coordinate the growth of multifaceted companies. As in Germany also, the sheer speed of the U.S. industrial explosion altered the world's economic context with dizzying rapidity. Indeed, it was through industrial expansion that the United States began to make an independent mark in world history by the 1870s. Several U.S. companies began establishing branches abroad; two American firms, in sewing machines and agricultural equipment, respectively, were the largest industrial enter-

Skyscrapers, the giant buildings that have dominated the urban skylines of the 20th century, were pioneered in the U.S. midwestern metropolis of Chicago, not in London, Paris, or New York. This photo of the Carson, Pirie, Scott building under construction gives a sense of the dramatic increase in scale that the skyscraper represented.

siderable resources for expansion. Huge firms strengthened their hold in heavy industry and chemicals. Newer industrial sectors, such as the burgeoning automobile industry, initially opened the way for newer, small-scale industrialists.

U.S. workers showed less interest than their European counterparts in socialism, especially its revolutionary variants, such as Marxism. Nonetheless, in the late 19th century Americans participated actively in industrial campaigns and protest movements similar to those in Europe. These were peak decades of factory conflict. Strike rates rose steadily, with strikes focusing on improving wages and hours. Workers also showed an increasing ability to articulate progressive demands, asking for a shorter working day and other conditions they were convinced they deserved but had not existed before. Workers were increasingly represented by labor unions, such as the American Federation of Labor, in their struggles with factory, mine, and railway owners. In the decades that shaped U.S. entry into the 20th century, workers also derived great benefit from the spread of elementary education among both the urban and rural laboring classes and the extension of the vote to virtually the entire male population.

DIPLOMATIC TENSIONS AMONG THE WESTERN POWERS

American growth added to the force of Western imperialism. By the 1890s the United States had completed its transcontinental expansion and subjugation of native Americans. Attention then turned to becoming a world power, particularly through industrial and naval strength. The nation seized island territories including Hawaii, Puerto Rico, and the Philippines, and pressed for a greater role in China.

Western expansion had its limits, however, and these limits were beginning to tell on the Western heartland by 1900. The rise of new parts of the Western world, particularly the growing strength and assertiveness of the United States, added to the sense of national competition. Along with Germany's newfound muscle, the U.S. presence on the world diplomatic scene made rivalries for empire and trade more intense.

More important still at this point was the fact that by 1900 there were few parts of the world available for Western seizure. Latin America was independent but

prises in Russia by 1900. More than in Germany, much U.S. public opinion remained committed to a rhetoric of free enterprise, even as big business grew and the government actively contributed to industrial expansion through not only grants of land but also high protective tariffs.

Larger and more sophisticated organization meant, finally, the spread of giant corporations—again a trend already intrinsic to industrial economies by the 1880s but extended steadily thereafter. Hundreds of new corporations formed each year in France, the United States, and other countries. Some of the companies were small, but they had, through the sales of shares to the public, con-

ANALYSIS

The United States in World History

World history surveys often have some problems in integrating the United States, after some coverage of colonial origins as part of Western explorations and trade. World history already offers a full menu. American high school students always take some separate U.S. history courses. So why not simplify life and leave the United States out of world surveys?

This approach gains added support from the fact that until the late 19th century the United States, relatively isolated save for the arrival of immigrants, was not particularly important in the larger stream of world history. American preoccupation lay in internal development, including westward expansion. This brought clashes with Mexico, an important foretaste of the rebalancing in power between the United States and Latin America. Westward expansion also brought some posturing against European nations tempted to interfere in the Western hemisphere. The Monroe Doctrine (1820) warned against meddling in Latin America. In fact it was British policy and naval power that kept the hemisphere largely free from new colonialism.

The United States long counted for little in world diplomacy. The nation's population, though growing, was small. Its economy, though developing, exported little until the great surge of agricultural exports followed by an industrial outflow in the 1870s and 1880s. The United States was a debtor nation, depending on loans from European banks for much of its development until 1914. The nation did play an important role in receiving European immigrants, just as it earlier had affected African history through its role in the slave trade. And the nation symbolized, especially to some Europeans, a land of freedom and prosperity; revolutionaries in 1848, for example, invoked American institutions, just as Latin American independence fighters had done around 1820. Although the United States depended on world currents of immigration, loans, and culture, it had yet to contribute much in detail.

By the end of the 19th century the tentativeness and isolation of the United States in world affairs had passed. U.S. agriculture poured goods into the markets of Europe. U.S. industry was rising, along with that of Germany, to the top of world output rankings. The United States had clearly become, along with western Europe, part of the dominant economic core in world trade. U.S. naval power led to the acquisition of important colonies in Asia and the West Indies. As it gained in international impact, the United States, while retaining some of its earlier image as a revolutionary new nation, became increasingly similar to major western European powers in defending existing world power alignments.

There is a legitimate historical question about whether to treat the United States as a separate civilization (along, perhaps, with Canada and other places that mixed dominant Western settlement with frontier conditions). A number of historians argue for American *exceptionalism*—that is, the United States as its own civilization, not part of larger Western patterns. American exceptionalism need not contend that the United States was immune from contact with western Europe, which would be ridiculous, but it argues that this contact was incidental to the larger development of the United States on its own terms.

American exceptionalists can point to a number of factors that caused the development of a separate U.S. civilization. The Atlantic colonies gained political and cultural characteristics in relative isolation—they were, among other things, unusually democratic (among white males) compared with Europe at the time. Though colonial immigrants often intended to duplicate European styles of life, the vastness and wealth of the new land quickly forced changes. As a result U.S. families gave greater voice to women and children, and abundant land created a class of independent farmers rather than a traditionalist peasantry with its tight-knit villages. Even after the colonial era, distinctive institutions, created by the successful revolution and its federal Constitution, continued to shape a political life different from that of western Europe. The frontier, which lasted until the 1890s and had cultural impact even beyond that date, continued to make Americans unusually mobile and restless, while draining off some of the social grievances that arose in western Europe.

There was less political fragmentation and extremism than in western Europe and more stability. No strong socialist movement took shape. Religion was more important in the United States than in Europe by the late 19th century. Religion served immigrants as a badge of identity and helped all Americans to retain some sense of foundation as they built a new society. The absence of established churches in the United States kept religion out of politics, in contrast to Europe, where churches got caught up in more general attacks on the political establishment.

The American exceptionalist argument often appeals particularly to those things Americans like to believe about themselves—more religious, less socialistic, full of the competence that came from taming a frontier—but it must embrace some less savory distinctiveness as well. The existence of slavery, and then the racist attitudes and institutions that arose following its abolition, created ongoing issues in American life that had no full counterpart in western Europe. Europe, correspondingly, had less direct contact with African culture; jazz was one of the key products of this aspect of U.S. life.

Yet from a world history standpoint, the United States must be seen also, and perhaps primarily, as an offshoot of Western civilization. The colonial experience showed the powerful impact of Western political ideas, culture, and even family styles. U.S. history in the 19th century followed patterns common in western Europe. The development of parliamentary life and the spread of democracy, though unusually early in the United States, fits a larger Western trajectory. U.S. industrialization was a direct offshoot of Europe and followed a basically common dynamic. U.S. intellectuals kept in close contact with European developments, and there were few purely American styles. Conditions for women and wider patterns of family life, in areas such as birth control or disciplining children, were similar on both sides of the North Atlantic, which shows that the United States not only imitated western Europe but also paralleled it.

Because the United States was freer from peasant and aristocratic traditions, in some important cases it pioneered developments that would soon surface in western Europe. This was true to an extent in politics; it was true in the development of mass consumer culture and mass media (for example, the popular press and popular films). In these areas the United States can be seen not as distinctive to the point of forming a separate civilization but as anticipating some developments that would become common in Western civilization in part because of American example.

Questions: Which argument has the greater strength in describing 19th-century history: the United States as a separate civilization or the United States as part of the West? Have the United States and western Europe become more or less similar in the 20th century? Why?

A Challenge: Take a major topic around 1900—family life, nature of the political party system, the labor movement, foreign policy—and compare the United States and western Europe. What stands out more, the differences or the shared patterns? And what best explains the differences or commonalities?

---

under extensive U.S. influence, so that a new intrusion of colonialism was impossible. Africa was almost entirely carved up. The few final colonies taken after 1900—Morocco by France and Tripoli (Libya) by Italy—caused great diplomatic furor on the part of other colonial powers worried about the balance of force on that continent. China and the Middle East were technically independent but were in fact crisscrossed by rivalries among the Western powers and Russia (and in China's case, Japan). No agreement was possible on further takeovers.

Yet for several decades the growth of empire had served as a vital outlet for Western diplomatic and military energies. The tensions among the Western nation-states had escalated dangerously after the unifications of Italy and Germany. Bismarck, the architect of German unity, cleverly devised an alliance system during the 1870s and 1880s that neutralized France, a "natural enemy" that feared the growing power of the German neighbor and resented the loss of territories after the war in 1870–1871. Germany allied directly with Austria and Italy and had

had a separate understanding with Russia. This intricate alliance system was in fact preserved by the interest key nations took in overseas expansion. France worried less about the rivalry with Germany than about gaining new colonies in Africa and Indochina, and Germany entered the imperialist game by seizures in Africa and East Asia. Britain remained preoccupied with colonial expansion.

Imperialist expansion, however, fed the sense of rivalry among key nation-states. Britain, in particular, grew worried about Germany's overseas drive, supplemented after 1890 by the construction of a larger navy. Economic competition between a surging Germany and a lagging Britain added fuel to the fire. France, eager to escape the Bismarck-engineered isolation, was willing to play down traditional rivalries with Britain. The French also took the opportunity to ally with Russia, when after 1890 Germany dropped this particular alliance because of Russian-Austrian enmity.

By 1907 most major European nations were paired off in two alliance systems: Germany, Austria-Hungary, and

Italy formed the Triple Alliance, while Britain, Russia, and France constituted the new Triple Entente. Three against three seemed fair, but in fact Germany grew increasingly concerned about facing potential enemies to both the east (Russia) and west (France). All the powers steadily built up their military arsenals in what turned out to be the first of several arms races in the 20th century. All powers save Britain had instituted peacetime military conscription to provide large armies and even larger trained reserves. Artillery levels and naval forces built steadily—the addition of a new kind of battleship, the Dreadnought, to naval arsenals was a key escalation—while discussions about reducing armament levels got nowhere.

Furthermore, each alliance system was dependent on an unstable partner. Russia suffered a revolution in 1905, and its allies worried that any further diplomatic setbacks might paralyze the eastern giant. Austria-Hungary was plagued by nationalist disputes, particularly by minority Slavic groups; German leaders fretted that a diplomatic setback might bring chaos. Both Austria and Russia were heavily involved, finally, in maneuverings in the Balkans—the final piece in what became a nightmare puzzle.

Small Balkan nations had won independence from the Ottoman Empire during the 19th century; as Turkish power declined, local nationalism rose, and Russian support for its Slavic neighbors paid off. But the nations were intensely hostile to each other. Furthermore, Balkan nationalism threatened Austria, which had a large southern Slav population. Russia and Austria nearly came to blows on several occasions over Balkan issues, for Austria felt that it must keep the Slavs in line, whereas Russia looked to the Balkans as a place where it might pick up needed diplomatic prestige. Then in 1912 and 1913 the Balkan nations engaged in two internal wars, which led to territorial gains for several states but satisfied no one. Serbia in particular, which bordered Austria to the south, had hoped for greater gains. At the same time, Austria grew nervous over the gains Serbia had achieved. In 1914 a Serbian nationalist assassinated an Austrian archduke on behalf of Serbian claims. Austria vowed to punish Serbia. Russia rushed to the defense of Serbia and mobilized its troops against Austria. Germany, worried about Austria and also eager to be able to strike against France before Russia's cumbersome mobilization was complete, called up its reserves and then declared war on August 1. Britain hesitated briefly, then joined its allies. World War I had begun, and with it came a host of new problems for Western society.

CONCLUSION: DIPLOMACY AND SOCIETY

The tensions that spiraled into major war are not easy to explain. Diplomatic maneuverings can seem quite remote from the central concerns of most people, if only because key decisions—for example, with whom to ally—are made by a specialist elite. Even as the West became more democratic, few ordinary people placed foreign affairs high on their election agendas.

The West had long been characterized by political divisions and rivalries. By comparison with some other civilizations, this was an endemic weakness of the Western political system. In a sense what happened in the first phase of the 20th century was that the nation-state system got out of hand, encouraged by the absence of serious challenge from any other civilizations. The details of this development, involving the rise of Germany and the new tensions in the Balkans, are obviously important, but the link with a longer-term Western problem area should not be forgotten.

At the same time, the diplomatic escalation also had some links with the strains of Western society under the impact of industrialization. Obviously the fact that modern war proved so horrible, as had already been suggested in the American Civil War, stemmed directly from the destructive power of modern factory-produced weaponry, from massive new guns and ships to steady improvements in the explosive power of chemical combinations. The causes of war, also, related to industrial patterns.

Most obviously, established leaders in the West continued to worry about social protest and the growing visibility of the masses. Politicians tended as a result to seek diplomatic successes in order to distract. This procedure worked nicely for a few decades when imperialist gains came easily. But then it proved a straitjacket. Around 1914 German officials, fearful of the power of the socialists, wondered if war would not aid national unity; British leaders, beset by feminist as well as labor unrest, failed to think through their own diplomatic options. Leaders also depended on military buildups for economic purposes. Modern industry, pressed to sell the soaring output of its factories, found naval purchases and army equipment a vital supplement.

The masses themselves had some role to play. Though some groups, particularly in the socialist camp, were hostile to the alliance system and to imperialism, many workers and clerks found the diplomatic successes of their nations exciting. In an increasingly disciplined and organized society, with work frequently routine if not downright boring, the idea of violence and energy, even of war, could find appeal. Mass newspapers that fanned nationalist pride with stories of conquest and tales of the evils of rival nations helped shape this belligerent popular culture.

The consolidation of industrial society in the West, in other words, had continued to generate strain at various levels. Consolidation meant more powerful armies and governments, a more potent industrial machine. It also meant continued social frictions and an ongoing tug of war between rational restraint and a desire to break out, to dare something wild.

Thus, just a few years after celebrating a century of material progress and relative peace, ordinary Europeans went to war almost gaily in 1914. Troops departed for the front, convinced that war would be exciting with quick victories, their departure hailed by enthusiastic civilians who draped their trains with flowers. Four years later almost everyone agreed that war had been unmitigated hell. The complexities of industrial society were such, however, that war's advent initially seemed almost a welcome breath of the unexpected, a chance to get away from the disciplined stability of everyday life.

Because of Europe's importance in the world as a whole, its crisis in 1914 quickly became a global crisis, though it would also provide new opportunities for independent developments in places like Japan and the Middle East. It is vital, at the same time, not to focus too exclusively on the crisis. European industrialization and its social consequences, the major new political patterns, and the rise of the United States had introduced durable new elements into world history. Other societies had been affected by these developments before 1914, and the ongoing impact of these forces for change, and the various interactions with them, would shape much of the 20th and 21st centuries.

FURTHER READING

Two excellent studies survey Europe's industrial revolution: Sidney Pollard, *Peaceful Conquest: The Industrialization of Europe, 1760–1970* (1981) and David Landes, *The Unbound Prometheus: Technological Change and Industrial Development in Western Europe from 1750 to the Present* (1969). See also Phyllis Deane, *The First Industrial Revolution* (1980), on Britain. On the demographic experience,

see Thomas McKeown, *The Modern Rise of Population* (1977); Eric Hobsbawm, *The Age of Capital, 1848–1875* (1984) and *The Age of Empire 1875–1914* (1989); and Susan Cotts Watkins, *From Provinces into Nations: Demographic Integration in Western Europe, 1870–1960* (1991).

Major developments concerning women and the family are covered in Louise Tilly and Joan Scott, *Women, Work and Family* (1989), and Steven Mintz and Susan Kellogg, *Domestic Revolutions: A Social History of American Family Life* (1989). See also R. Evans, *The Feminists: Women's Emancipation Movements in Europe, America and Australasia, 1840–1920* (1989). An important age group is treated in John Gillis's *Youth and History* (1981).

For an overview on social change, see Peter Stearns and Herrick Chapman, *European Society in Upheaval* (1991). On labor history, see Michael P. Hanagan, *The Logic of Solidarity* (1981) and Albert Lindemann, *A History of European Socialism* (1983). Eugene Weber, *Peasants into Frenchmen: The Modernization of Rural France, 1870–1914* (1976), and Harvey Graff, ed., *Literacy and Social Development in the West* (1982) deal with important special topics.

On political and cultural history, see Gordon Wright, *France in Modern Times* (1981); Louis Snyder, *Roots of German Nationalism* (1978); and David Blackbourn, *The Long Nineteenth Century: A History of Germany, 1780–1918* (1998). J. H. Randall, *The Making of the Modern Mind* (1976), is a useful survey; see also O. Chadwick, *The Secularization of the European Mind in the Nineteenth Century* (1976). On major diplomatic developments, see David Kaiser, *Politics and War: European Conflict from Philip II to Hitler* (1990). J. W. Burrow, *The Crisis of Reason: European Thought, 1848–1914* (2000), surveys European thought, connecting philosophy to its social and political contexts.

Other recent work includes Brenda Scalcup, *The Industrial Revolution* (2002); Norman Birnbaum, *After Progress: American Social Reform and European Socialism in the Twentieth Century* (2003); and Carolyn Tuttle, *Hard at Work in Factories and Mines: The Economics of Child labor During the British Industrial Revolution* (1999).

ON THE WEB

An overview of the Industrial Revolution, with articles on inventions, cartoons, the slums of London, and a game called "Who wants to be a Millionaire" illustrating the rise and fall of cotton merchants can be found at

http://www.bbc.co.uk/history/society_culture/
industrialisation/index.shtml

Related sites offer an animated ride on Stephenson's Rocket, the forerunner of all steam locomotives

http://www.bbc.co.uk/history/society_culture/
industrialisation/launch_ani_rocket.shtml

a virtual visit to an early iron bridge

http://www.bbc.co.uk/history/society_culture/
industrialisation/launch_vr_ironbridge.shtml

and a voyage through a blast furnace

http://www.bbc.co.uk/history/society_culture/
industrialisation/launch_ani_blast_furnace.shtml

Several Web sites are devoted to James Watt, whose life and re-conception of the steam engine can be found at

http://www.geocities.com/Athens/Acroolis/6914/
watte.htm
http://www.sartacus.schoolnet.co.uk/SCwatt.htm
http://homeages.westminster.org.uk/hooke/issue10/
watt.htm

Many sites are devoted to the lives of other key figures in the Industrial Revolution, such as Eli Whitney

http://www.eliwhitney.org

and Richard Arkwright

http://www.britainexress.com/History/bio/
arkwright.htm
http://www.bbc.co.uk/history/historic_figures/
arkwright_richard.shtml

The major works of Isambard Kingdom Brunel, the most famous British architect and builder of the early Industrial Age, can be found at

http://www.greatbuildings.com/architects/
Isambard_Kingdom_Brunel.html
http://www.spartacus.schoolnet.co.uk/RAbrunel.htm

The life of industrial workers in 19th century England is examined at

http://www.history.rochester.edu/pennymag
http://www.bbc.co.uk/history/lj/victorian_britainlj/
earning_a_living_1.shtml?site=history_victorianlj_
earning

The transformation of sports from brutal competitions to leisure activities suitable for middle class men and women is traced at

http://www.bbc.co.uk/history/society_culture/society/
sort_01.shtml
http://www.victorianweb.org/art/costume/nunn2.html

The Industrial Revolution's larger social and political effects and the literary response it engendered can be examined through links found at

http://www.fordham.edu/halsall/mod/modsbook14.html

which includes a selection from Emile Zola's Germinal, a work written as a protest against working conditions in nineteenth century mines. Other Web sites explore the world of working women, including

http://www.nettlesworth.durham.sch.uk/time/
victorian/vindust.html
http://home.earthlink.net/~womenwhist/lesson7.html
http://www.fordham.edu/halsall/mod/
1842womenminers.html

The lives of working children are addressed at

http://www.spartacus.schoolnet.co.uk/IRchild.main.htm

The Web offers resources for examining the writings of Karl Marx and others whose critiques and assessments of industrialization and the future of capitalism formed the basis of many 19th- and 20th-century revolutionary movements. A brief essay at

http://landow.stg.brown.edu/victorian/religion/html

illuminates key forms of Marxian analysis, including the role of ideology in human society. Two of the best sites for accessing and comparing the ideas of Marxist writers are

http//csf.colorado.edu/mirrors/marxists.org/admin/
intro/index.htm
http://www.anu.edu.au/polsci/marx/marx.html

which includes a RealAudio file of the revolutionary anthem, "The Internationale" sung by an Irish folksinger accompanied on the guitar.

Chapter 2

Extending the Industrial Core: The Emergence of Russia and Japan as 20th-Century Powers

This silk factory, based on imported technology and designed mainly for the burgeoning export trade to the West, is representative of early Japanese industrialization.

Chronology

1853–1854	Perry expedition to Edo Bay
1854–1856	Crimean War
1860–1868	Civil strife
1860s–1870s	Alexander II reforms
1861	Russian emancipation of serfs
1865–1876	Russian conquests in central Asia
1868–1912	Meiji period
1870	Ministry of Industry established (Japan)
1872	Universal military service established
1875–1877	Russian-Ottoman War, Russia wins new territory
1878	Bulgaria gains independence
1884–1914	Beginnings of Russian industrialization; near completion of trans-Siberian railway (full linkage 1916)
1889–1890	New constitution and legal code (Japan)
1892–1903	Sergei Witte, minister of finance
1894–1895	Sino-Japanese War
1898	Formation of Marxist Social Democratic Party
1904–1905	Russo-Japanese War
1905–1906	Revolution results in peasant reforms and Duma (Russia)
1910	Annexation of Korea by Japan
1912–1913	Balkan Wars
1912	Growing party strife in Japanese Parliament
1914	World War I
1916–1918	Japanese seizure of former German holdings in the Pacific and China
1917	Revolution and Bolshevik victory

INTRODUCTION

For most areas of the world in the 19th century, including the most populous societies, Western industrialization meant increasing Western economic and military pressure in the form of heightened imperialism. But in two significant exceptions to this pattern Western pressure resulted in substantial reform programs, including early industrialization. These responses, in Russia and Japan, did not produce new versions of Western society—in this the two nations differed markedly from the United States or Australia, for they already had well-established prior cultures. Their responses did, however, trigger new dynamism, bringing Russia and Japan into the network of expanding, aggressive nations by the end of the 19th century.

Economic changes in Russia and Japan by 1900, while not matching Western industrial levels, made it clear that industrialization was going to be a global experience, not just a Western one. They brought Japan into world affairs as never before. They also revealed different patterns of tradition and change from those that had developed in the West. Japan altered in many ways, but it did not become Western. This kind of balance, which had durable results in Japan itself, would become a global phenomenon as the 20th century wore on.

Russia and Japan had very little in common prior to the late 19th century. Japan had spent several centuries in virtual isolation from the rest of the world. It had an ongoing feudal tradition, though a centralized government, the Tokugawa shogunate, had imposed considerable order during the 17th and 18th centuries by pacifying the samurai warrior class. Russia featured a much more strongly centralized regime under the tsar, or emperor. It had been expanding territorially into Siberia, Central Asia, and eastern Europe for several centuries. It had a tightly constructed system of serfdom, with forced peasant labor sustaining much of its agricultural production. Though less urbanized and commercial than Japan, Russia had established more extensive contacts with western

Europe and by the 19th century was contributing literature and music to a common European elite culture.

Both Russia and Japan maintained reasonably vigorous governments prior to 1850, which gave them an advantage in meeting the new challenge of Western industrialization. Also, both had a tradition of successful imitation—Japan from China from the first centuries C.E., Russia from the West since the 17th century—that provided object lessons in how to borrow without losing identity. This, too, served as an important basis for response, differentiating these countries from China or the Middle East, for example, where assumptions of cultural superiority limited openness to the possibility of imitation.

Neither Russia nor Japan generated massive change during the first half of the 19th century. Russia responded to the tide of political revolution in the West by tightening tsarist controls, expanding the secret police, and imprisoning or exiling intellectuals eager to copy Western political ideas. Their system of serfdom remained rigorous, with work service increased to spur grain production for export in a highly agricultural economy. The early 1800s were relatively uneventful in Japan, though the shogunate had recurrent difficulties in raising sufficient tax revenue. Most intellectual activity centered on various schools of Confucianism, urging attention to traditional values and obedience to authority. Only the so-called Dutch school, formed around translators who dealt with Dutch merchants in the port of Nagasaki (Japan's only contact with the outside world), pushed for a cultural reorientation, calling for attention to the scientific and medical advances that were occurring in the West. Education expanded rapidly in the first part of the century, via private Confucian or Buddhist schools, reaching well beyond the elite.

Both Japan and Russia received rude reminders of the cost of their cautious policies during the 1850s, when the imperialistic West drove home its growing superiority in power over all societies that were not industrializing—that is, over literally all the other civilizations in the world. Russia, continuing its policy of territorial expansion in central Asia, had won a war with the Turkish Ottoman Empire in 1853 and claimed a big chunk of territory in the Crimea, north of the Black Sea. Britain and France objected to these gains, wanting to advance their own interests in the Middle East and, in Britain's case, to prevent any Great Power from getting too close to its holdings in India. The ensuing Crimean War, 1854–1856, was fought literally in Russia's backyard, yet the Western nations won, forcing Russia to return most of its Crimean gains to the Turks. The Western edge was industrial: With the factories to produce modern equipment and the ships to send them expeditiously, Britain and France were able to beat back the tsarist forces. Russian leadership reluctantly concluded that the time had come for major reforms that would open the possibility for economic change.

Japan's rude awakening began when a U.S. fleet sailed into Tokyo Harbor in 1853 and demanded that the nation open its markets to Western goods. Other fleets followed, from Britain as well as the United States, and some violence occurred as Westerners began to enter Japan. The crisis triggered internal unrest in Japan, with some aristocrats urging that Japan do its best to keep Westerners out and other samurai arguing for major reforms that would allow Japan to retain independence through change. Fighting between the two groups broke out in 1866, with reform-minded samurai arming themselves with surplus weapons from the American Civil War. The conservatives around the shogun were finally defeated, and with a restored emperor (long a symbol of legitimacy but now emerging as a political actor) Japan embarked on a major period of reform in 1868—the onset of the Meiji era, from the formal title for the new emperor, "enlightened one."

REFORMS IN RUSSIA, 1861–1914

The cornerstone of Russia's reform structure involved freeing the masses of serfs, a process necessary to make Russia's social structure more like that of the West (where a lighter manorial system had been fully removed some decades before) and, above all, to increase the mobility of labor. The final decision to emancipate the serfs, in 1861, came at roughly the same time that the United States decided to free slaves. Neither slavery nor rigorous serfdom suited the economic needs of a society seeking an independent position in Western-dominated world trade.

In some ways the emancipation of the serfs was more generous than the liberation of slaves in the Americas. Although aristocrats retained part of the land, including the most fertile holdings, the serfs got most of it—in contrast to slaves, who received their freedom but nothing else. Russian emancipation, however, was careful to preserve essential aristocratic power; the tsar was not interested in destroying the nobility, who remained his

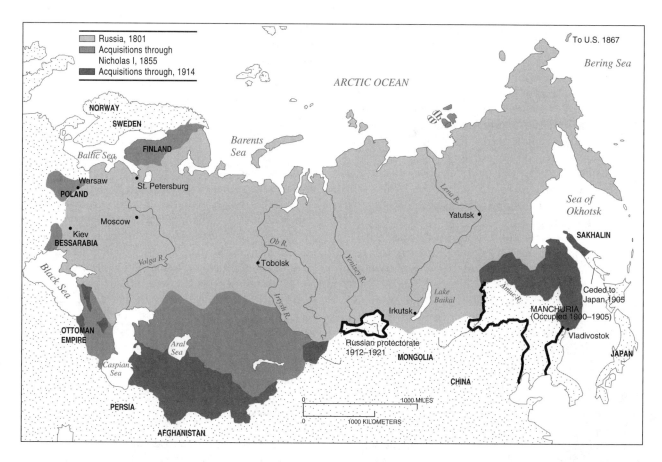

Russian Expansion, 1815–1914

most reliable political ally and the source of most bureaucrats. Even more, emancipation was designed to retain the tight grip of the tsarist state. The serfs obtained no new political rights at a national level. They were still tied to their villages until they could pay for the land they were given—the redemption money going to the aristocrats to help preserve this class. High redemption payments, in addition to state taxes that increased as Russia sought funds to build railroads and factories, kept most Russian peasants miserably poor. Peasant uprisings became more common as hopes for a brighter future now seemed dashed by the limits of change.

To be sure, the reform movement did not end with emancipation. Alexander II introduced a host of further measures in the 1860s and early 1870s. New law codes reduced traditional punishments now that serfs were legally free in the eyes of the law (though subject to important transitional restrictions). The tsar created local political councils, the *zemstvoes,* that had a voice in regulating roads, schools, and other regional policies. The councils, however, had no influence on national policy; the tsar resolutely maintained his own authority and that of his extensive bureaucracy. Another important area of change was the army, where the Crimean War had shown the need for reform. Some strides were made also in providing state-sponsored basic education, though schools spread unevenly.

The move toward industrialization was part of the wider process of change. The tsar's government was not always in agreement over industrialization goals, with some conservatives rightly fearing the impact of economic change on the existing social and political structure. On the whole, however, state support for industrialization continued even after the reform era ended in the late 1870s. And state support was vital, for Russia lacked a preexisting middle class and substantial capital; state enterprises had to make up part of the gap, in the tradition of economic activity that went back to Peter the Great.

The first step toward industrialization came with railroads, a clear necessity for military and political coordination as well as economic development in the vast land. Russia began to create an extensive railroad network in the 1870s. The establishment of the trans-Siberian railroad, which connected European Russia with the Pacific, was the crowning achievement of this drive when it was substantially completed by the end of the 1890s. The railroad boom directly stimulated expansion of Russia's iron and coal sectors.

By the 1880s, when Russia's railroad network had almost quintupled compared to 1860, modern factories were beginning to spring up in Moscow, St. Petersburg, and several Polish cities, and an urban working class was growing apace. Printing factories and metalworking shops greatly expanded the skilled artisanry in the cities, while huge new works in metallurgy and textiles created a still newer, semiskilled industrial labor force recruited from the troubled countryside.

Under Count Sergei Witte, minister of finance from 1892 to 1903 and an ardent economic modernizer, the government enacted high tariffs to protect new Russian industry, improved its banking system, and encouraged Western investors to build great factories with advanced technology. Witte and others were confident that strong government controls could keep the foreigners in line rather than converting Russia into a new imperialist playground, and certainly foreign influence over basic government policy was not extensive. Although the foreign presence and foreign profit taking created resentments from workers and conservatives alike, there was some clear payoff. By 1900, Russia had surged to rank fourth in the world in steel production and was second to the United States in the newer area of petroleum production and refining. Russian textile output was also impressive. Longstanding Russian economic lags were beginning to yield, though Russia's industrial revolution remained in its early stages.

Changes in Russia produced various reactions. The most important, a new wave of popular protest, set the basis for later revolution. But a new conservatism was also important. Many Russian intellectuals urged Russia to resist becoming like the West, which they saw as too secular, materialistic, disorderly, and individualistic. Russian values, they argued, were superior. The effort to preserve and idealize a separate identity from the West was an important part of the process of change, and it would show up in other parts of the world as well during the 20th century.

PROTEST AND REVOLUTION

A rising tide of unrest accompanied Russia's period of transformation. The reforms of Alexander II as well as economic change with the greater population mobility it involved, helped encourage demands by minority nationalists in the great empire. Intellectuals explored the cultural traditions of Ukrainians and other groups.

This cultural nationalism could lead to political demands, particularly when state power, through military recruitment and school expansion, was beginning to increase. Nationalist beliefs were initially imported from western Europe, but here, and elsewhere in eastern Europe, they encouraged divisive minority agitation of a sort that multinational states, such as Russia or Austria-Hungary, found very difficult to handle. Nationalist pressures were not the main problem in Russia, but in combination with other kinds of protest and given Russia's mainstream nationalist insistence on the distinctive superiorities of a Russian tradition, they did cause tensions.

Social protest was more vigorous still, heightened by not only the limitations of reform but also industrialization itself. Peasant discontent was not a constant force, but it continued to burst forth. Recurrent famines regularly provoked uprising. Peasants deeply resented redemption payments and taxes and frequently attacked and burned the records that indicated what they "owed" for the land. Peasants' sense of natural justice, heightened by population pressure, also turned them against aristocratic estates.

Many educated Russians, including some aristocrats, also clamored for revolutionary change. Two strands developed. Although not extremely aggressive, many business and professional people began to seek a fuller political voice and new rights, such as greater freedom in the schools and press; they thus argued for liberal reforms. At the same time, a group of radical *intelligentsia* (a Russian term denoting articulate intellectuals as a class) became increasingly active, building on earlier intellectual discontent. This kind of intellectual radicalism, capable of motivating outright terrorism, would characterize other societies caught in uncompleted change during the 20th century. The goals and motives of the Russian intelligentsia varied, but in general they wanted political freedom and deep social reform while maintaining a Russian culture different from that of the West, which they saw as hopelessly plutocratic and materialistic. Their radicalism may have stemmed from the demanding task they set themselves: simultaneously to attack key Russian institutions while building a new society that would not reproduce the injustices and crippling limitations of the Western world.

Not surprisingly, the recurrent waves of violent protest sponsored by radical intellectuals and students merely strengthened the tsarist regime's resolve to avoid further political change, in what became a vicious circle in 19th-century Russian politics. By the late 1870s Alexander II was retreating from his reform interest, fearing that change was getting out of hand. Censorship of newspapers and political meetings tightened; many dissidents were arrested and sent to Siberia. Alexander II was assassinated by a terrorist bomb in 1881, after a series of botched attempts. His successors, while escalating the effort to industrialize, continued to oppose further political reform. New measures of repression were also directed against minority nationalities, partly to dampen their unrest and partly to gain the support of upper-class conservatives who were wary of the industrialization process and could be satisfied only by vigorous backing for Russian dominance in language and culture. The Poles and other nationalities were carefully supervised. Russian-language instruction was forced on other people, such as the Ukrainians. Persecution of the large Jewish minority was stepped up, resulting in many executions—called *pogroms*—and seizures of property; as a consequence, many Russian Jews emigrated.

By the 1890s the protest currents were complemented by two other developments. In the first place, Marxist doctrines spread from the Western socialist movement to a segment of the Russian intelligentsia. One of the most active Marxist leaders was Vladimir Ilyich Ulyanov. Lenin, as he was known, came from a bureaucratic family; his brother had been killed by the political police. Lenin introduced important innovations in Marxist theory to make it more appropriate for the Russian scene. He argued that the spread of international capitalism was leading to the development of a proletariat worldwide in advance of industrialization. Russia, then, could have a proletarian revolution without going through a distinct middle-class phase. Lenin also insisted on the importance of disciplined revolutionary cells that could maintain doctrinal purity and effective action even amid severe police repression. Small but dedicated revolutionary cadres, not the mass electioneering of the Western socialist parties whose revisionism Lenin detested, would be the path to the future. Lenin's approach animated the group of Russian Marxists known as *Bolsheviks*, or majority party; ironically, however, they were a minority in the Russian-Marxist movement as a whole, much of which remained more wedded to the idea of an initial middle-class revolution. The Leninist approach proved ideal for Russian conditions.

Working-class unrest in the cities developed apace with the new currents among the intelligentsia. Russian workers became far more radical than their Western counterparts. They formed unions and conducted strikes—all illegal—but many of them also had firm political goals in mind. Their radicalism stemmed partly from rural unrest, for those new workers pulled in peasant grievances against the existing order. They stemmed partly from the severe conditions of early industrialization, exacerbated by large factories and frequent foreign ownership. Although many workers were not linked to any particular doctrine, some became interested in one of the revolutionary agendas—including bolshevism—and they were urged on by passionate organizers.

The Revolution of 1905

Military defeats in 1904 and 1905 finally lit this tinderbox. Russia had maintained its expansionist foreign policy through the later 19th century, in part because of tradition and in part because diplomatic success might draw the venom from some internal unrest. Russia also wanted to match the imperialist strides of the Western powers. A war with the Ottoman Empire in the 1870s brought substantial gains, which were then pushed back at the insistence of France and Britain. Russia also successfully aided the creation of new Slavic nations in the Balkans, such as Serbia and Bulgaria, the "little Slavic brothers" that filled nationalist hearts with pride. Some conservative writers even talked in terms of a Pan-Slavic movement that would unite the Slavic people, under Russian leadership of course. Russia participated vigorously in other Middle Eastern and central Asia areas. Russia and Britain both increased their influence in Persia and Afghanistan, reaching some uneasy truces that divided spheres of activity early in the 20th century. Russia was also active in China. The development of the trans-Siberian railroad encouraged Russia to incorporate some northern portions of Manchuria, violating the 18th-century Amur River

DOCUMENT

Conditions Under Russian Industrialization

Russia passed several laws protecting workers, but enforcement was minimal. The Ministry of Finance established a factory inspectorate in the 1880s, which dutifully reported on conditions; these reports usually were ignored. The following passages deal with a number of Moscow factories in the 1880s.

> In the majority of factories there are no special quarters for the workers. This applies to workers in paper, wool, and silk finishing. Skilled hand craftsmen like brocade weavers can earn good wages, and yet most of them sleep on or under their looms, for lack of anything else. Only in a few weaving factories are there special sleeping quarters, and these are provided not for the weavers, but for other workers—the winders and dyers, etc. Likewise, the velveteen cutters almost always sleep on the tables where they work. This habit is particularly unhealthy, since the work areas are always musty and the air is saturated with dye fumes—sometimes poisonous ones. Carpenters also generally sleep on their workbenches. In bastmatting factories, workers of both sexes and all ages sleep together on pieces and mats of bast which are often damp. Only the sick workers in these bast factories are allowed to sleep on the single stove. . . . Work at the mill never stops, day or night. There are two 12-hour shifts a day, which begin at 6:00 A.M. and 6:00 P.M. The men have a half-hour for breakfast (8:30–9:00) and one hour for dinner (1:00–2:00).
>
> The worst violations of hygienic regulations were those I saw in most of the flax-spinning mills where linen is produced. . . . Although in western Europe all the dust-producing carding and combing machines have long been covered and well ventilated, I saw only one Russian linen mill where such a machine was securely covered. Elsewhere, the spools of these machines were completely open to the air, and the scutching apparatus is inadequately ventilated. . . .
>
> In many industrial establishments the grounds for fines and the sizes of fines are not fixed in advance. The factory rules may contain only one phrase like the following: "Those found violating company rules will be fined *at the discretion of the manager.*" The degree of arbitrariness in the determination of fines, and thus also in the determination of the worker's wages, was unbelievably extreme in some factories. In Podolsk, for instance, in factories No. 131 and No. 135, there is a ten-ruble forfeit for leaving the factory before the expiration of one's contract. But as applied, this covers much more than voluntary breach of contract on the worker's part. This fine is exacted from every worker who for any reason has to leave the factory. Cases are known of persons who have had to pay this fine three times. Moreover, fines are levied for so many causes that falling under a severe fine is a constant possibility for each

agreement. Russia also joined Western powers in obtaining long-term leases to Chinese territory during the 1890s.

These were important gains, but they did not satisfy growing Russian ambitions, and they also brought trouble. Russia now risked an overextension, as its diplomatic aspirations were not backed by increases in military power. The problem first came to a head in 1904. Japan, increasingly powerful in its own right, became worried about further Russian expansion in northern China and efforts to extend influence into Korea. War broke out in 1904. Against all expectation save Japan's, the Japanese won. Russia could not move its fleet quickly to the Pacific, and the Russian military organization in general proved too cumbersome to oppose more effective Japanese maneuvers. Japan gained the opportunity to move into Korea, as the balance of power in the Far East began to shift.

Unexpected defeat in war unleashed massive protests on the home front in the Revolution of 1905. Urban workers mounted well-organized general strikes designed above all for political gains. Peasants produced a tumultuous series of insurrections, while liberal groups also agitated. After first trying brutal police repression—which only infuriated the urban crowds—and worried about the reliability of the peasant-based army, the tsarist regime had to change course. It granted little to the workers, for new rights for unions and Marxist political parties were almost immediately removed—though not before worker organizations gained further ground. But liberals were wooed through the creation of a national parliament, the *duma*. And the minister Stolypin introduced an important series of reforms for the peasantry. The emancipation system was greatly loosened. Peasants gained greater freedom from redemption payments and village controls. They could buy and sell land quite liber-

worker. For instance, workers who for any reason came into the office in a group, instead of singly, would be fined one ruble. After a second offense, the transgressors would be dismissed—leaving behind, of course, the ten-ruble fine for breach of contract. In factory No. 135 the workers are still treated as serfs. Wages are paid out only twice a year, even then not in full but only enough to pay the workers' taxes (other necessities are supplied by the factory store). Furthermore this money is not given to the workers directly, but is sent by mail to their village elders and village clerks. Thus the workers are without money the year around. Besides they are also paying severe fines to the factory, and these sums will be subtracted from their wages at the final year-end accounting.

Extreme regulations and regimentation are very common in our factories—regulations entangle the workers at every step and burden them with more or less severe fines which are subtracted from their often already inadequate wages. Some factory administrators have become real virtuosos at thinking up new grounds for fines. A brief description of a few of the fines in factory No. 172 is an excellent example of this variety: On October 24, 1877, an announcement was posted of new fines to be set at the discretion of the office for 14 different cases of failure to maintain silence and cleanliness.

There were also dozens of minor fines prescribed for certain individual offenses: For example, on August 4, 1883, a huge fine of five rubles was set for singing in the factory courtyard after 9:30, or at any time in any unauthorized place. On June 3, 1881, a fine was to be levied from workers who took tea and sugar, bread, or any kind of foodstuffs into the weaving building, "in order to avoid breeding any insects or vermin." On May 14, 1880, a fine was set for anyone who wrote with pencil, chalk, or anything else on the walls in the dyeing or weaving buildings.

Questions: What were the worst features of Russian factories? Were conditions worse than in western Europe during early industrialization, and if so in what ways and why? (Relatedly, what conditions probably were common in the first stages of factory industry everywhere?) How did working conditions and management attitudes help create a revolutionary mood among Russian workers? Think also about the nature of this source. Why would a conservative government sponsor such a critical report? What does the report suggest about tensions at the top of Russian society, between government and business? Would a conservative government be more likely to undertake this kind of inquiry than the more reform-minded regime that had existed a decade earlier? What do you think the results of such a report would be in the Russian context, or indeed in any early industrial context?

Source: From Basil Dmytrishyn ed., *Imperial Russia: A Sourcebook, 1700–1917* (New York: Holt, Rinehart & Winston, 1967), v. II, pp. 246–248.

ally. The goal here was to create a stratified, market-oriented peasantry in which successful farmers would move away from the peasant masses, becoming rural capitalists. Indeed, peasant unrest did die down, and a minority of aggressive entrepreneurs, called *kulaks*, began to increase agricultural production and buy additional land. Yet the overall reform package quickly came unglued. Not only were workers' rights withdrawn, triggering a new series of strikes and underground activities, but also the duma was progressively stripped of power. Nicholas II, a weak man who was badly advised, simply could not surrender the tradition of autocratic rule, and the duma became a hollow institution, representing and satisfying no one. Police repression also resumed, creating new opponents for the regime.

Pressed in the diplomatic arena by the closing of the Far Eastern theater through Japanese advance, yet eager to counter paralyzing internal pressures by some foreign policy success, the Russian government turned once again to the Ottoman Empire and the Balkans. Various stratagems to acquire new rights of access to the Mediterranean and to back Slavic allies in the Balkans yielded no concrete results, but they did stir the pot in this vulnerable area and helped lead to World War I. And this war, in which Russia participated in order to maintain its diplomatic standing and live up to the billing of Slavic protector while hoping for new territorial gains, brought on one of the great revolutions of modern times.

JAPAN: REFORM, INDUSTRIALIZATION, AND RISE TO GLOBAL POWER

Like Russia, Japan faced new pressures from the West during the 1850s, in the form of the demands for more open trade and admission of foreigners rather than

Early Russian industrialization is depicted in this 1888 photo of the commercial department of the Abrikosova and Son factory.

outright military conflict. Japan's response was more direct than Russia's and, on the whole, more immediately successful. Despite its long history of isolation, Japanese society was better adapted than Russia's to the challenge of industrial change. Market forms were more extensive, reaching into peasant agriculture; levels of literacy were higher. Nevertheless, Japan had to rework many of its institutions during the final decades of the 19th century, and the process produced significant strain. The result, by 1900, was different both from purely Western patterns and from the more obvious tensions of Russian society.

The Meiji government, which had been established in 1868 mainly in response to the threats posed by Western intrusion, promptly set about abolishing feudalism. In 1871 it replaced the domains of the feudal lords with a system of nationally appointed prefects (carefully chosen from different regions). Political power was effectively centralized and, from this base in turn, the Meiji rulers—the emperor and his close advisors drawn from loyal segments of the upper *samurai*, or military classes—began to expand the power of the state to effect economic and social change.

Soon after these reforms were initiated the Japanese government sent samurai officials to western Europe and the United States to study economics, political institutions, and technology. These samurai, deeply impressed by what they saw, pulled back from their earlier antiforeign mood and gained increasing voice over domestic development, accompanied by a diplomatic policy that carefully avoided antagonizing the Western powers.

Political Change

The restructuring of the state and its new policy commitments were accompanied by a fundamental improvement in government finance. Between 1873 and 1876 the Meiji ministers introduced a true social revolution, abolishing the samurai class and the stipends this group had received. The samurai were compensated with government-backed bonds, but these decreased in value, and most samurai became impoverished. The tax on agriculture was converted to a wider tax, payable in money. The government also introduced an army based on national conscription, and by 1878 the nation was militarily secure.

The final capping of the process of political reconstruction came in the 1890s, when Meiji leaders traveled abroad to gather suggestions about appropriate modern political forms. In 1884 they created a new conservative

A drawing of the first meeting of the Japanese Parliament in 1890. Note the Western dress and layout of the legislative or diet chamber.

nobility, stocked by former aristocrats and Meiji leaders, that would operate a British-style House of Peers. Next the bureaucracy was reorganized, insulated from political pressures, and opened to talent on the basis of civil service examinations. The bureaucracy simultaneously began to expand rapidly; it grew from 29,000 officials in 1890 to 72,000 in 1908. Finally, the constitution, issued in 1889, ensured major prerogatives for the emperor along with limited powers for the lower house of the Diet (as the new Parliament was called), which was elected by the wealthiest 5 percent of the male population.

Japan's political structure thus came to involve centralized imperial rule, wielded by a handful of Meiji advisors, combined with limited representative institutions copied from the West. This combination gave great power to an oligarchy of wealthy business leaders and former nobles, who influenced the emperor and also pulled strings within Parliament. Political parties arose, but a coherent oligarchy overrode their divisions into the 20th century. Japan thus followed its new policy of imitating the West, but it retained its own identity. It devised a structure that appeased many former samurai by giving them a voice in Parliament, while also creating the effective central government necessary to reorganize military and economic affairs. Finally, the Japanese political solution compared interestingly to Russian institutions after the reforms of Alexander II. Both states were centralized and authoritarian, but Japan had incorporated business leaders into its governing structure, whereas Russia defended a more traditional social elite.

Japan's Industrial Revolution

As Japan shaped its new political system, it also focused attention on creating the conditions necessary for industrialization. The government established new banks to fund growing trade and to provide capital for industry. State-built railroads spread across the country, and the islands were connected by rapid steamers. The market emphasis in agriculture increased, as new methods were introduced to raise output to feed the people of the growing cities.

Government initiative dominated manufacturing not only in the creation of transportation networks but also in state operation of mines, shipyards, and metallurgical plants. Scarce capital and the unfamiliarity of new technology seemed to compel state direction—as occurred in

Russia at the same time. Government control also helped check the many foreign advisors early Japanese industry required, and here Japan maintained closer supervision than its Russian neighbor. Japan established the Ministry of Industry in 1870, and it quickly became one of the key government agencies, setting overall economic policy and operating specific sectors. By the 1880s, model shipyards, arsenals, and factories, though not yet capable of substantial output, provided many Japanese with experience in new technology and disciplined works systems. Finally, by expanding technical training and education, setting up banks and post offices, and regularizing commercial laws, the government provided a structure within which Japan could develop on many fronts. Measures in this area largely copied established practices in the West but with adaptation suitable for Japanese conditions; thus, well before any European university, Tokyo Imperial University had a faculty of agriculture.

Private enterprise quickly played a role in Japan's growing economy, particularly in the vital textiles sector. Some business leaders came from older merchant families, though some of the great houses had been ruined along with the financial destruction of the samurai class. There were also newcomers, some rising from peasant ranks. Shuibuzawa Eiichi, for example, born a peasant, became a merchant and then an official of the Finance Ministry. He turned to banking in 1873, using other people's money to set up cotton-spinning mills and other textile operations. Chemicals, construction materials, and food products (including beer) were other areas dominated by private entrepreneurs, many of whom, however, had government experience. By the 1890s huge new industrial combines, later known as *zaibatsu,* were being formed as the result of accumulations of capital and far-flung merchant and industrial operations.

By 1900 the Japanese economy was fully launched in an industrial revolution. It rested on a political and social structure different from that of Russia, one that had in most respects changed more substantially. Japan's success in organizing industrialization, including its careful management of foreign advice and models, proved to be one of the great developments of later 19th-century history. Toward the end of the 20th century many Americans, pressed by Japanese competition, would fondly imagine that Japan's economic success was due to U.S. guidance and generosity after 1945. The fact was that industrialization came about through largely Japanese efforts, as indeed must be the case given the fundamental transformation involved.

It is important to keep these early phases of Japanese industrialization in perspective. Pre–World War I Japan was far from the West's equal. It depended on substantial imports of Western equipment and also of raw materials such as coal—for Japan was, for industrial purposes, a resource-poor nation. Although economic growth and careful government policy allowed Japan to avoid Western domination, Japan was newly dependent on world economic conditions and often at a disadvantage in the process. Exports were vital to pay for machine and resource imports, and these in turn required hordes of inexpensive labor. Silk production grew rapidly, the bulk of it destined for Western markets. Much of this production was based on poorly paid women workers laboring at home or in sweatshops, not in mechanized factories. Correspondingly the Japanese economy, in this fragile transition period, had little leeway for expansive social measures. A few big companies provided social organizations and other benefits for their employees, which helped maintain low-wage policies but also translated group-loyalty traditions from the feudal past. Most workers, however, were given a poor salary and nothing more. Efforts at labor organization or other means of protest were greeted by vigorous repression. This exploitative mood was not a permanent feature of Japanese industrialization, but it was widely characteristic of this first period, which meant that the social impact of Japan's industrial revolution had much in common with its earlier counterpart in the West or in contemporary Russia.

In some respects Japan's early industrialization was distinctive, compared with either the West or Russia. The need to rely on low-paid labor to produce manufacturing exports had some similarity to Western practice during the 18th century, but the fact that Japan had no prior capital built up from earlier foreign trade sharpened this characteristic. The export momentum also differed from the Russian case, for Russia's industrialization could utilize earnings from grain exports. Japan's industry was not geared in that direction. The Russian focus rested on heavy industry and production for domestic use, including government purchases for rails and military expansion. Japan produced ships and heavy industrial goods and built up its military forces, but because of its lack of domestic energy sources, it was inevitably more involved in a vigorous drive to sell manufactured goods abroad, even though this was a very new enterprise for the Japanese. These differences between Japanese and Russian industrial patterns would have ongoing implications in the 20th century, affecting relationships with the wider world as well.

The Separate Paths of Japan and China

Japan's ability to change in response to new Western pressure contrasted strikingly with the sluggishness of Chinese reactions into the 20th century. The contrast draws particular attention because China and Japan had been part of the same civilization orbit for so long, which means that some of the assets Japan possessed in dealing with change were present in China as well. Indeed by the mid-19th century Japan turned out to benefit from having become more like China in key respects during the Tokugawa period. The link between Chinese and Japanese traditions should not be overdrawn, of course, and earlier differences help explain the divergence that opened so clearly in the later 19th century. A problem of interpretation remains, however, as the East Asian world now split apart, with Japan seizing eagerly on Chinese weakness to target a series of attacks from the 1890s to 1945—which of course merely made China's troubles worse.

Japan and China had both chosen some degree of isolation from larger world currents from about 1600 until the West forced new openings between 1830 and 1860. Japan's isolation was more complete. Both countries changed less rapidly than the West between 1500 and 1800, which was why Western industrialization caught them unprepared. China's power and wealth roused Western greed and interference first, which gave Japan some relative leeway.

China, however, surpassed Japan in some areas that should have aided it in reacting to the Western challenge. Its leadership, devoted to Confucianism, was more thoroughly secular and bureaucratic in outlook. There was no need to brush aside otherworldly commitments or feudal distractions in order to deal with the West's material and organizational power. Government centralization, still an issue in Japan, had a long tradition in China. China had also traded very advantageously with the West until the 19th century. With a rich history of technological innovation and scientific discovery in its past as well, China might appear to be a natural to lead the Asian world in responding to the West.

That role, however, fell to Japan. Several aspects of Japanese tradition turned out to give it a flexibility that China lacked. It already knew the benefits of imitation, which China, save for a period of attraction to Buddhism, had never acknowledged. Japan's slower government growth had allowed a stronger, more autonomous merchant tradition, even as both societies became more com-

mercial in the 17th and early 18th centuries. Feudal traditions, though declining under the Tokugawa shogunate, also limited the heavy hand of government controls while stimulating some sense of competitiveness—as in the West. China's government, in contrast, probably tried to control too much by the 18th century and squashed initiative in the process.

China was also oppressed by massive population growth from the 17th century onward. This population pressure consumed great energy, leaving scant capital for more fundamental economic initiatives. Japan's population stability into the 19th century, though a sign of economic sluggishness, was more manageable and pressed resources less severely. Japan's island status made the nation more sensitive to Western naval pressures.

Finally, China and Japan were enmeshed in somewhat different trajectories when the Western challenge intruded in the mid-19th century. China was suffering one of its recurrent dynastic declines. Government became less efficient, intellectual life stagnated, and popular unrest surged. Quite possibly a cycle of renewal would have followed, with a new dynasty seizing more vigorous reins. But Western interference distorted this process, complicating reform and creating various new discontents that ultimately overturned the imperial office. China's sluggish leadership, convinced of the nation's superiority, finally provoked reformers to radical action as they saw their country torn apart by foreign imperialists.

Japan, in contrast, maintained considerable political and economic vigor into the 19th century. There were some new political challenges and an increase of peasant revolt. Whereas by the late 19th century China ironically needed Western guidance simply to handle such bureaucratic affairs as tariff collection or repression of peasant rebellion, Japan suffered no such breakdown of authority, using foreign advisors far more selectively.

Once a different pattern of response was established, every decade increased the gap. Western exploitation of Chinese assets as well as dilution of government power made conditions more chaotic, while Japanese strength steadily grew after a very brief period of uncertainty. By the 20th century the two nations were not only enemies—with Japan, for the first time, the stronger—but seemed to be in different orbits. Japan was an increasing industrial success, with a conservative state that would yield after World War II to a more fully parliamentary form. China, after decades of revolution, finally reached its 20th-century political solution, in communism.

Yet today, past the arrival of the 21st century, it becomes possible to wonder if East Asia was split as permanently as 19th- and early 20th-century developments had suggested. Japan's industrial lead remains, but China's economy is growing vigorously. Along with other innovations in Asia's Pacific Rim, a fruitful shared heritage continues to operate—a partly Confucian heritage quite different from that of the West but seemingly fully adaptable to the demands of economic change. And so Westerners begin to wonder if a Pacific century is about to dawn.

Questions: What civilization features had Japan and China shared before the 19th century? In what ways were Japanese political institutions more adaptable than Chinese institutions? Why was Russia also able to change earlier and more fundamentally than 19th-century China?

A Challenge: Comparison is an essential skill in dealing with world history. What characteristics did Japan and Russia share, that allowed them to respond more vigorously to the rise of Western power than China initially did? But also: how did Japanese and Russian responses differ?

Social and Economic Effects of Industrialization

The Industrial Revolution and the wider extensions of manufacturing and commercial agriculture, along with political change, had significant ramifications within Japanese culture and society. The government introduced a universal education system, providing primary schools for all. This education stressed science and technical subjects along with political loyalty to the nation and emperor. Elite students at the university level also emphasized science, many of them studying technical subjects abroad. The rapid assimilation of a scientific outlook built on the earlier secularization of Japanese elite culture, but it was a major new ingredient.

As in the West, industrialization altered social structure. Although an important group of aristocrats and people from the samurai warrior class entered the ranks of successful business leaders and officials, a new elite was formed that embraced leading entrepreneurs for the first time. Among the masses, a huge and growing propertyless class of urban workers endured low wages and high taxes, as Japanese leaders required profits and tax revenue to amass the capital needed for further investment. Japan's industrial success did not come easily as far as the lower classes were concerned. And although the new elite did not cultivate the luxurious lifestyle of Western business magnates, being content with lower profit rates, it did insist on retaining power. Unions and lower-class political parties began to emerge by 1900 but made only slow headway, and a militant socialist movement was outlawed. Periodic strike movements were brutally repressed, though a legacy of serious class bitterness remained.

Japanese society was also disrupted by massive population growth. Better nutrition and new medical provisions reduced death rates, and the upheaval of the rural masses cut into traditional restraints on births. The result was a steady population surge that strained Japanese resources and stability, though it also ensured an ongoing supply of low-cost labor.

Many Japanese copied Western fashions as part of the effort to become modern. Western-style haircuts replaced the samurai shaved head with a topknot—another example of the fascinating pattern of the Westernization of hair in world history. Western standards of hygiene spread, and the Japanese became enthusiastic tooth brushers and consumers of patent medicines. Japan also adopted the Western calendar and the metric system. Few Japanese converted to Christianity, however, and despite fads for Western popular culture, the Japanese managed to preserve an emphasis on their own values. Nevertheless, many conservatives lamented the changes that had occurred, setting up tensions that would long persist in Japan. Emphasis on nationalism and loyalty to the emperor helped preserve unity and motivation amid change, as Japanese virtues of obedience and harmony were touted over Western individualism.

Japanese family life retained many traditional emphases. The birthrate dropped as rapid population growth forced increasing numbers of people off the land. Meanwhile the rise of factory industry, separating work from home, made the labor of children less useful. Here was a trend, developed earlier in the West, that seems inseparable from successful industrialization. There were new signs of family instability as well. Many men moved to cities, leaving wives behind in rural manufacturing. The result, until legal changes made procedures more difficult, was the highest divorce rate in the world in 1900.

On the more traditional side, however, the Japanese were eager to maintain the inferiority of women in the home. The position of Western women repelled them. Japanese government visitors to the United States were appalled by what they saw as the bossy ways of women: "The way women are treated here is like the way parents are respected in our country." Standards of Japanese courtesy also contrasted with the more open and boisterous behavior of Westerners—particularly Americans. "Obscenity is inherent in the customs of this country," noted another samurai visitor to the United States.

Other basic features of Japanese life, including diet, were maintained in the face of Western influence. Certain Japanese religious values were also preserved. Buddhism lost some ground, though it remained important, but Shintoism, which appealed to the new nationalistic concerns with Japan's distinctive mission and the religious functions of the emperor, won new interests.

Japan's transformation had not brought the country to Western levels, and the Japanese remained intensely fearful for their independence. Economic change and the tensions as well as the power it generated did, however, produce a shift in Japanese foreign policy. With only one previous exception, the Japanese had never before been interested in territorial expansion, but by the 1890s they joined the ranks of imperialist powers. This shift was partly an imitation of Western models and at the same time an effort to prevent

Western encroachment. Imperialism also relieved some strains within Japanese society, giving displaced samurai a chance to exercise their military talents elsewhere and providing symbols of nationalist achievement for the populace as a whole. The Japanese economy also required access to markets and raw materials. Because Japan was poor in many basic materials, including coal and oil for energy, the pressure for expansion was particularly great.

In the quarrel for influence over Korea in 1894 and 1895, Japan's quick victory over China was a first step toward expansion. Japan convincingly demonstrated its new superiority over all other purely Asian powers. Humiliated by Western insistence that it abandon the Liaodong Peninsula it had just won, the Japanese planned a war with Russia as a means of striking out against the nearest European power. A 1902 alliance with Britain was an important sign of Japan's arrival as an equal nation in the Western-dominated world diplomatic system. The Japanese were also eager to dent Russia's growing strength in East Asia, after the development of the trans-Siberian railroad. Disputes over Russian influence in Manchuria and Japanese influence in Korea led to the Russo-Japanese War in 1904, which Japan won handily

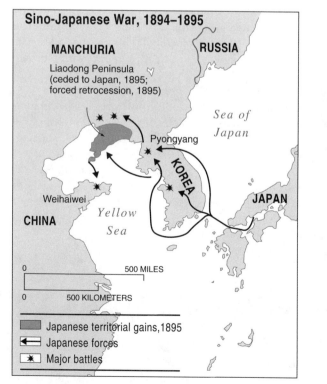

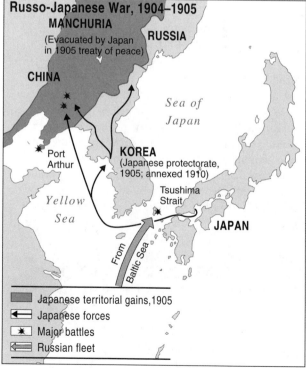

Japanese Colonial Expansion to 1914

on the basis of its superior navy. Japan annexed Korea in 1910; it was now not only a modern industrial power but a new imperialist power as well.

Japan, Russia, and World War I

The beginnings of serious industrialization in Russia and Japan and the unprecedented entry of Japan into world affairs contributed important new ingredients to the world diplomatic picture by the early 20th century. Developments in both countries, along with the rise of the United States, added to the growing sense of rivalry among the established Western powers. Japan's surge, and particularly its surprising military victories, promoted a fear in the West of a new "yellow peril" that should be opposed through greater imperialist efforts. Outright colonial acquisitions by the new powers added directly to the competitive atmosphere, particularly in the Far East. Japan, to be sure, was not yet a major world player, but it was beginning to make its muscle felt.

Furthermore, the strains of early industrialization, including the need to appease embittered conservative aristocrats as well as aggrieved masses, made both Russia and Japan increasingly dependent on diplomatic success. After 1912, for example, Japan faced growing political party competition in Parliament, with frequent if futile parliamentary defiance of the emperor's ministers. Massive popular protest added fuel to the fire as Japanese workers and peasants developed new political expectations and allegiances. It was in this setting that Japan joined the Allied side in World War I, hoping not for a significant military role but for the chance to seize German colonies in the Pacific—which it quickly gobbled up. Russia, of course, launched into the war from the outset as a central actor, as its narrowing diplomatic options combined with internal pressures to preclude any alternative. Japan and Russia were not unique in finding diplomacy affected by new domestic rifts—the Western industrial leaders faced some similar tensions—but they were unquestionably caught up in a new spiral.

CONCLUSION: RESPONSES TO THE WEST AND THE QUESTION OF AUTONOMY

Russia and Japan both reacted quickly to signs of the new Western power advantage. They realized that it was important to imitate some aspects of the West, including military technology and industrialization. They thus responded to Western example.

They did not, however, become Western, nor did they have any desire to do so. Conservatives in both societies found many Western features objectionable; the leading Russian revolutionaries wanted a new order but they also did not want it to be Western.

More fundamentally, even as they copied the West they developed distinctive combinations, blending imitation, tradition, and some new developments of their own. Changes in Japanese childhood illustrate this complexity. As we have seen, reformers quickly adopted aspects of Western education, including state-run schools for the masses (girls as well as boys) plus the new emphasis on science. Education helped lead to a broader revision of Japanese ideas about childhood, again influenced by Western thinking. By the 1900s Japan was developing special playgrounds for children, and a separate system of juvenile justice and reformatories, all based on new ideas about children's vulnerability and the importance of protecting children. These were far-reaching changes. But the Japanese carefully worked against introducing too much Western-style individualism among children. They insisted on traditional manners and group loyalty, and of course they preached the new mixture of nationalism and devotion to the emperor. In 1880 a memorandum to teachers, insisted that "Loyalty to the Imperial House, love of country, filial piety toward parents, respect for superiors, faith in friends . . . constitute the great path of human morality." This was not a Western recipe: imitation was bounded, combined with independent developments.

Finally, changes in Japan and Russia themselves constituted new forces in world history, alongside the more obviously important policies of the West. Both countries exercised new influence in China, and the two interacted with each other in novel ways. Japan's economic as well as military power would gain even more significance in the future, while Russia's response to social instability would have profound effects through the 20th century. The West helped galvanize these developments, but they gained a life of their own.

FURTHER READING

Several studies deal with Russian industrialization. W. Blackwell's *The Industrialization of Russia* (1982) provides a useful overview. Economic backwardness and latecomer reactions are taken up in A. Gerschenkron's *Economic Backwardness in Historical Perspective* (1962).

A number of historians have advanced understanding of Russia's workers. See R. Zelnik, *Labor and Society in Tsarist Russia, 1855–1870* (1971); Victoria Bonnell, ed., *The Russian Worker: Life and Labor Under the Tsarist Regime* (1983); and S. McCaffray, *The Politics of Industrialization: The Association of Southern Coal and Steel Producers, 1874–1914* (1996). R. Zelnik, *Law and Disorder on the Narova River: A Case Study of the Kreenholm Strike of 1872* (1995), is an interesting regional study. On rural conditions, see T. Emmons, *The Russian Landed Gentry and the Peasant Emancipation of 1861* (1968). Political agitation is discussed in A. B. Ulam's *Russia's Failed Revolution* (1981). Army service and protest form the subject of John Bushnell's *Mutiny Amid Repression: Russian Soldiers in the Revolution of 1905–1906* (1983). Barbara Engel's *Mothers and Daughters: Women of the Intelligentsia in Nineteenth Century Russia* (1983) takes up another vital topic. Finally, on popular culture, see Jeffrey Brooks's *When Russia Learned to Read: Literacy and Popular Culture* (1987). Rex Wade's The Russian Revolution, 1917 (2000) has excellent background material; see also Don Rawson, *Russian Rightists and the Revolution of 1905* (1995), and Robert Allen, Farm to Factory: A Reinterpretation of the Soviet Industrial Revolution (2003), again with background coverage.

For general coverage of Japan during this period, consult G. Akita's *Foundations of Constitutional Government in Modern Japan, 1868–1900* (1967) and W. G. Beasley's *The Meiji Restoration* (1973). On economic trends, see W. W. Lockwood, *The Economic Development of Japan* (1954).

Japanese industrial structure has received much recent attention from worried Americans. See J. C. Abegglen's *The Japanese Factory: Aspects of Its Social Organization* (1985). On culture, E. O. Reischauer's *Japan, the Story of a Nation* (1981) is usually readable, and M. Miyoshi's *Accomplices of Silence: The Modern Japanese Novel* (1974) is good. See also R. H. Myers and M. R. Peattie, eds., *The Japanese Colonial Empire, 1895–1945* (1984). Ann Waswo's *Modern Japanese Society, 1868–1994* (1996) is an accessible social and economic history. Andrew Gordon's *Labor and Imperial Democracy in Prewar Japan* (1991) is a political history that reveals the development of the labor movement along with the process of industrialization. Mikiso Hane's *Modern Japan: A Historical Survey* (1992) has a solid introduction, especially useful for its insights on the economically deprived, women, and minorities. See also Merle Goldman, ed., *Historical Perspectives on Contemporary East Asia* (2000) and Rudra Sil, *Managing Modernity: Work, Community and Authority in Late-Industrialization Japan and Russia* (2002).

ON THE WEB

The glories of Tsarist Russia are revealed by a virtual tour of the Alexander Palace at

http://www.alexanderplace.org/palace

However, the riches of the Tsars could not conceal the dismal world of the Russian peasantry whose lot was little improved by Russian economic modernization. The Crimean War receives treatment at

http://www.geocities.com/Broadway/Alley/5443/kerry .htm

a site that includes a history and audio file song of Irish soldiers who fought that conflict. Other sites focusing on documents, poems, photographic collections, and classroom activities include

http://www.crimeantexts.org.uk/
http://www.nationalcenter.org/ChargeoftheLightBrigade .html
http://www.loc.gov/rr/print/coll/251_fen.html
http://www.btinternet.com/~james.mckay/crimea01 .htm

Russian liberalism reached its high-water mark with the abolition of serfdom, an institution whose rise and demise is described at

http://www.yale.edu/lawweb/avalon/econ/koval6.htm

A copy of the Emancipation Manifesto can be viewed at

http://www.dur.ac.uk/~dml0www/emancipn.html

Subsequent economic reforms were pioneered by Count Sergei Witte, whose policies are discussed at

http://www.alexanderpalace.org/palace/wittebio.html
http://members.tripod.com/~american_almanac/witte92a .htm
http://www.spartacus.schoolnet.co.uk/RUSwitte.htm

which offers many links to related sites. Leon Trotsky's lively brief evaluation of Witte's place in history is reproduced at

http://www.marxists.org/archive/trotsky/works/1905/ ch10.htm

The failure of the Revolution of 1905

http://web.mit.edu/napoli/www/guided.html

to achieve any significant degree of political and social reform paved the way for those favoring more radical change, such as the Bolsheviks, led by Vladimir Ilyich Ulanov, whose life is examined at

http://www.marxists.org/archive/lenin/

http://www.soften.ktu.lt/~kaleck/Lenin/

which offers an audio file of a speech by Lenin.

Meiji Japan is surveyed at

http://www.japan-guide.com/e/e2130.html

A virtual tour of Meiji culture and politics is offered at

http://www.virtualmuseum.ca/Exhibitions/Meiji/
    english/html/index.html

This tour includes an examination of the Russo-Japanese War of 1905

http://www.virtualmuseum.ca/Exhibitions/Meiji/
    english/html/war3.html

that features rare lithographs and other illustrations.

Meiji life can be seen through contemporary woodblock art at

http://www.loc.gov/exhibits/ukiyo-e/
http://www.pbs.org/empires/japan/woodblock.html

where instructions are provided for making woodblock art. The life of Iwasaki Yataro, founder of Japanese industrial giant Mitsubishi, and his role in Japan's modernization are discussed at

http://www.mitsubishi.or.jp/e/h/his.html
http://www.mitsubishielectric.com/about/history.html

A key to understanding the process of modernization in Japan is the Constitution of the Empire of Japan (1889) which is reproduced at

http://history.hanover.edu/texts/1889con.html

A short essay exploring why Japan (and other Asian societies influenced by Confucian values) adapted rapidly to Western or modern industrial society can be found at

http://www.academiclibrary.com/view/History/2322
    .htm.

Chapter 3

Industrialization and Imperialism: The Making of a Global Colonial Order

A rather romantic depiction of the 1879 battle of Isandhlwana in the Natal province of South Africa. The battle demonstrated that, despite their superior firepower, the Europeans could be defeated by well-organized and determined African or Asian resistance forces. But like other well-publicized victories by Africa or Asian peoples over European or European-led armies, these defeats were soon avenged by even larger and better armed European forces that were dispatched into contested areas across the globe.

Chronology

1815	British annex Cape Town and surrounding area
1835	Decision to give state support for English education in India; English adopted as the language of Indian law courts
1836	Start of the Boers' Great Trek in South Africa
1850s	Boer republics established in the Orange Free State in Transvaal
1850s–1870s	Maori wars in New Zealand
1853	First railway line constructed in India
1853–1854	Perry Embassy to Japan
1857	Calcutta, Madras, and Bombay universities founded
1857–1858	"Mutiny" or Great Rebellion in north India
1867	Diamonds discovered in the Orange Free State
1869	Opening of the Suez Canal
1879	Zulu victory over British at Isandhlwana; Zulu defeat at Rourke's Drift
1882	British invasion of Egypt
1885	Indian National Congress Party founded in India; gold discovered in the Transvaal
1894–1895	Sino-Japanese War; Japan annexes Korea
1898	British-French crisis over Fashoda in the Sudan; U.S. annexation of Hawaiian Islands; Spanish-American War; U.S. annexation of Puerto Rico and the Philippines
1899–1902	Anglo-Boer War in South Africa
1890s	Partition of East Africa
1904–1905	Russo-Japanese War
1910	Japan annexes Korea
1914	Outbreak of World War I

INTRODUCTION

The process of industrialization that began to transform western European societies in the last half of the 18th century fundamentally altered the nature and impact of European overseas expansion. In the centuries of expansion before the industrial era, Europeans went overseas because they sought material things they could not produce themselves and because they felt threatened by powerful external enemies. They initially sought precious metals, for which they traded in Africa, and waged wars of conquest to control the Americas. In the Americas, they also seized land on which they could grow high-priced commercial crops such as sugar and coffee. In Asia, European traders and adventurers sought either manufactured goods, such as cotton and silk textiles (produced mainly in India, China, and the Middle East), or luxury items, such as spices, that would improve the living standards of the aristocracy and rising middle classes.

In the Americas, Africa, and Asia, missionaries from Roman Catholic areas, such as Spain and Portugal, sought to convert what were regarded as "heathen" peoples to Christianity. Both the wealth gained from products brought home from overseas and the souls won for Christ were viewed as ways of strengthening Christian Europe in its long struggle with the Muslim empires that threatened Europe from the south and east.

In the industrial era, from roughly 1800 onward, the things that Europeans sought in the outside world as well as the source of the insecurities that drove them there changed dramatically. Raw materials—metals, vegetable oils, dyes, cotton, and hemp—needed to feed the machines of Europe, not spices or manufactured goods, were the main products the Europeans sought overseas. Industrialization began to transform Europe into the manufacturing center of the world for the first time. As a result, overseas markets for machine-made European products became a key concern of those who pushed for colonial expansion.

Christian missionaries, by then as likely to be Protestant as Roman Catholic, still tried to win converts overseas. But unlike the rulers of Portugal and Spain in the early centuries of expansion, European leaders in the industrial age rarely took initiatives overseas to promote Christian proselytization. In part, this reflected the fact that western Europe itself was no longer seriously threatened by the Muslims or by any other non-European people. The fears that fueled European imperialist expansion in the industrial age arose from internal rivalries between the European powers themselves. Overseas peoples might resist the European advance, but different European national groups feared each other far more than even the largest non-European empires.

The contrast between European expansion in the preindustrial era and in the age of industrialization was also reflected in the extent to which the Europeans were able to "go ashore," or build true empires overseas. In the early centuries of overseas expansion, European conquests were concentrated in the Americas, where long isolation had left the indigenous peoples particularly vulnerable to the technology and diseases of the expansive Europeans. In much of the rest of the world, European traders and conquistadores were confined largely to the sea-lanes, islands, and coastal enclaves. Now, industrial technology and the techniques of organization and discipline associated with the increasing mechanization of the West gave the Europeans the capacity to reach and infiltrate any foreign land. From the populous, highly centralized, and technologically sophisticated Chinese Empire to small bands of hunters and gatherers struggling to survive in the harsh environment of Tierra del Fuego on the southern tip of South America, few peoples were remote enough to be out of reach of the steamships and railways that carried the Europeans to and across all continents of the globe. No culture was strong enough to remain untouched by the European drive for global dominance in this era. None could long resist the profound changes unleashed by European conquest and colonization.

The shift from the preindustrial to the industrial phase of European overseas expansion was gradual and cumulative, extending roughly from 1750 to 1850. By the middle decades of the 19th century, few who were attuned to international events could doubt that a watershed had been crossed. The first section of this chapter will explore the forces in Europe and the outside world that led to the great burst of imperialist expansion, which was a dominant feature of global history in the last decades of the 19th century. The middle sections will examine the patterns of European conquest and rule in the tropical dependencies in Asia, Africa, and Oceania, which made up the bulk of European empires in this era. The third section is focused on different types of settler colonization, which involved much higher levels of European migration to areas colonized overseas than was the case in the tropical dependencies.

INDUSTRIAL RIVALRIES AND THE PARTITION OF THE WORLD, 1870–1914

The spread of the Industrial Revolution from the British Isles to continental Europe and North America greatly increased the already considerable advantages the Western powers possessed in manufacturing capacity and the ability to wage war relative to all other peoples and civilizations. These advantages resulted in ever higher levels of European and American involvement in the outside world and culminated in the virtually unchallenged domination of the globe by industrial nations or empires. By the last decades of the 19th century, Russia and Japan had joined the Euro-American expansionist powers in the quest for colonial territories. Beginning in the 1870s, rival European powers had embarked on an orgy of overseas conquests that had reduced most of Africa, Asia, and the Pacific Ocean region to colonial possessions by the time of the outbreak of World War I in 1914. In these empires, there were major shifts from the early stages of European expansion in the social interaction between colonizers and subject peoples, in the means by which the industrial powers extracted wealth from their overseas possessions, and in the conquerors' attitudes toward the diffusion of what they regarded as their superior ideas and institutions.

Although science and industry gave the great powers capacity to run roughshod over the rest of the world, they also heightened economic competition and political rivalries between them. In the first half of the 19th century, industrial Britain, with its seemingly insurmountable naval superiority, was left alone to dominate overseas trade and empire building. By the last decades of the century, Belgium, France, and especially Germany, the United States, and increasingly Japan were challenging Britain's industrial supremacy and actively building (or in the case of France, adding to) colonial empires of their own. Many of the political leaders of these expansive nations viewed the possession of colonies as an essential attribute of states that aspired to status as great powers. Colonies were also seen as insurance against raw material shortages and the loss of overseas market outlets to industrial rivals in Europe and North America as well as Japan.

The concerns of the political leaders of industrial or industrializing nations were thus both political and economic. The last decades of the 19th century were a period of recurring economic depressions, especially in Europe and the United States. The leaders of the newly industrialized nations had little experience in handling the overproduction and unemployment that came with each of these economic crises. They were understandably deeply concerned about the social unrest, and in some cases what appeared to them to be stirrings of revolution, that each phase of depression engendered. Some political theorists at the time also argued that as destinations to which unemployed workers might migrate and as potential markets for surplus goods, colonial possessions could serve as safety valves to release the pressure built up in times of industrial slumps.

During the era of the scramble for colonial possessions, political leaders in Europe, the United States, and Japan played a much more prominent role in decisions to annex overseas territories than they had earlier—even in the first half of the 19th century. This was due in part to improved communications. Telegraphs and railways not only made it possible to transmit orders much more rapidly from the capitals of industrial nations to men on the spot in the tropics, but also allowed ministers back home to play a much more active role in the ongoing governance of the colonies. But more than politicians were involved in late 19th-century decisions to add to the colonial empires. The jingoistic "penny" press and the extension of the vote to the lower middle and working classes through much of industrial Europe, the United States, and Japan made public opinion a major factor in foreign policy. Though stalwart explorers might on their own initiative make treaties with local African or Asian potentates who assigned their lands to France, Germany, or Japan, these annexations had to be ratified by the home government. In most cases, ratification meant fierce parliamentary debates, which often spilled over into press wars and popular demonstrations. Empires were now only rarely (as in the case of King Leopold's fiefdom in the Congo before the early 1990s) the personal projects of private trading concerns and ambitious individuals; they were the property and pride of the industrial nations.

The Partition of Africa after 1870

Quarrels over the division of the colonial spoils were cited by those who sought to justify the arms buildup and general militarism of the age. Colonial rivalries greatly intensified the growing tension and paranoia that dominated great power interaction in the decades before World War I. As Europe divided into armed camps, successive crises over control of the Sudan, Morocco, and the Balkans (which the great powers treated very much like colonies) had much to do with the alliances that formed and the crisis mentality that contributed so much to the outbreak of the conflict in August 1914.

Unequal Combat: Colonial Wars and the Apex of European Imperialism

Industrial change not only justified the industrial powers grab for colonial possessions but made them much easier to acquire. By the last decades of the 19th century, scientific discoveries and technological innovations had catapulted industrial nations far ahead of all other peoples in the capacity to wage war. The great powers could tap mineral resources that most peoples did not even know existed, and Western-trained chemists mixed ever more deadly explosives. Advances in metallurgy made possible the mass production of light, mobile artillery pieces that rendered suicidal the massed cavalry or infantry charges that were the mainstay of Asian and African armies. Advances in artillery were matched by great improvements in hand arms. Much more accurate and faster-firing, breech-loading rifles replaced the clumsy muzzle-loading muskets of the first phase of empire building.

By the 1880s, after decades of experimentation, the machine gun had become an effective battlefield weapon. Railroads gave the industrial military forces the mobility of the swiftest African or Asian horsemen as well as the ability to supply large armies in the field for extended periods of time. On the sea, Europe's already formidable advantages were greatly increased by industrial transformations, and the United States and Japan also built powerful navies. After the opening of the Suez Canal in 1869, steam power supplanted the sail, iron hulls replaced wood, and massive guns, capable of hitting enemy vessels miles away, were introduced into the fleets of the great powers.

The dazzling array of new weaponry with which the industrial rivals set out on their expeditions to the Indian frontiers, Manchuria, and the African "bush" made the wars of colonial conquest very lopsided affairs. This was particularly true when the industrial forces encountered resistance from peoples such as those in the interior of Africa or the Pacific Islands. These areas had been cut off from most preindustrial advances in technology, and thus their peoples were forced to fight European machine guns with spears, arrows, and leather shields. One African leader, whose followers struggled with little hope to halt the German advance into East Africa, resorted to natural imagery to account for the power of the invaders' weapons:

On Monday we heard a shuddering like Leviathan, the voice of many cannon; we heard the roar like waves of the rocks and rumble like thunder in the rains. We heard a crashing like elephants or monsters and our hearts melted at the number of shells. We

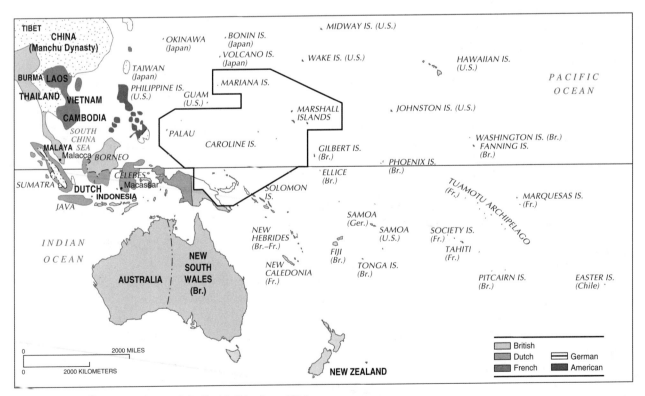

The Partition of Southeast Asia and the Pacific Islands to 1914

knew that we were hearing the battle of Pangani; the guns were like a hurricane in our ears.

Not even peoples with advanced preindustrial technology and sophisticated military organization, such as the Chinese and the Vietnamese, could stand against, or really comprehend, the fearful killing devices of the Europeans. In advising the Vietnamese emperor to give in to European demands, one of his officials, who had led the fight against the French invaders, warned:

Nobody can resist them. They go where they choose. . . . Under heaven, everything is feasible to them, save only the matter of life and death.

Despite the odds against them, African and Asian peoples often fiercely resisted the imposition of colonial rule. West African leaders, such as Mahmadom Lamine and Ahmadou Sekou, held back the European advance for decades. When rulers such as the Vietnamese emperors refused to fight, local officials organized guerrilla resistance in defense of the indigenous regime. Martial peoples, such as the Zulus in South Africa, had the courage and discipline to face and defeat sizable British forces in set piece (or conventional) battles, such as that at Isandhlwana in 1879 (which is depicted in the illustration that opens this chapter). But conventional resistance eventually ended in defeat. The guerrilla bands in Vietnam were eventually run to the ground. Even at Isandhlwana, 3000 Zulus lost their lives in defeating 800 British and 500 African troops. In addition, within days of the Zulu victory, a tiny force of 120 British troops at a nearby outpost held off an army of three or four thousand Zulus.

Given the advantages of industrialized military forces in conventional battles, guerrilla resistance, sabotage, and in some cases banditry proved the most effective means of fighting the great powers' attempts to assert political control. Religious leaders were often in the forefront of these struggles, which occurred across the globe from the Ghost Dance religion in the late 19th-century American West to the Maji Maji risings in German East Africa in 1907 and the Boxer Rebellion in China in 1898. The magic potions and divine assistance they offered for the protection of their followers seemed to be the only way to offset the demoralizing killing power of industrial weaponry.

However admirable the courage of those who resisted the advance of colonialism, and despite temporary setbacks, by the eve of World War I in 1914, very little of the earth was left for the Europeans to conquer. Excepting Ethiopia, all of Africa had been divided between the European powers (see map on page 55). Maps of the continent became a patchwork of colors: red for Great Britain, green for France, blue for Germany, and so on. In Southeast Asia (see map on page 56), only Siam remained independent, in part because Britain and France could not decide which of them should have it. The Americans had replaced the Spanish as the colonial overlords of the Philippines, and the Dutch were completing the conquest of the "outer islands" of the Indonesian archipelago. The Japanese had annexed Formosa and Korea, and they carved out a sphere of influence in southern Manchuria. Even the island clusters of the Pacific had been divided among the hungry industrial powers. China, Persia, and the Middle East had not yet been occupied, but many believed that the "informal" political and economic influences the industrial powers exerted in these areas were the prelude to formal annexation.

Patterns of Dominance: Continuity and Change

Widespread conquests were only the most dramatic manifestation of the great disparity in power that industrialization had created between the Europeans (including the North Americans) and all of the other peoples of the globe. The Europeans' sense of their own uniqueness and superiority, which was heightened by their unparalleled scientific and technological achievements, also led to major changes in their economic, social, and cultural relations with the colonized. Europeans living in the colonies increasingly distanced themselves in terms of everyday social interaction from the peoples they ruled. Europe and North America became even more dominant in the world market system, with much of the rest of the globe supplying them with low-priced raw materials in return for the more highly priced, mass-produced consumer goods of the West. The demand for Western learning on the part of the elite and middle classes of colonized peoples in Africa and Asia rose sharply. Ironically, these same groups who invested so heavily in acquiring aspects of Western culture would soon lead a global revolt against European colonial domination, in part by turning Western ideas and ideals back on the Europeans themselves.

By the end of the 19th century, the European colonial order was made up of two quite different kinds of colonies. The greater portion of the colonial empires consisted of the so-called *tropical dependencies* in Africa,

An engraving from the popular *Illustrated London News* shows British warships and gunboats bombarding the East African port of Mombasa in 1874. As in the early centuries of European expansion, sea power remained a critical way for the British and other colonizers to project their strength throughout the 19th century. Raids, such as the one shown in the illustration, were so heavily relied upon to control local rulers that the term "gunboat diplomacy" became a staple of international parlance in the mid-19th century.

Asia, and the South Pacific. In these colonies small numbers of Europeans ruled large populations of non-Western peoples. The tropical dependencies represented a vast extension of the pattern of dominance the British, Dutch, and French had worked out earlier in India, Java, and African enclaves such as Senegal. Most of these colonies had been brought, often quite suddenly, under European rule in the last decades of the 19th century and the first years of the 20th century.

Settlement colonies made up the second major type of European overseas possession, but within this type there were two different patterns of European occupation and indigenous response. The first pattern was exhibited by colonies such as Canada and Australia, which the British labeled the *White Dominions*. The White Dominions accounted for a good portion of the land area but only a tiny minority of the population of Britain's global empire. The descendants of European settlers made up the overwhelming majority of the population in these colonies, in which the native inhabitants had been decimated by diseases and wars of conquest. These patterns of substantial European settlement and the precipitous decline of the indigenous population were also found in those portions of North America that came to form the United States. Though colonies like Canada and Aus-

tralia remained within the British Empire, each moved steadily toward self-government and parliamentary rule in the late 19th century.

In some of the areas where large numbers of Europeans had migrated, a second major variation on the settlement colony developed. Both in regions that had been colonized as early as North America, such as South Africa, and in those the Europeans and Americans had begun to occupy only in the mid- or late 19th century, such as Algeria, Kenya, New Zealand, and Hawaii, the key demographic characteristics of both the settler colonies and tropical dependencies were combined. Temperate climates and relatively mild disease environments in these areas made it possible for tens or hundreds of thousands of Europeans to settle on a permanent basis. Despite the Europeans' arrival, large indigenous populations survived and then began to increase rapidly. As a result, in these areas for which the label *mixed settler colonies* seems most apt, Europeans and indigenous peoples increasingly clashed over land rights, resource control, social status, and cultural differences. From the 19th century onward, the history of mixed settler societies has been dominated by the interaction between European settlers and indigenous peoples. The last sections of this chapter are devoted to case studies of three of the most important and representative examples of the mixed settler colony variation on the settlement colony pattern: South Africa, New Zealand, and Hawaii.

COLONIAL REGIMES AND AFRICAN AND ASIAN PEOPLES

As the Europeans imposed their rule over tens of millions of additional Africans and Asians in the late 19th century, they drew heavily on precedents set in older colonies, particularly India, in establishing administrative, legal, and educational systems. As they had earlier in India (or in Java and Senegal), the Europeans exploited long-standing ethnic and cultural divisions between the peoples of their new African or Asian colonies to put down resistance and maintain control. In West and East Africa in particular, they used the peoples who followed animistic religions (those that focused on the propitiation of nature or ancestral spirits) or those who had converted to Christianity against the Muslim communities that existed in most colonies. In official reports and censuses, colonial administrators rigidified and enhanced existing ethnic differences by dividing the peoples in each colony into "tribes." The label itself, with its connotations of primitiveness and backwardness, says a great deal about general European attitudes toward the peoples of sub-Saharan Africa. In Southeast Asia, the colonizers attempted to use hill-dwelling "tribal" minorities against the majority populations that lived in the lowlands. In each colonial area, favored minorities, often Christians, were recruited into the civil service and police. Their collaboration not only resulted in a sense of loyalty to the colonizers but antagonized less-favored ethnic and religious groups, thus bolstering the divide-and-rule strategy of the Europeans.

As had been the case in India, Java, and Senegal, small numbers of Europeans lived mainly in the capital city and major provincial towns. From these urban centers they oversaw the administration of the African and Asian colonies, which was actually carried out at the local level mainly by hundreds or thousands of African and Asian subordinates. Some of these subordinates—normally those in positions of the greatest authority—were Western educated. But the majority were recruited from indigenous elite groups, including village headmen, local notables, and regional lords. In Burma, Malaya, and East Africa, numerous Indian administrators and soldiers assisted the British in ruling new additions to their empire. The Europeans also recruited promising male youths in the newly colonized areas for Western schooling that would make them fit for jobs as government clerks or railway mechanics. In the Philippines, American colonizers also adopted these patterns by building alliances with the Filipino *ilustrado* elite and recruiting policemen and soldiers among the indigenous peoples. On Formosa and in Korea, the Japanese also made use of groups willing to cooperate, but favored far more extensive staffing of the colonial regime with Japanese officers and bureaucrats.

In contrast to Java and India, the Philippines and Korea, where schools were heavily state-supported, Western-language education in Africa was left largely to Protestant and Catholic missionaries. As a result of deep-seated racial prejudices held by virtually all the colonizers, higher education was not promoted in Africa. As a result, college graduates were few in Africa compared with India, the Dutch East Indies, or even smaller Asian colonies such as Burma, the Philippines, and Vietnam. This policy stunted the growth of a middle class in black Africa—a consequence that European colonial officials increasingly intended. As nationalist agitation spread among the Western-educated classes in India and other Asian colonies, colonial policymakers warned against the dangers posed by college graduates. Those with advanced educations among the colonized, according to this argument, aspired to jobs that were beyond their capacity and were understandably disgruntled when they could not find employment.

ANALYSIS

Western Education and the Rise of an African and Asian Middle Class

To varying degrees and for many of the same reasons as the British in India, all Western colonizers educated the children of African and Asian elite groups in Western-language schools. The early 19th-century debate over education in India was paralleled, for example, by an equally hard-fought controversy among French officials and missionaries regarding the proper schooling for the peoples of Senegal in West Africa. The Dutch did not develop European-language schools for the sons of the Javanese elite until the middle of the 19th century, and many young Javanese males continued

Edward Blyden was a model product of European—in this case British—efforts to produce a Westernized middle class through education. Born in St. Thomas in the Caribbean, Blyden was the son of slaves, who excelled in the missionary schools on the island. He later become the editor of Liberia's most prominent newspaper, and the author of numerous books and articles. In his published work and in a lively correspondence with leading British and American politicians, he became one of Africa's most outspoken defenders and a much-quoted opponent of racism.

to be educated in the homes of the Dutch residing in the colonies until the end of the century. Whatever their particular views on education, all colonial policymakers realized that they needed administrative assistants and postal clerks and that they could not begin to recruit enough Europeans to fill these posts. Therefore, all agreed that Western education for some segments of the colonized population was essential for the maintenance of the colonial order.

One of the chief advantages of having Western-educated African and Asian subordinates—for they were always below European officials or traders—was that their salaries were considerably lower than what Westerners would have been paid for doing the same work. The Europeans and Americans had no trouble rationalizing this inequity. Africans and Asians served in their own lands and were thus accustomed to life in the hot, humid, insect- and disease-ridden tropics. For the Europeans and Americans who worked in the colonies, life in these environments was deemed difficult, even dangerous. Higher pay was thought to compensate them for the "sacrifices" involved in colonial service. The Europeans and Americans also had a higher standard of living than Africans or Asians, and colonial officials assumed that European employees would be more hardworking and efficient.

Beyond the need for government functionaries and business assistants, each European colonizer stressed different objectives in designing Western-language schools for the children of upper-class families. The transmission of Western scientific learning and production techniques was a high priority for the British in India. The goal of educational policymakers, such as Thomas Macaulay, was to teach the Indians Western literature and manners and to instill in them a Western sense of morality. As Macaulay put it, the British hoped that English-language schools would turn out brown "English gentlemen," who would in turn teach their countrymen the ways of the West.

The French, at least until the end of the 19th century, went even further. Because they conceived of French nationalism as a matter of culture rather than birth, it was of prime importance that Africans and other colonial students master the French language and the subtleties of French cuisine, dress, and etiquette. The French also saw the process of turning colonial subjects into black, brown, and yellow French citizens as a way to increase their stagnant population to keep up with rival nations, especially Germany and Great Britain. Both of these rivals and the United States had much higher birth rates in this period.

When the lessons had been fully absorbed and the students fully assimilated to French culture, they could become full citizens of France, no matter what their family origins or the color of their skin. Only a tiny minority of the population of any French colony had the opportunity for the sort of schooling that would qualify them for French citizenship. But by the early 20th century, there were thousands of Senegalese and hundreds of Vietnamese and Tunisians who could carry French passports, vote in French elections, and even run for seats in the French Parliament. Other European colonial powers adopted either the British or the French approach to education and its aims. The Dutch and the Germans, for example, followed the British pattern, while the Portuguese pushed assimilation for even smaller numbers of the elite classes among the peoples they colonized. In the Philippines, the American colonizers were determined to introduce widespread mass schooling in English as well as more limited opportunities for higher education. The Japanese also promoted mass elementary education in Japanese in their colonies, but sharply curtailed possibilities for college attendance on the part of the colonized in Korea or Formosa.

Western education in the colonies succeeded in producing clerks and railway conductors, brown Indian gentlemen, and black French citizens. It also had effects that those who shaped colonial educational policy, with the exception of American officials in the Philippines, did not intend—

effects that within a generation or two would produce major challenges to the continuation of European colonial dominance.

The population of most colonized areas was divided into many different ethnic, religious, and language groups with separate histories and identities. Western-language schools gave the sons (and, in limited instances, the daughters) of the leading families a common language in which to communicate. The schools also inculcated common attitudes and ideas and imparted to the members of diverse groups a common body of knowledge. In all Western colonial societies, Western education led to similar occupational opportunities: in government service, with Western business firms, or as professionals (lawyers, doctors, journalists, etc.). Thus, within a generation after their introduction, Western-language schools had in effect created a new middle class in the colonies that had no counterpart in precolonial African or Asian societies.

Occupying social strata and economic niches in the middle range between the colonizers and the old aristocracy on one hand, and the peasantry and urban laborers on the other, Western-educated Africans and Asians within each colony became increasingly aware of the interests and grievances they had in common. They often found themselves at odds with the traditional rulers or the landed gentry, who, ironically, were often their fathers or grandfathers. Members of the new middle class also felt alienated from the peasantry, whose beliefs and way of life were so different from those they had learned in Western-language schools.

For more than a generation they clung to their European and American tutors and employers. Eventually, however, they grew increasingly resentful of their lower salaries, and of European competition for scarce jobs. They were also angered by their social segregation from the Europeans (which intensified in the heightened racist atmosphere of the late-nineteenth century), who often made little effort to disguise their contempt for even the most accomplished, Western-educated Africans and Asians. Thus, members of the new middle class in the colonies were caught between two worlds: the traditional ways and teachings of their fathers and the "modern" world of their European masters. Finding that they would be fully admitted to neither world, they rejected the first and set about supplanting the colonizers and building their own versions of the modern world.

Questions: Why did the Europeans continue to provide Western-language education for Africans and Asians once it was clear they were creating a class that might challenge their position of dominance? Why were challenges from this new class much more effective than resistance on the part of the peasantry or movements led by the traditional religious and political elites? What factors prevented the Europeans from doing a better job to satisfy the demands of the new middle classes? Would the colonized have been satisfied in the long run by concessions by the Europeans in salaries, more jobs, and less racial discrimination? Do you think the European colonial order would have lasted longer if Western-language education had been denied to colonized peoples?

Changing Social Relations Between Colonizer and Colonized

In both long-held and newly acquired colonies, the growing tensions between the colonizers and the rising African and Asian middle classes reflected a larger shift in the colonizers' social interaction with the colonized peoples. This shift had actually begun long before the scramble for colonies in the late 19th century. Its causes are complex, but the growing size and changing makeup of European communities in the colonies were critical factors. As more and more Europeans went to the colonies, they tended to keep to themselves on social occasions rather than mixing with the "natives." New medicines and increasingly segregated living quarters made it possible to bring to the colonies the wives and families of government officials and European military officers (but

not of the rank and file until well into the 20th century). Wives and families further closed the social circle of the colonized, and European women looked disapprovingly on liaisons between European men and Asian or African women. Brothels were put off limits for upper-class officials and officers, and mixed marriages or living arrangements met with more and more vocal disapproval within the constricted world of the colonial communities and back home in Europe. Although there were no pre-19th century patterns to reverse, Japanese and American colonizer elites also exhibited these tendencies toward social segregation and exclusiveness. The growing numbers of missionaries and pastors for European congregations in the colonies obviously served to strengthen these taboos.

Historians of colonialism once put much of the blame on European women for the growing social gap between colonizer and colonized. But recent research has shown

A pointedly dramatized engraving of the submission in 1896 of King Prempeh of the powerful Asante kingdom in present-day Ghana. The picture underscores the importance the European colonizers placed on alliances with or the forced submission of indigenous African rulers and local leaders. It also shows a rare case of the public humiliation of indigenous leaders, who in this case had recently conspired to drive the British out by force. Normally, indigenous elites who cooperated with the colonizers were included in pageants celebrating the colonizers' power and were treated with respect, lest their hold over the mass of the colonized peoples be undermined.

that male officials bore most of the responsibility. They established laws restricting or prohibiting miscegenation and other sorts of interracial liaisons. They also pushed for housing arrangements and police practices designed specifically to keep social contacts between European women and the colonized at a minimum. These measures locked European and American women in the colonies into an almost exclusively Western world. They had many native servants and native nannies for their children, but they rarely came into contact with men or women of their own social standing from the colonized peoples. Occasions when they did were highly public and strictly formal.

The trend toward social exclusivism on the part of colonizers in the colonies and their open disdain for the culture of colonized peoples were reinforced by notions of white racial supremacy, which peaked in acceptance in the decades before World War I. It was widely believed that the mental and moral superiority of whites over the rest of humankind, which was usually divided into racial types according to the crude criterion of skin color, had been demonstrated by what were then believed to be scientific experiments. Because the inferior intelligence and weak sense of morality of non-Europeans were seen to be inherent and permanent, there seemed to be little motivation for Europeans or Americans to socialize with the colonized. A rather different sort of racism motivated the Japanese to distance themselves from the peoples they colonized in similar ways.

There were also lots of good reasons for fighting the earlier tendency to adopt elements of the culture and lifestyle of subject peoples. As photos from the late 19th century reveal, clothing such as stiff collars and ties for men, and corsets and long skirts for women, became obligatory for respectable colonial functionaries and their wives. The colonizers' houses were filled with the overstuffed furniture and bric-a-brac that the late Victorians loved so dearly. Western social life in the colonies revolved around the infamous clubs, where the only natives allowed were the servants. In the heat of the summer months, most of the administrators and virtually all of the colonizers' families retreated to the hill stations, where the cool air and the quaint architecture made it seem almost as if they were home again—or at least in a Swiss mountain resort.

DOCUMENT

Contrary Images: The Colonizer Versus the Colonized on the "Civilizing Mission"

Each of the following passages from novels written in the colonial era expresses a different view of the reasons behind European colonization in Africa and Asia and the consequences of it. The first is taken from an adventure story written by John Buchan entitled *Prester John,* a favorite in the pre–World War I decades among English schoolboys—many of whom would go out as young men to be administrators in the colonies. Davie, the protagonist in the story, is a "tall, square-set lad . . . renowned [for his] prowess at Rugby football." In the novel, Davie summarizes key elements of the "civilizing mission" credo by which so many European thinkers and political leaders attempted to justify their colonization of most of the rest of the world:

I knew then [after his struggle to thwart a "native" rising in South Africa] the meaning of the white man's duty. He has to take all the risks, reck[on]ing nothing of his life or his fortunes and well content to find his reward in the fulfillment of his task. That is the difference between white and black, the gift of responsibility, the power of being in a little way a king; and so long as we know this and practise it, we will rule not in Africa alone but wherever there are dark men who live only for the day and their own bellies. Moreover the work made me pitiful and kindly. I learned much of the untold grievances of the natives and saw something of their strange, twisted reasoning.

The second passage is taken from René Maran's *Batouala*, which was first published in 1921 just after World War I. Though a French colonial official in West Africa, like Edward Blyden, Maran was an African American, born in Martinique, who was highly sensitive to the plight of the colonized in Africa. Here his protagonist, a local African leader named Batouala, complains of the burdens rather than the benefits of colonial rule and mocks the self-important European agents of the vaunted civilizing mission:

But what good does it do to talk about it? It's nothing new to us that men of white skin are more delicate than men of black skin. One example of a thousand possible. Everyone knows that the whites, saying that they are "collecting taxes," force all blacks of a marriageable age to carry voluminous packages from when the sun rises to when it sets.

These trips last two, three, five days. Little matter to them the weight of these packages which are called "sandoukous." They don't sink under the burden. Rain, sun, cold? They don't suffer. So they pay no attention. And long live the worst weather, provided the whites are sheltered.

Whites fret about mosquito bites. . . . They fear mason bees. They are also afraid of the "prankongo," the scorpion who lives, black and venomous, among decaying roofs, under rubble, or in the midst of debris.

In a word, everything worries them. As if a man worthy of the name would worry about everything which lives, crawls, or moves around him.

Questions: What sorts of roles does Davie assume that the Europeans must play in the colonies? What benefits accrue to colonized peoples from their rule? What impression does he convey of the thinking and behavior of the colonized peoples? In what ways do Batouala's views of the Europeans conflict with Davie's assumptions about himself and other colonizers? Does Batouala agree with Davie's conviction that colonial rule is beneficial for the Africans? What sorts of burdens does Batouala believe it imposes? According to Batouala, what advantages do Africans have over Europeans?

Shifts in Methods of Economic Extraction

The relationship between the colonizers and the mass of the colonized remained much as it had been before. District officers, with the help of many native subordinates, continued to do their paternal duty to settle disputes between peasant villagers, punish criminals, and collect taxes. European planters and merchants still relied on African or Asian overseers and brokers to manage laborers and purchase crops and handicraft manufactures. But late 19th-century colonial bureaucrats and managers tried to instruct African and Asian peasants in scientific farming techniques and to compel the colonized peoples more generally to work harder and more efficiently. These efforts involved an important extension of dependent status in the Western-dominated world economy. Pressure for new work habits supported the drive for cheap raw materials (exports) and drew in a growing segment of the colonial labor force.

A wide range of incentives was devised to promote the expansion of export production. Some of these benefited the colonized peoples, such as the cheap consumer goods that could be purchased with cash earned producing marketable crops or laboring on European or American plantations or in Japanese factories overseas. In many instances, however, colonized peoples were simply forced to produce, for little or no remuneration, the crops or raw materials that the Europeans desired. Head and hut taxes were imposed that could be paid only in ivory, palm nuts, or wages earned working on European estates. Under the worst of these forced-labor schemes, such as those inflicted on the peoples of the Belgian Congo in the final decades of the 19th century, villagers were flogged and killed if they failed to meet production quotas, and women and children were held hostage to ensure that their menfolk would deliver the products demanded on time. Whether appealing to the colonized peoples self-interest or using terror tactics, the colonial overlords were determined to draw their subjects into fuller participation in the European-dominated global market economy.

As increasing numbers of the colonized peoples were drawn into the production of crops or minerals intended for export, the economies of most of Africa, India, and Southeast Asia were reorganized to serve the needs of the industrializing economies. Roads and railways were built primarily to facilitate the movement of farm produce and raw materials from the interior of colonized areas to port centers from which they could be shipped to Europe, North America, or Japan. Benefiting from technological advances in the metropoles, mining sectors grew dramatically in most of the colonies. Vast areas that had previously been uncultivated or (more commonly) had been planted in food crops were converted to the production of commodities—such as cocoa, palm oil, rubber, and hemp—in great demand in the markets of Europe and, increasingly, the United States and Japan.

The profits from the precious metals and minerals extracted from Africa's mines and the rubber grown in Malaya went mainly to European, American, and Japanese merchants and industrialists. The raw materials themselves were shipped to Europe to be processed and sold or used in the manufacture of industrial products. The finished products were intended mainly for Western, and in some cases Japanese, consumers: members of middle- and working-class families and government contractors. The African and Asian laborers who produced these products were generally poorly paid—if indeed they were paid at all. The laborers and colonial economies as a whole were steadily reduced to dependence on a global marked dominated by the industrial powers. Economic dependence complemented the political subjugation and social subordination of colonized African and Asian peoples in a world order loaded in favor of the expansionist nations of western Europe, North America, and Japan.

WHITE DOMINIONS AND MIXED SETTLER COLONIES

The mixed settler colonies that developed in Africa and the Pacific in the 19th century were similar to the White Dominions in important ways. In fact, the early history of South Africa, one of the largest of the mixed settler colonies, exhibited interesting comparisons and contrasts with that of Canada and Australia, the largest of the White Dominions. European settlers began to move into the southwest corner of South Africa and eastern Canada in the middle decades of the 17th century, long before the settlement of Australia got under way in the 1840s. The initial Dutch colony at Cape Town was established to provide a way station where Dutch merchant ships could take on water and fresh food in the middle of their long journey from Europe to the East Indies. In contrast to Canada, where French fur trappers and missionaries quickly moved into the interior, the small community of Dutch settlers stayed near the coast for decades after their arrival. But like the settlers in Australia, the Boers (or farmers), as the Dutch in South Africa came to be called, eventually began to move into the vast interior regions of the continent. Though the settlers in each of the three areas were confronted by uncharted and in some ways inhospitable frontier regions, they also found a temperate climate in which they could grow the crops and raise the livestock they were accustomed to in Europe. Equally important, they encountered a disease environment they could withstand.

The Boers and Australians found the areas into which they moved sparsely populated. In this respect their experience was somewhat different from that of the settlers in Canada, where the American Indian population, though far from dense, was organized into powerful tribal confederations. The Boers and Australians faced much less resistance as they took possession of the lands once occupied by hunting-and-gathering peoples. The Boer farmers and cattle ranchers enslaved these peoples, the Khoikhoi, while at the same time integrating them

In both New Zealand and Australia, sheepherding was a major impetus for the spread of European settlement into interior areas, thus paralleling the role of cattle raising in South Africa. In Australia, the sparse indigenous population and vast land area meant that there was ample room for the large herds that became a dominant feature of the landscape. On the smaller island of New Zealand, the advance of the herding frontier was often at the expense of the more populous Maori peoples and the cause of tension and a series of wars.

into their large frontier homesteads. Extensive miscegenation between the Boers and Khoikhoi in these early centuries of European colonization produced the sizable "colored" population that exists in South Africa today. The coloreds came to be regarded as quite distinct from the black African majority. The Australian and Canadian settlers drove the aborigines they encountered into the interior, eventually leaving those who survived their invasions the uneasy occupants of remote tracts of waste, which did not seem to be worth settling. In both cases, but particularly in Canada, the indigenous population was also decimated by many of the same diseases that had turned contacts with the Europeans into a demographic disaster for the rest of the Americas in the early centuries of expansion.

Thus, until the first decades of the 19th century, the process of colonization in South Africa paralleled that in Canada and Australia quite closely. Small numbers of Europeans had migrated into lands that they considered "empty" or "undeveloped." After driving away or subjugating the indigenous peoples, the Europeans farmed, mined, and grazed their herds on these lands, which they claimed as their own. But while the settler societies in Canada and Australia went on to develop, rather peace-

fully, into loyal and largely self-governing Dominions of the British empire, the arrival of the same British overlords in South Africa in the early 19th century sent the Boers reeling onto a very different historical course. The British captured Cape Town during the wars precipitated by the French Revolution in the 1790s, when Holland was overrun by France, thus making its colonies subject to British attack. The British held the colony during the Napoleonic conflicts that followed, and they annexed it permanently in 1815 as a vital link on the route to India.

Made up mainly of people of Dutch and French Protestant descent, the Boer community differed from the British newcomers in almost every way possible. The Boers spoke a different language, and they lived mostly in isolated rural homesteads that had missed the scientific, industrial, and urban revolutions that had transformed British society and attitudes. Most critically, the evangelical missionaries who entered South Africa under the protection of the new British overlords were deeply committed to eradicating slavery. They made no exception for the domestic pattern of enslavement that had developed in Boer homesteads and communities. By the 1830s, missionary pressure and increasing British interference in their lives drove a handful of Boers to open, but futile, rebellion, and many of the remaining Boers fled the Cape Colony.

In the decades of the Great Trek that followed, tens of thousands of Boers migrated in covered wagons pulled by oxen, first east across the Great Fish River and then over the mountains into the *veld,* or rolling grassy plains that make up much of the South African interior. In these areas, the Boers collided head-on with populous, militarily powerful, and well-organized African states built by Bantu peoples, such as the Zulus and the Xhosa. Throughout the middle decades of the 19th century, the migrating Boers clashed again and again with the Bantu peoples, who were determined to resist the seizure of the lands where they pastured their great herds of cattle and grew subsistence foods. The British, in effect, followed the Boer pioneers along the southern and eastern coast, eventually establishing a second major outpost at Durban in Natal. Tensions between the Boers and Britain remained high, but the British were often drawn into the frontier wars against the Bantu peoples, even though they were not always formally allied to the Boers.

In the early 1850s, the hard-liners among the Boers established two Boer Republics in the interior, named the Orange Free State and the Transvaal, which they tried to keep free of British influence. For over a decade, the Boers managed to keep the British out of their affairs. But when diamonds were discovered in the Orange Free State in 1867, British entrepreneurs, such as Cecil Rhodes, and prospectors began to move in, and tensions between the Boers and the British began to build anew. In 1880–1881, these tensions led to a brief war in which the Boers were victorious. The tide of British immigration into the republics, however, rose even higher after gold was discovered in the Transvaal in 1885.

Though the British had pretty much left the Boers to deal with the African peoples who lived in the republics as they pleased, British migrants and financiers grew more and more resentful of Boer efforts to limit their numbers and curb their civil rights. British efforts to protect the settlers and bring the feisty and independent Boers into line led to the republics' declaration of war against the British in late 1899 and to Boer attacks on British bases in Natal, the Cape Colony, and elsewhere. The Anglo-Boer War (1899–1902) that followed began the process of decolonization for the European settlers of South Africa. At the same time, it opened the way for the dominance of the Boer minority over the African majority that would become the central problem in South African history for most of the 20th century.

Pacific Tragedies

The territories that the Europeans, the Americans, and the Japanese claimed throughout the South Pacific in the 19th century were in some cases outposts of true empire and in others mixed settler colonies. In both situations, however, the coming of colonial rule resulted in demographic disasters and social disruptions of a magnitude that had not been seen since the first century of European expansion into the Americas. Like the American Indian peoples of the New World, the peoples of the South Pacific had long lived in isolation. This meant that, like the American Indians, they had no immunities to many of the diseases European explorers and later merchants, missionaries, and settlers carried to their island homes from the 1760s onward. In addition, their cultures were extremely vulnerable to the corrosive effects of outside influences, such as new religions, different sexual mores, more lethal weapons, and sudden influxes of cheap consumer goods. Thus, whatever the intentions of the incoming Europeans and Americans—and they were by no means always benevolent—their contacts with the peoples of the Pacific Islands almost invariably ushered in periods of social disintegration and widespread human suffering.

Of the many cases of contact between the expansive peoples of the West and the long-isolated island cultures of the South Pacific, the confrontations in New Zealand and Hawaii are among the most informative. Quite sophisticated cultures and fairly complex societies had developed in each of these areas. In addition, the two island groups contained, at the time of the European explorers' arrivals, some of the largest concentrations of population in the whole Pacific region. Both areas were subjected to European influences carried by a variety of agents, from whalers and merchants to missionaries and colonial administrators. After the first decades of contact, the peoples of New Zealand and Hawaii experienced a period of crisis so severe that their continued survival was in doubt. In both cases, however, the threatened peoples and cultures rebounded and found enduring solutions to the challenges from overseas. Their solutions combined accommodation to outside influences with revivals of traditional beliefs and practices.

New Zealand. The Maoris of New Zealand actually went through two periods of profound disruption and danger. The first began in the 1790s, when timber merchants and whalers established small settlements on the

New Zealand coast. Maoris living near these settlements were afflicted with alcoholism and the spread of prostitution. In addition, they traded wood and food for European firearms, which soon revolutionized Maori warfare—in part by rendering it much more deadly—and upset the existing balance among different tribal groups. Even more devastating was the impact of diseases, such as smallpox, tuberculosis, and even the common cold, that ravaged Maori communities throughout the north island. By the 1840s, only 80,000 to 90,000 Maoris remained of a population that had been as high as 130,000 less than a century earlier. But the Maoris survived these calamities and began to adjust to the imports of the foreigners. They took up farming with European implements, and they grazed cattle purchased from European traders. They cut timber, built windmills, and traded extensively with the merchants who frequented their shores. Many even converted to Christianity, which the missionaries began to proselytize after their first station was established in 1814.

The arrival of British farmers and herders in search of land in the early 1850s and the British decision to claim the islands as part of their global empire again plunged the Maoris into misery and despair. Backed by the military clout of the colonial government, the settlers occupied some of the most fertile areas of the north island. The warlike Maori fought back, sometimes with temporary successes, but they were steadily driven into the interior of the island. In desperation in the 1860s and 1870s, they flocked to religious prophets who promised them magical charms and supernatural assistance in their efforts to drive out the invaders. When the prophets also failed them, the Maoris seemed for a time to face extinction. In fact, some British writers predicted that within generations the Maoris, like the Arawaks and Tasmanians before them, would die out.

The Maoris displayed surprising resilience. As they built up immunities to new diseases, they also learned to use European laws and political institutions to defend themselves and preserve what was left of their ancestral lands. Because the British had in effect turned the internal administration of the islands over to the settlers' representatives, the Maoris' main struggle was with the invaders who had come to stay. Western schooling and a growing ability to win British colonial officials over to their point of view eventually enabled the Maoris to hold their own in their ongoing legal contests and daily exchanges with the settlers. A multiracial society has now evolved in which there is a reasonable level of European and Maori accommodation and interaction, and which has allowed the Maori to preserve much of value in their traditional culture.

Hawaii. The conversion of Hawaii to settler colony status followed familiar basic imperialist patterns but with specific twists. Hawaii did not become a colony until the United States proclaimed annexation in 1898, though an overzealous British official had briefly declared the islands for his nation in 1843. Hawaii came under increasing Western influence, however, from the late 18th century onward—politically at the hands of the British, culturally and economically from the United States, whose westward surge quickly spilled into the Pacific Ocean.

While very occasional contact with Spanish ships during the 16th and 17th centuries probably occurred, Hawaii was effectively opened to the West through the voyages of Captain James Cook from 1777 to 1779. Cook was first welcomed as a god, partly because he had the good luck to land during a sacred period when war was forbidden. A later and less well-timed visit brought Cook's death as Hawaiian warriors attempted to take over his ship with its metal nails. These humble objects were much prized by a people whose elaborate culture rested on a Neolithic technology and thus was without iron or steel. The Cook visit and later British expeditions convinced a young Hawaiian prince, Kamehameha, that some imitation of Western ways could produce a unified kingdom under his leadership, replacing the small and warring regional units that had previously prevailed. A series of vigorous wars, backed by British weapons and advisors, won Kamehameha his kingdom between 1794 and 1810. The new king and his successors promoted economic change, encouraging Western merchants to establish export trade in Hawaiian goods in return for increasing revenues to the royal treasury.

Hawaiian royalty began to imitate Western habits, in some cases traveling to Britain and often building Western-style palaces. Two powerful queens advanced the process of change by insisting that traditional taboos subordinating women be abandoned. In this context, vigorous missionary efforts from Protestant New England, beginning in 1819, brought extensive conversions to Christianity. As with other conversion processes, religious change had wide implications. Missionaries railed against traditional Hawaiian costumes, insisting that women cover their breasts, and a new garment, the muumuu, was fashioned from homespun American nightgowns with

The extent to which Hawaii had come under Western influence by the late 19th century is dramatically illustrated by the dress of the female attendants and the table settings at a feast given for U.S. and British naval officers by the ruler of the islands.

the sleeves cut off. Backed by the Hawaiian monarchy, missionaries also quickly established an extensive school system, which by 1831 served 50,000 students from a culture that had not previously developed writing.

The combination of Hawaiian interest and Western intrusion produced creative political and cultural changes, though inevitably at the expense of previous values. Demographic and economic trends had more insidious effects. Western-imported diseases, particularly venereal disease and tuberculosis, had the usual tragic consequences for a previously isolated people: By 1850 only about 80,000 Hawaiians remained of a prior population of about half a million. Westerners more consciously exploited the Hawaiian economy. Whalers helped create raucous seaport towns. Western settlers from various countries (called *haoles* by the Hawaiians) experimented with potential commercial crops, soon

concentrating particularly on sugar. Many missionary families, impatient with the subsistence habits of Hawaiian commoners, turned to leasing land or buying it outright. Most settlers did not entirely forget their religious motives for migrating to the islands, but it remained true that many families who came to Hawaii to do good ended by doing well.

Western businesses were mainly encouraged by the Hawaiian monarchy, eager for revenues and impressed by the West's military power. In 1848, an edict called the Great Mahele imposed Western concepts of property on Hawaiian land, which had previously been shared by commoners and aristocrats. Most of the newly defined private property went to the king and the nobles, who gradually sold most of it to investors from the West. As sugar estates spread, increasing numbers of Americans moved in to take up other commercial and professional positions—hence, an increasingly "settler" pattern developed in a technically independent state. Because of the Hawaiian population decline, it was also necessary to import Asian workers to staff the estates. The first Chinese contract workers had been brought in before 1800, and after 1868, a larger current of Japanese swelled the immigrant throng.

Literal imperialism came as an anticlimax. The abilities of Hawaiian kings declined after 1872, in one case because of disease and alcoholism. Under a weakened state, powerful planter interests pressed for special treaties with the United States that would promote their sugar exports, and the American government claimed naval rights at Pearl Harbor by 1887. As the last Hawaiian monarchs turned increasingly to the promotion of culture, writing a number of lasting Hawaiian songs but also spending considerable money on luxurious living, American planters concluded that their economic interests required outright United States control. An annexation committee persuaded American naval officers to "protect American lives and property" by posting troops around Honolulu in 1893. The Hawaiian ruler was deposed, and an imperialist-minded U.S. Congress obligingly took over the islands in 1898.

As in New Zealand, Western control was combined with considerable respect for Polynesian culture. Because Hawaians were not enslaved and soon ceased to threaten those present, Americans in Hawaii did not apply the same degree of racism that had described earlier relations with African slaves or with North American Indians. Hawaii's status as a settler colony was further complicated by the arrival of many Asian immigrants. Nevertheless, Western cultural and particularly economic influence extended steadily, and the ultimate political seizure merely ratified the colonization of the islands.

CONCLUSION: THE PATTERN OF THE AGE OF IMPERIALISM

Though the basic patterns of domination in the colonial empires in the decades prior to World War I remained similar to those worked out in Java and India in the early industrial period, the style of colonial rule and patterns of social interaction between colonizer and colonized changed considerably. Racism and social snobbery became pervasive in contacts between the colonizers and their African and Asian subordinates. Europeans, Amer-

icans, and Japanese consciously renounced the ways of dressing, eating habits, and pastimes that had earlier been borrowed from or shared with the peoples of the colonies. The colonizers no longer saw themselves simply as the most successful competitors in a many-sided struggle for political power. They were convinced that they were inherently superior beings—citizens of the most powerful, civilized, and advanced societies on earth. Colonial officials in the age of "high imperialism" were much more concerned than earlier administrators to pull Asian and African peasants into the market economy and to teach them the value of hard work and discipline. Colonial educators were determined to impress upon the children of the colonized elite classes the superiority of Western learning and of everything Western, from political organization to clothing fashions.

In striving for these objectives, the colonizers assumed that it was their God-given destiny to remake the world—insofar as the abilities of the natives would allow—in the image of industrial societies from which they went forth. But in pushing for change within colonized societies that had ancient, deeply rooted cultures and patterns of civilized life, the colonizers frequently aroused resistance to specific policies and to colonial rule more generally. The colonial overloads were able to put down protest movements led by displaced princes and religious prophets. But much more enduring and successful challenges to their rule came, ironically, from the very leaders their social reforms and Western-language schools had done so much to nurture. These nationalists reworked imported ideas and resurrected those of their own cultures. They borrowed European or American organizational techniques and made use of the communications systems and common language the colonizers had introduced to mobilize the resistance to colonial domination that was to become one of the dominant themes of global history in the 20th century.

FURTHER READING

The literature on various aspects of European imperialism is vast. Interesting comparisons between the preindustrial and nineteenth century ages of colonization are explored in detail in David Abernathy's *The Dynamics of Global Dominance* (2000). Useful general histories on the different empires include Bernard Porter, *The Lion's*

Share: *A Short History of British Imperialism, 1850–1995* (1996); Raymond Betts, *Tricouleur* (1978); James J. Cooke, *The New French Imperialism, 1880–1910* (1973); and Woodruff D. Smith, *The German Colonial Empire* (1978). There is no complete general history of the growth of Dutch power on Java or of the British Empire in India, but Edward Thompson and G. T. Garratt provide a reasonably lively chronology in the *Rise and Fulfillment of British Rule in India* (1962), which can be supplemented by the essays in R. C. Majumdar, ed., *British Paramountcy and Indian Renaissance, Part I* (1963). Most recent accounts of specific aspects of the rise of British power in India are available in C. A. Bayley, *Indian Society and the Making of the British Empire* (1988) and P. J. Marshall, *Bengal: The British Bridgehead, 1740–1828* (1987), both part of *The New Cambridge History of India*.

Of the many contributions to the debate over late 19th-century imperialism, some of the most essential are those by D. C. M. Platt, Hans-Ulrich Wehler, William Appleman Williams, Jean Stengers, D. K. Fieldhouse, and Henri Brunschwig, as well as the earlier works by V. I. Lenin and J. A. Hobson. Winfried Baumgart's *Imperialism* (1982) provides a good overview of the literature and conflicting arguments. Very different perspectives on the partition of Africa can be found in Jean Suret-Canale's *French Colonialism in Tropical Africa, 1900–1945* (1971) and Ronald Robinson and John Gallagher's *Africa and the Victorians* (1961).

Most of the better studies on the impact of imperialism and social life in the colonies are specialized monographs, but Percival Spear's *The Nabobs* (1963) is a superb place to start on the latter from the European viewpoint, while the works of Frantz Fanon, Albert Memmi, and O. Mannoni provide much information on the plight of the colonized. Fictional accounts, including Joseph Conrad's *Heart of Darkness*, E. M. Forster's *Passage to India*, Chinua Achebe's *Things Fall Apart*, and Wole Soyinke's *Death and the King's Horseman*, provide superb insights into the social and cultural life of colonial societies.

The introductory essay to the volume on *Tensions of Empire* (1997), edited by Frederick Cooper and Ann Stoler, provides an overview of recent trends in the history of colonialism. The impact of industrialization and other changes in European attitudes toward the colonized are treated in several works, including Philip Curtin, *The Image of Africa* (1964); William B. Cohen, *The French Encounter with Africans* (1980); Alice Conklin, *A Mission to Civilize* (1997); and Michael Adas, *Machines as the Measure of Men* (1989). Ester Boserup's *Women's Role in Economic Development* (1970) provides a good overview of the impact of colonization on African and Asian women and families, but it should be supplemented by more recent monographs on the position of women in colonial settings. One of the best of these is Jean Taylor's *The Social World of Batavia* (1983).

ON THE WEB

The Web offers sites that illuminate the causes of imperialism in the 19th century

http://www.fordham.edu/halsall/mod/modsbook34.html
http://www.loyno.edu/~seduffy/imperialism.html

and provide the means to more closely examine the trends, events and personalities involved in imperialism by region, such as Africa

http://pw2.netcom.com/~giardina/colony.html
http://www.fordham.edu/halsall/africa/book.html

American imperialism in the Philippines and in the rest of Asia

http://smplanet.com/imperialism/toc.html

Japanese imperialism in Korea

http://socrates.berkeley.edu/~korea/colony.html

which included the exploitation of Korean women as chôngsindae ("Comfort Women").

The role of the Suez Canal in the expansion of European trade and power in Asia is examined at

http://ce.eng.usf.edu/pharos/wonders/Modern/
    suezcanal.html
http://i-cias.com/e.o/suez_can.htm

A history of late, 19th-century Egypt and the building of the Suez Canal as seen by a former American Confederate soldier is offered at

http://home.earthlink.net/~atomic_rom/soldier/
    preface.htm

The onset of British imperialism in India, including studies of key personalities such as Robert Clive and events such as the Battle of Plassey receives careful treatment at

http://www.sscnet.ucla.edu/southasia/History/British/
    EAco.html

The British defeat at the hands of the Zulus at Isandhlwana and the Zulu wars are given fulsome treatment from a leading British historian at http://www.kwazulu.co.uk/

Imperialist notions of race and empire embodied in the writings of Rudyard Kipling are examined at

http://www.host.cc.utexas.edu/ftp/pub/das/forbidden
.html/south.asia/sagar/spring.1994.issue/nandi.bhatia
.art.html

The American anti-imperialist attack on Kipling's famous poem, "White Man's Burden," is presented at

http://www.boondocksnet.com/kipling/

Jomo Kenyata's African nationalist perspective on the anti-imperialist struggle is offered at

http://www.africawithin.com/kenyatta/imperialism.htm
http://flag.blackened.net/revolt/africa/wsfpp/
    imperialism6.html

while a Latin American perspective on that subject by Augusto Caesar Sandino of Nicaragua is offered at

http://flag.blackened.net/revolt/africa/wsfpp/
    imperialism6.html

Chapter 4

Precarious Sovereignty: Western Informal Empire and Constricted Development in Latin America, the Middle East, and China

In the late 19th century, the Chinese were forced to concede port and warehouse areas, such as the one in this painting, to rival imperialist powers. These areas were, in effect, colonial enclaves—guarded by foreign troops, flying foreign flags, and administered by Western or Japanese merchant councils.

Chronology

1798	French invasion of Egypt
1808–1825	Spanish-American Wars of Independence
1821	Mexico declares independence
1822	Brazil declares independence
1823	Monroe Doctrine indicates U.S. opposition to European ambitions in the Americas
1826	Ottoman Janissary corps destroyed
1839–1841	Opium War in China
1839–1876	*Tanzimat* reforms in the Ottoman Empire
1839–1897	Life of Islamic thinker Al-Afghani
1846–1848	Mexican-American War
1849–1905	Life of Muhammad Abduh
1862–1867	French intervention in Mexico
1850–1864	Taiping rebellion in China
1866	First railway begun in Ottoman Empire
1869	First school for girls in Mexico
1869	Opening of the Suez Canal
1870	Ottoman legal code reformed
1876–1911	Porfirio Díaz rules Mexico
1876–1908	Reign of Ottoman Sultan Abdul Hamid
1876	Constitution promulgated for Ottoman Empire
1882	British invasion and occupation of Egypt; failed revolt led by Orabi in Egypt
1886–1888	Cuba and Brazil abolish slavery
1889	Fall of Brazilian Empire; republic established
1895–1898	Cuban Spanish-American War; United States acquires Puerto Rico and Philippines
1898–1901	Boxer Rebellion in China; 100 Days of Reform in China
1898	British-Egyptian army defeats the Mahdist army at Omdurman
1903	Panamanian independence; beginning of Panama Canal (opens in 1914)
1908	Young Turks seize power in Istanbul

INTRODUCTION

For varying reasons a number of non-Western societies managed to escape conquest and formal colonization by the industrialized powers of Europe and North America in the decades before the outbreak of World War I. In both Siam and Persia, for example, European rivals chose to leave local rulers in power in order to maintain buffer states between their respective colonies. As we have seen in Chapter 2, Russia and Japan were able to "Westernize" sufficiently to ward off the threat of direct colonization by any of the industrial powers. Russia was, in any case, too large and had too long been a great power to be a serious candidate for conquest. In fact, Russia's tsarist rulers continued their centuries-old policy of expansion in Central Asia, which was an overland version of the pattern of empire building that western Europeans and the Americans pursued overseas. By contrast, Japan was too isolated from the European state system and was considered by imperial strategists in the West to be too poor in market and natural resource potential to justify the heavy costs of colonizing such a highly militarized society. For rather different reasons, the imperial powers found it much easier to manipulate politically and exploit economically the new states of Latin America and the vast Qing Empire of China through sporadic applications of gunboat diplomacy rather than outright conquest. As a result, each area was divided into informal spheres of influence among interested industrial powers. Within these spheres, the designated power (or powers) enjoyed special preferences in trade and investment and periodically applied diplomatic pressure or military force to bring recalcitrant indigenous leaders into line.

There were similar interventions in what remained of the Ottoman Empire as well. But the Islamic peoples of North Africa and the eastern Mediterranean had long been more directly involved in the wars and diplomatic maneuvering of the European powers. A combination of loss of territory to Balkan peoples, who overthrew Turkish control in the 19th century, and outright European conquests, particularly in North Africa and Egypt, raised the possibility that what was left of the battered Ottoman Empire would be partitioned into formal colonies like those in Africa or Southeast Asia.

In this chapter, we explore the ways in which informal dominance by the Western industrial powers worked in Latin America, the Middle Eastern heartlands of Islamic civilization, and China. We focus on both the ways that outside interventions skewed and often constricted the social, economic, and political development of these three critical areas, and on the efforts of targeted societies to resist Euro-American domination and reform their societies from within. To understand fully the important repercussions of these confrontations for world history in the 20th century, we need to look at both these internal developments and the impact of ongoing interventions by the Western imperialist powers.

NATIONAL CONSOLIDATION IN LATIN AMERICA

By 1830, the former Spanish and Portuguese colonies had become independent nations. The roughly 20 million inhabitants of these nations looked hopefully to the future. Many of the leaders of independence had shared ideals: representative government, careers open to talent, freedom of commerce and trade, the right to private property, and a belief in the individual as the basis of society. There was a general belief that the new nations should be sovereign and independent states, large enough to be economically viable and integrated by a common set of laws.

On the issue of freedom of religion and the position of the church, however, there was less agreement. Roman Catholicism had been the state religion and the only one allowed by the Spanish crown. While most leaders attempted to maintain Catholicism as the official religion of the new states, some tried to end the exclusion of other faiths. The defense of the Church became a rallying cry for the conservative forces.

The ideals of the early leaders of independence were often egalitarian. Bolívar had received aid from Haiti and had promised in return to abolish slavery in the areas he liberated. By 1854, slavery had been abolished everywhere except in Spain's remaining colonies, Cuba and Puerto Rico, as well as in Brazil; all were places where the economy was profoundly based on it. Early promises to end Indian tribute and taxes on people of mixed origin came much slower because the new nations still needed the revenue such policies produced. Egalitarian sentiments were often tempered by fears that the mass of the population was unprepared for self-rule and democracy. Early constitutions attempted to balance order and popular representation by imposing property or literacy restrictions on voters. Invariably, voting rights were reserved for men. Women were still disenfranchised and were usually not allowed to hold public office.

The lack of trust of the popular classes exhibited by the elite Creoles—American-born descendants of Europeans—was based on the fact that in many places the masses had not demonstrated a clear preference for the new regimes and had sometimes fought in royalist armies mobilized by traditional loyalties and regional interests. While some mestizos (people of mixed origin) had risen to leadership roles in the wars of independence, the old color distinctions did not disappear easily. In Mexico, Guatemala, and the Andean nations, the large Indian population remained mostly outside of national political life. The mass of the Latin American population, Indians and people of mixed origins, waited to see what was to come, and they were suspicious of the new political elite who were often drawn from the old colonial aristocracy but were now also joined by a new commercial and urban bourgeoisie.

Political Fragmentation

We can group the new Latin American nations into regional blocks. Some of the early leaders for independence had dreamed of creating a unified nation in some form, but regional rivalries, economic competition, and political divisions soon made that hope impossible. Mexico emerged as a short-lived monarchy until a republic was proclaimed in 1823, but its government remained unstable until the 1860s because of military coups, financial

ATLANTIC
OCEAN

MEXICO
1821
Mexico
City

Gulf of
Mexico

CUBA   HAITI 1804
BR.   PUERTO RICO
HONDURAS
Guatemala   TRINIDAD
UNITED PROVINCES OF   CARIBBEAN SEA
CENTRAL AMERICA   Panama
1823–1839   Caracas   BR. GUIANA
                  Bogotá   DUTCH GUIANA
                              FR. GUIANA
         GRAN COLOMBIA
         1819–1830
         Quito   Amazon R.

PACIFIC
OCEAN   PERU   EMPIRE OF BRAZIL
             1821   1822
             Lima   Bahia

             BOLIVIA
             1825
             Sucre   PARAGUAY
                     1813   Rio de Janeiro
                     Asunción
         CHILE
         1817
             Buenos   URUGUAY 1828
         Santiago Aires   Montevideo
             UNITED PROVINCES
             OF LA PLATA
             1816

Independent Nations of Latin America

failures, foreign intervention, and political turmoil. Central America broke away from the Mexican monarchy and did form a union, but regional antagonisms and resentment of Guatemala, the largest nation in the region, eventually led to dissolution of the union in 1838. Spain's Caribbean colonies, Cuba and Puerto Rico, suppressed early movements for independence and remained outwardly loyal. The Dominican Republic was occupied by its neighbor Haiti, and after resisting its neighbor, as well as France and Spain, it finally gained independence in 1844. The Dominican example and the fear of a Haitian-style slave revolt tended to keep the Creole leaders of Cuba and Puerto Rico quiet.

In South America, as mentioned previously, the old colonial viceroyalty of New Granada became the basis for Gran Colombia, the large new state created by Bolívar that included modern Ecuador, Colombia, Panama, and Venezuela. The union, made possible to some extent by Bolívar's personal reputation and leadership, disintegrated as his own standing declined, and it ended in

1830, the year of his death. In the south, the viceroyalty of the Rio de la Plata served as the basis for a desired state that the peoples of Argentina hoped to lead. Other parts of the region resisted. Paraguay declared and maintained its autonomy under Dr. José Rodríguez de Francia, who ruled his isolated and landlocked country as a dictator until 1840. Modern Uruguay was formed by a revolution for independence against the dominant power of its large neighbors, Argentina and Brazil. It became an independent buffer between those two nations in 1828. The Andean nations of Peru and Bolivia, with their large Indian populations and conservative colonial aristocracies, flirted with union from 1829 to 1839 under the mestizo general Andrés Santa Cruz, but once again regional rivalries and the fears of their neighbors undermined the effort. Finally, Chile, somewhat isolated and blessed by the opening of trade in the Pacific, followed its own political course in a relatively stable fashion.

Most attempts at consolidation and union failed. Enormous geographical barriers and great distances separated nations and even regions within nations. Roads were poor and transportation rudimentary. Geography, regional interests, and political divisions were too strong to overcome. The mass of the population remained outside the political process. The problems of national integration were daunting. What is striking is not that Spanish America became 18 separate nations but that it did not separate into even more.

Caudillos, Politics, and the Church

The problems confronting the new nations were many. Over a decade of warfare in places such as Venezuela, Colombia, and Mexico had disrupted the economies and devastated wide areas. The mobilization of large armies whose loyalty to regional commanders was often based on their personal qualities, rather than their rank or politics, led to the rise of *caudillos,* independent leaders who dominated local areas by force in defiance of national policies and who sometimes seized the national government itself to impose their concept of rule. In situations of intense division between civilian politicians, a powerful regional commander of the army became the arbiter of power, leading sometimes to a situation in which the army made and unmade governments. Keeping the army in the barracks became a preoccupation of governments, and the amount of money spent on the military in national budgets far exceeded the needs.

Military commanders and regional or national caudillos were usually interested in power for their own sake, but they could represent or mobilize different groups in society. Many often defended the interests of regional elites, usually landowners, but others were populists who mobilized and claimed to speak for Indians, peasants, and the poor and sometimes received their unquestioning support. A few, such as the conservative Rafael Carrera who ruled Guatemala from 1839 to 1865, sincerely took the interest of the Indian majority to heart, but other personalist leaders disregarded the normal workings of an open political system and the rule of law.

Other common issues confronted many of the new nations. Most political leaders were agreed on the republic as the basic form of government, but what kind of republic? A struggle often developed between centralists, who wished to create strong, centralized national governments with broad powers, and federalists, who wanted tax and commercial policies to be set by regional governments. Other tensions developed between liberals and conservatives. Liberals stressed the rights of the individual and attacked the corporate (membership in a group or organization) structure of colonial society. They dreamed of a secular society and looked to the United States and France as models. Often they wanted a decentralized, or federalist, form of government. Conservatives usually believed in a strong centralized state, and they often wished to maintain aspects of colonial life such as an emphasis on corporate groups like guilds.

Society, for the conservatives, was not based on open competition and individualism but was organic: each group was linked to the other like parts of a body whose health depended on the proper functioning of each part. Not all conservatives resisted change, and some—such as the Mexican intellectual and politician Lucas Alamán—were among the most "enlightened" leaders in terms of economic and commercial reforms. But as a group the conservatives were skeptical of secularism and individualism and strove to keep the Catholic Iberian heritage alive.

The role of the Church became a crucial issue in politics. It divided pro-clerical conservatives from the more secular liberals. In Mexico, for example, the Church had played a major role in education, the economy, and politics. Few questioned its dogma, but liberals tried to limit its role in civil life. The Church fought back with the aid of its pro-clerical supporters and with the power of the papacy, which until the 1840s refused to fill vacant positions in the hierarchy or to cooperate with the new governments.

Political parties, often calling themselves Liberal or Conservative, sprang up throughout Latin America.

They struggled for power and tried to impose their vision of the future on society. Their leaders, however, were usually drawn from the same social class of landowners and urban bourgeoisie, with little to differentiate them except their position in the Church or on the question of federalism versus centralization. The general population might be mobilized by the force and personality of a particular leader such as Juan Manuel de Rosas in Argentina or Antonio López de Santa Anna in Mexico, but political ideology was rarely an issue for most of the population.

The result was political turmoil and insecurity in much of Latin America in the first 50 years following independence. Presidents came and went with sad rapidity. Written constitutions, which both liberals and conservatives thought were a positive thing, were often short-lived and were overturned with a change in government because the margin for interpretation of the constitution was slight. Great efforts were made to make constitutions precise, specific, and definitive, but this resulted in an attempt to change or at least modify them each time there was a change in government. Some nations avoided the worst aspects of instability. Chile, after enacting a constitution in 1833 that gave the president broad powers, established a functioning political system that allowed for compromise. Brazil, with its monarchical rule, despite a period of turmoil from 1832 to 1850, was able to maintain a political system of compromise, although it was dominated by the Conservatives, who were favored by the emperor. Its 1824 constitution remained in force until 1889.

It is fair to say that in much of Latin America the basic questions of government and society remained unresolved after independence. Some observers attributed these problems to personalism, a lack of civic responsibility, and other defects in the "Latin" character. Nevertheless, the parallel experience of later emerging nations in the 20th century suggests that these problems were typical of former colonial dependencies searching for order and economic security in a world in which their options were constrained by their own potential and by external conditions.

Economic Resurgence and Liberal Politics

By the last quarter of the 20th century, as the world economy entered into a phase of rapid expansion, there was a shift in attitude and possibilities in Latin America. Liberals returned to power in many places in Latin America and initiated a series of changes that began to transform their nations. The ideological basis of the new liberal surge was also changing. Based on the ideas of *positivism* from the French philosopher Auguste Comte, who stressed observation and a scientific approach to the problems of society, Latin American politicians and intellectuals found a guiding set of principles and a justification of their quest for political stability and economic growth.

This shift was due in large part to the general economic expansion of the "second" Industrial Revolution and the age of imperialism. The application of science to industry created new demands for Latin American products, such as copper and rubber, to accompany the increasing demand for its consumer products, such as wheat, sugar, and coffee. The population of Latin America doubled to more than 43 million inhabitants in the 60 years between 1820 and 1880. After 1850, economies grew rapidly; the timing, of course, varied greatly, but the expansion of exports in places such as Colombia, Argentina, and Brazil stimulated prosperity for some and a general belief in the advantages of the liberal programs. The desire to participate in the capitalist expansion of the Western economy dominated the thinking of Latin American leaders. Foreign entrepreneurs and bankers joined hands with philosophical liberals, landowners, and urban merchants in Latin America to back the liberal programs, which now became possible because of the increased revenues generated by exports.

The leaders of the post-1860 governments were a new generation of politicians who had matured during the chaotic years of postindependence politics. Their inspiration came from England, France, and the United States. They were firm believers in progress, education, and free competition within a secular society, but they were sometimes distrustful of the mass of their own people, who seemed to represent an ancient "barbarism" in contrast to the "civilization" of progress. That distrust and their sometimes insensitive application of foreign models to a very different reality in their own countries—what one Brazilian author has called "ideas out of place"—prevented many from achieving the progress they so ardently desired.

Economic growth and "progress" were costly. Responding to international demand, landowners increased their holdings, often aided by the governments they controlled or influenced. Peasant lands were expropriated in Chile, Peru, and Bolivia; small farmers were displaced in Brazil and Costa Rica; and Church lands were seized in Mexico. Labor was needed. Immigrants from Europe flooded into Argentina and Brazil, while in other countries new forms of tenancy, peonage, and disguised servitude emerged.

Cultural Life and Politics

In the 1830s, the generation that came of age after independence turned to romanticism and found the basis of a new nationality in historical images, the Indian, and local customs. This generation often had a romantic view of liberty. They emphasized the exotic as well as the distinctive aspects of American society. In Brazil, for example, the poet Antônio Gonçalves Dias (1823–1864) used the Indian as a symbol of Brazil and America. In Cuba, novels sympathetic to slaves began to appear by midcentury. In Argentina, writers celebrated the pampas and its lonely open spaces. Sarmiento's critical account of the caudillos in *Facundo* described in depth the life of the gauchos, but it was José Hernández who in 1872 wrote *Martín Fierro*, a romantic epic poem about the end of the way of the gaucho. Historical themes and the writing of history itself became a political act, because the analysis of the past became a way of setting out a proper program for the present. Many of Latin America's leading politicians were also excellent historians: Mitre in Argentina, Alamán in Mexico, and a remarkable group of liberal Chilean historians deeply influenced by positivism.

By the 1870s, a new realism emerged in the arts and literature that was more in line with the scientific approach of positivism and the modernization of the new nations. As the economies of Latin America surged forward, novelists appeared who were unafraid to deal with human frailties such as corruption, prejudice, and greed. The Chilean Alberto Blest Gana and the Brazilian mulatto Machado de Assis (1839–1908) wrote critically about the social mores of their countries during this era.

Throughout the century, the culture of the mass of the population had been little affected by the trends and taste of the elite. Popular arts, folk music, and dance flourished in traditional settings, demonstrating a vitality and adaptability to new situations that was often lacking in the more imitative fine arts. Sometimes authors in the romantic tradition or poets like Hernández turned to traditional themes for their subject and inspiration, and in that way they brought these traditions to the greater attention of their class and of the world. For the most part, however, popular artistic expressions were not appreciated or valued by the traditional elites, by the modernizing urban bourgeoisie, or by the newly arrived immigrants.

Gender, Class, and Race

Although significant political changes make it appealing to deal with the 19th century as an era of great change and transformation in Latin America, it is necessary to recognize the persistence of old patterns and sometimes their reinforcement. Changes took place, to be sure, but their effects were not felt equally by all classes or groups in society, nor were all groups attracted by the promises of the new political regimes and their views of progress.

Women, for example, gained little ground during most of the century. They had participated actively in the independence movements. Some had taken up arms or aided the insurgent forces, and some such as the Colombian Policarpa (La Pola) Salvatierra, whose final words were "Do not forget my example," had paid for their activities on the gallows. Following independence, there was virtually no change in the predominant attitudes toward women's proper roles. Expected to be wives and mothers, women could not vote, hold public office, become lawyers, or in some places testify in a court of law. While there were a few exceptions, unmarried women younger than 25 remained under the power and authority of their fathers. Once married, they could not work, enter into contracts, or control their own estates without the permission of their husbands. As in the colonial era, marriage, politics, and the creation of kinship links were essential elements in elite control of land and political power, and thus women remained a crucial resource in family strategies.

Lower-class women had more economic freedom, often controlling local marketing, and also more personal freedom than elite women under the constraints of powerful families. In legal terms, however, their situation was no better—and in material terms, much worse—than that of their elite sisters. Still, women were by the 1870s an important part of the workforce.

Only in public education did the situation of women begin to change significantly. There had already been a movement in this direction in the colonial era. At first, the idea behind it was that since women were responsible for the education of their children, they should be educated so that the proper values could be passed to the next generation. By 1842, Mexico City required girls and boys aged 7 to 15 to attend school, and in 1869 the first girls' school was created in Mexico. Liberals in Mexico wanted secular public education to prepare women for an enlightened role within the home, and similar sentiments were expressed by liberal regimes elsewhere. Public schools appeared throughout Latin America, although their impact was limited. Brazil, for example, had a population of 10 million in 1873, but only about 1 million men and half that number of women were literate.

The rise of secular public education created new opportunities for women. The demand for teachers at the primary level created the need for schools in which to train teachers. Since most teachers were women, these teacher training schools provided women access to advanced education. While the curriculum often emphasized traditional female roles, an increasing number of educated women began to emerge who were dissatisfied with the legal and social constraints on their lives. By the end of the 19th century, these women were becoming increasingly active in advocating women's rights and other political issues.

In most cases, the new nations legally ended the old "society of castes" in which legal status and definition depended on color and ethnicity, but in reality much of that system continued. The stigma of skin color and former slave status created barriers to advancement. Indians in Mexico, Bolivia, and Peru often continued to labor under poor conditions and to suffer the effects of government failures. There was conflict. In Yucatan, a great rebellion broke out, pitting the Maya against the central government and the whites, in 1839 and then again in 1847. It smoldered for ten years. Despite the intentions of governments, Indians proved resistant to changes imposed from outside their communities and were willing to defend their traditional ways. The word Indian was still an insult in most places in Latin America. For some mestizos and others of mixed origin, the century presented opportunities for advancement in the army, professions, and commerce, but these cases were exceptions.

In many places, expansion of the export economy resulted in continuation and intensification of old patterns. Liberalism itself changed during the century, and once its program of secularization, rationalism, and rights of property were implanted as law, it displayed a more restrictive nature. Positivists of the end of the century still hoped for economic growth, but some were willing to gain it at the expense of individual freedoms. The positivists were generally convinced of the benefits of international trade for Latin America, and large landholdings increased in many areas at the expense of small farms and Indian communal lands as a result. A small, white Creole, landed upper class controlled the economies and politics in most places, and they were sometimes joined in the political and economic functions by a stratum of urban middle-class merchants, bureaucrats, and other bourgeois types. The landed and mercantile elite tended to merge over time to create one group that, in most places, controlled the government. Meanwhile, there were new social forces at work. The flood of immigration, beginning in earnest in the 1870s, to Argentina, Brazil, and a few other nations began to alter the social composition of those places. Increasingly, rapid urbanization also changed the nature of these societies. Still, Latin America, though politically independent, began the 1880s as a group of predominantly agrarian nations with rigid social structures and a continuing dependency on the world market.

Explaining Underdevelopment

Whether we use the word *underdeveloped,* the more benign *developing,* or the old-fashioned *backward,* it is usually clear that the term describes a large number of nations in the world that are beset by a series of economic and social problems. Because Latin America was the first part of what came to be called the Third World to establish its independence and begin to compete within the world economy, it had to confront the reasons for its relative position and problems quite early and without many alternative models to follow. Cultural explanations for Latin American problems were popular among 19th-century intellectuals and political leaders, and they continue today, though other general theories based on economics and politics have become more accepted.

At the time of Latin-American independence, the adoption of European models of economy, government, and law seemed to offer great hope. But as "progress," republican forms of government, free trade, and liberalism failed to bring about general prosperity and social harmony, Latin Americans and others began to search for alternative explanations of their continuing problems as a first step in solving them. Some critics condemned the Hispanic cultural legacy; others saw the materialism of the modern world as the major problem and called for a return to religion and idealism. By the 20th century, Marxism provided a powerful analysis of Latin America's history and present reality though Marxists themselves could not decide whether Latin American societies were essentially feudal and needed first to become capitalist, or whether they were already capitalist and were ready for socialist revolution.

Throughout these discussions and debates, Latin Americans often implicitly compared their situation with that of the United States and tried to explain the different economic positions of the two regions. At the beginning of the 19th century, both regions were still primarily agricultural, and while a few places in North America were starting small industries, the mining sector in Latin America was far stronger than that of its northern neighbor. In 1850, Latin America had a population of 33 million in comparison with 23 million in the United States, and the per capita income in both regions was roughly equal. By 1940, however, Latin America's population was much larger, and its economic situation was far worse than in the United States. Observers were preoccupied by why and how this disparity arose. Was there some flaw in the Latin American character, or were the explanations to be found in the economic and political differences between the two areas? How could these differences be explained? The answers to these questions were not easy to obtain, but increasingly they were sought not in the history of individual countries but in analyses of a world economic and political system.

While there had long been a Marxist critique of colonialism and imperialism, the modern Latin American analysis of underdevelopment grew from different origins. During the 1950s, a number of European and North American scholars developed the concept of "modernization," or "westernization." Basing their ideas on the historical experience of western Europe, they believed that development was a matter of increasing per capita production in any society, and that as development took place various kinds of social changes would follow. The more industrialized, urban, and modern a society became, the more social change and improvement were possible as traditional patterns and attitudes were abandoned or transformed. Technology, communications, and the diffusion of material goods were the means by which the transformation would take place. Some scholars also believed that as this process occurred there would be a natural movement toward more democratic forms of government and popular participation.

Modernization theory held out the promise that any society could move toward a brighter future by essentially following the path taken earlier by western Europe. Its message was one of improvement through gradual rather than radical or revolutionary change, and thus it tended to be politically conservative. It also tended to disregard cultural differences, internal class conflicts, and struggles for power within nations. Moreover, it was sometimes adopted by military regimes that believed that imposing order was the best way to promote the economic changes necessary for modernization.

The proponents of modernization theory had a difficult time convincing many people in the "underdeveloped" world, where the historical experience had been considerably different from that of western Europe. In 19th-century Latin America, for example, early attempts to develop industry had been faced with competition from the cheaper and better products of already industrialized nations such as England and France, and so a similar path to development was impossible. Critics argued that each nation did not operate individually but was part of a world system that functioned to keep some areas "developed" at the expense of others.

These ideas were first and most cogently expressed in Latin America. After World War II, the United Nations established an Economic Commission for Latin America (ECLA). Under the leadership of the Argentine economist Raul Prebisch, the ECLA began to analyze the Latin American economies. Prebisch argued that "unequal exchange" between the developed nations at the center of the world economy and those like Latin America created structural blocks to economic growth. The ECLA suggested various policies to overcome the problems, especially the development of industries that would overcome the region's dependence on foreign imports.

From the structural analysis of the ECLA and from more traditional Marxist critiques, a new kind of explanation, usually called *dependency theory,* began to emerge in the 1960s. Rather than seeing underdevelopment or the lack of economic growth as the result of failed modernization, some scholars in Latin America began to argue that development and underdevelopment were not stages but part of the same process. They believed that the development and growth of some areas, such as western Europe and the United States, were achieved at the expense of, or because of, the underdevelopment of dependent regions such as Latin America. Agricultural economies at the periphery of the world economic system were always at a disadvantage in dealing with the industrial nations of the center, and thus they would become relatively poorer as the industrial nations got richer. The industrial nations would continually draw products, profits, and cheap labor from the periphery.

This basic economic relationship of dependency meant that production, capital accumulation, and class relations in a dependent country were all essentially determined by external forces. Some theorists went even further and argued that Latin America and other nations of the Third World were also culturally dependent in their consumption of ideas and concepts. Both modernization theory and Mickey Mouse were seen as the agents of a cultural domination that was simply an extension of economic reality. These theorists usually argued that socialism offered the only hope for breaking out of the dependency relationship.

These ideas, which dominated Latin-American intellectual life, were broadly appealing to other areas of Asia and Africa that had recently emerged from colonial control. Forms of dependency analysis became popular in many areas of the world in the 1960s and 1970s. By the 1980s, however, dependency theory was losing its appeal. As an explanation of what had happened historically in Latin America, it was useful; but as a theory that could predict what might happen elsewhere and what to do, it provided little help. Marxists argued that it overemphasized the circulation of goods (trade) rather than how things were produced and that it ignored the class conflicts they believed were the motor force of history. Moreover, with the rise of multinational corporations, the nature of capitalism itself was changing, and thus an analysis based on trade relationships between countries became somewhat outdated.

Whether development can be widely diffused, as modernization theory argued, or whether the underdevelopment of some countries is inherent in the nature of the world economy, as the dependency theorists believed, is still a matter of dispute.

Now the debate centers on globalization, the increasing integration of the economies of advanced and developing nations as labor, capital, ideas, and jobs are exchanged. Some countries have seen faster growth and better living standards as a result of this global integration, but the economies of other nations have stagnated in the face of high unemployment. Globalization has its advocates and its detractors and while the context of the world economy has changed, the old debates on how best to achieve economic growth and to make its benefits available to as many people as possible remains as heated as they have been since the days of dependency theory.

Questions: In what sense was 19th-century Latin America a dependent economy? Which explanation or prediction about dependency best fits world economic trends today?

THE GREAT BOOM, 1880-1920

Between 1880 and 1920, Latin America, like certain areas of Asia and Africa, experienced a tremendous spurt of economic growth, stimulated by the increasing demand in industrializing Europe and the United States for raw materials, foodstuffs, and specialized tropical crops. Latin America was well prepared for export-led economic expansion. The liberal ideology of individual freedoms, an open market, and limited government intervention in the operation of the economy had triumphed in many places. Whereas this ideology had been the expression of the middle class in Europe, in Latin America it was adopted not only by the small urban middle class but also by the large landowners, miners, and export merchants linked to the rural economy and the traditional patterns of wealth and landowning. In a number of countries, a political alliance was forged between the traditional aristocracy of wealth and the new urban elements. Together they controlled the presidential offices and the congresses and imposed a business-as-usual approach to government at the expense of peasants and a newly emerging working class.

The expansion of Latin American economies was led by exports. Each nation had a specialty: bananas and coffee from Central America; tobacco and sugar from Cuba; rubber and coffee from Brazil; hennequen (a fiber for making rope), copper, and silver from Mexico; wool, wheat, and beef from Argentina; and copper from Chile. In this era of strong demand and good prices, these nations experienced high profits. This allowed them to import large quantities of foreign manufactures, and it provided funds for the beautification of cities and other government projects. But export-led expansion was always risky because the world market prices of Latin American commodities were ultimately determined by conditions outside the region. In that sense, these economies were particularly vulnerable and in some ways dependent.

The expansion of Latin American trade was remarkable. It increased by about 50 percent between 1870 and 1890. Argentina's trade was increasing at about 5 percent a year during this period, one of the highest rates of growth ever recorded for a national economy. "As wealthy as an Argentine" became an expression in Paris, reflecting the fortunes that wool, beef, and grain were earning for some in Argentina. In Mexico, an "oligarchic dictatorship," which maintained all the outward attributes of democracy but imposed "law and order" under the dictator Porfirio Díaz, created the conditions for un-restrained profits. Mexican exports doubled between 1877 and 1900. Similar figures could be cited for Chile, Costa Rica, and Bolivia.

This rapidly expanding commerce attracted the interest of foreign investors eager for high returns on their capital. British, French, German, and North American businessmen and entrepreneurs invested in mining, railroads, public utilities, and banking. More than half the foreign investments in Latin America were British, which alone were ten times more in 1913 than they had been in 1870. But British leadership was no longer uncontested; Germany and, increasingly, the United States provided competition. The United States was particularly active in the Caribbean region and Mexico, but not until after World War I would U.S. capital predominate in the region.

Foreign investments provided Latin America with needed capital and services but tended to place key industries, transportation facilities, and services in foreign hands. Foreign investments also constrained Latin American governments in the social, commercial, and diplomatic policies that they could follow.

Mexico and Argentina

We can use two large Latin American nations—Mexico and Argentina—as examples of different responses within the same general pattern. In Mexico, the Liberal triumph of Juarez had set the stage for economic growth and constitutional government. In 1876, Porfirio Díaz, one of Juarez's generals, was elected president, and for the next 35 years he dominated politics. Díaz suppressed regional rebellions and imposed a strong centralized government. Financed by foreign capital, the railroad system grew rapidly, providing a new way of integrating Mexican regional economies, moving goods to the ports for export and allowing the movement of government troops to keep order. Industrialization began to take place. Foreign investment was encouraged in mining, transportation, and other sectors of the economy, and financial policies were changed to promote investments—with U.S. investments, for example, expanding from about 30 million pesos in 1883 to over 1 billion by 1911.

Although the forms of liberal democracy were maintained, they were subverted in order to keep Díaz in power and to give his development plans an open track. Behind these policies were a number of advisors, who were strongly influenced by positivist ideas and who wished to impose a scientific approach on the national economy. These *cientificos* set the tone for Mexico while the government suppressed any political opposition to these policies. Díaz's Mexico projected an image of modernization led by a Europeanized elite who greatly profited from the economic growth and the imposition of order under Don Porfirio.

Growth was often bought at the expense of Mexico's large rural peasantry and its growing urban and working classes. This population was essentially native, since unlike Argentina and Brazil, Mexico had received few immigrants. Indigenous peoples participated very little in the prosperity of export-led growth. Economic expansion at the expense of peasants and Indian communal lands created a volatile situation.

Strikes and labor unrest increased, particularly among railroad workers, miners, and textile workers. In the countryside, a national police force, the *rurales,* maintained order, and the army was mobilized when needed. At the regional level, political bosses linked to the Díaz regime in Mexico City delivered the votes in rigged elections.

For 35 years, Díaz reigned supreme and oversaw the transformation of the Mexican economy. His opponents were arrested or driven into exile, while the small middle class, the landowners, miners, and foreign investors celebrated the progress of Mexico. In 1910, however, a middle-class movement with limited political goals seeking electoral reform began to mushroom into a more general uprising in which the frustrations of the poor, the workers, the peasants, and nationalist intellectuals of various political persuasions erupted in a bloody ten-year civil war, the Mexican Revolution.

At the other end of the hemisphere, Argentina followed an alternative path of economic expansion. By 1880, the Indians on the southern pampa had finally been conquered, and vast new tracts of land were opened to ranching. The strange relationship between Buenos Aires and the rest of the nation had finally been resolved when Buenos Aires was made a federal district. With a rapidly expanding economy, it became "the Paris of the Americas," an expression that reflected the drive by wealthy Argentines to establish their credentials as a modern nation. By 1914, Buenos Aires had over two million inhabitants, or about one-fourth of the national population. Its political leaders, the "Generation of 1880," were the inheritors of the liberal program of Sarmiento and Mitre, and they were able to enact their programs because of the high levels of income generated by the expanding economy.

Technological changes contributed to Argentine prosperity. Refrigerated ships allowed fresh beef to be sent directly to Europe, and this along with wool and wheat provided the basis of expansion. Labor was provided by a flood of immigrants. Some were *golondrinas* (literally, "swallows"), who were able to work one harvest in Italy and then a second in Argentina because of the differences in seasons in the two hemispheres, but many immigrants elected to stay. Almost 3.5 million immigrants

The tremendous boom in the Argentine economy was reflected in the growth of Buenos Aires, the so-called Paris of the Americas, as a cosmopolitan urban center.

stayed in Argentina between 1857 and 1930, and unlike the Mexican population, by 1914 about one-third of the Argentine population was foreign born. Italians, Germans, Russians, and Jews came to "hacer America"— that is, "to make America"—and remained. In a way, they really did Europeanize Argentina, introducing the folkways and ideologies of the European rural and working classes. This did not happen in Mexico. The result was a fusion of cultures that produced not only a radical workers' movement but also the distinctive music of the tango, which combined Spanish, African, and other musical elements in the cafe and red-light districts of Buenos Aires. The tango became the music of the Argentine urban working class.

As the immigrant flood increased, workers began to seek political expression. A Socialist party was formed in the 1890s and attempted to elect representatives to office. Anarchists hoped to smash the political system and called for strikes and walkouts. Inspired to some extent by European ideological battles, the struggle spilled into the streets. Violent strikes and government repression characterized the decade after 1910, culminating in a series of strikes in 1918 that led to extreme repression. Development had its social costs.

The Argentine oligarchy was capable of some internal reform, however. A new party representing the emerging middle class began to organize. It was aided by an electoral law in 1912 that called for secret ballots, universal male suffrage, and compulsory voting. With this change, the Radical party, promising political reform and more liberal policies for workers, came to power in 1916, but faced with labor unrest it acted as repressively as its predecessors. The oligarchy made room for middle-class politicians and interests, but the problems of Argentina's expanding labor force remained unresolved, and Argentina's economy remained closely tied to the international market for its exports.

With considerable variations, similar patterns of economic growth, political domination by oligarchies formed by traditional aristocracies and "progressive" middle classes, and a rising tide of labor unrest or rural rebellion can be noted elsewhere in Latin America. Modernization and "progress" were not welcomed by all sectors of society. Messianic religious movements in Brazil, Indian resistance to the loss of lands in Colombia, and banditry in Mexico were all to some extent reactions to the changes being forced on the societies by national governments tied to the ideology of progress and often insensitive to its effects.

Uncle Sam Goes South

After its Civil War, the United States began to take a more direct and active interest in the politics and economic situation of Latin America. Commerce and investments began to expand rapidly in this period, especially in Mexico and Central America. American industry was seeking new markets and raw materials, while the growing population of the United States created a demand for Latin American products. Attempts were made to create inter-American cooperation. A major turning point came in 1898 with the outbreak of war between Spain and the United States, which now began to join the nations of western Europe in the age of imperialism.

The war centered on Cuba and Puerto Rico, Spain's last colonies in the Americas. The Cuban economy had boomed in the 19th century on the basis of its exports of sugar and tobacco grown with slave labor. A ten-year civil war for independence, beginning in 1868, had failed in its main objective but had won the island some autonomy. A number of ardent Cuban nationalists, including the journalist and poet José Marti, had gone into exile to continue the struggle. Fighting erupted again in 1895, and the United States joined in 1898, declaring war on Spain and occupying Cuba, Puerto Rico, and the Philippines.

In fact, U.S. investments in Cuba had been rapidly increasing before the war, and the United States had become a major market for Cuban sugar. The Cuban Spanish-American War now opened the door to direct U.S. involvement in the Caribbean. The Cuban army was treated poorly by its American allies, and a U.S. government of occupation was imposed on Cuba as well as Puerto Rico, which had witnessed its own stirrings for independence in the 19th century. When the occupation of Cuba ended in 1902, a series of onerous conditions was imposed on independent Cuba that made it a virtual American dependency, a status that was in fact legally imposed in Puerto Rico.

For strategic, commercial, and economic reasons, Latin America, particularly the Caribbean and Mexico, began to attract American interest at the turn of the century. These considerations lay behind the drive to construct a canal across Central America that would shorten the route between the Atlantic and Pacific. When Colombia proved reluctant to meet American proposals, the United States backed a Panamanian movement for independence and then signed a treaty with its representative that granted the United States extensive rights over a transisthmus canal. President Theodore Roosevelt was a major force behind the canal, which was opened to traffic in 1908.

The Panama Canal was a remarkable engineering feat and a fitting symbol of the technological and industrial strength of the United States. North Americans were proud of these achievements and hoped to demonstrate the superiority of the "American way," a feeling fed to some extent by racist ideas and a sense of cultural superiority. Latin Americans were now wary of American power and intentions in the area. Many intellectuals cautioned against the expansionist designs of the United States and against what they viewed as the materialism of American culture. The Uruguayan José Enrique Rodó, in his essay *Ariel* (1900), contrasted the spirituality of Hispanic culture to the materialism of the United States. Elsewhere in Latin America, others offered similar critiques.

Latin American criticism had a variety of origins: nationalism, a Catholic defense of traditional values, and also some socialist attacks on expansive capitalism. In a way, Latin America, which had achieved its political independence in the 19th century and had been part of European developments, was able to articulate clearly the fears and the reactions of the areas that had become the colonies and semicolonies of western Europe and the United States in the age of empire.

FROM EMPIRE TO NATION: OTTOMAN RETREAT AND THE BIRTH OF TURKEY

Despite almost two centuries of unrelieved defeats on the battlefield and steady losses of territory, the Ottoman Empire somehow managed to survive into the 20th century. Its survival was due in part to divisions between the European powers, each of which feared that the others would gain more from the total dismemberment of the empire. In fact, the British concern to prevent the Russians from controlling Istanbul—thus gaining direct access to and threatening British naval dominance in the Mediterranean—led them to prop up the tottering Ottoman regime repeatedly in the last half of the 19th century. Ultimately, the Ottomans' survival depended on reforms from within—reforms initiated by the sultans and their advisors at the top of the imperial system and carried out in stages over most of the 19th century. At each stage, reform initiatives intensified tensions within the ruling elite. Some factions advocated far-reaching change along European lines, others argued for reforms

based on precedents from the early Ottoman period, and other elite groups had a vested interest in blocking change of any sort.

These deep divisions within the Ottoman elite rendered reform a dangerous enterprise. Though modest innovations, including the introduction of the first printing press in 1727, had been enacted in the 18th century, Sultan Selim III (1789–1807) believed that bolder initiatives were required if the dynasty and empire were to survive. But his reform efforts, which were aimed at improving administrative efficiency and building a new army and navy, angered powerful factions within the bureaucracy. They were also viewed by the Janissary corps, which had long been the dominant force within the Ottoman military, as a direct and vital threat. Selim's modest initiatives cost him his throne—he was toppled by a Janissary revolt in 1807—and his life.

Two decades later, a more skillful sultan, Mahmud II, succeeded where Selim III had failed. After secretly building a small professional army with the help of European advisors, in 1826 Mahmud II ordered his agents to incite a mutiny of the Janissaries. This began when the angry Janissaries overturned the huge soup kettles in their mess area. With little thought given to planning their next move, the Janissaries poured into the streets of Istanbul—more a mob than a military force. Once on the streets, they were shocked to be confronted by the sultan's well-trained new army. The confrontation ended in the slaughter of the Janissaries as well as their families and religious allies.

After cowing the ayan, or provincial notables, into at least formal submission to the throne, Mahmud II launched a program of much more far-reaching reforms than Selim III had attempted. Though the ulama, or religious experts, and some of Mahmud's advisors argued for self-strengthening through a return to the Ottoman and Islamic past, Mahmud II patterned his reform program on Western precedents. After all, the Western powers had made a shambles of his empire. He established a diplomatic corps on Western lines and exchanged ambassadors with the European powers. The Westernization of the army was expanded from Mahmud's secret force to the whole military establishment. European military advisors, both army and navy, were imported to supervise the overhaul of Ottoman training, armament, and officers' education.

In the decades that followed, Western influences were pervasive at the upper levels of Ottoman society, particularly during the period of the Tanzimat reforms between 1839 and 1876. University education was reorganized on

The Ottoman Empire in the Late 18th Century

Western lines, and training in the European sciences and mathematics was introduced. State-run postal and telegraph systems were introduced in the 1830s, and railways were begun in the 1860s. Newspapers were established in the major towns of the empire. Extensive legal reforms were enacted, and in 1876 a constitution, based heavily on European prototypes, was promulgated. These legal reforms greatly improved the position of minority religious groups, whose role in the Ottoman economy increased steadily.

Some groups were adversely affected by these changes, which opened the empire more and more to Western influences. This was especially true of the artisans, whose position was gravely weakened by an 1838 treaty with the British that removed import taxes and other barriers to foreign trade that had protected indigenous producers from competition from the West. Other social groups gained little from the Tanzimat reforms. This was particularly true of women. Proposals for women's education and an end to seclusion, polygamy, and veiling were debated in Ottoman intellectual circles from the 1860s onward. But few improvements in the position of women—even among the elite classes—were

won until after the last Ottoman sultan was driven from power in 1908.

Repression and Revolt

The reforms initiated by the sultans and their advisors did improve somewhat the Ottomans' ability to fend off, or at least deflect, the assaults of foreign aggressors. But they increasingly threatened the dynasty responsible for them. Western-educated bureaucrats, military officers, and professionals came increasingly to view the sultanate as a major barrier to even more radical reforms and the full transformation of society. The new elites also clashed with conservative but powerful groups, such as the ulama and the ayan, who had a vested interest in preserving as much as possible of the old order.

The Ottoman Sultan Abdul Hamid responded to the growing threat from Westernized officers and civilians by attempting a return to despotic absolutism during his long reign from 1878 to 1908. He nullified the constitution, and restricted civil liberties, particularly the freedom of the press. These measures deprived Westernized elite groups of the considerable initiative they had gained in the formulation of imperial policies. Legal safeguards were flouted as dissidents or even suspected troublemakers were summarily imprisoned and sometimes tortured and killed. But the deep impact that decades of reform had made upon the empire was demonstrated by the fact that even Abdul Hamid continued to push for Westernization in certain areas. The military continued to adopt European arms and techniques, increasingly under the instruction of German advisors. In addition, railways, including the famed line that linked Berlin to Baghdad, and telegraph lines were constructed between the main population centers. Western-style educational institutions grew and judicial reforms continued.

The despotism of Abdul Hamid came to an abrupt end in the nearly bloodless coup of 1908. Resistance to his authoritarian rule had led exiled Turkish intellectuals and political agitators to found the Ottoman Society for Union and Progress, in Paris in 1889. Professing their loyalty to the Ottoman regime, the Young Turks, as members of the society came to be known, were determined to restore the 1876 constitution and resume far-reaching reforms within the empire. Clandestine printing presses operated by the Young Turks turned out tracts denouncing the regime and outlining further steps to be taken to modernize and thus save the empire. Assassinations were attempted and coups plotted, but until 1908 all were undone by a combination of divisions within the ranks of the Westernized dissidents and police countermeasures.

Sympathy within the military for the 1908 coup had much to do with its success. Perhaps even more important was the fact that only a handful of the sultan's supporters were willing to die defending the regime. Though a group of officers came to power, they restored the constitution and press freedoms and promised reforms in education, administration, and even the status of women. The sultan was retained as a political figurehead and the highest religious authority in Islam.

Unfortunately, the officers soon became embroiled in factional fights that took up much of the limited time remaining before the outbreak of World War I. In addition, their hold on power was shaken when they lost a new round of wars in the Balkans and a conflict against Italy over Libya, the Ottomans' last remaining possession in North Africa. Just as the sultans had before them, however, the Young Turk officers managed to stave off the collapse of the empire by achieving last-gasp military victories and by playing the hostile European powers against each other.

Taken after Turkey's defeat in World War I and the successful struggles of the Turks to prevent the partition of their heartlands in Asia Minor by the victorious Greeks, this photo features members of the Young Turk group who have survived these challenges and grown a good deal older. The man in the business suit in the center is Mustafa Kemal, or Ataturk, who emerged as a masterful military commander during and after the war, and went on to become the founder of the modern nation of Turkey.

Though it is difficult to know how the Young Turks would have fared if it had not been for the outbreak of World War I, their failure to resolve several critical issues did not bode well for the future. They had overthrown the sultan, but they could not bring themselves to give up the empire ruled by Turks for over 600 years. The peoples most affected by their decision to salvage what was left of the empire were the Arabs of the Fertile Crescent and coastal Arabia, who still remained under Ottoman control. Arab leaders in Beirut and Damascus had initially favored the 1908 coup because they believed it would bring about the end of their long domination by the Turks. To their dismay, the Arabs discovered that the Young Turks not only meant to continue their subjugation but were determined to enforce state control to a degree unthinkable to the later Ottoman sultans.

The quarrels between the leaders of the Young Turk coalition and the growing resistance in the Arab portions of what was left of the Ottoman Empire were quite suddenly cut short in August 1914. The Young Turks' ineptitude was again demonstrated as they allowed the empire to become unnecessarily embroiled in the global conflict brought on by the outbreak of general war in Europe. Turkish entry into World War I on the side of the Germans in October, and its defeat several years later, brought about the dissolution of the Ottoman Empire. These reversals also gave rise to a leader, Mustafa Kemal, or Ataturk, who was able to galvanize his people for the formidable tasks involved in building the modern nation of Turkey from the ruins of defeat and the dismantling of the empire.

WESTERN INTRUSIONS AND THE CRISIS IN THE ARAB ISLAMIC HEARTLANDS

By the early 1800s, the Arab peoples of the Fertile Crescent, Egypt, coastal Arabia, and North Africa had lived for centuries under Ottoman-Turkish rule. Though most Arabs resented Turkish domination, they could identify with the Ottomans as fellow Muslims, who were both ardent defenders of the faith and patrons of Islamic culture. Still, the steadily diminishing capacity of the Ottomans to defend the Arab Islamic heartlands left them exposed to the danger of conquest by the aggressive European powers. The European capture of outlying, but highly developed, Islamic states from those in the In-

donesian archipelago and India to Algeria in North Africa engendered a sense of crisis among the Islamic faithful in the Middle Eastern heartlands. From the main adversaries of Christendom and the encirclers of its European bastion, the Muslims had become the besieged. The Islamic world had been displaced by the West as the leading civilization in a wide range of endeavors from scientific inquiry to monumental architecture. Much of the Muslim community was forced to live under infidel European overloads; what remained was threatened by European conquest.

The profound crisis of Islamic confidence brought on by successive reverses and the ever-increasing strength of their old European rivals elicited a wide variety of responses in the Islamic world. Islamic thinkers debated the best way of reversing the decline and driving back the Europeans. Some argued for a return to the Islamic past; others favored a large-scale adoption of Western ways; still others tried to find ways to combine the two approaches. Reformist leaders, such as Muhammad Ali in Egypt, tried to graft on elements of Western culture while preserving the old state and society pretty much intact. Religious leaders, most spectacularly the Mahdi of the Sudan who was regarded by his followers as a divinely appointed prophet, rose up to lead jihads, or holy wars, against the advancing Europeans.

Muhammad Ali and the Failure of Westernization in Egypt

Egypt provided the entering wedge for the advance of European imperialism in the Arab heartlands of the Middle East. The region was first conquered by Napoleon's armies in 1798, but the British navy and growing internal resistance soon ousted the French forces. In the chaos that followed the French invasion and eventual withdrawal in 1801, a young officer of Albanian origins named Muhammad Ali emerged as the effective ruler of Egypt. Deeply impressed by the weapons and discipline of the French armies, the Albanian upstart devoted his energies and the resources of the land that he had brought under his rule to building an up-to-date European-style military force. He introduced Western-style conscription among the Egyptian peasantry, hired French officers to train his troops, imported Western arms, and adopted Western tactics and modes of organization and supply. Within years he had put together the most effective fighting force in the Middle

East. With it, he flaunted the authority of his nominal overlord, the Ottoman sultan, by successfully invading Syria and building a modern war fleet that threatened Istanbul on a number of occasions.

Although Muhammad Ali's efforts to introduce reforms patterned after Western precedents were not confined to the military, they fell far short of a fundamental transformation of Egyptian society. To shore up his economic base, he ordered the Egyptian peasantry to expand their production of cotton, hemp, indigo, and other crops that were in growing demand in industrial Europe. Efforts to improve Egyptian harbors and extend irrigation works met with some success and led to modest increases in the revenues that could be devoted to the continuing modernization of the military. Attempts to reform education were ambitious but limited in what was actually achieved. His numerous schemes to build up an Egyptian industrial sector were eventually frustrated by the opposition of the European powers and by the intense competition from imported, Western-manufactured goods.

To secure his home base, Muhammad Ali also found that he had little choice but to ally with the powerful rural landlords, the *ayan*, to control the peasantry. He sought to eliminate nonofficial middlemen who collected taxes from the peasants, and he claimed all land as state property. But despite these measures, a hereditary landlord class was still firmly entrenched in the rural areas decades later. His forcible confiscations of the peasants' produce to pay for the rising costs of the military establishment and for his foreign entanglements further impoverished an already hard-pressed rural population.

The limited scope of Muhammad Ali's reforms ultimately checked his plans for territorial expansion and left Egypt open to inroads by the European powers. He died in 1848, embittered by the European opposition that had prevented him from mastering the Ottoman sultans and well aware that his empire beyond Egypt was crumbling. Lacking Muhammad Ali's ambition and ability, his successors were content to confine their claims to Egypt and the Sudanic lands that stretched away from the banks of the Upper Nile to the south (see map on p. 85). Intermarrying with Turkish families that had originally come to Egypt to govern in the name of the Ottoman sultans, Muhammad Ali's descendants provided a succession of rulers who were known as *khedives* after 1867. The khedives were the formal rulers of Egypt until they were overthrown by the military coup that brought Nasser to power in 1952.

Bankruptcy, European Intervention, and Strategies of Resistance

Muhammad Ali's successors made a muddle of his efforts to reform and revitalize Egyptian society. While cotton production increased and the landlord class grew fat, the great majority of the peasants went hungry or starved. The long-term consequences of these developments were equally troubling. The great expansion of cotton production at the expense of food grains and alternative market crops rendered Egypt dependent on a single export. This meant that it was vulnerable to sharp fluctuations in demand (thus price) on the European markets to which most of it was exported. Some further educational advances were made, but these were mainly at elite schools where French was the language of instruction. Therefore, the advances were too limited to benefit the broader populace by making government more efficient or stimulating public works projects and improved health care.

Much of the revenue the khedives managed to collect, despite the resistance of the ayan, was wasted on the extravagant pastimes of the mostly idle elite connected to the palace. Most of what was left was squandered on fruitless military campaigns to assert Egyptian authority over the Sudanic peoples along the upper Nile. The increasing inability of the khedives to balance their books led to their growing indebtedness to European financiers in the middle decades of the 19th century. The latter lent money to the profligate khedives and members of the Turkish elite because the financiers desired continued access to Egypt's cheap cotton. By the 1850s, they had a second motive—a share in the potentially lucrative schemes to build a canal across the Isthmus of Suez that would connect the Mediterranean and Red Seas. The completion of the Suez Canal in 1869 (see illustration on p. 89), transformed Egypt into one of the most strategic places on earth. The canal soon became a vital commercial and military link between the European powers and their colonial empires in Asia and East Africa. Controlling it became one of the key objectives of their peaceful rivalries and wartime operations through the first half of the 20th century.

The ineptitude of the khedival regime and the Ottoman sultans, who were their nominal overlords, prompted a good deal of discussion among Muslim intellectuals and political activists as to how they might ward off the growing European menace. In the middle decades of the 19th century, Egypt, and particularly Cairo's ancient Muslim University of al-Azhar, became key meeting places of these thinkers from throughout the

Building a canal across the desert Isthmus of Suez was a remarkable engineering feat. As this contemporary photo illustrates, a massive investment in up-to-date technology was needed. By creating a water route between the Mediterranean and Red seas, the canal greatly shortened the travel time between Europe and maritime Asia as well as the east coast of Africa. Combined with the growing predominance of steamships, it helped to expand global commerce as well as tourism, which became a major middle-class activity in the late 19th century.

Islamic world. Some prominent Islamic scholars called for a jihad to drive the infidels from Muslim lands. They also argued that the Muslim world could be saved only by a return to the patterns of religious observance and social interaction that they believed had existed in the "golden age" of the Prophet.

Other thinkers, such as al-Afghani (1839–1897) and his disciple Muhammad Abduh (1849–1905), stressed the need for Muslims to borrow scientific learning and technology from the West and to revive their earlier capacity to innovate. They argued that Islamic civilization had once taught the Europeans much in the sciences and mathematics, including such critical concepts as the Indian numerals. Thus it was fitting that Muslims learn from the advances the Europeans had made with the help of Islamic borrowings. Those who advocated this approach also stressed the importance of the tradition of

rational inquiry in Islamic history. They strongly disputed the views of religious scholars who contended that the Quran was the source of all truth and should be interpreted literally.

Though both religious revivalists and those who stressed the need for imports from the West agreed on the need for Muslim unity in the face of the growing European threat, they could not reconcile their very different approaches to Islamic renewal. Their differences and the uncertainties that these injected into Islamic efforts to cope with the challenges of the West, remain central problems in the Muslim world today.

The mounting debts of the khedival regime and the strategic importance of the canal gave the European powers, particularly Britain and France, a growing stake in the stability and accessibility of Egypt. French and British bankers, who had bought up a good portion of the khedives' shares in the canal, urged their governments to intervene militarily when the khedives proved unable to meet their loan payments. At the same time, French and British diplomats quarreled over how much influence each of their nations should exercise within Egypt.

In the early 1880s, a major challenge to the influence of foreign interests was mounted by the supporters of a charismatic young Egyptian officer named Ahmad Orabi. The son of a small farmer in lower Egypt, Orabi had attended Quranic school and studied under the reform-minded Muhammad Abduh at al-Azhar. Though a native Egyptian, Orabi had risen in the ranks of the khedival army and had become increasingly critical of the fact that the officer corps was dominated by Turks with strong ties to the khedival regime. An attempt by the khedive to save money by disbanding Egyptian regiments and dismissing Egyptian officers sparked a revolt led by Orabi in the summer of 1882. Riots in the city of Alexandria, associated with mutinies in the Egyptian armies, drove the frightened khedive to seek British assistance. After bombarding the coastal batteries set up by Orabi's troops, the British sent ashore an expeditionary force that crushed Orabi's rebellion and secured the position of the khedive. Though Egypt was not formally colonized, the British intervention began decades of dominance by both British consuls, who ruled through the puppet khedives, and British advisors to all high-ranking Egyptian administrators. British officials controlled Egypt's finances and foreign affairs; British troops ensured that their directives were heeded by Egyptian administrators. Direct European control over the Islamic heartlands had begun.

Jihad: The Mahdist Revolt in the Sudan

As Egypt fell under British control, the invaders were inevitably drawn into the turmoil and conflict that gripped the Sudanic region to the south (see map on p. 85). Egyptian efforts to conquer and rule the Sudan, beginning in the 1820s, were fiercely resisted. The opposition forces were led by the camel- and cattle-herding nomads who occupied the vast, arid plains that stretched west and east from the Upper Nile. The sedentary peoples who worked the narrow strip of fertile land along the river were more easily dominated. Thus, Egyptian authority, insofar as it existed at all, was concentrated in these areas and in river towns such as Khartoum, which was the center of Egyptian administration.

Even in the riverine areas, Egyptian overlordship was greatly resented. The Egyptian regime was notoriously corrupt, and its taxes placed a heavy burden on the peasants compelled to pay them. The Egyptians were clearly carpetbagging outsiders, and the favoritism they showed some of the Sudanic tribes was guaranteed to alienate the others. In addition, virtually all groups in the Muslim areas in the north Sudan were angered by Egyptian attempts in the 1870s to eradicate the slave trade. The trade had long been a great source of profit for both the merchants of the Nile towns and the nomads, who raided in areas occupied by non-Muslim peoples, such as the Dinka in the south, in order to capture slaves.

By the late 1870s, Egyptian oppression and British intervention had aroused deep resentment and hostility. But a leader was needed to unite the diverse and often divided peoples of the region and to provide an ideology that would give focus and meaning to rebellion. Muhammad Achmad proved to be that leader. He was the son of a boat builder and had been educated by the head of a local Sufi (mystical) brotherhood. The fact that his family claimed descent from the Prophet and that he had the physical signs—a cleft between his teeth and a mole on his right cheek—that the local people associated with the promised deliverer, or *Mahdi,* did much to advance his reputation. The visions he began to experience, after he had broken with his Sufi master and established his own sectarian following, also suggested that a remarkable future was in store. What was seen to be a miraculous escape from a bungled Egyptian effort to capture and imprison Muhammad Achmad soon led to his widespread acceptance as a divinely appointed leader of revolt against the foreign intruders.

The jihad that Muhammad Achmad, who came to be known to his followers as the Mahdi (the promised deliverer), proclaimed against both the Egyptian heretics and British infidels was one of a number of such movements that had swept through sub-Saharan Africa since the 18th century. It represented the most extreme and violent Islamic response to what was perceived as the dilution of Islam in the African environment and the growing threat of Europe. Muhammad Achmad promised to purge Islam of what he viewed as superstitious beliefs and degrading practices that had built up over the centuries, thus returning the faith to what he believed to be its original purity. He led his followers in a violent assault on the Egyptians, whom he believed professed a corrupt version of Islam, and on the European infidels. At one point, his successors dreamed of toppling the Ottoman sultans and invading Europe itself.

The Mahdi's skillful use of guerrilla tactics and the confidence his followers placed in his blessings and magical charms earned his forces several stunning victories over the Egyptians. Within a few years the Mahdist forces were in control of an area corresponding roughly to the present-day nation of Sudan (see map on p. 55). At the peak of his power, the Mahdi fell ill with typhus and died. In contrast to many movements of this type, which have collapsed rapidly after the death of their prophetic leaders, the Mahdists found a capable successor for Muhammad Achmad. The Khalifa Abdallahi had been one of the Mahdi's most skillful military commanders. Under Abdallahi, the Mahdists built a strong, expansive state. They also sought to build a closely controlled society, where smoking, dancing, and alcoholic drink were forbidden, and theft, prostitution, and adultery were severely punished. Islamic religious and ritual practices were rigorously enforced. In addition most foreigners were imprisoned or expelled, and the ban on slavery was lifted.

For nearly a decade, Mahdist armies attacked or threatened neighboring states on all sides, including the Egyptians to the north. But in the fall of 1896, the famed British General Kitchener was sent with an expeditionary force to put an end to what was one of the most serious threats to European domination in Africa. The spears and magical garments of the Mahdist forces proved no match for the machine guns and artillery of Kitchener's columns. At the battle of Omdurman in 1898, thousands of the Mahdist cavalry and Abdallahi himself were slaughtered. The Mahdist state collapsed, and British power advanced yet again into the interior of Africa.

Retreat and Anxiety: Islam Imperiled

The 19th century was a time of severe reverses for the peoples of the Islamic world. Outflanked and outfought by their old European rivals, either Islamic leaders became puppets of European overlords or their lands passed under the rule of infidel colonial rulers. Diverse forms of resistance, from the reformist path taken by the Ottoman sultans to the prophetic rebellions of leaders such as Muhammad Achmad, slowed but could not halt the European advance. European products and demands steadily eroded the economic fabric and heightened social tensions in Islamic lands. The stunning military and economic successes of the Christian Europeans cast doubts on Muslim claims that they possessed the one true faith. By the century's end, it was clear that neither the religious revivalists, who called for a return to a purified Islam free of Western influences, nor the reformers, who argued that some borrowing from the West was essential for survival, had come up with a successful for-

mula for dealing with the powerful challenges posed by the industrial West. Failing to find adequate responses and deeply divided within, the Islamic community grew increasingly anxious over the dangers that lay ahead. Islamic civilization was by no means defeated. But its continued viability was clearly threatened by its powerful neighbor, which had become master of the world.

THE LAST DYNASTY: THE SLOW DEATH OF THE QING EMPIRE IN CHINA

Though China had been strong enough to get away with its policies of isolation and attitudes of disdain in the early centuries of European expansion, by the late 18th century, these policies were outmoded and dangerous. Not only had the Europeans grown incomparably stronger than they had been in the early centuries of expansion, but Chinese society was crumbling from within. Over a century of strong rule by the Manchus and a high degree of social stability, if not prosperity, for the Chinese people gave way to rampant official corruption, severe economic dislocations, and social unrest by the last decades of the 18th century. With the British in the lead, the Western powers took advantage of these weaknesses over the course of the 19th century, to force open China's markets, humiliating its military defenders, and reducing its Qing rulers to little more than puppets. By century's end, Chinese intellectuals were locked in heated debates over how to check the power of the advancing "barbarians" from the West and how to restore China's collapsing political and social order.

Rot from Within: Bureaucratic Breakdown and Social Disintegration

By the late 18th century, it was clear that like so many Chinese dynasties of the past, the Qing was in decline. The signs of decline were pervasive and familiar. The bureaucratic foundations of the Chinese empire were rotting from within. The exam system, which had done well in selecting able and honest bureaucrats in the early decades of the dynasty, had become riddled with cheating and favoritism. Despite formal restrictions, sons of high officials were often ensured a place in the ever-growing bureaucracy. Even more disturbing was the fact that virtually anyone with enough money could buy a post for sons or brothers. Impoverished scholars could be paid to take the exams for poorly educated or not-so-bright relatives. Examiners could be bribed to approve

China during the Qing Era

ingly this resulted in a noticeable drop in the training and armament of the military. Even more critical for the mass of the people were reductions in spending on public works projects. Of these, the most vital were the great dikes that confined the Yellow River in northern China. Over the millennia, the silting of the river bottom and the constant repair of and additions to the dikes had created a situation where river and dikes were raised high above the densely populated farmlands through which they passed. Thus, when these great public works were neglected for lack of funds and proper official supervision of repairs, leaking dikes and the rampaging waters of the great river meant catastrophe for much of northeastern China.

Nowhere was this disaster more apparent than in the region of the Shandong Peninsula (see map opposite). Before the mid-19th century, the Yellow River emptied into the sea south of the peninsula. By the 1850s, however, the neglected dikes had broken down over much of the area, and the river had flooded hundreds of square miles of heavily cultivated farmland. By the 1860s, the main channel of the river flowed north of the peninsula. The lands in between had been flooded and the farms wiped out. Peasants in the millions were left without livestock or land to cultivate. Tens—perhaps hundreds—of thousands of peasants died of famine and disease.

As the condition of the peasantry deteriorated in many parts of the empire, further signs of dynastic decline appeared. Food shortages and landlord exactions prompted mass migrations. Vagabond bands clogged the roads and beggars crowded the city streets. Banditry, long seen by the Chinese as one of the surest gauges of the extent of dynastic decline, became a major problem in many districts. As the following verse from a popular ditty of the 1860s illustrates, the government's inability to deal with the bandits was seen as a further sign of Qing weakness:

> When the bandits arrive, where are the troops?
> When the troops come, the bandits have vanished.
> Alas, when will the bandits and troops meet?

The assumption then widely held by Chinese thinkers—that the dynastic cycle would again run its course and the Manchus would be replaced by a new and vigorous dynasty—was belied by the magnitude of the problems confronting the leaders of China. The belief that China's future could be predicted by the patterns of its past history ignored the fact that, in a number of ways,

weak credentials or look the other way when candidates consulted cheat sheets while taking their exams. In one of the most notorious cases of cheating, a merchant's son won high honors despite the fact that he had spent the days of testing in a brothel hundreds of miles from the examination site.

As early as the first decades of the 18th century, cheating had become so blatant that in 1711 students who had failed the exams at Yangzhou held a public demonstration to protest bribes given to the exam officials by wealthy salt merchants. The growing influx of merchant and poorly educated landlords' sons into the bureaucracy was particularly troubling because few of them had received the classical Confucian education that stressed the responsibilities of the educated ruling classes and their obligation to serve the people. Increasingly, positions in the bureaucracy were regarded by the wealthy as a means of exerting influence over local officials and judges as well as a way of enhancing family fortunes. Less and less concern was expressed for the effects of bureaucratic decisions on the peasantry and urban laborers.

Over several decades, the diversion of revenue from state projects to the enrichment of individual families had a devastating impact on Chinese society. For example, funds needed to maintain the armies and fleets that defended the huge empire fell off sharply. Not surpris-

there were no precedents for the critical changes that had occurred in China under Manchu rule. Some of these changes had their roots in the preceding Ming era in which, for example, food crops from the Americas, such as corn and potatoes, had set in motion a population explosion. An already large population had nearly doubled to reach a total of over 200 million in the first century (c. 1650–1750) of Manchu rule; in the following century, it doubled again to reach from 410 to 415 million. However successful they had been in the past, Chinese social and economic systems were simply not capable of carrying such a large population. China desperately needed innovations: breakthroughs in technology and organization that would increase its productivity to the point where its exploding population could be supported at a reasonable level. The corrupt and highly conservative late-Manchu regime was increasingly an obstacle to, rather than a source of, these desperately needed changes.

Barbarians at the Southern Gates: The Opium War and After

A second major difference between the forces sapping the strength of the Manchus and those that had brought down earlier dynasties was the nature of the "barbarians" who threatened the empire from outside. Though the Manchu rulers and their Chinese administrators, out of ignorance, treated the Europeans much like the nomads and other peoples whom they regarded as barbarians, the Europeans presented a very different sort of challenge. They came from a civilization that was China's equal in sophistication and complexity. In fact, though European nation-states like Great Britain were much smaller in population (in the early 19th century, England had 7 million people to China's 400 million), they could, thanks to the scientific and industrial revolutions, compensate for their smaller numbers with better organization and superior technology. These advantages proved critical in the wars between China and Britain and the other European powers that broke out in the middle decades of the 19th century.

The issue that was responsible for the initial hostilities between China and the British did little credit to the latter. For centuries, British merchants had eagerly exported silks, fine porcelains, tea, and other products from the Chinese Empire. Finding that they had little in the way of manufactured goods or raw materials that the Chinese were willing to take in exchange for these prod-

ucts, the British were forced to surrender growing amounts of silver bullion to obtain the products they wanted. Unhappy about the unfavorable terms of trade in China, British merchants hit on a possible solution in the form of opium, which was grown in the hills of eastern India. Though opium was also cultivated in China, the Indian variety was far more potent and was soon in great demand in the Middle Kingdom. By the first decades of the 19th century, an average of 4500 chests of opium, each weighing 133 pounds, were sold, either legally or illicitly, to merchants on the south China coast. By 1839, on the eve of the Opium War, nearly 40,000 chests were imported by the Chinese.

Although the British had found a way to reverse the trade balance in their favor, the Chinese soon realized that the opium traffic was a major threat to their economy and social order. Within years, China's favorable trade balance with the outside world was reversed, and silver began to flow in large quantities out of the country. As sources of capital for public works and trade expansion decreased, agricultural productivity stagnated or declined, and unemployment spread, especially in the hinterlands of the coastal trading areas. Wealthy Chinese, who could best afford it, squandered increasing amounts of China's wealth to support their opium habits. Opium dens spread in the towns and villages of the empire at an alarming rate. By 1838, it has been estimated, 1 percent of China's more than 400 million people were addicted to the drug. Strung-out officials neglected their administrative responsibilities, the sons of prominent scholar-gentry families lost their ambition, and even laborers and peasants abandoned their work for the debilitating pleasures of the opium dens.

From early in the 18th century, Qing emperors had issued edicts forbidding the opium traffic, but little had been done to enforce them. By the first years of the 19th century, it was clear to the court and high officials that the opium trade must be stopped. When serious efforts were finally undertaken in the early 1820s, they only served to drive the opium dealers from Canton to nearby islands and other clandestine locations on the coast. Finally, in the late 1830s, the emperor sent one of the most distinguished officials in the empire, Lin Zexu, with orders to use every means available to stamp out the trade. Lin, who was famed for his incorruptibility, took his charge quite seriously. After being rebuffed in his attempts to win the cooperation of European merchants and naval officers in putting an end to the trade, Lin ordered the European trading areas in Canton blockaded, their warehouses searched, and all the opium confiscated destroyed.

Not surprisingly, these actions enraged the European merchants, and they demanded military action to avenge their losses. Arguing that Lin's measures violated both the property rights of the merchants and principles of free trade, the British ordered the Chinese to put an end to their anti-opium campaign or risk military intervention. When Lin persisted, war broke out in late 1839. In the conflict that followed, the Chinese were first routed on the sea, where their now-antiquated war junks were no match for British gunboats. They were then soundly defeated in their attempts to repel an expeditionary force that the British sent ashore. With British warships and armies threatening the cities of the Yangtze River region, the Qing emperor was forced to sue for peace and send Lin into exile in a remote province of the empire.

Their victories in the Opium War and a second conflict, which erupted in the late 1850s, allowed the European powers to force China to open trade and diplomatic exchanges. After the first war, Hong Kong was established as an additional center of British commerce. European trade was also permitted at five other ports, where the Europeans were given land to build more warehouses and living quarters. By the 1890s, 90 ports of call were available to over 300,000 European and American traders, missionaries, and diplomats. Britain, France, Germany, and Russia had won long-term leases over several ports and the surrounding territory (see map on p. 92).

Although the treaty of 1842 made no reference to the opium trade, following China's defeat the drug poured unchecked into China. By the middle of the century, China's foreign trade and customs were overseen by British officials. They were careful to ensure that European nationals had favored access to China's markets and that no protective tariffs, such as those the Americans were using at the time to protect their young industries, were established by the Chinese. Most humiliating of all for the Chinese was the fact that they were forced to accept European ambassadors at the Qing court. Not only were ambassadors traditionally (and usually quite rightly) regarded as spies, but the exchange of diplomatic missions was a concession that European nations were equal in stature to China. Given the deeply entrenched Chinese conviction that their Middle Kingdom was the civilized center of the earth and that all other peoples were barbarians, this was indeed a very difficult concession to make. European battleships and firepower gave them little choice.

A Civilization at Risk: Rebellion and Failed Reforms

Though it was not immediately apparent, China's defeat in the Opium War greatly contributed to a building crisis that threatened not just the Qing dynasty but Chinese civilization as a whole. Defeat and the dislocations brought on by the growing commercial encroachments of the West spawned a massive rebellion that convulsed much of southern China in the 1850s and early 1860s, and at one point threatened to overthrow the Qing dynasty. Led by a mentally unstable, semi-Christianized prophet named Hong Xiuquan, the Taiping rebellion exacerbated the already considerable stresses within Chinese society and further drained the diminishing resources of the ruling dynasty. Widespread peasant uprisings, incited by the members of secret societies like the White Lotus, had erupted as early as the 1770s. But the Taiping movement was the first to pose a serious alternative not only to the Qing dynasty but to Confucian civilization as a whole. The Taipings offered sweeping programs for social reform, land redistribution, and the liberation of women. They also attacked the traditional Confucian elite and the learning on which its claims to authority rested. Taiping rebels smashed ancestral tablets and shrines, and they proposed a simplified script and mass literacy that would have undermined one of the scholar-gentry's chief sources of power.

Their attack on the scholar-gentry, in fact, was one of the main causes of the Taipings' ultimate defeat. Left no option but to rally to the Manchu regime, the provincial gentry became the focus of resistance to the Taipings. Honest and able Qing officials, such as Zeng Guofan, raised effective, provincially based military forces just in time to beat off the Taiping assault on northern China. Zeng and his allies in the government also worked to carry out much-needed reforms to root out corruption in the bureaucracy and revive the stagnating Chinese economy.

In the late 1800s, these dynamic provincial leaders were the most responsible for China's self-strengthening movement, which was aimed at countering the challenge from the West. They encouraged Western investment in railways and even factories in the areas they governed, and modernized their armies. Combined with the breakdown of Taiping leadership and the declining appeal of a movement that could not deliver on the promises it made to its followers, the efforts of the gentry brought about the eventual but very bloody suppression of the Taiping rebellion. Other movements were also crushed, and banditry was brought under control for a time. But like the Ottoman sultans and their advisors, the Chinese gentry introduced changes that they viewed as limited. They wished to preserve the existing order, not fundamentally transform it. They continued to profess loyalty to the gravely weakened Manchu regime because they saw it as a defender of the traditional order. At the same time, their own power grew to such a point that the Manchus could control them only with great difficulty. Resources were increasingly drained from the court center to the provincial governors, whose growing military and political power posed a potential threat to the Qing court. The basis of China's political fragmentation was building behind the crumbling facade of Manchu rule.

Despite their clearly desperate situation by the last decades of the 19th century, including a shocking loss in a war with Japan in 1894–1895, the Manchu rulers stubbornly resisted the far-reaching reforms that were the only hope of saving the regime and, as it turned out, Chinese civilization. Manchu rulers on occasion moved to back those officials who pushed for extensive political and social reforms, some of which were inspired by the example of the West. But their efforts were repeatedly frustrated by the backlash of members of the imperial household and their allies among the scholar-gentry, who were determined to preserve the old order with only minor changes and to make no major concessions to the West.

With German officers supervising, Chinese executioners are about to behead Boxer insurgents accused of involvement in the murder of the German ambassador in Beijing. The European powers and Japan imposed harsh penalties on China after the Boxer Rebellion was crushed in 1901.

Revolutionary Impulses and the Breakdown of the Confucian Order

In China, as in areas like India and Africa that were actually occupied and ruled by the European powers, a new elite emerged that found itself caught between long-established, indigenous cultural norms and new modes of thinking and organizing associated with influences from the industrialized West. As China's great and ancient Confucian civilization plunged into political division and social turmoil at the turn of the 20th century, young students in particular were divided by loyalties: on the one hand to their extended families, and on the other hand to student organizations and the revolutionary enthusiasm of those who sought to strengthen China by using imports from the West and Japan and to prevent the takeover of their land by these intruders. In the following excerpts from Ba Jin's semiautobiographical novel *Family*, one of the main characters, Chueh-hui, is berated by his grandfather who epitomizes all that the Chinese youth see wrong with older generations who are trying to preserve the old Confucian order.

"Come back here. I have something to say to you."

Chueh-hui turned and walked back.

"Where have you been? We've been looking all over for you." The old man's low voice was dry and harsh. He was sitting up now.

The question took Chueh-hui by surprise. He knew he couldn't say he had been at a Students' Federation meeting, but for the moment his quickness of wit failed him and he was unable to think of an answer. His grandfather's stern eyes were scrutinizing him, and Chueh-hui felt his face reddening. "I went to see a classmate," he finally managed, after some hesitation.

The old man laughed coldly. His eyes swept Chueh-hui's face. "Don't lie," he snapped. "I know all about you. People have told me. The students and the soldiers have been brawling the last few days, and you've been in it. . . . School is over, but you're out every day at some students' federation or other. . . . Mistress Chen just told me she heard from one of my sedan-chair carriers that he saw you handing out leaflets on the street. . . .

"You students have been much too reckless right along—checking stores for Japanese goods, seizing merchants and parading them through the streets—completely lawless! The soldiers would be quite right to beat you. Why do you provoke them with such nonsense? . . . I hear the authorities are planning to take strong measures against the students. If you keep rioting around like this you're liable to riot your young fool lives away!"

After each few sentences, the old man paused or coughed. But whenever Chueh-hui tried to answer, he went on with his lecture. Now he concluded his remarks with a veritable fit of coughing. Mistress Chen hastened in from the next room to drum her fists lightly on his back.

Yeh-yeh's coughing slowly subsided. But the old man's anger was again aroused when he saw Chueh-hui, still standing before him.

The last decades of the dynasty were dominated by the ultraconservative dowager empress Cixi, who became the power behind the throne. In 1898, she and her faction crushed the most serious move toward reform from the top. Her nephew, the emperor, was imprisoned in the Forbidden City, and leading advocates for reform were executed or driven from China. On one occasion, Cixi flaunted the Westernizers by rechanneling funds that had been raised to build modern warships to defend China into the building of a huge marble boat in one of the lakes in the imperial gardens. With genuine reform blocked by Cixi and her faction, the Manchus relied on various divisions among the provincial officials as well as among the European powers to maintain their position. Members of the Qing household also secretly backed popular outbursts aimed at forcibly expelling the foreigners from China. Most notable was the Boxer Rebellion, which broke out in 1898 and was put down only through the intervention of the imperialist powers in 1901. Its failure led to even greater control over China's internal affairs by the Europeans and a further devolution of power to provincial officials.

The Fall of the Qing

By the first years of the 20th century, the days of the Manchus were clearly numbered. With the defeat of the Taipings, resistance to the Qing came to be centered in rival secret organizations such as the Triads and the Society of Elders and Brothers. These underground organizations inspired numerous local uprisings against the dynasty in the last decades of the 19th century. All of these

"You students don't study, you just make trouble. The schools are in a terrible state. They produce nothing but rioters. I didn't want you boys to go to school in the first place. The schools make you all go bad. Look at your uncle Ke-ting. He never went to school, he only studied at home with a tutor. But he reads the classics very well, and he writes better than any of you."

"It's not that we want to make trouble. We've been concentrating on our studies right along. We only started this drive in self-defence. The soldiers attacked us for no reason at all. Naturally, we couldn't let them get away with it," Chueh-hui replied evenly, repressing his anger.

"How dare you argue! When I talk, you listen! . . . From now on, I forbid you to go out brawling again! . . . Mistress Chen, call his Big Brother in." The old man's voice was trembling, and he began to cough again. Gasping, he drew long, shuddering breaths.

"Third Young Master, look at the state you've got your *Yeh-yeh* in! Please stop arguing with him and let him get a little rest," rasped Mistress Chen, her face darkening. Her frown made her long face look even longer.

Though stung by the unfairness of her implication, in the presence of his coughing grandfather Chueh-hui could only hold back his retort and hang his head in silence, biting his lips.

"Call his brother, Mistress Chen," the old man said in a calmer voice. He had stopped coughing.

Mistress Chen assented and went out, leaving Chueh-hui standing alone before his grandfather. The old man did not speak. His misty old eyes stared vacantly around the room. Then he half closed them again.

Chueh-hui gazed at his grandfather stubbornly. He examined the old man's long, thin body. A peculiar thought came to him. It seemed to him that the person lying in the cane reclining chair was not his grandfather but the representative of an entire generation. He knew that the old man and he—the representative of the grandson's generation—could never see eye to eye. He wondered what could be harboured in that long thin body that made every conversation between them seem more like an exchange between two enemies than a chat between grandfather and grandson. Gloomy and depressed, Chueh-hui shook himself defiantly.

Questions: As the eldest male in Chueh-hui's extended household what sort of relationship does his grandfather have with his grandson? What does this suggest about how authority was exercised within families in prerevolutionary China? Was this sort of exchange likely to have occurred in prerevolutionary China? If not, why not? If so, why? What sorts of activities on the part of Chueh-hui and his brothers does the grandfather find upsetting? Why is the grandfather so pessimistic about the future of China? What factors make the divisions between the generations in early 20th century China seem so impossible to bridge? How does Chueh-hui resolve the quarrel with his grandfather? Why do you think he is so nonconfrontational, despite his obvious dislike for the old man?

Source: Ba Jin, *Family* (Garden City, NY: Anchor Books, 1972), pp. 66–67.

---

efforts failed because of lack of coordination and sufficient resources. But some of the secret society cells became a valuable training ground that prepared the way for a new sort of resistance to the Manchus. By the end of the 19th century, the sons of some of the scholar-gentry and especially of the comprador merchants in the port cities were becoming more and more involved in secret society operations and other activities aimed at the overthrow of the regime. Because many of these young men had received European-style educations, their resistance was aimed at more than just getting rid of the Manchus. They envisioned power passing to Western-educated, reformist leaders who would build a new, strong nation-state in China patterned after those of the West, rather than simply establishing yet another imperial dynasty. For aspiring revolutionaries such as Sun Yat-sen, who emerged as one of their most articulate spokesmen, their seizure of power was also seen as a way of enacting desperately needed social programs to relieve the misery of the peasantry and urban workers.

Although they drew heavily on the West for ideas and organizational models, the revolutionaries from the rising middle classes were deeply hostile to the involvement of the imperialist powers in Chinese affairs. They also condemned the Manchus for their failure to control the foreigners. The young rebels cut off their queues in defiance of the Manchu order that all ethnic Chinese wear their hair in this fashion. They joined in uprisings fomented by the secret societies or plotted assassinations and acts of sabotage on their own. Attempts to coordinate an all-China uprising floundered on several occasions because of personal animosities or amateurish incompetence. But in late 1911, opposition to the government's reliance on the Western powers for railway loans led to secret society uprisings, student demonstrations, and mutinies on the part of imperial troops. When key provincial officials refused to put down the spreading rebellion, the Manchus had no choice but to abdicate. In February 1912, the last emperor of China, a small boy named Puyi, was deposed, and one of the more powerful of the provincial lords was asked to establish a republican government in China.

The End of a Civilization?

The revolution of 1911 toppled the Qing dynasty, but in many ways a more important watershed for Chinese civilization was crossed in 1905. In that year, the civil service exams were given for the last time. Reluctantly, even the ultraconservative advisors of the empress Cixi had concluded that solutions to China's predicament could no longer be found in the Confucian learning that the exams tested. In fact, the abandonment of the exams signaled the end of a pattern of civilized life that the Chinese had nurtured, improved, and held to for nearly 2500 years. The mix of philosophies and values that had come to be known as the Confucian system, the massive civil bureaucracy, rule by an educated and cultivated scholar-gentry elite, and even the artistic accomplishments of the old order were to come under increasing criticism in the early years of the 20th century. Many of these hallmarks of the most enduring civilization that has ever existed would be vehemently discarded and violently destroyed.

Even though Confucian civilization passed into history like so many before it, many of its ideas, attitudes, and ways of approaching the world survived. Some of them played critical roles in the violent and painful struggle of the Chinese people to build a new civilization to replace the one that had failed them. The challenge of blending and balancing the two remains to the present day.

CONCLUSION: ISLAMIC AND CHINESE RESPONSES TO THE CHALLENGE OF THE WEST

Though both Chinese and Islamic civilizations were severely weakened by internal disruptions in the 18th and 19th centuries, each was thrown into prolonged crisis by the growing challenges posed by the West. Several key differences in the interaction between each civilization and the West do much to explain why Islam, though badly shaken, survived, while Chinese civilization collapsed under the burden of domestic upheavals and foreign aggression. For the Muslims, who had been warring and trading with Christian Europe since the Middle Ages, the Western threat had long existed. What was new was the much greater strength of the Europeans in the ongoing contest, which resulted from their global expansion and their scientific and industrial revolutions.

For China, the challenges from the West came suddenly and brutally. Within decades, the Chinese had to revise their estimate of their empire as the center of the world and the source of civilization itself to take into account severe defeats at the hands of peoples they once dismissed as barbarians. The Muslims could also take comfort from the fact that in the Judeo-Christian and Greek traditions they shared much with the ascendant Europeans. As a consequence, elements of their own civilization had played critical roles in the rise of the West. This made it easier to justify Muslim borrowing from the West, which in any case could be set in a long tradition of exchanges with other civilizations.

Though some Chinese technology had passed to the West, Chinese and Western leaders were largely unaware of early exchanges and deeply impressed by the profound differences between their societies. For the Chinese, borrowing from the barbarians required a painful reassessment of their place in the world—a reassessment many were unwilling to make.

In countering the thrusts from the West, the Muslims gained from the fact that they had many centers to defend—the fall of a single dynasty or regime did not mean the end of Islamic independence. The Muslims also gained from the more gradual nature of the Western advance. They had time to learn from earlier mistakes and to try out different responses to the Western challenges. For the Chinese, the defense of their civilization came to be equated with the survival of the Qing dynasty—a line of thinking that the Manchus did all they could to promote. When the dynasty collapsed in the early 20th century, the Chinese lost faith in the formula for civilization that they had successfully followed for more than two millennia. Again, timing was critical. The crisis in China seemed to come without warning. Within decades, the Qing went from being the arrogant controller of the barbarians to being a defeated and humbled pawn of the European powers.

When the dynasty failed and it became increasingly clear that the barbarians had outdone the Chinese in so many fields of civilized endeavor, the Chinese had little to fall back on. Like the Europeans, they had excelled in social and political organization and in mastery of the material world. Unlike the Hindus and the Muslims, they had no great religious tradition with which to counter the European conceit that worldly dominance could be equated with inherent superiority. In the depths of their crisis, Muslim peoples clung to the conviction that they possessed the true faith, the last and fullest of God's revelations to humankind. That faith became the basis of their resistance and of their strategies for renewal, the key to the survival of Islamic civilization and its continuing efforts to meet the challenges of the West in the 20th century.

FURTHER READING

The best general introductions to the Ottoman decline and the origins of the nation of Turkey are Bernard Lewis's *The Emergence of Modern Turkey* (1961) and the chapter "The Later Ottoman Empire" by Halil Inalcik in *The Cambridge History of Islam*, vol. 1 (1973). Other recent studies of importance on specific aspects of this process include C. V. Findley, *Studies of Ottoman Bureaucratic Reform and the Development of a Modern Civil Service in What is Today Turkey*; Ernest Ramsaur, *The Young Turks* (1957); Stanford Shaw, *Between Old and New* (1971); and David Kusher, *The Rise of Turkish Nationalism* (1977).

On Egypt and the Islamic heartlands in this period, see P. M. Holt's *Egypt and the Fertile Crescent, 1516–1922* (1965) or P. J. Vatikiotis's *The History of Egypt* (1985). On the Mahdist movement in the Sudan, see P. M. Holt's *The Mahdist State in the Sudan* (1958) or the fine summary by L. Carl Brown in Robert Rotberg and Ali Mazrui, eds., *Protest and Power in Black Africa* (1970). The latter also includes many informative articles on African resistance to European conquest and rule. For a broadly based analysis of anticolonial, messianic movements similar to the Mahdi's, see Michael Adas, *Prophets of Rebellion* (1979). On women and changes in the family in the Ottoman realm, see Nermin Abadan-Unat, *Women in Turkish Society* (1981), and in the Arab world, see Nawal el Saadawi, *The Hidden Face of Eve* (1980).

On the Manchu takeover in China, see Frederic Wakeman Jr., *The Great Enterprise* (1985) and Jonathan Spence and John E. Willis, eds., *Ming to Ch'ing* (1979). On dynastic decline under the Qing among the most readable and wide-ranging works are the relevant sections in Jonathan Spence's *The Search for Modern China* (1990) and the essays in John Fairbank, ed., *The Cambridge History of China: Late Ch'ing, 1800–1911* (1978). A good survey of the causes and course of the Opium War is provided by Hsin-pao Chang, *Commissioner Lin and the Opium War* (1964). The Taiping rebellion is covered in Jen Yu-wen's *The Taiping Revolutionary Movement* (1973), and the first stages of the Chinese nationalist movement are examined in the essays in Mary Wright, ed., *China in Revolution: The First Phase, 1900–1913* (1968). The early sections of Elisabeth Croll's *Feminism and Socialism in China* (1980) provide an excellent overview of the status and condition of women in the Qing era.

ON THE WEB

The life and politics of the liberators of South America Simon Bolivar and Jose de San Martin are explored at

http://www.emory.edu/COLLEGE/CULPEPER/
   BAKEWELL/thinksheets/thsh-bolivar.html
http://pachami.com/English/ressanmE.htm
http://www.geocities.com/TimesSquare/1848/martin.html

For Father Hildalgo's later ill-fated revolutionary movement in Mexico, see

http://www.mexconnect.com/mex_/history/jtuck/
   jthidalgo.html
http://www.mexonline.com/person1.htm

The best Web site addressing the life and work of Cuba's Jose Marti is

http://www.josemarti.org/

(Access through google.com search engine for automatic English translation). See also

http://library.thinkquest.org/18355/jose_marti.html
http://www.fiu.edu/~fcf/jmarti.html

The concept of Manifest Destiny as it relates to world history beyond the U.S.-Mexican conflict is discussed at

http://odur.let.rug.nl/~usa/E/manifest/manifxx.htm
http://www.pbs.org/kera/usmexicanwar/dialogues/
   prelude/manifest/d2aeng.html

For U.S. and Latin American relations generally, see
http://darkwing.uoregon.edu/^caguirre/uslatam.html
For a discussion of dependency theory, see
http://www.mtholyoke.edu/acad/intrel/depend.htm
http://en.wikipedia.org/wiki/Dependency_theory
http://www.tutor2u.net/economics/content/topics/
    development/development_models_dependency.htm
The decline of the Qing Dynasty in China
http://library.thinkquest.org/26469/history/1900.html
was accelerated by the failure of a reform effort which
climaxed in the 103 days between June 11 to September
21, 1898 is explored at
http://www-chaos.umd.edu/history/modern3.html
This failure magnified the negative impact of the
Opium Wars, overviews of which are provided at
http://historyliterature.homestead.com/files/
    extended.html
http://www.serendipity.li/wod/hongkong.html
http://kizuna.ins.cwru.edu/asia110/projects/projects/
    Tang 3/tang3.html
Discussions of the Opium Wars as seen through related
documents can be found at
http://acc6.its.brooklyn.cuny.edu/~phalsall/texts/
    com-lin.html
http://web.jjay.cuny.edu/~jobrien/reference/ob36.html
The anti-foreign, anti-Qing Taiping Rebellion
http://www-chaos.umd.edu/history/modern2.html
had earlier gravely weakened 2000 years of traditional
Chinese government. The Boxer Rebellion
http://www.gcocities.com/CollegePark/Pool/6208/
    title_page.htm
provided the coup de grâce. For a discussion of the suppression of the Boxer Rebellion by foreign troops and
their motivation, see
http://www.h-net.msu.edu/~german/gtext/kaiserreich/
    china.html

http://www.awm.gov.au/atwar/boxer.htm
For a virtual tour of China at the time of the Boxer Rebellion, go to http://www.chinaexhibit.org/
After Major General Charles "Chinese" Gordon whose
life is examined at
http://www.cis.upenn.edu/~homeier/interests/heros/
    gordon4.html
took part in the suppression of the Taiping Rebellion, he
found himself addressing another uprising of indigenous
people, an Arab revolt in Egypt led by Muhammad
Ahmad ibn as Sayyid abd Allah, known as al- Madhi
http://countrystudies.us/sudan/12.htm
Unlike al-Mahdi, who sought the path of militant
Islamic revivalism. Mohammad Abduh and Jamal al-din
Afghani
http://www.ghazali.net/book2/chapter6/body_chapter6
    .html
http://www.afghan-web.com/bios/yest/afghani
    .html
http://sitemaker.umich.edu/emes/sourcebook/da.data/
    82631/FileSource/1884_al-afghani.pdf
sought Western-style modernization within the context
of Islam.
Earlier, Mohammad Ali, ruler of Egypt, had sought the
same goal through economic transformation, but even
the efforts of his successors to build the Suez Canal
backfired due to European control over capital flow and
ultimately led to increased European control over Egypt
http://www.emayzine.com/lectures/egypt1798-1924
    .html
Much the same fate befell the reform effort (Tanzimat)
of the Ottoman Empire
http://landow.stg.brown.edu/victorian/history/dora/
    dora9.html

PART II

A HALF-CENTURY OF CRISIS, 1914–1945

The depths of despair to which Europe had sunk after two world wars and a global depression are captured in Max Ernst's surrealist painting Europe After the Rain, II, 1940–1942, *which depicts the barbaric condition into which the 20th century's once preeminent civilization had fallen under the Nazi reign of terror.*

Chronology

1910–1920s	Mexican Revolution
1912	African National Congress party formed in South Africa
1914–1918	World War I
1917	Russian Revolutions
1919	Revolt in Egypt; first Pan-African Congress
1919	Versailles peace settlement; League of Nations
1920s	Jazz Age in United States and Western Europe; Dadaism, surrealism, expressionism dominate art world
1921	Foundation of Chinese Communist Party
1927–1928	Stalin heads the Soviet Union; Five-Year Plans and collectivization begin
1929–1933	Height of Great Depression
1930s	Great age of Mexican mural painting
1931–1947	Gandhi-led resistance in India
1931	Japan invades Manchuria
1933–1939	New Deal in United States
1933	Nazis sieze power in Germany
1934–1940	Cárdenas reform period in Mexico
1935	German rearmament; Italy conquers Ethiopia
1937	Army officers in power in Japan; invasion of China
1939–1945	World War II
1942–1945	Holocaust
1943–1945	Manhattan Project to develop atomic bomb

DECADES OF TURMOIL

Two world wars of unprecedented extent and ferocity and a prolonged global depression provided the context for what can be seen as the second major phase of 20th-century history. Beginning with the outbreak of what contemporaries called the Great War in August of 1914, and ending with the surrender in August 1945 of Japan—the last of the Axis powers to be defeated by the Allies in World War II—this period is rightly seen as an era of intensifying global crisis. Because of the strong linkages between the First World War from 1914 to 1918 and the Second, which raged from 1939 to 1945, historians have often referred to these decades as the era of the "30 years' war." This allusion to an earlier, 17th-century conflict that ravaged much of Europe is apt because the 1914–1945 period witnessed armed conflicts, revolutions, civil wars, and state repression that produced destruction and human death and suffering on a scale that was inconceivable in any earlier century. But unlike the earlier Thirty Years' War that was largely confined to Europe, the three decades of crisis that mark the middle period of the 20th century affected much of the globe, though direct involvement in the world wars and the impact of the Great Depression varied considerably in different regions.

Historians of these decades have, not surprisingly, tended to be preoccupied with the suffering and destruction that marred the second phase of 20th-century history. But an exclusive emphasis on disasters or the causes of disasters can result in dangerous oversimplification, including an excessive preoccupation with the woes and excesses of the Western nations. Global wars and depressions led to important and enduring political, social, and economic innovations in many regions of the world and opened up opportunities for advancement by some nations and social groups, albeit usually at the expense of others. In World War I, for example, both the United States and Japan emerged as global economic powers and the United States was suddenly, if temporarily, catapulted to the status of the world's most powerful military nation. As a result of the 1914–1918 war, regions in Africa and Asia that were colonized by the Western powers in the 18th and 19th centuries found new openings for intellectual and political resistance to European domination, and movements for independence gathered strength in many colonial areas. The weakness of China's new military leadership in the face of Japan's demands during the war and at the Paris Peace Conference led to the student and worker protest that sent the ongoing process of revolution in China in new and more radical directions. The collapse of the autocratic regimes of central and eastern Europe as a result of defeat in World War I led to revolutions—both successful and frustrated—that opened up new possibilities for the liberation of formerly oppressed or disadvantaged ethnic minorities and social groups like workers, peasants, and women.

These revolutionary gains were largely reversed by the totalitarian dictatorships of the 1930s and early 1940s (and the 1920s as well, in the case of Italy and much of eastern Europe), but lasting improvements remained in areas like mass health care and education. In addition, the legitimacy of governments was increasingly judged according to the novel standard of how well they provided for the welfare of the citizens they ruled. Though the Great Depression proved devastating to the United States, Japan, and much of western Europe, its shocks were less harmful to the relatively isolated Soviet Union and some colonized areas that were not fully tied into the global market system. In addition, in some European countries, and particularly the United States, the Depression led to necessary state regulation of banking and securities; long overdue welfare measures, such as social security; and massive public works projects that brought lasting infrastructural improvements, such as dams, bridges, and highways. Some areas, such as Latin America, were profoundly shaken by the worldwide economic downturn, but new and constructive political forces and government policies emerged to meet the crisis. These not only made for major shifts in Latin American politics and society, they resulted in some reduction in the longstanding handicaps that skewed the participation of Latin American nations in international trade.

World War II saw great gains for the United States in global economic and military power. Despite enormous human suffering, it also enlarged the Soviet Union's sphere of direct control and influence, particularly in eastern Europe and Asia. And even in western Europe, the region of the globe most devastated by the succession of war, revolution, depression, and war, recovery from the decades of crisis was in many ways stunningly successful. The second phase of the 20th century did result in a significant diminution of western Europe's dominance over the rest of the globe and a complex rebalancing among civilizations after 1945. But Western society rebounded

in many ways, creating a political, cultural, and economic vitality that contrasted markedly with the agonies of the 1914–1945 era. Thus, while some Europeans who lived through the decades of crisis thought that civilization was coming to an end, their pessimism was countered by the rebirth of Europe from the late 1940s which defied the seemingly intractable problems that had plagued earlier generations.

FOUNDATIONS OF AN ERA OF REVOLUTIONS AND TOTALITARIAN STATES

The global ramifications of wars begun in Europe and an economic downturn triggered by the 1929 stock market collapse in the United States illustrate the extent to which the world network had intensified as a result of industrialization and Western imperialism. There had been previous wars with theaters of combat spread across the globe. The Seven Years' War (1756–1763), for example, had been fought in North America, the Caribbean, and India as well as Europe itself, and the same was true for the Napoleonic struggles of the early 19th century. But the two world wars of the 20th century were more genuinely international conflicts because they not only spread over a larger portion of the globe, they directly involved as both combatants and victims the peoples of the Europeans' vast colonial empires, as well as the citizens of rising powers, such as Japan and the United States.

Though different regions of the globe had long been tied to the ever-expanding world market system centered on Europe and increasingly the United States, the intensity and extent of the shock waves set off by the Great Depression were unprecedented. A complex meshing of import-export exchanges, international monetary linkages, and loan agreements had bound the industrialized West to its African and Asian colonies, Japan, China, and Latin America. This meant that a severe financial crisis in one part of the global economic system eventually threatened the entire international order. In fact, the tariff wars and the sharp decrease in lending that marked the years of depression fragmented the global economy into increasingly closed economic blocs that corresponded ominously with the political adversaries that fought World War II.

The technological and organizational transformations that had linked the peoples of the globe together were also critical to key transformations within specific regions and nations in the decades of crisis. The quantum leap in killing power that accompanied the mass production of the new weaponry that was developed in the 19th and early 20th centuries made possible the slaughter or maiming of millions of European and allied soldiers during World War I. The prevailing ineptitude of Europe's political and military leaders, most of whom had little idea of how to employ the new weapons, rendered the slaughter tragically senseless since neither side could decisively defeat the other despite the appalling casualties. But the national rivalries and patriotic sentiments, whose intensification in the decades before 1914 had done much to bring on the conflict, made it possible for the hostile powers to mobilize tens of millions of conscripts and to keep most of them fighting, despite the futility of the conflict, for four long years. Industrial transportation (particularly the railway) and communication systems were essential to supplying and deploying these massive armies, and the mobilization of the civilian populations of the combatant societies proved necessary to the continuation of the war effort. Military and civilian mobilization efforts led in turn to a dramatic increase in the power and functions of the state—a trend that would prove one of the central themes of global history in the 20th century.

The relentless demands of the war effort also produced severe dislocations that provided opportunities for some social groups while proving deeply detrimental to others. Women, for example, in European societies, as well as in the British Dominions and the United States, found their occupational prospects greatly enhanced, even in spheres like heavy industry that had been all but closed to them in the 19th century. They also experienced a latitude of social and sexual freedom and openings for personal expression that would have been unthinkable in the Victorian era. By contrast, the power and reputation of the aristocratic classes of Europe, which had played leading roles in the diplomatic corps that had been unable to control the crisis that led to war and in the failed military leadership that had rendered the conflict so costly, fell dramatically in the interwar era.

Although the war brought a sharp decline in the numbers and importance of the household servant classes in western Europe and the United States, it greatly strengthened the position of the working classes in most of the combatant societies. In wartime and in the postwar decades, socialist and labor parties shared power in most of western Europe. In the United States the legitimacy of workers' organizations, such as the American Federation of Labor, was greatly enhanced. In Russia and Germany, the urban working classes provided the bulk of support for Marxist-Leninist inspired revolution-

ary movements that sought to seize power from defeated regimes in 1917 and 1918–1919, respectively. The disconnected risings in Germany failed (as did a postwar revolution in Hungary), but the more disciplined and centralized Bolshevik Party managed to seize power in Russia in October 1917. Its ascendancy and survival in the bloody civil war that followed made for a major division that persisted through much of the rest of the 20th century in the international community between a revolution-minded communist camp, and the bourgeois democracies, whose leaders were very often preoccupied with containing and ultimately crushing the radical menace. From the early 1920s onward, the Russian revolution also provided inspiration and material support for leftist revolutionaries in societies as diverse as China, British India, and the nations of Latin America and the Caribbean.

The Bolshevik victory also marked another great leap in state power and control over its subjects. Bolshevik efforts to survive the assaults of both domestic and external enemies and a party philosophy that espoused state-directed programs for social and economic transformation led to the growth of a massive bureaucracy, military establishment, and secret police apparatus. After Stalin's consolidation of power over the Soviet state in the late 1920s, these trends toward centralization and bureaucratic control were accelerated in all spheres, marking a turn toward totalitarianism that distinguished the 1930s and early 1940s in Europe, eastern Asia, and parts of Latin America. The rise of Stalin's despotism had particularly tragic consequences for the peoples of the Soviet Union in the 1930s, as the manmade "famines" in the Ukraine and elsewhere, the succession of party purges, and the spread of concentration camps or *gulags* in Siberia amply testify. Partly in response to the perceived threat of the industrializing Soviet Union and the spread of communism, and taking full advantage of the dislocations and human suffering brought on by the Great Depression, fascist parties seized or shared power in Germany, Spain, and Argentina. Like Mussolini, who had used the threat of revolution from the left to gain power in Italy in the early 1920s, the Nazis in Germany and Falangists in Spain moved to destroy all political opposition and establish party control over all aspects of economic and cultural life.

The external aggressiveness of the fascist regimes in Germany and Italy, as well as that of their uncertain ally in Japan, led to World War II in which the Axis powers were pitted against the unlikely alliance of the Soviet Union and the Western democracies. The war not only demonstrated the daunting capacity of 20th-century states to regiment and mobilize their subject populations, it underscored the awesome productive capacity of advanced industrialized societies. Nowhere was this combination more brutally apparent than in the assembly-line approach to genocide adopted by the Nazi bureaucracy that resulted in the imprisonment and then the systematic murder of millions of Jews, as well as large numbers of gypsies, ethnic minorities, political dissidents, and other "undesirables," such as homosexuals. As Walter Frankel so movingly relates in his account of the struggle to survive in the Nazi death camps, by the mid-20th century the state had the power to deprive individual subjects of their jobs, their rights as citizens, their homes and families, their clothing, and the very hairs on their heads and bodies. Never before in history had the power of handfuls of leaders been so great; never before had the suffering of humanity been so massive.

The unprecedented growth of state power that was a central feature of the decades of crisis that make up the second phase of 20th-century history did not take place without resistance. Somewhat predictably, the most powerful and enduring forces that countered trends toward centralization and bureaucratic interference in the everyday lives of ordinary people emerged in areas where industrial technology was less established and appeals to patriotism and ideologies of racial supremacy rang hollow. In the colonized areas of Africa and Asia and the economically dominated informal colonies of China and Latin America resistance to European and increasingly U.S. global dominance surged in the second phase of the 20th century.

In all of these areas, this resistance was built primarily on the support of peasants, or subsistence-oriented farmers, who have been the largest of all social groups in most societies for much of human history. Long-exploited Amerindian communities and landless agricultural laborers played critical roles in the complex combination of regional upheavals that converged to produce the Mexican revolution. Begun four years before the outbreak of World War I, the Mexican conflict raged into the late 1920s and continued to produce aftershocks for decades thereafter. It was the first of the great revolutions of the 20th century, and much more than the Russian upheavals of 1917, it gave voice—however fleetingly—to the peasant masses. Though Marxist ideology would play a much greater role in most of the revolutions that followed later in the 20th century than it had in Mexico, the central role of the peasantry was reflected in revolutionary upheavals from China and Vietnam to Angola and Bolivia.

In the decades of crisis, peasant struggles became caught up over much of Africa and Asia in broader movements of resistance to Western colonial dominance. Led mainly by Western-educated individuals from well-to-do families, these movements of liberation and nation-building gave rise to the two most powerful approaches to resistance to state power to emerge in the 20th century. Guerrilla tactics had been very effectively used by the white Afrikaner farmers of South Africa to counter the superior numbers and firepower of the British colonizers as early as the Anglo-Boer war from 1899 to 1902. They had also been employed by regional leaders like Emiliano Zapata in the Mexican revolution. But Chinese revolutionaries, especially Mao Zedong, crafted tactics employed rather haphazardly for millennia by the weak and poorly armed into comprehensive strategies for waging guerrilla warfare.

The violent thrust of the guerrilla response to Western political dominance and weapons superiority contrasted sharply with the techniques of civil disobedience and nonviolent resistance developed by Mahatma Gandhi and his followers. In their struggles against racial discrimination and colonial rule in South Africa and India from the early 1900s, Indian nationalists forged the second major option developed in the 20th century for those who wished to challenge the unprecedented power of the state. Though associated mainly with anticolonial movements in the decades of crisis, civil disobedience in the Gandhian mode was to play a major role in struggles against discrimination and injustice in the United States and western Europe in the post–World War II era.

Growing resistance to European global dominance underscores one of the key trends of the decades of crisis after 1914—the growing number of significant actors in world affairs after an era in which western European nations had monopolized center stage. This trend was sometimes masked by the continuing prominence of British, French, and German leaders in world councils and their ability to shore up European colonial regimes in most areas. Nonetheless, the shift in economic power and political influence was very real. Not only were the Europeans increasingly under siege in their colonial bastions, but new rivals rose to challenge their global leadership. As we have seen, the Soviet Union and the social revolutions it sought to foment abroad provided the most obvious and threatening of these rivals. But in the decades after World War I, the most potent contender for world power proved to be the United States, which came to dominate the international economy in many sectors and experimented cautiously and often inconsistently with global political leadership as well.

Many Americans, to be sure, oscillated between serious commitments to highly profitable international commercial exchanges and an inclination to retreat into political and military isolation. Americans also vacillated between conventional great power maneuvers and a desire to inject idealism, which some leaders argued was peculiarly American, into the diplomatic process. It was not always easy for other peoples to adjust to the American style, and in the 1930s in particular deep disagreements developed between the United States and other rivals for international influence, such as Japan and a remilitarized Germany. Whatever the quarrels and great powers involved, it was apparent that the decades of crisis that spanned the middle period of the 20th century marked the end of over a century of European global dominance. From the 1920s onward, world dramas involved a more and more varied cast, and western European actors—for all of their pretensions to imperial grandeur—were steadily pushed from center stage to the wings and increasingly relegated to what amounted to bit parts.

PART OVERVIEW

Chapter 5, which opens this section on the second main phase of the 20th century, focuses on the causes, conduct, and impact of World War I. This chapter also deals with the rise of nationalism in India, Africa, and the Middle East in the decades leading up to the war, and the ways in which the conflict gave great impetus to these movements and the weakening of the European world order. Efforts to restore the pre–World War I global order in Europe and the United States are explored in Chapter 6, which also looks at the powerful new challenges to those efforts posed by the rise of Fascism in Italy and the success of the Bolshevik revolution in Russia. The coming of the Great Depression with the collapse of the New York stock market in the fall of 1929, sets the stage for the decade of economic crisis and social turmoil that is analyzed in Chapter 7. Revolutionary struggles and political repression in Latin America and East Asia are highlighted in this chapter as well as the turn to state despotism under Stalin in the Soviet Union. World War II is the focus of Chapter 8, which deals with the forces that gave rise to the conflict in both the European-Mediterranean and the Pacific theaters that emerged. This final chapter in Part II also examines the major ways in which this second global conflagration was vital to the process of decolonization that dominated the decades after the war ended in 1945.

Chapter 5

Descent into the Abyss:
World War 1 and
the Crisis of the European
Global Order

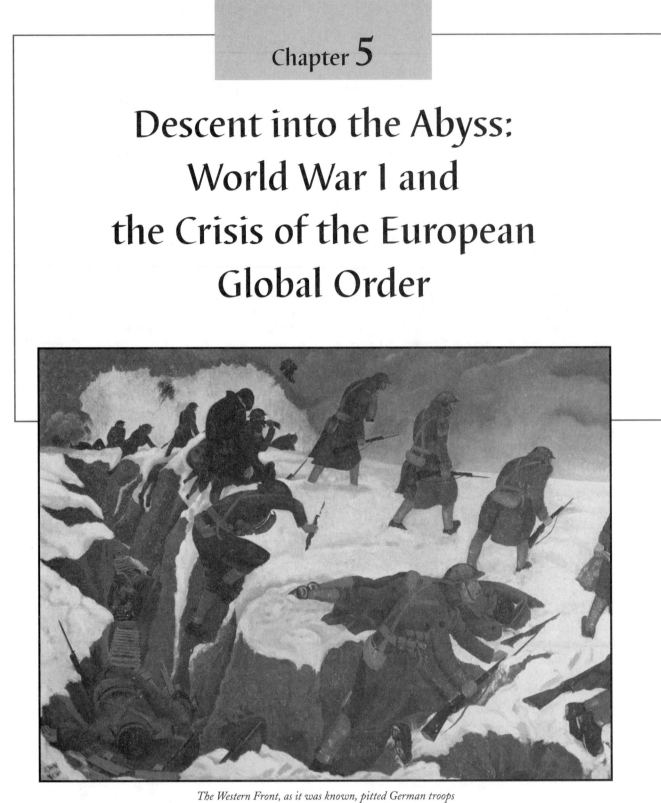

The Western Front, as it was known, pitted German troops against French, British, and soldiers drawn from each power's vast overseas empires. Trench warfare, depicted in this painting, employed the formidable technology of modern war.

1870–1890	Cycle of depressions in Europe and the United States
1890	End of the Three Emperor's Alliance (Russia, Austria-Hungary, Germany)
1894	Franco-Russian Alliance
1899–1901	Anglo-Boer war in South Africa
1904–1905	Japanese victory over Russia
1906	Dinshawai incident in Egypt
1909	Morley-Minto reforms in India
1910	Union of South Africa formed
1914–1918	World War I
1916	Beginning of Arab revolt against Ottoman Empire
1917	Russian Revolution
1917	United States enters war
1918	Treaty of Brest-Litovsk; Russia withdraws from war
1919	Versailles conference and Treaty of Paris, League of Nations established
1919	Gandhi leads first nonviolent protest movements in India; revolt in Egypt; Rowlatt Act in India
1920	French and British mandates set up in Middle East
1920s	Pan-African Congresses in Paris
1923	Treaty of Lausanne recognizes independence of Turkey

INTRODUCTION

The First World War—or the Great War as it was called by those who lived through it and did not know that a second conflict of this magnitude lay in their future—was one of several key turning points of world history in the 20th century. Because of the colonial domination and pervasive influence that the industrial powers of Europe had achieved throughout the globe by the late 1800s, a war that in an earlier era might have been confined to Europe spread within weeks to the Middle East and parts of Africa as well as (on a much reduced scale) to East Asia and over the oceans of the world. The epicenters of the conflict in northern France and east-central Europe sucked in manpower and resources from across the globe. Distant Dominions within the British Empire, such as New Zealand, Australia, and Canada, were soon involved directly in combat. And the two great industrial nations outside of Europe, Japan and ultimately the United States, became active participants in a struggle for global supremacy (again, with very different levels of intensity) that raged for four devastating years.

The immediate causes of the outbreak of the war in August 1914 had mainly to do with the fears and miscalculations of the leaders of the European powers. But decades of crises, and in some instances actual military clashes between European rivals, over overseas territories and international influence proved critical long-term factors in the march to war. Again and again in the decades leading up to 1914 (which we have argued make up the first phase of 20th-century history), colonial quarrels increased tensions between the great powers of Europe. Over time, these recurring crises solidified the hostile alliances between the Triple Entente states (Russia, France, and Great Britain) and the Central Powers (Germany and Austria-Hungary) that were the initial and enduring adversaries in World War I. The succession of diplomatic and military clashes in the Balkans that occurred in the years leading up to the war were in important ways the direct product of colonial rivalries. Although geographically located in Europe, Serbia and the other areas of the Balkans displayed most of the attributes of colonial enclaves. And like overseas colonies, they were treated by the great powers as pawns in the struggle for supremacy in Europe and across the globe.

Four years of massive slaughter, with the European imperial powers suffering the bulk of the casualties, severely weakened or utterly shattered existing global systems. The long war also generated new historical forces that dominated the history of the decades that followed and in important ways persist to the present day. In this chapter we will examine the forces that led to the outbreak of the war and the nature of the conflict on the Western Front, central and eastern Europe, the Middle East, and a number of key locations in sub-Saharan Africa. In the second half of the chapter, we will explore the ways in which the war undermined the colonial empires of the European powers and led to the decline of a European-dominated global order. In the remaining chapters of Part II, we will trace the connections between World War I and critical political upheavals—driven by forces on both the right and left of the political spectrum—in key areas of the world. And we will look at the ways in which the Great Depression of the 1930s exacerbated the ongoing crises brought on by the war and pushed the world to a second, and even more horrific and extensive, global conflict.

THE COMING OF THE GREAT WAR

By 1914 diplomatic tensions had escalated fairly steadily among the major European powers. Colonial rivalries and arms races had led to the formation, beginning in the 1890s, of two increasingly hostile alliances. Each of the alliances was anchored on secret treaties that committed those who joined to come to each other's assistance in case of attack by an outside rival power. The participants in each alliance also made plans to coordinate both military preparations and operations should war break out in Europe.

Hostile Alliances and Armaments Races

Fear of Germany's growing economic and military power had driven autocratic Russia to ally first with republican France and then with the even more democratic Britain. Germany's growing power also menaced its neighbor to the west, France. In both cases, from the early 1890s the arrogance and aggressive posturing of Germany's new ruler, Kaiser Wilhelm II, only magnified the threat the emerging colossus seemed to pose for the rest of Europe. The French also hoped that their alliance with Russia would lead to a two-front war that would brake Germany's rising supremacy and allow France to recover the provinces of Alsace and Lorraine, which France had lost to Germany through defeat in the Franco-Prussian War of 1870. Eclipsed by Germany economically and increasingly threatened overseas by a growing German navy, Britain joined with Russia and France to form the Triple Entente alliance in the early 1900s.

In the same years, the Entente powers increasingly confronted a counteralliance consisting of Germany, Austria-Hungary, and (nominally at least) Italy. With the accession of Kaiser Wilhelm II to power, Germany had moved away from a defensive triple alliance with Russia and Austria-Hungary to a growing dependence on the latter alone. Germany had also sought to draw Italy into its coalition with promises of support for its efforts at colonial expansion. But Italian hostility to Austria-Hungary, which still controlled lands the Italians claimed as their own, kept Italy's role as one of the Central Powers tentative and liable to shift with changing international circumstances. Italian ambivalence became all too clear after the outbreak of war when they not only refused to support Germany and Austria-Hungary, but in 1915 entered the conflict on the side of the Triple Entente.

The alliance system, menacing in itself, was embittered by the atmosphere generated by imperial rivalries that were played out over most of the globe. As we have seen in Chapters 3 and 4, in the decades leading up to World War I, most of the European powers had been involved in empire building overseas and they came to equate the prestige of great power status with the possession of colonies. Rivalries over areas to colonize heightened nationalist sentiments in each country. But by 1900, most of the world's available territories had been colonized by one or another of the states in the two alliance systems. As a result, the scramble in the early 1900s for the few areas as yet unclaimed produced much greater tensions in the European diplomatic system. France maneuvered to annex Morocco to its North African colonies, which already included Algeria and Tunisia. Germany twice threatened war if the French advance continued, only to back off when it was clear that none of the other European powers would support it. In the second of the international crises over Morocco in 1911, the Germans had to be bought off by a French concession of a strip of territory from their possessions in the Congo in central Africa. In the same year, Italy sought to conquer Tripoli (today's Libya) to the chagrin of the Young Turks who had seized power in the moribund Ottoman Empire. Italian success encouraged a number of the small states, such as Bulgaria and Serbia, to attack the Ottomans, which led to two bitter Balkan wars in 1912 and 1913 and further losses of territory for the Turks.

Imperialist rivalries solidified the growing divisions between the two alliances, and fed the jingoism (warlike nationalist sentiments that spread widely among the middle and working classes throughout Europe) that had much to do with the coming of the war. Most European leaders of both the great powers and smaller states like

Europe and the Middle East during World War I

those in the Balkans were eager to vie for increased territories and obsessed with keeping their rivals from advancing at their country's expense.

Imperialism and the alliance system were both linked to ever more intense and costly arms races. Naval rivalry was the most apparent and fiercely contested. The Germans decision to build a navy that could threaten Great Britain's longstanding control of the world's oceans was one of the key reasons for the British moves for military cooperation with France and (more grudgingly) Russia.

It also touched off the greatest arms race in all of history to that time. Huge new warships, such as the Dreadnought battleship launched in 1906 and the German ships built in response, kept the naval rivalry at a fever pitch. Serious hopes for arms limitations, much less reductions, faded. Armies grew steadily in size and firepower, and practiced massive maneuvers that national leaders were prepared to implement in the event of the outbreak of a general war. Not surprisingly, the military buildup helped pave the way to war, as some in the

German military in particular pushed for a preemptive strike before army reforms in Russia made it too powerful to overcome.

Diplomatic and military competition tied foreign policy to spiraling domestic tensions. All of the major industrial nations, and those in the process of industrializing like Russia, faced growing labor unrest after 1900. Strikes, the growth of trade unions, and votes for socialist parties mounted steadily in the decade and a half before 1914. The business classes and the political elites were alarmed by these challenges to their dominance. They sought diplomatic successes and confrontations with rival powers to distract their subjects from social problems at home. British ministers and the German Kaiser were notable examples, appealing for labor peace in the name of national unity in the face of the threat of attack by powerful rivals. Those in power also supported military buildups because they provided employment for the working classes and huge profits to industrialists who were pillars of support for each of the European regimes.

The Outbreak of the War

In the years just before 1914, decades of rivalry and mounting tensions within the European state system were increasingly centered on the Balkans, where Russia sought to back Serbia in its determined resistance to the steady advance of the Austro-Hungarian empire. The complex ethnic divisions and interstate rivalries of the Balkan area mirrored the growing crisis of Europe as a whole. It was not surprising, then, that the event that precipitated World War I occurred in the Balkans. In July 1914, a Serbian nationalist, Gavriel Pricip, assassinated the heir apparent to the Austro-Hungarian throne, Archduke Ferdinand, and his wife in Sarajevo, the administrative center of the Bosnian province of the Austrian empire. Bolstered by the infamous "blank check" promised by German leaders for reprisals against Serbia, the Austro-Hungarians drew up a list of demands that was impossible for the Serbs to accede to without surrendering their nation's sovereignty. The ruling circles of Austria-Hungary were determined to put an end to decades of Serbian challenges to their control over portions of the Balkans, and thus they were clearly intent on forcing a war.

When the Russians vowed to support their Slavic brethren in Serbia should war break out with the Austrians, the alliance systems that had been forged in the preceding decades quickly came into play. Within months the confrontation of the two blocs had transformed what

THE BOILING POINT.

The obvious fear displayed by an assortment of European leaders in this 1912 *Punch* cartoon is eerily prescient of the bafflement and concern that later seized European and world leaders in the midst of the Balkan wars of the 1890s.

might have been a regional war among the Balkan states and their Austrian or Russian backers into the threat of a general European war. Inept diplomacy and a widespread sense of resignation to the eventual outbreak of war, which some believed would sort out the quarrels and tensions that had been building for decades, led to the mobilization of the armies of the great powers in late July 1914.

Although the leaders of most of the powers had long regarded mobilization as a way of applying diplomatic pressure, for the Germans mobilization meant war. Because they had faced the possibility of massive combat on two fronts since the 1890s, the Germans had devised an intricate plan to first attack in the west and defeat France before turning to the more backward, and thus slower to mobilize, Russians in the east. Once Russia mobilized against Germany and the German armies moved to mobilize in retaliation according to a rigid railway timetable that plotted an invasion of neutral Belgium on the way to an all-out assault on France, the alliance systems were locked into a massive war. When the British entered the conflict, officially to defend tiny Belgium which they had long before pledged to protect, a European conflict was transformed into a global one. Britain's naval ally—Japan—quickly jumped into the fray. And British-ruled colonial territories, from the "white" dominions of Canada, Australia, and New Zealand to Britain's extensive imperial possessions in India and across Africa and Southeast Asia, were brought directly into the war. After nearly a century's lapse, Europe was again consumed by a general war that rapidly spread to other parts of the world. But nationalist passions, the new power of Western states, and industrial weaponry would mean destruction and disruption on a far larger and more fundamental scale than those of any previous conflict. And these outcomes would be globalized with an intensity unprecedented in the human experience to that time.

A WORLD AT WAR

Part of the reason European leaders let their nations blunder into war in 1914 was that most of them expected the conflict to come to be brief and decisive. They saw a war between the European powers as a way to break the logjam of tension and unresolved disputes built up by decades of confrontations between the two alliance systems. Many were also convinced that because the economies of the industrial powers, particularly Britain and Germany, were so interdependent, Europe could simply not remain at war for more than several months or at best a year. Thus, the soldiers of the combatant powers, and most of the leaders who sent them off to war in August 1914, were convinced that the troops would be home by Christmas. But as early as September, with offensives crushed or bogged down on both the Western Front and in the east, it was beginning to be clear that Europe and the world had been plunged into a conflict that was likely to go on for a good deal longer, perhaps many years. As this expectation was realized in more horrific ways than most contemporaries could imagine, the conflict spread far beyond Europe and grew into one of the great watersheds of 20th-century global history.

The War in Europe

Perhaps more than any other single factor, the failure of Germany's ambitious plan for a quick victory over France

ensured that there would be a long war of stalemate and attrition. German political and military leaders counted on their country's superb railway system and huge armies to overwhelm the Belgians and defeat the French before they could even fully mobilize. And the French obliged them by launching offensives against deeply entrenched German forces in Alsace-Lorraine that ended in the near destruction of some of France's best armies. But Belgium resisted bravely, slowing the German goliath, and the small but superbly trained British army suddenly appeared to contest the momentum of three German armies, each of which was larger than the total British forces. By the time they reached the frontiers of northern France, the German soldiers were tired and, having left the railways behind in southern Belgium, growing short of boots, food, and ammunition. Reeling from their defeats by the Germans in Alsace-Lorraine, the French forces fled toward Paris, where they were regrouped, reinforced (in part by a famous convoy of Parisian cab drivers), and prepared for the German onslaught. During a five-day battle along the Marne River in early September, the German advance was halted, then thrown back. Paris had been saved and the stage set for more than three years of bloody stalemate on the Western Front.

To protect themselves from the withering firepower of the artillery and machine guns of the opposing armies, British and German soldiers began to dig into the ground during and after the clashes along the Marne. Soon northern and western France was crisscrossed by miles and miles of entrenchments that frustrated—with staggering levels of dead and wounded—all attempts to break the stalemate between the opposing forces until well into 1918. The almost unimaginable killing power of the industrial technology wielded by the opposing European armies favored the defensive. Devastating artillery, the withering fire of machine guns, barbed-wire barriers, and the use of poison gas turned the Western Front into a killing ground that offered no possibility of decisive victory to either side. The carnage reached unimaginable levels, with the Germans losing 850,000 men, the French 700,000, and the British over 400,000 in the single year of 1916 on just the Western Front. This mechanized mass slaughter was to have lasting effects in the decades that followed in part because many of the soldiers who survived it, and in the process hardened themselves against the carnage, later joined the shock troops of both the fascist and Nazi movements. These trends increased the reach of total warfare, which World War I introduced into global history, and later led to devastating losses among civilian populations in World War

II and paved the way for the mass, assembly-line slaughter of 12 million noncombatants in the Holocaust.

By the millions, the youths of Europe were killed, maimed, and driven insane, or waited for the next offensive catastrophe in rat- and lice-infested trenches. Like the so-called "primitive" peoples the Europeans had come to dominate overseas, soldiers were exposed to rain and cold and deprived of virtually all of the material comforts that large sections of western European societies had come to regard as their birthright. A German soldier, and later novelist, captured the constant fear, the almost unendurable anxiety the soldiers experienced:

> The front is a cage in which we must await fearfully whatever may happen. We lie under the network of arching shells and live in a suspense of uncertainty. Over us chance hovers.

In so many ways, the war in Europe was centered on the ongoing and senseless slaughter in the trenches. Levels of dead and wounded that would have been unimaginable before the war rose ever higher between 1915 and 1918. And they were all the more tragic because neither side could break the stalemate; hundreds of thousands were killed or maimed to gain small patches of ground that were soon lost in counterattacks. Years of carnage made all too evident the lack of imagination and utter incompetence of most of the generals on both sides of the conflict. Few understood that mass assaults on mechanized defenses had become suicidal at this point in the industrial age. And the aged officers in the higher commands and overmatched politicians soon demoted or dismissed those who sought to find creative ways out of the trench morass. As the years passed, a British war poet observed:

> *Neither [side] had won or could win the war*
> *The war had won and would go on winning.*

The War in the East and in Italy

In the first weeks of the conflict, the Germans were alarmed by the rapidity with which the Russians were able to mount major offensives against both Austria-Hungary and eastern Germany itself. Having committed most of their forces to their own offensives against France, the German high command felt obliged to divert critical resources and manpower to check the advancing Russian armies. In late August the reorganized German forces virtually destroyed an entire Russian army (and

sent a second into headlong retreat). In defeat, the Russian forces exhibited many of the weaknesses that resulted in, by far, the highest levels of casualties of any of the combatants and the ultimate and utter defeat of the Tsarist armies. Aristocratic generals dispatched millions of mostly illiterate and poorly trained peasants to certain death in repeated assaults on better armed and led German forces. Commands in critical battles were sent in uncoded format, and readily picked up by their adversaries. Russian artillery, manned by upper-class personnel, usually provided little cover for massed peasant forces, which were reduced to little more than cannon- and machine-gun fodder in assaults on the entrenched Germans.

Although the lines shifted over large areas in the east, they inexorably, with horrific human cost, moved east into the provinces of the Russian empire. The poor showing of the Russian commanders, including the hapless Tsar Nicholas II who insisted on taking control at the front, did much to spark the mutinies and peasant revolts that were critical forces in the revolutionary waves that destroyed the Tsarist regime in 1917.

The Russians fared somewhat better on the Austro-Hungarian front (see map on p. 111), where they faced even more inept generals and multiethnic armies whose soldiers' loyalty to the Austrian emperor was often lukewarm or nonexistent. But the Russians could not prevent the Austrians from crushing Serbia, which held out until the end of 1915. And thanks largely to timely interjections of German soldiers, the Austro-Hungarians managed, again at the cost of millions of casualties, to check repeated Russian offensives. The Austrian forces generally fought much better against the Italians, who entered the war in May 1915. Nine months earlier, Italian leaders had declined to march to war with their Central Power allies, whom the Italians claimed had attacked first and thus nullified what was a defensive treaty. Having wrested British promises of substantial territorial gains, mostly at Austria-Hungary's expense, the Italians launched a series of offensives against the Austrians.

With the Austrians enjoying the high ground in the eastern Alps, the assaults all ended in disaster. Incompetent and corrupt generals; soldiers increasingly disgusted by costly campaigns that went nowhere; and venial politicians double dealing behind the lines resulted in the near collapse of the Italian front in 1917. Although British and French reinforcements rushed from the Western Front eventually stalled the Austrian advance, Italian soldiers deserted in droves and the war plunged Italy into social and political turmoil. One of the Italian soldiers, who was briefly at the front and slightly wounded, Benito

Mussolini, would soon exploit this unrest to the fullest in his postwar drive to impose a fascist dictatorship on Italy.

The Home Fronts in Europe

As the war dragged on without any sign that decisive victories could be won by either side, soldiers at the fronts across Europe grew resentful of the civilians back home. Their anger was focused on political leaders who cheered them on from the safety of the sidelines far to the rear. But the soldiers were also disturbed, more generally, by the patriotic zeal and insensitivity of the civilian populace that had little sense of the horrors they were forced to endure at the front. In fact, the commitment of the civilians behind the lines and their hatred for the enemy were usually far more pronounced than those of the soldiers actually in combat. Each of the powers remained able to mobilize ever larger numbers of soldiers and military resources, despite growing food shortages and privations on the home fronts. Governments responded by rationing resources and regulating production to head off potentially crippling labor disputes.

Whole industrial sectors, such as railways, were administered directly by the state. Executive branches of the combatants' governments gradually took over the power of elected parliaments—particularly in Germany, where by late 1916 the General Staff virtually ran the country. Dissent was suppressed, often by force, and newspapers and other media outlets (as well as the letters of the soldiers) were strictly censored. Governments developed propaganda departments that grew more sophisticated and strident as the war dragged on. The British proved the most adept at propaganda. Much of this was aimed at the United States in the hope that the Americans would be drawn into the war. The British and American public were bombarded with stories of German atrocities. As the war went into its second and third years, news of severe setbacks was increasingly denied to the German people. As a consequence, most Germans were stunned by what seemed their sudden defeat in 1918. The extent of the involvement of the civilian population (in some cases as targets of bombardments and aerial assaults) and the power of governments to mobilize men *and* women and control the information they received about the conflict made "The Great War" truly the first total war in human history.

The war in essence sped up many developments already visible in industrial societies. The power of organization increased, particularly through the new interventions of governments. To maintain unified backing of the civilian population, socialists and trade union chiefs were given new recognition and allowed to serve on governing boards in charge of industrial production and negotiate improved working conditions. As their leaders became ever more drawn into the existing governmental system, some labor groups rejected their leadership and became ever more vocal critics of the war. As the war lumbered on, seemingly out of control, these trends became more pronounced, particularly in Russia and Germany. Labor protests in Moscow and St. Petrograd gave powerful momentum to the wave of discontent and mass protest that brought down the Tsarist regime in February 1917 and propelled the Bolsheviks to power in October of the same year. In Germany, labor agitation, very often sparked by growing shortages of food and fuel that were intensified by the British naval blockade, also loomed as a threat to the military commanders who ran the country in the last years of the conflict. As the German front in France and Belgium collapsed in the early summer of 1918, leftist leaders and angry laborers pushed the nation to the brink of revolution in late 1918 and 1919.

As a direct consequence of the war, women's participation in the labor force increased greatly, particularly in Germany, Britain, and the United States. Defying prevailing prewar notions about the "natural" gender roles, women proved very able to work even in heavy industry where many were engaged in the very dangerous production of munitions. Better wages and the confidence they gained from their mastery of such demanding and critical roles as factory workers and nurses at the front sparked a broader liberation for women during the war years. From the rising hemlines of their dresses and their ability to smoke in public to unchaperoned dating and greatly increased political activism, many women sought to recast gender roles and images. At war's end, the loss of many of their jobs to men returning from the front and government programs consciously designed to force them back into the home reversed many of the gains that women had achieved during the conflict. But in Britain, Germany, and the United States, they gained the vote, which they had struggled for in the decades before 1914. And the visibility and influence of the career-oriented and sophisticated "new women" of the 1920s, though a small minority even in Germany and the United States, gave promise of broader advances in the decades to come.

The War Outside of Europe

Except for Austria-Hungary, all of the major powers that went to war in 1914 had colonies outside of Europe. When it became clear that the war was not to be the quick, decisive clash that most had anticipated, the

The drastic shortage of farm and factory workers caused by the insatiable military manpower needs of World War I generals provided abundant (but often dangerous, as the munitions work shown here suggests) job outlets for young women.

manpower and resources of these imperial possessions were increasingly sucked into the spreading conflict. By 1915, fighting had spread to the Middle East, West and East Africa, across most of the seas and oceans of the world, and even to China and the islands of the Pacific. Troops from Canada, Australia, New Zealand, and throughout much of Africa had been recruited, mainly to fight for the Triple Entente allies. And by 1917, the United States had entered the war, leaving only the nations of South America alone of all of the continents not directly engaged in the struggle.

More than any other power, Britain's participation in the war contributed to its globalization. The British navy not only cut off Germany from its colonies in Africa, China, and the Pacific islands, it hunted down German ships still on the high seas at the outbreak of war. Perhaps most critically, British naval supremacy meant that an effective blockade could be maintained that would deprive the Central Powers of supplies of food and raw materials from overseas throughout the war. Because the British also controlled transatlantic cable links, they could easily outdo the Germans in propaganda efforts to convince the neutral United States to side with them in the war. The expensive and highly touted German navy fully engaged the British Grand Fleet only once during the war, in 1916 off Jutland in Denmark. Though the Germans sank more ships and killed more British sailors, the High Seas fleet was driven back into port and proved of little use to the larger German effort for the rest of the war.

The British entry into the war also meant that its empire and allies were drawn into the fray. Japan, which had joined Britain in a naval pact in 1902, eagerly attacked German colonies in China and the Pacific. These acquisitions, especially the seizure of the Shandong Peninsula, would provide great impetus to Japan's imperialist aspirations in China in the 1930s. The islands they captured from the Germans in World War I proved components of the defense perimeter they sought to build in the Pacific during World War II. The British Dominions—Canada, Australia, and New Zealand—quickly marshalled considerable resources to support the war effort. These areas not only supplied food and critical raw materials, in defiance of the German U-boat fleet in the Atlantic, they swelled the initially meager ranks of Britain's armed forces. Dominion troops were a mainstay of British operations in the Middle East, including the defense of the vital Suez Canal link and the ill-fated assault at Gallipoli in 1915. And they fought valiantly on the Western Front throughout the war, at times bolstering British lines that were crumbling under massive German assaults. White settler colonials in South Africa also joined those from the Dominions in support of the British, despite bitter opposition from some segments of the Afrikaner population, which had suffered so greatly as a result of draconian British repression in the Anglo-Boer war just over a decade earlier.

The British and the French also received vital support from their nonsettler colonies in Africa, India, and

Southeast Asia. The massive army, which the British had recruited in India for over a century and a half, did much of the fighting in sub-Saharan Africa and the Middle East. The French deployed tens of thousands of non-European soldiers, recruited mainly in North and West Africa, on the Western Front, where many served with distinction but with scant reward. Unlike the British, who turned mainly to women to replace the millions of farmers and factory workers who went off to war, the French relied heavily on laborers recruited in their colonies from Africa to Vietnam.

Although the Germans quickly lost most of their colonies in Africa and the Far East, superbly led African soldiers recruited and trained in German East Africa (Tanzania today) held off hundreds of thousands of British-led Indian and South African troops until two weeks after the end of hostilities in Europe itself! But Germany's main support from outside of Europe came from the Ottoman Empire (see map on p. 111), which entered the war in the fall of 1915. The Young Turk leaders, who had consolidated their power in Constantinople in the decade leading up to the war (see Chapter 4), had continued the Ottoman sultan's reliance on German military advisors and financiers. After fending off the British-led campaign to capture the Gallipoli peninsula, the Turks opened up fronts in southern Russia, where they suffered severe defeats, and the Middle East, where their fortunes were more mixed and they remained for years a threat to the British in Egypt and the Suez Canal zone.

The Young Turk leaders sought to transfer blame for the reverses on the Russian front to the Christian Armenian minority that was concentrated in areas that spanned the two empires in eastern Anatolia and the Caucasus. In fact, remembering earlier pogroms launched by the Turks against them, some of the Armenians living in Turkish areas had backed the Russians. But most of the minority was loyal or neutral, and poor generalship and bad planning were the main causes of the Turkish military disasters. Struggling to cover their blunders, the Young Turk leaders launched a genocidal assault in 1915 against the Armenians, which claimed as many as a million lives and sent hundreds of thousands of Armenians in flight to Russia and the Middle East.

The last major combatant to enter the global conflagration was the United States, which declared war on Germany in the spring of 1917. The war made the United States into a major global power, culminating developments that had been underway for decades. By 1914, the United States had become an active force in international diplomacy and power politics. It had built a modest Pacific empire, centering on Hawaii and the Philippines, and had become increasingly forceful in its interventions in Central America and the Caribbean. The outbreak of the war was greeted with considerable ambivalence on the part of American leaders and the citizenry more generally. Distant from the battlefields, Americans disagreed over which side was in the right and whether or not they should intervene in quarrels that seemed to have little to do with them. But American businesses profited greatly from the war by selling food, raw materials, and eventually weapons, mainly (due to the British blockade) to the Entente allies. American mercantile interests, like their counterparts in Japan, also took advantage of the Europeans' need to concentrate their industrial production on the war effort by taking over new markets in Latin America and Asia. Rapidly rising exports, combined with huge loans to Britain, France, and Russia, which all needed credit to buy American goods, transformed the United States from an international debtor to the world's largest creditor and strongest economy.

Despite all of the gains that the United States had accrued through neutrality, American leadership and a majority of the American public were pro-British. British successes in the propaganda war and ever growing economic ties to the Entente allies did much to explain this sentiment. But clumsy German attempts to influence American opinion and, most critically, the German need to use submarines to counter the British blockade and control of sea access to Europe, did much to drive the United States into the war. Following the resumption of unrestricted submarine warfare in the Atlantic, which President Woodrow Wilson had earlier warned would force military retaliation by the United States, America entered the conflict in April 1917. American warships were immediately joined with the British to create a convoy system that eventually offset an intensified German submarine campaign designed to starve the British isles into submission. For much of 1917, the number of American troops sent to Europe was small and largely symbolic. But by early 1918, millions of young Americans were in training and hundreds of thousands arriving in Europe each week. The growing buildup of American reinforcements, and American-produced arms and supplies, convinced the German high command that they must launch a massive strike for a quick victory, before the full manpower and resources of the United States could be brought to bear against their weary soldiers.

Endgame: The Return of Offensive Warfare

For several weeks in March and April of 1918, the massive offensives launched by the Germans on the Western Front looked as if they might bring victory to the Central Powers. An entire British army had been shattered and another was in full retreat; the already demoralized French forces were also falling back toward Paris. Nearly a million German soldiers transferred from the Eastern Front after Russia was knocked out of the war, and new assault tactics and the deployment of storm troopers had restored the offensive and broken three long years of bloody stalemate. But just as Paris was again within the range of the great German guns, the advance slowed. Mounting casualties and sheer fatigue on the German side, counteroffensives, new weapons like tanks, and a rapidly increasing influx of fresh and enthusiastic American soldiers stalled the German drive and then began to push the German armies out of northern France. At the same time, the Austrian fronts broke down in both northeast Italy and the Balkans. As the Austro-Hungarian empire fragmented along national lines, the heir to the Hapsburg throne abdicated as separate republics in Austria and Hungary sued the Entente allies for peace.

Fearing that their armies were on the verge of collapse and menaced by widespread rebellions at home, the German commanders agreed to an armistice on November 11, 1918. The generals sought to shift the blame for defeat to a civilian government that they had abruptly installed in Berlin. Made up of members of the Center and Socialist parties, Germany's new civilian leaders were forced to both sue the Entente allies for peace and consent to an armistice agreement delivered by two British admirals and two French generals. Assuming that their armies were on the verge of victory just months before, the German people were stunned by the sudden reversal. And many accepted the myth that Germany had been betrayed by socialist and Jewish politicians, whose alleged "stab in the back" would become a rallying cry for Hitler and the Nazis' drive for power from the early 1920s.

After four years of slaughter, the casualty totals were staggering (see Table 5.1). At least 10 million soldiers were dead and 20 million more wounded. The losses were, by far, the heaviest among the great powers of Europe who had been the main adversaries in the conflict. From France to Russia, virtually every European family had a death to mourn. As the fighting ended, an additional calamity struck. Hundreds of thousands of soldiers and millions of civilians died in an influenza pandemic that began in Asia and spread like wildfire around the

TABLE 5.1
World War I Losses

	Dead[*]	Wounded	Prisoner
Great Britain	947,000	2,122,000	192,000
France	1,385,000	3,044,000	446,000
Russia	1,700,000	4,950,000	500,000
Italy	460,000	947,000	530,000
United States	115,000	206,000	4,500
Germany	1,808,000	4,247,000	618,000
Austria-Hungary	1,200,000	3,620,000	200,000
Turkey	325,000	400,000	unknown

[*]The number of known dead (round numbers) was placed at about 10 million and the wounded at about 20 million, distributed among chief combatants.

globe. Though the direct costs of the long and widespread war and the indirect economic losses it inflicted are almost impossible to calculate with certainty, both totals reached hundreds of billions of dollars. In Belgium and northern France, northern Italy and across east-central Europe, extensive swaths of fertile farmlands and bustling cites were reduced to smoldering ruins. This devastation and a postwar economic downturn that followed the armistice dislocated economies across the globe until well into the mid-1920s and fed into the Great Depression that was to follow a decade later.

FAILED PEACE

The widespread bitterness evoked by unprecedented cost in lives and destruction of the war was redoubled by the utter failure of the peace conference convened by the victorious allies at Versailles in 1919. The Germans' willingness to negotiate an armistice owed much to their faith in Woodrow Wilson's frequent promises that he would seek a peace that was not aimed at punishing the defeated powers but focused on establishing a viable new world order in which such a war could never again occur. Whatever Wilson's intentions, his vision of a nonpunitive peace was soon done in by America's Entente allies, who viewed Wilson and his advisors as ill-informed idealists with little grasp of the realities of European power politics. While the Italians and Japanese scrambled to obtain maximum advantage from their support for the allied cause, the French insisted that they had suffered the most and their losses had to be avenged. Georges Clemenceau, the French Premier, pushed for the conference to brand the Germans the aggressors and thus to force them to pay huge reparations to France and the other nations assaulted. He also worked to cut down the size of Germany and funnel its resources to France and the other powers.

Fearing that a reduced Germany would prove fertile ground for the spread of communist revolution, David Lloyd George, the British Prime Minister attempted, with little success, both to mediate between Clemenceau and Wilson and to win enough reparations to satisfy a disgruntled electorate at home. And all of the leaders of the victorious Entente powers, including Wilson, soon closed ranks against the demands welling up from peoples in colonized areas, from the Middle East to Vietnam. Dashing the expectations that he had aroused by his ringing call for the right of peoples to self-determination. Wilson soon made it clear that the peoples he had in mind were white folk like the Poles, not Arabs or Vietnamese. With Wilson's blessing, the British and French set about shoring up, and in fact expanding, their battered empires, while the Japanese solidified their beachhead in China and island enclaves in the western Pacific. The triumvirate of Wilson, Lloyd George, and Clemenceau, which dominated the proceedings at Versailles, also made certain that a mild antiracist clause never made it into the final draft of the treaty.

The Peace of Paris, which was the most important of a series of treaties that emerged from the gathering at Versailles, was nothing less than the diktat (dictated peace, without negotiations) that German politicians across the political spectrum sought to reverse in the postwar era. The German delegation was allowed no part in drafting the treaty, and they were given no opportunity to amend or refuse it. The German representatives were even humiliated by being brought in by the servants' entrance for the signing and being required to stand for hours while the entire draft of the treaty was read aloud before the assembled delegates. The Germans' main allies—the Austrians—were also major targets of the treaties that emerged from the conference. The Austro-Hungarian Empire was dismembered, as nationalist groups carved out the new nations of Czechoslovakia, Hungary, and Yugoslavia. Poland was also reborn, and like Czechoslovakia, it was given substantial chunks of what had been German territory before the war. This left a somewhat fragile Germanic Austria, cut off from its traditional markets, as one of many weak countries between a smaller Germany and a massive Soviet Union to the east.

The fatal flaws of the peace process extended far beyond calculated insults to the Germans. The new Bolshevik leaders of Russia, who would be treated as pariahs

At the Paris Peace Conference of 1919, the Arabs sought a new voice. The Arab representatives included Prince Feisal of Jordan and an Iraqi general. A British delegation member, T. E. Lawrence (third from the right), was a long-time friend of the Arabs. The Arabs failed to win full national self-determination for their homelands.

for decades, were not even invited to the conference. Wartime promises to the Arabs in return for their support for the Entente allies in the war were forgotten, as Britain and France divided the Arab heartlands of the Middle East between themselves. China's pleas for protection from Japanese occupation of the Shandong Peninsula were dismissed, and a youthful Ho Chi Minh was rudely refused an audience with Woodrow Wilson. Denied their demand that Germany be permanently partitioned, French leaders turned inward on each other and waited despondently for the next German assault they were convinced was inevitable. Even the United States, whose President Wilson had opened the peace conference with such exuberant expectations, repudiated what had been wrought at Versailles. Despite Wilson's literally near-fatal efforts to win popular support for the treaty, the American Congress voted down the critical clauses establishing a League of Nations and later made a separate peace with Germany. Even as the delegates were still at work, it was clear to knowledgeable observers that Versailles was a disaster. As one of the most perceptive chroniclers of the war years and their aftermath, Vera Brittain, wrote as the terms of the treaty began to be made public in the press:

> The Big Four were making a desert and calling it peace. When I thought about these negotiations . . . they did not seem to me to represent at all the kind of "victory" that the young men whom I had loved would have regarded as sufficient justification for their lost lives.

WORLD WAR I AND THE NATIONALIST ASSAULT ON THE EUROPEAN COLONIAL ORDER

Four long years of intra-European slaughter severely disrupted the systems of colonial domination that had been expanded and refined in the century leading up to the war. The conflict also gave great impetus to the forces of resistance that had begun to well up in the decades before the war. Though the European colonizers had frequently quarreled over colonial possessions in the late 19th century, during the war they actually fought each other in the colonies for the first time. African and Asian soldiers and laborers in the hundreds of thousands served both on the Western Front and in the far-flung theaters of war from Egypt, Palestine, and Mesopotamia to East

Africa. The colonies also supplied food for the home populations of the Triple Entente powers, as well as vital raw materials such as oil, jute, and cotton. Contrary to long-standing colonial policy, the hard-pressed British even encouraged a considerable expansion of industrial production in India to supplement the output of their overextended home factories. Thus, the war years contributed to the development in India of the largest industrial sector in the colonized world.

World War I presented the subjugated peoples of Africa and Asia with the spectacle of the self-styled civilizers of humankind sending their young men by the millions to be slaughtered in the horrific and barbaric trench stalemate on the Western Front. For the first time, African and Asian soldiers were ordered by their European officers to kill other Europeans. In the process, the vulnerability of the seemingly invincible Europeans and the deep divisions between them were starkly revealed. During the war years, European troops in the colonies were withdrawn to meet the need for manpower on the many war fronts. The garrisons that remained were dangerously understaffed. The need to recall administrative personnel from both British and French colonies meant that colonial officials were compelled to fill their vacated posts with African and Asian administrators, many of whom enjoyed real responsibility for the first time.

To maintain the loyalty of their traditional allies among the colonized and to win the support of the Western-educated elites or new allies such as the Arabs, the British and French made many promises regarding the postwar settlement. Because these concessions often seriously compromised their prewar dominance or their plans for further colonial expansion, the leaders of the victorious Allies repeatedly reneged on them in the years after the war. The betrayal of these pledges understandably contributed a great deal to postwar agitation against the continuance and spread of European colonial domination.

For intellectuals and political leaders throughout Africa and Asia, the appalling devastation of World War I cast doubt on the claims that the Europeans had made for over a century that they were, by virtue of their racial superiority, the fittest of all peoples to rule the globe. The social and economic disruptions caused by the war in key colonies, such as Egypt, India, and the Ivory Coast, made it possible for nationalist agitators to build a mass base for their anticolonial movements for the first time. But in these and other areas of the colonized world, the war gave added impetus to movements and processes already underway rather than initiating new responses to

European global domination. Therefore, it is essential to place wartime developments in the colonies and the postwar surge in anticolonial resistance in a longer-term context that takes into account African and Asian responses that extend in some cases back to the last decades of the 19th century. Since it is impossible to relate the history of the independence struggles in all of the European colonies, key movements, such as those that developed in India, Egypt, and British and French West Africa, will be considered in some depth. These specific movements will then be related to broader patterns of African and Asian nationalist agitation and the accelerating phenomena of decolonization worldwide.

India: The Makings of the Nationalist Challenge to the British Raj

Because India and much of Southeast Asia had been colonized long before Africa, movements for independence arose in Asian colonies somewhat earlier than in their African counterparts. By the last years of the 19th century, the Western-educated minority of the colonized in India and the Philippines had been organized politically for decades. Their counterparts in Burma and the Netherlands Indies were also beginning to form associations to give voice to their political concerns. Because of India's size and the pivotal role it played in the British Empire (by far the largest of the European imperialist empires) as a whole, the Indian nationalist movement pioneered patterns of nationalist challenge and European retreat that were later followed in many other colonies. Though it had been under British control for only a matter of decades, Egypt also proved an influential center of nationalist organization and resistance in the pre–World War I era.

Local conditions elsewhere in Asia and in Africa made for important variations on the sequence of decolonization worked out in India and Egypt. But key themes—such as the lead taken by Western-educated elites, the importance of charismatic leaders in the spread of the anticolonial struggle to the peasant and urban masses, and a reliance on nonviolent forms of protest—were repeated again and again in other colonial settings.

The Indian Congress party led the Indians to independence and governed through most of the early decades of the postcolonial era. It grew out of regional associations of Western-educated Indians that were originally more like study clubs than political organizations in any meaningful sense of the term. These associations were centered in the cities of Bombay, Poona, Calcutta,

and Madras. The Congress party that Indian leaders formed in 1885 had the blessing of a number of high-ranking British officials. These officials viewed it as a forum through which the opinions of educated Indians could be made known to the government, thereby heading off potential discontent and political protest.

For most of its first decades, the Congress party served these purposes quite well. The organization had no mass base and very few ongoing staff members or full-time politicians who could sustain lobbying efforts on issues raised at its annual meetings. Some members of the Congress party voiced concern for the growing poverty of the Indian masses and the drain of wealth from the subcontinent to Great Britain. But the Congress party's debates and petitions to the government were dominated by elite-centric issues, such as the removal of barriers to Indian employment in the colonial bureaucracy and increased Indian representation in all-Indian and local legislative bodies. Most of the members of the early Congress party were firmly loyal to the British rulers and confident that once their grievances were made known to the government, they would be remedied.

Many Western-educated Indians were increasingly troubled, however, by the growing virulence of British racism. This they were convinced had much to do with their poor salaries and limited opportunities for advancement in the colonial administration. In their annual meetings, members of the Congress, who were now able to converse and write in a common English language, discovered that no matter where they came from in India, they were treated in a similar fashion. The Indians' shared grievances, their similar educational and class backgrounds, and their growing contacts through the Congress party gave rise to a sense of common Indian identity that had never before existed in a South Asian environment that was more diverse linguistically, religiously, and ethnically than the continent of Europe.

Social Foundations of a Mass Movement

By the last years of the 19th century, the Western-educated elites had also begun to grope for causes that would draw a larger segment of the Indian population into their growing nationalist community. More than a century of British rule had generated in many areas of India the social and economic disruptions and the sort of discontent that produced substantial numbers of recruits for the nationalist campaigns. Indian businessmen, many of whom would become major financial backers of the Congress

Lessons for the Colonized from the Slaughter in the Trenches

The prolonged and senseless slaughter of the youth of Europe in the trench stalemate on the Western Front did much to erode the image of Europeans as superior, rational, and more civilized beings that they had worked hard to propagate among the colonized peoples in the decades before the Great War. The futility of the seemingly endless slaughter cast doubts on the Europeans' rationality and fitness to rule themselves, much less the rest of the world. The destructive uses to which their science and technology were put brought into question the Europeans' long-standing claims that these material advancements tangibly demonstrated their intellectual and organizational superiority over all other peoples. The following quotations, taken from the writings of some of the leading thinkers and political leaders of the colonized peoples of Africa and Asia, reflect their disillusionment with the West as a result of the war and the continuing turmoil in Europe in the postwar era.

1. Rabindranath Tagore, Bengali poet, playwright, and novelist, who was one of the earliest non-European recipients of the Nobel Prize for literature:

   Has not this truth already come home to you now when this cruel war has driven its claws into the vitals of Europe? When her hoard of wealth is bursting into smoke and her humanity is shattered on her battlefields? You ask in amazement what she has done to deserve this? The answer is, that the West has been systematically petrifying her moral nature in order to lay a solid foundation for her gigantic abstractions of efficiency. She has been all along starving the life of the personal man into that of the professional.

2. Mohandas Gandhi, who emerged in the years after the war as India's leading nationalist figure:

   India's destiny lies not along the bloody way of the West, but along the bloodless way of peace that comes from a simple and godly life. India is in danger of losing her soul. . . . She must not, therefore, lazily and help-

party, were angered by the favoritism the British rulers showed to British investors in establishing trade policies in India. Indian political leaders increasingly stressed these inequities and the more general loss to the Indian people resulting from what they termed the "drain" of Indian resources under colonial rule. Though the British rebuttal was that a price had to be paid for the peace and good government that had come with colonial rule, nationalist thinkers pointed out that the cost was too high.

A large portion of the government of India's budget went to cover the expenses of the huge army that mainly fought wars elsewhere in the British Empire. The Indian people also paid for the generous salaries and pensions of British administrators, who occupied positions that the Indians themselves were qualified to assume. Whenever possible, as in the purchase of railway equipment or steel for public works projects, the government bought goods manufactured in Great Britain. This practice served to buttress a British economy that was fast losing ground to the United States and Germany. It also ensured that the classic colonial relationship between a manufacturing European colonizer and its raw-material-producing overseas dependencies was maintained.

In the villages of India, the shortcomings of British rule were equally apparent by the last decades of the 19th century. The needs of the British home economy had often dictated policies that pushed the Indian peasantry toward the production of cash crops such as cotton, jute, and indigo. The decline in food production that invariably resulted played a major role in the regional famines that struck repeatedly in the pre–World War I era. Radical Indian nationalists frequently charged that the British were callously indifferent to the suffering caused by food shortages and outbreaks of epidemic disease, and that they did far too little to alleviate the suffering that resulted. In many areas, landlessness and chronic poverty, already problems before the establishment of British rule, increased markedly. In most places, British measures to control indebtedness and protect small landholders and tenants were too little and came too late.

The Rise of Militant Nationalism

Some of the issues that Indian nationalist leaders stressed in their early attempts to build a mass base had great appeal for devout Hindus. This was particularly true of campaigns for the protection of cows, which had long had a special status for the Hindu population of South Asia. But these religiously oriented causes often strongly alienated the adherents of other faiths, especially the

lessly say, "I cannot escape the onrush from the West." She must be strong enough to resist it for her own sake and that of the world. I make bold to say that the Europeans themselves will have to remodel their outlooks if they are not to perish under the weight of the comforts to which they are becoming slaves.

3. Léopold Sédar Senghor, Senegalese poet and political leader, who is widely regarded as one of the finest writers in the French language of the 20th century:

> Lord, the snow of your Peace is your proposal to a divided world
>   to a divided Europe
> To Spain torn apart. . . .
> And I forget
> White hands that fired the shots which brought the empires
>   crumbling
> Hands that flogged the slaves, that flogged You [Jesus Christ]
> Chalk-white hands that buffeted You, powdered painted hands
>   that buffeted me
> Confident hands that delivered me to solitude to hatred
> White hands that felled the forest of palm trees once com-
>   manding Africa, in the heart of Africa. . . .

(From *Snow Upon Paris*)

4. Aimé Cesaire, West Indian poet and founder of the Négritude (assertion of black culture) movement in the late 1920s:

> Heia [Praise] for those who have never invented anything
> those who never explored anything
> those who never tamed anything
> those who give themselves up to the essence of all things
> ignorant of surfaces but struck by the movement of all things

(From *Return to My Native Land*)

Questions: On the basis of this sample, what aspects of the West's claims to superiority would you say were called into question by the suicidal conflict of the leading powers within European civilization? What aspects of their own civilizations do these writers, both implicitly and explicitly, champion as alternatives to the ways of the West? Are these writers in danger of stereotyping both the West and their own civilizations?

Muslims. Not only did Muslims eat beef, and thus slaughter cattle, they made up nearly one fourth of the population of the Indian Empire. Some leaders, such as B. G. Tilak, were little concerned by this split. They believed that since Hindus made up the overwhelming majority of the Indian population, nationalism should be built on appeals to Hindu religiosity. Tilak worked to promote the restoration and revival of what he believed to be the ancient traditions of Hinduism. On this basis, he opposed women's education and the raising of the very low marriage age for women. Tilak also turned festivals for Hindu gods into occasions for mass political demonstrations. He broke with more moderate leaders of the Congress party by demanding the boycott of British-manufactured goods. Tilak also sought to persuade his fellow Indians to refuse to serve in the colonial administration and military. Tilak demanded full independence, with no deals or delays, and threatened violent rebellion if the British failed to comply.

Tilak's oratorical skills and religious appeal made him the first Indian nationalist leader with a genuine mass following. Nonetheless, his popularity was confined mainly to his home base in Bombay and in nearby areas in western India. At the same time, his promotion of a very reactionary sort of Hinduism offended and fright-ened moderate and progressive Hindus, Muslims, and followers of other religions, such as the Sikhs. When evidence was found connecting Tilak's writings to underground organizations that advocated violent revolt, the British, who had grown increasingly uneasy about his radical demands and mass appeal, arrested and imprisoned him. Six years of exile in Burma for Tilak had a dampening effect on the mass movement he had begun to build among the Hindu population.

The other major threat to the British in India before World War I also came from Hindu communalists who advocated the violent overthrow of the colonial regime. But unlike Tilak and his followers, those who joined the terrorist movement favored clandestine operations over mass demonstrations. Though terrorists were active in several parts of India by the last decade of the 19th century, those in Bengal built perhaps the most extensive underground network. Considerable numbers of young Bengalis, impatient with the gradualist approach advocated by moderates in the Congress party, were attracted to underground secret societies. These were led by quasi-religious, guru-style leaders who exhorted them to build up their physiques with Western-style calisthenics and learn how to use firearms and make bombs. British officials and government buildings were the major targets of terrorist assassination plots and sabotage. On occasion the young revolutionaries also struck at European civilians and collaborators among the Indian population. But the terrorists' small numbers and limited support from the colonized populace as a whole rendered them highly vulnerable to British repressive measures. The very considerable resources the British devoted to crushing these violent threats to their rule had checked the terrorist threat by the outbreak of World War I.

Tilak's removal and the repression campaigns against the terrorists strengthened the hand of the more moderate politicians of the Congress party in the years before the war. Western-educated Indian lawyers came to be the dominant force in nationalist politics, and—as the careers of Gandhi, Jinnah, and Nehru demonstrate—they would provide many of the movement's key leaders throughout the struggle for independence. The approach of those who advocated a peaceful, constitutionalist route to decolonization was given added appeal by timely political concessions on the part of the British. The Morley-Minto reforms of 1909 provided educated Indians with considerably expanded opportunities both to vote for and serve on local and all-India legislative councils.

The Emergence of Gandhi and the Spread of the Nationalist Struggle

In the months after the outbreak of the war, the British could take great comfort from the way in which the peoples of the empire rallied to their defense. Though already well on the way to independence, their subjects in the White Dominions, lost no time in declaring war on the Central Powers and in raising armies. Dominion troops served with distinction in both the Middle Eastern and European theaters of war. But botched campaigns like those at Gallipoli and the costly offensives on the Somme severely strained relations between the British high command and the colonials. Of the many colonies among the tropical dependencies, none played as critical a role in the British war effort as India. The Indian princes offered substantial war loans; Indian soldiers bore the brunt of the war effort in East Africa and the Middle East; and nationalist leaders, including Gandhi and Tilak, toured India selling British war bonds. But as the war dragged on and Indians died on the battlefields or went hungry at home to sustain a conflict that had little to do with them, signs of unrest spread throughout the subcontinent.

Wartime inflation had adversely affected virtually all segments of the Indian population. Indian peasants were angered at the ceilings set on the price of their market produce, despite rising costs. They were also often upset by their inability to sell what they had produced because of shipping shortages linked to the war. Indian laborers saw their already meager wages drop steadily in the face of rising prices. At the same time, their bosses grew rich from profits earned in war production. Many localities suffered from famines, which were exacerbated by wartime transport shortages that impeded relief efforts.

After the end of the war in 1918, moderate Indian politicians were frustrated by the British refusal to honor wartime promises. Hard-pressed British leaders had promised the Indians that if they continued to support the war effort, India would move steadily to self-government within the empire once the conflict was over. Indian hopes for the fulfillment of these promises were raised by the Montagu-Chelmsford reforms of 1919. These measures increased the powers of Indian legislators at the all-India level and placed much of the provincial administration of India under their control. But the concessions granted in the reforms were offset by the passage later in the same year of the Rowlatt Act, which placed severe restrictions on key Indian civil rights, such as the freedom of the press. These conditions fueled local protest during and immediately after the war. At the same time, Mohandas Gandhi emerged as a new leader who soon forged this localized protest into a sustained all-India campaign against the policies of the colonial overlords.

Gandhi's remarkable appeal to both the masses and the Western-educated nationalist politicians was due to a combination of factors. Perhaps the most important was the strategy for protest that he had worked out a decade earlier as the leader of a successful movement of resistance to the restrictive laws imposed on the Indian migrant community in South Africa. Gandhi's stress on nonviolent, but quite aggressive, protest tactics endeared him both to the moderates and to more radical elements within the nationalist movement. His advocacy of peaceful boycotts, strikes, noncooperation, and mass demonstrations—which he labeled collectively *satyagraha,* or truth force—proved an effective way of weakening British control while limiting opportunities for violent reprisals that would allow the British to make full use of their superior military strength.

It is difficult to separate Gandhi's approach to mass protest from Gandhi as an individual and a thinker. Though physically unimposing, he possessed an inner confidence and sense of moral purpose that sustained his followers and wore down his adversaries. He combined the career of a Western-educated lawyer with the attributes of a traditional Hindu ascetic and guru. The former had given him considerable exposure to the world beyond India and a rather astute understanding of the strengths and weaknesses of the British colonizers. These qualities and his soon legendary skill in negotiating with the British made it possible for Gandhi to build up a strong following among middle-class, Western-educated Indians, who had long been the dominant force behind the nationalist cause. But the success of Gandhi's protest tactics also hinged on the involvement of ever-increasing numbers of the Indian people in anticolonial resistance. The image of a traditional mystic and guru that Gandhi projected was critical in gaining mass support from peasants and laborers alike. Many of these "ordinary" Indians would walk for miles when Gandhi was on tour. Many did so in order to honor a saint rather than listen to a political speech. Gandhi's widespread popular appeal, in turn, gave him even greater influence among nationalist politicians. The latter were very much aware of the leverage his mass following gave to them in their ongoing contests with the British overlords.

Egypt and the Rise of Nationalism in the Middle East

Egypt is the one country in the Afro-Asian world in which the emergence of nationalism preceded European conquest and domination (see map on this page). Risings touched off by the mutiny of Ahmad Orabi and other Egyptian officers, which led to the British occupation in 1882, were aimed at the liberation of the Egyptian people from their alien Turkish overlords as well as the meddling Europeans. British occupation meant, in effect, double colonization for the Egyptian people by the Turkish khedives (who were left in power) and their British advisors.

In the decades following the British conquest, government policy was dominated by the strong-willed and imperious Lord Cromer. As High Commissioner of Egypt, he pushed for much-needed economic reforms that reduced but could not eliminate the debts of the puppet khedival regime. Cromer also oversaw sweeping reforms in the bureaucracy and the construction of irrigation systems and other public works projects. But the prosperity the British congratulated themselves for having brought to Egypt by the first decade of the 20th century was enjoyed largely by tiny middle and elite classes, often at the expense of the mass of the population. The leading beneficiaries included foreign merchants, the

The Middle East after World War I

Turco-Egyptian political elite, a small Egyptian bourgeoisie in Cairo and other towns in the Nile delta, and the ayan, or the great landlords in the rural areas.

The latter were clearly among the biggest gainers. The British had been forced to rely heavily on local, estate-owning notables in extending their control into the rural areas. As a result, the ayan, not the impoverished mass of rural cultivators and laborers, received most of the benefits of the new irrigation works, the building of railways, and the increasing orientation of Egyptian agriculture to the production of raw cotton for the export market. Unfettered by legal restrictions, the ayan greedily amassed ever larger estates by turning smallholder owners into landless tenants and laborers. As their wealth grew, the contrast between the landlords' estate houses and the thatch and mud-walled villages of the great mass of the peasantry became more and more pronounced. Bored by life in the provinces, the well-heeled landed classes spent most of their time in the fashionable districts of Cairo or in resort towns such as Alexandria. Their estates were run by hired managers, who were little more than rent collectors as far as the peasants were concerned.

With the khedival regime and the great landlords closely allied to the British overlords, resistance to the occupation was left mainly to the middle class. Since the middle of the 19th century, this relatively new and small social class had been growing in numbers and influence, mainly in the towns in the Nile delta. With the memory of Orabi's revolt in 1882 still fresh, the cause of Egyptian independence was taken up mainly by the sons of the *effendi*, or the prosperous business and professional families that made up much of this new middle class. Even nationalist leaders who came from rural ayan families built their following among the urban middle classes. In contrast to India, where lawyers predominated in the nationalist leadership, in Egypt, journalists (a number of them educated in France) led the way.

In the 1890s and early 1900s, numerous newspapers in Arabic (and to a lesser extent French and English) vied to expose the mistakes of the British and the corruption of the khedival regime. Egyptian writers also attacked the British for their racist arrogance and their monopolization of well-paying positions in the Egyptian bureaucracy. Like their Indian counterparts, Egyptian critics argued that these could just as well have been filled by university-educated Egyptians. In the 1890s, the first nationalist party was formed. But again in contrast to India, where the Congress party dominated the nationalist movement from the outset, a variety of rival parties proliferated in Egypt. There were three main alternatives by 1907, but none could be said to speak for the great majority of the Egyptians, who were illiterate, poorly paid, and largely ignored urban laborers and rural farmers.

In the years before the outbreak of World War I in 1914, heavy-handed British repression was necessary on several occasions to put down student riots or retaliate for assassination attempts against high British and Turco-Egyptian officials. Despite the failure of the nationalist parties to unite or build a mass base in the decades before the war, the extent of the hostility felt by the Egyptian masses was demonstrated by the Dinshawai incident in 1906. This confrontation between the British and their Egyptian subjects exemplified the racial arrogance displayed by most of the European colonizers. Though the incident at Dinshawai was seemingly a small clash resulting in only limited numbers of fatalities, the excessive British response to it did much to undermine whatever support remained for their continued presence in Egypt.

Most Egyptian villages raised large numbers of pigeons, which served as an important supplement to the meager peasant diet. Over the years, some of the British had turned the hunting of the pigeons of selected villages into a holiday pastime. A party of British officers on leave were hunting the pigeons of the village of Dinshawai in the Nile delta when they accidentally shot the wife of the prayer leader of the local mosque. The angry villagers mobbed the greatly outnumbered shooting party, which in panic fired on the villagers. Both the villagers and the British soldiers suffered casualties in the clashes that followed. In reprisal for the death of one of the officers, the British summarily hung four of the villagers. Although the actual hanging was not shown, the building of the scaffolding was captured in the photograph shown on the facing page. The British also ordered that other villagers connected to the "incident" be publicly flogged or sentenced to varying terms of hard labor.

The harsh British reprisals aroused a storm of protest in the Egyptian press and among the nationalist parties. Some Egyptian leaders later recounted how the incident convinced them that cooperation with the British was totally unacceptable and fixed their resolve to agitate for an end to Egypt's occupation. Popular protests in several areas, and the emergence of ayan support for the nationalist cause, also suggested the possibility of building a mass base for anti-British agitation. More than anything else, the incident at Dinshawai had galvanized support for nationalist agitation across the communal and social boundaries that had so long divided the peoples of Egypt.

By 1913, the British had been sufficiently intimidated by the rising tide of Egyptian nationalism to grant a constitution and representation in a parliament elected indirectly by the men of wealth and influence. World War I and the British declaration of martial law put a temporary end to nationalist agitation. But, as in India, the war unleashed forces in Egypt that could not be stopped and that would soon lead to the revival of the drive for independence with even greater strength than before.

War and Nationalist Movements in the Middle East

In the years after World War I, resistance to European colonial domination, which had been confined largely to Egypt in the prewar years, spread to much of the rest of the Middle East. Having sided with the Central Powers in the war, the Turks now shared in their defeat. The Ottoman Empire disappeared from history, as Britain and France carved up the Arab portions that had revolted against the Young Turk regime during the war. Italy and Greece attacked the Turkish rump of the empire around Constantinople and in Anatolia (Asia Minor) with the intent of sparking a partition of these areas in concert

This photograph, probably taken without the knowledge of the British authorities, shows the construction of the gallows that were used to hang the four peasants who were executed in reprisal for the attacks on British soldiers at Dinshawai in 1906. The conical tower in the distance behind the scaffold was the roost for the pigeons that were the intended targets of the ill-fated hunting party. The Dinshawai incident exemplified the colonizers' tendency to overreact to any sign of overt resistance on the part of the colonized. Their frequent resort to execution and other violent reprisals in these situations was clearly linked to an undercurrent of paranoia that many commentators observed in the tiny communities of European officials, merchants, and planters who lived among large numbers of Africans or Asians.

with the other Entente allies. But a skilled military commander, Mustafa Kemal or Ataturk, had emerged from the Turkish officer corps during the war years. Ataturk rallied the Turkish forces and gradually drove back the forces intent on colonizing the Turkish homeland. By 1923, an independent Turkish republic had been established, but at the cost of the expulsion of tens of thousands of ethnic Greeks. As an integral part of the effort to establish a viable Turkish nation, Ataturk launched a sweeping program of reforms. Many of the often radical changes his government introduced in the 1920s and 1930s were modeled on Western precedents. But in important ways his efforts to secularize and develop Turkey also represented the culmination of transformations made under the Ottomans over the preceding century (see Chapter 4).

With Turkish rule in the Arab heartlands ended by defeat in the war, Arab nationalists in Beirut, Damascus, and Baghdad turned to face the new threat presented by the victorious Entente powers, France and Britain. Betraying promises to preserve Arab independence that the British had made in 1915 and early 1916, French and British forces occupied much of the Middle East in the years after the war. Hussein, the *sherif* of Mecca, had used these promises to convince the Arabs to rise in support of Britain's war against the Turks, despite the fact that the latter were fellow Muslims. Consequently, the allies' postwar violation of these pledges humiliated and deeply angered Arabs throughout the Middle East. The occupying European powers faced stiff resistance from the Arabs in each of the mandates they carved out in Syria, Iraq, and Lebanon under the auspices of the League of Nations. The Arabs' sense of humiliation and anger was greatly intensified by the disposition of Palestine, where British occupation was coupled with promises of a Jewish homeland.

The fact that the British had appeared to promise Palestine, for which they received a League of Nations mandate in 1922, to both the Jewish Zionists and the Arabs during the war greatly complicated an already confused situation. Despite repeated assurances to Hussein and other Arab leaders that they would be left in control of their own lands after the war, Lord Balfour, the British foreign secretary, promised prominent Zionist leaders in 1917 that his government would promote the establishment of a Jewish homeland in Palestine after the war. This pledge fed existing Zionist aspirations for the Hebrew people to return to their ancient Middle Eastern lands of origin, which had been nurtured by the Jews of the diaspora for millennia. In the decades before World War I, these dreams led to the formation of a number of organizations. Some of these were dedicated to promoting Jewish emigration to Palestine; others were committed to the eventual establishment of a Jewish state there.

These early moves were made in direct response to the persecution of the Jews of eastern Europe in the last decades of the 19th century. Particularly vicious *pogroms,* or violent assaults on the Jewish communities of Russia and Romania in the 1860s and 1870s, convinced Jewish intellectuals such as Leon Pinsker that assimilation of the Jews into, or even acceptance by, Christian European nations was impossible. Pinsker and other thinkers called for a return to the Holy Land. Likeminded individuals founded Zionist organizations, such as the Society for the Colonization of Israel, to promote Jewish migration to Palestine in the last decades of the 19th century. Until World War I, the numbers of Jews returning to Palestine were small—in the tens of thousands—though Zionist communities were established on lands purchased in the area.

Until the late 1890s, the Zionist effort was generally opposed by Jews in Germany, France, and other parts of western Europe who enjoyed citizenship and extensive civil rights. In addition, many in these communities had grown prosperous and powerful in their adopted lands. But a major defection to the Zionists occurred in 1894. Theodor Herzl, an established Austrian journalist, was stunned by French mobs shouting "Death to the Jews" as they taunted the hapless army officer Alfred Dreyfus. Dreyfus was a French Jew who had been falsely accused of passing military secrets to the Germans. His subsequent mistreatment, including exile to the infamous penal colony on Devil's Island, became the flashpoint for years of bitter debate between the left and right in France. Soon after this incident in 1897, Herzl and a number of other prominent, western European Jews joined with Jewish leaders from eastern Europe to form

the World Zionist Organization. As Herzl made clear in his writings, the central aim of this increasingly well-funded organization was to promote Jewish migration to and settlement in Palestine until a point was reached when a Zionist state could be established in the area. Herzl's nationalist ambitions, as well as his indifference to the Arabs already living in the area, were captured in the often-quoted view of one of his close associates that Palestine was "a land without people for a people [the Jews] without a land."

Lord Balfour's promises to the Zionists and the British takeover of Palestine struck the Arabs as a double betrayal of wartime assurances that Arab support for the Entente powers against the Turks would guarantee them independence after the war. This sense of betrayal was a critical source of the growing hostility the Arabs felt toward Jewish emigration to Palestine and their purchase of land in the area. Rising Arab opposition convinced many British officials, especially those who actually administered Palestine, to severely curtail the rather open-ended pledges that had been made to the Zionists during the war. This shift led in turn to Zionist mistrust of British policies and open resistance to them. It also fed the Zionists' determination to build up their own defenses against the increasingly violent Arab resistance to the Jewish presence in Palestine. But British attempts to limit Jewish emigration and settlement were not matched by efforts to encourage, through education and consultation, the emergence of strong leadership among the Arab population of Palestine. Consequently, in the critical struggles and diplomatic maneuvers of the 1930s and 1940s, the Arabs of Palestine were rarely able to speak for themselves. They were represented by Arab leaders from neighboring lands, who did not always understand Palestinian needs and desires. These non-Palestinian spokespersons also often acted more in the interests of Syrian or Lebanese Arabs than those of the Christian and Muslim Arab communities in Palestine.

Revolt in Egypt, 1919

Because Egypt was already occupied by the British when the war broke out, and it had been formally declared a protectorate in 1914, it was not included in the promises made by the British to the sherif Hussein. As a result, the anticolonial struggle in Egypt was rooted in earlier agitation and the heavy toll the war had taken on the Egyptian people, particularly the peasantry. During the war, the defense of the Suez Canal was one of the top priorities for the British. To guard against possible Muslim uprisings in response to Turkish calls for a holy war, martial law was declared soon after hostilities began. Throughout the war, large contingents of Entente and empire forces were garrisoned in Egypt. These created a heavy drain on the increasingly scarce food supplies of the area. Forced labor and confiscations by the military of the precious draft animals of the peasantry also led to widespread discontent. As the war dragged on, this unrest was further inflamed by spiraling inflation as well as by food shortages and even starvation in some areas.

By the end of the war, Egypt was ripe for revolt. Mass discontent strengthened the resolve of the educated nationalist elite to demand a hearing at Versailles, where the victorious Allies were struggling to reach a postwar settlement. When a delegation (*Wafd* in Arabic) of Egyptian leaders was denied permission to travel to France to put the case for Egyptian self-determination to the peacemakers at Versailles, most Egyptian leaders resigned from the government and called for mass demon-

strations. What followed shocked even the most confident British officials. Student-led riots touched off outright insurrection over much of Egypt. Especially noteworthy among the demonstrators were large numbers of women, some of whom were from Westernized households but joined the majority of women participating by wearing veils and long robes as a sign of their liberation from British cultural domination. At one point, Cairo was cut off from the outside world, and much of the countryside was hostile territory for the occupying power. Though the British army was able, at the cost of scores of deaths, to restore control, it was clear that some hearing had to be given to Egyptian demands. The emergence of the newly formed Wafd party under its hard-driving leader Sa'd Zaghlūl, provided the nationalists with both a focus for unified action and a mass base that far exceeded any they had attracted in the prewar decades.

ANALYSIS

Women in Asian and African Nationalist Movements

One important but often neglected dimension of the liberation struggles that Asian and African peoples waged against their colonial overlords was the emergence of a stratum of educated, articulate, and politically active women in most colonial societies. In this process, the educational opportunities provided by the European colonizers often played as vital a role as they had in the formation of male leadership in nationalist movements. Missionary girls' schools were confined in the early stages of European involvement in Africa and Asia to the daughters of lower-class or marginal social groups. But by the end of the 19th century these schools had become quite respectable for women from the growing Westernized business and professional classes. In fact, in many cases, some degree of Western education was essential if Westernized men were to find wives with whom they could share their career concerns and intellectual pursuits.

The seemingly insurmountable barriers that separated Westernized Asian and African men from their traditional—and thus usually without formal education—wives became a stock theme in the novels and short stories of the early nationalist era. This concern was perhaps best exemplified by the works of Rabindranath Tagore. The problem was felt so acutely by the first generation of Indian nationalist leaders that many took up the task of teaching their wives English

and Western philosophy and literature at home. Thus, for many upper-class Asian and African women, colonization proved a liberating force. This trend was often offset by the male-centric nature of colonial education and the domestic focus of much of the curriculum in women's schools.

Although women played a small role in the early, elitist stages of Asian and African nationalist movements, they frequently became more and more prominent as the early study clubs and political associations reached out to build a mass base. In India, women who had been exposed to Western education and European ways, such as Tagore's famous heroine in the novel *The Home and the World*, came out of seclusion and took up supporting roles, though they were still usually behind the scenes. Gandhi's campaign to supplant imported, machine-made British cloth with homespun Indian cloth, for example, owed much of whatever success it had to female spinners and weavers. As nationalist leaders moved their anticolonial campaigns into the streets, women became involved in mass demonstrations. Throughout the 1920s and 1930s, Indian women braved the *lathi*, or billy club, assaults of the Indian police; suffered the indignities of imprisonment; and launched their own newspapers and lecture campaigns to mobilize female support for the nationalist struggle.

In Egypt, the British made special note of the powerful effect that the participation of both veiled women and more Westernized upper-class women had on mass demonstrations in 1919 and the early 1920s. These outpourings of

Both the British colonizers and many Egyptians were caught off guard by the very active participation of veiled Egyptian women from both the elite and working classes in the post-World War I mass protests that convinced the British to relinquish direct control over much of Egypt in 1922.

popular support did much to give credibility to the Wafd's demands for British withdrawal. In both India and Egypt, female nationalists addressed special appeals to British and American suffragettes to support their peoples' struggles for political and social liberation. In India in particular, their causes were advanced by feminists such as the English champion of Hinduism, Annie Besant, who became a major figure in the nationalist movement both before and after World War I.

When African nationalism became a popularly supported movement in the post–World War II period, women, particularly the outspoken and fearless market women in West Africa, emerged as a major political force. In settler colonies, such as Algeria and Kenya, where violent revolt proved necessary to bring down deeply entrenched colonial regimes, women took on the dangerous tasks of messengers, bomb carriers, and guerrilla fighters. As Frantz Fanon argued decades ago, and as was later beautifully dramatized in the film *The Battle of Algiers*, this transformation was particularly painful for women who had been in seclusion right up to the time of the revolutionary upsurge. The cutting of their hair, as well as the wearing of lipstick and Western clothes, often alienated them from their own fathers and brothers, who equated such practices with prostitution.

In many cases, women's participation in struggles for the political liberation of their people was paralleled by campaigns for female rights in societies that, as we have seen, were dominated by males. Upper-class Egyptian women founded newspapers and educational associations that pushed for a higher age of marriage, educational opportunities for women, and an end to seclusion and veiling. Indian women took up many of these causes and also developed programs to improve hygiene and employment opportunities for lower-caste women. These early efforts, as well as the prominent place of women in nationalist struggles, had much to do with the granting of basic civil rights to women. These included suffrage and legal equality that were key features of the constitutions of many newly independent Asian and African nations. The great majority of women in the new states of Africa and Asia have yet to enjoy most of these rights. Yet, their inclusion in constitutions and postindependence laws provides crucial backing for the struggles for women's liberation in the nations of the postcolonial world.

Questions: Why might missionary education for women in the colonies have stressed domestic skills? In what ways do you think measures to "modernize" colonial societies were oriented to males? Can you think of women who have been or are major political figures in contemporary Africa and Asia? Why have there not been more? What sorts of traditional constraints hamper the efforts of women to achieve economic and social equality and major political roles in newly independent nations?

When a special British commission of inquiry into the causes of the upheaval in Egypt met with widespread civil disobedience and continuing violent opposition, it recommended that the British begin negotiations for an eventual withdrawal from Egypt. Years of bargaining followed, which led to a highly qualified independence for the Egyptians. British withdrawal occurred in stages, beginning in 1922 and culminating in the British withdrawal to the Suez Canal zone in 1936. But though they pulled out of Egypt proper, the khedival regime was preserved and the British reserved the right to reoccupy Egypt should it be threatened by a foreign aggressor.

Though they had won a significant degree of political independence, the Egyptian leaders of the Wafd party, as well as its rivals in the Liberal Constitutionalist and Union parties, did little to relieve the increasing misery of the great majority of the Egyptian people. Most Egyptian politicians regarded the winning of office as an opportunity to increase their own and their families' fortunes. Many politicians, both those from ayan households and those from the professional and merchant classes, used their influence and growing wealth to amass huge estates, which were worked by landless tenants and laborers. Locked in personal and interparty quarrels, as well as the ongoing contest with the khedival regime for control of the government, few political leaders had the time or inclination to push for the land reforms and public works projects that the peasantry so desperately needed.

The utter social bankruptcy of the 40 years of nationalist political dominance that preceded the military coup and social revolution led by Gamal Abdul Nasser in 1952 is suggested by some revealing statistics compiled by the United Nations in the early 1950s. By that time, nearly 70 percent of Egypt's cultivable land was owned by 6 percent of the population. Some 12,000 families alone controlled 37 percent of the farmland. As for the mass of the people, 98 percent of the peasants were illiterate, malnutrition was chronic among both the urban and rural populations, and an estimated 95 percent of rural Egyptians suffered from eye diseases. Such was the legacy of the very unrevolutionary process of decolonization in Egypt.

The Beginnings of the Liberation Struggle in Africa

Most of Africa had come under European colonial rule only in the decades before the outbreak of World War I. Nonetheless, precolonial missionary efforts had produced small groups of Western-educated Africans in parts of West and south-central Africa by the end of the 19th century. Like their counterparts in India, most Western-educated Africans were staunchly loyal to their British and French overlords during World War I. With the backing of both Western-educated Africans and the traditional rulers, the British and especially the French were able to draw on their African possessions for manpower and raw materials throughout the war. But this reliance took its toll on their colonial domination in the long run. In addition to local rebellions in response to the forcible recruitment of African soldiers and laborers, the war effort seriously disrupted newly colonized African societies. African merchants and farmers suffered from shipping shortages and the sudden decline in demand for crops, such as cocoa. African villagers were not happy to go hungry so that their crops could feed the armies of the Allies. As Lord Lugard, an influential colonial administrator, pointed out, the desperate plight of the British and French also forced them to teach tens of thousands of Africans

> how to kill white men, around whom [they had] been taught to weave a web of sanctity of life. [They] also know how to handle bombs and Lewis guns and Maxims—and [they have] seen the white men budge when [they have] stood fast. Altogether [they have] acquired much knowledge that might be put to uncomfortable use someday.

The fact that the Europeans kept few of the promises of better jobs and public honors, which they had made during the war to induce young Africans to enlist in the armed forces or serve as colonial administrations, contributed a good deal to the unrest of the postwar years. This was particularly true of the French colonies, where opportunities for political organization, much less protest, were severely constricted before, during, and after the war. Major strikes and riots broke out repeatedly in the interwar period. In the British colonies, where there was considerably more tolerance for political organization, there were also strikes and a number of outright rebellions. Throughout colonized Africa, protest intensified in the 1930s in response to the economic slump brought on by the Great Depression.

Though Western-educated politicians did not link up with urban workers or peasants in most African colonies until the 1940s, disenchanted members of the emerging African elite began to organize in the 1920s and 1930s. In the early stages of this process, charismatic African American political figures, such as Marcus Garvey and

W. E. B. Du Bois had a major impact on emerging African nationalist leaders. In the 1920s, much effort was placed into attempts to arouse all-Africa loyalties and build pan-African organizations. The fact that the leadership of these organizations was mainly African American and West Indian, and that delegates from colonized areas in Africa itself faced very different challenges under different colonial overlords, had much to do with the fact that pan-Africanism proved unworkable. But its well-attended conferences, especially the early ones in Paris, did much to arouse anticolonial sentiments among Western-educated Africans.

By the mid-1920s, nationalists from French and British colonies were pretty much going separate ways. Because of restrictions in the colonies, and because small but well-educated groups of Africans were represented in the French Parliament, French-speaking West Africans concentrated their organizational and ideological efforts in Paris during this period. The Négritude literary movement nurtured by these exiles did much to combat the racial stereotyping that had so long held the Africans in psychological bondage to the Europeans. Writers such as Léopold Senghor, Léon Damas, and the West Indian Aimé Césaire celebrated the beauty of black skin and the African physique. They argued that in the precolonial era African peoples had built societies where women were freer, old people were better cared for, and attitudes toward sex were far healthier than they had ever been in the so-called civilized West.

Except in settler colonies, such as Kenya and Rhodesia, Western-educated Africans in British territories were given greater opportunities to build political associations within Africa itself. In the early stages of this process, African leaders sought to nurture organizations that linked the emerging nationalists of different British colonies, such as the National Congress of British West Africa. By the late 1920s, these pan-colony associations gave way to political groupings concerned primarily with issues within individual colonies such as Sierra Leone, the Gold Coast, or Nigeria. After the British granted some representation in colonial advisory councils to Western-educated Africans in this period, emphasis on colony-specific political mobilization became even more pronounced. Though most of these early political organizations were too loosely structured to be considered true political parties, there was a growing recognition by some leaders of the need to build a mass base. In the 1930s a new generation of leaders made much more vigorous attacks on the policies of the British. Through their newspapers and political associations, they also reached out to ordinary African villagers and the young, who had hitherto played little role in nationalist agitation. Their efforts to win a mass following would come to full fruition only after European divisions plunged humanity into a second global war.

CONCLUSION: AFTER CATASTROPHE

In a multitude of ways World War I set the global historical agenda for the 20th century. The long war, particularly the horrific and increasingly senseless slaughter in the trenches, did much to undermine Europe's prewar position of global dominance. The war severely disrupted Europe's economy and bolstered already emerging rivals, especially the United States and Japan, for preeminence in world trade and finance. Over much of Europe, the hardships endured by the civilian populations on the home front reignited longstanding class tensions. In Russia, but also elsewhere in east-central Europe, growing social divisions sparked full-scale revolutions. In Britain, France, Germany, and other liberal democracies in western Europe, labor parties, some socialist or communist, emerged with much greater power after the conflict. And many shared power, both in coalitions with center parties or in their own right in the 1920s and 1930s. The war saw major changes in gender roles and the relationships in spheres ranging from employment and marriage to sex and fashion. It also generated growing challenges to the rigid racial hierarchies that had dominated both scientific theorizing and popular attitudes in the decades leading up to the conflict.

The victorious Entente allies, especially the British and French but also the Belgians and Japanese, managed to hold on to, and in fact enlarge, their empires. But the hardships endured by colonized peoples and the empty promises made by their desperate colonial overloads during the war gave great impetus to resistance to their empires that spread from the Middle East and India to Vietnam and China. For African and Asian intellectuals at least, the psychological advantages that racial thinking and scientific and technological superiority had given the Europeans began to dissipate. And the essential cooperation of nationalist leaders like Gandhi gave them and their ideologies of liberation access to ever larger numbers of colonized peoples. In the postwar decades, mass civil disobedience campaigns in India and Egypt, and peasant risings in Vietnam and China, established the protest techniques and demands that would ultimately bring down all of the European colonial empires. And the revolutionary regime in Russia, which had come to power as a direct consequence of the war, actively abetted efforts to advance the cause of decolonization around the world. Two other industrial nations whose power had been greatly enhanced by the war, the United States and Japan, sought in rather different ways both to supplant the European colonizers and replace them as the economic and political power centers of the 20th century.

FURTHER READING

There is a vast literature on the origins of World War I. A somewhat dated but still very readable introduction, is available in Laurence Lafore's *The Long Fuse* (1965). James Joll's *The Origins of the First World War* (1984) includes a much fuller treatment of the many and highly contested interpretations of the causes of the conflict. Fritz Fisher's *Germany's Aims in the First World War* stirred great controversy by arguing that Germany's leaders purposely provoked the conflict, while Paul Kennedy's *The Rise of the Anglo-German Antagonism, 1860–1914* covers one of the key rivalries and especially the naval race with a good deal more balance. The impact of colonial disputes on the coming of the war is concisely and convincingly treated in L. F. C. Turner, *Origins of the First World War* (1970).

Of the many general histories of the war on land and sea, the more reliable and readable include *The World in the Crucible, 1914–1919* (1984) by Bernadotte Schmitt and Harold Vedeler and more recently and globally Hew Strachan's encyclopedic *The First World War*, Vol. 1 (2001). Marc Ferro's *The Great War* (1973) remains one of the most stimulating analyses of the conduct of the war. Three of the most successful attempts to understand the war from the participants' perspectives are Paul Fussell's *The Great War and Modern Memory* (1975) and John Cruickshank's *Variations on Catastrophe* (1982), which draw on literary works and memoirs, and Richard Cork's magisterial exploration of artistic images of the conflict in *A Bitter Truth: Avant-Garde Art and the Great War*. Omer Bartov's *Murder in Our Midst* (1996) explores key linkages between the slaughter in the trenches and genocide in the 20th century. Some of the better accounts by the participants include Erich Remarque's classic *All Quiet on the Western Front* (1929); Frederic Manning's *The Middle Parts of Fortune* (1929); Vera Brittain's *Testament of Youth* (1933), and Wilfred Owen's *Poems* (1920; reprinted in 1964 as *The Collected Poems of Wilfred Owen*).

The disasters at Versailles and some of their consequences are also chronicled in numerous books and articles. Two of the most readable are Harold Nicholson's *Peace Making, 1919* (1965) and Charles L. Mee, Jr.'s *The End of Order: Versailles, 1919* (1980). Samples of varying views on the many controversies surrounding the conference can be found in Ivo J. Lederer, ed., *The Versailles Settlement* (1960). The best book on the wider ramifications of the decisions made at or in connection with the conference is Arno Mayer's *Politics and Diplomacy of Peace-Making, 1918–1919* (1967).

A good general historical narrative of the impact of the war on the struggle for Indian independence can be found in Sumit Sarkar's *Modern India, 1885–1947* (1983). The war also figures importantly in the early sections of Mohandas Gandhi's autobiographical *The Story of My Experiments with Truth* (1927). Louis Fischer's biography, *Gandhi* (1950), still yields valuable insights into the personality of one of the great nationalist leaders and the workings of nationalist politics. Judith Brown's studies of Gandhi as a political leader, including *Gandhi's Rise to Power* (1972), and her recent biography of his life and career provide an approach more in tune with current research. The poems and novels of Rabindranath Tagore yield wonderful insights into the social and cultural life of India through much of this era.

P. J. Vatikiotis's *The History of Egypt* (especially the 1985 edition) has excellent sections on the war and early nationalist era in that country. Interesting, but often less reliable, is Jacque Berque's *Colonialism and Nationalism in Egypt* (1972). Leila Ahmed's *Women and Gender in Islam* (1992) has excellent chapters on the roles of women at various stages of the nationalist struggle and in the postindependence era. George Antonius's *The Arab Awakening* (1946) is essential reading on British double dealing in the Middle East during the war, especially as this affected the Palestine question. Alternative perspectives are provided by Aaron Cohen's *The Arabs and Israel* (1970). David Fromkin's *A Peace to End All Peace* provides a more recent and superb account of wartime and postwar events in the Middle East as a whole.

The early stages of the nationalist struggle, including the war years in West Africa, are well covered by Michael Crowder's *West Africa Under Colonial Rule* (1982). A narrative of the history of World War I as a whole in sub-Saharan Africa can be found in Byron Farwell's *The Great War in Africa* (1986). The continued advance of European colonialism in the Middle East and Africa in the postwar years is analyzed in *France Overseas* (1981) by Christopher Andrew and A. S. Kanya-Forstner.

ON THE WEB

Recent interactive overviews of the Great War and its legacies are provided at

http://www.bbc.co.uk/history/war/wwone/index.shtml
http://www.worldwar1.com/index.html
http://www.geocities.com~worldwar1/default.html

and at the Wilfred Owen multimedia archive at

http://www.hcu.ox.ac.uk/jtap/

Wilfred Owen joined the British Army to help relieve the suffering of soldiers in the field "directly by leading them as well as an officer can; indirectly, by watching their sufferings that I may speak of them as well as a pleader can." He accomplished both tasks. His life and war poetry are movingly presented at sites such as

http://home.tiscali.be/ericlaermans/cultural/owen.html
http://www.rjgeib.com/heroes/owen/owen.html
http://www.pitt.edu/~pugachev/greatwar/owen.html
http://www.bbc.co.uk/history/3d/trench.shtml

The latter site includes a host of useful links to a wide variety of related subjects, including a virtual tour of a trench. Life in the trenches, including related weapons such as chemical agents, is also explored at

http://www.worldwar1.com/

But even this excellent site cannot compare in impact with the personal account of trench warfare found in the diary of Private Donald Fraser of the Canadian Expeditionary Force at

http://www.fordham.edu/halsall/mod/1918fraser.html
http://www.archives.ca/05/0518/05180105/
    0518010504_e.html

which also provides resources for the study of the Battle of Vimy Ridge. Other sites illuminating this battle near Arras include

http://www.spartacus.schoolnet.co.uk/FWWvimy.htm
http://www.cbc.ca/news/background/vimy/

The First, Second, and Third Battles of Ypres (Passchendaele) are examined at

http://www.firstworldwar.com/battles/ypres1.htm
http://www.worldwar1.com/sf2ypres.htm
http://www.spartacus.schoolnet.co.uk/
    FWWpasschendaele.htm
http://www.geocities.com/Athens/Acropolis/2354/
    ypres3.html

Two of the greatest battles in the trenches, the Somme and Verdun, are illuminated at

http://www.stemnet.nf.ca/beaumont/somme2.htm
http://www. achtungpanzer.com/blitz.htm

The home fronts of the combatant nations, from food rationing to the impact of the related influenza epidemic, are discussed at

http://www.spartacus.schoolnet.co.uk/ FWWhome.htm
    (scroll down to "War and the Home Front")

The text of the Zimmerman Telegram that provided the proximate cause of the U.S. entry into World War I can be found at

http://www.firstworldwar.com/source/ zimmerman.htm

The roles of Canada and Latin American in the war and the war's impact on them are explored at

http://www.archives.ca/05/0518_e.html
http://www.worldwar1.com/sfla.htm

The text of the Treaty of Paris and many ancillary materials are offered at

http://history.acusd.edu/gen/text/versaillestreaty/
    vercontents.html

A vast collection of other major documents related to the war is offered at

http://www.lib.byu.edu/~estu/wwi/
http://www.ku.edu/~kansite/ww_one

Postwar colonial issues such as Négritude is the subject of analysis at

http://www.postcolonial.org/ (go to Search Tool, enter
    "negritude" for links on this subject)
http://www.stg.brown.edu/projects/hypertext/landow/
    post/poldiscourse/negritude.html

The African National Congress party homepage provides not only current information about the party but also materials on the freedom struggle in South Africa, such as the life histories, speeches, and writings of African National Congress anti-apartheid freedom fighters:

http://www.anc.org.za/ (click on "documents" at left)

Insight into the casual brutality of imperialism that fueled postwar nationalist revolts can be derived from an account of the Dinshawai incident in Egypt

http://touregypt.net/denshwaymuseum.htm

and the Amritsar massacre in India

http://www.scholars.nus.edu.sg/landow/post/india/
    history/colonial/massacre.html
http://www.geocities.com/Broadway/Alley/5461/
    AMRITSAR.htm
http://lachlan.bluehaze.com.au/churchill/am-man.htm

The place in the history of the attempt to send an Egyptian delegation (Wafd) to the Versailles Peace Conference is described at

http://countrystudies.us/egypt/28.htm

The Balfour Declaration

http://www.fordham.edu/halsall/mod/balfour.html and the McMahon-Hussein Correspondence

http://www.mideastweb.org/mcmahon.htm
http://www.wzo.org.il/home/politic/mac.htm
http://www.fordham.edu/halsall/mod/1915mcmahon .html
http://www.arab2.com/biography/conflict/ McMahon-Letters-aa.htm

figured greatly in the postwar debates over Arab and Jewish homelands.

Theodor Herzl's leadership of the early Jewish nationalist movement can be seen from the Zionist perspective at

http://www.jewishvirtuallibrary.org/jsource/biography/ Herzl.html
http://www.jafi.org.il/education/100/people/BIOS/ herzl.html
http://www.us-israel.org/isource/biography/Herzl.htm

Palestinian nationalist perspectives on Herzl and Zionism can be found at

http://www.arab2.com/biography/Arab-Israeli- Conflict.htm

The life of one of the early leaders of the Indian nationalist movement, B. G. Tilak, is briefly examined at

http://www.kamat.com/kalranga/itihas/tilak.htm

Mohandas Gandhi's leadership of that movement is explored at

http://dwardmac.pitzer.edu/anarchist_archives/bright/ gandhi/Gandhi.html

His famous Salt March

http://www.sscnet.ucla.edu/southasia/History/Gandhi/ Dandi.html
http://www.algonet.se/~jviklund/gandhi/ENG.MKG .salt.html

is the subject of a film at

http://harappa.com/wall/1930.html

His "Quit India" speech of 1942 is offered at

http://www.ibiblio.org/pha/policy/1942/420427a.html

An audio file of one of Gandhi's speeches can be accessed at

http://www.harappa.com/sounds/gandhi.html

The character of Gandhi's close associate, Jawaharlal Nehru, is offered at

http://www.itihaas.com/modern/nehru-profile.html

Rabindranath Tagore, the poet laureate of the Indian independence movement, is discussed at

http://www.itihaas.com/modern/tagore-profile.html

A review of the life of Muhammad Ali Jinnah, the Indian Muslim nationalist who led the campaign for the creation of the state of Pakistan and became its first president, is provided at

http://www.rediff.com/news/1998/sep/10jinnah.htm

Short audio files of him delivering key speeches are available at

http://www.harappa.com/sounds/jinnah.html

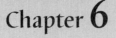

Chapter 6

The Postwar World: The Unfolding of Revolutionary Challenges

The construction of a strong nation built on socialist principles was the message conveyed after the Mexican Revolution in public murals such as this one by David Siqueros.

Chronology

1917	Tsarist regime overthrown in February; Bolshevik revolution in October; Mexican constitution includes revolutionary changes
1918	Armistice ends World War I in November
1919	Versailles conference; Treaty of Paris; leftist revolution defeated in Germany; May Fourth movement in China
1920–1940	Muralist movement in Mexico
1921	Albert Einstein wins the Nobel Prize; Chinese Communist Party founded; Lenin's New Economic Policy in USSR
1922	Mussolini/Fascists seize power in Italy; first commercial radio station in Pittsburgh
1923–1924	Hyperinflation in Germany
1923	Defeat of Japanese bill for universal suffrage; Tokyo earthquake
1927	Charles Lindbergh's solo transatlantic flight; Guomindang (Nationalists) capture north China, purge Communist Party
1927–1928	Stalin pushes the first five-year plan in the Soviet Union; collectivization begins
1929	Women given the right to vote in Ecuador
1931	Statute of Westminster gives full autonomy to British Dominions of Canada, Australia, New Zealand, South Africa, and the Irish Free State

INTRODUCTION

The 1920s saw pathbreaking developments in a number of international centers. Superficially, Western power seemed to be restored. France and Britain maintained their great colonial empires. Efforts to exploit Africa for European economic benefit accelerated. New semicolonial mandates extended British and French power in the Middle East. A new international organization, the League of Nations, provided some hope for the maintenance of peace, but it was dominated by the major Western powers.

Yet both war and the peace settlement opened important new stresses in Western society. Europe had trouble regaining its balance, while the United States pulled away into diplomatic isolation, its international commitment not matching its growing strength. A number of innovations occurred in the West, but some, in the cultural field, combined creativity with a certain sense of despair or desperation.

Many new initiatives developed outside the Western orbit. Far more fundamental changes were occurring in places like Russia, Japan, and Mexico than in western Europe or the United States during the postwar decade. The unfolding of the Russian Revolution, deeply feared by the Western powers, was the single most important innovation, pulling Russia into significant innovation and, ultimately, new dynamism. Japan gained new strength as its industrial economy entered a second, more powerful phase. Revolutionary stirrings in China did not bring solutions to the long quest for an appropriate system for China in the contemporary world, but they did reduce Western controls. The same held for the ongoing revolution in Mexico, where assertion of the national independence was a leading theme. New uncertainties in the West and powerful new movements outside began a process of realignment that clearly suggested a new stage in world history.

World War I had immediate repercussions around the world. Even before the war, challenges to the established order had emerged in Mexico and China, along with rumblings in Russia. The war influenced these developments, particularly in China, and spurred an even greater revolution in Russia. Challenges to colonial rule gained momentum as well. This chapter focuses on these upheavals, running from a few years before 1914 through the 1920s.

Deficiencies in the peace settlements added to confusion. Nationalists in many regions were dissatisfied, either because they gained nothing or gained too little. A fierce new kind of nationalism emerged in Italy. Tensions between France and Germany made recovery more difficult. The United States had become a world power, but pulled back from full engagement, while Japan sought new recognition.

THE DISARRAY OF WESTERN EUROPE, 1918–1929

World War I quickly shattered the confidence many Europeans had maintained around the turn of the century. The war also caused serious structural damage to the European economy, diplomatic relations among Western states, and political systems in many countries.

Although the ultimate effects of World War I involved Europe's world position, the war also brought tremendous dislocation within Europe. Though some of the damage was quickly repaired, much persisted for the subsequent two decades. The key battlegrounds for four bloody years had been in Europe. The sheer rate of death and maiming, as well as the frustration of long periods of virtual stalemate, had had a devastating material and psychological impact on the European combatants. More than 10 million Europeans had died. In Britain, France, and Germany the percentage killed had severely reduced the number of young men available. Vast amounts of property had been destroyed. Most governments had failed to tax their populations enough to pay for the war effort—lest they weaken domestic support—so huge debts accumulated, leading to inflationary pressure even before the war was over. Key prewar regimes were toppled when the German emperor abdicated and the Hapsburg Empire collapsed.

Germany, indeed, was close to revolution in 1918 and 1919, as worker soviets were proclaimed in some cities and a separate Socialist government briefly emerged in Bavaria. The extreme left was put down, and the moderate Socialists ushered in Germany's new Weimar Republic, but the atmosphere of political extremes, far right as well as far left, would continue to complicate German development.

The Roaring Twenties

Despite all the disruptions, a brief period of stability, even optimism, emerged in the mid-1920s. Diplomatic tensions eased somewhat within Europe, as Germany made some moves to accommodate its reduced position in return for partial relief from the reparations payments.

Although Germany refused to accept its new eastern boundaries, it did promise friendship all around. Hopes that the Versailles settlement could be permanent ran so high that an American and a French leader coauthored a treaty outlawing war forever (the Kellogg-Briand Pact of 1928, which a number of nations dutifully ratified)—a sign of the shallow hopes of the decade.

Internal politics also seemed to calm. The war's end and immediate economic dislocations, as well as the impact of the Russian Revolution, had inspired a new political polarization in many western European countries. Many veterans joined groups on the far right that wanted an authoritarian government and recovery of national honor; the labor movement on the left split, with a minority wing becoming Communist, taking cues from the revolutionary regime in the Soviet Union. Both radical factions scared each other, further complicating parliamentary life. Germany produced an admirable constitution for its new democratic republic, but many groups did not accept it and there were understandable fears for its life. Even Britain, long known for its political stability, saw a major shift as the Labour Party replaced the Liberals as the second major political force. Generally, the liberal middle sector of European politics was weakened. Nevertheless, the middle years of the 1920s brought a brief respite, as the extremist groups declined in force.

Economic prosperity buoyed hopes in the middle of the decade. The worst inflationary pressures were resolved at the cost of wiping out the value of savings for many propertied groups. Industrial production boomed, though more markedly in the United States than in western Europe. Mass-consumption standards rose for several years. New products, such as the artificial fiber rayon and radios, spread widely. Household appliances proliferated, as technology's impact on daily life reached a new height.

Finally, the 1920s saw a burst of cultural creativity in many parts of the West. Filmmakers experimented with the motion picture genre for both artistic expression and mass entertainment. Avant-garde artists developed cubist styles and other innovations. Writers, poets, and playwrights pioneered new literary forms, fragmenting plot lines and often seeking audience involvement in live theater. In retrospect the mood of the 1920s, in terms of high culture and popular culture alike, seemed somewhat frenzied. The defiance of traditional styles—the growing abstraction of modern art and novelists' efforts to capture the unconscious mind rather than to structure neat plots—attempted to convey some of the menacing tensions beneath the surface of modern life.

Women, particularly those in the middle class, registered important gains. Women's involvement in the labor

Consumer society, 1920s style: cars, cosmetics, a "new woman," and more open pleasure seeking.

dustries, both in Europe and in the United States, and managers learned new ways to coordinate and discipline masses of workers in factories, offices, and sales outlets. Major new product lines developed with artificial fibers and other consumer goods.

Western Culture: Innovations and Tensions

Despite new political and economic tensions, or perhaps because of them, Western culture in the first half of the 20th century displayed important creativity and change. The early decades of the 20th century saw fundamental new developments in various facets of intellectual and artistic endeavor. Artists and composers stressed stylistic innovation, rejecting older traditions and even the efforts of the previous generation. Complex discoveries in science, such as the principle of relativity in physics, qualified older ideas that nature can be captured in a few sweeping scientific laws. And the sheer specialization of scientific research removed much of it from ready public understanding. Because no clear unifying assumptions captured the essence of formal intellectual activity in the contemporary West, neutral terms, such as *modern,* were used even in the artistic field. Disciplines that had once provided an intellectual overview, such as philosophy, declined in the 20th century or were transformed into specialized research fields; many philosophers, for example, turned to the scientific study of language, and sweeping political theory virtually disappeared. And although work in theology continued among both Catholic and Protestant thinkers, it no longer commanded center stage in intellectual life. No emphasis was placed on an integrated approach, as Western intellectual life developed with specialized branches, and no agreement was reached on what constitutes an essential understanding of human endeavor.

The dynamism of scientific research continued to form the clearest central thread in Western culture after 1920. Growing science faculties commanded greatest prestige in the expanding universities. Individual scientists made striking discoveries, and a veritable army of researchers cranked out more specific findings than scientists had ever before produced. In addition, the wider public continued to maintain a faith that science held the keys to understanding nature and society and to improving technology and human life. Finally, although scientific findings varied widely, a belief in a central scientific method persisted: Form a rational hypothesis, test through experiment or observation, and emerge with a generalization that will show regularities in physical behaviors and thus provide human reason with a means of

force during the war was short-lived, as men pushed them out at war's end. However, postwar legislation granted women suffrage in Britain, Germany, and the United States. Further, prosperity and the declining birthrate gave many women the chance to develop new leisure habits and less restrictive fashions. Young women in the United States began to date more freely, as a preliminary to courtship. Wives in Britain wrote of new interests in sexual pleasure, while maintaining commitment to marriage. Women began to smoke and drink in public and to enjoy new dance crazes and other leisure activities. Here were developments, like the more general rise of consumerism, that would gain momentum later on. These developments also produced reaction from people who thought women should stay in traditional roles with traditional modesty.

Industrialization continued to advance. The 1920s saw continued gains for assembly-line production and big-business forms. Huge combines developed in key in-

systematizing and even predicting such behaviors. No other approach to understanding Western culture has had such power or widespread adherence.

By the 1930s physicists began to experiment with bombarding basic matter with *neutrons,* or particles that carry no electric charge; this work culminated during World War II in the development of the atomic bomb. Astronomers made substantial progress in identifying additional galaxies and other phenomena in space; the debate also continued about the nature of matter.

Breakthroughs in biology primarily involved genetics. The identification in the 1860s of the principles of inheritance received wide attention only after 1900. By the 1920s researchers who used the increasingly familiar fruit fly had exact rules for genetic transmission. Medical research advanced in a variety of areas, including new discoveries about human tissues.

Fundamental discoveries in physics and biology, though difficult for even the educated public to grasp, promoted the idea of science as penetrating the mysteries of the universe. They also furthered the relationship between science and technology. Physicists spearheaded research into atomic weaponry and atomic power. During and after World War II, they helped develop missiles and other spacecraft. Biologists produced major improvements in health care. New drugs, beginning with penicillin in 1928, revolutionized the treatment of common diseases, and immunization virtually eliminated such scourges as diphtheria.

The new science displayed some troubling features, even apart from its use in the weapons of destruction or its sheer complexity. The physical world was no longer considered to be neatly regulated, as it had been by Newtonian physics. Many other phenomena came to be perceived as relative and unpredictable. Genetics made it clear that evolution proceeded by a series of random accidents, not through any consistent pattern. A major eugenics movement developed, urging attention to the breeding of "superior" people. The movement had wide influence, and it encouraged the later racist policies of the German Nazis.

The scientific method, broadly conceived, also advanced in the social sciences from 1920 onward. In economics, sweeping theories were downplayed while quantitative models of economic cycles or business behavior increasingly gained ground. In psychology, the work by Sigmund Freud on the human unconscious and its role in mental disturbance gained increasing attention; although no single psychological theory predominated, the idea of using research to probe both conscious thought and irrational impulse won growing acceptance.

As in the physical sciences, many social scientists sought practical applications for their work. Psychologists became involved, for example, not only in dealing with mental illness but also in trying to promote greater work efficiency.

Most 20th-century artists, seeking to capture the world through impressions and abstract forms rather than through reason or the confinements of literal reality, worked against the grain of science and social science. Painting became increasingly nonrepresentational. The cubist movement, headed by Pablo Picasso, rendered familiar objects as geometrical shapes; after cubism, modern art moved even farther from normal perception, stressing purely geometrical design or wild swirls of color. The focus was on mood, the individual reaction of viewers to the individual reality of the artist. Musical composition involved the use of dissonance and experimentation with new scales. In poetry, the use of unfamiliar forms, ungrammatical constructions, and sweeping imagery continued the movement of the later 19th century. In literature, the novel remained dominant, but it turned toward the exploration of mood and personality rather than the portrayal of objective events or clear story lines.

The arts in the 20th-century West were thus characterized by unprecedented diversity, by a conscious effort to seek new forms, and by a focus on the individual and mood rather than on some agreed-upon objective reality. These emphases provided the artistic equivalent of relativity, and they certainly stressed the importance of the unconscious. But a vast gulf grew between the scientific approach and the artistic framework as to how reality can be captured and even, to an extent, what constitutes reality.

Many people ignored the leading modern artists and writers in favor of more commercial artistic productions and popular stories. The gap that had opened earlier between avant-garde art and public taste generally continued. Some politicians, including Adolf Hitler, campaigned against what they saw as the decadence and immorality of modern art, urging a return to more traditional styles. And certainly art did not hold its own against the growing prestige of science.

Yet the artistic vision was not simply a preoccupation of artists. Designs and sculptures based on abstract art began to grace public places from the 1920s onward; furnishings and films also reflected the modernist themes. Most revealing of a blend of art, modern technology, and public taste was the development of a characteristic 20th-century architectural style, the "modern," or "international," style. Use of new materials, such as reinforced concrete and massive sheets of glass, allowed the abandonment of much that was traditional in architecture. The need for new kinds of buildings, particularly for office use, and the growing cost of urban space also encouraged the introduction of new forms, such as the skyscraper, pioneered in the United States. In general the modern style of architecture sought to develop individually distinct buildings—sharing the goal of modern art to defy conventional taste and cultivate the unique—while conveying a sense of space and freedom from natural constraints. Soaring structures, free-floating columns, and new combinations of angles and curves were features that described leading Western buildings in the 20th century.

Artistic innovation thus played an important role in Western society in the 20th century. Inherently controversial, it seemed to provide an alternative to the regularized world of mechanized industry and rationalistic science. The result has been no unified culture but rather a set of tensions and options that can be creative for society as a whole, as well as meaningful to many individuals.

There were a few unifying themes between the artistic and the scientific approaches, as both explored elements of the human unconscious or reflected a growing uncertainty about the benevolence and clear rationality of nature and human nature. A continual quest for the new was another feature, as artists sought new styles and scientists sought new discoveries. Furthermore, Western culture in the 20th century, both in art and in science, became increasingly secular. Individual artists, writers, and scientists might proclaim religious faith, but the churches generally lost control over basic style or content.

Western culture was not a monopoly of European civilization in the 20th century. Western art forms, particularly in architecture, spread widely, because of their practicality and their currency in what remained a highly influential society. The achievements of Western science, at least those related to technology and medicine, often had to be taken into account by societies seeking their own industrial development. Although the internationalization of 20th century Western culture quickened after 1950, outreach developed in the interwar decades as well. No other culture, not even the Japanese, created quite the same balance between an overwhelming interest in science and a frenzied concern for stylistic innovation and individual expression in the arts.

Fascism in Italy

Shortly after the Russian Revolution began, and partly because of a growing fear of communism, another kind of political upheaval occurred in Italy: fascism.

In 1919 a former Socialist and (very briefly) a former soldier, Benito Mussolini, formed the *fascio di combattimento,* or union for struggle. Italian Fascists vaguely advocated a corporate state that would replace both capitalism and socialism with a new national unity. They pointed to the need for an aggressive, nationalistic foreign policy. Above all, however, Fascists worked to seize power by any means and to build a strong state under a strong leader. They violently attacked rival political groups, seeking to promote an atmosphere of chaos.

Fascism had its roots in the late 19th century, with groups disenchanted with liberal, parliamentary systems and with social conflict. Various intellectuals, in many countries, began to urge the need for new, authoritarian leadership and devotion to nationalist values over capitalist profit-seeking and socialist class struggle alike.

Conditions in postwar Italy gave these impulses a huge boost. Nationalists resented the fact that Italy had gained so little new territory in World War I. Veterans often felt abandoned by civilian society, and some thirsted for new action. Labor unrest increased, which convinced some conservatives that new measures were essential against ineffective liberal leadership. The Italian parliament seemed incapable of decisive measures, as political factions jockeyed for personal advantage. These were the conditions where Mussolini, a former socialist but now fascism's leading exponent, could make his mark even with a minority of direct supporters.

Amid growing political divisions and a rising threat from the working-class left, the Italian king called on Mussolini to form a new government in 1922. Though the Fascists themselves had only limited popular support, they seemed the only hope to stem left-wing agitation and parliamentary ineptitude.

Once in power, Mussolini eliminated most opposition, suspending elections outright in 1926, while seeking greater state direction of the economy and issuing strident propaganda about the glories of military conquest. This first Fascist regime moved with some caution, fitting into the briefly hopeful negotiations among European states in the 1920s, but the principles it espoused suggested how far European politics had been unseated from the widespread prewar agreements on parliamentary rule.

Italian fascism shared some of the grievances that spurred communism in Russia. Both movements were directed against capitalist excess, at least in principle (Mussolini did little to hinder big business, in fact). Both sought to create a new artistic culture, different from the modern art styles gaining ground elsewhere: Mussolini promoted architecture in a grandiose neoclassical style

One of the most ominous acts of Mussolini's fascist regime was the burning of books and other literature deemed "subversive."

that came to be associated with fascist triumph. Both communists and fascists boosted the authority of the state over liberal institutions and individual freedoms. But the two movements differed profoundly as well. Italian fascism did not attack Italy's basic social structure, as the revolution did in Russia. It compromised more readily with Christianity. It was more open in its embrace of military values and the glories of war. It vaunted nationalism instead of the virtues of working-class revolution.

The New Nations of East-Central Europe

Many of the problems and reactions visible in western Europe after World War I also affected the new nations of east-central Europe, though here the challenge of building new political regimes and the predominantly agrarian character of the economy complicated the situation even in the 1920s. Most of the new nations looked to western Europe for political inspiration at first, and all were hostile to the new Communist regime in the Soviet Union. "Westernization," however, proved difficult, particularly when the West itself was so troubled.

Most of the new nations, from the Baltic states to Yugoslavia, were consumed by nationalist excitement at independence but also harbored intense grievances about territories they had not acquired. Hence there were bitter rivalries among the small eastern European states, which weakened them both diplomatically and economically.

Most of the new nations began the interwar period with some form of parliamentary democracy, in imitation of the West, but soon converted to authoritarian rule, either through a dictator (as in Poland) or by a monarch's seizure of new power (as in Yugoslavia, the new nation expanded from Serbia). This political pattern resulted from more underlying social tensions. Most eastern European countries remained primarily agricultural, heavily dependent on sales to western Europe. They were hard-hit by the collapse of agricultural prices in the 1920s and then further damaged by the Depression. Furthermore, most countries also refused to undertake serious land reform, despite widely professed intentions. Aristocratic estate owners thus sought desperately to repress peasant movements, which brought them to support authoritarian regimes, which often had vaguely fascist trappings. Peasant land hunger and continued problems of poverty and illiteracy were simply not addressed in most cases.

The massive political and economic power of the landlords combined with low agricultural prices and economic pressure to maintain social tensions throughout the period. In Hungary 0.7 percent of the population owned 48.3 percent of the land; in Poland 0.6 percent owned 43 percent. Overall, 70 percent of the peasants in eastern Europe possessed less than 12.5 acres of land, enough for a bare subsistence at best. In Romania, the one non-Communist country where land reform did occur after 1918 (only 7 percent of the land remained in

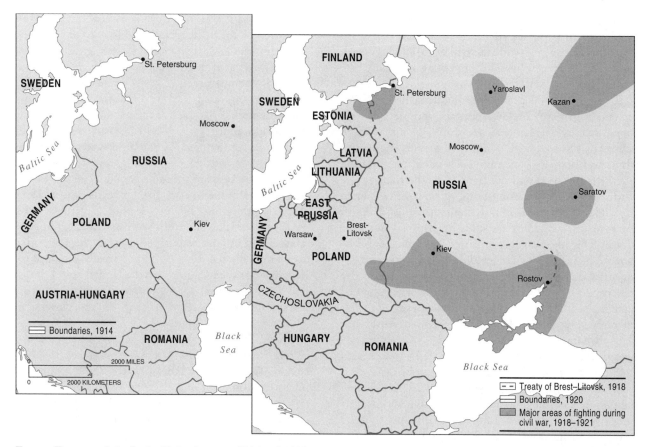

Eastern Europe and the Soviet Union between 1914 and 1939

large holdings), 50 percent of the peasantry held less than 7.5 acres. Without capital or education, Romanian peasants were unable to produce for the market and returned to a near-subsistence economy. Here and elsewhere up to one-third of all children died before reaching two years of age, reflecting the impoverished housing and diet available.

Only Czechoslovakia stood as an exception to these regional patterns. Here an unusually advanced industrialization process and extensive urban culture, combined with substantial land reform, produced the basis for an effective parliamentary-democratic regime. Only Czechoslovakia clearly maintained the east-central European borderland impulse to look primarily to the West for models and interaction. Most of the rest of eastern Europe remained caught between Western patterns that seemed impossible or irrelevant and a revolutionary Soviet Union now feared for both its communism and its Russian strength. The situation was predictably impossible. Although interwar experience served to enhance na-

tionalist loyalties, it did not create a viable economic or diplomatic system for the region.

THE WEST OUTSIDE EUROPE: THE BRITISH COMMONWEALTH AND THE UNITED STATES

By 1900 societies profoundly shaped by Western institutions and culture had developed in several parts of the world distant from Europe. These extensions of the West were not, of course, mere European replicas. They embraced different populations, such as the native Maoris in New Zealand and both Native Americans and African Americans in the United States, and were affected by their recent frontier experiences. Nevertheless, Canada, Australia, New Zealand, and the United States were Western in basic respects, beginning with the fact that the population majority in each case was of European origin; all aligned closely with the diplomatic and economic conflicts of Western society during the first half of the 20th century. All, finally, came into new world prominence, starting with their roles in World War I, providing a vital new ingredient to both world and Western history.

Canada, Australia, and New Zealand had all been colonial territories of Great Britain and were heavily populated by British and Irish immigrants (though Canada also had a large minority of French origin). All three had developed increasing self-government during the 19th century. From this trend came the concept of a British commonwealth of nations, which would maintain the links that derived from a common British colonial background but adjust for effective national independence. This idea was first broached in an imperial conference in London in 1887 and discussed further subsequently. By 1914 all three regions had won effective independence—Australia, for example, became a unified and independent federation in 1901—with strong parliamentary governments. Their participation in World War I, at Britain's side, furthered the idea of a commonwealth, and another imperial conference in 1921 agreed that the self-governing dominions should be considered coequals with Britain in international affairs. A 1926 resolution defined the dominions as "autonomous communities" within the British Empire, equal in status, in no way subordinate one to another in any aspect of their domestic or external affairs, though united by a common allegiance to the (British) crown, and freely associated as members of the British Commonwealth of Nations. British representation in the dominions, aside from the symbolic monarchy, consisted of a governor-general with no real authority.

Canada was developing not only its national politics but also an increasingly vibrant economy during the early years of the 20th century. Completion of the Canadian Pacific Railway by 1905 spurred rapid development in the western prairie provinces. Exploitation of mineral and forest resources joined with abundant production of wheat, as Canada exported food widely to Europe, as well as minerals and wood pulp to various areas, particularly the United States. Canadian development was marked also by rapid immigration, particularly from eastern Europe. Between 1903 and 1914, 2.7 million immigrants entered Canada, and as late as 1941, 40 percent of the population of the prairie provinces was of central or eastern European origin. French Canadians, centered in the province of Quebec, also increased their representation through one of the highest birthrates in the world, becoming a full quarter of the total Canadian population.

Vibrant as it was, the Canadian economy was overshadowed by that of its giant neighbor to the south. By 1914 almost one-quarter of all U.S. foreign investments were concentrated in Canada, and although British investments loomed larger, U.S. involvement cut a growing swath. Concentrated initially in Canadian mines and transportation, U.S. capital expanded into manufacturing during and after World War I. Canadian automobile production, for example, was simply an extension of U.S. corporations. Outright diplomatic relations with the United States eased in the same period. A joint commission was established between the two nations in 1909, charged with issuing binding decisions regarding water use (in shared lakes and rivers) and any other controversy referred to it by both countries. Boundary disputes, often contentious in the 19th century, virtually disappeared. Relations between Canada and the United States settled into a pattern of substantial harmony combined with a marked disparity in economic and cultural power that left many Canadians uneasy.

World War I brought Canada international status as a mature democracy. The Ottawa government immediately backed Britain in the war, and 600,000 Canadians (of a population of 9 million) served in the nation's military forces. Canada gained a seat at the Versailles peace conference and subsequently participated actively in the League of Nations.

Australia's independence brought important developments in parliamentary institutions early in the 20th century. Like Canada, the new nation consisted of a federation of provinces. More than Canada, Australia strongly emphasized leadership in the field of social legislation. Welfare measures current in Britain and Germany were enacted during the 1890s and pressed forward in subsequent decades. A strong trade union movement prompted increasing attention to government-sponsored arbitration procedures. The government was also active in economic planning, for the country had limited arable land but depended heavily on agricultural exports. Government ownership included railways and shipping lines, banks, and power plants. Participation in World War I gave Australia a new international role and a new sense of national pride. Rapid immigration contributed to a vigorous economy that was, however, severely damaged by the 1930s depression.

The Rise of the American Colossus

Outside the evolving British Commonwealth, the United States served as a final extension of many aspects of Western society. Because of its size, population, and

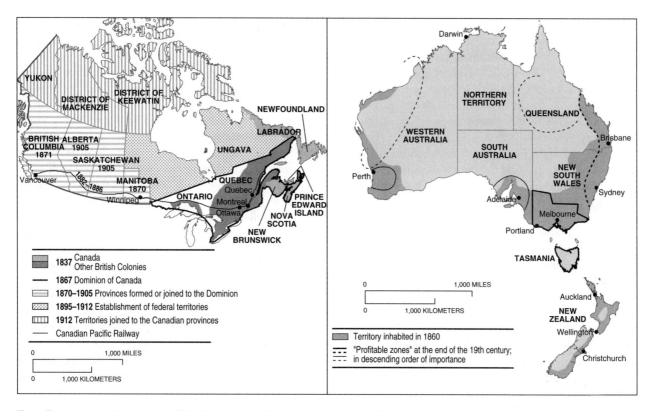

From Dominions to Nationhood: The Formation of Canada, Australia, and New Zealand

economic strength, the growing international role of the United States had even greater significance than the emergence of Canada, Australia, and New Zealand. Like these nations, the United States had developed extensive agricultural exports to western Europe, based on its rich and highly mechanized farms. More than the other nations, however, the United States had also emerged as a formidable industrial power, rivaling and then surpassing the rise of Germany in the later 19th century. Active imperialism, in the acquisition of territory in the Caribbean and the Pacific during the 1890s, further revealed the new stature of the United States as a world power.

The United States was late entering World War I, reflecting strong traditions of isolation. The war catapulted the United States into a leadership position, and the nation guided many of the provisions of the Versailles treaty. But the U.S. Senate rejected the treaty, and the United States retreated into an isolationist policy between the world wars, leavened only by participation in international economic and disarmament conferences. Interventionism in Latin America continued, though by the 1930s the United States tried to improve its relations with its southern neighbors and attempted to substitute negotiation for big-stick diplomacy.

The U.S. presence in world affairs accelerated during the 1920s, however, in the economic and cultural realms. After a brief postwar readjustment, the U.S. economy boomed during the 1920s. Industrial production doubled between 1921 and 1929. Republican administrations fostered business growth through high tariffs and low taxes on corporations and personal incomes. Many corporations merged into larger and more efficient conglomerates, and technological innovations spawned an increasing array of consumer goods for U.S. and world markets. Within the United States a new level of consumerism developed, as growing numbers of the middle class bought automobiles and electric appliances. Radios and telephones spread even more widely. Humbler products, such as soap and cosmetics, won a growing mass market, and advertising reached new audiences to spur demand. Credit buying expanded, with enhanced reliance on installment buying.

Besides their sheer growth and their involvement in mass consumerism, U.S. corporations were innovators. Many corporations set up research and development programs, which helped generate new product lines, such as rayon and nylon—artificial fibers that soon rivaled silk in popularity. Organization of work systems combined with new technology to boost productivity. Henry Ford had introduced the assembly line in 1913, using conveyor belts to move automobile assembly through various routine stages, with semiskilled workers continuously repeating small tasks as the products moved toward completion. Engineers in the United States promoted efficiency studies, which treated workers like additional machinery to be rationalized as fully as possible. During the 1920s industrial psychologists found additional ways to boost output, studying the impact of piped-in music, for example, in unconsciously prompting workers to speed up their pace. Such methods were widely imitated abroad, not only in western Europe but also in the Soviet Union. With growing exports of grain and manufactured products, increasing international investment, and literal world leadership in organizational innovation, the international economic role of the United States gained ground steadily, in marked disparity to its isolationist diplomacy.

The 1920s also formed an important period in U.S. cultural development. For several decades U.S. artists had been participating actively in such Western painting styles as impressionism. This process continued, but U.S. artists increasingly experimented with abstraction. Major literary figures such as T. S. Eliot and Ernest Hemingway did most of their work in Europe, expressing a certain alienation from mainstream U.S culture but also contributing to the national booklist. During the 1920s, as the Great Migration of African Americans from southern farms to northern cities reached a crescendo, an important black cultural movement arose—the Harlem Renaissance. Poets and novelists, such as Langston Hughes, worked to capture the culture of their people. The rise of jazz, which originated in New Orleans, contributed a vital new musical genre. Architects also contributed new themes, building on the skyscrapers first introduced in Chicago before World War I. Frank Lloyd Wright pioneered a variety of modern architectural designs.

Its culture was increasingly exported, as the United States began to give as well as to receive in this vital area. Jazz quickly caught on in Europe; U.S. artists and writers participated in an increasingly internationalized Western culture. But it was in the area of popular culture that the United States made it greatest mark. As the first mass-consumer society, the United States led the way in a number of marketing and advertising developments. The dime store, for example, spread to England and was copied in France and Germany as a major outlet for low-cost mass merchandise. Hollywood became the world capital of the popular movie industry during the 1920s.

Movies quickly began to play a vital role in U.S. culture, with 40 million viewers attending a film at least once a week in 1922; by 1929 that number had risen to 100 million. Hollywood stars—some born in Europe, such as Charlie Chaplin, Greta Garbo, and Rudolph Valentino—became symbols of comedy or sexuality throughout the Western world and beyond. Just as Britain had served as an international source of new sports in the later 19th century, so the United States now led in provision of commercial spectacles. Even its dance crazes, such as the Charleston, quickly spread to European centers, in an increasingly fad-conscious culture.

With all these signs of vigor, the United States also showed the symptoms of disturbingly rapid change. New relations between the genders were furthered by the granting of female suffrage in 1920. Women began to participate more fully in public entertainments, wearing new and more daring dresses and often smoking and drinking. Novel behaviors, such as teenage dating, challenged 19th-century notions of strict sexual decorum in public. Although "going all the way" remained atypical, gradations of "necking" and "petting" became increasingly liberal. The continued growth of big cities posed another kind of challenge to rural and small-town populations. Emotional standards were changing as well. The nineteenth-century middle-class American man had been urged toward assertiveness and courage. Now the emphasis on management harmony within a corporation and the growth of sales jobs stressed a more plastic, controlled personality. Dale Carnegie began a successful career in teaching Americans how to be cheerful salespeople in the 1920s, arguing that people-pleasing, not sincere conviction, was the key to the economic kingdom.

Many people responded to change by casting about for new ways to slow the pace. The Ku Klux Klan, previously a southern organization directed mainly against political claims by blacks, now spread to other parts of the country as a means of shoring up more traditional values through intimidation and often violence. The United States acted to shut down immigration, with a restrictive law of 1923. A "red scare" focused new anxieties about political radicalism amid the aftermath of the Russian Revolution. Hostility to labor strikes and trade unionism, a common theme of Western capitalism in the 1920s, was particularly fierce in the United States. The Socialist movement, a small but promising third party before World War I, withered in this attack against "un-American" politics. The United States became the only Western nation without a significant labor party. And, of course, isolationism expressed a fervent desire for a re-

The interwar decades saw the rise of the star system in Europe and North America and the emergence of mass audiences for films, big bands, and (as this photo from a 1942 production attests) a succession of dance crazes.

turn to a simpler past—what in the 1920s was called "normalcy"—in foreign policy. A series of lackluster Republican presidents reassured the country that significant political and diplomatic change could be avoided.

Japan and Its Empire

One final area of the world participated in many of the same trends as did western Europe, the Commonwealth nations, and the United States during the first decades of the 20th century. Japan was decidedly not a Western nation, either by origin or adoption. It had, however, become an industrial power and had replaced its traditional, feudal government with a regime in which ministers appointed by the emperor combined, sometimes uneasily, with a parliament. The Japanese government in 1900 was not totally unlike that of Germany, except that the vote was much more restricted. Like Germany and other Western nations, Japan would see its new political institutions tested by war and depression; like Germany and Italy, its commitment to the parliamentary form would decline under this test. In the 1930s Japan turned to a more adventurous foreign policy in re-

sponse to economic challenge and political change—again, like many nations in the West.

The interwar years were not simply a time of crisis for Japan, however. During the 1920s, particularly, new cultural developments, an expanding economy, and a growing commitment to liberal democracy produced important currents as well—currents that could be called on after the crisis period had ended.

During the initial decades of the 20th century, Japan concentrated heavily on diplomatic and military gains, as well as the difficult process of adjusting to the parliamentary, constitutional government established during the Meiji period. During the 1890s, the various branches of the central government had faced serious problems of cooperation, as opposition parties in the Parliament tried to gain ground at the expense of the executive ministries. In 1900 the government leaders formed their own political party, winning a majority in the lower house of Parliament. Over the next 22 years the leadership party struggled to maintain a working majority against various opposition factions. Japan was by this point an expansionist power, having formally annexed Korea in 1910. Japan ruled its new Asian colonies firmly, exacting considerable taxes and raw materials while securing markets for its growing industrial output. In no sense did the new Japanese empire lead directly to a united or vigorous Pacific Rim, though the disruption of established dependence on China did add an important new ingredient to Korean development.

Along with international gains came continued industrial advance. Japanese industry continued to lag behind Western levels, relying heavily on low-wage labor and the export of a relatively small number of items, such as silk cloth; silk production, at 16 million pounds in 1900, soared to 93 million pounds in 1929. Agricultural productivity improved steadily, led by progressive landlords who introduced fertilizers and new equipment. Rice production more than doubled between the 1880s and the 1930s. Modern industry advanced more slowly, though it passed well beyond the pilot phase of the late 19th century. Great industrial combines—the *zaibatsu*—sponsored rapid expansion in such fields as shipbuilding, usually relying heavily on tight links with the government bureaucracy, but there were daring individual entrepreneurs as well. Between 1905 and 1918 Japan enjoyed a considerable industrial boom, with rapid advances not only in light industries, such as silk, but also in electrical power, iron, and coal. Japanese life expectancy began to improve, fueled by a higher standard of living. A popular consumer culture emerged, at least in the cities, as workers began to attend movies and read newspapers. Education advanced rapidly, with primary-school attendance universal in the relevant age groups by 1925. Enrollments in secondary schools and technical colleges swelled, improving the nation's capacity to assimilate the newer Western technologies.

Limits on Japanese economic advance included vulnerability to economic conditions abroad. Because Japan exported relatively few items to the West but continued to require considerable imports of raw materials, including fuels and sophisticated equipment, a slump in demand for a product such as silk cloth could be disastrous. In this sense Japan bore some resemblance to dependent economies in the world, despite industrial progress. Population growth was another burden, or at least a mixed blessing. Japan's population soared from 30 million in 1868 to 45 million in 1900 and then to 73 million by 1940. This was a tribute to agricultural advance, as the size of the farm population remained constant, and it facilitated a low-wage industrial economy. It also restricted further improvements in the standard of living and created considerable social dislocation in the crowded, migrant-filled cities. Periodic protests through strikes,

demonstrations, and some Socialist agitation were met with vigorous police response.

Japan experienced ongoing difficulties in assimilating a generally accepted political structure—difficulties that had not been resolved during the first decades of the 20th century. Military leaders began to take a growing role in setting general diplomatic policy from the mid-1920s onward, at the expense of the civilian parties and politicians. Japan's oligarchic political structure, in which elite groups negotiated with one another for appropriate policy rather than fully yielding to any single agency, such as Parliament, permitted this kind of realignment. From the Meiji period onward, military leaders, though largely weaned from the samurai tradition, had remained separate from the civilian bureaucracy. They were trained in separate schools and regarded themselves as true guardians of the modern Japanese state as well as older traditions. They reported not to civilian authority but directly to the emperor. Like military leaders in the West during the 1920s but with greater vigor, they resented what they regarded as the selfishness and accommodation to special interests of the political parties, as the latter increasingly resorted to mass political campaigns and vote-getting strategies. Reduction of military budgets during the 1920s hit military leaders hard, and army prestige declined to the point that officers wore civilian clothing when off base. In essence Japan experimented during the 1920s with a liberal political pattern, which seemed to give primacy to party maneuverings and electoral appeals but which also antagonized the military (and other conservative elite groups) while failing to subject them to new controls. Voting rights were extended to all adult males, but this did not produce agreement on political forms.

Patterns in the West and Japan

The 1920s produced two kinds of change in industrial societies: first, some superficial adjustments that did not take deep root or erase some fundamental weaknesses; and second, some more basic innovations.

In the first category, democracy came to Germany and Japan, but the political systems in both countries remained fragile, not strong enough to weather severe difficulty. France and Germany reconciled on the surface, but deep fears and grievances remained. American isolationism did not really protect the country from world influence, but it did poison experiments like the League of Nations, which the United States refused to join. Europe's economic prosperity suffered from sectors of real weakness and from new levels of international competition, and it did not last long.

At the same time, developments in science and modern art, the expansions of popular consumerism, and new activities for women set up more durable themes for the future. So did the growing voice of the United States, Canada, and Japan. Advances in mass production were also fundamental. The rise of Italian fascism was a genuine innovation of another sort.

REVOLUTION: THE FIRST WAVES

Outside the industrial societies of the West and Japan, more fundamental developments occurred through a striking series of revolutions. Each of the revolutions had its own character, but all challenged not only the existing social and political structure within the societies involved, but also Western claims to world dominance. Two of the revolutions began before World War I, but all contributed to the global climate of the 1920s.

Mexico's Upheaval

Two cataclysmic events launched Latin America into the 20th century and set in motion trends that would determine much of the region's subsequent history. The first of these events was the 10-year civil war and political upheaval of the Mexican Revolution, caused primarily by internal forces. Eventually, the Mexican Revolution was also influenced by another major event: the outbreak of World War I. Although most Latin American nations avoided direct participation in World War I, the disruption of traditional markets for Latin American exports and the elimination of European sources of goods caused a realignment of the economies of several nations in the region. They were forced to rely on themselves. A spurt of manufacturing continued the process begun after 1870, and some small steps were taken to overcome the traditional dependence on outside supply. Finally, at the end of World War I, the United States emerged as the dominant foreign power in the region, replacing Great Britain in both economic and political terms. That position created a reality that Latin Americans could not ignore and that greatly influenced the economic and political options in the region.

The regime of Porfirio Díaz had been in power since 1876 and seemed unshakable. During the Díaz dictatorship, tremendous economic changes had been made, and foreign concessions in mining, railroads, and other sectors of the economy had created a sense of prosperity among the Mexican elite. However, this progress had been bought at considerable expense. Foreigners controlled large sectors of the economy. The hacienda system of extensive landholdings by a small elite dominated certain regions of the country. The political system was corrupt, and any complaint was stifled. The government took repressive measures against workers, peasants, and Indians who opposed the loss of their lands or the unbearable working conditions. Political opponents often were imprisoned or forced into exile. In short, Díaz ruled with an iron fist through an effective political machine.

By 1910, however, Díaz was 80 years old and seemed willing to allow some political opposition. Francisco Madero, a wealthy son of an elite family, proposed to run against Díaz. Madero believed that some moderate democratic political reforms would relieve social tensions and allow the government to continue its economic development with a minimum of popular unrest. This was more than Díaz could stand. Madero was arrested, a rigged election put Díaz back in power, and things returned to normal. When Madero was released from prison, he called for a revolt.

A general rebellion developed. In the north, small farmers, railroaders, and cowboys coalesced under the colorful former bandit and able commander Pancho Villa. In the southern province of Morelos, an area of old conflicts between Indian communities and large sugar estates, a peasant-based guerrilla movement began under Emiliano Zapata, whose goal of land reform was expressed in his motto "Tierra y Libertad" (Land and Liberty). Díaz was driven from power by this coalition of forces, but it soon became apparent that Madero's moderate programs would not resolve Mexico's continuing social problems. Zapata rose in revolt, demanding a sweeping land reform, and Madero steadily lost control of his subordinates. In 1913, with at least the tacit agreement of the American ambassador in Mexico, who wanted to forestall revolutionary changes, a military coup removed Madero from government and he was then assassinated.

General Victoriano Huerta sought to impose a Díaz-type dictatorship supported by the large landowners, the army, and the foreign companies, but the tide of revolution could not be stopped so easily. Villa and Zapata rose again against the government and were joined by other middle-class political opponents of Huerta's illegal rule. By 1914 Huerta was forced from power, but the victorious leaders now began to fight over the nature of the new regime and the mantle of leadership. An extended period of warfare followed, and the tides of battle shifted constantly. The railroad lines built under Díaz now moved large numbers of troops, including *soldaderas,* women who sometimes shouldered arms. Matters were also complicated by U.S. intervention, aimed at bringing order to the border regions, and by diplomatic maneuverings after the outbreak of World War I in Europe. Villa and Zapata remained in control in their home territories, but they could not wrest the government from the control of the more moderate political leaders in Mexico City. Alvaro Obregón, an able general who had learned the new tactics of machine guns and trenches from the war raging in Europe and had beaten Villa's cavalry in a series of bloody battles in 1915, emerged as leader of the government.

As much as the Mexican Revolution had its own internal dynamic, it is interesting to note that it was roughly contemporaneous with revolutions in other agrarian societies that had also just undergone a period of rapid and disruptive modernization. The Boxer Rebellion in China (1899–1901) and the toppling of the emperor in 1911, the 1905 revolution in Russia, and a revolution in Iran in the same year underlined the rapid changes in these societies, all of which had received large foreign investments from either the United States or western Europe. In each of these countries, governments had tried to establish strong centralized control and had sought rapid modernization, but in doing so they had made their nations increasingly dependent on foreign investments and consequently on world financial markets. Thus, the world banking crisis of 1907 and 1908 cut Mexico and these other countries off from their needed sources of capital and created severe strains on their governments. This kind of dependency, and the fact that in Mexico more than 20 percent of the nation's territory was owned directly by citizens or companies from the United States, fed a growing nationalism that spread through many sectors of society. That nationalist sentiment played a role in each of these revolutions.

By 1920 the civil war had ended and Mexico began to consolidate the changes that had taken place in the previous confused and bloody decade. Obregón was elected president in that year. He was followed by a series of presidents from the new "revolutionary elite" who tried to consolidate the new regime. There was much to be done. The revolution had devastated the country; 1.5 million people had died, major industries were destroyed, and ranching and farming were disrupted. But there was great hope because the revolution also promised (although it did not always deliver) real changes.

What were some of these changes? The new Mexican Constitution of 1917 promised land reform, limited the foreign ownership of key resources, guaranteed the rights of workers, placed restrictions on clerical education and Church ownership of property, and promised educational reforms. The workers who had been mobilized were organized in a national confederation and were given representation in the government. The promised land reforms were slow in coming, but under President Lázaro Cárdenas (1934–1940), more than 40 million acres were distributed, most of them in the form of *ejidos,* or communal holdings. The government launched an extensive program of primary and especially rural education.

Culture and Politics in Postrevolutionary Mexico

Nationalism and *indigenism*—the concern for the Indians and their contribution to Mexican culture—lay beneath many reforms. Having failed to integrate the Indians into national life for a century, Mexico now attempted to "Indianize" the nation through secular schools that emphasized nationalism and a vision of the Mexican past that glorified its Indian heritage and denounced Western capitalism. Artists such as Diego Rivera and José Clemente Orozco recaptured that past and outlined a social program for the future in stunning murals on public buildings designed to inform, convince, and entertain at the same time. The Mexican muralist movement had a wide impact on artists throughout Latin America even though, as Orozco himself stated, it sometimes created simple solutions and strange utopias by mixing a romantic image of the Indian past with Christian symbols and Communist ideology. Novelists, such as Mariano Azuela, found in the revolution itself a focus for the examination of Mexican reality. Popular culture celebrated the heroes and events of the revolution in scores of ballads (*corridos*) that were sung to celebrate and inform. In literature, music, and the arts, the revolution and its themes provided a stimulus to a tremendous burst of creativity.

> *Gabino Barrera*
>   *rose in the mountains*
>   *his cause was noble,*
>   *protect the poor and give them the land.*
>   *Remember the night he was murdered*
>   *three leagues from Tlapehuala;*
>   *22 shots rang out leaving him time for nothing.*

Gabino Barrera and his loyal steed fell in the hail of
rounds,
the face of this man of the Revolution
finally rested, his lips pressed to the ground.

The gains of the revolution were not made without opposition. Although the revolution preceded the Russian Revolution of 1917 and had no single ideological model, many of the ideas of Marxist socialism were held by leading Mexican intellectuals and a few politicians. The secularization of society and especially education met strong opposition from the Church and the clergy, especially in states where socialist rhetoric and anticlericalism were extreme. In the 1920s, a conservative peasant movement backed by the church erupted in central Mexico. These *Cristeros,* backed by conservative politicians, fought to stop the slide toward secularization. The fighting lasted for years until a compromise was reached.

The United States intervened diplomatically and militarily during the revolution, motivated by a desire for order, fear of German influence on the new government, and economic interests. An incident provoked a short-lived U.S. seizure of Veracruz in 1914, and when Pancho Villa's forces had raided across the border, the United States sent an expeditionary force into Mexico to catch him. The mission failed. For the most part, however, the war in Europe dominated U.S. foreign policy efforts until 1918. The United States was suspicious of the new government, and a serious conflict arose when U.S.-owned oil companies ran into problems with workers. When President Cárdenas expropriated the companies in 1934, the companies called for U.S. intervention or pressure. An agreement was worked out, however, and Mexico nationalized its petroleum industry in a state-run monopoly. This nationalization of natural resources was considered a declaration of economic independence. It symbolized the nationalistic basis of many of the revolution's goals.

As in any revolution, the question of continuity arose when the fighting ended. The revolutionary leadership hoped to institutionalize the new regime by creating a one-party system. This organization, called the Party of the Institutionalized Revolution (PRI), developed slowly during the 1920s and 1930s into a dominant force in Mexican politics. It incorporated labor, peasant, military, and middle-class sectors and proved flexible enough to incorporate new interest groups as they developed. Although Mexico became a multiparty democracy in theory, in reality the PRI controlled politics and, by accommodation and sometimes repression, maintained its hold

on national political life. Some presidents governed much like the strongmen in the 19th century had done, but the party structure and the need to incorporate various interests within the government coalition limited the worst aspects of caudillo, or personalist, rule. The presidents were strong, but the policy of limiting the presidency to one six-year term ensured some change in leadership. The question of whether a revolution could be institutionalized remained in debate. By the end of the 20th century, many Mexicans believed that little remained of the principles and programs of the revolutionaries of 1910.

War and Revolution in Russia

The currents of revolution in Russia emerged somewhat gradually. By 1900 a variety of groups were seriously aggrieved, and several erupted in recurrent protest. Peasants resented their continuing obligations under the terms of the Emancipation of the Serfs of 1861. Many had to make annual payments for their rights to the land. Many were subjected to community restrictions on buying or selling land or even leaving the village. Furthermore, aristocratic landlords continued to hold some of the richest land. Russia's peasantry, pressed by a growing population, sought new access to the land and to freedom from obligatory payments. Russia also had a growing urban working class, fed by migrations from the peasantry and absorbing some peasant discontents. Life in the factories and in the crowded cities was harsh, which generated grievances of another sort; strikes and illegal unions formed amid many groups. Business and professional people, a nascent middle class, often sought new political rights against a tsarist government that resolutely banned dissident political expression at the national level. Intellectuals, some of upper-class origin, espoused a variety of revolutionary doctrines, from anarchist yearnings to destroy all government to the newer Marxist ideas of working-class revolt. They organized illegal agitation groups and sought to disseminate their ideas to the lower classes.

These varied grievances erupted into revolution in 1905, triggered by Russia's shocking loss in a war with Japan. The tsar in turn created a national parliament, the Duma, and confirmed peasant land tenure, removing the hated community controls and obligatory redemption payments. Although peasant discontent was alleviated, prohibition of working-class parties and, soon, of trade unions only exacerbated urban discontent. The Duma was progressively stripped of any real power, becoming a hollow institution as tsarist autocracy resumed its hold. Many historians believe that renewed revolution was virtually inevitable. It certainly became inevitable when Russia's arduous participation in World War I led to new levels of material misery for the bulk of the population.

In March 1917 strikes and food riots broke out in Russia's capital, St. Petersburg (subsequently renamed Leningrad until 1991, when it was renamed St. Petersburg as a gesture of defiance against the revolutionary legacy). The outbursts, spurred by wartime misery— including painful food shortages, but more basically protesting the conditions of early industrialization set against incomplete rural reform and an unresponsive political system—quickly assumed revolutionary proportions. The rioters called not just for more food and work but for a new political regime as well. A council of workers, called a soviet, took over the city government and arrested the tsar's ministers, after some brutal attempts at military repression. Unable to rely on his own soldiers, the tsar abdicated, thus ending the long period of imperial rule.

Liberalism to Communism

For eight months a liberal provisional government struggled to rule the country. Russia seemed thus to launch its revolution on a basis similar to France in 1789, where a liberal period set change in motion. Like Western liberals, Russian revolutionary leaders, such as Alexander Kerensky, were eager to see genuine parliamentary rule, religious and other freedoms, and a host of political and legal changes. But liberalism was not deeply rooted in Russia, if only because of the small middle class, so the analogies with the first phase of the French revolution cannot be pressed too far. Furthermore, Russia's revolution took place in much more adverse circumstances, given the pressures of participation in the world war. The initial liberal leaders were eager to maintain their war effort, which associated their link with democratic France and Britain. Yet the nation was desperately war weary, and prolongation drastically worsened economic conditions while public morale plummeted. Liberal leaders also held back from the massive land reforms expected by the peasantry, for in good middle-class fashion they respected existing property arrangements and did not wish to rush into social change before a legitimate new political structure could be established. Hence serious popular unrest continued, and in November (October, by the Russian calendar) a second revolution took place, which expelled liberal leadership and soon brought to power the radical, Bolshevik wing of the Social Democratic Party (soon renamed the Communist Party), and Lenin, their dynamic chief.

The revolution was a godsend to Lenin, who had long been writing of Russia's readiness for a Communist revolt because of the power of international capitalism and its creation of a massive proletariat, even in a society that had not directly passed through middle-class rule. Lenin quickly gained a strong position among the urban workers' councils in the major cities. This corresponded to his deeply rooted belief that revolution should come not from literal mass action but from tightly organized cells whose leaders espoused a coherent plan of action.

Once the liberals were toppled, Lenin and the Bolsheviks faced several immediate problems. One, the war, they handled by signing a humiliating peace treaty with Germany and giving up huge sections of western Russia in return for an end of hostilities. This treaty was soon nullified by Germany's defeat at the hands of the Western allies, but Russia was ignored at the Versailles peace conference—treated as a pariah by the fearful Western powers. Much former territory was converted into new nation-states. A revived Poland built heavily on land Russia had controlled for more than a century, and new, small Baltic states cut into even earlier acquisitions. Still, although Russia's deep grievances against the Versailles treaty would later help motivate renewed expansionism, the early end to the war was vital to Lenin's consolidation of power.

Although Lenin and the Bolsheviks had gained a majority role in the leading urban soviets, they were not the most popular revolutionary party, and this situation constituted the second problem faced at the end of 1917. The November seizure of power had led to the creation of the Council of People's Commissars, drawn from soviets across the nation and headed by Lenin, to govern the state. But a parliamentary election had already been called, and this produced a clear majority for the Social Revolutionary Party, which emphasized peasant support and rural reform. Lenin, however, shut down the parliament, replacing it with a Bolshevik-dominated Congress of Soviets. He pressed the Social Revolutionaries themselves to disband, arguing that "the people voted for a party which no longer existed." Russia was thus to have no Western-style, multiparty system but rather a Bolshevik monopoly in the name of the true people's will. Indeed, Communist control of the government apparatus persisted from this point to 1989, a record for continuity much different from the fate of revolutionary groups earlier in the Western past.

Moscow workers guard the Bolshevik headquarters during the Russian Revolution of 1917.

Russia's revolution did, however, produce a familiar backlash that revolutionaries in other eras would have recognized quite easily: foreign hostility and, even more important, domestic resistance. The world's leading nations—aside from Germany, now briefly irrelevant—were appalled at the Communist success, which threatened principles of property and freedom they cherished deeply. As settled regimes, they also disliked the unexpected, and some were directly injured by Russia's renunciation of its heavy foreign debts. The result was an attempt at intervention, recalling the attacks on France in 1792. Britain, France, the United States, and Japan all sent troops. But this intervention, although it heightened Russian suspicion of outsiders, did relatively little damage. The Western powers, exhausted by World War I, pulled out quickly, and even Japan, though interested in lingering in Asiatic Russia, stepped back fairly soon.

The internal civil war, which foreign troops slightly abetted, was a more serious matter, as it raged from 1918 to 1921. Tsarist generals, religiously faithful peasants, and many minority nationalities made common cause against the Communist regime. Their efforts were aided by continuing economic distress, the normal result of revolutionary disarray, but also heightened by earlier Communist measures. Lenin had quickly decreed a redistribution of land to the peasantry and also launched a nationalization, or state takeover, of basic industry. Many already landed peasants resented loss of property and incentive and in reaction lowered food production and the goods sent to markets. Industrial nationalization somewhat similarly disrupted manufacturing. Famine and unemployment created more economic hardship than the war had generated, which added fuel to the civil war fires. Even workers revolted in several cities, threatening the new regime's most obvious social base as well as ideological mainstay.

Stabilization of the New Regime

Order was restored, however, on several key foundations. First, the construction of the powerful new army under the leadership of Leon Trotsky recruited able generals and masses of loyal conscripts. This Red Army was an early beneficiary of two ongoing sources of strength for Communist Russia: a willingness to use people of humble background but great ability who could rise to great heights under the new order but who had been doomed to immobility under the old system, and an ability to inspire mass loyalty in the name of an end to previous injustice and a promise of a brighter future. Next, economic disarray was reduced in 1921 when Lenin issued his New Economic Policy. Intended as a stopgap measure

DOCUMENT

Socialist Realism

One of the most fascinating features of the Soviet system was the attempt to create a distinctive art, different from Western cultures (seen as decadent) and appropriate to the Communist mission. This effort involved censorship and forced orthodoxy, but it also was an attempt to resolve earlier Russian problems of relating formal culture to the masses and trying to preserve a national distinctiveness amid the seductions of Western influence. The following effort to define Soviet artistic policy was written by Andrey Zhdanov in 1934, the year Stalin made him the party's spokesperson at the Congress of Soviet Writers.

> There is not and never has been a literature making its basic subject-matter the life of the working class and the peasantry and their struggle for socialism. There does not exist in any country in the world a literature to defend and protect the equality of rights of the working people of all nations and the equality of rights of women. There is not, nor can there be in any bourgeois country, a literature to wage consistent war on all obscurantism, mysticism, hierarchic religious attitudes, and threats of hell-fire, as our literature does.
>
> Only Soviet literature could become and has in fact become such an advanced, thought-imbued literature. It is one flesh and blood with our socialist construction. . . .
>
> What can the bourgeois writer write or think of, where can he find passion, if the worker in the capitalist countries is not sure of his tomorrow, does not know whether he will have work, if the peasant does not know whether he will be working on his bit of land or thrown on the scrap heap by a capitalist crisis, if the working intellectual is out of work today and does not know whether he will have work tomorrow?
>
> What can the bourgeois author write about, what source of inspiration can there be for him, when the world, from one day to the next, may be plunged once more into the abyss of a new imperialist war?
>
> The present position of bourgeois literature is such that it is already incapable of producing great works. The decline and decay of bourgeois literature derives from the decline and decay of the capitalist system and are a feature and aspect characteristic of the present condition of bourgeois culture and literature. The days when bourgeois literature, reflecting the victories of the bourgeois system over feudalism, was in the heyday of capitalism capable of creating great works, have gone, never to return. Today a degeneration in subject matter, in talents, in authors and in heroes, is in progress. . . .
>
> A riot of mysticism, religious mania and pornography is characteristic of the decline and decay of bourgeois culture. The "celebrities" of that bourgeois literature which has sold its pen to capital are today thieves, detectives, prostitutes, pimps, and gangsters. . . .
>
> The proletariat of the capitalist countries is already forging its army of writers and artists—revolutionary writers, the representatives of whom we are glad to be able to welcome here today at the first Soviet Writers' Congress. The number of revolutionary writers in the capitalist countries is still small but it is growing and will grow with every day's sharpening of the class struggle,

in recognition of the real-life barriers to immediate construction of communism, the NEP promised considerable freedom of action for small business owners and peasant landowners. The state continued to set basic economic policies, but its efforts were now combined with individual initiative. Under this temporary policy, food production began to recover, and the regime gained time to prepare the more durable structures of the Communist system.

By 1923 the Bolshevik revolution was an accomplished fact. A new constitution set up a federal system of socialist republics. This system recognized the multinational character of the nation, which was called the Union of Soviet Socialist Republics. The dominance of ethnic Russians was preserved in the central state apparatus, however, and certain groups, notably Jews, were given no distinct representation. Since the separate republics were firmly controlled by the national Communist Party and since basic decisions were as firmly centralized, the impact of the new nationalities' policy was somewhat mixed; yet it was also true that direct nationalities' protest declined notably from the 1920s until the late 1980s.

The apparatus of the central state was another mixture of appearance and reality. The Supreme Soviet had many of the trappings of a parliament and was elected by universal suffrage. But competition in elections was normally prohibited, which meant that the Communist Party easily controlled the body, which served mainly to ratify decisions taken by the party's central executive.

with the growing strength of the world proletarian revolution.

We are firmly convinced that the few dozen foreign comrades we have welcomed here constitute the kernel, the embryo, of a mighty army of proletarian writers to be created by the world proletarian revolution in foreign countries. . . .

Comrade Stalin has called our writers "engineers of the human soul." What does this mean? What obligations does such an appellation put upon you?

It means, in the first place, that you must know life to be able to depict it truthfully in artistic creations, to depict it neither "scholastically" nor lifelessly, nor simply as "objective reality," but rather as reality in its revolutionary development. The truthfulness and historical exactitude of the artistic image must be linked with the task of ideological transformation, of the education of the working people in the spirit of socialism. This method in fiction and literary criticism is what we call the method of socialist realism.

Our Soviet literature is not afraid of being called tendentious, for in the epoch of class struggle there is not and cannot be "apolitical" literature.

And it seems to me that any and every Soviet writer may say to any dull-witted bourgeois, to any philistine or to any bourgeois writers who speak of the tendentiousness of our literature: "Yes, our Soviet literature is tendentious and we are proud of it, for our tendentiousness is to free the working people—and the whole of mankind—from the yoke of capitalist slavery."

To be an engineer of the human soul is to stand four-square on real life. And this in turn means a break with old-style romanticism, with the romanticism which depicted a nonexistent life and nonexistent heroes, drawing the reader away from the contradictions and shackles of life into an unrealizable and utopian world. Romanticism is not alien to our literature, a literature standing firmly on a materialistic basis, but ours is a romanticism of a new type, revolutionary romanticism. We say that socialist realism is the fundamental method of Soviet fiction and literary criticism, and this implies that revolutionary romanticism will appear as an integral part of any literary creation, since the whole life of our Party, of the working class and its struggle, is a fusion of the hardest, most matter-of-fact practical work, with the greatest heroism and the vastest perspectives. The strength of our Party has always lain in the fact that it has united and unites efficiency and practicality with broad vision, with an incessant forward striving and the struggle to build a communist society.

Soviet literature must be able to portray our heroes and to see our tomorrow. This will not be utopian since our tomorrow is being prepared by planned and conscious work today.

Questions: What were the reasons for culture according to Stalinist intellectuals? How did Soviet cultural leaders analyze Western intellectual life? What were the proper tasks of an artist in Soviet society? How were these tasks expressed in socialist realism? What would the Soviet response be to a Western intellectual claiming objectivity for his work?

Parallel systems of central bureaucracy and party bureaucracy further confirmed the Communist monopoly on power and the ability to control major decisions from the center. The Soviet political system was elaborated over time. A new constitution in the 1930s spoke glowingly of human rights. In fact, the Communists had quickly reestablished an authoritarian system, making it more efficient than its tsarist predecessor had been, complete with updated versions of political police to ensure loyalty.

A Period of Experimentation

The mid-1920s constituted a lively, experimental period in Soviet history, partly because of the jockeying for power at the top of the power pyramid. Despite the absence of Western-style political competition, a host of new groups found a voice. The Communist Party, though not eager to recruit too many members lest it lose its tight organization and elite status, encouraged all sorts of subsidiary organizations. Youth movements, women's groups, and particularly organizations of workers all actively debated problems in their social environment and directions for future planning. Workers were able to influence management practices; women's leaders helped carve legal equality and new educational and work opportunities for their constituents.

The atmosphere of excited debate spilled over into such areas as family policy. At various points Soviet policy seemed to downplay the importance of family in favor of individual rights, thus making it easy to obtain divorces or abortions. Ultimately, by the 1930s the pendulum swung back toward greater conservatism, featuring protection of the family unit and an effort to encourage the birthrate, but only after some fascinating experimentalism. One key to the creative mood of these years was the rapid spread of education promoted by the government, as well as educational and propaganda activities sponsored by various adult groups. Literacy gained ground quickly. The new educational system was also bent on reshaping popular culture away from older peasant traditions and, above all, religion, and toward beliefs in Communist political analysis and science. Access to new information, new modes of inquiry, and new values encouraged controversy.

The Soviet regime grappled with other key definitional issues in the 1920s. Rivalries among leaders at the top had to be sorted out. Lenin became ill and then died in 1924, creating an unexpected leadership gap. A number of key lieutenants jostled for power, including the Red Army's flamboyant Trotsky and a Communist Party stalwart of worker origins who had taken the name Stalin, meaning steel. After a few years of jockeying, Joseph Stalin emerged as undisputed leader of the Soviet state, his victory a triumph also for party control over other branches of government.

Stalin's accession was more than a personal bureaucratic issue, however. Stalin represented a strongly nationalist version of communism, in contrast to the more ideological and international visions of many of his rivals. At the revolution's outset Lenin himself had believed that the Russian rising would be merely a prelude to a sweeping Communist upheaval throughout the Western industrial world. Many revolutionary leaders actively encouraged Communist parties in the West and set up an organization that they named Comintern (Communist International) to guide this process. But revolution did not spill over, despite a few brief risings in Hungary and Germany right after World War I. Under Stalin, the revolutionary leadership, although still committed in theory to an international movement, pulled back to concentrate on Russian developments pure and simple—building "socialism in one country," as Stalin put it. Stalin in many ways represented the anti-Western strain in Russian tradition, though in new guise. Rival leaders were killed or expelled, rival visions of the revolution downplayed.

The Russian Revolution was one of the most successful risings in human history, at least for several decades. Building on widespread if diverse popular discontent and a firm belief in centralized leadership, the Bolsheviks

beat back powerful odds to create a new, though not totally unprecedented, political regime. They used features of the tsarist system but managed to propel a wholly new leadership group to power not only at the top but also at all levels of the bureaucracy and army. The tsar and his hated ministers were gone, mostly executed, but so was the overweening aristocratic class that had loomed so large in Russian history for centuries. And after the first years, the revolutionaries never had to look backward; they avoided even a partial restoration of the "old regime" as had occurred in England after its 17th-century Civil War and in France after Napoleon. The Bolsheviks, in contrast, managed to create a new political, economic, and cultural structure without serious internal challenge between the initial, chaotic years and the late 1980s.

Serious revolutions, however, do not end quickly. Although the formal revolutionary period consumed but a few vivid years, the force of the revolution continued easily until the middle of the 1930s—that is, through a period of fascinating experimentation during the 1920s and into the establishment of a full Stalinist regime from 1928 onward.

Toward Revolution in China

The abdication of Puyi, the Manchu boy-emperor in 1912, marked the end of a century-long losing struggle on the part of the Qing dynasty to protect Chinese civilization from foreign invaders and revolutionary threats from within, such as the massive Taiping movement (see Chapter 4). The fall of the Qing opened the way for an extended struggle over which leader or movement would be able to capture the mandate to rule the ancient society that had for millennia ordered the lives of at least one-fifth of humankind. The loose alliance of students, middle-class politicians, secret societies, and regional military commanders that overthrew the Manchus quickly splintered into several hostile contenders for the right to rule China. Both internal factors and foreign influences paved the way for the ultimate victory of the Chinese Communist Party under Mao Zedong.

After the fall of the Qing dynasty, the best-positioned of the contenders for power were regionally based military commanders or warlords, who would dominate Chinese politics for the next three decades. Many of the warlords combined in cliques or alliances, both to protect their own territories and to crush neighbors and annex their lands. The most powerful of these cliques, centered in north China, was headed by the unscrupulous Yuan Shikai who hoped to seize the vacated Manchu throne and found a new dynasty. By virtue of their wealth, the merchants and bankers of coastal cities like Shanghai and Canton made up a second power center in post-Manchu China. Their involvement in politics resulted from their willingness to bankroll both favored warlords and Western-educated, middle-class politicians like Sun Yat-sen.

Sometimes supportive of the urban civilian politicians, and sometimes wary of them, university students and their teachers, as well as independent intellectuals, provided yet another factor in the complex post-Qing political equation. Though the intellectuals and students played critical roles in shaping new ideologies to rebuild Chinese civilization, they were virtually defenseless in a situation in which force was essential to those who hoped to exert political influence. Deeply divided, but very strong in some regions, secret societies represented another contender for power. Like many in the military, members of these societies envisioned the restoration of monarchical rule, but under a Chinese, not a foreign, dynasty. As if the situation were not confused enough, it was further complicated by the continuing intervention of the Western powers, eager to profit from China's divisions and weakness. Their inroads, however, were increasingly overshadowed by the entry into the contest for the control of China by the newest imperialist power, Japan. From the mid-1890s, when the Japanese had humiliated their much larger neighbor by easily defeating it in war, until 1945, when Japan's surrender ended World War II, the Japanese were a major factor in the long and bloody contest for mastery of China.

The May Fourth Movement and the Rise of the Marxist Alternative

Sun Yat-sen headed the Revolutionary Alliance, a loose coalition of anti-Qing political groups that had spearheaded the 1911 revolt. After the Qing were toppled, Sun claimed that he and the parties of the alliance were the rightful claimants to the mandate to rule all of China. But he could do little to assert civilian control in the face of warlord opposition. The Revolutionary Alliance had little power and virtually no popular support outside the urban trading centers of the coastal areas in central and southern China. Even in these areas, they were at the mercy of the local warlords. The alliance formally elected Sun president at the end of 1911, set up a parliament modeled after those in Europe, and chose cabinets with great fanfare. But their decisions had little effect on warlord-dominated China.

Sun Yat-sen conceded this reality when he resigned the acting presidency in favor of the northern warlord Yuan Shikai in 1912. As the most powerful of the northern clique of generals, Yuan appeared to have the best chance to unify China under a single government. He at first feigned sympathy for the democratic aims of the alliance leaders but soon revealed his true intentions. He took foreign loans to build up his military forces and buy out most of the bureaucrats in the capital at Beijing. When Sun and other leaders of the Revolutionary Alliance called for a second revolution to oust Yuan in the years after 1912, he made full use of his military power and more underhanded methods, such as assassinations, to put down their opposition. By 1915, it appeared that Yuan was well on his way to realizing his ambition of becoming China's next emperor. His schemes were foiled, however, by the continuing rivalry of other warlords, republican nationalists like Sun, and the growing influence of Japan in China. The latter increased dramatically as a result of World War I.

As England's ally according to terms of a 1902 treaty, Japan immediately entered the war on the side of the Entente (or Western allied) powers. Moving much too quickly for the comfort of the British and the other Western powers, the Japanese seized German-held islands in the Pacific and occupied the Germans' concessionary areas in China. With all the great powers except the United States embroiled in war, the Japanese sought to establish a dominant hold over their giant neighbor. In early 1915, they presented Yuan's government with Twenty-One Demands, which, if accepted, would have reduced China to the status of a dependent protectorate. Though Sun and the Revolutionary Alliance lost much support by refusing to repudiate the Japanese demands, Yuan was no more decisive. Neither accepting nor rejecting the demands, he concentrated his energies on an effort to trump up popular enthusiasm for his accession to the throne. Disgusted by Yuan's weakness and ambition, one of his warlord rivals plotted his overthrow. Hostility to the Japanese won Yuan's rival widespread support, and in 1916, Yuan was forced to resign the presidency. His fall was the signal for a free-for-all power struggle between the remaining warlords for control of China.

As one of the victorious allies, Japan managed to solidify its hold on northern China by winning control of the former German concessions in the peace negotiations at Versailles in 1919. But the Chinese had also allied themselves to the Entente powers during the war. Enraged by what they viewed as a betrayal by the Entente powers, students and nationalist politicians organized mass demonstrations in numerous Chinese cities on May 4, 1919. The demonstrations began a prolonged period of protest against Japanese inroads. This protest soon expanded from marches and petitions to include strikes and mass boycotts of Japanese goods.

The fourth of May in 1919, the day when the resistance began, gave its name to a movement in which intellectuals and students played a leading role. Initially at least, the May Fourth movement was aimed at transforming China into a liberal democracy. Its program was enunciated in numerous speeches, pamphlets, novels, and newspaper articles. Confucianism was ridiculed and rejected in favor of a wholehearted acceptance of all that the Western democracies had to offer. Noted Western thinkers, such as Bertrand Russell and John Dewey, toured China, extolling the merits of science, industrial technology, and democratic government and basking in the cheers of enthusiatic Chinese audiences. Chinese thinkers called for the liberation of women, the simplification of the Chinese script in order to promote mass literacy, and the promotion of Western-style individualism. Many of these themes are captured in the literature of the period. In the novel *Family* by Ba Jin, for example, a younger brother audaciously informs his elder sibling that he will not accept the marriage partner the family has arranged for him. He clearly sees his refusal as part of a more general revolt of the youth of China against the ancient Confucian social code.

> Big Brother, I'm doing what no one in our family has ever dared do before—I'm running out on an arranged marriage. No one cares about my fate, so I've decided to walk my own road alone. I'm determined to struggle against the old forces to the end. Unless you cancel the match, I'll never come back. I'll die first.

However enthusiastically the program of the May Fourth movement was adopted by the urban youth of China, it was soon clear that mere emulation of the liberal democracies of the West could not provide effective solutions to China's prodigious problems. Civil liberties and democratic elections were meaningless in a China that was ruled by warlords. Gradualist solutions were folly in a nation where the great mass of the peasantry was destitute, much of it malnourished or dying of starvation. Even if fair elections could be held and a Western-style parliament installed as an effective ruling body, China's

crisis had become so severe that there was little time for legislators to squabble and debate. The ministers of an elected government with little military clout would hardly have been able to implement well-meaning programs for land redistribution and subsidies for the poor in the face of deeply entrenched regional opposition from the landlords and the military. It soon became clear to many Chinese intellectuals and students, as well as to some of the nationalist politicians, that more radical solutions were needed. In the 1920s, this conviction gave rise to the Communist left within the Chinese nationalist movement.

The example of the Russian Revolution, rather than careful reading of the writings of Karl Marx and Friedrich Engels, made a number of Chinese thinkers aware of possible Marxist solutions to China's ills. The Bolshevik victory and the programs launched to rebuild Russia prompted Chinese intellectuals to give serious attention to the works of Marx and other socialist thinkers and the potential they offered for the regeneration of China. But the careful study of the writings of Marx, Engels, Lenin, and Trotsky in the wake of the Russian Revolution also impressed a number of Chinese intellectuals with the necessity for major alterations in Marxist ideology if it was going to be of any relevance to China or other peasant societies. Marx, after all, had foreseen socialist revolutions occurring in the more advanced industrial societies with well-developed working classes and a strong proletarian consciousness. He had thought that there would be little chance for revolution in Russia. In China, with its overwhelmingly rural, peasant population (and Marx viewed the peasantry as a reactionary or, at best, a conservative, petty bourgeois social element), the prospects for revolution looked even more dismal.

The most influential of the thinkers who called for a reworking of Marxist ideology to fit China's situation was Li Dazhao. Li was from peasant origins, but he had excelled in school and eventually become a college teacher. He headed the Marxist study circle that developed after the 1919 upheavals at the University of Beijing. His interpretation of Marxist philosophy placed heavy emphasis on its capacity for promoting renewal and its ability to harness the energy and vitality of a nation's youth. In contrast to Lenin, Li saw the peasants, rather than the urban workers, as the vanguard of revolutionary change. He justified this shift from the orthodox Marxist emphasis on the working classes, which made up only a tiny fraction of China's population at the time, by characterizing the whole of Chinese society as proletarian. All of China, he argued, had been exploited by the bourgeois, industrialized West. Thus, the oppressed Chinese as a whole needed to unite and rise up against their exploiters.

Li's version of Marxism, with alterations or emphasis on elements that made it suitable for China, had great appeal for the students, including the young Mao Zedong, who joined Li's study circle. They too were angered by what they perceived as China's betrayal by the imperialist powers. They shared Li's hostility (very much a throwback to the attitudes of the Confucian era) to merchants and commerce, which appeared to dominate the West. They, too, longed for a return to a political system, like the Confucian, in which those who governed were deeply committed to social reform and social welfare. They also believed in an authoritarian state, which they felt ought to intervene constructively in all aspects of the peoples' lives.

The Marxist study club societies that developed as a result of these discoveries soon spawned a number of more broadly based, politically activist organizations. The Marxists' capture of prominent periodicals, such as the *New Youth* magazine, did much to spread the ideas of Marx and Lenin among the politically active youth of China's coastal cities. With support from Sun Yat-sen, Marxist intellectuals established the Socialist Youth Corps in 1920, which was dedicated to recruiting the urban working classes to the revolutionary movement. Students like Mao returned to their provincial bases to win supporters for the leftist cause and to foment resistance to the oppressive rule of the local warlords.

In the summer of 1921, in an attempt to unify the growing Marxist wing of the nationalist struggle, a handful of leaders from different parts of China met in secret in the city of Shanghai. At this meeting, closely watched by the agents of the local warlord and rival political organizations, the Communist Party of China was born. In Paris a year earlier, Zhou Enlai, who like Mao was later to become one of the main Communist leaders, and several other Chinese expatriate students had founded the Communist Youth Corps. In Paris and inside China itself, the development of Communist organizations was supported by both the advisors and funds of the Comintern, the international arm of the Bolshevik or Communist Party of the Soviet Union. The Communist Party was minuscule in terms of the numbers of its supporters, and at this time it was still dogmatically fixed on a revolutionary program oriented to the small and scattered working class. But the Communists at least offered a

clear alternative to fill the ideological and institutional void left by the collapse of the Confucian order.

The Seizure of Power by the Guomindang, or Nationalist Party

In the years when the Communist movement in China was being put together by urban students and intellectuals, the *Guomindang*, or Nationalist Party, which was to prove the Communists' great rival for the mandate to rule in China, was struggling to survive in the south. Sun Yat-sen, who was the acknowledged head of the nationalist struggle from the 1911 revolution until his death in early 1925, had gone into exile in Japan in 1914, while warlords, such as Yuan Shikai, consolidated their regional power bases. After returning to China in 1919, Sun and his followers attempted to unify the diverse political organizations struggling for political influence in China by reorganizing the revolutionary movement and naming it the Nationalist Party of China (the Guomindang).

The Nationalists began the slow process of forging alliances with key social groups and building an army of their own, which they now viewed as the only way to rid China of the warlord menace. Sun strove to enunciate a nationalist ideology that gave something to everyone. It stressed the need to unify China under a strong central government, to bring the imperialist intruders under control, and to introduce social reforms that would alleviate the poverty of the peasants and the oppressive working conditions of laborers in China's cities. Unfortunately for the great majority of the Chinese people, for whom social reforms were the main concern, the Nationalist leaders concentrated on political and international issues, such as relations with the Western powers and Japan, and failed to implement most of the domestic programs they proposed, most especially land reform.

In this early stage Sun and the Nationalists built their power primarily on the support provided by urban businessmen and merchants in coastal cities such as Canton. Though it received little publicity at the time, the Nationalist Party also drew support from local warlords and the criminal underworld, especially the notorious Green Gang headquartered in Shanghai. After much factional infighting, Sun had more or less secured control over the party, if not the warlords in the neighborhood of Canton. He forged an alliance with the Communists that was officially proclaimed at the first Nationalist Party conference in 1924. For the time being at least, the Nationalist leaders were content to let the Communists serve as their major link to the peasants and the urban workers.

Disappointed in their early hopes of assistance from the Europeans and the United States, Nationalist leaders turned to Soviet Russia. Lenin and the Bolsheviks were eager to support a revolutionary movement in neighboring China. The Bolsheviks sent advisors and gave material assistance. They also encouraged the fledgling Communist Party to join with the larger and richer Nationalists in a common struggle to seize power.

In 1924, the Whampoa Military Academy was founded with Soviet help and partially staffed by Russian instructors. The academy gave the Nationalists a critical military dimension to their political maneuvering. The first head of the academy was an ambitious young military officer named Chiang Kai-shek. The son of a poor salt merchant, Chiang had made his career in the military and by virtue of connections with powerful figures in the Shanghai underworld. He had received some military training in Japan, and managed by the early 1920s to work his way into Sun Yat-sen's inner circle of advisors. Chiang was not happy with the Communist alliance. But he was willing to bide his time until he had the military strength to deal with both the Communists and the warlords, who remained the major obstacles to the Nationalist seizure of power.

Absorbed by all these political machinations, Sun and other Nationalist leaders had little time left for serious attention to the now severe deterioration of the Chinese economy or providing relief for the huge population whose sufferings mounted as a result. Urban laborers worked for pitiful wages and lived in appalling conditions. But the social condition of the peasantry, which made up nearly 90 percent of China's population, was perhaps the most pressing issue facing China's aspiring national leaders. Patterns of landowning varied considerably in different parts of China. Over a century of corruption, weak Manchu rule, the Qing collapse in 1911, and the depredations of the warlords had left the peasantry in many regions of China in misery. Big landlords and rich peasants rapaciously amassed great landholdings, which they rented out at exorbitant rates that left the tenants who worked them little to feed and clothe their families. In times of flood and drought when the crops failed, tenants, landless laborers, and even small landowners simply could not make ends meet. Tenants and smallholders were turned off their lands, and landless laborers could not find crops to harvest. Famine and disease stalked China's heavily populated provinces, while its ancient irrigation systems fell into disrepair. Corrupt warlords and bureaucrats, including those allied to the Nationalist Party, colluded with the landlords to extract the maximum taxes and labor services from the peasantry.

As they had for millennia, dispossessed peasants took to banditry or vagabondage to survive. Many joined the hordes of beggars and unemployed in the towns; many more perished—swept away by floods, famine, disease, or the local warlord's armies. Children were sold into slavery by their parents so that both might have a chance to survive. A growing number of cases of cannibalism were reported, which occurred after the bark and leaves had been stripped off all the trees to make the scarcely digestible "stew" that the peasants ate to put something in their bellies. Many peasants were too poor to perform the most basic of social duties, such as burying their deceased parents, whose bodies were often left to be devoured by vultures and packs of wild dogs. Given the great reverence for family and parents that had been instilled for millennia by Confucian teachings, the psychological scars left by the nonperformance of such critical obligations must have been deep and lasting.

Though rural China cried out for strong leadership and far-reaching economic and social reform, China's leaders bickered and plotted but did little. Sun gave lip service to the Nationalist Party's need to deal with the peasant problem. But his abysmal ignorance of rural conditions was revealed by statements in which he denied that China had exploitative landlords and his refusal to believe that there were "serious difficulties" between the great mass of the peasantry and the landowners.

Mao and the Peasant Option

Though the son of a fairly prosperous peasant, Mao Zedong had rebelled early in his life against his father's exploitation of the tenants and laborers who worked the family fields. Receiving little assistance from his estranged father, Mao was forced to make his own way in the world. Through much of his youth and early adulthood, he struggled to educate himself in the history, philosophy, and economic theory that most other nationalist and revolutionary leaders mastered in private schools. Having moved to Beijing in the post–May Fourth era, Mao came under the influence of thinkers such as Li Dazhao, who placed considerable emphasis on solutions to the peasant problem as one of the keys to China's survival. As the following passage from Mao's early writings

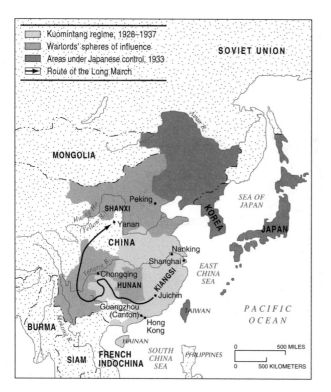

China in the Era of Revolution

reveals, almost from the outset he was committed to revolutionary solutions that depended on peasant support:

> A revolution is an insurrection, an act of violence by which one class overthrows another. A rural revolution is a revolution by which the peasantry overthrows the power of the feudal landlord class. Without using the greatest force, the peasants cannot possibly overthrow the deep-rooted authority of the landlords which has lasted for thousands of years.

Throughout most of the 1920s, however, Mao's vision of a rural revolution remained a minority and much-repudiated position even with the Communist Party. Rivals such as Li Lisan, who favored a more orthodox Marxist strategy based on the urban working classes, dominated party policymaking. Ironically, the move by Chiang and the Nationalist leaders to destroy all the Communists in the late 1920s would pave the way for Mao's rise to leadership in the party.

The Nationalists' successful drive for national power began only after Sun Yat-sen's death in 1925, which

opened the way for Chiang Kai-shek and his warlord allies to seize control of the party. After winning over or eliminating the military chiefs in the Canton area, Chiang marched north with his newly created armies. His first campaign culminated in the Nationalists' seizure of the Yangtze River valley and Shanghai in early 1927. Later his forces also captured the capital at Beijing and the rest of the Yellow River basin. The refusal of most of the warlords to end their feuding meant that Chiang could defeat them or buy them out, one by one. By the late 1920s, he was the master of China in name and international standing, if not in actual fact. He was, in effect, the head of a warlord hierarchy. But most political leaders within China and in the outside world recognized him as the new president of China.

Since there were no elections, the people had no say in the matter. Nor had Chiang's political rivals, whom he ruthlessly purged even while he was still settling scores with the warlords. The most fateful of these purges came while Chiang's armies were occupying Shanghai in the spring of 1927. First the Nationalists cleared the Communists out of the Nationalist central committee, where they had been represented since 1924. Chiang then ordered his troops and gangster allies in Shanghai to round up the workers, despite the fact that their mass demonstrations had done so much to make possible the city's capture by the Nationalist armies. In some of the most brutal scenes of an era when violence and human suffering were almost commonplace, Chiang's soldiers and hired toughs machine-gunned and beheaded Communist supporters wherever they could be found throughout the city. Though the Communists' Soviet advisors continued to insist that they cooperate with the Nationalists, Chiang's extension of the bloody purge to other cities and into the countryside precipitated an open civil war between the two main branches of the nationalist movement. Despite temporary and halfhearted truces, this civil war ended only with the Communist victory in 1949.

Reaction Versus Revolution and the Communist Victory

At the outset, all signs appeared to favor the Nationalist party in its violent contest with the Communists for control of China. Despite the fact that Chiang did not fully control the more powerful regional warlords, as the heir of Sun Yat-sen and the architect of the victorious northern

The Guomindang's brutal suppression of the workers' organizations in Shanghai in 1927 was a turning point in the history of modern China. The Guomindang–Communist Party alliance was shattered, and Mao Zedong's call for a peasant-based revolution became imperative as the vulnerability of the small Chinese working class was exposed.

campaign he had the support of the richest and most powerful social groups in China. These included the urban businessmen and merchants, most of the intellectuals, and a large portion of the university students, the rural landlords, and the military. Chiang could also count on the services of the bureaucrats and police throughout China, and he launched a calculated public relations campaign to win sympathy in the United States and the other Western democracies. The urban workers, who preferred the Communists or other radical parties, had been beaten into submission. The peasants, who longed for stable government and state-sponsored relief, were willing, for the time being at least, to wait and see whether the Nationalists would act to alleviate their distress.

Despite his ruthless betrayal of the Communists, Chiang continued to receive assistance from the Soviet Union, where Stalin had emerged as the unchallenged dictator of a totalitarian state. Possibly because he preferred a weak China under the Nationalist Party to a revolutionary one under the Communists, Stalin gave little assistance to his alleged comrades and continued to push policies that left them at the mercy of Chiang and his henchmen. With what seemed to be insurmountable advantages, Chiang moved to eliminate his few remaining rivals for power, most especially the shattered remnants of the Communist Party.

The smashing of the workers' movement in Shanghai and other urban centers greatly strengthened Mao's hand in his ongoing struggle with Li Lisan and other orthodox ideologues within the Communist Party. Mao and much of what was left of the Communist leadership retreated into the countryside and set to work carrying out land reform and improving life in China's tens of thousands of impoverished villages.

In the late 1920s, the center of Communist operations came to be the south-central province of Hunan where the Communists established soviets (named after the revolutionary workers' and soldiers' organizations in Russia) and "liberated" zones. This area became the main target of a succession of military campaigns that Chiang launched against the Communists in the early 1930s. Though the Communists successfully resisted the early campaigns, Chiang's reliance on German military advisors and his command of the resources and manpower of the rest of China eventually wore the Communists down. By the autumn of 1934, it was clear that if the remaining Communists did not break out of the Nationalist encirclement and escape from Hunan, they would be eliminated. At the head of over 90,000 party stalwarts, Mao set off on the Long March across thousands of miles of the most difficult terrain in China to Shanxi in northwestern China, where a smaller number of peasant soviets had been established earlier. At the end of the following year, Mao and only about 20,000 followers who had managed to survive fought their way into the rugged, sparsely populated terrain of Shanxi. From that moment until the mid-1940s, Shanxi with its capital at Yanan became the center of the Communist movement in China.

By the end of the Long March, Mao was firmly established as the head of the Chinese Communist Party. The heroic and successful struggle for survival in the Long March on the part of those who supported his peasant-based strategy of revolution greatly enhanced his stature and inspired his followers with the conviction that whatever the odds, they could not be defeated. Chiang obviously did not agree. Soon after the Communists were established in Shanxi, he launched a new series of extermination campaigns. Again, the peasant supporters of the Communists fought valiantly, but Chiang's armies were beginning to get the upper hand by early 1937.

Just as Chiang was convinced that he was on the verge of total victory, his anti-Communist crusade was rudely interrupted by the all-out Japanese invasion of the Chinese mainland. Obsessed with the Communists, Chiang had done little to block the steady advance of Japanese forces in the early 1930s into Manchuria and the islands along China's coast. Even after the Japanese launched their massive assaults aimed at the conquest of all of China, Chiang wanted to continue the struggle against the Communists.

Forced by his military commanders to concentrate on the Japanese threat, Chiang grudgingly formed a military alliance with the Communists. Though he did all he could to undermine the alliance and continue the anti-Communist struggle by underhanded means, for the next seven years the war against Japan took priority over the civil war in the contest for control of China.

Though it brought still further suffering to the Chinese people, the Japanese invasion proved enormously advantageous for the Communist Party. This turned out to be so vital to the ultimate Communist victory that some writers have speculated Mao chose Shanxi in the northwest partly out of the calculation that it would put his forces in the probable path of the anticipated Japanese advance. Whatever his thinking, the war against the Japanese greatly strengthened his cause while weakening his Nationalist rivals. The Japanese invaders captured much of the Chinese coast, where the cities were the centers of the business and mercantile backers of the Nationalists. Chiang's conventional military forces were pummeled by the superior air, land, and sea forces of the Japanese. The Nationalists' attempts to meet the Japanese in conventional, set-piece battles led to disaster; their inability to defend the coastal provinces lowered their standing in the eyes of the Chinese people. Chiang's hasty and humiliating retreat to Chongqing in the interior of China further eroded his aura as the savior of the nation and rendered him more dependent than ever on his military allies, the rural landlords, and—perhaps most humiliating—foreign powers like the United States.

ANALYSIS

A Century of Revolutions

Not since the late 18th and early 19th centuries has there been a succession of revolutions like those of the first quarter of the 20th century. In contrast to the revolutionary movements of the earlier period, however, the mid-20th century upheavals were just the first waves of a revolutionary tide that struck with renewed fury after 1945. A number of factors account for successive surges of revolution in the 20th century. To begin with, vast increases in the power and reach of the state, which were made possible by industrial weaponry and advanced communications systems, greatly reduced the effectiveness of traditional tactics of resistance employed by key social groups, especially the peasantry. Larger, better-trained bureaucracies made cheating or running away from the tax collector increasingly difficult. Well-disciplined armies proved more and more able to foil such time-honored protest options as banditry and food or tax riots. As a result, popular protest increasingly aimed at the state itself.

The ever greater growth of the commercial and working classes and their concentration in urban centers also contributed substantially to the propensity of disgruntled groups to openly confront what they viewed as the oppressive or indifferent agents of the state, who were also concentrated in the cities. The growth of the size and power of state institutions made government functionaries increasingly obvious targets. And, somewhat ironically, rebel leaders and their followers increasingly counted on the seizure of the very state apparatuses and national communications systems they had once found so oppressive to carry out their revolutionary programs.

Equally fundamentally, the rise of revolutionary movements was fed by the underlying disruptions caused by the spread of the Industrial Revolution and the

Western-centered, global market system. Handicraft producers thrown out of work by an influx of machine-manufactured goods, and peasants, such as those in central Mexico, who lost their land to moneylenders frequently rallied to calls to riot and, at times, ultimately became caught up in revolutionary currents. In the colonies, unemployed Western-educated African and Asian secondary school and college graduates became deeply committed to struggles for independence that promised them dignity and decent jobs. Urban laborers, enraged by the appalling working and living conditions that were characteristic of the early stages of industrialization in countries such as Russia and China, provided key support for revolutionary parties in many countries.

Although global economic slumps did much to fire the revolutionaries' longings, world wars proved to be even more fertile seedbeds of revolutions. Returning soldiers and neglected veterans provided the shock troops for leftist revolutionaries and fascist pretenders alike. Defeated states witnessed the rapid erosion of their power to suppress internal enemies and floundered as their armies refused to defend them or joined movements dedicated to their overthrow. In this regard, the great increase in global interconnectedness in the 20th century was critical. The economic competition and military rivalries of the industrial powers drew them into unwanted wars that they could not sustain without raw materials and manpower drawn from their colonies and other neutral states.

Another key factor that contributed to the sharp rise in the incidence of revolutions in the 20th century was the underlying intellectual climate. Notions of progress and a belief in the perfectibility of human society, which were widely held in the 19th century, deeply influenced such Communist theorists as Marx, Lenin, Mao Zedong, and Ho Chi Minh.

These and other revolutionary ideologues sought, in part, to overthrow existing regimes, which they viewed as exploitative and oppressive. But they were also deeply committed to building radically new societies that would bring justice and a decent livelihood to previously downtrodden social groups, especially the working classes, peasantry, and urban poor. Visions of the good life in peasant communes or workers' utopias have proved a powerful driving force for revolutionary currents throughout the century from Mexico to China. One measure of their influence is the extent to which highly competitive capitalist societies have developed social welfare programs to curb social discontent that could spiral into active protest, and perhaps even revolutionary challenges to the existing social order.

All 20th-century revolutions were also to some degree anti-Western. Early risings in China and Mexico aimed at reducing Western property control. Communist revolutions utilized some Western ideas, but directly attacked Western-style capitalism and cultural influence. Later in the 20th century the Iranian revolution reflected even more sweeping grievances against Western cultural and political models.

Questions: Discuss the internal and external forces that weakened the governments of Mexico and China in the opening decades of the 20th century and unleashed the forces of revolution. Identify the key social groups behind the revolutions in Mexico, China, and Russia, and discuss the reasons why they were so important in each case. Discuss the similarities and differences among these three early revolutions in the 20th century. Why did all the major 20th century revolutions occur outside the West? How different were independence movements, such as those in India, from revolutions, such as those in China?

CONCLUSION: THE ENDURING IMPACT OF A CATASTROPHIC GLOBAL WAR

When Woodrow Wilson and the other leaders of the victorious allied coalition met at Versailles in the months after the end of World War I, they sought to find ways to preserve the Western-dominated global order that had existed before the outbreak of 1914. But four years of global conflict had proved so devastating to the social and political fabric of European societies and the structures of colonial dominance overseas, and had so stunningly enhanced the power of overseas nations, particularly the United States and Japan, that nothing resembling the prewar order could be put back together again. Realizing the profundity of these shifts, key leaders, especially Wilson and the British Prime Minister, David Lloyd George, also sought to forge innovative international institutions and alter great power relationships in ways that would both correct the flaws of the prewar system and provide a solid foundation for a new world order that would endure through the 20th century.

In many cases given impetus by the ill-considered and vengeful Versailles settlement, challenges to the pre-1914 global order came from both the Left and the Right as well as from rapidly proliferating anticolonial movements in Asia and Africa. On the Left, the Bolsheviks' seizure of power in 1917 and their survival in the civil war that followed, installed a Marxist-inspired regime, dedicated to the overthrow of the capitalist and colonial systems, in what for centuries had been one of the major power centers of the European system. In the years after that war, similar Marxist-inspired revolutions very nearly came to power in Hungary and Germany, and their aftershocks destabilized east-central Europe through all of the 1920s and 1930s. From the Right, the postwar order was menaced from 1919 by the emergence of Mussolini and the Fascist alternative in 1919, which like the Bolsheviks were committed to the destruction of the prewar state system and bourgeois class structure. Mussolini and the Fascist leaders who emerged after him in Germany, Spain, Argentina, and elsewhere were contemptuous of the old diplomacy and the sanctity of treaties and alliances that it stressed. His corporatist, dictatorial state also had little use for the human rights, individualism, and democratic institutions that had begun to flourish in the decades before the cataclysm of 1914–1918.

Beyond Europe, equally critical forces were reshaping the global order. Although Great Britain and France actually expanded their colonial domains by annexing former German colonies under the guise of League of Nations Mandates, from India to Egypt and Vietnam to Senegal, nationalist movements had been strengthened by the spectacle of Europe's suicidal war. A new generation of charismatic nationalist leaders, including Gandhi and Nehru in India, Ho Chi Minh in French Indochina and Sukarno in the Dutch East Indies, Blaise Diagne and—more enduringly—Léopold Senghor in West Africa, emerged to provide organizational focus and international voice for the diverse groups determined to throw off Western dominance. Above all in China, the loose coalition of students, intellectuals, and workers which came together in the May Fourth movement was determined to free China from the informal colonialism of the West and the increasing threat of Japan. They also sought to forge a new, even revolutionary, political and social order, based at first on Western democratic precedents but over time relying more and more on Marxist-Leninist models.

Along with these very considerable forces eroding the prewar order, however, the emergence of two new global powers, Japan and the United States, doomed the restoration efforts of leaders like Lloyd George. Initially, Japan seemed content to go along with the victorious allies, despite its greatly increased industrial capacity and its wartime territorial gains in China and the Pacific. But the coming of the Depression and persistent opposition by other powers, particularly the United States, to its great power pretensions, drove a new generation of Japanese leaders to protectionism and military dictatorship at home, and imperialist expansionism abroad. Japan's Pacific rival, the United States, emerged from the war, the uncontested economic hegemon of a patchwork global order. But America's efforts to retreat from the diplomatic and military burdens that were inevitable given its new international standing, were increasingly frustrated as a massive global depression in the 1930s and armaments races in Europe and East Asia dramatically put an end to Wilson's failed schemes to build a new world order on the ruins of the one that had come apart between 1914 and 1918.

FURTHER READING

Good overall studies of revolution in the 20th century include Eric Wolf's *Peasant Wars of the Twentieth Century* (1965), Theda Skocpol's *States and Social Revolutions* (1970), and John Dunn's *Modern Revolutions* (1972). Mark N. Katz's *Reflections on Revolutions* (1999) is an accessible survey of historical theories of revolution. On Japan in the period and beyond, see Marlene Mayo et al., *Occupation and Creativity: Japan and East Asia, 1920–1960* (2001). On American developments in the 1920s, see Kathleen Drowne, *1920's* (2004).

On the Russian Revolution, Sheila Fitzpatrick's *The Russian Revolution* (1994) is an overview with a rich bibliography. See also E. H. Carr, *The Bolshevik Revolution, 1917–1923* (1978), and Rex Wade, *The Bolshevik Revolution and Russian Civil War* (2001). Edmund Wilson's *To the Finland Station* (1972) offers a dramatic account of the revolution's early phase and the philosophical currents that informed Bolshevik thinking. On specific social groups in the revolution, see John Keep's *The Russian Revolution: A Study in Mass Mobilization* (1976) and Victoria Bonnell's *Roots of Rebellion: Workers' Politics and Organizations in St. Petersburg and Moscow, 1900–1914* (1983). Leon Trotsky's *History of the Russian Revolution* is a gripping narrative by a key participant, surveying social, economic, and political dimensions of the revolution.

On fascism in Italy, R. J. B. Bosworth's *The Italian Dictatorship: Problems and Perspectives in the Interpretation of Mussolini and Fascism* (1998) traces changing historical thinking. Philip Morgan's *Italian Fascism, 1919–1945* (1995) provides a general overview. Emilio Gentile's *The Sacralization of Politics in Fascist Italy*, trans. Keith Botsford (1996), examines popular political culture. C. F. Delzell's *Mediterranean Fascism, 1919–1945* (1970) provides documents and primary sources. An important general work is Robert Paxton, *The Anatomy of Fascism* (2004).

The economic history of Latin America is summarized in the classic by Brazilian economist Celso Furtado, *Economic Development of Latin America* (1976), and in John Sheahan's *Patterns of Development in Latin America* (1987). Two excellent studies of labor that have different emphases are Hobart Spalding Jr., *Organized Labor in Latin America* (1977) and Charles Berquist, *Labor in Latin America* (1986). An overview is provided by Richard Salvucci, ed., in *Latin America and the World Economy* (1996).

There are many good studies of Latin American politics, but Guillermo O'Donnell's *Modernization and Bureaucratic Authoritarianism* (1973) has influenced much recent scholarship. The role of the United States is discussed in Abraham Lowenthal's *Partners in Conflict: The United States and Latin America* (1987). Lester D. Langley's *The United States and the Caribbean in the Twentieth Century* (1989) gives a clear account of the recent history in that region, and Walter La Feber's *Inevitable Revolutions* (1984) is a critical assessment of U.S. policy in Central America. Lars Schoultz's *Human Rights and United States Policy Toward Latin America* (1981) details the influence of human rights on foreign policy.

A few good monographs on important topics represent the high level of scholarship on Latin America. Alan Knight's *The Mexican Revolution*, 2 vols. (1986), and John M. Hart's *Revolutionary Mexico* (1987) provide excellent analyses of that event. Freidrich Katz's *The Life and Times of Pancho Villa* (1998) is an outstanding biography. Florencia Mallon's *The Defense of Community in Peru's Central Highlands* (1983) looks at national change from a community perspective. Robert Potash's *The Army and Politics in Argentina 1945–1962* (1980) is one of the best in-depth studies of a Latin American military establishment, and Richard Gott's *Guerilla Movements in Latin America* (1972) presents analysis and documents on the movements seeking revolutionary change. On the

cultural aspects of the U.S. influence on Latin America there is Gilbert Joseph et. al., eds., *Close Encounters Empire* (1998).

Some of the best general studies on China in the 20th century include Lucian Bianco's *The Communist Revolution in China* (1967), C. P. Fitzgerald's *Birth of Communist China* (1964), Wolfgang Franke's *A Century of Chinese Revolution, 1851–1949* (1970), and Jonathan Spence's *The Search for Modern China* (1990). Maurice Meisner's *Li Ta-Chao and the Origins of Chinese Marxism* (1967) provides a detailed account of the transformations of Marxist thought in the Chinese revolutionary context. For first-hand accounts of conditions in the revolutionary era, see especially Graham Peck's *Two Kinds of Time* (1950), Edgar Snow's *Red Star over China* (1938), and Theodore White and Analee Jacoby's *Thunder Out of China* (1946). Mark Selden's *The Yenan Way in Revolutionary China* (1971) provides the fullest account of the development of the Communist movement after the Long March.

ON THE WEB

The BBC provides a very user-friendly guide for studying the origins of the Russian Revolution, including how global historical forces such as World War I shaped its course:

http://www.bbc.co.uk/education/modern/russia/
    russihtm.htm

The initial political program of the Russian Provisional Government is accessible on the Web at

http://www.dur.ac.uk/~dml0www/provgov1.html

Its worst political blunders are discussed at

http://www.historylearningsite.co.uk/provisional_
    government.htm

and the revealing lyrics of its national anthem at

http://www.national-anthems.net/~davidk/ruf2-txt.htm

The Lenin Archive is a good place to find the works, a biography, and various images of the Bolshevik leader.

http://www.marxists.org/archive/lenin/

Other useful sites for further study of Lenin and other leaders of the early communist movement are

http://www2.cddc.vt.edu/marxist/archive/index.html
http://www.campus.northpark.edu/history/
    WebChron/EastEurope/OctRev.html

http://www.marxist.com/Russia/rev-betrayed.html

Benito Mussolini's vision of fascism can be glimpsed at

http://www.fordham.edu/halsall/mod/mussolini-fascism.html

Italian fascism and life in fascist Italy is explained at

http://www.library.wisc.edu/libraries/dpf/Fascism/Intro.html

An internal link at this site

http://www.library.wisc.edu/libraries/dpf/Fascism/Youth.html

offers a vivid look into the manner in which young fascists were indoctrinated via a magazine, a glimpse of whose front covers are alone worth a visit to the site.

The politics of Latin Americans in the early 20th century are traced at sites exploring the lives of Pancho Villa, such as

http://ojinaga.com/villa/
http://www.mexconnect.com/mex_/history/panchovilla1.html

Life in the United States in the 1920s is illuminated at

http://www.cvip.fresno.com/~jsh33/roar.html
http://www.webtech.kennesaw.edu/jcheek3/roaring_twenties.htm

Other sites examine in detail the Scopes "Monkey Trial," prohibition, and Harlem in the "Jazz Age"

http://www.xroads.virginia.edu/~UG97/inherit/1925home.html
http://www.prohibition.history.ohio-state.edu/
http://www.etext.lib.virginia.edu/harlem/index.html

The path that led to the winning of voting rights for women is traced at

http://www.memory.loc.gov/ammem/naw/nawshome.html

while the role of women peace activists during the Red Scare is examined at

http://www.womhist.binghampton.edu/wilpf/intro.htm

Links to sites illuminating key figures in the fall of the Qing Empire can be found in a useful biography of Yuan Shikai at

http://www.wikipedia.org/wiki/Yuan_Shikai

The emergence of Republican China, including Sun Yat-sen's early political platform, is treated at

http://www.chaos.umd.edu/history/republican.html

The life of Chiang Kai-shek as seen against the background of nationalist politics is provided at

http://www.wsu.edu:8001/~dee/MODCHINA/NATIONAL.HTM

An interesting reflection on the legacy of the student-led May Fourth movement is offered at

http://www.fas.harvard.edu/~asiactr/haq/199903/9903a003.htm

An excellent introduction to the life of Mao Zedong is provided at

http://www.asiasource.org/society/mao.cfm

The revolution in Mexico inspired both joy and deadly reaction:

http://ac.acusd.edu/History/projects/border/page01.html

Insight into Mexico's best known revolutionaries is presented at various sites. Emiliano Zapata is discussed at

http://www.cs.utk.edu/~miturria/project/zapata.html
http://www.mexconnect.com/mex_/history/ezapata1.html

and Pancho Villa at

http://ojinaga.com/villa/
http://www.mexconnect.com/mex_/history/panchovilla1.html

The desire of many Latin Americans for a more egalitarian society was celebrated in the works of artists such as Diego Rivera:

http://www.arts~history.mx/museomural.html
http://www.diegorivera.com/index.htm

Chapter 7

Global Depression and the Challenge of Totalitarianism

*In this example of Socialist realism, heroic women workers labor
at a bustling, productive factory.*

Chronology

1927–1928	Agricultural slump in the United States.
1928–1929	Skyscraper "craze" in New York; Empire State Building begun
1929	New York stock market crashes
1930	U.S. Congress passes the Smoot-Hawley Tariff Act; economic downturn in western Europe, especially Germany, and throughout European colonial empires; rapid rise of the Nazi Party in Germany
1931	Statute of Westminster grants full autonomy to the British Dominions of Canada, Australia, New Zealand, South Africa, and the Irish Free State
1931	Failed rebellion against Japanese rule in Korea; poor harvests and severe economic dislocations in Japan; Japanese invasion of Manchuria
1932	Franklin Roosevelt begins four-term tenure as U.S. President and launches the New Deal
1932–1934	Forced collectivization at height in the U.S.S.R.; genocidal famine inflicted on the Ukraine and other areas
1933	Adolf Hitler becomes Chancellor of Germany
1934–1940	Cardenas serves as President in Mexico, extensive land reform
1935	Nuremberg laws deprive Jews of German citizenship; Mussolini's armies invade Ethiopia; outbreak of the Civil War in Spain
1936	Popular Front government formed in France; junior army officers "revolt" in Japan, key political leaders assassinated
1936–1938	Height of Stalinist purges in the Soviet Union
1937	Full-scale Japanese invasion of China
1938	*Kristallnacht* begins intensification of attacks on Jews in Germany; Munich agreement allows Hitler to begin the destruction of Czechoslovakia
1938	Japan's military leaders impose state control over economy and social system, Diet approves a war budget
1939	Outbreak of World War II
1940s	Era of Perónista dominance in Argentina

INTRODUCTION

The worldwide depression that began in 1929 changed conditions in many parts of the world. Its most dramatic impact involved the emergence of new states built on a combination of internal power and external aggression, headed by Nazi Germany. Relatedly, national tensions increased as economic conditions worsened. Many Western powers, though able to maintain parliamentary democracies, found themselves both wounded and powerless. Creative adjustments emerged as well in many parts of the world, but they were eclipsed by the clouds of authoritarianism and war.

The Depression helped trigger an array of new regimes, many of them bent on military expansion. Nazism in Germany was the centerpiece, but other fascist or semifascist regimes developed in other parts of Europe. Japan created its own version of a military, authoritarian state and began a concerted effort at territorial expansion in Asia. Russian communism, under Stalin, launched a fuller police state, and it, too, ultimately turned to expansion. Key nations in Latin America, though less aggressive, introduced new forms of one-man rule. They also worked at creating more independent economies. China's revolution, beset by internal strife and war, turned away from democracy. Finally depression and political challenge modified Europe's colonial hold in other parts of the world.

Depression and political change dominated the 1930s and led directly to a new world war. If some responses pointed in more promising directions, they were overshadowed by the escalation of human suffering and raw assertions of power.

Analysts offered various explanations for the political trends of the decade. Fascism combined political innovation with an appeal to traditional social values as opposed to more modern trends. But other new systems seemed designed to accelerate economic and social modernization. Some observers talked of a "flight from freedom" in which people sought to escape choice and complexity by embracing strongman rule. Whatever the mix of factors, the pressures of this particular period, in the aftermath of war and amid tremendous economic dislocation, played a crucial role.

Depression triggered a return to various efforts at military expansion. Germany, under its fascist regime, focused on Europe itself, but Italy mounted a new imperialist effort in Africa. Japan, with a new authoritarian regime, launched a series of efforts to gain more territory in China.

Responses to the Depression directly involved new kinds of initiatives in places like Latin America, designed to respond to growing economic hardship. The whole phenomenon of the Depression and its political aftermath conditioned world affairs throughout the 1930s.

THE GLOBAL GREAT DEPRESSION

Coming barely a decade after the turmoil of World War I, the onset of global economic depression constituted a crucial next step in the mounting spiral of international crisis. The crash of the New York stock market hit the headlines in 1929, but in fact a depression had begun, sullenly, in many parts of the world economy even earlier. The Depression resulted from new problems in the industrial economy of Europe and the United States, combined with the long-term weakness in economies, like those of Latin America, that depended on sales of cheap exports in the international market. The result was a worldwide collapse that spared only a few economies and brought political as well as economic pressures on virtually every society.

Causation

The 1920s had seemed to offer a return to prosperity, after some severe dislocations immediately after World War I. But key societies, like Great Britain, did not really recover from wartime expenditures and loss of exports. Most of the new, small nations created in east-central Europe were not economically viable, and trade patterns were disrupted as a result. Weak prices for agricultural goods affected both the industrial countries of the West and huge regions like Africa and Latin America. The overall global structure was shaky, and speculative fever in places like the United States inflated stock prices well beyond the actual performance of the economy. Loans from U.S. banks for various European enterprises helped sustain demand for goods but on condition that additional loans pour in to help pay off the resultant debts.

Farmers throughout much of the Western world, including the United States, faced almost chronic overproduction of food and resulting low prices. Food production had soared in response to wartime needs; during the postwar inflation many farmers, both in western Europe and in North America, borrowed heavily to buy new equipment, overconfident that their good markets would be sustained. But rising European production combined with large imports from the Americas and New Zealand sent prices down, which made debts harder to repay. One response was continued population flight from the countryside, as urbanization continued. Remaining farmers were hard-pressed and unable to sustain high demand for manufactured goods.

Furthermore, most of the dependent areas in the world economy, colonies and noncolonies alike, were suffering badly. Pronounced tendencies toward overproduction developed in the smaller nations of eastern Europe, which sent agricultural goods to western Europe, as well as among tropical producers in Africa and Latin America. Here, continued efforts to win export revenue pressed local estate owners to drive up output in coffee, sugar, and rubber. As European governments and businesses organized their African colonies for more profitable exploitation, they set up large estates devoted to goods of this type. Again, production frequently exceeded demand, which drove prices and earnings down in both Africa and Latin America. This meant, in turn, that many colonies and dependent economies were unable to buy many industrial exports, which weakened demand for Western products precisely when output tended to rise amid growing U.S. and Japanese competition. Several food-exporting regions, including many of the new eastern European nations, fell into a depression, in terms of earnings and employment, by the mid-1920s, well before the full industrial catastrophe.

Governments of the leading industrial nations provided scant leadership during the emerging crisis of the 1920s. Knowledge of economics was often feeble within a Western leadership group not noteworthy for its quality even in more conventional areas. Nationalistic selfishness predominated. Western nations were more concerned about insisting on repayment of any debts owed to them or about constructing tariff barriers to protect their own industries than about facilitating balanced world economic growth. Protectionism, in particular, as practiced even by traditionally free-trade Great Britain and by the many nations in eastern Europe simply reduced market opportunities and made a bad situation worse. By the later 1920s employment in key Western industrial sectors—coal (also beset by new competition from imported oil), iron, and textiles—began to decline, the foretaste of more general collapse.

The Debacle

The formal advent of depression occurred in October 1929, when the New York stock market collapsed. Stock values tumbled as investors quickly lost confidence in issues that had been pushed ridiculously high. Banks, which had depended heavily on their stock investments, rapidly echoed the financial crisis, and many institutions failed, dragging their depositors along with them. Even before this crash, Americans had begun to call back earlier loans to Europe. Yet the European credit structure depended extensively on U.S. loans, which had fueled some industrial expansion but also less productive investments, such as German reparations payments and the construction of fancy town halls and other amenities. In Europe, as in the United States, many commercial enterprises existed on the basis not of real production power but of continued speculation. When one piece of the speculative spiral was withdrawn, the whole edifice quickly collapsed. Key bank failures in Austria and Germany followed the U.S. crisis. Throughout most of the industrial West, investment funds dried up as creditors went bankrupt or tried to pull in their horns.

This photo of a woman in the United States exemplifies unemployment and poverty during the Great Depression.

With investment receding, industrial production quickly began to fall, beginning with the industries that produced capital goods and extending quickly to consumer products fields. Falling production—levels dropped by as much as one-third by 1932—meant falling employment and lower wages, which in turn withdrew still more demand from the economy and led to further hardship. The existing weakness of some markets, such as the farm sector or the nonindustrial world, was exacerbated as demand for foods and minerals plummeted. New and appalling problems developed among workers, now out of jobs or suffering from reduced hours and reduced pay, as well as among the middle classes. The Depression, in sum, fed on itself, growing steadily worse from 1929 to 1933. Even countries initially less hard hit, such as France and Italy, saw themselves drawn into the vortex by 1931.

In itself the Great Depression was not entirely unprecedented. Previous periods had seen slumps triggered by bank failures and overspeculation, yielding several years of falling production, unemployment, and hardship. But the intensity of the Great Depression had no precedent in the brief history of industrial societies. Its duration was also unprecedented; in many countries full recovery came only after a decade and only with the forced production schedules provoked by World War II. Unlike earlier depressions, this one came on the heels of so much other distress—the economic hardships of war, for example, and the catastrophic inflation of the 1920s—and caught most governments totally unprepared.

The Depression was more, of course, than an economic event. It reached into countless lives, creating hardship and tension that would be recalled even as the crisis itself eased. Loss of earnings, loss of work, or simply fears that loss would come devastated people at all social levels. The suicides of ruined investors in New York were paralleled by the vagrants' camps and begging that spread among displaced workers. The statistics were grim; up to one-third of all blue-collar workers in the West lost their jobs for prolonged periods. White-collar unemployment, though not quite as severe, was also unparalleled. In Germany 600,000 of 4 million white-collar workers had lost their jobs by 1931. Graduating students could not find work or had to resort to jobs they regarded as insecure or demeaning. Six million overall unemployed in Germany and 22 percent of the labor force unemployed in Britain were statistics of stark misery and despair. Families were disrupted, as men felt emasculated at their inability to provide and women and children were disgusted at authority figures whose authority was now hollow. In some cases wives and mothers found it easier to gain jobs in a low-wage economy than their husbands did, and although this development had some promise in terms of new opportunities for women, it could also be confusing for standard family roles. For many the agony and personal disruption of the Depression were desperately prolonged, with renewed recession around 1937 and with unemployment still averaging 10 percent or more in many countries as late as 1939.

Inevitably, the Depression affected popular culture, reducing the excitement and experimentation of the 1920s. Women's fashions became more sedate, with skirt lengths dropping. Movies emphasized escapist themes, as consumer culture continued amid growing poverty. In the United States the comic book character Superman was introduced in the late 1930s to provide an alternative to the constraints of normal life.

The Depression, like World War I, was an event that blatantly contradicted the optimistic assumptions of the later 19th century. To many it showed the fragility of any idea of progress and of the belief that Western civilization was becoming more humane. To still more it challenged the notion that the parliamentary democracies of the West were able to control their own destinies. And because it was a second catastrophic event within a generation, the Depression led to even more extreme results than the war itself had done—more bizarre experiments, more paralysis in the face of deepening despair. Just as the Depression had been caused by a combination of specifically Western problems and wider weaknesses in the world economy, so its effects had both Western twists and international repercussions.

A few economies were buffered from the Depression. The Soviet Union, busy building an industrial society under Communist control and under the heading "socialism in one country," had cut off all but the most insignificant economic ties with any other nations. The result placed great hardships on many Russian people, called to sustain rapid industrial development without outside capital, but it did prevent anything like a depression during the 1930s. Soviet leaders pointed with pride to the steadily rising production rates and lack of serious unemployment, in a telling contrast with the miseries of Western capitalism at the time. For most of the world, however, the Depression worsened an already bleak economic picture. Western markets could absorb fewer commodity imports as production fell and incomes dwindled. Hence the nations that produced foods and raw materials saw prices and earnings drop even more than before. Unemployment rose rapidly in the export sectors of the Latin American economy, creating a major political challenge not unlike that faced by the Western nations. Japan, a new industrial country, still heavily depended on export earnings for financing its imports of essential fuel and raw materials. The Japanese silk industry, an export staple, was already suffering from the advent of artificial silklike fibers produced by Western chemical giants. Now Western luxury purchases collapsed, leading to severe unemployment in Japan and a crucial political crisis. Between 1929 and 1931, the value of Japanese exports plummeted by 50 percent. Workers' real income dropped by almost one-third, and more than three million people were unemployed. Depression was compounded by poor harvests in several regions, leading to rural begging and near starvation.

The Great Depression, though most familiar in its Western dimensions, was a truly international collapse, a sign of the tight bonds and serious imbalances that had developed in world trading patterns. The results of the collapse, and particularly the varied responses to it, are best traced in individual cases. For Latin America the Depression stimulated new kinds of effective political action, particularly greater state involvement in economic planning and direction. New government vigor did not cure the economic effects of the Depression, which escaped the control of most individual states, but it did set an important new phase in this civilization's political evolution. For Japan the Depression increased suspicions of the West and helped promote new expansionism designed, among other things, to win more assured markets in Asia. In the West the Depression led to new welfare programs that stimulated demand and helped restore confidence, but it also led to radical social and political experiments, such as German Nazism. What was common in this welter of reactions was the intractable global quality of the Depression itself, which made it impossible for any purely national policy to restore full prosperity. Even Nazi Germany, which boasted of regaining full employment, continued to suffer from low wages and other dislocations aside from its obvious and growing dependence on military production. The reactions to the Depression, including a sense of weakness and confusion in many quarters inside and outside policy circles, helped to bring the final great crisis of the first half of the 20th century: a second, and more fully international, world war.

Responses to the Depression in Western Europe

In western Europe and the United States, the Great Depression revealed that neither the economic nor the political achievements of the mid-1920s had been as solidly based as had been hoped. Political consequences were inevitable with so many people out of work or threatened with unemployment. The relatively weak Western governments responded to the onset of the catastrophe counterproductively. National tariffs were raised to keep out the goods of other countries, but this merely worsened the international economy and curbed sales for everyone. Most governments tried to cut spending, reflecting the decline in revenues that accompanied falling production. They were concerned about avoiding renewed inflation, but in fact their measures further reduced economic stimulus and pushed additional workers—government employees—out of jobs. Confidence in the normal political process deteriorated. In many coun-

tries the Depression heightened political polarization. People sought solutions from radical parties or movements, both on the left and on the right. Support for Communist parties increased in many countries, and in important cases the authoritarian movement on the radical right gained increased attention. Even in relatively stable countries such as Britain, battles between conservative and labor movements made decisive policy difficult. Class conflict rose to new levels, in and out of politics.

In key cases, the Great Depression led to one of two effects: either a parliamentary system that became increasingly incapacitated, unable to come to grips with the new economic dilemma and too divided to take vigorous action, even in foreign policy, or the outright overturning of the parliamentary system.

France was a prime example of the first pattern. The French government reacted sluggishly to the Depression. Voters responded by moving toward the political extremes. Socialist and then Communist parties expanded. Rightist movements calling for a strong leader and fervent nationalism grew, their adherents often disrupting political meetings in order to discredit the parliamentary system. In response Liberal, Socialist, and Communist parties formed the Popular Front in 1936 to win the election. The Popular Front government, however, was unable to take strong measures of social reform because of the ongoing strength of conservative republicans and the authoritarian right. The same paralysis crept into foreign policy, as Popular Front leaders, initially eager to support the new liberal regime in Spain that was attacked by conservative army leaders in the Spanish Civil War, found themselves forced to pull back. The Popular Front fell in 1938, but even before this France was close to a standstill.

There were more constructive responses. Scandinavian states, most of them directed by moderate Socialist parties, increased government spending, providing new levels of social insurance against illness and unemployment. This foreshadowed the welfare state. British policy was more tentative, but new industrial sectors emerged under the leadership of innovative businessmen. The world's first television industry, for example, took shape in southern England in the late 1930s.

The New Deal

After a few years of floundering, the United States generated another set of creative responses. Initial American policies, under President Herbert Hoover, resembled those of western Europe, in seeking higher tariffs and attempting to cut spending in reaction to falling revenues. The United States also sought to accelerate war debt repayments from Europe, which also made matters worse internationally. In 1933 a new administration took over, under Franklin Roosevelt, offering a "new deal" to the American people.

New Deal policies, as they unfolded during the 1930s, offered more direct aid to Americans at risk, through increased unemployment benefits and other measures. Many unemployed people were given jobs on public works projects. A crucial innovation was the Social Security system, based on contributions from workers and employers and designed to provide protection during unemployment and old age. The New Deal also undertook some economic planning and stimulus, for both industry and agriculture, while installing new regulations on banking.

The New Deal ushered in a period of rapid government growth, a watershed in American history particularly as it was followed by the massive expansion of military operations in World War II. The regime did not solve the Depression, which sputtered on until wartime spending ended it in the early 1940s. It also did not install a full welfare state, holding back, for example, from plans to offer a health insurance system. But the New Deal did restore the confidence of most Americans in their political system, preempting more extremist political movements and minimizing the kind of paralysis that afflicted Britain and France in the same years.

ANALYSIS

Learning from the 1930s

So many things went wrong in the 1930s, or as a result of failures in the 1930s, that it is not surprising that many groups and nations vowed they would never repeat such crucial mistakes.

- Many Western governments were completely unprepared for such a devastating economic collapse as the Depression turned out to be. Most governments at that time received little advice from economic experts. Many responded to the Depression by raising tariffs and taking other measures that harmed international trade. As tax revenues declined, many laid off government workers and cut budgets. Measures of this sort would later be criticized as precisely the wrong reactions, destined to make matters worse.
- Aggressive actions by Italy, Germany and Japan—including the invasions of Ethiopia and China, and the fascist interference in the Spanish Civil War—were not met by strong responses from other countries. Internal divisions, including the debate about whether fascism or communism was the greater problem, plus exhaustion after World War I as well as a strong strain of pacifism that argued against military response, seemed to paralyze action. While many groups did oppose the aggressions, in the name of international morality, and the League of Nations passed condemnatory resolutions, no strong action resulted, and the belligerents went on to the additional attacks that became World War II. The ineffectiveness of

government response and of world opinion would later be criticized as ultimately making problems worse.

- A specific symbol of failure, the agreement at Munich to let Hitler take over part of Czechoslovakia, long served as an apparent warning that aggressors should never be met with compromise. "Avoiding Munich" was a rallying cry for many actions during the Cold War.
- Horrible events occurred in the 1930s that led to the deaths of millions of people. Stalin's purges costs millions of lives. Hitler began his systematic attacks on the Jews, and while the worst slaughters of the Holocaust occurred after World War II began, the branding of Jews as unwanted outsiders and depredations against their property were well underway beforehand. Other nations, and world opinion more generally, did little or nothing in opposition. This inaction would later be criticized as unworthy of proper civilized standards.

Specific efforts to avoid the mistakes of the 1930s help explain a wide number of developments during and after World War II. The United Nations was supposed to correct some of the weaknesses of the League of Nations. New institutions were set up to combat global depression and avoid purely nationalistic tariff responses. Latin American governments, intervening more actively in the economy to encourage manufacturing, also took measures to prevent such great vulnerability to economic collapse. European reformers introduced new state planning mechanisms and many also worked toward a kind of European unity that would prevent renewed warfare on the continent and particularly that would heal the conflict between Germany and

The adulation that the German masses felt for Adolph Hitler in the mid-1930s is evident in this rally photo. Hitler's popularity rested primarily on his promises to rebuild Germany's deeply depressed economy and restore its world power status by reversing the 1919 Treaty of Paris ending World War I.

France. American decisions to go to war in Korea and then in Vietnam were prompted partly by the desire to avoid Munich-like concessions to communist aggression. More generally, systematic pacificism, of the sort that in the 1930s had inhibited military response to military action, also declined. New agencies of world opinion—for example, the efforts of Amnesty International, founded in 1961—along with the United Nations attempted to identify human rights abuses and call for international action, to avoid the kind of ignorance and avoidance that had greeted the Holocaust. Specific institutions like the Catholic Church also decided that more active policies against racism and violations of human rights were essential.

Different parts of the world, of course, had different reactions to the 1930s. For many areas, the continuation of European imperialism was the dominant fact of the 1930s, rather than the problems that more obviously preoccupied people in the West. Communists, already convinced that capitalism was a misguided system, tended to see the 1930s as a confirmation of their views, though they too made later adjustments to counter political and economic problems.

It remains true that a decade has seldom generated such a widespread desire to learn from recent history. Whether the lessons were identified correctly and whether they were learned well, of course, are open to discussion.

Questions: Why did so many problems accumulate in the 1930s? Is the sense that the 1930s constitute a particularly dark decade unduly Western, or is it an accurate judgment from the standpoint of world history? What kinds of groups and institutions would take a lead in trying to institute reforms that would prevent the key problems of the 1930s?

A Challenge: Which of the problems of the 1930s have been more effectively corrected? Which of the problems have persisted or recurred in the past half century? Pick one area where problems have been reduced and explain how and why this occurred. Pick one area where 1930s-type problems have recurred and explain why reform has not worked.

Nazism and Fascism

German patterns differed markedly from the wavering responses of its neighbors, and from democratic welfare innovation as well. In Germany the impact of the Depression led directly to a new fascist regime. Germany had suffered the shock of loss in World War I, enhanced by treaty arrangements that cast primary blame for the war on the German nation, which had only recent and shaky parliamentary traditions. A number of factors, in sum, combined to make Germany a fertile breeding ground for fascism, though it took the Depression to bring this current to the fore.

Fascism in Germany, as in Italy, was a product of the war. The movement's advocates, many of them former veterans, attacked the weakness of parliamentary democracy and the corruption and class conflict of Western capitalism. They proposed a strong state ruled by a powerful leader who would revive the nation's forces through vigorous foreign and military policy. Fascists vaguely promised social reforms to alleviate class antagonisms, and their attacks on trade unions as well as Socialist and Communist parties pleased landlords and business groups. Although fascism won outright control only in Italy in the movement's early years, Fascist parties complicated the political process in a number of other nations during the 1920s and beyond. But it was the advent of the National Socialist, or Nazi, regime in Germany under Adolf Hitler that made this new political movement a major force in world history. Here, a Western commitment to liberal, democratic political forms was challenged and reversed.

In his vote-gathering campaigns in the later 1920s and early 1930s, Hitler repeated standard Fascist arguments about the need for unity and the hopeless weakness of parliamentary politics. The state should provide guidance, for it was greater than the sum of individual interests, and the leader should guide the state. Hitler promised many groups a return to more traditional ways; thus many artisans voted for him in the belief that preindustrial economic institutions, such as the guilds, would be revived. Middle-class elements, including big-business leaders, were attracted to Hitler's commitment to a firm stance against socialism and communism. Hitler also focused grievances against various currents in modern life, from big department stores to feminism, by attacking what he claimed were Jewish influences in Germany. And he promised a glorious foreign policy to undo the wrongs of the Versailles treaty. Finally, Hitler represented a hope for effective action against the Depression. Although the Nazis never won a majority vote in a free

election, his party did win the largest single slice in 1932, and this enabled Hitler to make arrangements with other political leaders for his rise to power legally in 1933.

Once in power, Hitler quickly set about constructing a *totalitarian* state—a new kind of government that would exercise massive, direct control over virtually all the activities of its subjects. Hitler eliminated all opposition parties; he purged the bureaucracy and military, installing loyal Nazis in many posts. His secret police, the *Gestapo*, arrested hundreds of thousands of political opponents. Trade unions were replaced by government-sponsored bodies that tried to appease low-paid workers by offering full employment and various welfare benefits. Government economic planning helped restore production levels, with particular emphasis on armaments construction. Hitler cemented his regime by continual, well-staged propaganda bombardments, strident nationalism, and an incessant attack on Germany's large Jewish minority.

Hitler's hatred of Jews ran deep; he blamed them for various personal misfortunes and also for socialism and excessive capitalism—movements that in his view had weakened the German spirit. Obviously, anti-Semitism served as a catchall for a host of diverse dissatisfactions, and as such it appealed to many Germans. Anti-Semitism also played into Hitler's hands by providing a scapegoat that could rouse national passions and distract the population from other problems. Measures against Jews became more and more severe; they were forced to wear special emblems, their property was attacked and seized, and increasing numbers were sent to concentration camps. After 1940 Hitler's policy insanely turned to the literal elimination of European Jewry, as the Holocaust raged in the concentration camps of Germany and conquered territories.

Hitler's foreign and military policies were based on preparation for war. He wanted to not only recoup Germany's World War I losses but also create a land empire that would extend across much of Europe, particularly toward the east against what he saw as the inferior Slavic peoples. Hitler progressively violated the limits on German armaments and annexed neighboring territories, provoking only weak response from the Western democracies.

Hitler first suspended German reparation payments, thus renouncing this part of the Versailles settlement; he walked out of a disarmament conference and withdrew from the League of Nations. In 1935 he announced German rearmament and in 1936 brought military forces into the Rhineland both moves in further violation of the Versailles treaty. When France and Britain loudly

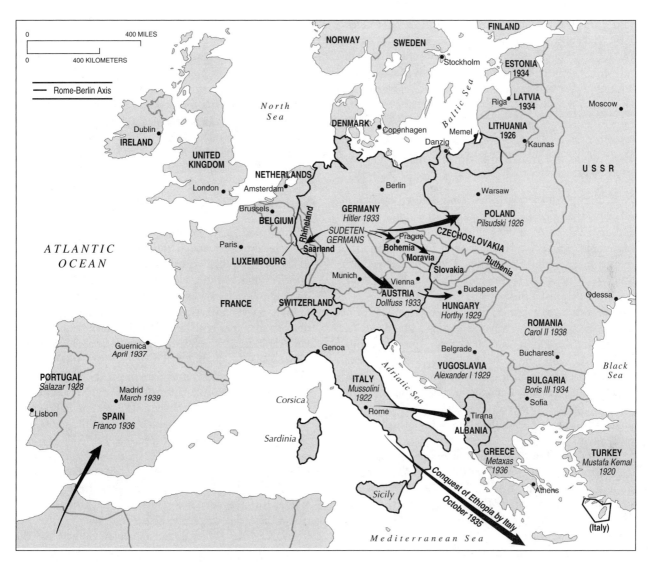

The Spread of Fascism and Nazism in the 1930s

protested but did nothing more, and the isolationist United States said even less, Hitler was poised for the further buildup of German strength and further diplomatic adventures that would ultimately lead to World War II.

In 1938 Hitler proclaimed a long-sought union, or Anschluss, with Austria as a fellow German nation. Western powers complained and denounced but did nothing. That year Hitler marched into a German-speaking part of Czechoslovakia. War threatened, but a conference at Munich convinced French and British leaders that Hitler might be satisfied with acquiescence. Czechoslovakia was dismembered, and the western (Sudeten) region

turned over to Germany. The British prime minister, Neville Chamberlain, seizing on Hitler's apparent eagerness to compromise, proclaimed that his appeasement had won "peace in our time." ("Our time" turned out to be slightly more than a year.) Emboldened by Western weakness, Hitler took over all of Czechoslovakia in March 1939 and began to press Poland for territorial concessions. He also concluded an agreement with the Soviet Union, which was not ready for war with Germany and had despaired of Western resolve. The Soviets also coveted parts of Poland, the Baltic states, and Finland for their own, and when Hitler invaded Poland, Russia launched its own war to undo the Versailles settlement.

Hitler attacked Poland on September 1, 1939, not necessarily expecting general war but clearly prepared to risk it; Britain and France, now convinced that nothing short of war would stop the Nazis, made their own declaration in response. War had been an integral part of Nazism all along; now it moved to center stage.

The Spread of Fascism and the Spanish Civil War

Nazi triumph in Germany inevitably spurred fascism in other parts of Europe. Many east-central states, already authoritarian, took on fascist trappings. Explicit fascist movements emerged in Hungary and Romania. Fascism in Austria was vindicated when Hitler proclaimed the union of Austria and Germany in 1938, quickly spreading the apparatus of the Nazi party and state.

Hitler's advent galvanized the authoritarian regime of a nearby power, Italy, where a fascist state had been formed in the 1920s, led by Benito Mussolini. Like Hitler, Mussolini had promised an aggressive foreign policy and new nationalist glories, but in fact his first decade had been rather moderate diplomatically. With Hitler in power, however, Mussolini began to experiment more boldly, if only to avoid being overshadowed completely.

In 1935 Mussolini attacked Ethiopia, planning to avenge Italy's failure to conquer this ancient land during the imperialist surge of the 1890s. The League of Nations condemned the action, but neither it nor the democratic powers in Europe and North America took action. Consequently, after some hard fighting, the Italians won their new colony. Here, then, was another destabilizing element in world politics.

Fascism also spread into Spain. Here, polarization between forces supporting a parliamentary republic plus social reform, and advocates of a military-backed authoritarian state had feuded since 1931. In 1936 outright civil war broke out. Spanish military forces were led by a general, Francisco Franco. They were also backed by an explicitly fascist party, the Falange, as well as more conventionally conservative landowners and Catholic leaders.

Republican forces included various groups, with support from peasants and workers in various parts of the country. Communists and a large anarchist movement played a crucial role. They won some support also from volunteers from the United States and Western Europe, and also from the Soviet Union.

Bitter fighting consumed much of Spain for three years. German and Italian forces bombed several Spanish cities, a rehearsal for the bombing of civilians in World War II. France, Britain, and the United States made vague supporting gestures to the republican forces but offered no concrete aid, fearful of provoking a wider conflict and paralyzed by internal disagreements about foreign policy. Franco's forces won in 1939. The resultant regime was not fully fascist, but it did maintain authoritarian controls and catered to landlords, church, and army for the next 25 years.

THE 1930s IN LATIN AMERICA

During and after World War I, Latin American economies had expanded and the population continued to increase, especially in the cities. The growth of middle-class and working-class populations challenged traditional oligarchies and resulted in new political parties, often populist and nationalist. These new parties and the traditional elites both attacked liberalism and laissez-faire capitalism, which were clearly in crisis by the time of the world economic crash in 1929. The Mexican Revolution had a limited immediate impact beyond the borders of Mexico, but the outbreak of World War I affected most of Latin America directly. The economic boom of the late 19th century had continued into the early 20th century. Each nation had its specialized crop or set of exports: coffee from Colombia, Brazil, and Costa Rica; minerals from Bolivia, Chile, and Peru; bananas from Ecuador and Central America; and sugar from Cuba. As long as European demand remained high, groups in control of these exports profited greatly.

World War I had some immediate effects on the Latin American economies. Cut off from supplies of traditional imports, these countries experienced a spurt of industrial growth in what economists call *import substitution industrialization*. Latin Americans had to produce for themselves some of what they had formerly imported. Most of this involved light industry such as textiles. Latin America continued to suffer from a lack of capital, limited markets (because so many people had so little to spend), and low technological levels. Still, changes took place. Moreover, during the war European demand for some products increased. World War I had stimulated the economy, but it was a false start. After the war, a general inflation meant that the real wages of the working classes declined and their worsening condition contributed to increasing political unrest.

That unrest also resulted from population growth, which was rapid in some countries. Immigrants continued to pour into Argentina, Brazil, and some of the other countries with a temperate climate, swelling the ranks of the rural and urban working classes. Cities grew in size and importance. Some, such as Lima, Montevideo, Quito, and Mexico City, so dominated the economic and political resources of their countries that growth outside the capital was difficult. Rapid urban growth created a series of social problems that reflected the transformation of Latin America from agrarian to industrializing societies.

Labor and the Middle Class

The rising importance of urban labor and the growth of an urban middle class led to changes in the political structure of some Latin American nations. The traditional land-owning oligarchy in countries such as Argentina, Chile, and Brazil began to open up the political system to meet the desire of the growing middle class to share political power. In Argentina, for example, a new electoral law in 1912 resulted in the 1916 triumph of the middle-class–based Radical party. After some preliminary attempts to forge an alliance with workers, however, that strategy was abandoned in favor of closer ties with the traditional elites. In Brazil, after the establishment of a republic in 1889, a series of conservative presidents from the Republican party in the wealthiest and most powerful states held control of the government. This alliance of traditional landed interests and urban middle classes maintained political stability and a business-as-usual approach to government, but it began to encounter a series of opponents during the 1920s. Reformist military officers, disaffected state politicians, bandits, and millenarian peasant movements seeking a return to a golden age all acted in different ways against the political system and the system of export–import capitalism that seemed to produce increasing inequality while it produced great wealth. Similar criticisms were voiced throughout Latin America.

As in western Europe, the growing industrial and urban labor forces in Latin America began to exert some influence on politics during the first decades of the century. Not surprisingly, many workers were engaged in export production or in related transportation activities. Immigrants from Spain, Italy, and elsewhere in Europe sometimes came with well-developed political goals and ideologies. These ideologies ranged from *anarchism,* which aimed to smash the state entirely by using the general strike to gain power, to *syndicalism,* which aimed to use the organization of labor to achieve that goal. Railroad, dock, and mining workers often were among the most radical and the first to organize; usually they

were met with force. Hundreds of miners in Iquique, Chile, striking against awful conditions in 1907, were shot down by government forces. Between 1914 and 1930, a series of general strikes and labor unrest swept through much of Latin America. Sometimes, as in Argentina in 1919 during the *Tragic Week,* the government reaction to "revolutionary workers," many of whom were foreign born, led to brutal repression under the guise of nationalism.

A growing sense of class conflict developed in Latin America as in western Europe during this period. Some gains were made, however, as it became increasingly clear that governments now had to consider organized labor as a force to be confronted or accommodated. It should be emphasized that most workers in Latin America, unlike those in western Europe, were still agrarian and for the most part were not organized. Thus, the history of the labor movement tells only a small part of the story.

Ideology and Social Reform

In the 1920s and 1930s, the failures of liberalism were becoming increasingly apparent. A middle class had emerged and had begun to enter politics, but unlike its western European counterpart, it gained power only in conjunction with the traditional oligarchy or the military. In Latin America, the ideology of liberalism was not an expression of the strength of the middle class but rather a series of ideas not particularly suited to the realities of Latin America, where large segments of the population were landless, uneducated, and destitute. Increasing industrialization did not dissolve the old class boundaries, nor did public education and other classic liberal programs produce as much social mobility as had been expected.

Disillusioned by liberalism and World War I, artists and intellectuals who had looked to Europe for inspiration turned to Latin America's own populations and history for values and solutions to Latin American problems. During the 1920s, intellectuals complained that Latin America was on a race to nowhere. In literature and the arts, the ideas of rationality, progress, and order associated with liberalism and the outward appearances of democracy were under attack.

Ideas of reform and social change were in the air. University students in Cordoba, Argentina, began a reform of their university system that gave the university more autonomy and students more power within it. This movement soon spread to other countries. Movements for social reform gathered strength in Brazil, Chile, and Uruguay. Many of those who criticized the failure of the liberal regimes claimed that Latin America should seek its own solutions rather than import ideas from Europe. There were other responses as well. Socialist and Communist parties were formed or grew in strength in several Latin American nations during this period, especially after the Russian Revolution of 1917. The strength of these parties of the left originated in local conditions but sometimes was aided by the international Communist movement. Although criticism of existing governments and of liberalism as a political and economic philosophy came from these left-leaning parties, it also came from traditional elements in society such as the Roman Catholic Church, which disliked the secularization represented by a capitalist society.

Populist Politics: The Case of Peru

We can use Peru as an example of this ferment. That Andean nation, with its predominantly Indian population, followed the general trend of export-oriented development based on nitrates and a few agricultural products. The foreign capital invested there controlled many crucial transportation facilities and vital industries. The elites profited from economic expansion, but a war with Chile (the War of the Pacific, 1879–1883) led to the loss of territory and nitrate resources. Many peasants were landless, and government corruption was rampant. By the 1920s critics had emerged. José Carlos Mariateguí (1895–1930), a young essayist, wrote nationalistic analyses of Peru's ills from a socialist perspective that glorified the Indian past and denounced political and economic conditions in Peru. His *Seven Essays of Peruvian Reality* (1928) became a classic of social criticism.

Another young Peruvian, Victor Raul Haya de la Torre (1895–1979) created a new party, the American Popular Revolutionary Alliance (APRA), in 1924. Drawing on the models of the Mexican Revolution, socialism, and nationalism, as well as on some aspects of Mussolini's fascism, this party aimed at being an international party throughout the hemisphere. However, its greatest success was in Peru itself, where by the 1930s its members had made an impact on politics. Anti-imperialist, nationalistic, and in favor of nationalizing lands and basic industries, APRA's program won wide support. Haya de la Torre depended on his own personal charisma and on middle-class and proletarian support for the success of APRA. This was a mix of personal qualities and programs that could be seen in a number of Latin American regimes in the period. Electoral battles and political strife between right and left in the 1930s kept APRA from power. Although opposed by the military and other

sectors of society, *Apristas* remained a force in Peruvian politics and finally gained the presidency in 1985 with the victory of Alan García, but the origins of the movement were tied to the political disillusionment of the period between the wars.

APRA represented the new populist political parties in Latin America that began to mobilize mass support among workers, small farmers, and urban sectors under the direction of personalist leaders. Populism usually was nationalist and seemingly antiestablishment. It gained broad support from urban masses and rural peasants, but it was often led by politicians from the military or the elites, who channeled this support into policies that did not challenge the government structure. With an emphasis on personal charisma, direct appeals to the masses, and the political mobilization of people previously excluded from politics, populist leaders, such as Juan Perón in Argentina, became powerful forces in the region.

The Great Crash and Latin American Responses

The economic dependency of Latin America and the internal weaknesses of the Liberal regimes were made clear by the great world financial crisis of interests of different social groups. This philosophy often appealed to conservative groups and to the military because it stressed cooperation and the avoidance of class conflict and because it placed the state at the center of power. Moreover, the fact that corporatism was adopted by Catholic European regimes, such as Italy, Spain, and Portugal, contributed to its popularity in Latin America. Aspects of Italian and later German fascism also appealed to conservatives in Latin America. During the 1930s Fascist groups formed, complete with their own militant rhetoric and uniforms, and sometimes gained political power in Brazil, Mexico, and Chile.

Unrestrained capitalism had created deep social divisions. By the 1930s many Western societies, including Latin America, began to moderate the principles and policies of unbridled laissez-faire capitalism by trying to bring about some kind of social reform to provide a broader basis for governments. The New Deal in the United States and the corporatist governments of Italy and Spain were responses to the failures and problems of capitalism. Latin America also participated in this trend.

Promises of Social Reform

New regimes, as well as a new concern with social problems, characterized much of Latin America in the 1930s.

One such reforming administration was that of President Cárdenas (1934–1940) in Mexico, when land reform and many of the social aspects of the revolution were initiated on a large scale. Cárdenas distributed more than 40 million acres of land and created communal farms and a credit system to support them. He expropriated foreign oil companies that refused to obey Mexican law and created a state oil monopoly. He expanded rural education programs. These measures made him broadly popular in Mexico and seemed to give the promise of the revolution substance.

Cárdenas was perhaps the most successful example of the new political tide that could be seen elsewhere in Latin America. In Cuba, for example, the leaders of a nationalist revolution in 1933 aimed at social reform and breaking the grip of the United States took power, and although their rule soon was taken over by moderate elements, important changes and reforms did take place. To some extent, such new departures underlined both the growing force of nationalism and the desire to integrate new forces into the political process. Nowhere was this more apparent than in the populist regimes of Brazil and Argentina.

The Vargas Regime in Brazil

In Brazil, a contested political election in 1929, in which the state elites could not agree on the next president, resulted in a short civil war and the emergence of Getúlio Vargas (1872–1954) as the new president. The Brazilian economy, based on coffee exports, had collapsed in the 1929 crash. Vargas had promised liberal reforms and elimination of the worst abuses of the old system. Once in power, he launched a new kind of centralized political program, imposing federal administrators over the state governments. He held off attempted coups by the communists in 1935 and by the green-shirted Fascist "Integralists" in 1937. With the support of the military, Vargas imposed a new constitution in 1937 that established the *Estado Novo* (New State), based on ideas from Mussolini's Italy. It imposed an authoritarian regime within the context of nationalism and economic reforms, limiting immigration and eliminating parties and groups that resisted national integration or opposed the government.

For a while, Vargas played off Germany and the Western powers in the hope of securing armaments and favorable trade arrangements. Despite Vargas's authoritarian sympathies, he eventually joined the Allies, supplied bases to the United States, and even sent troops to fight against the Axis powers in Italy. In return, Brazil obtained arms, financial support for industrial development, and trade advantages. Meanwhile, Vargas ran a corporatist government, allowing some room for labor negotiations under strict government supervision. Little open opposition to the government was allowed. The state organized many other aspects of the economy. Opposition to Vargas and his repressive policies was building in Brazil by 1945, but by then he was turning increasingly to the left, seeking support from organized labor and coming to terms with the Communist Party leaders whom he had imprisoned.

In 1945 Vargas was deposed by a military coup, but he did not disappear from Brazilian political life. After an interim of five years, Vargas returned to the presidency, this time on a program of nationalism and with support from the left and from a new Workers' Party. Under his supporter João Goulart, the party mobilized the urban labor force. Limitations were put on foreign profit making in Brazil. As in Mexico and Argentina, a state monopoly of petroleum was established. Vargas's nationalist and populist stance had a broad appeal, but his policies were often more conservative than his statements. Under criticism from both the right and the left, Vargas committed suicide in 1954. His suicide note emphasized his populist ties and blamed his death on Brazil's enemies:

> Once more the forces and interests which work against the people have organized themselves again and emerge against me. . . . I was a slave to the people, and today I am freeing myself for eternal life. But this people whose slave I was will no longer be slave to anyone. My sacrifice will remain forever in their souls and my blood will be the price of their ransom. . . .

Much of Brazilian history since Vargas has been a struggle over his mantle of leadership. In death, Vargas became a martyr and a nationalist hero, even to those groups he had repressed and imprisoned in the 1930s.

Argentina: Populism, Perón, and the Military

Argentina was something of an anomaly. There, the middle-class Radical Party, which had held power during the 1920s, fell when the economy collapsed in 1929. A military coup backed by a strange coalition of nationalists, fascists, and socialists seized power, hoping to return Argentina to the golden days of the great export boom of the 1890s. The coup failed. Argentina became more dependent as foreign investments increased and markets for Argentine products declined. However, industry was growing, and with it grew the numbers and strength of industrial workers, many of whom had migrated from

The growing labor force that resulted from Latin American industrialization began to change the nature of urban life and politics around the time of World War I. Here, women in Orizaba, Mexico, are making sacks for coffee.

the countryside. By the 1940s the workers were organized in two major labor federations. Conservative governments backed by the traditional military held power through the 1930s, but in 1943 a military group once again took control of the government.

The new military rulers were nationalists who wanted to industrialize and modernize Argentina and make it the dominant power of South America. Some were admirers of the Fascist powers and their programs. Although many of them were distrustful of the workers, the man who became the dominant political force in Argentina recognized the need to create a broader basis of support for the government. Colonel Juan D. Perón (1895–1974) emerged as a power in the government. Using his position in the Ministry of Labor, he appealed to workers, raising their salaries, improving their benefits, and generally supporting their demands. Attempts to displace him failed, and he increasingly gained popular support, aided by his wife, Eva Duarte, known as Evita. She became a public spokesperson for Perón among the lower classes. During World War II, Perón's admiration for the Axis powers was well known. In 1946, Perón successfully manipulated an attempt by the United States to discredit him, because of his pro-Fascist sympathies, into nationalist support for his presidential campaign.

Perón forged an alliance between the workers, the industrialists, and the military. Like Vargas, he learned the effectiveness of the radio, the press, and public speeches in mobilizing public support. He depended on his personal charisma and on repression of opponents to maintain his rule. The Peronist program was couched in nationalistic terms. The government nationalized the foreign-owned railroads and telephone companies, as well as the petroleum resources. The foreign debt was paid off, and for a while the Argentine economy boomed in the immediate postwar years. But by 1949 there were economic problems again. Meanwhile, Perón ruled by a combination of inducements and repression, while his wife, Evita, became a symbol to the *descamisados,* or the poor and downtrodden, who saw in Peronism a glimmer of hope. Her death in 1952 at age 33 caused national mourning.

Perón's regime was a populist government with a broader base than had ever been attempted in Argentina. Nevertheless, holding the interests of the various components of the coalition together became increasingly difficult as the economy worsened. A democratic opposition developed and complained of Perón's control of the press and his violation of civil liberties. Industrialists disliked the strength of labor organizations. The military worried that Perón would arm the workers, and would begin to cut back on the military's gains. The Peronist Party became more radical and began a campaign against the Catholic church. In 1955, anti-Perón military officers drove him into exile.

Argentina spent the next 20 years in the shadow of Perón. The Peronist Party was banned, and a succession of military-supported civilian governments tried to resolve the nation's economic problems and its continuing political instability. But Peronism could survive even without Perón, and the mass of urban workers and the strongly Peronist unions continued to agitate for his programs, especially as austerity measures began to affect the living conditions of the working class. Perón and his new wife, Isabel, returned to Argentina in 1973, and they won the presidential election in that year—she as vice president. When Perón died the next year, however, it was clear that Argentina's problems could not be solved by the old formulas. Argentina slid once more into military dictatorship.

THE MILITARIZATION OF JAPAN

Authoritarian military rule had taken over in Japan even earlier. Not fascist outright, it had some clear affinities with the new regimes in Europe, including its aggressive military stance. As early as 1931, as the Depression hit Japan hard, military officials completed a conquest of the Chinese province of Manchuria, without the backing of the civilian government.

As political divisions increased in response to the initial impact of the depression, a variety of nationalist groups emerged, some advocating a return to Shintoist or Confucian principles against the more Western values of urban Japan. This was more than a political response to the Depression. As in Germany, a variety of groups used the occasion for a more sweeping protest against parliamentary forms; nationalism here seemed a counterpoise to alien Western values. Older military officers joined some bureaucrats in urging a more authoritarian state that could ignore party politics; some wanted further military expansion to protect Japan from the uncertainties of the world economy by providing secure markets.

In May 1932 a group of younger army officers attacked key government and banking officers and murdered the prime minister. They did not take over the state directly, but for the next four years moderate military leaders headed the executive branch, frustrating both the military firebrands and the political parties. Another attempted military coup in 1936 was put down by forces controlled by the established admirals and generals, but this group, including General Tojo Hideki, increasingly interfered with civilian cabinets, blocking the appointment of most liberal bureaucrats. The result, after 1936, was a series of increasingly militaristic prime ministers.

The military superseded civilian politics, particularly when renewed wars broke out between Japan and China in 1937. Japan, continuing to press the ruling Chinese government lest it gain sufficient strength to threaten Japanese gains, became involved in a skirmish with Chinese forces in the Beijing area in 1937. Fighting spread, initially

During the early stages of World War II in Asia, the Japanese bombed Shanghai, China, in 1937.

quite unplanned. Most Japanese military leaders opposed more general war, arguing that the nation's only interest was to defend Manchuria and Korea. However, influential figures on the General Staff held that China's armies should be decisively defeated to prevent trouble in the future. This view prevailed, and Japanese forces quickly occupied the cities and railroads of eastern China. Several devastating bombing raids accompanied this invasion.

Although Japanese voters had continued to prefer more moderate policies, their wishes were swept away by military leaders in a tide of growing nationalism. By the end of 1938 Japan controlled a substantial regional empire, including Manchuria, Korea, and Taiwan, within which the nation sold half its exports and from which it bought more than 40 percent of all imports, particularly food and raw materials. Both the military leadership, eager to justify further modernization of Japan's weaponry and to consolidate political control, and economic leaders, interested in rich resources of other parts of Asia—such as the rubber of British Malaya or the oil of the Dutch East Indies—soon pressed for wider conquests as Japan surged into World War II.

As war in Asia expanded, well before the formal outbreak of World War II, Japan also tightened its hold over its earlier empire, particularly in Korea. Efforts to suppress Korean culture were stepped up, and the Japanese military brutally put down any resistance. Japanese language and habits were forced on Korean teachers. Japanese industrialists dominated Korean resources, while peasants were required to produce rice for Japan at the expense of nutrition in Korea itself. Young men were pressed into labor groups, as the population was exhorted to join the Japanese people in "training to endure hardship."

Japanese policies did quell the Depression, even more fully than did those of Hitler's Germany. While the Depression initially hit Japan hard—half of all factories were closed by 1931, children in some areas were reduced to begging for food from passengers on passing trains, and farmers were eating tree bark—active government policies quickly responded. As a result, Japan suffered far less than many Western nations did during the depression decade as a whole. Under the 1930s minister of finance, Korekiyo Takahashi, the government increased its spending to provide jobs, which in turn generated new demands for food and manufactured items, yielding not only the export boom but also the virtual elimination of unemployment by 1936. The same policy helped support

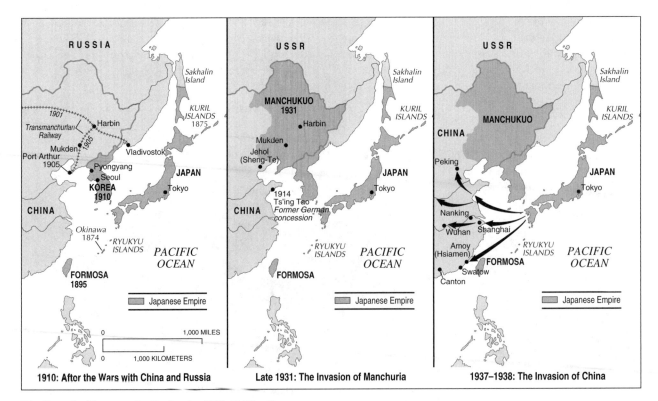

| 1910: After the Wars with China and Russia | Late 1931: The Invasion of Manchuria | 1937–1938: The Invasion of China |

The Spread of Japan to the Outbreak of World War II

government military purchasing, but it is not clear that this constituted an essential response.

Indeed, Japan made a full turn toward industrialization after 1931, its economy growing much more rapidly than that of the West and rivaling the surge of the Soviet Union. Production of iron, steel, and chemicals soared. The spread of electric power was the most rapid in the world. The number of workers, mainly men, in the leading industries rose sevenfold during the 1930s. Quality of production increased as assembly line methods were introduced, and Japanese manufacturing goods began to rival those of the West. As the level of Japanese industrial goods rose, the first Western outcry against Japanese exports was produced—even though in 1936 the Japanese controlled only 3.6 percent of world trade.

Japan also initiated a series of new industrial policies designed to stabilize the labor force and prevent social unrest. These paralleled the growing emphasis on mass patriotism and group loyalty developed by the government. Big companies began to offer lifetime contracts to a minority of skilled workers and to develop company entertainments and other activities designed to promote hard work and devotion. These distinctive Japanese policies, not part of its initial industrialization, proved to be a durable feature of Japanese society.

By 1937 Japan boasted the third largest and the newest merchant marine in the world. The nation became self-sufficient in machine tools and scientific equipment, the fruit of the growth in technical training. The basis had been set for the more significant economic surge of the later 20th century, delayed by Japan's dash into World War II.

STALINISM IN THE SOVIET UNION

Another totalitarian state emerged in the Soviet Union from the late 1920s onward. Here, under communism, the impetus was not the Depression, which the largely independent Soviet economy ignored. Rather, pressures to step up industrialization plus the autocratic hand of a new leader accounted for a new police state. Rhetoric and social policies differed from those of the Fascist regimes, but the political structure itself became uncannily similar.

The experimental mood of the mid-1920s faded quickly after 1927, when Joseph Stalin acquired full power over potential rivals. Stalin was eager both to have authoritarian control and to renew the momentum toward socialism, which had been deflected by the New Economic Policy and the surge of discussion among many mass organizations. By this point the bulk of the

land lay in the hands of the *kulaks*, a minority of wealthy, commercially oriented peasants who were particularly attuned to a profit-based market agriculture. Rural areas seemed inclined to parallel earlier Western experience in dividing the peasantry among relatively innovative owners and a mass of laborers—and this was not socialism. Even in industry, state-run enterprises and planning had only limited effect, as opposed to small private businesses. Stalin devoted himself to a double task: to make the Soviet Union a fully industrial society and to do so under full control of the state rather than through private initiative and individual ownership of producing property. In essence, Stalin wanted modernization but with a revolutionary, noncapitalist twist. And although he was willing to borrow Western techniques and advice, importing a small number of foreign engineers, for example, he insisted on Soviet control and largely Soviet endeavor.

Economic Policies

A massive program to collectivize agriculture began in 1928. Collectivization meant the creation of large, state-run farms, rather than individual holdings as in the West. Communist party agitators pressed peasants to join in collectives. In addition to being distinctly socialistic, the collectives movement also further offered, at least in theory, the chance to mechanize agriculture most effectively, as collective farms could group scarce equipment, such as tractors and harvesters. Collectivization also allowed more efficient control over peasants themselves, reflecting—though in radical new form—a traditional reluctance to leave peasants to their own devices. Government and party control was desirable not only for political reasons but also because Stalin's hopes for a speedup of industrialization required that resources be taken from peasants, through taxation, in order to provide capital for industry.

The peasantry responded to collectivization with a decidedly mixed voice. Many laborers, resentful of kulak wealth, initially welcomed the opportunity to have more direct access to land. But most kulaks refused to cooperate voluntarily, often destroying livestock and other property rather than submit to collectivization. Devastating famine resulted from Stalin's insistence on pressing forward. In addition, millions of kulaks were killed or deported to Siberia during the early 1930s, in one of the most brutal oppressions of what turned out to be a brutal century in world history. Gradually, rural resistance collapsed and production began to increase once again; the decimation of the kulaks may indeed have weakened opportunities to oppose Stalin's increasingly authoritarian

DOCUMENT

The Leader of the Soviet Union Evaluates the Depression

In March 1939 Joseph Stalin, uncontested leader of the Soviet state, spoke to the 18th Communist Party Congress on the state of the world and the implications for the Soviet Union. His evaluation of the nature of the Depression and its implications were central to his overall policy statement.

New Economic Crisis in the Capitalist Countries, Intensification of the Struggle for Markets and Sources of Raw Material, and for a New Redivision of the World

The economic crisis which broke out in the capitalist countries in the latter half of 1929 lasted until the end of 1933. After that the crisis passed into a depression, and was then followed by a certain revival, a certain upward trend of industry. But this upward trend of industry did not develop into a boom, as is usually the case in a period of revival. On the contrary, in the latter half of 1937 a new economic crisis began which seized the United States first of all and then England, France, and a number of other countries.

The capitalist countries thus found themselves faced with a new economic crisis before they had even recovered from the ravages of the recent one.

This circumstance naturally led to an increase of unemployment. The number of unemployed in capitalist countries, which had fallen from 30,000,000 in 1933 to 14,000,000 in 1937, has now again risen to 18,000,000 as a result of the new crisis.

A distinguishing feature of the new crisis is that it differs in many respects from the preceding one, and, moreover, differs for the worse and not for the better.

Firstly, the new crisis did not begin after an industrial boom, as was the case in 1929, but after a depression and a certain revival, which, however, did not develop into a boom. This means that the present crisis will be more severe and more difficult to cope with than the previous crisis.

Further, the present crisis has broken out not in time of peace, but at a time when a second imperialist war has already begun; when Japan, already in the second year of her war with China, is disorganizing the immense Chinese market and rendering it almost inaccessible to the goods of other countries; when Italy and Germany have already placed their national economies on a war footing, squandering their reserves of raw material and foreign currency for this purpose; and when all the other big capitalist powers are beginning to reorganize themselves on a war footing. This means that capitalism will have far less resources at its disposal for a normal way out of the present crisis than during the preceding crisis.

Lastly, as distinct from the preceding crisis, the present crisis is not universal, but as yet involves chiefly the economically powerful countries which have not yet placed themselves on a war economy basis. As regards the aggressive countries such as Japan, Germany, and Italy, who have already reorganized their economies on a war footing, they—because of the intense development of their war industry—are not yet experiencing a

hold for a generation or two. But collectivization, though increasingly thorough, was not a smash success, for even those peasants who participated often seemed fairly unmotivated. Although the collective farms allowed peasants small plots of their own, as well as job security and considerable propagandizing by the omnipresent Communist Party members, they created an atmosphere of factory-like discipline and rigid planning from above that antagonized many peasants. The centralized planning process allowed few incentives for special efforts and often complicated a smooth flow of supplies and equipment, a problem also exacerbated by the Stalinist regime's priority concentration on the industrial sector. Agricultural production remained a major weakness in the Soviet economy, demanding a higher percentage of the labor force than was common under industrialization.

The collective farms did, however, allow normally adequate if minimal food supplies once the messy transition period had ended, and they did free excess workers to be channeled into the ranks of urban labor. The late 1920s and early 1930s saw a massive flow of unskilled workers into the cities, as the Soviet Union's industrialization, already launched, shifted into high gear.

If Stalin's approach to agriculture had serious flaws, his handling of industry was in most ways a stunning success. A system of five-year plans under the state planning commission began to set clear priorities for industrial development, including expected output levels and new facilities. The government constructed massive factories in metallurgy, mining, and electric power to make the Soviet Union an industrial country independent of Western-dominated world banking and trading patterns,

Chapter 7 Global Depression and the Challenge of Totalitarianism

crisis of overproduction, although they are approaching it. This means that by the time the economically powerful, nonaggressive countries begin to emerge from the phase of crisis the aggressive countries, having exhausted their reserves of gold and raw material in the course of the war fever, are bound to enter a phase of very severe crisis. . . .

The Soviet Union is the only country in the world where crises are unknown and where industry is continuously on the upgrade. Naturally, such an unfavorable turn of economic affairs could not but aggravate relations among the powers. The preceding crisis had already mixed the cards and sharpened the struggle for markets and sources of raw materials. The seizure of Manchuria and North China by Japan, the seizure of Abyssinia [Ethiopia] by Italy—all this reflected the acuteness of the struggle among the powers. The new economic crisis was bound to lead, and is actually leading, to a further sharpening of the imperialist struggle. It is no longer a question of competition in the markets, of a commercial war, of dumping. These methods of struggle have long been recognized as inadequate. It is now a question of a new redivision of the world, of spheres of influence and colonies, by military action. It is a distinguishing feature of the new imperialist war that it has not yet become universal, a world war. The war is being waged by aggressor states, who in every way infringe upon the interests of the nonaggressive states, primarily Britain, France, and the U.S.A., while the latter drawback and retreat, making concession after concession to the aggressors.

Thus we are witnessing an open redivision of the world and spheres of influence at the expense of the nonaggressive states, without the least attempt at resistance, and even with a certain connivance, on their part.

Incredible, but true.

To what are we to attribute this one-sided and strange character of the new imperialist war?

How is it that the nonaggressive countries, which possess such vast opportunities, have so easily and without resistance abandoned their positions and their obligations to please the aggressors?

It is to be attributed to the weakness of the nonaggressive states? Of course not! Combined, the nonaggressive, democratic states are unquestionably stronger than the fascist states, both economically and militarily.

To what then are we to attribute the systematic concession made by these states to the aggressors?

It might be attributed, for example, to the fear that a revolution might break out if the nonaggressive states were to go to war and the war were to assume worldwide proportions. The bourgeois politicians know, of course, that the first imperialist world war led to the victory of the revolution in one of the largest countries. They are afraid that the second imperialist world war may also lead to the victory of the revolution in one or several countries.

Questions: How did Stalin compare his nation's economy to that of the capitalist leaders? How did he relate the Depression to the diplomatic crisis? Was his judgment accurate, or was it unduly biased by Communist theory? What would be the implications of this kind of analysis for Soviet foreign policy by 1939?

with the productive infrastructure also suitable for modern war. There was more than a hint of Peter the Great's policies here, in updating the economy without really Westernizing it, save that industrialization constituted a more massive departure than anything Peter had contemplated. The focus, as earlier, was on heavy industry, which built on the nation's great natural resources and also served to prepare for possible war with Hitler's anti-Communist Germany. This distinctive industrialization, which slighted consumer goods production, was to remain characteristic of the Soviet version of industrial society. Further, Stalin sought to create an alternative not simply to private business ownership but also to the profit-oriented market mechanisms of the West. Thus he relied not on price competition but on formal, centralized resource allocation to distribute equipment and sup-

plies. This led to many bottlenecks and considerable waste, as quotas for individual factories were set in Moscow, but there was no question that rapid industrial growth occurred. During the first two five-year plans, to 1937—that is, during the same period that the West was mired in the Depression—Soviet output of machinery and metal products grew 14-fold. The Soviet Union had become the world's third industrial power, behind only Germany and the United States. A long history of backwardness seemed to have ended.

Toward an Industrial Society

For all its distinctive features, the industrialization process in the Soviet Union produced many results similar to those in the West. Increasing numbers of people were crowded into cities, often cramped in inadequate housing stock—for Soviet planners, like earlier Western capitalists, were reluctant to put too many resources into mass housing. Factory discipline was strict, as Communist managers sought to instill new habits in a peasant-derived work force. Incentive procedures were introduced to motivate workers to higher production. Particularly capable workers received bonuses and also elaborate public awards for their service to society. At the same time, Communist policy quickly established a network of welfare services, surpassing the West in this area and reversing decades of tsarist neglect. Workers had meeting houses and recreational programs, as well as protection in cases of illness and old age. Soviet industrial society provided only modest standards of living at this point, but a host of collective activities compensated to some degree. Finally, although Soviet industry was directed from the top, with no legal outlet for worker grievances—strikes were outlawed, and the sole trade union movement was controlled by the Party—worker concerns were studied, and identified problems were addressed. The Soviet Union under Stalin used force and authority, but it also recognized the importance of maintaining worker support—so, informally, laborers were consulted as well.

Totalitarian Rule

Stalinism instituted new controls over intellectual life. In the arts, Stalin insisted on uplifting styles that differed from the modern art themes of the West, which he condemned as capitalist decadence. (Hitler and Stalin, bitter enemies, both viewed contemporary Western culture as dangerous.) Artists and writers who did not toe the line risked exile to Siberian prison camps, and party loyalists in groups like the Writers Union helped ferret out dissidents. Socialist realism was the dominant school, emphasizing heroic idealizations of workers, soldiers, and peasants. Science was also controlled. Stalin clamped down hard on free scientific inquiry, insisting for example that evolutionary biology was wrong because it contradicted Marxism. A number of scientists were ruined by government persecution.

Stalin also combined his industrialization program with a new intensification of government police procedures, as he used Party and state apparatus to monopolize power, even more thoroughly than Hitler's totalitarian state attempted. Real and imagined opponents of his version of communism were executed. During the great purge of Party leaders that culminated in 1937 and 1938, hundreds of people were intimidated into confessing imaginary crimes against the state, and most of them

In his 1949 painting *Creative Fellowship*, Shcherbakov shows the cooperation of scientists and workers in an idealized factory setting. The painting exemplifies the theories and purposes of Socialist realism.

were then put to death. Many thousands more were sent to Siberian labor camps. Any possibility of vigorous internal initiative was crushed, as both the state and the Communist Party were bent under Stalin's suspicious will. News outlets were monopolized by the state and the Party, and informal meetings also risked a visit from the ubiquitous secret police, renamed the MVD in 1934. Party congresses and meetings of the executive committee, or Politburo, became mere rubber stamps. An atmosphere of terror spread.

Stalin's purges, which included top army officials, ironically weakened the nation's ability to respond to growing foreign policy problems, notably the rising threat of Hitler. Soviet diplomatic initiatives after the Revolution had been unwontedly modest, given the nation's traditions, largely because of the intense concentration on internal development. Diplomatic relations with major nations were gradually reestablished, as the fact of Communist leadership was accepted, and the Soviet Union was allowed into the League of Nations. A few secret military negotiations, as with Turkey in the early 1920s, showed a flicker of interest in more active diplomacy, and of course the nations continued to encourage and often guide internal Communist Party activities in many other countries.

Hitler's rise was a clear signal that more active concern was necessary. A strong Germany was inevitably a threat to Russia from the west, and Hitler was vocal about his scorn for Slavic peoples and communism, about his desire to create a "living room" for Germany to the east. Stalin initially hoped that he could cooperate with the Western democracies in blocking the German threat. The Soviet Union thus tried to participate in a common response to German and Italian intervention during the Spanish Civil War, in 1936 and 1937. But France and Britain were incapable of forceful action and were in any event almost as suspicious of the Soviets as of the Nazis. So the Soviet Union, unready for war and greatly disappointed in the West, signed a historic agreement with Hitler in 1939. This pact bought some time for greater war preparation and also enabled Soviet troops to attack eastern Poland and Finland, in an effort to regain territories lost in World War I. Here was the first sign of a revival of Russia's long interest in conquest, which would be intensified by the experience of World War II.

CONCLUSION: ECONOMIC AUTARKY AND THE COMING OF ANOTHER WORLD WAR

As we have seen, the causes of the onset and spread of the Great Depression of the 1930s were complex and diverse. But the underlying pattern of the fragmentation of the global economy, which can be traced as far back as World War I, contributed to anxieties that gave rise to the economic crisis and accelerated its spread across much of the world. The goal of the allied leaders who met at Versailles to shape a postwar world order was to restore and revitalize the process of globalization that had reached unprecedented heights in the decades leading up to 1914. Woodrow Wilson's Fourteen Points had stressed the importance of promoting free trade, the unimpeded flow of capital, and market mechanisms rather than the state as the regulator of economic fluctuations. He correctly observed that among the major reverses inflicted by the war was the severe disruption or complete cessation of these exchanges between the adversary powers in the warring camps. Much more than the vindictive Versailles settlement that ended the war diplomatically, Wilson and his disciples intended that the League of Nations

would prove a major force for restoring a global economy based on free-market capitalist principles.

Even before the Treaty of Paris was signed, Wilson's schemes for reinvigorating globalization as it had developed in the prewar decades was profoundly challenged by the Bolshevik victory in Russia. As the anticapitalist policies of the new regime made clear, the Soviet Union would not only resist reintegration into the global market network, it was dedicated to the destruction of the capitalist economies that system was designed to link and render prosperous. The failure of the Bolsheviks to extend revolutionary communism beyond Russia to east and central Europe, compelled Lenin, and especially Stalin who succeeded him, to strive to create a autarkic, or self-contained, economy within the Soviet Union. The command communist system that developed was connected as little as possible with outside states or the international capitalist system for trade, investment, and natural resources.

The Soviet challenge was compounded in the mid-1920s by the determination of Mussolini and the Fascist leaders of Italy to also build an autarkic economy. In part their intent was to put an end to the economic domination of Italy by Great Britain, Germany, and the other more industrialized states of western Europe, which had been a major source of frustration for even Italy's parliamentary leaders before the war. But Italy's dependence on the import of such key resources as oil meant that the dream of autarky inevitably fed military buildups and schemes for imperialist expansion. External aggression, the fascists were convinced, would guarantee a reliable supply of cheap raw materials, secure market outlets for Italy's industries, and provide a reservoir of cheap labor. As Britain, France, and other democracies threatened to cut off Italy's imported oil and other materials in response to its attack on Ethiopia in the mid-1930s, the impetus for colonial expansion only intensified.

As the western European democracies—Britain, France, Belgium, and the Netherlands—struggled in the 1920s to break out of the economic slump that had followed on World War I, they also began to increase the domestic tariffs that had been erected to protect their home industries, investors, and workers in the decades before 1914. And, with Britain in the lead, they steadily closed in their colonial empires with preferential tariffs and trade regulations that made it difficult for competitors, such as the United States and Japan, to trade and invest over much of the globe that was still ruled by the European colonial powers. Even before Hitler came to power in the early 1930s, Germany, which had been stripped of its colonial possessions by Britain and France after World War I, bridled at the loss of investment and market outlets over much of Africa and Asia due to these restrictions. And once the Nazis were in control, they sought to make Germany as self-sufficient as possible. It soon became clear that this objective would require both Germany's remilitarization and aggression within Europe to create an ever-expanding reich that would have sufficient resources and market outlets to make autarky sustainable.

The crumbling of the global economic system turned to full collapse with the passage of the Smoot-Hawley Tariff Act by the U.S. Congress in 1930. Despite pleas from some of America's most distinguished economists and warnings from the civilian leaders of Japan, the bill restored the protectionist wall that had sheltered the domestic economy in the decades around 1900, when the United States grew into the largest and most advanced industrial society in the world. America's retreat from free trade and overseas investment after 1930 was particularly devastating because the United States had become the engine of the global capitalist system after World War I. Its withdrawal was particularly devastating for the Japanese, who depended heavily on American export markets for everything from toys to silk stockings and textiles. The slump in the latter products was particularly troublesome, because many Japanese farmers depended on the supplemental income from silk production to survive. Because the highly nationalistic junior officers in the army were drawn heavily from these peasant families, the deepening economic crisis in Japan was directly linked to the militarization of Japanese society in the 1930s. Leaders who pushed for overseas aggression and colonization found widespread acceptance of their call for a Japanese empire that would become a self-contained zone of economic exchange, secure from the misery spread by the collapse of the capitalist world order.

The importance of the fragmentation of the global economic system into increasingly disconnected trading blocs is clearly indicated by the configuration of alliances and adversary conflicts that led to World War II. Initially the British and French empires confronted the Fascist-Nazi alliance, which was seeking to extend its control over much of Europe and had designs on the Mediterranean. In the Pacific, the United States sought to thwart Japanese maneuvers to assert their hegemony over China, Southeast Asia, and the western Pacific. Having failed in his efforts to buy off the increasingly aggressive Nazi menace, Stalin eventually brought the massive, but underdeveloped, Soviet colossus into the war on the side of the beleaguered British, who were soon to be joined by

the Americans in both the European-Mediterranean and Pacific theaters of the war. The splintering of the global economy had not only intensified competition in a time of profound economic breakdown and human suffering, it had severed the economic linkages and dependencies that might have served to brake the march to another global war that seemed unavoidable by the late-1930s.

FURTHER READING

On the causes and onset of the Great Depression, C. Kindleberger's *The World in Depression, 1929–1939* (1973) is a solid introduction. See also J. Galbraith, *The Great Crash: 1929* (1980) and, for a useful collection of articles, W. Lacquer and G. L. Mosse, eds., *The Great Depression* (1970). Japan's experience is covered in I. Morris, ed., *Japan, 1931–1945: Militarism, Fascism, Japanism?* (1963). See also Dick Stegewerns, *Nationalism and Internationalism in Imperial Japan: Autonomy, Asian Brotherhood, or World Citizenship?* (2003).

On the Stalinist era/terror state, Robert Conquest's *The Great Terror: A Reassessment* (1990) and Roy Medvedev's *Let History Judge: The Origins and Consequences of Stalinism* (1989) are important studies of the period. Stephen Kotkin's *Magnetic Mountain: Stalinism as Civilization* (1995) assesses the cultural, social, and political impact of Stalin's industrialization program by looking at the experience of a planned industrial city. Sarah Davies's *Popular Opinion in Stalin's Russia: Terror, Propaganda, and Dissent, 1934–1941* (1997) has a revealing portrayal of everyday cultural life under Stalin.

For standard analyses of the Spanish Civil War, see Hugh Thomas's *The Spanish Civil War* (1977), Paul Preston's, *The Spanish Civil War, 1936–1939* (1994), and Raymond Carr's, *The Spanish Tragedy: The Civil War in Perspective* (1993). Peter Carroll's *The Odyssey of the Abraham Lincoln Brigade: Americans in the Spanish Civil War* (1994) deals with one of the civil war's many international aspects. Pamela Beth Radcliff's *From Mobilization to Civil War: The Politics of Polarization in the Spanish City of Gijon, 1900–1937* (1996) is a local case study. Sheelagh M. Ellwood's *Spanish Fascism in the Franco Era* (1987) provides a general treatment on the Falangist movement.

For the United States, William Leuchtenburg's *The Perils of Prosperity, 1914–1932* (1958) is an important account of the 1920s; for a more general view of basic changes, Morris Janowitz's *The Last Half Century: Political and Social Change in the United States* (1970) is useful.

For a case study of social and political change, see Lizabeth Cohen's *Making a New Deal: Industrial Workers in Chicago, 1919–1939* (1990). See also William Chafe's *Women and Equality: Changing Patterns in American Culture* (1984). Ronald Edsforth's *The New Deal: America's Response to the Great Depression* (2000) is a readable introduction to the political history of the New Deal. See also Caren Irr's *The Suburb of Dissent: Cultural Politics in the United States and Canada During the 1930s* (2003) and Jeff Singleton's *The American Dole: Unemployment Relief and the Welfare State in the Great Depression* (2000).

ON THE WEB

The causes of the Great Depression are examined at

http://www.sos.state.mi.us/history/museum/techstuf/
    depressn/teacup.html
http://www.escape.com/~paulg53/politics/
    great_depression.shtml

Photographic images and personal remembrances of the Great Depression are recorded at

http://memory.loc.gov/ammem/fsowhome.html
http://www.pbs.org/wgbh/amex/dustbowl/
    peopleevents/pandeAMEXO5.htm
http://www.sos.state.mi.us/history/museum/techstuf/
    depressn/teacup.html

The Franklin Delano Roosevelt Library offers a gateway to the study of America's longest serving president:

http://www.fdrlibrary.marist.edu/index.html

His response to the Great Depression, the New Deal, is examined at what is simply one of the finest of all Internet sites:

http://www.newdeal.feri.org/

For a review of the life of Lenin, the father of the Russian Revolution, go to

http://history.hanover.edu/modern/lenin.htm

For a critical view of Lenin set against more recent events in Russia, go to

http://flag.blackened.net/revolt/ws91/lenin31.html

The individuals and ideas responsible for the Soviet Union's rise to power, including Stalin and the New Economic Policy, are examined at

http://home.mira.net/~andy/bs/index.htm

The origins and course of Stalinism are explored at

http://home.mira.net/~andy/bs/index.htm

Stalinism is seen through declassified documents at

http://www.utoronto.ca/serap

Stalin's view of Soviet industrialization is offered at

http://artsci.shu.edu/reesp/documents/
    Stalin—industrialization.htm

A transcript of one of Stalin's purge trials can be found at

http://art-bin.com/art/omosc20e.html

Soviet constitutions and other early Soviet documents and pictures are found at

http://www.hutman.com/~nusides/Soviet

For Leon Trotsky's role as an exiled critic of Stalin's regime, see

http://www.anu.edu.au/polsci/marx/contemp/pamsetc/
    socfrombel/sfb_7.htm

Leon Trotsky's now classic critique of fascism is available at

http://eserver.org/history/fighting-fascism/
http://csf.colorado.edu/psn/marx/Other/Trotsky/
    Archive/1930-Ger/

It is possible to make a virtual visit to the house in Mexico where Trotsky was assassinated by a Stalinist agent:

http://old.myhouse.com/pub/bigjohn/STORY12.html

Soviet poster art can be viewed at

http://www.internationalposter.com/ru-text.cfm

The collections are organized by historical period, including a section devoted to New Economic Policy Posters. Other collections of Soviet poster art include

http://www.sweb.cz/posters/listy/russ6.htm
http://www.poster.s.cz/
http://www.funet.fi/pub/culture/russian/html_pages/
    posters1.html
http://www.raketa.f2s.com/pics/index.cgi?direct=
    Soviet_Posters

The Museum of Socialist Realist Art, comprised of examples drawn from Russian museums, offers good links to other sources:

http://www.stanford.edu/~gfreidin/courses/147/propart/
    propart.htm

Profiles of Nazi leaders and documents illustrating the rise of German fascism are offered at

http://fcit.coedu.usf.edu/holocaust/people/perps.htm

The origins of Hitler's anti-Semitism are revealed at

http://www2.h-net.msu.edu/~german/gtext/kaiserreich/
hitler1.html

A lesson plan that offers a good general introduction to
German National Socialism and its totalitarian state and
that includes useful definitions of key terms can be
found at

http://www.remember.org/guide/Facts.root.nazi.html

Life under Italian fascism is illustrated at

http://www.library.wisc.edu/libraries/dpf/Fascism/
Home.html
http://www.personal.psu.edu/faculty/c/i/cin1/
COMPLETE%20LECTURE%20ON%20
FASCISM.htm

The nature of the totalitarian state and the relationship
between politics and art can be explored at

http://www.calvin.edu/academic/cas/gpa/politart.htm
http://fcit.coedu.usf.edu/holocaust/arts/artReich.htm
http://www.humanities.uci.edu/~rmoeller/body/nazi_art
.html

The Spanish Civil War is analyzed at

http://www.geocities.com/CapitolHill/9820/

An excellent related photo file, including Robert Capra's
famous "Moment of Death" photograph, can be found at

http://history.sandiego.edu/cdr2/WW2Pics/13953.jpg

Some vivid accounts of the lives of notable Latin Americans in the 1930s are available at various sites. The life
of Fulgencio Batista is presented at

http://www.historyofcuba.com/history/batista.htm

and of Getulio Vargas at

http://historicaltextarchive.com/sections.php?op=
viewarticle&artid=428
http://historicaltextarchive.com

The followers of Juan Perón maintain their own Web
page at

http://www.falange.org/peron.htm

Though devoid of critical analysis, this site has excellent
contemporary photographs of Argentina.

Examinations of larger movements, such as the diplomacy of the interwar period, can be found at

http://www.mre.gov.br/acs/diplomacia/ingles/h_diplom/
ev003i.htm

Chapter 8

A Second Global Conflict and the End of the European World Order

Sober-faced and weeping Czechs watch the entry of the Nazi armies into Prague in the fall of 1938, as Hitler completes the takeover of the tiny democracy that was betrayed by the duplicity and cowardice of Allied leaders.

INTRODUCTION

World War II began officially on September 1, 1939, with the German invasion of Poland. But a succession of localized clashes, which were initiated by the Japanese seizure of Manchuria in 1931, can be seen as part of a global conflict that raged for well over a decade between the 1930s and 1945. In contrast to the coming of World War I, which, as we have seen, the leaders of Europe more or less blundered into, World War II was provoked by the deliberate aggressions of both Nazi Germany and its Italian ally, and a militarized and imperialist Japan. The failure on the part of both the leaders of the Western democracies and the Soviet Union to respond resolutely to these challenges simply fed the militarist expansionism of the Axis Powers. National rivalries and especially deep suspicions on the part of the Western democracies of the totalitarian Stalinist regime prevented effective co-ordination, much less alliances, between Britain

France and the Soviets, and thus limited their ability to counter the moves of the Axis leaders. Strong responses on the part of British and French leaders to repeated Nazi aggressions in particular were made all but impossible by the deep political divisions within each of these democracies, and lingering guilt about the way the Allies had mishandled the Versailles settlement after World War I. Some leaders—including, most infamously, Neville Chamberlain—long thought that there was some truth to Hitler's strident allegations that the Germans had been unjustly blamed for the war and punished by being stripped of parts of their homeland, colonies, and the means to rebuild a viable economy after the war.

As the 1930s progressed, it was increasingly clear that international security arrangements centered on the League of Nations were impotent. When Japan was censured for its invasion of Manchuria in 1931 or Italy for its brutal takeover of Ethiopia in 1935 and 1936, their leaders contemptuously withdrew from the League and easily fended off the feeble or failed attempts to apply sanctions to punish their aggressions. By the time of Germany's successive annexations in central and eastern Europe in the late 1930s and Japan's full-scale invasion of all of China, the League was little more than a joke shared by the fascist-militarist dictators. And the treaties worked out in good faith by statesmen like Chamberlain were not worth the paper they were written on. Leaders like Hitler and Mussolini scorned the old diplomacy, and viewed treaties as a way to cover their aggressions and delay reprisals while they strengthened their military forces for the general war they believed must eventually come.

OLD AND NEW CAUSES OF A SECOND WORLD WAR

The path to World War II was paved by major social and political upheavals in several of the nations that had fought in World War I and had either been defeated, as was the case with Germany, or, like Italy and Japan, had been on the winning side but disappointed by their share of the spoils. Grievances related to World War I were compounded in each case by the economic havoc, and resulting social tensions, brought on by the Depression. In Japan, these forces had given rise to highly militarist, ul-

tranationalist groups, whose violent outbursts werc covered whenever possible by high-ranking officers in the army. The secret societies that were associated with the parties of the far right, such as the Black Dragon Society, opposed Westernization and urged the restoration of Shintoism. Their adherents indulged in fanatical emperor-worship. They longed for a Nazi–style authoritarian government free from parliamentary restraints and empowered to quash individualism at home and the diplomatic cooperation with the Western powers abroad that they believed were key sources of Japan's decline. The younger army officers in particular pushed for a military dictatorship that would allegedly fully restore the emperor's authority. They violently assaulted those who had made treaties in the past or proposed new ones with the United States or other democracies. And they spearheaded Japanese advances, first into Manchuria and then into China south of the Great Wall in the late 1930s.

The gradual militarization of Japan proceeded despite the solid majorities that moderate political parties continued to win until the very end of the 1930s. And it developed in the context of a succession of regional diplomatic crises. During the later 1920s, nationalistic forces in China began to get the upper hand over the regional warlords who had dominated Chinese politics since the early 1900s. At the head of the Guomindang (or Nationalist)

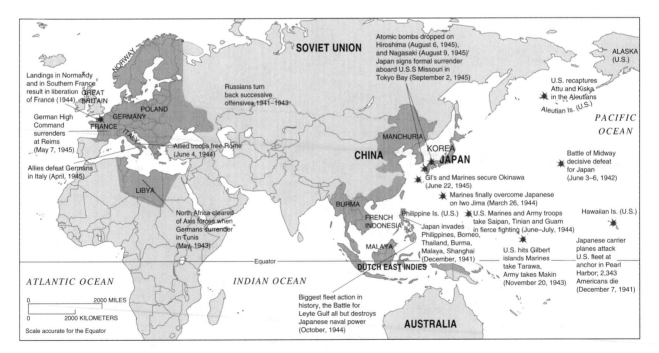

Main Theaters of Action, World War II, and the Axis Empires at Their Height

Party, General Chiang Kai-shek in particular was able to win the support of intellectuals, students, the business classes, the rural gentry, and even members of the largely discredited Confucian elites and rival military leaders. His military successes against first the southern and later the northern warlords seemed destined to unify China under a strong central government for the first time in decades.

The success of the Guomindang worried Japan's army officers who feared that a reunited China would move to resist the informal control the Japanese had exerted over Manchuria since their victory in the Russo-Japanese War in 1905. Fearful of curbs on their expansionist aims on the mainland and unimpeded by weak civilian governments at home, the Japanese military seized Manchuria in 1931, and proclaimed it the independent state of Manchukuo. The international crisis that resulted worked to the military's advantage because civilian politicians were reluctant to raise objections that might weaken Japan in negotiations with the United States and the other powers or undermine its armies of occupation in Manchuria and Korea, which the Japanese had declared a colony in 1910.

In contrast to the gradual shift of power to the military in Japan, the change of regimes in Germany was more abrupt and more radical. Parliamentary government in the Weimar era had been under siege from the time its civilian leaders had agreed to the armistice in 1918, and even more so after they signed the punitive treaty at Versailles. Weimar had survived these humiliations, civil war, and the hyperinflation of the mid-1920s, but just as economic recovery appeared to be gaining real momentum, the Depression struck. In the social discontent and political turmoil that followed, Adolf Hitler and the National Socialists (Nazis) captured a steadily rising portion of the votes and parliamentary seats in a rapid succession of elections. The Nazis promised to put the German people back to work, to restore political stability, and to set in motion a remilitarization program that would allow Germany to throw off the shackles of what Hitler branded the *diktat* of Versailles. Hitler also promised to turn back the Communist bid to capture power in Germany that had grown more and more serious as the Depression deepened. The threat of the Communists within was linked to that of the Soviet Union to the east. From the early 1920s, Hitler and his lieutenants had stressed the need to invade and destroy the Soviet empire, and a key part of Hitler's racist vision for the future was reducing the Russians and other Slavic peoples to virtual slaves in the service of the Aryan master race.

As we have seen in Chapter 7, a major part of the Nazis' political agenda once in power was a systematic dismantling of the political and diplomatic system created by the Versailles settlement. In many ways these objectives bolstered the willingness of British leaders, most infamously Neville Chamberlain, to appease or accede to Hitler's demands. British historians and contemporary participants had been highly critical of the punitive treaty imposed on the defeated Germans at Versailles and the allies insistence that the Central Powers assume all responsibility for the outbreak of the war. Therefore, British leaders, as well as some French statesmen, proved willing to accede to the Hitler's initial demands regarding heavily German populated territories lost in 1919. German rearmament from 1935, the militarization of the Rhineland in 1936, a forced union with Austria and the seizure of areas in Czechoslovakia where German-speakers were in the majority in 1938, and the occupation or dismantling of the rest of the Czechoslovak republic the following year made a shambles of the agreements that had ended World War I. Hitler's successes emboldened Mussolini to embark on military adventures of his own, most infamously in Ethiopia where Italian pilots bombed defenseless cities, and highly mechanized armies made extensive use of poisonous gases against resistance forces, armed with little more than rifles. The Fascists stunned much of the rest of the world by routinely unleashing these weapons on a civilian population that had no means of defending itself.

Hitler and Mussolini also intervened militarily in the Spanish civil war in the mid-1930s in the hope of establishing an allied regime. Once again, Mussolini's mechanized forces proved effective, this time against the overmatched, left-leaning armed forces of the Spanish republic. And both the Italian and German air forces used the Spanish conflict as a training ground for their air forces, though in the absence of enemy planes or pilots, their main targets were ground forces and ominously civilians in Spain's cities and villages. The support of Axis allies was critical to Franco's destruction of the elected republican government and seizure of power, particularly since the Western democracies had refused to counter the Nazi and Fascist interventions.

Excepting volunteer forces recruited in England, France, the United States, and other democracies, only the Soviet Union sought to provide military aid to the republicans. But though valiant, these relief attempts proved futile in the face of relentless assaults by Franco's well-supplied legions and the Axis forces. Despite the critical assistance provided by his fellow fascists, Franco refused to join them in the global war that broke out soon after he had crushed the republic and begun a dictatorial rule in Spain that would last for decades.

From Mechanized to High-Tech War and the Rise of Resistance to Both

No epoch of human history can begin to match the 20th century in terms of the pace and breadth of advances in weapons for waging war. Some of the technological innovations that made for the successive waves of military revolutions that transformed warfare from the late 1800s occurred as a result of the first industrial revolution that began in the late-18th century. But most of these weapons were brought to new levels in the extent to which they could be deployed in combat during the first decades of what we have identified as the long 20th century. Repeating, breech-loading rifles, machine guns, and the extensive use of railroads for moving troops and supplies had begun to transform the ways in which wars were conducted as early as the American Civil War, and these changes accelerated in the Franco-Prussian War of 1870, the Anglo-Boer War in South Africa between 1899 and 1901, and the Russo-Japanese War of 1904 and 1905. All of these transformations culminated in the cataclysm of World War I, in which a bewildering array of industrialized weapons with unprecedented firepower were deployed by armies far larger than those mobilized and supplied in any previous conflict for four brutal years of combat on fronts across Euroasia.

By 1918, and at the cost of appalling casualties, it had become clear to all but the most obtuse observers that killing machines had advanced beyond the capacity of the politicians and generals to put them to effective use by winning decisive victories. But the frustrations of the trench stalemate and indecisive war of attrition between 1914 and late 1917 spurred the development of a new generation of weaponry—which included tanks, flame throwers, and increasingly sophisticated warplanes—and corresponding strategies and tactics. These innovations restored maneuver and mobility to the fighting on the Western Front by early 1918. Even though the Germans had been responsible for many of these antidotes to the war of attrition in the trenches, the superior productivity of the Entente allies, now backed by the economic resources and fresh manpower of the United States, sealed the defeat of the Central Powers by the late fall of 1918. But in the postwar decades of the 1920s and 1930s, both the winners and losers strove to improve on the new weapons—particularly motorized vehicles and airplanes—and ways of waging war. And these more advanced versions of weapons introduced at the end of the Great War became central components

Americans and Europeans are generally aware that the Soviet Union lost between 20 and 30 million people in World War II. Fewer are aware, however, that when the Japanese invaded China in 1931, they opened up a series of conflicts that would result in more than 20 million Chinese deaths by 1945. It is hard to comprehend suffering on that scale. Here, in a more limited form, one can see the tragic results of the Japanese invasions.

of the armies of the Axis and Allied powers that clashed in a second global war between 1939 and 1945. This war was marked by the revival of Germany and Russia as formidable military powers as well as the ascendancy of the United States and Japan as key combatants in the Pacific theater of the conflict. It also saw America's emergence as a global colossus whose economic and military interventions were critical in Europe—where Soviet armies bore the brunt of Nazi assaults—and decisive in North Africa, Asia, and the Pacific.

Rather remarkably, in the final stages of World War II another new generation of weaponry and support technologies were introduced that made possible a quantum leap in warfare from the mechanized warfare that had been dominant for most of the 20th century to high-tech combat that would come into its own at the turn of the 21st. Jet airplanes, early large-frame computers, vastly improved communications systems, rocket-carrying explosives, and the first atomic bombs marked a second watershed shift in warfare in a matter of decades. As was the case after the end of World War I, the decades after 1945 were a time for testing, improving, and gradually introducing these weapons into the arsenals of the great powers, especially those of the so-called superpowers, the United States and the Soviet Union. Policymakers on both sides of the cold war divide between the communist and capitalist blocs, which grew ever more rigid in the 1950s and early 1960s, increasingly relied on the new technologies—especially computers, ballistic missiles, and nuclear bombs and warheads—in preparing for a global conflict that many on both sides deemed inevitable.

One of the more important, broader global effects of these dramatic advances in the killing power of weaponry was to put the civilian populations of combatant nations at ever greater risk. Air power enthusiasts touted the capacity of strategic bombing to destroy the industrial base of enemy nations and to demoralize civilian populations increasingly concentrated in vulnerable urban areas. The vast nuclear arsenals built up by the superpowers and the policy of mutual assured destruction (MAD) that was favored by communist and capitalist rivals alike in the opening decades of the cold war era meant that civilians on both sides would be the main targets of a global exchange. Ironically, one of the consequences of nuclear escalation was that the United States lost the immunity its noncombatant population and industrial base had enjoyed throughout most of the 20th century due to its isolation from other great powers and the protective barriers provided by the Atlantic and Pacific oceans. The sea was now the place where swift enemy nuclear submarines lurked that could launch missiles armed with multiple warheads directed at American cities along the coasts and even in the midwestern heartlands.

The newly decolonized states and peoples in what would come to be called the "Third World" could not afford to build these expensive new weapons systems. And many lacked the sophisticated scientific community and facilities that were essential to developing the new technologies that made them possible. As a result, the gap between the "developed" or highly industrialized nations and "underdeveloped" or (more politely) "developing" nations loomed even larger than that which had separated the imperialist powers of the late 19th century from the nonindustrial societies in Africa, the Middle East, Asia and the Pacific that had been subjected to Western, and later Japanese, dominance. But beginning in the late 1800s, leaders of different kinds of movements of non-Western resistance to colonial rule by the industrialized global powers began to develop techniques of both violent and nonviolent

confrontation that were specifically designed to offset the vastly greater killing power of the military forces of their industrial adversaries.

Mohandas Gandhi and his followers pioneered highly effective techniques of nonviolent protest—ranging from widespread economic boycotts and noncooperation to hunger strikes and mass protest marches—that would set the parameters for active resistance for most of the movements of decolonization from the 1920s through the 1970s. But the success of even the best-organized and most-disciplined, nonviolent protesters depended heavily on a reasonable degree of restraint on the part of colonial officials. And it hinged even more critically on access on the part of journalists and other media organizations to demonstrations against the policies of those in power. Under highly repressive regimes, such as those in Nazi Germany and Stalinist Russia, activists involved in peaceful, public mass protest could not only be rounded up and imprisoned (as was often the case in British India or the African colonies) they could be shot down in the streets or carted off to work/death camps with impunity. And in situations where free speech and the right of assembly were denied by government fiat, journalists and newscasters had little opportunity to make the grievances and activities of protesters known to a broader national or international audience. Without support from beyond the movements, which widespread media coverage was capable of generating, dissidents could readily be crushed or driven underground by the well-armed police and military forces serving the regimes in power.

In places such as 20th-century China, French-occupied Vietnam, and Afrikaner-ruled South Africa, where nonviolent protest was routinely met with brutal, violent repression, a second means emerged for dissident groups to counter the seemingly overwhelming advantages of industrialized states in conflict situations. Maoist-inspired guerrilla forces, which were in most instances based on the support of oppressed peasant populations in rural areas, provided the main source of protection and insurgent power directed against colonial overlords and reactionary regimes, including the Guomindang in China and the Batista dictatorship in Cuba. Often in alliance with intellectuals, students, and urban workers, peasant armies fought under charismatic leaders, such as Mao Zedong, Fidel Castro and Ho Chi Minh, to destroy government forces and alienate their supporters. Guerrilla forces moved through a series of clearly delineated stages from an initial emphasis on propaganda, recruitment, and terrorist attacks, through sustained hit-and-run resistance, to conventional combat aimed in the final phase at the seizure of government power. In all but the last of these, their political-military organizational hierarchy and fighting tactics were specifically designed to offset the superior weaponry, numbers, and resources incumbent regimes could deploy against them. Although guerrilla movements were in many instances crushed—for example, in French Algeria and British Kenya—the cost of suppressing the resistance they generated eventually led to the political liberation of colonized peoples. And often guerrilla warfare produced stunning victories, such as those won by the Maoists against the American-backed Guomindang in China in the 1940s, by the Vietnamese against the American superpower in the late-1960s and early 1970s, and by a loose alliance of militant Muslim organizations against the other cold war superpower, the Soviet Union, in the 1980s.

The introduction of a new generation of high-tech weaponry and computerized satellite surveillance systems in the post–cold war era has racheted up the already formidable advantages that industrial powers have long enjoyed in conflicts with colonial or developing societies. This further imbalance has led to several mutations in guerrilla warfare in the 1990s and early 2000s. As practiced by organizations such as, most infamously, al-Qaeda, guerrilla resistance has increasingly been focused on tactics associated with the terrorist/recruiting phase, has become far more internationalized in financing and organization, and has been based increasingly on hundreds of widely dispersed, semi-independent insurgent cells. The targets of guerilla assaults have shifted to an unprecedented extent from regimes in the developing world to civilian society in Europe, Russia, and the United States. After the decisive defeat of the Taliban and al-Qaeda alliance in the U.S.-led invasions of Afghanistan in late 2001 and the rout of Iraq's conventional forces in the spring of 2003, guerrilla insurgents have also concentrated their military operations in urban areas, most tellingly in the cities of Iraq. Whether or not the industrial powers will prove able to cope with these shifts and the devastation insurgents have demonstrated they can inflict in societies across the globe remains to be seen. But clashes between the high-tech world powers and guerrilla/terrorist insurgents are very likely to be a dominate force of disruption in global history for the foreseeable future of the twenty-first century.

Questions: In what specific ways did industrial technologies improve the killing capacity of the powers that possessed them? How have scientific breakthroughs and high-tech weapons enhanced these advantages over the last three or four decades? Has guerrilla warfare become more common than nonviolent resistance over much of the developing world in recent decades? If so, why? What are the costs of repressing movements of this sort to peoples and dissident groups in the developing world and to societies such as those in the United States, Japan, and Europe that are increasingly chosen as their targets?

UNCHECKED AGGRESSION AND THE COMING OF THE WAR IN EUROPE AND THE PACIFIC

By the late 1930s a number of patterns were clearly established in the interaction between the new totalitarian states and the democracies. The paramount lesson for the former was that aggression would succeed and at little cost. Hitler and Mussolini also discovered that Britain and France, and even more so the increasingly isolated United States, were quite willing to sacrifice small states, such as Spain and Czechoslovakia, in the false hope that Fascist and especially Nazi territorial ambitions would be satisfied and thus war averted. Leaders like Winston Churchill, who warned that a major war was inevitable given Hitler's insatiable ambitions, were kept from power by voters who had no stomach for another world war. Rival politicians, such as Neville Chamberlain and the socialist leaders of France, also feared correctly that rearming as Churchill proposed would put an end to their ambitious schemes to build welfare states as an antidote to further depressions. But in the late 1930s, another round of provocative aggressions pushed the democracies into a war that none had the stomach for or was prepared at that point to fight.

Although traditionally, Nazi aggressions have been stressed as the precipitants of World War II, the Japanese military actually moved first. In the second half of 1937, from their puppet state in Manchukuo, they launched a massive invasion of China proper. Exploiting a trumped-up incident in early July that led to a firefight between Japanese and Chinese troops, the army launched an ill-advised campaign to conquer the whole of China. Prominent naval leaders and civilian politicians had deep misgivings about this massive escalation of the war in China and were uneasy about American and British reactions to yet another major round of Japanese aggression. But they were largely cowed into silence by the threat of assassination by fanatical junior army officers and appeals to patriotic solidarity in a situation where Japanese soldiers were at risk.

At first, the advancing Japanese forces met with great success, occupying most of the coastal cities, including Shanghai and by the end of 1938 Canton, as well as the hinterlands behind cities in the north. The Japanese deployed extensive aerial bombing against Guomindang forces and especially the civilian population in the coastal cities. As Chinese resistance stiffened in some areas, Japanese soldiers resorted to draconian reprisals against both the Chinese fighters and civilians. In many instances—most infamously the capture in December 1937 of the city of Nanjing, the evacuated Guomindang capital—Japanese forces took out their frustrations on retreating Chinese troops and the civilian population. The wanton destruction and pillage, murder of innocent civilians, and rape of tens of thousands of undefended Chinese women that accompanied the Japanese occupation of the ancient city was but a prelude to the unparalleled human suffering of the world war that had now begun.

Deprived of the coastal cities and provinces that were the main centers of their power, Chiang and the Guomindang forces retreated up the Yangtze River, deep into the interior to the city of Chongqing, which became the nationalist capital for the rest of the war. Thus, long before the Japanese attack on Pearl Harbor in early December 1941, Japan and China were engaged in a massive and deadly contest for control of all of East Asia. With the advance of their forces into China seemingly unstoppable, the Japanese military began to shift their attention to plans for the conquest of much of Southeast Asia and the Pacific Islands. As they had in China, the Japanese justified their expanding aggressions as assaults on a decadent Euroamerican colonial order. Using the rubric of the Greater East Asia Co-Prosperity Sphere, they styled themselves as the liberators of colonized peoples from Burma and the Netherlands Indies to China and the Pacific outposts of the American empire. They concentrated their imperial drive beyond China against island Southeast Asia that was rich in the oil, tin, rice, and other resources they were well aware would prove vital to Japan's capacity to wage the war that would surely be precipitated after their surprise assault on Pearl Harbor and the Hawaiian Islands.

The Japanese had plunged into war without coordination, or even serious consultation with their likely allies, Germany and Italy. In fact the Tripartite Pact, which joined the three expansive states in a loose alliance, was not signed until September of 1940, when the war was well underway in both Europe and East Asia. And Nazi military advisors had contributed greatly to the training of the Guomindang officers and troops that fought to contain the Japanese invasion of China. But with a pause to consolidate his stunning gains in central Europe from 1936 to 1938, Hitler now concentrated his forces on the drive to the Slavic east, which he had longed staked out as the region that would provide living space for the Germanic master race. He bought time to prepare the way for the assault on the main target, the Soviet Union, by signing a nonaggression pact with Stalin in August 1939. Military emissaries of the two dictators negotiated a division of the smaller states that separated their empires, and Stalin was willing to share Poland with the Nazis in order to buy time for the Soviet Union to prepare for the German invasion that most observers were now convinced was inevitable. Within days of the signing of the agreement, Hitler ordered the Wehrmacht, or Nazi armies, to overrun western Poland, which in turn precipitated the Soviet occupation of the eastern half of the country which had been promised to them in the cynical pact just concluded with the Nazis.

The brutal Nazi invasion of Poland on September 1, 1939, put an end to any lingering doubts about Hitler's contempt for treaties and repeated assurances that Germany's territorial ambitions had been satisfied by the absorption of Czechoslovakia into the Nazi Reich. Although they were helpless to assist the overmatched Poles in their futile efforts to oppose the German advance, the British and French had no choice but to declare war on Germany. But the armies of both powers simply dug in along the defensive lines that had been established in eastern France in the late 1920s. There they waited for the Nazis to turn to the west for further conquests, and prepared for another defensive war like the one they had managed to survive, at such horrific cost, between 1914 and 1918. But a second major theater of what rapidly developed into a second world war had been opened, and this conflict would prove radically different in almost all major respects from the one to which the new configuration of powers in Europe and the Pacific believed they were committing themselves.

THE CONDUCT OF A SECOND GLOBAL WAR

The forces that gave rise to World War II meant that there would be more of a balance between a number of theaters spread across Europe, North Africa, and Asia, in contrast to World War I, whose outcome hinged on the battles on the Western Front. Within Europe, the largest and most costly front in lives lost and physical destruction was in the vast expanses of the Soviet Union, where huge, mechanized Nazi and Russian armies and air forces clashed in some of the largest battles in history from 1941 into 1945. The Nazis were also compelled to do battle with the democratic allies in North Africa (including Egypt), Italy, and—at both the beginning and end of the war—northern France and the Low Countries. After December 1941 the decade-long contest between Japan and China spread across Southeast Asia and much of the Pacific, as the United States and Great Britain emerged as the main obstacles to Japan's drive to become the hegemon of East Asia and the western rim of the Pacific.

The reluctance to rearm and react decisively displayed by both the Western democratic and the Soviet Union allies in the 1930s made possible crushing and almost unremitting victories and rapid territorial advances on the part of the main Axis powers, Germany and Japan, early in the war. But once the Nazis became bogged down in the expanses of the Russian steppes and the United States entered the war, the tide shifted steadily in favor of the Allies. Once the initial momentum of the Axis war machines was slowed, it became increasingly clear that the Anglo-American and Soviet alliance was decidedly more powerful in terms of population size, potential industrial production, technological innovation, and military capacity on land, under and above the seas, and in the air.

Nazi Blitzkrieg, Stalemate, and the Long Retreat

As the Japanese bogged down in China and debated the necessity of tangling with the United States and the European colonial powers, the Nazi war machine captured France and the Low Countries with stunning speed, forced the British armies to beat a fast retreat to their island refuge, and then rolled over eastern Europe and drove deep into the Soviet Union. For a time, Germany appeared to be unstoppable and the fate of a large chunk of humanity seemed destined to be a long period of tyrannical Nazi rule. From the outset, German strategy was centered on the concept of *Blitzkrieg* or "lightning war," which involved the rapid penetration of enemy territory by a combination of tanks and mechanized troop carriers, backup infantry, and supporting fighter aircraft and bombers. The effective deployment of these forces overwhelmed the Poles in 1939, and more critically routed the French and British within a matter of days in the spring

of 1940, thereby accomplishing what the Kaiser's armies failed to do through four long years of warfare between 1914 and 1918. German willingness to punish adversaries or civilian populations in areas that refused to yield greatly magnified the toll of death and destruction left in the wake of Hitler's armies. In early 1940, for example, the Dutch port of Rotterdam was virtually levelled by Nazi bombers, killing over 40,000 civilians.

The rapid collapse of France was in part a consequence of the divided and weak leadership that the republic had displayed in the successive crises of the 1930s. Governments had come and gone as contemporaries quipped that they were moving in revolving doors. Left and right quarreled and stalemated over rearming, responding to the Nazis and allying with the British and the Soviets. When the war broke out, the citizenry of France was thoroughly demoralized, and the nation's defenses were outdated and extremely susceptible to the Wehrmacht's blitzkrieg offensives. By the summer of 1940, all of north and central France was in German hands, and in the south, a Nazi puppet regime, centered on the city of Vichy, was in charge. With the Nazi occupations of Norway and Denmark in the following months, Britain alone of the western democracies in Europe survived. And what remained of the British armies had been driven from the continent, while the nation's people and cities were under heavy assault by a markedly superior German air force, which strove to open the way to cross-channel invasion by the much larger and more powerful land forces of the steadily growing Nazi empire.

Remarkably, under the courageous leadership of Winston Churchill, the British people weathered what their new Prime Minister had aptly pronounced the nation's "darkest hour." A smaller British air force proved able to withstand the Nazi air offensive, including saturation bombing of London and other British cities. Victory in what came to be known as the Battle of Britain was due to a mix of strong leadership by Churchill and a very able coalition cabinet; innovative air tactics, made possible by the introduction of radar devices for tracking German assault aircraft; and the bravery of Britain's royal family and the high morale of the citizenry as a whole that the bombing raids only seemed to enhance. Unable to destroy the British air defenses nor break the resolve of its people, Hitler and the Nazi high command had to abandon their plans for conquest of the British Isles. Without air superiority, the Germans could not prevent the Royal Navy from entering the channel and destroying the huge flotilla of landing craft that would be needed to carry the Nazi forces across the narrow but turbulent straits that

Erwin Rommel and German mechanized forces in North Africa. Rommel was perhaps the most astute and daring Nazi general. But he met his match in the desert war fought against British troops led by Bernard Montgomery.

had for nearly a millennium shielded Britain from outside invasion.

By mid-1941 the Germans controlled most of the continent of Europe and much of the Mediterranean. They had rescued the Italians' floundering campaign for the conquest of Albania, and overrun Yugoslavia and Greece. They had conquered, or in the case of Sweden forced the neutralization, of the Scandinavian countries. They continued on to capture most of the islands of the Mediterranean, and launched motorized offensives under the soon-to-be legendary commander, Erwin Rommel, across North Africa and on to Egypt, with the goal of seizing the Suez Canal and cutting Britain off from its Asian empire. Once conquered, the hundreds of millions of peoples subjugated by Nazi aggression were compelled to provide resources, war materials, soldiers, and slave labor to a German war machine then being directed against even more ambitious targets.

Frustrated by resolute British defiance, Hitler and the Nazi high command turned to the south and east to regain the momentum that had propelled them to so many victories in the first years of the war in Europe. As Nazi forces, numbering 3.5 million, drove the poorly prepared and understaffed Soviet forces out of Finland, Poland, the Baltic states, and much of Byelorussia and the Ukraine in the summer and early fall of 1941, Hitler's grandest victory of all—and unlimited access to cheap labor and such critical resources as oil—seemed within reach. The Soviet armies, despite appalling losses, did not collapse but retreated eastward rather than surrender. Stalin ordered So-

viet industry relocated across the Ural mountains to shield them from capture and German aerial attacks.

As with Napoleon's invasion nearly a century and a half earlier, Russian resistance stiffened as winter approached, and the German drive east stalled on the outskirts of Moscow and Leningrad. The harsh winter caught the German forces unprepared while their Russian adversaries used terrain and weather conditions they knew well to counterattack with ferocity on a wide front. The Nazis' mass killings and harsh treatment of the Slavic peoples, including the Ukrainians, many of whom initially were disposed to support the invaders, aroused guerrilla resistance by tens, then hundreds, of thousands of partisans who fought behind German lines throughout the rest of the war.

Renewed German offensives in the spring of 1942 again drove deep into Russia but failed a second time to capture key cities such as Moscow, Leningrad, and Stalingrad, and perhaps as critically, the great Baku oil fields in the southern steppes. The two sides clashed in some of the greatest battles of the entire war—in fact of all human history—including Kursk which featured thousands of tanks deployed (and destroyed) by each of the adversaries. As another winter approached, the Germans were further away from knocking the Soviets out of the war than the year before. In fact, the failed Nazi attempt to capture Stalingrad in the bitter winter of 1942 and 1943, ended in the destruction of an entire German army and proved a decisive turning point in the war in the East.

In 1943, the Red armies went over to the offensive at numerous points on the overextended, undermanned, and vulnerable German front. With staggering losses in lives and equipment, the Nazi forces, despite Hitler's rantings that they die in place, began the long retreat from the Soviet Union. By late 1944, Red armies had cleared the Soviet Union of Nazi forces, and captured Finland, Poland, and much of east-central Europe southward into the Balkans. As the Soviet forces advanced inexorably toward Germany itself, it was clear that the destruction of Hitler's "thousand-year reich" was only months away. And it was also apparent that the almost unimaginable sacrifices and remarkable resilience of Russian soldiers, which included many women, had contributed mightily to the destruction of the vaunted Nazi fighting machine.

From Persecution to Genocide: Hitler's War Against the Jews

As the Nazi war machine bogged down in Russia, Hitler and his Nazi henchmen stepped up their vendetta against the Gypsies, leftist politicians, homosexuals, and especially the Jews. Jews, Polish intellectuals, and Communists had been rounded up and killed in mass executions during the German offensives into eastern Europe and Russia in the early 1940s. But after a "final solution" for the "Jewish problem" was decided upon by prominent Nazi officials at the Wannsee Conference in February 1942, the regime directed its energies explicitly and systematically to genocide. The destruction, rather than the removal, of the Jewish people became the official policy of the Reich. In the three years that remained to Hitler and his henchmen, the concentration camps they had set up in the 1930s to incarcerate their political enemies and groups branded as racially inferior—thus polluting to the Aryan people—were transformed into factories for the mass production of death.

The more the war against the Allies turned against Hitler and the Nazi high command, the more they pressed the genocidal campaign against the largely defenseless Jewish peoples of Europe. In fact, vital resources were regularly diverted from the battlefronts to transport, imprison, and mass murder in the camps where the destruction of human life reached a frenetic pace in the last years of the regime. Jews and other "undesirables" were identified and arrested throughout the Nazi empire. Shipped to the camps in the east, those deemed physically fit were subjected to harsh forced labor regimes that themselves took a heavy toll in lives.

The less fortunate, including the vast majority of the women and children, were systematically murdered, sometimes in experiments carried out by German physicians with the callous disregard for human suffering and humiliation that was a hallmark of the Nazi regime.

As many as twelve million people were murdered in the genocidal orgy that has come to be known as the Holocaust, and which will perhaps prove to be what is remembered more than anything else about the Nazi regime. Of these, at least six million were Jews, and many millions of others were Slavic peoples mercilessly slaughtered on the Eastern Front. Without question, the Holocaust was by far the most lethal genocide of the 20th century, which had begun with the Armenian massacres in 1915, and had the horrors of Kampuchea, Rwanda, Bosnia, and Kosovo yet to come. With the possible exceptions of the massacres in the Soviet Ukraine in the 1930s and those carried out in the 1970s by the Khmer Rouge, the Holocaust—more than any of the other major episodes of the 20th-century genocide—was notable for the degree to which it was premeditated, systematic, and carried out by the Nazi state apparatus and functionaries, who until the very end kept precise and detailed records of their noxious deeds. But like later epidemics of human brutality and mass murder, the Holocaust was at least passively abetted by denial on the part of the German people and those of occupied countries, though the Danes and Italians were notable for their resistance to Nazi demands that they turn over "their" Jews for incarceration.

The plight of the Jews of Europe was also greatly exacerbated by the refusal of the Western Allies to accept as emigrants any but the most affluent or skilled Jews fleeing Nazi atrocities, and by the failure of those same Allies to use their military assets to strike at the railway lines and killing chambers they clearly knew were in operation by the last months of the war. These responses to the Nazi horror show only steeled the resolve of Zionist leaders in Palestine and elsewhere to facilitate, by negotiations with the hated Nazis if necessary, the flight of the European Jews. It also intensified their determination to establish a Jewish state in Palestine to ensure that there could never be another Holocaust.

Anglo-American Offensives, Encirclement, and the End of the 12-Year Reich

For nearly two years, the British were so absorbed in their own struggle for survival that they could provide little relief for their Soviet allies hard-pressed by what some have seen as Hitler's foolhardy invasion of Russia. Even before the attack on Pearl Harbor in December 1941, the United States was providing substantial assistance, including military supplies, to beleaguered Britain. In addition, Franklin Roosevelt was quite openly sympathetic to the British cause, and soon established a good working relationship with Churchill, the new British prime minister. American forces first entered the war in a major way in the campaigns to counter German U-boat attacks on shipping crossing the Atlantic. American tank divisions and infantrymen also joined the British in reversing Rommel's gains in North Africa in 1942 and 1943. Having all but cleared Nazi forces from Africa and the Middle East, Anglo-American armies next struck across the Mediterranean at Sicily and then Italy proper. Their steady, but often costly, advance up the peninsula lasted into early 1945, but eventually toppled the Fascist regime and prompted a Nazi takeover of northern Italy. Mussolini and the last of his many mistresses were captured and shot by partisans and enraged civilians and hung upside down on a lamp post near Lake Bellagio.

With significant German forces tied down on the Eastern Front and in Italy, the allied high command, with General Dwight Eisenhower at its head, prepared landings in northern France that would carry the war into the fortress the Nazis had been building in occupied Europe since their defeat in the Battle of Britain in 1940. In early June, against fierce resistance, the Allies established beachheads at Normandy, from which they launched liberation campaigns into the Low Countries and the rest of France. Despite Hitler's last-ditch effort to repel the invading Allied armies in what became known as the Battle of the Bulge in the winter of 1944–1945, by early in 1945, the Allies had invaded Germany itself from the west, while the Red armies were pouring in from the east.

In late April, Russian and American troops linked up at the Elbe River, where they became caught up in spontaneous celebrations. The genuine comradery and mutual respect widely displayed by troops on both sides would soon be lost in high-stakes maneuvers by the political leaders in each camp to shape the postwar world order. On April 30, after haranguing his closest advisors for his betrayal by the German people, Adolph Hitler committed suicide in his Berlin bunker. Less than two weeks later, German military leaders surrendered their forces, putting an end to the war in the European and Mediterranean theaters. But the contest between the Anglo-American and Soviet allies for control of Germany had already commenced, and it would soon be extended to Europe as a whole and to the rest of the world.

The United States advanced on Japan with the invasion and capture of Okinawa in March 1945. Note the huge stores of munitions, food, and other supplies provided for the Allied armies. This awesome material abundance touched off "cargo cult" movements in the Pacific Islands after the war.

Japan and the Defeat in World War II

Japan's defeat in World War II brought moral and material confusion. The government was so uncertain of the intentions of the victorious Americans that it evacuated its female employees to the countryside. The following excerpt from the 1945 diary of Yoshizawa Hisako (who became a writer on home economics) discusses the various factors that contributed to commonly held beliefs. The passage also reveals how the American occupation force tried to present itself and the reception it received.

August 15: As I listened to the Emperor's voice announcing the surrender, every word acquired a special meaning and His Majesty's voice penetrated my mind. Tears streamed down my cheeks. I kept on telling myself that we must not fight ourselves and work hard for our common good. Yes, I pledged myself, I must work [for Japan's recovery].

The city was quiet.

I could not detect any special expression in people's faces. Were they too tired? However, somehow they seemed brighter, and I could catch an expression showing a sign of relief. It could have been a reflection of my own feelings. But I knew I could trust what I saw. . . .

The voluntary fighting unit was disbanded, and I was no longer a member of that unit. Each of us burned the insignia and other identifications.

I cannot foresee what kind of difficulty will befall me, but all I know is that I must learn to survive relying on my health and my will to live.

August 16: People do not wear expressions any different from other days. However, in place of a "good morning" or "good afternoon," people are now greeting each other with the phrase "What will become of us?"

During the morning, the city was still placed under air-raid alert.

My company announced that until everything becomes clearer, no female employees were to come to work and urged all of us to go to the countryside, adding that we should leave forwarding addresses. This measure was taken to conform to the step already taken by governmental bureaus. Are they thinking that the occupation army will do something to us girls? There are so many important questions we have to cope with, I cannot understand why governmental officials are so worried about these matters.

We did not have enough power and lost the war.

The Army continued to appeal to the people to resist the enemy to the end. This poses a lot of problems. People can show their true colors better when they are defeated than when they win. I just hope we, as a nation, can show our better side now.

Just because we have been defeated, I do not wish to see us destroying our national characteristics when we are dealing with foreign countries.

August 17: It was rumored that a number of lower echelon military officers were unhappy with the peace, and were making some secret moves. There were other rumors, and with the quiet evacuation of women and children from the cities, our fear seemed to have intensified. After all we have never experienced a defeat before. Our fear may simply be the manifestation of fear of the unknown.

Our airplanes dropped propaganda leaflets.

One of the leaflets was posted at the Kanda Station which said: "Both the Army and Navy are alive and well. We expect the nation to follow our lead." The leaflet

The Rise and Fall of the Japanese Empire in the Pacific War

Long before their sneak attack on Pearl Harbor on December 7, 1941, the Japanese had been engaged in a major war on the Chinese mainland. And even after Pearl Harbor roughly one-third of all Japanese military forces would remain bogged down in China, despite the sudden extension of the Japanese empire over much of Southeast Asia and far out into the Pacific. With the American Pacific fleet temporarily neutralized by the Japanese assault, combined air, sea, and army assaults quickly captured the colonial territories of the British in Hong Kong in south China as well as Malaya and Burma. They also overran the Dutch East Indies, the Philippines—despite more determined resistance—and completed the takeover of French Indochina. The Thais managed to stave off the invasion and occupation of Siam by retreating into neutrality and cooperating with the ascendant Japanese. Although Great Britain remained a major combatant, and Australia and New Zealand provided important support, the United States quickly emerged as the major counterforce to Japan's ever-expanding Asian empire.

Though impressive in size and the speed with which it was captured, the Japanese empire soon proved to be highly vulnerable to the Allied forces committed to its destruction. The Japanese had risked alienating virtually all of the European colonial powers by their seizure of much of Southeast Asia. They did so because they calculated

was signed. I could understand how those military men felt. However, we already have the imperial rescript to surrender. If we are going to rebuild, we must open a new path. It is much easier to die than to live. In the long history of our nation, this defeat may become one of those insignificant happenings. However, the rebuilding after the defeat is likely to be treated as a far more important chapter in our history.

We did our best and lost, so there is nothing we have to say in our own defense. Only those people who did not do their best may now be feeling guilty, though.

Mr. C. said that everything he saw in the city was so repugnant that he wanted to retreat to the countryside. I was amazed by the narrowness of his thought process. I could say that he had a pure sense of devotion to the country, but that was only his own way of thinking. Beautiful perhaps, but it lacked firm foundation. I wish men like him would learn to broaden their perspectives.

August 18: Rationed bread distribution in the morning. I went to the distribution center with Mrs. A.

August 21: We heard that the Allied advance units will be airlifted and arrive in Japan on the 26th. And the following day, their fleet will also anchor in our harbors. The American Army will be airlifted and land in Atsugi airport.

According to someone who accompanied the Japanese delegation which went to accept surrender conditions, the Americans behaved like gentlemen. They explained to the Americans that certain conditions were unworkable in light of the present situation in Japan. The Americans immediately agreed to alter those conditions. They listened very carefully to what the Japanese delegation had to say.

An American paper, according to someone, reported that meeting as follows; "We cooked thick beef-steak expecting seven or eight Japanese would appear. But seventeen of them came, so we had to kill a turkey to prepare for them. We treated them well before they returned." . . . When I hear things like this, I immediately feel how exaggerated and inefficient our ways of doing things are. They say that Americans will tackle one item after another at a conference table, and do not waste even 30 seconds. . . .

In contrast, Japanese administration is conducted by many chairs and seals. For example when an auxiliary unit is asked to undertake a task for a governmental bureau, before anything can be done, twenty, or thirty seals of approval must be secured. So there is no concept of not wasting time. Even in war, they are too accustomed to doing things the way they have been doing and their many seals and chairs are nothing but a manifestation of their refusal to take individual responsibilities.

The fact of a defeat is a very serious matter and it is not easy to accept. However, it can bring some positive effects, if it can inculcate in our minds all the shortcomings we have had. I hope this will come true some day, and toward that end we must all endeavor. Even if we have to suffer hunger and other tribulations we must strive toward a positive goal.

Questions: How did Japanese attitudes in defeat help prepare Japan for postwar redevelopment? Did defeat produce new divisions in attitudes among the Japanese? What other kinds of reactions might have been expected? How would you explain the rather calm and constructive outlook the passage suggests? Would American reactions to a Japanese victory have been similar?

---

that since the European metropoles had been overrun or were hard-pressed by the Nazis, the Europeans would not be able to reinforce their colonial enclaves. The Japanese leadership was also aware that the homeland's wartime economy was in desperate need of critical raw materials, including oil and staple foods, that could be imported from Southeast Asia. But in their efforts to extract those resources, the Japanese imposed colonial regimes on the peoples of Southeast Asia that were a good deal more brutally oppressive than those of any of the displaced Western colonizers. Over time, this produced growing resistance movements from Burma to the Philippines, which drew Japanese soldiers and substantial resources from the war in the Pacific against the advancing Allied forces.

Resistance fighters also cooperated with British and American forces pushing into the area in the latter stages of the war. Southeast Asian guerrilla forces, which often had communist affiliations, played significant roles in sabotaging occupying forces and harassing retreating Japanese armies. The shipping lanes from distant colonial enclaves throughout Southeast Asia also proved highly vulnerable to American submarines, which by late 1944 were able to sink a high percentage of the tons of foodstuffs and war materials shipped back to Japan.

The main front of the Pacific theater of the war centered on the widely scattered islands that Japan had begun to occupy before, and especially after, World War I, as well as those seized from the British and Americans after Pearl Harbor. No sooner had the Japanese garrisoned these enclaves than a hastily but well-prepared American advance into the central Pacific put them on the defensive. Having attacked Pearl Harbor when all of the major American aircraft carriers were at sea, the Japanese missed the chance to cripple the most potent weapons in the United States arsenal. Within six months, the U.S. naval and air forces fought the Japanese to a standoff at the Battle of the Coral Sea. In June, less than one month later, off Midway Island, they won a decisive victory over a powerful carrier force, commanded by Admiral Yamamoto, the architect of the Pearl Harbor attack. Once the Allied forces had gained the upper hand in the air and on the sea through these engagements, they could begin the assault on the double ring of Pacific island fortresses that protected the Japanese homeland.

Keying their amphibious assaults on strategically vital islands, the joint air, sea, and land operations of the Allied forces had come within striking distance of Japan itself by early 1944, despite fierce and unrelenting Japanese resistance. In June of that year, the American Air Force began regular bomber assaults on the Japanese home islands. The high concentration of the Japanese population in urban areas and the wood and paper construction of most Japanese dwellings provided tempting targets for American bomber squadrons. In March 1945, General Curtis Le May, who was in charge of American air operations, ordered mass aerial bombardment of highly vulnerable Japanese cities. In Tokyo alone, these raids killed over 125,000 people, mostly civilians, and destroyed over 40% of the city within days. At the same time, Allied naval superiority and submarine attacks had largely cut the home islands off from what remained of the empire in China and Southeast Asia.

By early summer in 1945, Japanese leaders were sending out peace feelers, while the more fanatical elements in the army were promising to fight to the death. The end was sudden and terrifying. On August 6, and three days later, atomic bombs were dropped on Hiroshima and Nagasaki, respectively. In a matter of a few seconds these cities, which to this point had been spared bombing, were reduced to ashes, with short-term casualties in both well over 100,000, and deaths from radiation sickness increasing this total greatly in the years, and even decades, that followed. Even more than in the European theater, the end of this long and most destructive war in human history came swiftly. As they had in dealing with Germany, the Allies demanded unconditional surrender by the Japanese. With the exception of retaining the em-

peror, which was finally allowed, the Japanese agreed to these terms and began to disarm. With the division of Germany that had begun some months earlier, the Allied occupation of the islands set the stage for the third main phase of the 20th century, which would be dominated by the cold war between the Soviet and American superpowers that would be waged amid the collapse of the European colonial order.

WAR'S END AND THE EMERGENCE OF THE SUPERPOWER STANDOFF

World War II did not produce the sweeping peace settlements, misguided as most of them turned out to be, that had officially ended World War I. The leaders of the Allies opposed to the Axis powers met on several occasions in an attempt to build the framework for a more lasting peace free of the vindictiveness that was so prominent at the Versailles gathering. A key result of Allied discussions was agreement on establishing the United Nations. From the outset, this new international organization was more representative of the world's peoples, in both large and small nations, than the League of Nations. The United States pledged to join, played a major role in the UN's planning and finance, and ultimately provided the site on the East River in Manhattan where the organization's permanent headquarters was ultimately located. The Soviet Union was also a charter member, along with longstanding great powers, such as Britain and France. And China, represented in the first decades after 1945 by the Guomindang, was grouped with these other global powers as a permanent member of the Security Council, the steering committee for UN operations. In the decades after the end of the war, the vanquished Axis powers were eventually granted membership as were the former colonies, soon after each gained their independence.

With the successful establishment of the UN, international diplomacy and assistance moved beyond the orbit of the Western powers, who had all but monopolized them for centuries, but through their vetos in the Security Council retained considerable control. Like the League of Nations, the UN's primary mission was to provide a forum for negotiating international disputes. But it also took over the apparatus of more specialized international agencies, including the World Court of Justice, those concerned with human rights, and those that coordinated programs directed at specific groups and problems, ranging from labor organization and famine relief to agricultural development and women's concerns. Although UN interventions to preserve or restore peace to numerous regions have encountered much resistance by both the great powers and regional power brokers, they have repeatedly proved vital to reducing violent conflict and providing refugee relief throughout the globe. The UN has also sponsored initiatives, including critical international conferences, that have proved highly influential in shaping policies and programs including child labor, women's rights, and environmental protection.

From Hot War to Cold War

The final stages of World War II quickly led to a tense confrontation between the United States and the Soviet Union, each backed by allies. The cold war pitted two different political and economic systems—capitalist versus communist, each of which displayed missionary zeal in attempting to prescribe policies for the rest of the world. It pitted two military giants—the great victors of World War II, with vast territories, population, and resources—in a bitter rivalry for more territory and influence. After a brief pause immediately after World War II, each side in the cold war embarked on massive military buildups, soon featuring nuclear weaponry and missile delivery systems. Each side sought military alliances and bases almost everywhere.

The cold war would last until the late 1980s, with various points of crisis and confrontation. Direct conflict between the two superpowers, did not occur, despite dire forebodings. Much of world history, however, was shaped by the cold war's maneuverings for over four decades.

The cold war began when the World War II allies turned, in the war's final conferences, to debate the nature of the postwar settlement. It quickly became apparent that the Soviet Union expected massive territorial gains and that Britain and the United States intended to limit these gains through their own areas of influence. Unresolved disputes—for World War II was never ended with a clear set of peace negotiations—then led to the full outbreak of the cold war between 1945 and 1949.

Tensions had clearly opened during the 1944 Teheran conference, when the allies agreed on the invasion of Nazi-occupied France. The decision to focus on France rather than moving up from the Mediterranean in effect gave the Soviet forces a free hand to move through the smaller nations of eastern Europe as they pushed the Nazi armies back. Britain negotiated separately with the Soviets to ensure Western preponderance in postwar Greece as well as equality in Hungary and Yugoslavia, with Soviet control of Romania and Bulgaria, but the United States resisted this kind of un-Wilsonian scorn for the rights of small nations.

The next settlement meeting took place in Yalta in the Soviet Crimea early in 1945. President Franklin Roosevelt of the United States was eager to press the Soviet Union for assistance against Japan and to this end promised the Soviets important territorial gains in Manchuria and the northern Japanese islands. The organization of the United Nations was confirmed. As to Europe, however, agreement was more difficult. The three powers easily arranged to divide Germany into four occupation zones (liberated France getting a chunk), which would be disarmed and purged of Nazi influence. Britain, however, resisted Soviet zeal to eliminate German industrial power, seeing a viable Germany as a potential ally in a subsequent Western-Soviet contest. Bitter dispute also raged over the smaller nations of eastern Europe. No one disagreed that they should be friendly to their Soviet neighbor, but the Western leaders also wanted them to be free and democratic. Stalin, the Soviet leader, had to make some concessions by including non-Communist leaders in what was already a Soviet-controlled government in liberated Poland—concessions that he soon violated.

The final postwar conference occurred in the Berlin suburb of Potsdam in July 1945. Russian forces now occupied not only most of eastern Europe but eastern Germany as well. This de facto situation prompted agreement that the Soviet Union could take over much of what had been eastern Poland, with the Poles gaining part of eastern Germany in compensation. Germany was divided pending a final peace treaty (which was not to come for more than 40 years). Austria was also divided and occupied, gaining unity and independence only in 1956, on condition of neutrality between the United States and the Soviet Union. Amid great difficulty, treaties were worked out for Germany's other allies, including Italy, but the United States and, later, the Soviet Union signed separate treaties with Japan.

All these maneuvers had several results. Japan was occupied by the United States and its wartime gains stripped away. Even Korea, taken earlier, was freed but was divided between U.S. and Soviet zones of occupation (the basis for the North Korea–South Korea division still in effect today). Former Asian colonies were returned to their old "masters," though often quite briefly, as new independence movements quickly challenged the control of the weakened imperialist powers. China regained most of its former territory, though here, too, stability was promptly challenged by renewed fighting between Communist and nationalist forces within the nation, aided by the Soviet Union and the United States, respectively.

The effort to confirm old colonial regimes applied also to the Middle East, India, and Africa. Indian and African troops had fought for Britain during the war, as in World War I, though Britain imprisoned key nationalist leaders and put independence plans on hold. African leaders had participated actively in the French resistance to its authoritarian wartime government. The Middle East and North Africa had been shaken by German invasions and Allied counterattacks. Irritability increased, and so did expectations for change. With Europe's imperial powers further weakened by their war effort, adjustments seemed inevitable, as in those parts of Asia invaded by the Japanese.

In Europe the boundaries of the Soviet Union pushed westward, with virtually all the losses after World War I erased. Independent nations created in 1918 were for the most part restored (though the former Baltic states of Latvia, Lithuania, and Estonia became Soviet republics because they had been Russian provinces before World War I). Except for Greece and Yugoslavia, the new nations quickly fell under Soviet domination, with Communist governments forced on them and Soviet troops in occupation. The nations of western Europe were free to set up or confirm democratic regimes, but most of them lived under the shadow of growing U.S. influence, manifested in continued occupation by U.S. troops, substantial economic aid and coordination, and no small amount of outright policy manipulation.

The stage was set, in other words, for two of the great movements that would shape the ensuing decades in world history. The first comprised challenges by subject peoples to the tired vestiges of control by the great European empires—the movement known as "decolonization" that in a few decades would create scores of new nations in Asia, Africa, and the West Indies. The second great theme was the confrontation between the two superpowers that emerged from the war—the United States and the Soviet Union, each with new international influence and new military might. This confrontation was quickly dubbed the "cold war," and many believed it would soon become a war in a more literal and devastating sense.

That these trends constituted a peace settlement was difficult to imagine in 1945 or 1947, yet they seemed the best that could be done.

NATIONALISM AND DECOLONIZATION

The effects of a second global conflict, brought on by the expansionist ambitions of Hitler's Germany and of imperial Japan, proved fatal to the already badly battered European colonial empires. The sobering casualties of yet another war between the industrialized powers sapped the will of the Western colonizers to engage in further conflicts that would clearly be needed to crush resurgent nationalist movements throughout Africa and Asia. From India and Pakistan to West Africa, independence was won in most of the nonsettler colonies with surprisingly little bloodshed and remarkable speed. But in areas such as Algeria, Kenya, and South Africa, where large European settler communities tried to block nationalist agitation, liberation struggles were usually violent and costly and at times far from complete.

The Nazi rout of the French and the stunningly rapid Japanese capture of the French, Dutch, British, and United States colonies in Southeast Asia put an end to whatever illusions the colonized peoples of Africa and Asia had left about the strength and innate superiority of their colonial overlords. Because the Japanese were non-Europeans, their early victories over the Europeans and Americans played a particularly critical role in destroying the myth of the white man's invincibility. The fall of the "impregnable" fortress at Singapore on the southern tip of Malaya, and the American reverses at Pearl Harbor and in the Philippines proved to be blows from which the colonizers never quite recovered, even though they went on to eventually defeat the Japanese. The sight of tens of thousands of British, Dutch, and American troops, struggling under the supervision of the victorious Japanese to survive the "death marches" to prison camps in their former colonies, left an indelible impression on the Asian villagers who saw them pass by. The harsh regimes and heavy demands that the Japanese conquerors imposed on the peoples of Southeast Asia during the war further strengthened their determination to fight for self-rule and to look to their own defenses after the conflict was over.

The devastation of World War II—a total war fought in the cities and countryside over much of Europe—drained the resources of the European powers. This devastating warfare also sapped the will of the European populace to hold increasingly resistant African and Asian peoples in bondage. The war also greatly enhanced the power and influence of the two giants on the European periphery: the United States and the Soviet Union. In Africa and the Middle East, as well as in the Pacific, the United States approached the war as a campaign of liberation. American propagandists made no secret of Franklin Roosevelt's hostility to colonialism in their efforts to win Asian and African support for the Allied war effort. In fact American intentions in this regard were enshrined in the Atlantic Charter of 1941. This pact sealed an alliance between the United States and Great Britain that the latter desperately needed to survive in its war with Nazi Germany. In it Roosevelt persuaded a reluctant Churchill to include a clause that recognized the "right of all people to choose the form of government under which they live." The Soviets were equally vocal in their condemnation of colonialism and were even more forthcoming with material support for nationalist campaigns after the war. In the cold war world of the superpowers that emerged after 1945, there was little room for the domination that the much-reduced powers of western Europe had once exercised over much of the globe.

The Winning of Independence in South and Southeast Asia

The outbreak of World War II soon put an end to the accommodation between the Indian National Congress and the British in the late 1930s. Congress leaders offered to support the Allies' war effort if the British would give them a significant share of power at the all-India level and commit themselves to Indian independence once the conflict was over. These conditions were staunchly rejected both by the viceroy in India and at home by Winston Churchill, who headed the coalition government that led Britain through the war. Labour members of the coalition government, however, indicated that they were quite willing to negotiate India's eventual independence. As tensions built between nationalist agitators and the British rulers, Sir Stafford Cripps was sent to India in early 1942 to see whether a deal could be struck with the Indian leaders. Indian divisions and British intransigence led to the collapse of Cripps's initiative and the renewal of mass civil disobedience campaigns under the guise of the Quit India movement, which began in the summer of 1942.

The British responded with repression and mass arrests, and for much of the remainder of the war, Gandhi, Nehru, and other major Congress politicians were imprisoned. Of the Indian nationalist parties, only the Communists—who were committed to the anti-Fascist alliance—and, more ominously, the Muslim League rallied to the British cause. The League, now led by a former Congress party politician, the dour and uncompromising Muhammad Ali Jinnah, won much favor from the British for its wartime support. As their demands for a separate Muslim state in the subcontinent hardened, the links between the British and Jinnah and other League leaders became a key factor in the struggle for decolonization in South Asia.

World War II brought disruptions to India similar to those caused by the earlier global conflict. Inflation stirred up urban unrest, while a widespread famine in 1943 and 1944, brought on in part by wartime transport shortages, engendered much bitterness in rural India. Winston Churchill's defeat in the first postwar British election in 1945 brought a Labour government to power that was ready to deal with India's nationalist leaders. With independence in the near future tacitly conceded, the process of decolonization between 1945 and 1947 focused on what sort of state or states would be carved out of the subcontinent after the British withdrawal. Jinnah and the League had begun to build a mass following among the Muslims. In order to rally support they played on widespread anxieties among the Muslim minority that a single Indian nation would be dominated by the Hindu majority, and that the Muslims would become the targets of increasing discrimination. It was therefore essential, they insisted, that a separate Muslim state called Pakistan be created from those areas in northwest and east India where Muslims were the most numerous.

As communal rioting spread throughout India, the British and key Congress party politicians reluctantly concluded that a bloodbath could be averted only by partition—the creation of two nations in the subcontinent: one secular, one Muslim. Thus, in the summer of 1947, the British handed power over to the leaders of the majority Congress party, who headed the new nation of India, and to Jinnah, who became the first president of Pakistan.

In part because of the haste with which the British withdrew their forces from the deeply divided subcontinent, a bloodbath occurred anyway. Vicious Hindu-Muslim and Muslim-Sikh communal rioting, in which neither women nor children were spared, took the lives of

As this photo of Mahatma Gandhi beside his spinning wheel suggests, he played many roles in the Indian nationalist struggle. The wheel evokes India's traditional status as a textile center and the economic boycotts of British machine-made cloth that were central to Gandhi's civil disobedience campaigns. Gandhi's meditative position projects the image of a religious guru that appealed to large segments of the Indian populace. The simplicity of his surroundings evokes the asceticism and detachment from the material world that had long been revered in Indian culture.

hundreds of thousands in the searing summer heat across the plains of northwest India. Whole villages were destroyed; trains pulled into railway stations that were packed with corpses hacked to death by armed bands of rival religious adherents. These atrocities fed a massive exchange of refugee populations between Hindu-Sikh and Muslim areas that may have totaled 10 million people. Those who fled were so terrified that they were willing to give up their land, their villages, and most of their worldly possessions. The losses of partition were compounded by the fact that there was soon no longer a Gandhi to preach tolerance and communal coexistence. On January 30, 1948, he was shot by a Hindu fanatic while on his way to one of his regular prayer meetings.

In granting independence to India, the British in effect removed the keystone from the arch of an empire that spanned three continents. Burma (known today as Myanmar) and Ceylon (now named Sri Lanka) won their independence peacefully in the following years. India's independence and Gandhi's civil disobedience campaigns, which had done so much to win a mass following for the nationalist cause, also inspired successful struggles for independence in Ghana, Nigeria, and other African colonies in the 1950s and 1960s.

The retreat of the most powerful of the imperial powers could not help but contribute to the weakening of lesser empires such as those of the Dutch, the French, and the Americans. In fact, the process of the transfer of power from United States officials to moderate, middle-class Filipino politicians was well under way before World War II broke out. The loyalty to the Americans that most Filipinos displayed during the war, as well as the stubborn guerrilla resistance they put up against the Japanese occupation, did much to bring about the rapid granting of independence to the Philippines once the war was ended. The Dutch and French were less willing to follow the British example and relinquish their colonial possessions in the postwar era. From 1945 to 1949, the Dutch fought a losing war to destroy the nation of Indonesia, which nationalists in the Netherlands Indies had established when the Japanese hold over the islands broke down in mid-1945. The French struggled to retain Indochina. Communist revolutions in East Asia also emerged victorious in the postwar period. No sooner had the European colonizers suffered these losses than they were forced to deal with new threats to the last bastions of the imperial order in Africa.

The Liberation of Nonsettler Africa

World War II proved even more disruptive to the colonial order imposed on Africa than the first global conflict of the European powers. Forced labor and confiscations of crops and minerals returned, and inflation and controlled markets again cut down on African earnings. African recruits in the hundreds of thousands were drawn once more into the conflict and had even greater opportunities to use the latest European weapons to destroy Europeans. African servicemen had witnessed British and French defeats in the Middle East and Southeast Asia, and they fought bravely only to experience renewed racial discrimination once they returned home. Many were soon among the staunchest supporters of postwar nationalist campaigns in the African colonies of the British and French. The swift and humiliating rout of the French and Belgians by Nazi armies in the spring of 1940 shattered whatever was left of the colonizers' reputation for military prowess. It also led to a bitter and, in the circumstances, embarrassing struggle between the forces of the puppet Vichy regime and those of De Gaulle's Free French, who continued fighting the Nazis mainly in France's North and West African colonies.

The wartime needs of both the British and the Free French led to major departures from long-standing colonial policies that had restricted industrial development throughout Africa. Factories were established to process urgently needed vegetable oils, foods, and minerals in western and south-central Africa. These in turn contributed to a growing migration on the part of African peasants to the towns and a sharp spurt in African urban growth. The inability of many of those who moved to the towns to find employment made for a reservoir of disgruntled, idle workers that would be skillfully tapped by nationalist politicians in the postwar decades.

There were essentially two main paths to decolonization in nonsettler Africa in the postwar era. The first was pioneered by Kwame Nkrumah and his followers in the British Gold Coast colony, which, as the nation of Ghana, became the first independent black African state in 1957. Nkrumah epitomized the more radical sort of African leader that emerged throughout Africa after the war. Educated in African missionary schools and the United States, he had established wide contacts with nationalist leaders in both British and French West Africa and civil rights leaders in America prior to his return to the Gold Coast in the late 1940s. He returned to a land in ferment. The restrictions of government-controlled marketing boards and their favoritism for British merchants had led to widespread, but nonviolent, protest in the coastal cities. But after the police fired on a peaceful demonstration of ex-servicemen in 1948, rioting broke out in many towns.

Though both urban workers and cash crop farmers had supported the unrest, Western-educated African leaders were slow to organize these dissident groups into a sustained mass movement. Their reluctance arose in part from their fear of losing major political concessions, such as seats on colonial legislative councils, that the British had just made. Rejecting the caution urged by more established political leaders, Nkrumah resigned his position as chairman of the dominant political party in the Gold Coast and established his own Convention Peoples Party (CPP). Even before the formal break, he had signaled the arrival of a new style of politics by organizing mass rallies, boycotts, and strikes.

In the mid-1950s, Nkrumah's mass following, and his growing stature as a leader who would not be deterred by imprisonment or British threats, won repeated concessions from the British. Educated Africans were given more and more representation in legislative bodies, and gradually they took over administration of the colony. The British recognition of Nkrumah as the prime minister of an independent Ghana in 1957 simply concluded a transfer of power from the European colonizers to the Western-educated African elite that had been under way for nearly a decade.

The peaceful devolution of power to African nationalists led to the independence of the British nonsettler colonies in black Africa by the mid-1960s. Independence in the comparable areas of the French and Belgian empires in Africa came in a somewhat different way. Hard-pressed by costly military struggles to hold on to their colonies in Indochina and Algeria, the French took a much more conciliatory line in dealing with the many peoples they ruled in West Africa. Ongoing negotiations with such highly Westernized leaders as Senegal's Senghor and the Ivory Coast's Felix Houphouât-Boigny led to reforms and political concessions. The slow French retreat ensured that moderate African leaders, who were eager to retain French economic and cultural ties, would dominate the nationalist movements and the postindependence period in French West Africa. Between 1956 and 1960, the French colonies moved by stages toward nationhood—a process that sped up after de Gaulle's return to power in 1958. By 1960, all of France's West African colonies were free.

In the same year, the Belgians completed a much hastier retreat from their huge colonial possession in the Congo. Their virtual flight was epitomized by the fact that there was little in the way of an organized nationalist movement to pressure them into concessions of any kind. In fact, by design there were scarcely any well-educated Congolese to lead resistance to Belgian rule. At independence in 1960, there were only 16 African college graduates in a Congolese population that exceeded 13 million. Though the Portuguese still clung to their impoverished and scattered colonial territories, by the mid-1960s the European colonial era had come to an end in all but the settler societies of Africa.

Repression and Guerrilla War: The Struggle for the Settler Colonies

The pattern of relatively peaceful withdrawal by stages that characterized the process of decolonization in most of Asia and Africa proved unworkable in most of the settler colonies. These included areas like Algeria, Kenya, and Southern Rhodesia, where substantial numbers of Europeans had gone to settle permanently in the 19th and early 20th centuries. South Africa, which had begun to be settled by Europeans centuries earlier, provided few openings for nationalist agitation except that mounted by the politically and economically dominant colonists of European descent. In each case, the presence of European settler communities, varying in size from millions in South Africa and Algeria to tens of thousands in Kenya and Southern Rhodesia, blocked both the rise of indigenous nationalist movements and concessions on the part of the colonial overlords.

Because the settlers regarded the colonies to which they had emigrated as their permanent homes, they fought all attempts to turn political control over to the African majority or even to grant them civil rights. They also doggedly refused all reforms by colonial administrators that required them to give up any of the lands they had occupied, often at the expense of indigenous African peoples. Unable to make headway through nonviolent protest tactics—which were forbidden—or negotiations with British or French officials, who were fearful of angering the highly vocal settler minority, many African leaders turned to violent, revolutionary struggles to win their peoples' independence.

The first of these erupted in Kenya in the early 1950s. Impatient with the failure of the nonviolent approach adopted by Jomo Kenyatta and the leading nationalist party, the Kenya African Union (KAU), an underground organization, coalesced around a group of more radical leaders. After forming the Land Freedom Army in the early 1950s, the radicals mounted a campaign of terror and guerrilla warfare against the British, the settlers, and Africans who were considered collaborators. At the height of the struggle in 1954, some 200,000 rebels were in action in the capital at Nairobi and in the forest reserves of the central Kenyan highlands. The British responded with an all-out military effort to crush the guerrilla movement, which was dismissed as an explosion of African savagery and labelled the "Mau Mau" by the colonizers, not the rebels. In the process, the British, at the settlers' insistence, imprisoned Kenyatta and the KAU organizers, thus eliminating the nonviolent alternative to the guerrillas.

The rebel movement had been militarily defeated by 1956 at the cost of thousands of lives. But the British were now in a mood to negotiate with the nationalists, despite strong objections from the European settlers. Kenyatta was released from prison, and he emerged as the spokesman for the Africans of Kenya. By 1963, a multiracial Kenya had won its independence. Under what was in effect Kenyatta's one-party rule, it remained until the mid-1980s one of the most stable and more prosperous of the new African states.

The struggle of the Arab and Berber peoples of Algeria for independence was longer and even more vicious than that in Kenya. Algeria had for decades been regarded by the French as an integral part of France—a department just like Provence or Brittany. The presence of more than a million European settlers in the colony only served to bolster the resolve of French politicians to retain it at all costs. But in the decade after World War II, sporadic rioting grew into sustained guerrilla resistance. By the mid-1950s, the National Liberation Front (FLN) had mobilized large segments of the Arab and Berber population of the colony in a full-scale revolt against French rule and settler or *colon* dominance. High ranking French army officers came to see the defeat of this movement as a way to restore a reputation that had been badly tarnished by recent defeats in Vietnam (see Chapter 12). As in Kenya, the rebels were defeated in the field. But they gradually negotiated the independence of Algeria after de Gaulle came to power in 1958. The French people had wearied of the seemingly endless war, and de Gaulle became convinced that he could not restore France to great power status as long as its resources continued to be drained by the Algerian conflict.

Algerians celebrate in Oran as French barricades are torn down by members of the local Arab militia and Arab civilians just after independence is announced in July 1962. The barricades were erected throughout the colony to deny access to areas where Europeans were resident to the Arabs and Berbers, who made up the overwhelming majority of the population. Although cities such as Oran and Algiers had long been segregated into "native" and European quarters, the protracted and bloody war for independence fought by the Arab and Berber peoples had resulted in full-scale occupation by the French army and the physical separation of settler and Arab-Berber areas.

In contrast to Kenya, the Algerian struggle was prolonged and brutalized by a violent settler backlash. Led after 1960 by the Secret Army Organization (OAS), it was directed against the Arabs and Berbers as well as French settlers who favored independence for the colony. With strong support from elements in the French military, earlier resistance by the settlers had managed to topple the government in Paris in 1958, thereby putting an end to the Fourth Republic. In the early 1960s, the OAS came close to assassinating de Gaulle and overthrowing the Fifth Republic, which his accession to power had brought into existence. In the end, however, the Algerians won their independence in 1962. After the bitter civil war, the multiracial accommodation worked out in Kenya appeared out of the question as far as the settlers of Algeria were concerned. More than 900,000 left the new nation within months after its birth. In addition, tens of thousands of *harkis,* or Arabs and Berbers who had sided with the French in the long war for independence, fled to France. They, and later migrants, formed the core of the substantial Algerian population now present in France.

The Persistence of White Supremacy in South Africa

In southern Africa, violent revolutions also put an end to white settler dominance in the Portuguese colonies of Angola and Mozambique in 1975 and in Southern Rhodesia (now Zimbabwe) by 1980. Only in South Africa did the white minority manage to maintain its position of supremacy. Its ability to do so rested on several factors that distinguished it from other settler societies. To begin with, the white population of South Africa, roughly equally divided between the Dutch-descended Afrikaners and the more recently arrived English speakers, was a good deal larger than that of any of the other settler societies. Though they were only a small minority in a country of 23 million black Africans and 3.5 million East Indians and coloreds (mulattos, in American parlance), by the mid-1980s, South Africa's settler-descended population had reached 4.5 million.

Unlike the settlers in Kenya and Algeria, who had the option of retreating to Europe as full citizens of France or Great Britain, the Afrikaners in particular had no European homeland to fall back upon. They had lived in

South Africa as long as other Europeans had in North America, and they considered themselves quite distinct from the Dutch. Over the centuries, the Afrikaners had also built up what was for them a persuasive ideology of white racist supremacy. Though crude by European or American standards, Afrikaner racism was far more explicit and elaborate than that developed by the settlers of any other colony. Afrikaner ideology was grounded in selected biblical quotations and the celebration of their historic struggle to "tame a beautiful but hard land" in the face of opposition from both the African "savages" and the British "imperialists."

Ironically, their defeat by the British in the Anglo-Boer War from 1899 to 1902 also contributed much to the capacity of the white settler minority to maintain its place of dominance in South Africa. A sense of guilt, arising especially from their treatment of Boer women and children during the war—tens of thousands of whom died of disease in what the British called concentration camps—led the victors to make major concessions to the Afrikaners in the postwar decades. The most important of these was internal political control, which included turning over the fate of the black African majority to the openly racist supremist Afrikaners. Not surprisingly, the continued subjugation of the black Africans became a central aim of the Afrikaner political organizations that emerged in the 1930s and 1940s, culminating in the Afrikaner National Party. From 1948, when it emerged as the majority party in the all-white South African legislature, the National Party devoted itself to winning complete independence from Britain (which came without violence in 1961) and to establishing lasting white domination over the political, social, and economic life of the new nation.

A rigid system of racial segregation (which will be discussed more fully in Chapter 11), called "apartheid" by the Afrikaners, was established after 1948 through the passage of thousands of laws. Among other things, this legislation reserved the best jobs for whites and carefully defined the sorts of contacts permissible between different racial groups. The right to vote and political representation were denied to the black Africans, and ultimately to the coloreds and Indians. It was illegal for members of any of these groups to hold mass meetings or to organize political parties or labor unions. These restrictions, combined with very limited opportunities for higher education for black Africans, hampered the growth of black African political parties and their efforts to mobilize popular support for the struggle for decolo-

nization. The Afrikaners' establishment of a vigilant and brutal police state to uphold apartheid and their opportunistic cultivation of divisions between the diverse peoples in the black African population, also contributed to their ability to preserve a bastion of white supremacy in an otherwise liberated continent.

Conflicting Nationalisms: Arabs, Israelis, and the Palestinian Question

Although virtually all Arab peoples who were not yet free by the end of World War II were liberated by the early 1960s, the fate of Palestine continued to present special problems. Hitler's campaign of genocide against the European Jews had provided powerful support for the Zionists' insistence that the Jews must have their own homeland, which more and more was conceived in terms of a modern national state. The brutal persecution of the Jews also won international sympathy for the Zionist cause. This was in part due to the fact that the leaders of many nations, including the United States and Great Britain, were reluctant to admit Jews fleeing the Nazi terror into their own countries. As Hitler's henchmen stepped up their race war against the Jews, the tide of Jewish immigration to Palestine rose sharply. But growing Arab resistance to Jewish settlement and land purchases in Palestine, which was often expressed in communal rioting and violent assaults on Zionist communities, led to increasing British restrictions on the entry of Jews into the colony.

A major Muslim revolt swept Palestine between 1936 and 1939. The British managed to put down this rising but only with great difficulty. It both decimated the leadership of the Palestinian Arab community and further strengthened the British resolve to stem the flow of Jewish immigrants to Palestine. Government measures to keep out Jewish refugees from Nazi oppression led in turn to violent Zionist resistance to the British presence in Palestine. The Zionist assault was spearheaded by a regular Zionist military force, the Haganah, and several underground terrorist organizations.

By the end of World War II, the major parties claiming Palestine were locked into a deadly stalemate. The Zionists were determined to carve out a Jewish state in the region. The Palestinian Arabs and their allies in neighboring Arab lands were equally determined to transform Palestine into a multireligious nation in which the position of the Arab majority would be ensured. Having badly bungled their mandatory responsibilities,

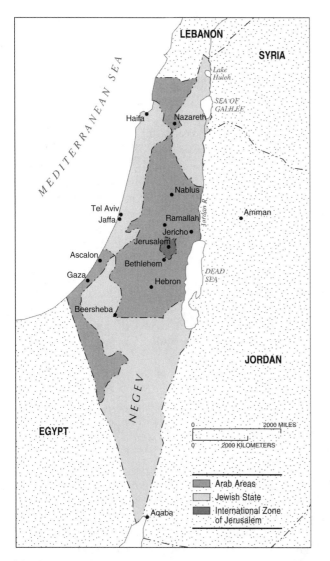

The Partition of Palestine after World War II

with the United States and the Soviet Union in rare agreement—approved the partition of Palestine into Arab and Jewish countries.

The Arab states that bordered the newly created nation of Israel had vehemently opposed the UN's action. Soon the two sides were engaged in all-out warfare. Though heavily outnumbered, the Zionists proved to be better armed and much better prepared to defend themselves than almost anyone could have expected. Not only did they hold onto the tiny, patchwork state they had been given by the United Nations, they expanded it at the Arabs' expense. The brief but bloody war that ensued created hundreds of thousands of Palestinian Arab refugees. It also sealed the persisting hostility between Arabs and Israelis that has been the all-consuming issue in the region and a major international problem to the present day. In Palestine, conflicting strains of nationalism had collided. As a result, the legacy of colonialism proved even more of a liability to social and economic development than in much of the rest of newly independent Africa and Asia.

CONCLUSION: THE LIMITS OF DECOLONIZATION

Given the fragile foundations on which it rested, the rather rapid demise of the European colonial order is not really surprising. The winning of political freedom in Asia and Africa also represented less of a break with the colonial past than the appearance of many new nations on the map of the world might lead one to assume. The decidedly nonrevolutionary, elite-to-elite transfer of power that was central to the liberation process in most colonies, even those where there were violent guerrilla movements, limited the extent of the social and economic transformation that occurred. The Western-educated African and Asian classes moved into the offices and took the jobs—and often the former homes—of the European colonizers. But social gains for the rest of the population in most new nations were minimal or nonexistent.

In Kenya, Algeria, and Zimbabwe (formerly Southern Rhodesia), abandoned European lands were distributed to Arab and African peasants and laborers. But in most former colonies, especially in Asia, the big landholders that remained were indigenous, and they have held on tenaciously to their holdings. Educational reforms were carried out to include more sciences in school curricula and the history of Asia or Africa rather than Europe. But

and under attack from both sides, the British wanted more than anything else to scuttle and run. The 1937 report of a British commission of inquiry supplied a possible solution: partition. The newly created United Nations provided an international body that could give a semblance of legality to the proceedings. In 1948, with sympathy for the Jews running high because of the postwar revelations of the horrors of Hitler's Final Solution, a majority of the member states of the United Nations—

Western cultural influences have remained strong in almost all of the former colonies. Indians and many West Africans with higher educations continue to communicate in English. Some of the most prominent of the leaders of former French colonies continue to pride themselves on their impeccable French, decorate their presidential palaces with French antiques, and keep in touch closely with trends in French intellectual circles.

The liberation of the colonies also did little to disrupt Western dominance of the terms of international trade or the global economic order more generally. In fact, in the negotiations that led to decolonization, Asian and African leaders often explicitly promised to protect the interests of Western merchants and businessmen in the postindependence era. As we shall see in the next chapter, these and other limits that sustained Western influence and often dominance, even after freedom was won, greatly reduced the options open to nationalist leaders struggling to build viable and prosperous nations. Though new forces have also played important roles, the postindependence history of colonized peoples cannot be understood without a consideration of the lingering effects of the colonial interlude in their history.

FURTHER READING

Two of the most genuinely global histories of World War II, which also include extensive accounts of the origins of the war in both Europe and the Pacific, are Gerhard L. Weinberg's *A World at Arms: A Global History of World War II* (1994) and Peter Calvocoressi and Guy Wint's *Total War: Causes and Courses of the Second World War* (1972). For a good overview of the coming of the war in Europe from the British perspective, see Christopher Thorne, *The Approach of War 1938–1939* (1967), and from the German viewpoint, Gerhard L. Weinberg, *Germany, Hitler, and World War II* (1995). A fine analysis of the underlying patterns in the European theater can be found in Gordon Wright, *The Ordeal of Total War, 1939–1945* (1968).

From a prodigious literature on the Holocaust, some good works to begin with are Hannah Arendt's brilliant *Eichmann in Jerusalem* (1963) and Raul Hilberg's *Destruction of the European Jews* (1985). Christopher Browning's *Ordinary Men* (1992) provides a chilling account of some of those who actually carried out the killings, while Viktor Frankl's *Man's Search for Meaning* (1959) is one of the most poignant of the numerous autobiographical accounts of the concentration camps. Omer Bartov provides a thoughtful meditation on the wider meanings of the Holocaust for 20th-century history in *Murder in Our Midst* (1996).

On the causes of the Pacific war, see Michael Barnhart's *Japan Prepares for Total War* (1987) and William O'Neill's *A Democracy at War* (1993). On the course of the war in the Pacific from differing perspectives, see Ronald Spector's *Eagle Against the Sun* (1985), Saburò Ienaga's *The Pacific War, 1931–1945* (1978), and John Dower's *War Without Mercy: Race and Power in the Pacific War* (1986). On the end of the war and the forces that led to the cold war, see Martin Sherwin's *A World Destroyed: The Atomic Bomb and the Grand Alliance* (1975), William Craig's *The Fall of Japan* (1967), Herbert Feis's *From Trust to Terror: The Onset of the Cold War, 1945–1950* (1970), and Melvyn Leffler's *A Preponderance of Power: National Security, the Truman Administration, and the Cold War* (1992).

A thoughtful overview of the process of decolonization in the British empire as a whole can be found in the works of John Darwin. In addition to P. J. Vatikiotis's general *History of Egypt*, mentioned in Chapter 5, Jacques Berque's, *Egypt: Imperialism and Revolution* (1972) and Peter Mansfield's, *The British in Egypt* (1971) provide detailed accounts of the nationalist revolt and early years of quasi independence. The struggles for decolonization in Africa are surveyed by Ali A. Mazrui and Michael Tidy, *Nationalism and New States in Africa* (1984); J. D. Hargreaves, *Decolonization in Africa* (1988); and W. R. Louis and P. Gifford, eds., *Decolonization in Africa* (1984).

From the very substantial literature on the rise of nationalism in settler societies, some of the best studies include C. Roseberg and J. Nottingham, *The Myth of "Mau Mau"* (1966) on Kenya; the writings of Terrence Ranger on Rhodesia; and Alastair Horne, *A Savage War of Peace* (1977) on Algeria. Of the many works on South Africa, the general histories of S. Throup, B. Bunting, T. D. Moodie, and Leonard Thompson provide a good introduction to the rise of Afrikaner power. The period of the partition and the first Arab-Israeli conflict have been the subject of much revisionist scholarship in recent years. Some of the best of this is included in important books by Benny Morris, Walid Khalidi, Ilan Pappé, and Tom Segev.

On the United States in the cold war decades, see Walter Lafeber's *America, Russia, and the Cold War, 1945–1980* (1993). Ronald Powaski's *The Cold War: The United States and the Soviet Union, 1917–1991* (1998) is a reliable and readable standard political history that synthesizes the historiography of the Cold War. Ellen Schrecker's *Many Are the Crimes: McCarthyism in America* (1998) has a broad social history of political and cultural legacy of the Red Scare. T. H. Etzold and J. L. Gaddis, eds., *Containment: Documents on American Policy and Strategy, 1945–1950* (1978), provides primary source material on the political history of the early cold war.

ON THE WEB

A superb starting point for the on-line study of World War II can be found at

http://www.historywiz.com/worldwartwo.htm

The site features links to battle histories, oral histories, and exhibits, and it offers an audio file of President Truman's speech announcing the use of the atomic bomb against Japan. Other useful links can be found at

http://history.acusd.edu/gen/ww2_links.html

This site leads to sources organized by battles and by countries, including the battle for Stalingrad and the role of Russia in the war. Yale University provides a digital library for World War II documents at

http://www.yale.edu/lawweb/avalon/wwii/wwii.htm

Rutgers University offers records of personal experiences at

http://fas-history.rutgers.edu/oralhistory/orlhom.htm

This can be supplemented by other collections at

http://www.ibiscom.com/w2frm.htm
http://clicksmart.co.uk/History/WW2/
http://www.geocities.com/Athens/Oracle/2691/links.htm
http://www.fsu.edu/~ww2/links.htm

A variety of links to sites ranging from combat stories to prisoner of war experiences can also be found here.

Dramatic recreations or virtual visits to key sites of World War II conflicts abound on the Web. Hiroshima is discussed at

http://titan.iwu.edu/~rwilson/hiroshima/

the siege of Leningrad at

http://www.cityvision2000.com/history/900days.htm

and Pearl Harbor at

http://execpc.com/~dschaaf/mainmenu.html
http://www.hawaii.navy.mil/cnbdata/cnbdata/7dec98/virtour.htm
http://plasma.nationalgeographic.com/pearlharbor/

The concept of blitzkrieg or "lightning war" is explained at

http://www.achtungpanzer.com/blitz.htm

The role of the American home front and American women in World War II is explored through photographs and interviews at

http://www.pomperaug.com/socstud/stumuseum/web/ARHhome.htm
http://www.u.arizona.edu/~kari/rosie.htm
http://www.wasp-wwii.org/
http://www.stg.brown.edu/projects/WWII_Women/WomenInWWII.html

The experience of internment and death camps for civilians and prisoners of war in German-, Russian-, and Japanese-held territories is examined at

http://www.vikingphoenix.com/public/rongstad/military/pow/pow.htm
http://www.mansell.com/pow-index.html

The removal of the Japanese American population in the United States to internment camps during World War II is discussed at

http://www.geocities.com/Athens/8420/main.html

The internment camp experience is examined through posters at

http://bss.sfsu.edu/internment/posters.html

Many Japanese internment camps in the United States have their own dedicated Web site, including

http://www.nps.gov/manz/
http://www.library.arizona.edu/wracamps/

Overviews and interactive digital databases for the Holocaust are provided at

http://www.remember.org
http://www.holocaust-history.org
http://www.ushmm.org

See also the excellent teacher's resource that offers study guides, documents, and essays at

http://fcit.coedu.usf.edu/holocaust/resource/document/DocPropa.htm

A map of Nazi concentration camps is provided at

http://history1900s.about.com/library/holocaust/
   blmap.htm

There are several sites devoted to those who struggled against the Holocaust, including Oskar Schindler at

http://auschwitz.dk/Schindler2.htm

and Raul Wallenberg at

http://www.usisrael.org/jsource/biography/wallenberg
   .html

The struggle against those who seek to deny the genocidal nature of the Nazi regime is addressed at

http://www.holocausthistory.org/

The search for meaning in the Holocaust has been pioneered by one of its victims, Simon Wiesenthal at

http://www.wiesenthal.com/

Information on Anne Frank lends a human face to both fascist oppression and the quest for a world without hatred at

http:// www.annefrank.nl/
http://www.annefrank.com
http://www.nicole-caspari.de/annefrank/e_links.html
http://www.coollessons.org/holocaust.htm

That this holocaust is but one of many human genocides is the subject of several sites that offer comparative analyses or links to other examples from Cambodia to Rwanda. These include

http://www.ess.uwe.ac.uk/genocide.htm
http://www.yale.edu/cgp/
http://www.webster.edu/~woolflm/holocaust.html
http://www.sage.edu/RSC/programs/globcomm/
   division/courses/history/wwwhol.html

Northwestern University offers a superb collection of American World War II posters at

http://www.library.northwestern.edu/govpub/
   collections/wwii-posters/

A Canada-based collection of Allied posters can be found at

http://www.pma.edmonton.ab.ca/vexhibit/warpost/
   english/home.htm

The Soviet Union's use of poster art to cast the war against Germany as the "Great Patriotic War" is illustrated at

http://www.funet.fi/pub/culture/russian/html_pages/
   posters1.html

Other sources for Soviet posters (including a small collection of Ukrainian posters) can be found at

http://www.brama.com/art/poster.html

A short film of Gandhi visiting London can be seen at

http://www.historychannel.com/speeches/index.html

The winning of India's independence as well as Gandhi's last years and his assassination are discussed at

http://www.colorado.edu/conflict/peace/example/
   wehr7496.htm
http://www.pbs.org/weta/forcemorepowerful/india/
   satyagraha.html

Many resource lists and examples of others who have followed the path of nonviolence in India and abroad are discussed at

http://www.pbs.org/weta/forcemorepowerful/classroom/
   resources.html
http://www.transnational.org/forum/Nonviolence/
   Nonviolence.html
http://nonviolenceinternational.net/seasia/
   Learn_%20nonviolence/Index.htm
http://edition.cnn.com/WORLD/9708/India97/india/
   gandhi.legacy/

Jawaharlal Nehru's life and role in the freedom movement is explored at

http://www.pbs.org/wgbh/commandingheights/shared/
   minitextlo/prof_jawaharlalnehru.html

His "tryst with destiny" speech that inaugurated a new chapter in the history of the Indian subcontinent can be read at

http://www.itihaas.com/independent/speech.html
http://www.fordham.edu/halsall/mod/1947nehru1.html

It can be heard at

http://www.harappa.com/sounds/nehru.html

A newsreel covering the birth of Pakistan can be viewed at

http://harappa.com/wall/pakistan.html

The birth of Bangladesh is traced at

http://www.virtualbangladesh.com/

The generation of leaders who helped secure Africa's freedom is well represented on the Internet. For Léopold Senghor, poet of négritude and president of Senegal, see

http://web.uflib.ufl.edu/cm/africana/senghor.htm

Links to Tanzania's Julius Nyerere's life and speeches can be found at

http://www.hartford-hwp.com/archives/30/index-fd.html

Jomo Kenyatta and his role in the Land Freedom Army and Mau Mau movements are discussed at

http://www.kenyaweb.com/history/struggle/
http://www.ccs.neu.edu/home/feneric/maumau.html

The anticolonial role of the African National Congress party as well its earliest beginnings with Nelson Mandela are discussed at

http://www.anc.org.za/

Apartheid in South Africa is discussed at

http://www-cs-students.stanford.edu/~cale/cs201/
    apartheid.hist.html

PART III

AFTER THE DELUGE: WORLD HISTORY IN THE ERA OF THE COLD WAR

Breaching the Berlin Wall in 1989:
West Germany and East Germany meet.

Chronology

1945–1948	Soviet takeover of Eastern Europe
1945	Formation of United Nations
1945	Atomic bomb
1947–1975	Cold war; Marshall Plan
1947	Peronism in Argentina
1947	India and Pakistan gain independence
1948	Israel-Palestine partition; first Arab-Israeli war
1949	Formation of NATO
1949	Communist victory in China
1950–1953	Korean War
1955	Warsaw Pact
1955	Bandung conference; Nonaligned Movement begins
1957	Ghana becomes first independent African nation
1957	Establishment of European Economic Community (Common Market)
1959	Cuban Revolution
1960s	Civil rights movement in United States; revival of feminism
1965–1968	Cultural Revolution in China
1965–1973	U.S. military intervention in Vietnam
1968–1973	Student protests in West
1973–1979	Oil crisis; height of OPEC power
1975–1989	Democratic regimes spread in Latin America
1975	Communist victory in Vietnam
1976	Death of Mao; new reform pattern in China
1978	China adopts more market-based economic policies
1979	Iranian revolution; spread of Islamic revivalism
1980–1988	Iran-Iraq war
1989	Chinese repression of democratic protest
1990–1991	Gulf War

COLD WAR TRANSFORMATIONS AND THE TRANSITION TO A NEW ERA

By the end of the "30 years war," which dominated global history in the middle decades of the 20th century, much of Europe and Asia was in ruins. From Great Britain to Japan, some of the key industrial and trading centers of the world had been reduced to smoldering rubble. A vast swath of death and destruction stretched from the Rhineland in Germany through central and southern Europe and the heartlands of the Soviet Union across northern and coastal China to the islands of the vanquished Japanese empire. Regions, such as the Middle East and much of Southeast Asia, which had been secondary theaters of World War II, had also suffered heavy losses of lives and property. Areas that were not actual sites for the massive campaigns of the war, such as the United States, Australia, India, and much of sub-Saharan Africa, had nonetheless poured vast amounts of resources and suffered sobering losses of young men and women sent overseas to wage war against the Axis powers.

The burden of these losses was compounded by revelations of the brutal excesses that had accompanied the war on virtually all fronts. This was especially true in eastern Europe and in the Pacific, where the struggle had degenerated into a race war, and in the concentration camps of the Nazi empire, where racist ideologies had inspired state-directed genocide that had claimed millions of defenseless civilian victims.

By conservative estimates, over 100 million people were dead, injured, or missing. Of these, a sizable major-

223

ity were civilians, who were either direct casualties of bombing and enemy assaults or victims of the death camps, epidemics, forced-labor schemes, and famines spawned by the greatest of all conflicts in human history. Tens of millions of additional people were homeless and displaced persons, the latter often uprooted forever from the lands of their birth. Throughout much of eastern Europe, the Middle East, South and Southeast Asia, and China, the collapse of the Axis regimes gave rise to costly civil wars or gave new impetus to sometimes violent struggles for liberation from European colonial rule. These conflicts were almost invariably caught up in a larger postwar clash between the Soviet Union and its former Western allies that the fall of their common Axis adversaries also made possible.

For the war's devastation virtually ensured that the major west European powers would no longer be able to claim the kind of world dominance they had aspired to even after World War I. Their new weakness encouraged two major changes in the postwar world: a wave of decolonization, creating new nations where once European empires had flourished; and the new struggle between the Soviet system and the United States. This cold war ultimately proved less important than decolonization, but it loomed larger initially, replacing the old conflicts within Europe with a new and global confrontation.

THE COLD WAR AND SHIFTS IN THE BALANCE OF GLOBAL POWER

Even before the guns had cooled and the bombs ceased to fall, a new kind of global war—a "cold war"—between a Soviet-built communist bloc and the capitalist West had begun. Though direct military clashes were for the most part avoided, none could rest easy as the tensions mounted between the emerging superpowers. The specter of unimaginable devastation caused by U.S. atomic bombs dropped in the last month of the war on Hiroshima and Nagasaki made the mounting contest between the United States and the Soviet Union an immediate concern for all the peoples of the globe. Incredibly, an even more destructive war than World War II was now possible—truly the war that would end war, and perhaps human history itself.

The cold war simmered for 40 years, occasionally breaking out into direct conflict, notably in Korea and later Vietnam. While the main focus involved the U.S.-Soviet rivalry, with allies on both sides of the Iron Curtain in Europe, the struggle had global dimensions. Both sides competed for allies in other parts of Asia and in

Africa and Latin America, often using economic and military aid as inducements. Although many nations resisted taking sides, the pressure was great. The fear of a direct nuclear clash, though most acute during the 1950s, affected people in many different regions as well. Even other developments, like decolonization, were shaped in part by the cold war framework.

Although the tense global contest for supremacy between the United States and the Soviet Union and their allies dominated the headlines in the decades after 1945, some of the more virulent sources of human misery and destructiveness had been removed or discredited. Isolated fascist regimes remained in Spain and Argentina, but the global threat of this strain of totalitarianism abated. Nazi excesses, the revolt by colonized peoples, and civil rights struggles in the United States and elsewhere dealt crippling blows to racist ideologies that had been prominent in the first two phases of the 20th century. Racist sentiments continued to justify discrimination and spark social conflict in many areas of the globe. But anthropologists and scientists alike rejected the "scientific" proofs of biological superiority or inferiority that racist thinkers had pushed throughout the 19th and early 20th centuries. The struggles for human rights and dignity on the parts of minorities and disadvantaged groups, such as women, which had surfaced in the first decades of the 20th century, were revitalized after 1945. In the United States, for example, President Truman's executive order of 1948 ended formal segregation in the military, while a civil rights movement aiming to end discrimination in U.S. society more generally gained momentum in the 1950s. At the same time, ancient ethnic rivalries and hatreds in many regions, particularly eastern and central Europe where communist regimes came to power, were submerged by monolithic regimes and the overarching ideological confrontations of the cold war adversaries.

In addition, within the global framework shaped by the cold war struggles between the capitalist and communist blocs, potent new forces of renewal and creativity soon emerged from the ruins of decades of war and turmoil. Though the settlement that followed World War II was dominated by the growing divisions between the Soviet Union and the United States, which had only recently been allied against the Axis powers, determined efforts were made to strengthen international organizations aimed at keeping the peace. Even before the war had ended, the partners of the victorious allied coalition had drawn up plans for and convened the first meetings of a new security organization, the United Nations. With Soviet and U.S. participation and thereby possessing greater powers in critical areas like peacekeeping and economic assistance, the United Nations was a much more effective and comprehensive force in world affairs than its failed predecessor, the League of Nations, which had been established after World War I. Though its initiatives have often been frustrated by the opposition of one or both of the superpowers at critical junctures—as, for example, in the Cuban missile crisis of 1962—the UN has provided a forum for debate and negotiation that has helped to head off violent clashes and on several occasions global nuclear war.

Perhaps the most remarkable rebirths after 1945 came in war-shattered Europe and Japan. Determined to avoid the devastating backlash that had resulted from the punitive peace imposed on Germany after World War I and eager for allies in the emerging cold war, the United States sought to bring the defeated Axis powers—Germany, Japan, and Italy—back into a reconstructed world community rather than isolate them as pariahs. Fearing that Communism might readily spread to these shattered and impoverished societies, the United States also provided massive economic support and technical assistance to spur their redevelopment as democracies within the Western, capitalist camp. Of all of the international projects undertaken by the United States in the last phase of the 20th century, these were by far the most successful. In the decade after 1945, the leaders of the revitalizing economies and stabilized polities of western Europe took steps to forge an economic union, the European Economic Community (EEC). It was hoped this would put an end to the recurring wars that had plagued western European civilization from its inception. Buoyed by the Common Market that resulted, western Europe entered into an era of unprecedented prosperity and launched a cultural renaissance that defied its much reduced position in global politics. Drawn into political and military alliance under the United States–led North Atlantic Treaty Organization (NATO), the nations of western Europe have enjoyed decades of internal peace that have in turn fed hopes of a lasting union of the European continent. The economic "miracle" of postwar Europe's revival and its cultural ramifications are the focus of Chapter 9, which leads off this section on the cold war decades of 20th-century history.

On the other side of the "iron curtain," which Winston Churchill famously proclaimed had come to divide eastern from western Europe in the years after 1945, the Soviets and their allies struggled to rebuild societies and economies devastated by the Nazi invasions of World War II. The magnitude of the Soviet losses is reflected in the widely accepted estimate that as many as 26 million people in the Soviet Union lost their lives in the conflict.

Having established, in effect, the sway of the Soviet empire in Poland, East Germany, Czechoslovakia, Hungary, and the Balkans (excepting Yugoslavia) in the years following the conflict, the Soviets formalized their dominance by establishing the Warsaw Pact in 1955. These developments and the efforts of the Soviets and other Eastern European societies to build viable societies under Command Communism, or state-directed economic and cultural development programs, dominated the decades of the cold war era, which are covered in Chapter 10.

GLOBAL ADJUSTMENTS: POSTCOLONIAL OPTIONS AND THE PERSISTENCE OF REVOLUTION

Though sometimes overshadowed by the fears and dramas of the cold war, the bigger story of the postwar decades involved the complex repositioning of western Europe and the United States in the world at large. The repositioning was affected by the cold war in turn.

In terms of population, this trend had begun in the first decades of the 20th century, as family planning and the availability of modern contraceptives led to a slowing or leveling off of population growth in the industrialized nations flanking the North Atlantic. This meant a declining share of world population overall. In the decades after 1945, the revolt against Western colonial dominance in Africa and Asia and the consequent formation of dozens of newly independent nations in these regions greatly diminished the global political influence of the former European powers, most notably France and Great Britain.

As will become clear in Chapter 11, which discusses the postcolonial era in Africa and Asia, despite the fall of the colonial empires, the economic and cultural influences of the West have, if anything, increased markedly in many areas. Not only have the new nations of Africa and Asia become even more dependent on a global market system, which is dominated by the West and in recent decades Japan, but none has found a viable path to development that diverges substantially from those pioneered in the western Europe and the United States. In addition, from Levi's jeans and Coca-Cola to rock music and stream-of-consciousness novels, the cultural hold of the West has grown steadily stronger as indigenous crafts and artistic traditions have been marginalized in many non-Western areas.

Efforts on the part of African, Asian, or Latin American peoples to forge independent paths to development were also greatly hampered by the fact that these regions were repeatedly drawn into cold war rivalries between the superpowers and their ideological allies. Attempts in the 1950s and 1960s by leaders like Egypt's Nasser and Nehru of India to build a meaningful bloc of nonaligned nations between the Western alliance and the Warsaw Pact nations floundered due to divisions within and pressing economic needs of most postcolonial nations. Throughout the cold war era, the communist and capitalist global rivalry repeatedly spilled over into the power struggles within and between recently decolonized societies. "Third World" countries, as they came to be known in cold war diplospeak, provided major outlets for the armaments industries of both West and East. Foreign aid and the assistance of international lending agencies like the International Monetary Fund (IMF) and the World Bank have often been contingent on the degree to which political and economic policies of leaders in "developing" countries were in line with communist or capitalist strategies. Attempts—such as those by OPEC (Organization of Petroleum Exporting Countries) or African or Asian producers of raw materials—to band together to gain leverage in international markets have been limited to specific products and a handful of countries, and they have usually been undermined by divisions within.

Revolutionary movements in Africa, Asia, and Latin America also frequently, and at the cost of countless lives, became caught up in cold war calculations and prolonged military interventions in postcolonial states by the superpowers or their surrogates. Several of these key confrontations, including the Cuban upheavals under Fidel Castro, the American debacle in Vietnam, and the ill-fated Soviet involvement in Afghanistan, are considered in Chapters 10 and 12. Most of these movements were inspired by Marxist-Leninist ideologies and programs for change, and most of them occurred in societies whose population consisted overwhelmingly of poor peasants. But, as we shall see, they varied considerably in their histories and outcomes due in large part to the often widely differing political and cultural situations in which they occurred. Responses to the meddling of the cold war superpowers also shaped the course of each of the major revolutions that were a dominant force in world history during the cold war decades.

THE NEW POSITION OF EAST ASIA

Along with the cold war and decolonization, the rise of powerful economies in East Asia progressively contributed to the new framework for world history overall.

Here was another way, of course, in which Western influence was partially diluted, as East Asia became a major, successful economic competitor on a global scale—and the source of some new cultural influence as well.

The revival of Japan in the 1950s and 1960s, discussed in Chapter 13, was even more impressive than the West European economic miracle. Japan lay in ruins in 1945. But partly because of cold war rivalries that argued for making Japan an ally, and partly because of a genuine desire to construct a viable democracy, Japan was not punished further for its wartime role. The allies did demand unconditional surrender, but they allowed the emperor to remain, though shorn of his symbols of divinity; here was an initial gesture to Japan's history and identity.

Like the Germans, the Japanese faced a huge job of economic rebuilding, but like the Germans they proved willing to work hard and to sacrifice, and their own past industrial success provided a basis for rapid gains. By the late 1960s, Japan's living standards passed all previous levels, and the nation was a global center for production of electronic equipment, automobiles, and other items. Democracy also took firm hold, though under the dominance of a single political party.

Japan's surge helped stimulate the wider Pacific Rim—South Korea, Taiwan, Singapore, and several Southeast Asian countries. Rapid economic growth exceeded Western rates, adding another dominant center for the global economy. Then, with new policies installed in 1978, China itself began to join the economic surge, adding further strength and potential to one of the big regional shifts in contemporary world history.

PORTENTS OF THE FUTURE OF THE GLOBAL COMMUNITY

For much of the cold war phase of 20th-century history, the maneuvers of the superpowers and the continuing nuclear arms race obscured other shifts in global history that may eventually be seen as more decisive. Beginning in the late 1960s there was an increasing awareness of the adverse environmental consequences of nearly two centuries of unchecked scientific experimentation and industrial growth. Subsequent revelations regarding the acceleration of plant and animal species' extinction in recent decades and the ecological devastation wrought by the "development" of hitherto sparsely populated regions—most dramatically the rain forests of the tropics—have underscored the global perils of pollution and resource exhaustion. Although still hotly debated, environmental trends such as global warming and the depletion of the ozone layer have become major concerns for government policymakers and ordinary citizens throughout the world. The environmental toll of Western-style development has raised doubts about the capacity of the planet to withstand the global spread of industrialization, particularly since few developing countries can afford the antipollution devices deployed in Europe, Japan, and the United States. At the very least, it has become essential to include environmental costs in schemes promoting economic growth.

These concerns are heightened by yet another global trend, the spiraling growth of the human population. Although birth rates in industrialized societies have fallen or leveled off and those in the largest countries, China and India, have abated somewhat, very high levels of net population increases persist in Africa, much of the Middle East, Latin America, and other regions of the world. Though it has taken humankind tens of thousands of years to reach a population of six billion by 1990, nearly four of those six billion have been added in the six decades since 1930! According to conservative estimates as many as four billion more people will be born in the first half of the 21st century.

In a world that is already threatened by overpopulation, pollution, and dwindling resources, these are indeed daunting trends. They are complicated by what appear to be countervailing tendencies of the most brutal Malthusian variety. Despite the great 20th-century advances of medicine and scientific farming, the spread of epidemic disease and massive famines have figured prominently in the last decades of the century. The resurgence of disease is epitomized by the AIDs epidemic, which is much more widespread in Africa, China, parts of the Caribbean, and Southeast Asia than more publicized areas like the United States and western Europe. Less spectacular, but perhaps equally threatening, has been the reemergence of diseases such as tuberculosis and smallpox, which international health agencies had once predicted were soon to be extinct. In addition, new strains of crop and animal diseases have surfaced, which may be linked to broader processes of environmental degradation. Shifting global weather patterns and inappropriate farming techniques often based on those in the West have done much to accelerate the spread of the

desert and precipitate famine in postcolonial areas. In some countries, such as Somalia, Ethiopia, and Mozambique, these conditions have been greatly exacerbated by local civil wars, which have disrupted food production and often frustrated international relief efforts.

The world's history in the four decades after World War II was dominated by the cold war. In the first few postwar years the most basic kinds of recovery from wartime dislocations and destruction were stressed, particularly but not exclusively in Europe and the Far East. Then as the rivalry between the United States and the Soviet Union and their respective allies intensified in 1947 and 1948, a number of other basic trends surfaced. Key among these were the decolonization struggle, which would continue through the 1970s, the revival of western Europe and Japan, the surge of East Asia more generally, and the growing influence of consumer cultures developed in the United States, Europe, and Japan. These global shifts were accompanied by the rise or renewal of human rights struggles across the globe from the United States and South Africa to Eastern Europe and those embedded in the peasant-based revolutions that were such a pronounced feature of the cold war decades. In some cases, particularly in Marxist-inspired revolutions, these movements were driven mainly by demands for such basic entitlements as jobs and living wages or education and health care. And though these demands also figured in contemporary mobilizations against discrimination and the resulting disadvantages endured by women, ethnic minorities, and still colonized peoples including those in Eastern Europe, the Middle East, and southern Africa, in these latter struggles rather different human rights were much more in evidence. Freedom of expression, fair and open elections, and the right to peaceful protest became the rallying cries of not just those living in affluent, industrialized societies but those struggling against repressive regimes and discriminatory social systems. Until the late 1980s, when a new phase of global history emerged, all of these struggles were waged in the shadow of the worldwide contests of the superpowers, each with massive nuclear stockpiles that in days, or perhaps hours, could reduce millennia of human achievement to radioactive rubble.

Chapter 9

The West and the World During the Cold War: Changing Definitions and Changing Roles

The letter sweaters, "box," and rock-and-roll dancing of these Japanese teenagers are all hallmarks of a youth culture that spread across the globe in the decades after 1945. Much of this culture originated in the United States, but rock groups, such as Great Britain's Beatles, and Japanese electronics shaped it in major ways.

Chronology

1945–1948	New constitutions in Italy, Germany, and France; Labour Party victory in Britain; basic measures of welfare states
1945	End of World War II
1947–1960s	Emergence and most intense phase of cold war
1947	Marshall Plan
1948	East and West German regimes established
1949	North Atlantic Treaty Organization established
1957	Establishment of European Economic Community (Common Market)
1958	Formation of De Gaulle's Fifth Republic in France
1960s	Civil rights movement in the United States
1960s	Emergence of new feminist movement
1968–1973	Massive student protests
1970s	Democratic regimes in Spain, Portugal, and Greece
1973, 1977	Oil crises
1979	Thatcher and new conservatism in Britain
1979	Significant recession
1981	Reagan president in United States
1992	End of economic restrictions within Common Market
1993	Division of Czechoslovakia; Clinton inauguration ends three-term Republican tenure in White House
2001	Euro currency introduced

INTRODUCTION

Four connections linked developments in western Europe and the United States to the rest of the world between 1945 and the end of the cold war, and their combination was complex. First, of course, was the cold war itself. The United States quickly assumed leadership of a Western effort to oppose the communist bloc headed by the Soviet Union. American cold war policies had great influence in western Europe, and the larger western cold war effort affected literally every part of the world.

Second, western Europe, and to some degree the United States, lost some key strengths in world affairs during these same decades. Western population growth lagged behind most of the rest of the world. The West was unable to retain colonial regimes in Asia, Africa, and the Americas. Adjustments to the new independence of states outside the West, and to new economic initiatives especially from parts of Asia, were an important part of the Western-world relationship in this period.

Third, western Europe regained considerable internal strength during the postwar decades. Economic and political changes and revival were both significant and, by contrast with the patterns of the 1920s and 1930s, quite surprising.

Finally, partly because of revival, partly because of cold war competition, Western political and particularly cultural patterns had wide global influence from 1945 onward, even as conventional imperialism receded. This meant that Western developments such as a renewed commitment to political democracy or changes in conditions for women, had impact beyond the West itself. Many Western innovations provoked both imitation and resistance in other parts of the world.

Amid the ashes of World War II, almost any observer of the West in 1947 would have been filled with dire forebodings about the region's future. After a previous war a scant 30 years before, European society had proved unable to invigorate an ailing economy or to deal with massive internal tensions among the major classes; political leadership had failed, and the only major innovations pointed toward the belligerence of fascism and renewed bloodshed. How could the results of this second devastating war be any better?

Yet after a brief recovery period, European society, along with its cousins in North America, moved into a new phase. Novel diplomatic policies joined with new domestic roles for the state. Europe's new lease on life and the firm establishment of the United States as the leading superpower formed key themes in the overall postwar history of Western society. Much of the West, furthermore, developed a new version of industrial society. The manufacturing sector declined in importance, in favor of the rise of service activities, such as information exchange and medical care. Gender roles were substantially altered by the new entry of women in the labor force. Popular culture reached for new expressions, from Europe's mania for vacations to the rock music that emerged from both sides of the North Atlantic. The striking and fundamental changes in the West's social forms constituted a final focus of the second half of the 20th century, emerging gradually amid initial postwar experimentation, then blossoming during the 1960s and 1970s.

AFTER WORLD WAR II: INTERNATIONAL SETTING FOR THE WEST

World War II was fully as total a war as its predecessor, and it left western Europe in shambles. The sheer physical destruction, caused particularly by bombing raids, disrupted housing and transportation. Downed bridges and rail lines complicated food shipments, leaving many people in France and Germany ill fed and unable to work at full efficiency. German use of forced foreign labor, as well as the many boundary changes resulting from the war, generated hundreds of thousands of refugees trying to return home or find a new home. For at least two years after 1945 it was unclear that recovery would be possible, as sheer survival proved difficult enough. Europe's postwar weakness after three decades of strife also helped trigger in the former colonial areas a crescendo of nationalist sentiment directed against the West, as well as the fuller emergence of the United States and the Soviet Union, whose size and building industrial strength finally overshadowed Europe's proud nation-states.

Europe and Its Colonies

The two larger changes provoked by the war—decolonization and the cold war—quickly intruded on the West. Colonies outside Europe, roused by the war, became increasingly restive. When the British returned to Malaya and the Dutch to Indonesia—areas from which

they had been dislodged—they found a more hostile climate, with well-organized nationalist resistance. It was soon clear that many colonies could be maintained only at great cost, and in the main the European nations decided that the game was not worth the candle. A few cases proved messy. France tried to defend its holdings in Vietnam against Communist guerrillas, yielding only in 1954 after some major defeats. The French clung even more fiercely to Algeria, the oldest African colony and one with a large European minority. The French military joined Algerian settlers in insisting on a war to the death against nationalist forces, and bitter fighting went on for years. The tension even threatened civil war in France, until a new president, Charles de Gaulle, realized the hopelessness of the struggle and negotiated Algeria's independence in 1962.

Overall, decolonization proceeded more smoothly than this between the late 1940s and the mid-1970s, without prolonged fighting that might drain the Western nations themselves, with Kenya and the Algerian morass bitter exceptions. Western governments typically retained important cultural relations with their former colonies. They sometimes intervened in cases of political instability. Both France and Belgium, for example, periodically sent troops to Africa after decolonization was officially complete. Finally, Western economic interests remained strong in most former colonies—particularly in Africa, which exploited mineral and agricultural resources in a pattern of trade not radically different from that of colonial days.

The impact of decolonization on the West should not, however, be minimized. Important minorities of former settlers and officials came home embittered, though, except briefly in France, they were not significant political forces. Europe's overt power in the world was dramatically reduced. Efforts by Britain and France to attack independent Egypt in 1956, to protest Egypt's nationalization of the Suez Canal, symbolized the new state of affairs. The United States and the Soviet Union forced a quick end to hostilities, and what was once a colonial lifeline came into non-Western hands. Yet although decolonization was a powerful change in world affairs, it did not, at least in the short run, overwhelm the West, as neither economic growth nor internal political stability suffered greatly.

The Cold War

The final new ingredient of Europe's diplomatic framework, the cold war between the United States and the Soviet Union, had a more durable influence on politics and society within the West, while significantly affecting the rest of the world. The conflict took shape between 1945 and 1947. The last wartime meetings among the leaders of Britain, the United States, and the Soviet Union had rather vaguely staked out the boundaries of postwar Europe, which were certainly open to varied interpretations. By the war's end, Soviet troops firmly occupied most eastern European countries, and within three years the Soviets had installed Communist regimes to their liking, while excluding opposition political movements. Thus an eastern bloc emerged that included Poland, Czechoslovakia, Bulgaria, Romania, and Hungary. And Soviet boundaries themselves had pushed west, reversing the decisions of the post–World War I Versailles conference. The Baltic states disappeared, and Poland lost territory to Russia, gaining some former German lands as compensation. Finally, Soviet occupation of the eastern zone of Germany gave Russia a base closer toward the heart of Europe than the tsars had ever dreamed possible.

Offended by the Soviet Union's heavy-handed manipulation of eastern Europe, including its zone in eastern Germany, U.S. and British policymakers tried to counter. The new American president, Harry Truman, was less eager for smooth relations with the Soviets than Franklin Roosevelt had been; Truman was emboldened by the U.S. development in 1945 of the atomic bomb. Britain's wartime leader, Winston Churchill, had long feared Communist aggression; it was he who in 1946 coined the phrase "iron curtain" to describe the division between free and repressed societies that he saw taking shape in Europe. But Britain frankly lacked the power to resist Soviet pressure, and under the Labour government it explicitly left the initiative to the United States.

The United States responded to Soviet power plays with vigor. It criticized Soviet policies and denied Soviet applications for reconstruction loans. It bolstered regimes in Iran, Turkey, and Greece that were under Soviet pressure. In Greece, particularly, the United States took over British resistance to a powerful Communist guerrilla campaign. Then in 1947 the United States proclaimed its Marshall Plan, a program of substantial loans that was designed to aid Western nations rebuild from the war's devastation. In Soviet eyes the Marshall Plan was a vehicle for U.S. economic dominance, and indeed there is little question that in addition to humanitarian motives the United States intended to beat back domestic communist movements in countries such as France and Italy by promoting economic growth.

The focal point of the cold war in these early years was in Germany. Soviet policy in Germany initially con-

centrated on seizing goods and factories as reparation. The Western Allies soon prevented Soviet intervention in their own zones and turned to some rebuilding efforts in the interests of playing a modest "German card" against growing Soviet strength in the east. That is, although the West, led by the United States, did not intend to resurrect a powerful Germany, it soon began to think in terms of constructing a viable political and economic entity. Allied collaboration started building a unified West Germany in 1946, and local political structures followed by more national ones were established through elections. When in 1947 the West moved to promote German economic recovery by creating a stable currency, the Soviet Union responded by blockading the city of Berlin, the divided former capital that sat in the midst of the Soviet zone. The United States responded with a massive airlift to keep the city supplied, and the crisis finally ended in 1948, with two separate Germanies—East and West—beginning to take clear shape along a tense, heavily fortified frontier.

Cold war divisions spread from Germany to Europe more generally with the formation of two rival military alliances. The North Atlantic Treaty Organization (NATO) was formed in 1949, under U.S. leadership, to group most of the western European powers and Canada in a defensive alliance against possible Soviet aggression. The NATO pact soon legitimated some rearmament of West Germany in the context of resistance to communism, as well as the continued maintenance of a substantial U.S. military presence in Germany and in other member nations. In response the Soviet Union organized the Warsaw Pact among its eastern European satellites. When in 1949 the Soviets developed their own nuclear capability, the world—particularly the European world—seemed indeed divided between two rival camps, each in turn dominated by its own superpower. Numerous U.S. and Soviet military units were permanently stationed in Europe on either side of the cold war divide.

The cold war had a number of implications for western Europe. It brought new influences from the United States on internal as well as foreign policy. Through the 1950s and beyond, the United States pressed for acceptance of German rearmament (though under some agreed on limits); it lobbied for higher military expenditures in its old allies France and Britain; and it pressed for acceptance of U.S. forces and weapons systems. The Americans' wishes were not always met, but the United States had vital negotiating leverage in the economic aid it offered (and might withdraw), in the troops it stationed in Europe, and in the nuclear "umbrella" it developed (and might, in theory, also withdraw). The nuclear weapons seemed to offer the only realistic protection should the Soviet Union venture direct attack. The Soviets, for their part, influenced western Europe not only through perceived aggressive intent but also by funding and supporting substantial Communist movements in France and Italy, which in turn affected but did not overwhelm the political process.

The cold war did not maintain within Europe the intensity it reached in the initial years. Centers of conflict shifted in part outside Europe as Korea, then Vietnam, and recurrently the Middle East became flashpoints. In special circumstances a few European states managed to stay out of strict cold war alignment. Sweden and Switzerland maintained traditions of neutrality; Finland, a capitalist democracy on Soviet borders, was neutral perforce. Austria regained independence in 1956—in a period of lessening cold war dispute—on condition of neutrality; and Yugoslavia, though Communist, increasingly pulled away from the Soviet camp. Finally, the main Western powers themselves, once launched on recovery, found increasing room to maneuver. After 1958, France became more and more restive under what it viewed as Anglo-U.S. dominance of NATO, and it finally withdrew its forces from the joint NATO command, requiring also that U.S. troops leave French soil. In the 1970s Germany opened new negotiations with the Soviet Union and eastern bloc countries, wanting increased export opportunities and reduced diplomatic tension. Nevertheless, the cold war and the resultant alliance system continued to describe much of the framework of East-West relations in Europe and elsewhere in the world.

By the late 1940s the cold war was spreading well beyond Europe, as later chapters will discuss. Communist victory in China by 1949 brought a new balance in Asia, and it was quickly followed by one of the few outright battles of the cold war—in Korea. Here the United States, worried about progressive losses to communism, intervened to save South Korea from a takeover by communist North Korea and from greater Chinese influence as well.

A vital feature of this diplomatic configuration obviously involved the rise of the United States to preeminence within the West. This development was long in the making. Its industrial surge had already brought the United States new influence by the late 19th century. Economic power was enhanced by agricultural exports and, after World War I, the powers of U.S. banking and credit. Following World War II, the economic supremacy of the United States among the Western na-

tions seemed assured, and for a time many experts worried that Europe would never regain economic autonomy, doomed always to poor-relative status vis-à-vis its giant U.S. cousin. This situation proved temporary, as we shall see, but even in the 1980s the economic power of the United States continued to surpass that of western Europe.

After 1941 the diplomatic and military ascendancy of the United States matched its economic power for the first time, save for the brief flicker between 1917 and 1919. The U.S. leadership role in the postwar Western alliance was never seriously challenged, although it produced grievances and protests within Europe from various groups, both conservative nationalists and leftist supporters of nuclear disarmament.

The shifting balance between the United States and Europe produced a crisscrossing of military relationships. As western Europe abandoned military preeminence, the United States, never before a major peacetime military power, devoted growing resources to its military capacity and gave an increasing voice to its military leaders. Regardless of the political party in power, the percentage of the U.S. government budget going to the military remained stable from the 1950s to the 1980s—when it went up. In contrast, some European leaders boasted that their societies had made a transition toward preeminence of civilian values and goals. Although U.S. and European values and institutions became more similar in key respects after World War II, the differences in military roles signaled ongoing distinctions within Western society.

THE RESURGENCE OF WESTERN EUROPE

Although the shifts in the West's external environment triggered by World War II were not catastrophic, they constituted major readjustments. Ironically, western Europe's domestic development in this same period was considerably more positive, a strong contrast not only to its reduction in world status but also to the massive troubles that had followed World War I. Immediately after the war, western Europe suffered tremendous dislocation, amid grinding poverty and painful rebuilding, made worse by the new cold war division of the European map and strong fears of a new superpower clash.

But though postwar problems left their marks, western Europe demonstrated surprising resiliency. A new set of leaders emerged in many countries, some from wartime resistance movements, eager to avoid the mistakes that had led to depression and war. Although their vision was not always realized, from 1945 onward western Europe did move onward on three important fronts: the extension of democratic political systems, a modification of nation-state rivalries within Europe, and a commitment to rapid economic growth that reduced previous social and gender tensions.

The Spread of Liberal Democracy

In politics, defeat in war greatly discredited fascism and other rightist movements that had opposed parliamentary democracy. Vestiges of these movements continued, periodically surfacing in France and Italy but rarely with much muscle. At the same time, key leftist groups, including the strong Communist movements that emerged from the war in France and Italy, were committed to democratic politics. Although social protest continued, outright revolutionary sentiment declined. Finally, several new political movements surfaced, notably an important Christian Democratic current, which was wedded to democratic institutions and moderate social reform. Despite national variations, in general western Europe experienced a shift in the political spectrum toward fuller support for democratic constitutions and greater agreement on the need for government planning and welfare activities.

New regimes had to be constructed in Germany and Italy after the defeat of Fascist and Nazi leaderships. France established a new republic once occupation ended. In Germany political reconstruction was delayed by the division of the nation by the victorious Allies. As the cold war took shape, however, France, Britain, and the United States progressively merged their zones into what became the Federal Republic of Germany (West Germany), encouraging a new constitution that would avoid the mistakes of Germany's earlier Weimar Republic by outlawing extremist political movements. The new constitutions set up after 1945 in many European countries varied in particulars but uniformly established effective parliaments with universal (now always including female) suffrage. And the regimes endured. Only France, pressed by the Algerian War, changed its constitution in 1958, forming a Fifth Republic, still democratic but with stronger presidential authority.

Western Europe's movement toward more consistent democracy continued in the 1970s, when Spain and Portugal moved from their authoritarian, semi-Fascist constitutions (following the deaths of longtime strongmen) to democratic, parliamentary systems. Greece, increasingly linked to the West, followed the same pattern. By the 1980s western Europe had become more politically uniform than ever before in history. Party dominance shifted, with conservatives, including Christian Democrats, alternating with Socialist coalitions, but all major actors agreed on the constitutional system itself. The relative vitality of democracy in the West, along with the strength of newer democracies in Japan and India, strongly influenced political choices elsewhere in the world, especially from the 1970s onward.

The Welfare State

The consolidation of democracy also entailed a general movement toward a welfare state. Resistance ideas and the shift leftward of the political spectrum helped explain the new activism of the state in economic policy and welfare issues. Wartime planning in the British government had pointed to the need for new programs to reduce the impact of economic inequality and to reward the lower classes for their loyalty. Not surprisingly, the governments that emerged at the war's end—Britain's Labour Party and the Communist-Socialist-Christian Democrat coalitions in France and Italy—quickly moved to set up a new government apparatus that would play a vigorous role in economic planning and develop new social activities as well. By 1948 the basic nature of the modern welfare state had been established throughout western Europe, as not only the new regimes but also established reformists (as in Scandinavia) extended a variety of governmental programs. The United States, though somewhat more tentative in welfare measures, added to its New Deal legislation in the 1960s, under President Lyndon Johnson's Great Society programs, creating medical assistance packages for the poor and the elderly. Canada enacted an even more comprehensive medical insurance plan.

The welfare state elaborated a host of social insurance measures. Unemployment insurance was improved. Medical care was supported by state-funded insurance or, as in Britain where it became a centerpiece to the new Labour program, the basic health care system was nationalized. State-run medical facilities provided free care to the bulk of the British population from 1947 onward, although some small fees were later introduced. Family assistance was another category, not entirely new, that was now greatly expanded. All western European governments provided payments to families with several children, the amount increasing with family size.

The great sacrifices of the ordinary people during World War II brought great pressure for the establishment of welfare states at war's end. Here orange juice and vitamins are distributed to children and mothers at a British health clinic in the mid-1950s.

Because the poor now tended to have the largest families, family-aid programs both encouraged population growth—of particular concern to countries such as France—and helped redistribute some of the general tax revenues toward the neediest groups. In the 1950s a French working-class family with low earnings and five children (admittedly an unusual brood by this point) could improve its income by as much as 40 percent through family aid. Governments also became more active in the housing field—a virtual necessity given wartime destruction and postwar population growth. Britain embarked on an ambitious program of "council housing," providing many single-family units that deliberately mixed working-class and middle-class families in new neighborhoods. By the 1950s over one fourth of the British population was housed in structures built and run by the government.

The welfare state that emerged in the postwar years was a compromise product. It recognized a substantial private sector and tried to limit and cushion individual initiative rather than replacing it with state action alone, as in the communist system. It provided aid for citizens at many income levels. Middle-class people might benefit from family assistance, and they certainly used state medical insurance. They also disproportionately benefited from the expanded educational systems and university scholarships that developed along with the welfare state. In other words, although the welfare state focused particularly on problems of workers and the poor, it won support from other groups by dealing with some of their special needs as well.

Relatedly, although some aspects of the welfare state redistributed income, the welfare state did not generally make a huge dent on western Europe's unequal class system. Though taxes rose, they were not always steeply graduated. Furthermore, starting with France, a supplementary tax system was installed, beginning in the late 1950s, that was not graduated at all. This value-added tax system, which quickly spread through Europe, levied taxes on each stage of the production process, operating essentially as a supra–sales tax ultimately paid by consumers. Here was a potent source of revenue that had little redistributive effect.

The welfare state was, in sum, an important new definition of government functions but hardly a device for social revolution. It cushioned citizens against major expenses and unusual hardships rather than rearranging overall social structure. It protected the purchasing power of the very poor against catastrophe, and it contributed to improved health conditions generally. It also, of course, increased contacts between government and citizen, and it produced a host of new regulations that framed European life.

Despite many criticisms from both the left and the right, the welfare state won wide acceptance from its inception. The British, for example, became quickly attached to their new health system, making major revision impossible. For the most part political debate centered on tinkering with the welfare state, not revolutionizing it in any particular direction. Socialist parties, when in power, extended welfare measures by expanding their coverage and benefits. Conservative parties, for their part, often cut back a bit and promised more efficient administration. Into the 1970s no major political movement attacked the new state root and branch.

The welfare state was undeniably expensive. It greatly enlarged government bureaucracies, in addition to channeling tax monies to new purposes. By the 1950s up to 25 percent of the gross national product of France and

Holland was going to welfare purposes, and the figure tended to rise with time. As military expenses began to stabilize, welfare commitments became far and away the largest component of Western government budgets outside the United States. Here was a clear indication of the extent to which the western European state had altered its relationship to the wider society.

An increased governmental role in economic policy paralleled the welfare state. Most postwar governments nationalized some sectors of industry outright. Most European countries also set up new planning offices, responsible for developing multiyear economic projections and for setting goals and the means to meet them. By coordinating tax concessions and directing the flow of capital from state banks, government planners had genuine power to shape, although not directly to run, economic activity. Planning extended to both agriculture and industry. Planning offices regulated crop sizes and encouraged consolidation of land for greater efficiency, and they could require farmers to participate in cooperatives that would improve marketing and purchasing procedures.

Planning involved European governments more directly than ever before in commitments to economic growth, full employment, and avoidance of damaging recessions. It was also aimed at improving the economic development of laggard regions. Italy thus tried to direct increasing industrialization toward the south, whereas France industrialized toward the west, in both cases with partial success.

Of the Western nations, only the United States shunned an economic planning office, though it maintained government regulation of the financial system. Rather, government growth consisted more of expanding military activities and piecemeal welfare measures, though U.S. elections, like European, usually hinged on the electorate's judgment of how well the nation was doing economically.

Despite important variations, the role of the state loomed unprecedentedly large throughout the West from the 1940s onward. A new breed of bureaucrat, often called a technocrat because of intense training in engineering or economics and because of a devotion to the power of national planning, came to the fore in the offices of the government. Some state initiatives undoubtedly reflected the potential overzealousness of the new breed. Housing authorities forced workers out of old but comfortable slums into anonymous high-rise structures that, however elegant on paper, never felt right to residents. Peasants, no friends of distant central governments even before, often lamented heavy-handed re-

quirements. Yet here as with the welfare state, no particularly coherent political disputes took shape, at least until the 1960s. The new state seemed to work well enough that it was difficult to attack categorically.

Political Stability and the Question Marks

The fact was that big, contentious political issues were notable for their absence through most of Europe during the 1950s and 1960s, except for the polarizing experience in France of the Algerian War. Reformist governments of the immediate postwar years tended to give way to more conservative regimes during the 1950s. Labour, for example, lost the 1951 election in Britain; even earlier, Communists had been forced out of coalitions in France and Italy. But the conservative regimes were generally content to support the existing definition of state functions. Also, when socialist or labor governments gained renewed access to power as in Britain in the 1960s, they, too, typically had no dramatic new programs to offer. For better or worse, Europeans seemed to accept the state's new social and economic roles as well as its constitutional structure. Political debates were often fierce, and partisan loyalties intense, but few sweeping issues were raised.

The Western pattern of political compromise around the mechanisms of parliamentary democracy and the welfare state were, however, severely jolted by a series of student protests that developed in the late 1960s. Even before this, in the United States a vigorous civil rights movement had developed to protest unequal treatment of African Americans. Massive demonstrations, particularly in Southern cities, attacked segregation and limitations on African-American voting rights.

Campus unrest was a Western-wide phenomenon in the 1960s. At major American universities, protests focused on the nation's involvement in the war in Vietnam. Young people in Europe and the United States also targeted the materialism of their societies, including the stodginess of the welfare state, seeking more idealistic goals and greater justice. Student uprisings in France in 1968 created a near revolution. By the early 1970s new rights for students and other reforms, combined with police repression, ended the most intense student protests, whereas passage of civil rights legislation in the United States ultimately reduced urban rioting and demonstrations. The flexibility of postwar Western democracy seemed triumphant. Some additional political concerns, including a new wave of feminism focusing on economic rights and dignity for women, and environmentalist movements entered the arena during the 1970s, partly as

Campus unrest was a Western-wide phenomenon in the 1960s. Student uprisings in France in 1968 created a near revolution. Here, students and workers demonstrate in Paris.

an aftermath of the student explosion. The rise of the Green movement in several countries in the 1970s signaled a new political tone, hostile to uncontrolled economic growth. Green parliamentary deputies in Germany even refused to wear coats and ties in their efforts to defy established political habits.

Observers in many countries speculated that a shift in basic political alignments might be in the making if old parties failed to deal adequately with the new issues. In some western European countries, a terrorist movement targeting political and business leaders also caused recurrent anxiety. As economic growth slowed in the 1970s and the Western world faced its greatest economic recession since the immediate postwar years, other signs of political change appeared. New leadership sprang up within the British Conservative Party and the U.S. Republican Party, seeking to reduce the costs and coverage of the welfare state. In 1979 British Conservative leader Margaret Thatcher began the longest-running prime-ministership in history, working to cut welfare and housing expenses and to promote free enterprise. Neither she nor her U.S. counterpart, Ronald Reagan, fully dismantled the welfare state, but they did reduce its impact.

In the 1990s a set of moderate socialist governments took over in Britain, France, and Germany, emphasizing economic growth but with a welfare safety net and strong environmental policies. Despite important adjustments, the main line of postwar government then persisted into the 21st century. Democratic institutions often failed to command great excitement, as voting levels went down throughout the West (particularly in the United States), but they roused no widespread, coherent resistance either. New political movements, although interesting, had yet to dislodge mainstream conservative and socialist (or, in the United States, liberal) parties. The Western world has unquestionably remained freer from major political upheavals than have most other civilizations in the postwar decades and freer than Western society itself had been during the 1920s and 1930s. Has Western society achieved a durable new harmony, or were the postwar decades a period of deceiving tranquility before some yet-to-be-defined storm?

The Diplomatic Context

Along with the extension of democracy and the development of the welfare state, the West showed postwar vigor in addressing some traditional diplomatic problems, notably recurrent nationalistic rivalry, as well as specific manifestations, such as French-German enmity. U.S. guidance combined with innovative thinking in the new European governments.

During the war, many resistance leaders had tempered their hatred of Nazism with a plea for a reconstruction of the European spirit. The Christian Democratic movement, particularly, produced important new advocates of harmony among European nations. Early postwar reforms, however, concentrated primarily on internal changes. Although cold war rivalries prevented a formal European peace settlement, initial impulses by the victorious Allies suggested a harsh treatment of Germany, possibly a permanent dismemberment, in order to avoid a repetition of the two previous world wars—not a more fundamental rethinking of Western conventions.

Yet the demands of the cold war and pressure from the United States forced second thoughts, which ultimately revived elements of resistance idealism. By 1947 U.S. leaders were eager to spur western Europe's economic recovery, for which they judged coordination across national boundaries an essential precondition. Thus the resulting Marshall Plan required discussion of tariffs and other development issues among recipient nations. With simultaneous U.S. insistence on the partial rearmament of Germany and German participation in NATO, the framework for diplomatic reform was complete.

Faced with these pressures and aware of the failure of nationalistic policies between the wars, several French statesmen took a lead in proposing coordination between France and Germany as a means of setting up a new Europe. The nations of the Low Countries and Italy were soon linked in these activities. The idea was to tie German economic activity to an international framework so that the nation's growing strength would not again threaten European peace. Institutions were established to link policies in heavy industry and later to develop atomic power. A measure to establish a united European military force proved too ambitious and collapsed under nationalist objections. But in 1957 the six western European nations (West Germany, France, Italy, Belgium, Luxembourg, and the Netherlands) set up the European Economic Community, or Common Market, to begin to create a single economic entity across national political boundaries. Tariffs were progressively reduced among the member nations, and a common tariff policy was set for the outside world. Free movement of labor and investment was encouraged. A Common Market bureaucracy was established, ultimately in Brussels, to oversee these operations. The Common Market set up a court system to adjudicate disputes and prevent violations of coordination rules; it also administered a development fund to spur economic growth in such laggard regions as southern Italy and western France.

The Common Market (later called the European Union) did not move quickly toward a single government. Important national disputes limited the organization's further growth. France and Germany, for example, routinely quarreled over agricultural policy, with France seeking more payments to farmers as a matter of obvious self-interest. The establishment of the Fifth Republic in France, under Charles de Gaulle, indeed signaled an increase of French nationalism. But although the European Union did not turn into full integration, it did survive and, on the whole, prosper. It even established an advisory international parliament, ultimately elected by direct vote. Furthermore, in the 1980s firm arrangements were made to dismantle all trade and currency exchange barriers among member states in 1992, creating essentially complete economic unity. A single currency, the euro, was set up in many member countries by 2001. The European Union's success expanded its hold within western Europe. After long hesitations Britain, despite its tradition of proud island independence, decided to join, as did Ireland, Denmark, and later Greece, Spain, Portugal, Austria, Sweden, Denmark, and Finland. By 2001, other nations near to central Europe were pressing for membership, and in 2004 a number of new countries were admitted, from the new Baltic states to Malta and Cyprus.

Nationalist tensions within Europe receded to a lower point than ever before in modern European history. After the worst scares of the cold war, focused mainly on the division between the Communist East and semicapitalist West, Europe became a diplomatically placid continent, enjoying one of the longest periods of substantial internal peace in its history.

Economic Expansion

After a surprisingly short, if agonizing, postwar rebuilding, striking economic growth accompanied political and diplomatic changes. The welfare state and the European Union may have encouraged this growth by improving purchasing power for the masses and facilitating market expansion across national boundaries; certainly economic growth encouraged the success of new political and diplomatic systems.

There was no question that by the mid-1950s western Europe had entered a new economic phase. Agricultural production and productivity increased rapidly as peasant farmers, backed by the technocrats, adopted new equipment and seeds. European agriculture was still less efficient than that of North America, which necessitated some much-resented tariff barriers by the Common

DOCUMENT

Youth Culture in the 1960s

The explosion of youth unrest throughout the West in the 1960s was directed against a host of grievances—problems in finding jobs, opposition to the Vietnam War, concerns about the basic trends of corporate life and consumerism in Europe and the United States alike. Some observers predicted that youth would become the central protest group of advanced industrial society, replacing the working class. In key respects, however, youth protest turned out to be a vivid but short-lived phenomenon. It generated larger cultural outlooks and new behaviors that continued to excite young people and that outlasted the protest current itself. Rock music, for example, maintained high levels of popularity. New kinds of sexual behavior, involving the younger ages of those engaging in sexual intercourse, emerged in the 1960s and continued at a substantial pace thereafter, though modified in the early 1990s by new disease concerns.

The following three selections deal with the two kinds of youth rebellion. The first is a recollection by a former U.S. student radical, reflecting after the fact on his protest activities during his college years.

When I felt really good was during a sit-in, when there was a drawing together, a unity. . . . The marches I went

on, they made me feel like I was doing something. When I saw it wasn't going anywhere it started turning me off. All I was doing was stretching my legs. People would yell and shake their fist, and the government would once in a while come out and throw them a bone or push them around, then pass them off.

From the way that I felt when I was on acid, I thought that everyone else would feel like that, too. So if we all felt like that, how could there be any violence or evil? Because when I was on acid, I didn't feel like being hassled. All I wanted to do was sit and rap or just think about something. Just sit down between the stereo speakers and put on Janis [Joplin] singing "Summertime" and just watch the fish swim in the aquarium. That was the most mellow state I could be in.

I didn't know what I wanted. No, I wanted happiness, but I didn't know what it was. I thought it was being high twenty-four hours a day, and I couldn't get it. Now I know it's being contented. In the world that's impossible—there's always something wrong with you, but the Lord takes you just the way you are and if you've got something wrong in your heart, he'll deliver you from it. All you have to do is obey His Word.

Source: From Steven M. Tipton, *Getting Saved from the Sixties* (Berkeley: University of California Press, 1982), pp. i, 39, 86

The second selection (on the facing page) offers a different kind of evidence: statistics on youth political attitudes, also in the United States, during the same time period.

Market. But food production easily met European needs, often with some to spare for export. Retooled industries poured out textiles and metallurgical products. Expensive consumer products, such as automobiles and appliances, supported rapidly growing factories. Western Europe also remained a leading center of weapons production, trailing only the United States and the Soviet Union in exports.

Overall growth in gross national product surpassed the rates of any extended period since the Industrial Revolution began; it also surpassed the growth rates of the U.S. economy during the 1950s and 1960s. The German economy, after some basic reconstruction and a currency stabilization in 1948, expanded at 6 percent a year during the 1950s; with few modest setbacks this pace continued into the early 1970s. France's growth rate reached 8 percent by the late 1950s, maintained almost this level during the 1960s, and returned to rates of over 7 percent an-

nually by the early 1970s. By 1959 the Italian economy, a newcomer to the industrial big leagues, was expanding at an annual rate of 11 percent. These were, admittedly, the clearest success stories. Scandinavian growth was substantial but more modest, and Britain, also expanding but falling rapidly in rank among the European national economies, managed an increase of 4 percent at best. Even this, however, contrasted markedly with the stagnation of the 1920s and early 1930s.

Growth rates of the sort common in western Europe, their impact heightened by the absence of major depressions, depended on rapid technological change. Europe's rising food production was achieved with a steadily shrinking agricultural labor force. France's peasant population—16 percent of the labor force in the early 1950s—fell to 10 percent two decades later, but overall output was much higher than before. During the 1950s the industrial workforce grew as part of factory expansion, but

This poll divided American college students into two groups: "high prestige" students from upper-middle-class backgrounds and "vocational," students from lower status families, who looked on college as providing a set of job-relevant skills.

A 1998 Poll on Political Attitudes

| | Percentages | |
| | "Vocational" Students | "High Prestige" Students |
Beliefs		
U.S. a "sick" society	32	50
Against war in Vietnam	43	69
Civil disobedience may be justified	32	68
Too little done for blacks	38	71
Dislike business	26	46
Containing communism worth fighting for	59	28
Need more law and order	78	39
More respect for authority	73	41
Should prohibit marijuana	69	37
Technology good	75	56
Factors in career choice:		
Family	48	25
Money	58	21
Job prestige	33	13

Source: Adapted from "What They Believe: A Fortune Yankelovich Survey," *Fortune*, January 1999, 34–36. Copyright © Time Inc.

The third selection, also statistical, moves to one of the other areas of innovation—sexuality—picking up on trends that had begun during the 1960s but continued to amplify during the 1970s.

The Sexual Revolution: Percentage of Women 15–19 Years of Age Who Had Premarital Intercourse

Current Age	1971	1976
15	14.2	18.5
16	22.3	27.9
17	28.6	43.6
18	40.7	54.0
19	49.5	60.4
15–19	30.1	40.9

Source: Adapted from Melvin Zelnik, John F. Kantner, Kathleen Ford, *Sex and Pregnancy in Adolescence* (Beverly Hills, CA: Sage, 1981), p. 65.

Questions: What were the common themes of youth culture that emerged in the 1960s? Was sex related to politics? What were some of the divisions among youth? How can the new youth culture be explained? Why did it ultimately turn away from collective protest? How much of it survives in the West today?

by the 1960s, the relative proportion of factory workers also began to drop, despite rising production. Workers in the service sector, filling functions as teachers, clerks, medical personnel, insurance and bank workers, and performers and other "leisure industry" personnel, rose rapidly in contrast. Europe, like the United States, began to convert technological advance into the provision of larger bureaucracies and service operations without jeopardizing the expanding output of goods. In France half of all paid workers were in the service sector by 1968, and the proportion rose steadily thereafter.

The high rates of economic growth also ensured relatively low unemployment after the immediate postwar dislocations passed. Even Britain, with lagging development, averaged no more than 4 percent unemployment a year during the 1950s and 1960s, whereas France and Germany featured rates of 2 percent to 3 percent a year. Indeed, many parts of the Continent were labor-short and had to seek hundreds of thousands of workers from other areas—first from southern Europe, then, as this region industrialized, from Africa, the Middle East, and parts of Asia. The rise of immigrant minorities was a vital development in western Europe and also the United States, where the influx of Asian and Latin American immigrants stepped up markedly.

Unprecedented economic growth and low unemployment meant unprecedented improvements in incomes, even with the taxation necessary to sustain welfare programs. Per capita disposable income rose 117 percent in the United States between 1960 and 1973 and soared 258 percent in France, 312 percent in Germany, and 323 percent in Denmark. Indeed, Scandinavia, Switzerland, and the Federal Republic of Germany surpassed the United States in standards of living by the 1980s, whereas France, long an apparent laggard in modern economic development, pulled even. New spending money

Chevy puts the purr in performance!

That new V8 in the '57 Chevrolet is as quiet as a contented cat and as smooth as cream. And it's cat-quick in response when you ask for action!

No household tabby sitting in a sunny window ever purred more softly than Chevy's new V8 engine. It's so kitten-quiet and cream-smooth that you can scarcely even tell when it's idling.

But when you judge the accelerator, you know it's there, all right! It pours out the kind of velvety action that helps you be a surer, safer driver. Its right-now response keeps you out of highway emergencies. It over-

powers steep hills with such ease they seem like level landscape.

New Chevrolet V8 engine options put up to 245* horsepower under your command. With 203 cubic inches of displacement, this beautifully designed V8 is a new, bigger and better edition of the engines that have put Chevrolet at the top of the performance ladder. It's sassy, sure—but as tame to your touch as a purring pussycat.

Try the smoothest V8 you ever put a toe to, and all the good things that go with it. It's available in any one of the bright new Chevrolet models you choose—all with Chevy's own special savvy and solid way of going. Stop by your Chevrolet dealer's . . . soon!

SEE YOUR AUTHORIZED CHEVROLET DEALER

CHEVROLET

1 USA
'57 CHEVROLET

270-h.p. high-performance V8 also available at extra cost.

In the United States, as well as in Japan and western Europe, advertisements increasingly evoked a good life to be achieved by buying the right goods. The newest car was associated with a prosperous home, a loving family, and even happy pets.

rapidly translated into huge increases in the purchase of durable consumer goods, as virtually the whole of Western civilization became an "affluent society." By 1969, two out of every ten people in Britain, Sweden, West Germany, and France owned an automobile, and rates continued to climb. Ownership of television sets became virtually universal (See Table 9.1). France and other countries indulged in a mania for household appliances. Shopping malls and supermarkets, the agents of affluence and extensive but efficient shopping that had first developed in the United States, spread widely, at the expense of more traditional, small specialty shops. A West German company, in fact, took over a key U.S. grocery chain in the late 1970s, on grounds that Europeans now knew mass marketing as well as or better than the U.S. consumer pioneers.

Europe had unquestionably developed a framework of affluent consumerism as fully as had the United States, with at least as much impact on basic social patterns and

TABLE 9.1
Two Measures of Rising Consumer Prosperity in Europe, 1957 and 1965

Automobiles	1957	1965
France	3,476,000	7,842,000
Germany (Federal Republic)	2,456,288	8,103,600
Italy	1,051,004	5,469,981
The Netherlands	375,676	1,272,890
Sweden	796,000	1,793,000

Televisions	1957	1965
France	683,000	6,489,000
Germany	789,586	11,379,000
Italy	367,000	6,044,542
The Netherlands	239,000	2,113,000
Sweden	75,817	2,110,584

Source: Adapted from *The Europa Year Book 1959* (London: Europa Publications, 1959) and *The Europa Year Book 1967*, vol. 1 (London: Europa Publications, 1967).

habits of thought. Advertising was not quite as ubiquitous in Europe as across the Atlantic, particularly because most television channels were state-run and noncommercial. But promptings to buy, to smell good, to look right, to express one's personality in the latest car style began quickly to describe European life. The frenzy to find good vacation spots was certainly intense. Literally millions of Germans poured annually into Italy and Spain, seeking the sun. Britons thronged to Spanish beaches. Europeans were bent on combining efficient work with indulgent leisure.

The West's economic advance was not without some dark spots. Inflation was a recurrent headache when demand outstripped production. Inflation in the 1970s, affecting even the cautious Germans, who were particularly eager to avoid this specter from the past, caused serious dislocation. Pockets of unemployment were troubling. Many immigrant workers from Turkey, North Africa, Pakistan, and the West Indies suffered very low wages and unstable employment. These immigrants, euphemistically labeled "guest workers," were often residentially segregated and victims of discrimination by employers and police, as racism continued to be an important factor in Western society.

More troubling still was the slowing of economic growth in the 1970s. In 1973 the oil-producing states of the Middle East cut their production and raised prices, initially in response to a Middle Eastern war with Israel.

Many nations were hit hard by higher energy prices, but western Europe, heavily dependent on imports, was particularly pressed. A second orchestrated oil crisis in 1979 led to a severe recession throughout Western society, with unusually high rates of unemployment. By now growing competition from East Asia and other areas cut into traditional staples, such as steel and automobile production, making it difficult to recover the dynamism of the two postwar decades.

Western leaders were able to respond to new crises with some success. Conservation measures reduced dependence on imported oil, and by the 1980s energy prices fell back. Several European nations embarked on rapid development of nuclear energy production. European productivity rates continued to improve; some nations, such as France, introduced the use of robots on assembly lines at a particularly rapid pace. The economic climate had become tighter, however. This spurred some renewed labor agitation, directed, for example, at governments that closed inefficient factories.

The Results of Western Vitality

Comparative political stability and economic prosperity in western Europe and the United States obviously had global implications. Both sides of the North Atlantic attracted new waves of immigrants from Asia, Africa and Latin America, a significant change particularly from Europe. Some societies, like France, became as much as 10 percent Muslim. Economic vigor gave the West, along with the Pacific Rim, a leading role in economic globalization, with Western-based corporations expanding their activities throughout the world. At various points from the 1970s onward, Western achievements convinced leaders in other nations that they should imitate the West's market-based economy, or its democracy, or both. The West's role in the world certainly changed and became more complicated with the decline of colonialism, but its economic role and political and cultural influences still loomed large

COLD WAR ALLIES: THE UNITED STATES, CANADA, AUSTRALIA, AND NEW ZEALAND

Developments in the so-called overseas West in many ways paralleled those in western Europe, but without the sense of grappling with prior collapse. The sheer level of innovation in domestic policy was less great, in part because the crises of the first half of the 20th century had

been less severe. Crucial adjustments occurred, however, in foreign policy. The United States led the way in making the changes in its own tradition that were necessary to develop a massive peacetime military force and a global set of alliances. With the decline of European, and particularly British, international power and the emergence of the cold war context, Australia, New Zealand, and Canada tightened their links with the United States and developed new contacts with other areas of the world.

The Former Dominions

Canada forged ahead in welfare policies after World War II, establishing a greater stake in economic planning and in state-run medical insurance than did the United States. At the same time, however, Canadian economic integration with the United States continued, with U.S. investments in Canadian resources and mutual exports and imports soaring steadily into the 1970s. By 1980 the Canadian government took some measures to limit further U.S. penetration, and a sense of Canadian nationalism sparked resentment of the giant to the south. In 1988, however, the two nations signed a free-trade agreement, creating a North American trading bloc at a time when European unity was increasing rapidly.

Continued emigration to Canada pointed in new directions also, with growing numbers of people arriving from various parts of Asia. Canada's most distinctive issue, however, involved growing agitation by French Canadians in Quebec for regional autonomy or even national independence. A new separatist party, founded in 1967, took control of the provincial government during the 1970s. Subsequent legislation limited the use of the English language in Quebec's public and commercial life, though referendums for full independence failed during the 1980s. A new constitution in 1982, however, granted greater voice to the provinces, both to counter French Canadian demand and also to recognize the growing economic strength of the resource-rich western provinces. Separatist tensions continued to simmer, however, into the 21st century.

From 1945 onward, Australia and New Zealand moved steadily away from their traditional alignment with Great Britain and toward horizons around the Pacific. The two commonwealths joined a mutual defense pact with the United States in 1951, directed against potential Communist aggression in the Pacific. Both nations cooperated with the United States in the Korean War, and Australia backed U.S. intervention in Vietnam. In 1966 the Australian prime minister declared, "Wherever the United States is resisting aggression . . . we will go a-waltzing Matilda with you." In the later 1970s and 1980s Australia and especially New Zealand began to distance themselves somewhat from U.S. foreign policy. New Zealand barred U.S. nuclear-armed vessels in 1985.

As Great Britain aligned with the European Union, Australian and New Zealand exports were increasingly directed toward other Pacific nations, notably Japan, whereas investment capital came mainly from the United States and Japan. Indeed, Australia became Japan's chief raw-materials supplier aside from oil. Asian emigration also increasingly altered the population mix, again particularly in Australia. Despite a long-held whites-only immigration policy, the Australian government was powerless to resist growing regional emigration, particularly from Indochina. By 1983 Asians accounted for 60 percent of the total immigrant population in Australia.

The "U.S. Century"?

Amid a host of domestic issues, the big news in U.S. history after 1945 was its assumption—in many ways, its eager assumption—of the superpower mantle, opposing the Soviet Union and serving as the world's leading defender of democratic and capitalistic values. The United States hesitated briefly after 1945, demobilizing its World War II forces rather quickly with some hope that world peace would provide some respite from further international engagement. However, Great Britain's inability to continue to police the world for the West, together with rapid Soviet successes in installing Communist governments in Eastern Europe, prompted a decisive U.S. stance. In 1947 President Harry Truman promised support for "free peoples who are resisting subjugation by armed minorities or by outside pressures." The doctrine, specifically directed against Communist pressures on Greece and Turkey, soon extended into the elaboration of Marshall Plan aid to rebuild the economies of western Europe against the possibility of Communist subversion in these war-torn countries. The Republican Party was initially tempted to resist these new international engagements, but the 1948 Communist takeover of Czechoslovakia checked that impulse. For many decades basic U.S. foreign policy proceeded amid wide bipartisan agreement.

The plunge into the cold war took a toll on the home front, however. The United States entered a period of intense, even frenzied concern about internal Communist conspiracies, ferreting out a host of suspected spies and subjecting people in many fields to dismissal from their jobs on grounds of suspected radical sympathies.

Cold war engagement prompted other policy changes in the federal government. The Defense Department was set up in 1947 to coordinate military policy, and the Central Intelligence Agency was established to organize a worldwide information-gathering and espionage network. Military spending increased considerably, with the formation of the Strategic Air Command to stand in constant readiness in case of a Soviet bombing attack. A massive U.S. airlift thwarted Soviet pressure on the western sectors of occupied Berlin. The United States resisted the invasion of South Korea by the Communist North, beginning in the 1950s; U.S. troops stationed in Japan were sent in to support the South Koreans. Under General Douglas MacArthur and backed by several allies under a hastily arranged UN mandate, the North Korean invasion was repulsed within a few months. The United States then authorized an invasion into North Korea, which brought a retaliatory intervention from Communist China. The United States was pushed back, and more than two years of additional fighting ensued before peace was negotiated in 1953—with the earlier boundary line between the two Koreas restored. In the meantime annual U.S. spending on the military had increased further, from $13.5 billion to $50 billion.

During the 1950s, under the presidency of Dwight D. Eisenhower, the United States settled into a policy of containment of the Soviet Union, which involved maintenance of large peacetime military forces. The United States also arranged alliances not only with western Europe, in NATO, but also with Australia and New Zealand, with several southeast Asian nations, and with several nations in the Middle East; this alliance system virtually surrounded the Soviet Union. Less novel was recurrent U.S. intervention in Central America against suspected Communist movements; thus U.S. aid toppled a new Guatemalan government in 1954. The United States was unable to prevent a takeover in Cuba that eventually propelled Cuba into the Communist camp, despite a U.S.-backed invasion attempt by anti-Communist Cuban rebels. Nonetheless, the United States maintained its policy of vigilance (under President John Kennedy, in 1962) by forcing the Soviet Union to back down on plans to install missile sites on the island.

The U.S. containment policy yielded a final test that took shape during the 1960s, when intervention against Communist revolutionaries in South Vietnam gradually escalated. The U.S. Air Force began bombing Communist North Vietnam in 1965. Later that year troops were sent in, reaching a total of 550,000 by 1968. By this time the United States was spending $2 billion a week on a war that never produced convincing success and gradually bogged down in horrendous bloodshed on both sides. By 1970 more bombs had been dropped on Vietnam than had been dropped by anyone, anywhere previously in the 20th century. By 1968 domestic pressure against the war, centered particularly on U.S. college campuses, began to force changes in strategy. A new U.S. president, Richard Nixon, tried to expand the war to other parts of Indochina, to increase pressure on North Vietnam. Simultaneously, peace negotiations with North Vietnam were launched, resulting finally in an agreement on a ceasefire, in 1973. By 1975, as the United States speedily withdrew, all Vietnam lay in Communist hands.

Furor over the Vietnam War led to agonizing policy reassessments in the United States. Some observers judged that new directions might be forged, as the United States had discovered that its massive military might could be stalemated by fervent guerrilla tactics. Both the U.S. military and the public grew more wary of regional wars. Although the national mood sobered, however, decisive policy changes did not ensue. A socialist government in Chile, for example, was ousted with the aid of covert U.S. pressure even as the Vietnam conflict wound down. The socialist government was replaced by a brutal military regime. Then in 1980 the United States overwhelmingly elected a new president, Ronald Reagan, who combined conservative domestic policies with a commitment to bolster military spending and make sure that the United States would "ride tall" again in world affairs. The 1980s saw no major new international involvements, but several punitive raids were conducted against suspected terrorists in the Middle East, and the small West Indian island of Grenada was invaded to topple a leftist regime. President Reagan sponsored a number of expensive new weapons systems, which helped press an afflicted Soviet economy to virtual collapse as its leaders attempted to keep pace. The next president, George Bush, continued an interventionist policy by sending U.S. troops into Panama to evict and arrest an abrasive dictator and then by spearheading a Western and moderate Arab alliance against Iraq's invasion of Kuwait, in 1990 and 1991. The United States also led participation in military action against forces in the Balkans in the 1990s, and led an invasion of Iraq in 2003.

Domestic Dislocations

Amid the extensive overseas commitments and recurrent crises linked to the new U.S. role as anti-Soviet leader and self-appointed world police officer, domestic innovations took something of a back seat. In the ongoing economic prosperity of the 1950s and 1960s the United States had been able to combine its growing military budget with several new initiatives: a massive highway program and then the extension of the limited welfare state under Great Society initiatives in the mid-1960s. Federal involvement in preschool programs and health assistance to the needy and elderly expanded notably. New civil rights legislation was introduced in the mid-1960s, following a decade of mounting pressure from various African American organizations and inspired particularly by the leadership of Martin Luther King Jr. Dr. King's preaching of nonviolence moved many people to support the cause of racial equality; a series of major urban riots between 1965 and 1968 pressed the need for change as well. Protection for African Americans' voting rights in the South and new legislation against discrimination in housing and public facilities combined with court-sponsored school integration measures to ease racial tensions somewhat.

With more difficult economic times in the 1970s, however, domestic initiatives dwindled. Many observers faulted not only government but also private business for insufficient attention to research and development and even to application of existing technologies. Concern mounted that the United States, though still a massive economic powerhouse, was lagging behind its industrial competitors both in western Europe and the Pacific Rim. Material standards suffered as well; from 1973 onward families improved their average standard of living only through additional work of family members, usually a wife and mother. Individual real wages stagnated into the 1990s. Certain groups, including inner-city African Americans, suffered particularly, as outright unemployment mounted. However, little collective violence resulted after both civil rights and youth unrest subsided in the early 1970s. Under conservative presidents in the 1980s and again after 2000, government protections were scaled back, especially for the unemployed and for impoverished children—as one third of all the nation's children now fell below the poverty line.

The 1990s saw higher unemployment in much of Europe, while the United States picked up new vigor through the rapid growth of the information technology sector. The United States economy zoomed forward in the 1990s, on the strength of national leadership in information technology. Leading businessmen acquired vast fortunes, as economic inequality increased despite full employment. American leaders vaunted a new commitment to free markets and entrepreneurship.

Amid fluctuations, the impact of heightened prosperity continued to define much of Western life. It helped explain why the West remained a compelling model for other parts of the world, as well as a major economic player in world affairs even as imperialism receded.

The United States and Western Europe: Convergence and Complexity

The relationship between the United States and western Europe has been important both historically and analytically for at least two centuries. Many people in the United States have tried to establish a distinctive identity while acknowledging special relationships with Europe; isolationism was one response earlier in this century. Europeans, for their part, have groped for definition of their U.S. "cousins," particularly as U.S. military and cultural influences grew in the 20th century. Were U.S. innovations to be welcomed, as stemming from a kindred society with a special flair for technology and modern mass taste, or should they be resisted as emblems of a superficial, degenerate, and essentially un-European society?

Analytically, comparison of the United States with western Europe is essential in order to organize a civilization roster for world history. If the United States forms a separate civilization, related to but different from the West, the list of important civilizations obviously grows. If, however, the United States is "Western," albeit with some undeniably distinctive features, the civilization roster is simpler. Both cases can be argued; both depend, however, on careful comparison.

The United States–western Europe relationship is, furthermore, not a constant. It is easy to draw distinctions at some points, as when the United States established universal male suffrage for nonslaves in the early 19th century but Europe remained locked in older political systems; when the aristocracy still loomed large in European but not in U.S. society, or when there was slavery in U.S. society but not European. Over time, however, and particularly since 1945, U.S. and European societies have in many important respects converged. Because of heightened imitation and shared advanced industrial economies, some earlier differences have receded.

Western Europe, for example, no longer has a very distinct peasantry. Its farmers, though smaller scale than their U.S. agribusiness counterparts, are commercialized and simply so few in numbers that they no longer set their society apart. European workers, though less likely than those in the United States to call themselves middle class, are now relatively prosperous. They have moved away from some of the political radicalism that differentiated them from their U.S. counterparts earlier in the 20th century. Europe does not, to be sure, have as deep-seated a racial issue as the United States inherited from slavery, but the growing influx of people from the West Indies, North Africa, and Asia has duplicated in Europe some of the same racial tensions and inner-city problems that bedevil the United States. At the other end of the social scale, trained managers and professionals now form a similar upper class in both societies, the fruit of systems of higher education that differ in particulars but resemble each other in producing something of a meritocratic elite.

A shared popular culture has certainly emerged. Although it stemmed mainly from U.S. innovations before World War II, more recently it has involved mutual borrowing. The United States, for example, embraced miniskirts and rock groups from Britain in the 1960s, and not only British but also French youth raced to buy the latest style in blue jeans.

Differences remain, of course, some of them going back to earlier historical traditions. The United States has relied more fully on free-market capitalism than did western Europe, with the United States possessing a less complete planning, fewer environmental regulations, and more modest welfare apparatus. The difference was heightened during the 1990s. The United States proved much more religious than did western Europe. Only a minority of people in most western European countries professed religious belief by the 1990s, with less than 10 percent in most cases attending church with any regularity. In contrast the United States remains highly religious, with up to 40 percent regular church attendance, and 70 to 80 percent of its people professing religious belief. The United States made a less complete conversion to a new leisure ethic after World War II than did western Europe; European vacation time advanced toward more than a month a year, whereas the average in the United States remained two weeks or less. Europeans were franker also about teenage sexuality, following the 1960 sexual revolution. They distributed birth control materials to adolescents much more commonly than did their more prudish U.S. counterparts, reducing

The skyscraper, developed first in the United States, became a major expression of artistic innovation and dramatic new structural materials, including novel uses of glass. This Chicago tower was designed by European master Ludwig Mies van der Rohe.

rates of teenage pregnancy in the process. In certain important respects, then, the United States constituted a more traditional society, in terms of values, in the latter 20th century than did western Europe. Some of the variations between the two societies related to long-established distinctions (as in the degree of suspicion of government power); others emerged for the first time, sometimes surprisingly, after World War II.

The biggest distinctions between the two societies in recent decades, however, followed from their increasingly divergent world roles. Western Europe, though still highly influential in culture and trade on a global scale, concentrated increasingly on its own regional arrangements, including the European Union trading bloc, and decreasingly on military development. The United States moved in the opposite direction. Thus a traditional distinction was reversed; the United States became the more military (and, some would argue, militaristic) society, and many Europeans became committed to more strictly civilian goals.

Other signs of new divergence gained attention by the early 21st century. European opposition to the death penalty—the European Union insisted that any entrant abolish the death penalty—contrasted with American policy. European governments seemed to embrace more environmental regulation than their American counterparts. The opposition of a considerable majority of Europeans to United States intervention in Iraq in 2003 revealed other policy tensions. Was another new trend emerging?

Questions: Why did the United States and western Europe converge in new ways during the 20th century? Do the two societies remain part of a common civilization? What are the most important issues to resolve in making this judgment?

A Challenge: Pick one of the differences between the United States and western Europe, such as religion, military policy, attitudes toward immigrants, or the death penalty. Explain why the difference has arisen and discuss its seriousness in relations between the two societies. Does the difference outweigh key similarities?

CULTURE AND SOCIETY IN THE WEST

Political and economic changes in Western society progressively altered the contours of earlier industrial development. The West became the first example of an advanced industrial society, especially from the 1950s onward, and both the United States and western Europe shared in leading facets of change.

Social Structure

Economic growth, bringing increasing prosperity to most groups, eased some earlier social conflicts throughout the West. Workers were still propertyless, but they had substantial holdings as consumers, and their sense of social inferiority often declined as a result. Social lines were also blurred by increasing social mobility, as educational

Protests by women increased in different parts of the world after the 1960s, spurred by the rise of new feminist movements in various places. Here, an Egyptian woman shouts slogans during an anti-war demonstration outside the Arab League in Cairo in March 2003. Nearly 100 women gathered on International Women's Day to protest the imminent American strike against Iraq and the Palestinian situation.

opportunities opened further and the size of the white-collar sector expanded. Much unskilled labor was left to immigrants. Economic and political changes also altered conditions for western Europe's peasantry and not only by cutting its size. Peasants became increasingly commercial, eager for improvements in standards of living, and participant, through car trips and television, in urban culture. They also became more attuned to bureaucracies, as state regulations pushed them into cooperative organizations.

Social distinctions remained. The middle class had more abundant leisure opportunities and a more optimistic outlook than did most workers. Signs of tension continued. Crime rates went up throughout Western society after the 1940s, though the levels were particularly high in the U.S. Race riots punctuated U.S. life in the 1950s and

1960s and exploded in immigrant sections of British cities in the 1980s and Germany in the early 1990s.

There were strong signs that what was happening in Western society, at least by the 1960s, was not so much a resolution of older issues—how to fit peasants into modern society or what to do about worker grievances—as the establishment of a new social system, a second version of industrial society or, as some held, a postindustrial society. The majority of workers in the West was now engaged in services and management hierarchies, not working either on farms or in factories. The new labor force was drawn less to the older ethic of hard work than to new ideas of high consumption and expressive leisure. The West continued to change, whether for good or ill.

The Women's Revolution

A key facet of postwar change involved women and the family, and again both western Europe and the United States participated fully in this upheaval. Although family ideals persisted in many ways—with workers, for example, urging that "a loving family is the finest thing, something to work for, to look to and to look after"—the realities of family life changed in many ways. Family leisure activities expanded. Extended family contacts were facilitated by telephones and automobiles. More years of schooling increased the importance of peer groups for children, and the authority of parents undoubtedly declined.

The clearest innovation in family life came through the new working patterns of women. World War II brought increased factory and clerical jobs for women, as the earlier world war had done. After a few years of downward adjustment, the trends continued. From the early 1950s onward, the number of working women, particularly married women, rose steadily in western Europe, the United States, and Canada. Women's earlier educational gains had improved their work qualifications; the growing number of service jobs created a need for additional workers—and women, long associated with clerical jobs and paid less than men, were ideal candidates. Many women also sought entry into the labor force as a means of adding to personal or family income, to afford some of the consumer items now becoming feasible but not yet easy to buy, or as a means of personal fulfillment in a society that associated worth with work and earnings.

The growing employment of women, which by the 1970s brought the female segment of the labor force up to 44 percent of the total in most Western countries, represented particularly the employment of adult women, most of them married and many with children. Teenage employment dropped as more girls stayed in school, but long-term work commitments rose steadily. This was not, to be sure, a full stride to job equality. Women's pay lagged behind men's pay. Most women were concentrated in clerical jobs rather than spread through the occupational spectrum, despite a growing minority of middle-class women who were entering professional and management ranks. Clearly, however, the trends of the 19th-century Industrial Revolution, to keep women and family separate from work outside the home, had yielded to a dramatic new pattern.

Other new rights for women accompanied this shift. Where women had lacked the vote before, as in France, they now got it; of the western European nations, only Switzerland doggedly refused this concession at the national level until 1971. Gains in higher education were considerable, though again full equality remained elusive. Women constituted 23 percent of German university students in 1963, and under Socialist governments in the 1970s the figure rose. Preferred subjects, however, remained different from those of men, as most women stayed out of engineering, science (except medicine), and management. Family rights improved, at least in the judgment of most women's advocates. Access to divorce increased, which many observers viewed as particularly important to women. Abortion law eased, though more slowly in countries of Catholic background than in Britain or Scandinavia; it became increasingly easy for women to regulate their birthrate. Development of new birth control methods, such as the contraceptive pill introduced in 1960, as well as growing knowledge and acceptability of birth control, decreased unwanted pregnancies. Sex and procreation became increasingly separate considerations. Although women continued to differ from men in sexual outlook and behavior—more than twice as many French women as men, for example, hoped to link sex, marriage, and romantic love, according to 1960s polls—more women than before tended to define sex in terms of pleasure.

Predictably, of course, changes in the family, including the roles of women, brought new issues and redefined ideals of companionship. The first issue involved children. A brief increase in the Western birthrate ended in the early 1960s and a rapid decline ensued. Women working and the desire to use income for high consumer standards mitigated against children, or very many children, particularly in the middle class, where birthrates were lowest. Those children born were increasingly sent, often at an early age, to day-care centers, one of the amenities pro-vided by the European welfare state and particularly essential where new fears about population growth began to surface. European families had few hesitations about replacing maternal care with collective care, and parents often claimed that the result was preferable for children. At the same time, however, some observers worried that Western society, and the Western family, were becoming indifferent to children in an eagerness for adult work and consumer achievements. American adults, for example, between the 1950s and 1980s, shifted their assessment of family satisfaction away from parenthood by concentrating on shared enjoyments between husbands and wives.

Family stability also opened new cracks. Pressures to readjust family roles, women working outside the family context, and growing legal freedoms for women caused men and women alike to turn more readily to divorce. In 1961, 9 percent of all British marriages ended in divorce; by 1965 the figure was 16 percent and rising. By the late 1970s, one third of all British marriages ended in divorce, and the U.S. rate was higher still.

Finally, even aside from divorce, the changing roles of women raised questions about family values. Expectations lagged behind reality. Polls taken of German women in the 1960s indicated that a solid majority believed that mothers with children under 12 should stay home; yet a solid majority of such mothers were working. Gaps of this sort, between ideals and practice, suggested that, like Western society generally, the family was in a new transition, its end state far from clear.

The development of a new surge of feminist protest, although it reflected much wider concerns than family life alone, showed the strains caused by women's new activities and continued limitations. Growing divorce produced many cases of impoverished women combining work and child care. New work roles revealed the persistent earnings gap between men and women. More generally, many women sought supporting values and organizations as they tried to define new identities less tied to the domestic roles and images of previous decades.

A new feminism began to take shape with the publication in 1949 of *The Second Sex* by the French intellectual Simone de Beauvoir. Echoed in the 1950s and 1960s by other works, such as Betty Friedan's *The Feminine Mystique* in the United States, a new wave of women's rights agitation rose after three decades of relative calm. The new feminism tended to emphasize a more literal equality that would play down special domestic roles and qualities; therefore, it promoted not only specific reforms but also more basic redefinitions of what it meant to be male and female.

The new feminism did not win all women, even in the middle class, which was feminism's most avid audience. It also did not cause some of the most sweeping practical changes that were taking place, as in the new work roles. But it did support the revolution in roles. From the late 1960s onward it pressed Western governments for further change, raising issues that were difficult to fit into established political contexts. The movement both articulated and promoted the gap between new expectations and ongoing inequalities in gender. And the new feminism expressed and promoted some unanswered questions about family functions. In a real sense later 20th-century feminism seemed to respond to the same desire for individuality and work identity in women that had earlier been urged on men as part of the new mentality suitable for a commercialized economy. Family remained important in the evolving outlook of women, although some feminist leaders attacked the institution outright as hopelessly repressive. Even for many less ideological women, however, family goals were less important than they had been before.

Other Social Disruptions in the West

By the 1960s and 1970s what seemed to be happening in the West was a major realignment of protest issues and groups, accompanying the larger structural changes in society and economy. Working-class unrest persisted but at a reduced rate. Aside from a brief surge at the end of the 1960s, strike rates and union membership fell from 1958 onward, both in Europe and the United States. Class-based politics also became less divisive, as working-class parties accepted moderate reforms and middle-class groups accepted basic premises of the welfare state. There was no guarantee that class division would not surge again in the future, if economic growth stagnated, for example, but for the moment, at least, other currents seemed more vigorous.

Feminism was one of these; environmentalism was another. Although youth unrest had declined by the early 1970s, it left a legacy of concern about aspects of industrial society and rampant consumerism that spawned more durable protest movements. In many European countries, and to a slightly lesser extent in the United States, environmental issues moved steadily forward on the social and political agendas. Environmentalists in Germany, Austria, and Scandinavia, as well as in the United States, forced curtailment of nuclear power programs, for example. "Green" parties, pushing for greater environmental protection, gained an important political role in countries like Germany and the Netherlands.

Ethnic nationalisms generated another set of protest issues, as regional minorities pressed for greater autonomy from the pressures of political and cultural centralization, sometimes using violence to drive their point home. Ethnic conflicts in Northern Ireland, Quebec, and the Basque region of Spain formed recurrently bitter centers of unrest, but there were other movements as well. Old identities combined with new grievances about the homogenizing, impersonal qualities of modern industrial society.

Finally, racial issues generated important conflict. By the 1980s western Europe housed about 15 million immigrant workers. Since the early 1960s the United States had witnessed the largest immigration in its history, and like western Europe, most of its newcomers came from non-Western sources. A disproportionate number of immigrants, together with the African Americans in U.S. inner cities, constituted a largely segregated labor force, holding low-paying, transient, unskilled jobs. African Americans in Chicago, for example, were 40 percent less likely than working-class whites to be employed by the 1980s, although a decade earlier their rates had been roughly equal. The decline in the number of factory jobs, racism on the part of employers, and increased competition from immigrants led to a new structure within the labor force and a new set of problems. The result was recurrent unrest in the cities, as in the British race riots of the 1980s. Another result was the formation of new anti-immigrant and racist organizations. Many Germans turned against the Muslim minority in the country. According to one extremist faction: "Two million foreign workers equals two million German unemployed, so send them all home." A new political party in France, the National Front, argued for expulsion of many immigrants; by 1984 it was winning 11 percent of the total French vote. Here, clearly, was a set of issues of vital importance for the future of the West and, more broadly, for the future of the West's relationship to the wider world.

Western Culture

Amid great innovations in politics, the economy, and social structure—including some pressing new problems—Western cultural life in many respects proceeded along established lines. A host of specific new movements arose, and a wealth of scientific data was assimilated, but basic frameworks had been set earlier, often in the more turbulent but intellectually creative decades of the early 20th century. The partial cooling of Western intellectual life raised interesting issues for those who promote cultural activity as ultimately the most accurate measurement of a society and its prospects. It is also possible that intellectual life reflected a channeling of creative energies in other directions, including those of mass culture, where Europe in fact displayed new spark.

One key factor in Europe's relative intellectual lag was a shift of focus toward the United States. Greater political stability in the United States during the 1930s and 1940s, as well as Hitler's persecutions, had driven many prominent intellectuals to U.S. shores, where they often remained even as western Europe revived. As U.S. universities expanded, their greater wealth fueled more scientific research; what was called a "brain drain," based on dollar power, drew many leading European scientists to the United States even during the 1950s and 1960s. European science remained active, but the costliness of cutting-edge research produced a durable U.S. advantage. Money also mattered in art, as patronage became increasingly important, and thus New York replaced Paris as the center of international styles.

Europeans did participate in some of the leading scientific advances of the postwar years. Francis Crick, of Cambridge University in England, shared with the American James Watson key credit for the discovery of the basic structure of the genetic building block deoxyribonucleic acid (DNA), which in turn opened the way for rapid advances in genetic knowledge and industries based on artificial synthesis of genetic materials. By 2000 work on the human genome project was proceeding rapidly on both sides of the Atlantic. Europeans also participated in nuclear research, often through laboratories funded by the European Union or other inter-European agencies. European space research, slower to develop than Soviet or U.S. initiatives, nevertheless also produced noteworthy achievements by the 1970s, and again there were important commercial spin-offs in communications satellites and other activities.

The Western commitment to science certainly did not flag. Scientific research everywhere consisted increasingly of largely incremental additions to the knowledge store, rather than sweeping breakthroughs of the Newtonian or Einsteinian sort. But there was a massive expansion of knowledge and information links to technology, as in the growing area of genetic engineering.

Developments in the arts maintained earlier 20th-century themes quite clearly. Most artists continued to work in the "modern" modes set before World War I, which featured unconventional self-expression and a wide array of nonrepresentational techniques. The clearest change involved growing public acceptance of the modern styles. The shock that had greeted earlier innovations disappeared, and the public, even when preferring older styles

displayed in museums or performed by symphony orchestras devoted to the classics, now seemed reconciled to the redefinition of artistic standards. New names were added to the roster of leading modern artists. In Paris Bernard Buffet scored important successes with gaunt, partially abstract figures. The British sculptor Henry Moore produced rounded figures and outright abstractions that conveyed some of the horrors of wartime life and postwar dislocations. A new group of "pop" artists in the 1960s tried to bridge the gap between art and commercial mass culture by incorporating cans and their products, comic strips, and advertisements into paintings, prints, and collages. As also held true in the realm of fully abstract painting, U.S. artists increasingly took the lead.

Europeans retained clearer advantages in art films. Italian directors produced a number of gripping, realistic films in the late 1940s, portraying both urban and peasant life without frills. Italy, France, and Sweden became centers of experimental filmmaking again in the 1960s. Jean-Luc Godard and Michelangelo Antonioni portrayed the emptiness of urban life, and Swedish director Ingmar Bergman produced a series of dark psychological dramas. Individual directors in Spain, Britain, and Germany also broke new ground, as Europeans remained more comfortable than their U.S. counterparts in producing films of high artistic merit, relatively free from commercial distractions.

Developments in literature and in painting generally continued prewar directions. A variety of French writers concocted the "new novel," which focused on concrete details and descriptions of surfaces and objects, without plot, character development, or a clear sense of the observer's identity. Some German novelists were more realistic, using the novel to satirize the frenzied commercial society around them. In music, composers continued to search for new sounds to liberate themselves from conventional tone and harmony. New electronic techniques were added to earlier experimentation, as computers and synthesizers joined instrumentation developed in Europe in the 1930s.

Overall, the arts reflected significant levels of activity, but a substantial acceptance of stylistic statements developed as much as a century before. In several fields Europeans at least shared eminence with practitioners in the United States, in what was increasingly a transatlantic high culture.

Fragmentation also occurred in the social sciences, with no commanding figure arising to succeed the Marxes or Webers of previous generations, willing to posit fundamental social dynamics or sweeping theories. Many specific fields in the social sciences turned to massive data collections and pragmatic, detailed observations; in many of these, U.S. practitioners in turn developed a decided advantage. Economics, in particular, became something of an American specialty in the post-Keynesian decades and focused on massive quantitative studies of economic cycles and money supplies.

Basic innovation and European leadership did conjoin in the structuralist movement in the social sciences and related literary criticism. Here the leading figure was the French anthropologist Claude Lévi-Strauss. Starting with fieldwork among Indian tribes in Brazil, Lévi-Strauss set out to discover basic, common ingredients in thought processes among primitive peoples generally. By analyzing rituals and myths concerning food and other fundamental activities, Lévi-Strauss believed he could decipher and catalog a limited number of thought processes applicable to all human societies, primitive or not, featuring the logic of pairing, determining opposites, and similar activities.

French intellectuals also contributed to a redefinition of historical study, building on innovations launched between the world wars. Social history, or the focus on changes in the lives of ordinary people, became increasingly the order of the day, giving a great spur to historical research throughout western Europe and the United States. Some French social historians were attracted to a structural approach that downplayed fundamental change, but others retained a vigorous interest in periodization and the discovery of basic alterations of human and social modes.

A Lively Popular Culture

Western society displayed more vitality in its popular culture than in formal intellectual life, which reflected the results of economic and social changes. Here, too, as in previous decades and as in high culture, U.S. influence was strong in what was in so many respects a common North Atlantic pattern. As European economies struggled to recover from the war and as U.S. military forces spread certain enthusiasms more widely than before, some observers indeed spoke of a U.S. "Coca-cola-niza-tion" of Europe. U.S. soft drinks, blue-jeaned fashions, chewing gum, and other artifacts became increasingly common. U.S. films continued to wield substantial influence, although the lure of Hollywood declined somewhat. More important was the growing impact of U.S. television series. Blessed with a wide market and revenues generated from advertising, American television was quite simply "slicker" than its European counterparts, and the western drama *Bonanza*, the soap opera

Dallas, and many other shows appeared regularly on European screens to define, for better or worse, an image of the United States.

In contrast to the interwar decades, however, European popular culture had its own power, and it even began to influence the United States as well. The most celebrated figures of popular culture in the 1960s were unquestionably the Beatles, from the British port city of Liverpool. Although they adopted popular music styles of the United States, including jazz and early rock, the Beatles added an authentic working-class touch in their impulsiveness and their mockery of authority. They also expressed a good-natured desire to enjoy the pleasures of life, which is a characteristic of modern Western popular culture regardless of national context. British popular music groups continued to set the standard in the 1970s and had wide impact on western Europe more generally.

Other facets of popular culture displayed a new vigor. Again in Britain, youth fashions, separate from the standards of the upper class, showed an ability to innovate and sometimes to shock. Unconventional uses of color and cut, as in the punk hairstyles of the latter 1970s, bore some resemblance to the anticonventional tone of modern painting and sculpture.

Sexual culture also changed in the West, building on earlier trends that linked sex to a larger pleasure-seeking mentality characteristic of growing consumerism and to a desire for personal expression. Films and television shows demonstrated increasingly relaxed standards about sexual display. In Britain, Holland, and Denmark sex shops sold a wide array of erotic materials and products.

Like the United States, western Europe experienced important changes in sexual behavior starting around 1960, particularly among young people. Premarital sex became more common. The average age of first sexual intercourse began to go down. For a time as a result, the rates of illegitimate births began to rise once more, after a long period of stability since 1870. But Europeans adjusted relatively easily to the new habits and began urging teenagers to use birth control devices; in contrast, reactions in the United States were more tentative and prudish, with the result that teenage ignorance of birth control measures remained more widespread. Expressive sexuality in western Europe was also evident in the growing number of nude bathing spots, again in interesting contrast to more hesitant initiatives in the United States. Although the association of modern popular culture with sexuality and body concern was not novel, the openness and diversity of expression unquestionably reached new levels and also demonstrated western Europe's new confidence in defining a vigorous, nontraditional mass culture of its own.

Cultural innovation, like social change, brought disturbance as well as enthusiasm. Although critics of changing tastes were less numerous and less political than between the wars—there was no counterpart to the earlier Nazi attack on modern styles or women's fashions—there was concern about the disparity between formal intellectual life, where energies might be flagging, and the vibrancy of youth-oriented popular styles. Other observers wondered whether enthusiasms for new fashions and antiestablishment lyrics misleadingly distracted ordinary people in what was still a hierarchical society—but this, of course, was a complex subject that had emerged with the birth of modern popular culture itself.

CONCLUSION: ADJUSTING TO ADVANCED INDUSTRIAL SOCIETY

Changes in Western society in the late 20th century set part of the framework for the world as a whole; they generated new tensions within the West itself; and they even suggested a new kind of society that might in turn have its own global consequences.

Under U.S. leadership, Western policies in the cold war helped generate important military interventions (as in Korea and Vietnam) and war scares during the four decades after World War II. They—along with the Soviet Union—also contributed to a growing international armament level. Increasingly sophisticated weapons combined with a desire to win loyalties and make sales. Countries like the United States and France, and their communist counterparts like the Soviet Union and Czechoslovakia, became major arms suppliers to countries throughout the world.

At the same time, Western prosperity created growing interest in many aspects of Western culture, from democracy and science to consumerism. Along with Japan, the West became the world's major supplier of international popular culture and standards. This same role, of course, inspired resistance from groups that resented Western economic prominence and cultural influences in such areas as conditions for women or sexuality in the media.

Tensions within the West were also important, though they were less raw than the class warfare of the 1930s. Many observers commented on the relationship between the high levels of rationality and emotional control required at work, and growing spectator interest in violence and pornography noted the dualism present in formal culture and popular outlook since the 19th century. There were other pressures. On the one hand,

Western society encouraged children to think of themselves as individuals, whereas the growing leisure interests also appealed to individual pleasure seeking. But individualism was severely curtailed by the growing bureaucratization of society. Most jobs involved routine activities, controlled by an elaborate supervisory apparatus; individual initiative counted for little in factories or in the offices of giant corporations. Leisure, appealing to individual self-expression in one sense, generally in practice meant mass, commercially manipulated outlets for all but a handful of venturesome souls. By the 1950s television watching had become far and away the leading recreational interest of Western peoples, and most television fare was deliberately standardized. Ironically, individualism and its outlets in consumer behavior often made collective protest against bureaucratization and routine extremely difficult. One reason for the decline of organized labor in the West was the growing need of workers to spend time earning money to buy new cars or to go places with their new cars.

To Western and non-Western critics alike, Western society at times seemed badly confused. Poverty and job boredom coexisted with affluence and continued appeals to the essential value of work. Youth protest—including defiant clothing and hairstyles and pulsating rock music, family instability, and growing crime—might be signs of a fatally flawed society. The rising rates of suicide and increasing incidence of mental illness were other troubling symptoms. At the least, Western society continued to display the strains of change.

By the 1970s, many people in Western society believed that they were facing greater changes than ever before, whether for better or for worse. A new concept of a postindustrial society took shape both in western Europe and in North America. The idea was that Western society was leading in a transformation as fundamental as the Industrial Revolution had been. The rise of a service economy, according to this argument, promised as many shifts as the rise of an industrial economy had done. Control of knowledge, rather than control of goods, would be the key to the postindustrial social structure. Technology would allow expansion of factory production with a shrinking labor force, and attention would shift to the generation and control of information. The advent of new technology, particularly the computer, supported the postindustrial concept by applying to knowledge transmission the same potential technological revolution the steam engine had brought to manufacturing.

Changes in the roles of women paralleled the postindustrial concept, and some observers began to talk of a postindustrial family in which two equal spouses would pool their earnings in a high-consumption lifestyle. Postindustrial cities would increasingly become entertainment centers, as most work could now be decentralized in suburbs, linked by the omnipresent computer. Postindustrial politics were less clearly defined, though some commentators noted that the old party structure might loosen as new, service-sector voters sought issues more appropriate to their interests. The rise of environmental and feminist concerns, which cut across older political alignments, thus might prove an opening wedge to an unpredictable future for the West.

The postindustrial society is not established fact, of course. Important continuities with earlier social forms, including political values and cultural directions, suggest that new technologies might modify rather than revolutionize Western industrial society. It is clear, however, that Western society has taken on important new characteristics, ranging from age brackets to occupational structure, that differentiate it from the initial industrial patterns generated in the 19th century. And this fact, even if more modest than the visions of some postindustrial forecasters, raises a vital question for the West and the world: How would a rapidly changing, advanced industrial society fit into a world that has yet fully to industrialize? How could the concerns of an affluent, urban, fad-conscious Westerner coexist with the values of the world's peasant majority?

For there was a final complication in the developments in the West in the decades after World War II. The prosperity of Western economies, along with those in the Pacific Rim, contrasted with growing poverty in many parts of the world. Global economic inequality increased. The West provided a huge and growing market not just for foods and raw materials, but for manufactured goods like textiles, produced by badly paid workers in factories in Southeast Asia, Latin America, and Africa. Western living standards, disseminated around the world through tourism and the media, helped define aspirations for many people in almost all of the world's societies, but growing economic gaps constituted the stark realities for many of these same people.

FURTHER READING

Important overviews of recent European history are found in Walter Laqueur, *Europe Since Hitler* (1982); John Darwin, *Britain and Decolonization* (1988); Helen

Wallace et al., *Policy-Making in the European Community* (1983); and Alfred Grosser, *The Western Alliance* (1982).

Some excellent national interpretations provide vital coverage of events since 1945 in key areas of Europe. See A. F. Havighurst's *Britain in Transition: The Twentieth Century* (1982) and John Ardagh's highly readable *The New French Revolution: A Social and Economic Survey of France* (1968) and *France in the 1980s* (1982). Volker Berghahn's *Modern Germany: Society, Economy and Politics in the 20th Century* (1983) is also useful.

On post–World War II social and economic trends, see C. Kindleberger, *Europe's Postwar Growth* (1967); V. Bogdanor and R. Skidelsky, eds., *The Age of Affluence, 1951–1964* (1970); R. Dahrendorf, ed., *Europe's Economy in Crisis* (1982); and Peter Stearns and Herrick Chapman, *European Society in Upheaval* (1991). On the welfare state, see Stephen Cohen's *Modern Capitalist Planning: The French Model* (1977) and E. S. Einhorn and J. Logue's *Welfare States in Hard Times* (1982).

On the relevant Commonwealth nations, see Charles Doran, *Forgotten Partnership: U.S.-Canada Relations Today* (1983); Edward McWhinney, *Canada and the Constitution, 1979–1982* (1982); and Stephen Graubard, ed., *Australia: Terra Incognita?* (1985).

ON THE WEB

Stalin's death heralded much political infighting, discussed at

http://www.1upinfo.com/country-guide-study/
    soviet-union/soviet-union65.html

This eventually saw the installation of Nikita Khrushchev, discussed at

http://www.cnn.com/SPECIALS/cold.war/kbank/
    profiles/khrushchev/

Khrushchev's famous "We will bury you" remarks are offered at

http://www.em.doe.gov/timeline/nov1956.html

Soviet attacks on dissidents can be found at

http://www.ibiblio.org/expo/soviet.exhibit/attack.html

The life and work of Russian cold war leader Leonid Brezhnev and the speech that established what became known as the Brezhnev Doctrine can be found at

http://www.cnn.com/SPECIALS/cold.war/episodes/14/
    documents/doctrine/

http://www.cnn.com/SPECIALS/cold.war/kbank/
profiles/brezhnev/

Links for the study of the Soviet space program are
offered at

http://www.slavweb.com/eng/Russia/space-e0.html

The role of that program in the cold war is examined at

http://www.pbs.org/newshour/forum/october97/
sputnik_10-13.html

http://socstudy.onysd.wednet.edu/academics/history/us/
coldwar.html

Excellent overviews of the Cold War in text, images,
and documents are available at

http://cwihp.si.edu/
http://www.coldwar.org/
http://www.fas.harvard.edu/~hpcws/index2.htm
http://www.stmartin.edu/~dprice/cold.war.html
http://history.acusd.edu/gen/20th/coldwar0.html

American President John F. Kennedy's famous "Ich bin
ein Berliner" speech is presented in written and audio
formats at

http://www.coldwar.org/museum/berlin_wall_exhibit
.html

This site also traces the Berlin Wall's rise and demise.

The Cold War's impact on American domestic politics is
presented at

http://www.spartacus.schoolnet.co.uk/USAmccarthyism
.htm

American intervention in Latin America during the cold
war is examined at

http://web.mit.edu/cascon/cases/case_els.html
http://www.hartford-hwp.com/archives/47/index-ca
.html
http://www.coha.org/WRH_issues/wrh_21_15_nic.htm
http://www.hartford-hwp.com/archives/47/index-fba
.html

The National Security Archives offers audio tapes of
related intelligence briefings, images of Soviet missile
bases in Cuba, and minute-by-minute chronologies of
the crisis at

http://www.gwu.edu/~nsarchiv/nsa/cuba_mis_cri/

Sites devoted to the women's liberation movement
include

http://scriptorium.lib.duke.edu/wim/wlm
http://lists.village.virginia.edu/sixties/1960s

Feminism and the place of Betty Friedan in the American feminist movement is discussed at

http://womenshistory.about.com/od/quotes/a/
betty_friedan.htm

A militant view of the alleged ills of the affluent society
and the growing dominance of multinational and non-
state organizations in the postmodern era is presented at

http://www.socialconscience.com/

A less radical view that nonetheless suggests that the
twin pillars of Western Civilization (the market economy and democracy) are more likely to undermine than
support each other can be found at

http://www.mtholyoke.edu/acad/Intrel/attali.html

Chapter 10

The Eastern Bloc, the Cold War, and Global Repercussions

Successful competition in international athletic events, such as those at the Olympics, were among the great accomplishments of the states of the Soviet bloc. At the 1988 Summer Olympics in Seoul, the Soviet men's gymnastic team celebrates its long-standing monopoly of the team gold medals.

Chronology

1945–1948	Soviet takeover of Eastern Europe
1949	Soviet Union develops atomic bomb
1953	Stalin dies
1955	Formation of Warsaw Pact
1956	Stalinism attacked by Khrushchev
1956	Hungarian revolt and its suppression
1961	Berlin Wall erected
1962	Cuban missile crisis
1968	Revolt in Czechoslovakia and its repression; Soviet policy (Brezhnev Doctrine) proclaims right to intervene in any Socialist country
1979	Uprisings in Poland and their suppression
1979	Soviet invasion of Afghanistan

INTRODUCTION

From the vantage point of the early 21st century, it is obvious that developments in the Soviet Union and Eastern Europe, in the years after World War II, had far less lasting global importance than those in the West. For several decades, however, the Soviet Union maintained the other side of the cold war, thus contributing to rivalries, arms sales, and other global developments whose significance persists. This was a vital period in Soviet history, as the heritage of the 1917 revolution was refined, and also in the east-central European countries that fell under Soviet control. Even today, as both Russia and east-central Europe have cast off communism, they continue to grapple with changes that the Soviet system introduced. On the whole while rejecting this system they also show no desire to go back to the regimes that the system displaced.

Soviet influence also had an unprecedented importance in wider world history during the 20th century, for several reasons. The Russian Revolution and the success of the Soviet state seemed to many people, in many parts of the world, a vital beacon. The example of the revolution and the rise of Communist movements to some extent patterned after and guided by Russian leadership played a vital role in world history both before and after 1945. China and Cuba used Russian models, though adding their own twists. Revolutionaries elsewhere in Latin America, Asia, Africa, and the West drew inspiration from the Soviet system.

Global influence went beyond outright communist movements. Many governments developed welfare programs in part to compete with communist social goals.

Concern about communism encouraged some of the new movements for greater racial justice within the United States. Communist example also promoted new approaches to international sports, with ramifications that still echo today. The Soviet system could also encourage science—many students from Africa and Asia attended Soviet scientific and technical institutions. Humankind's ventures into space—and the rivalries that then followed—owe much to Soviet initiatives.

Spurred by the revolution and ongoing industrialization, the new Soviet Union emerged, after 1945, as one of the two great world powers. Soviet economic and military influence burst beyond Europe and Asia, to have direct effects literally around the globe, as the rivalry between the Soviet Union and the United States set a basic framework for world diplomacy in the post–World War II decades. The Soviet role must thus be added to the factors considered in the intensifying world exchange of the 20th century. For several decades after 1945, as Western colonial controls receded, Soviet ideological influence seemed to rival the West's cultural outreach in the world at large.

One means of sorting out the complex history of the Soviet Union and its global impact after 1945 involves division into three subperiods. Between 1945 and 1955 the Soviet Union seized on new opportunities as a World War II victor, while also attempting to prevent a recurrence of outside attack and grappling with the superpower activities of the United States. Stalinism survived, but it was altered by the growing international role. The years between 1956 and 1985, as Stalinism was modified, saw the consolidation of the Soviet Union as world superpower and the development of Eastern Europe into what was effectively a new Soviet empire. Finally, since 1985 a host of innovations and uncertainties have shaken the Soviet system, dissolved its empire, and raised questions about the survival of the Russian state itself.

THEMES IN EASTERN EUROPEAN HISTORY SINCE 1945

By 1945 Soviet foreign policy had several ingredients. Desire to regain tsarist boundaries (though not carried through regarding Finland) joined with traditional interest in expansion and in playing an active role in European diplomacy. The genuine fear inspired by Germany's two consecutive invasions, in the two world wars, prompted a feverish desire to set up buffer zones, under Soviet control. As a result of Soviet industrialization and its World War II push westward, the nation also emerged as a world power, like the newcomer United States. Continued concentration on heavy industry and weapons development, combined with strategic alliances and links to Communist movements in various parts of the world, helped maintain this status.

The Soviet Union as Superpower

Soviet participation in the late phases of the war against Japan provided an opportunity to seize some islands in the northern Pacific. The Soviet Union established a protectorate over the Communist regime of North Korea, to match the U.S. protectorate in South Korea. Soviet aid to the victorious Communist Party in China brought new influence in that country for a time and in the 1970s the Soviet Union gained a new ally in Communist Vietnam, which provided naval bases for the Soviet fleet. Its growing military and economic strength gave the postwar Soviet Union new leverage in the Middle East, Africa, and even parts of Latin America; alliance with the new Communist regime in Cuba was a key step here, during the 1960s. The Soviet Union's superpower status was confirmed by its development of the atomic and then hydrogen bombs, from 1949 onward, and by its deployment of missiles and naval forces to match the rapid expansion of U.S. arsenals.

The New Soviet Empire in Eastern Europe

As a superpower, the Soviet Union developed increasing worldwide influence, with trade and cultural missions on all inhabited continents and military alliances with several Asian, African, and Latin American nations. Russia had long affected developments in the neighboring Middle East and China, and this obviously continued: initially cordial relations with communist China turned into considerable rivalry, while the Soviet Union ventured various alliances with Middle Eastern states while also developing new concerns about Islamic movements.

The clearest extension of the Soviet sphere, however, developed right after World War II, in Eastern Europe. Here the Soviets made it plain that they intended to stay, pushing the Soviet effective sphere of influence farther to the west than ever before in history. Soviet insistence on this empire helped launch the cold war, as the Soviet Union displayed its willingness to confront the West rather than relax its grip.

The small nations of Eastern Europe, mostly new or revived after World War I, had gone through a troubled period between the world wars. Other than democratic Czechoslovakia, they had failed to establish vigorous, independent economies or solid political systems. Then came the Nazi attack, and ineffective Western response, as Czechoslovakia, Poland, and Yugoslavia were seized by German or Italian forces. Eastern Europe fell under Nazi control for four years. Although anti-Nazi governments formed abroad, only in Yugoslavia was a resistance movement strong enough to seriously affect postwar results.

By 1945 the dominant force in Eastern Europe was the Soviet army, as it pushed the Germans back and remade the map of Eastern Europe. Through the combination of the Soviet military might and collaboration with local Communist movements in the nations that remained technically independent, opposition parties were crushed and non-Communist regimes forced out by 1948. The only exceptions to this pattern were Greece, which moved toward the Western camp in diplomatic alignment and political and social systems; Albania, which formed a rigid Stalinist regime that ironically brought it into disagreement with Soviet post-Stalinist leaders; and Yugoslavia, where a Communist regime formed under the resistance leader Tito quickly proclaimed its neutrality in the cold war, resisting Soviet direction and trying to form a more open-ended, responsive version of the Communist economic and social systems.

After what was in effect the Soviet takeover, a standard development dynamic emerged throughout most of Eastern Europe by the early 1950s. The new Soviet-sponsored regimes attacked possible rivals for power, including, where relevant, the Roman Catholic church. Mass education and propaganda outlets were quickly developed. Collectivization of agriculture ended the large

Legend:
- Warsaw Pact
- Boundaries, 1939
- Post–World War II boundaries
- Soviet Union, 1939
- Lands gained by Soviet Union

Soviet and East European Boundaries by 1948

estate system, without creating a property-owning peasantry. Industrialization was pushed through successive five-year plans, though with some limitation due to Soviet insistence on access to key natural resources (such as Romanian oil) on favorable terms. Finally, a Soviet-Eastern European trading zone became largely separate from the larger trends of international commerce.

After the formation of NATO in western Europe, the relevant Eastern European nations were also enfolded in a common defense alliance, the Warsaw Pact, and a common economic planning organization. Soviet troops continued to be stationed in most Eastern European states both to confront the Western alliance and to ensure the continuation of the new regimes and their loyalty to the common cause.

Although it responded to many social problems in the smaller nations of Eastern Europe, as well as to the desire of the Soviet Union to expand its influence and guard against German or more general Western attack, the new Soviet system created obvious tensions. Dissatisfaction with particularly tight controls in East Germany brought a workers' rising in 1953, vigorously repressed by Soviet troops, and widespread exodus to West Germany until a wall was built in Berlin in 1961 to stem the flow. All along the new borders of Eastern Europe, barbed wire fences and armed patrols kept the people in. In 1956 a relaxation of Stalinism within the Soviet Union created new hopes that controls might be loosened. More liberal Communist leaders arose in Hungary and Poland, with massive popular backing, seeking to create states that, although Communist, would permit greater diversity and certainly more freedom from Soviet domination. In Poland the Soviets accepted a new leader more popular with the Polish people. Among other results, Poland was allowed to halt agricultural collectivization, establishing widespread peasant ownership in its place, and the Catholic Church, now the symbol of Polish independence, gained greater tolerance. But a new regime in Hungary was cruelly and quickly crushed by the Soviet army in 1956 and a hard-line Stalinist leadership set up in its place.

Yet Soviet control over Eastern Europe did loosen slightly overall, for the heavy-handed repression cost considerable prestige. Eastern European governments were given a freer hand in economic policy and were allowed limited room to experiment with greater cultural freedom. Several countries thus began to outstrip the prosperity of the Soviet Union itself. Contacts with the West expanded in several cases, with greater trade and tourism. Eastern Europe remained with the Soviet Union as a somewhat separate economic bloc in world trade, but there was room for limited diversity. Individual nations, such as Hungary, developed new intellectual vigor and experimented with slightly less centralized economic planning. The Communist political system remained in full force, however, with its single-party dominance and strong police controls; diplomatic and military alignment with the Soviet Union remained essential.

The limits of experimentation in Eastern Europe were brought home again in 1968, when a more liberal regime came to power in Czechoslovakia. Again the Soviet army responded, expelling the reformers and setting up a particularly rigid leader. A challenge came from Poland once more in the late 1970s, in the form of widespread Catholic unrest and an independent labor movement called Solidarity, all against the backdrop of a stagnant economy and low morale. Here response was slightly more muted, though key agitators were arrested; the Polish army took over the state, under careful Soviet supervision.

By the 1980s Eastern Europe had been vastly transformed by several decades of Communist rule. Important national diversity remained, visible both in industrial

As Soviet troops moved into Hungary to crush the revolt of 1956, freedom fighters in Budapest headed for the front with whatever weapons they could find. This truckload of supporters is being urged on by the crowd.

levels and in political styles. Catholic Poland thus differed from hard-line, neo-Stalinist Bulgaria or Romania. Important discontents remained as well. Yet a Communist-imposed social revolution had brought considerable economic change and real social upheaval, through the abolition of the once-dominant aristocracy and the remaking of the peasant masses through collectivization, new systems of mass education, and industrial, urban growth. Earlier cultural ties with the West, though still greater than in the Soviet Union itself, had been lessened; Russian, not French or English, was the first foreign language learned.

The expansion of Soviet influence answered important Soviet foreign policy goals, both traditional and new. The Soviets retained a military presence deep in Europe, which among other things reduced very real anxiety about yet another German threat. Eastern European allies aided Soviet ventures in other parts of the world, providing supplies and advisors for activities in Africa, Latin America, and elsewhere. Yet the recurrent unrest in Eastern Europe served as something of a check on Soviet policy as well. The need for continued military presence may have diverted Soviet leaders from emphasizing expansionist ambitions in other directions, particularly where direct commitment of troops might be involved.

Evolution of Domestic Policies

Within the Soviet Union the Stalinist system remained intact during the initial postwar years. The war encouraged growing use of nationalism as well as appeals for Communist loyalty, as millions of Russians responded heroically to the new foreign threat. Elements of this mood were sustained as the cold war with the United States developed after 1947, with news media blasting the United States as an evil power and a distorted society. Many Soviets, fearful of a new war that U.S. aggressiveness seemed to them to threaten, agreed that strong government authority remained necessary. This attitude helped sustain the difficult rebuilding efforts after the war, which proceeded rapidly enough for the Soviet Union to regain its prewar industrial capacity and then proceed, during the 1950s, to impressive annual growth rates. The attitude also helped support Stalin's rigorous efforts to shield the Soviet populations from extensive contact with foreigners or foreign ideas. Strict limits on travel, outside media, or any uncensored glimpse of the outside world kept the Soviet Union unusually isolated in the mid-20th-century world—its culture, like its economy, largely removed from world currents.

Stalin's political structure continued to emphasize central controls and the omnipresent party bureaucracy, leavened by the adulation accorded to Stalin and by the aging leader's endemic suspiciousness. Moscow-based direction of the national economy, along with the steady extensions of education, welfare, and police operations, expanded the bureaucracy both of the government and of the parallel Communist Party. Recruitment from the ranks of peasant and worker families continued into the 1940s, as educational opportunities, including growing secondary school and university facilities, allowed talented young people to rise from below. Party membership, the ticket to bureaucratic promotion, was deliberately kept low, at about 6 percent of the population, to ensure selection of the most dedicated elements. New candidates for the party, drawn mostly from the more broadly based Communist youth organizations, had to be nominated by at least three party members. Party members vowed unswerving loyalty and group consciousness. A 1939 Communist party charter stated the essential qualities:

> The Party is a united militant organization bound together by a conscious discipline which is equally binding on all its members. The Party is strong because of its solidarity, unity of will and unity of action, which are incompatible with any deviation from its program and rules, with any violation of Party discipline, with fractional groupings, or with double dealing. The Party purges its ranks of persons who violate its program, rules or discipline.

Through the party apparatus, the Soviet system became one of careful hierarchy and elaborate bureaucracy. The Communist Party itself was run by the Politburo, a top political bureau consisting of 20 people who were the real power brokers in the nation—operating, of course, under Stalin's watchful eye. Most Politburo members also held key ministries or top positions in the secret police or army. The Politburo apparatus helped coordinate these various branches and balance their interests and ambitions. Both party and state, as overlapping governing bodies, spread gradations of authority from the top committees through the state governments to local industries, cities, and collective farms. Decisions were made at the top, often in secret, and then transmitted to lower levels for execution; little reverse initiative, with proposals coming from lower bureaucratic agencies, was encouraged.

The Stalinist version of this system, indeed, engendered particular bureaucratic caution. Innovative proposals, much less criticisms, were risky. Top officials who kept their posts tended to be colorless figures, competent but above all extremely loyal both to official ideology and to Stalin as a leader. For example, one durable foreign minister, Molotov, was described by Stalin himself as having a "mind like a file clerk."

The Communist government built on the precedent of tsarist authoritarianism. As with the tsars, political contests and open-ended agencies, much less multiparty parliaments, were shunned. Carefully worded constitutions gave citizens the vote, and indeed required participation in elections, but mainly to rubber-stamp official candidates and policies. The Supreme Soviet, like the earlier Duma, had no power to initiate legislation or block official decisions; it served to ratify and praise.

SOVIET CULTURE: PROMOTING NEW BELIEFS AND INSTITUTIONS

The Soviet government was a source of major innovations in both society and culture, not just a renewal of tsarist autocracy. It carried on a much wider array of functions than the tsars had ventured, not only in fostering industrialization but also in reaching out for the direct loyalties of individual citizens.

The government and the party maintained an active cultural agenda, and although this had been foreshadowed by the church-state links of tsarist days, it had no full precedent. The regime declared war on the Orthodox Church and other religions soon after 1917, seeking to shape a secular population that would maintain a Marxist, scientific orthodoxy; vestigial church activities remained but under tight government regulation. Artistic and literary styles, as well as purely political writings, were carefully monitored to ensure adherence to the party line. The educational system was used not only to train and recruit technicians and bureaucrats but also to create a loyal, right-thinking citizenry. Mass ceremonies, such as May Day parades, stimulated devotion to the state and to communism.

Although the new regime did not attempt to abolish the Orthodox Church outright, it greatly limited the church's outreach. Thus the church was barred from giving religious instruction to anyone under 18, and state schools vigorously preached the doctrine that religion was mere superstition. The Soviet regime also limited freedom of religion for the Jewish minority, often holding up Jews as enemies of the state in what was in fact a manipulation of traditional Russian anti-Semitism. The larger Muslim minority was given greater latitude, on condition of careful loyalty to the regime. On the whole, the traditional religious orientation of Soviet society declined in favor of a scientific outlook and Marxist explanations of history in terms of class conflict. Church attendance dwindled under government repression; by the 1950s only the elderly seemed particularly interested.

The Soviet state also continued to attack modern Western styles of art and literature, terming them decadent, while maintaining some earlier Western styles, which were appropriated as Russian. Thus Russian orchestras performed a wide variety of classical music, and the Russian ballet, though rigid and conservative by 20th-century Western norms, commanded wide attention and enforced rigid standards of excellence. Soviet culture emphasized a new style of "socialist realism" in the arts, bent on glorifying heroic workers, soldiers, and peasants through grandiose neoclassical paintings and sculpture. Soviet architecture, though careful to preserve older buildings, emphasized functional, classical lines, with a pronounced taste for the monumental. Socialist realist principles spread to Eastern Europe after World War II, particularly in public displays and monuments. With some political loosening and cold war thaw after 1950, however, Soviet and Eastern European artists began to adopt Western styles to some extent. At the popular level, jazz and rock music bands began to emerge by the 1980s, though official suspicion persisted.

Literature in the Soviet Union remained diverse and creative, despite official controls sponsored by the Communist-dominated Writers' Union. Leading authors wrote movingly of the travails of World War II, maintaining the earlier tradition of sympathy with the people, great patriotism, and concern for the Russian soul. The most creative Soviet artists, particularly the writers, often skirted a fine line between conveying some of the sufferings of the Russian people in the 20th century and courting official disapproval. Their freedom also depended on

leadership mood; thus censorship eased after Stalin and then tightened again somewhat in the late 1960s and 1970s, though not to previous levels. Yet even authors critical of aspects of the Soviet regime maintained distinctive Russian values. Aleksandr Solzhenitsyn, for example, exiled to the United States after the publication of *The Gulag Archipelago*, his trilogy on Siberian prison camps, found the West too materialistic and individualistic for his taste. Though barred from his homeland, he continued to seek an alternative both to Communist policy and to Westernization, with more than a hint of a continuing belief in the durable solidarity and faith of the Russian common people and a mysterious Russian national soul.

Along with interest in the arts and a genuine diversity of expressions despite official party lines, Soviet culture continued to place great emphasis on science and social science. Scientists enjoyed great prestige and wielded considerable power. Social scientific work, heavily colored by Marxist theory, nonetheless produced important analyses of current trends and of history. Scientific research was even more heavily funded, and Soviet scientists generated a number of fundamental discoveries in physics, chemistry, and mathematics. At times scientists themselves felt the heavy hand of official disapproval. Biologists and psychiatrists, particularly, were urged to reject Western theories that called human rationality and social progress into question, though here as in other areas controls were most stringent in the Stalinist years. Thus Freudianism was banned, and under Stalin biologists who overemphasized the uncontrollability of genetic evolution were jailed. But Soviet scientists overall enjoyed considerable freedom and great prestige. As in the West, their work was often linked with advances in technology and weaponry. After the heyday of Stalinism, scientists gained greater freedom from ideological dictates, and exchanges with Western researchers became more common in what was, at base, a common scientific culture.

Shaped by substantial state control, 20th-century Soviet culture overall proved neither traditional nor Western. Considerable ambivalence about the West remained, as Soviets continued to utilize many art forms they developed in common with the West, such as the ballet, while instilling a comparable faith in science. Fear of cultural pollution—particularly, of course, through non-Marxist political tracts but also through modern art forms—remained lively, as Soviet leaders sought a culture that would enhance their goals of building a socialist society separate from the capitalist West.

Economy and Society

The Soviet Union became a fully industrial society between the 1920s and the 1950s. Rapid growth of manufacturing and the rise of urban populations to more than 50 percent of the total were measures of this development. Most of the rest of Eastern Europe was also heavily industrialized by the 1950s. Eastern European modernization, however, had a number of distinctive features. State control of virtually all economic sectors was one key element; no other industrialized society gave so little leeway to private initiative. The unusual imbalance between heavy industrial goods and consumer items was another distinctive aspect. The Soviet Union lagged in the priorities it placed on consumer goods—not only such Western staples as automobiles but also housing construction and simple items, such as bathtub plugs. Consumer-goods industries were poorly funded and did not achieve the advanced technological level that characterized the heavy-manufacturing sector.

The Soviet need to amass capital for development in a traditionally poor society helped explain the inattention to consumer goods; so did the need to create, in a society that remained poorer overall, a massive armaments industry to rival that of the United States. Thus despite an occasional desire to beat the West at its own affluent-society game, Eastern Europe did not develop the kind of consumer society that came to characterize the West. Living standards improved and extensive welfare services provided security for some groups not similarly supported in the West—state-sponsored vacations for workers, for example, became a valued feature of Soviet society—but complaints about poor consumer products and long lines to obtain desired goods remained a feature of Soviet life.

Soviet industrialization also caused an unusual degree of environmental damage. The drive to produce at all costs created bleak zones around factories, where waste was dumped, and in agricultural mining areas up to one quarter of all Soviet territory (and that of the Eastern bloc) was environmentally degraded, often with severe health damages as well.

The Communist system throughout Eastern Europe also failed to resolve problems with agriculture. Capital that might have gone into farming equipment was often diverted to armaments and heavy industry. The arduous climate of northern Europe and Asia was a factor as well, dooming a number of attempts to spread grain production to Siberia, for example. But it seemed clear that the Eastern European peasantry continued to find the constraints and lack of individual incentive in collectivized agriculture deterrents to maximum effort. Thus Eastern Europe had to retain a larger percentage of its labor force in agriculture than was true of the industrial West, but it still encountered problems with food supply and quality.

Despite the importance of distinctive political and economic characteristics, Eastern European society echoed a number of the themes of contemporary Western social history—simply because of the shared fact of industrial life. Work rhythms, for example, became roughly similar. Industrialization brought massive efforts to speed the pace of work and to introduce regularized supervision. The incentive systems designed to encourage able workers resembled those used in Western factories. Along with similar work habits came similar leisure activities. For decades, sports has provided excitement for the peoples of Eastern Europe, as have films and television. Family vacations to the beaches of the Black Sea became cherished respites. Here, too, there were some distinctive twists, as the Communist states boosted sports efforts as part of their political program (in contrast to the Western view of sports as a combination of leisure and commercialism). East Germany, along with the Soviet Union, developed particularly extensive athletic programs under state sponsorship, winning international competitions in a host of fields.

Eastern European social structure also grew closer to that of the West, despite the continued importance of the rural population and despite the impact of Marxist theory. Particularly interesting was a tendency to divide urban society along class lines—between workers and a better-educated, managerial middle class. Wealth divisions remained much less great than in the West, to be sure, but the perquisites of managers and professional people—particularly for Communist Party members—set them off from the standard of living of the masses.

Finally, the Soviet family reacted to some of the same pressures of industrialization as did the Western family. Massive movements to the cities and crowded housing enhanced the nuclear family unit, as ties to a wider network of relatives loosened. The birthrate dropped. Official Soviet policy on birthrates varied for a time, but the basic pressures became similar to those in the West: Falling infant death rates, with improved diets and medical care, together with increased periods of schooling and some increase in consumer expectations, made large families less desirable than before. Wartime dislocations contributed to birthrate decline at points as well. By the 1970s the Soviet growth rate was about the same as that of the West. As in the West, also, some minority groups—particularly Muslims in the southern Soviet

DOCUMENT

1986: A New Wave of Reform

The following document (from a speech to the Communist Party in Khabarovsk) reflects a wave of reform introduced in 1986 by a new Soviet leader, Mikhail Gorbachev. Gorbachev's policies ultimately ushered in a major new era of Russian history. At the time, however, they represented an attempt to save the key features of the Soviet state while recognizing ominous new problems. (We will take up the unanticipated changes in Chapter 14.) The document obviously invites analysis around several issues, including what features of the Soviet state Gorbachev sought to preserve, what new problems he identified, and how he intended to deal with them. You might also speculate about why the reforms turned out to spin out of Soviet control.

> None of us can continue living in the old way. This is obvious. In this sense, we can say that a definite step toward acceleration has been made.
>
> However, there is a danger that the first step will be taken as success, that we will assume that the whole situation has been taken in hand. I said this in Vladivostok. I want to say it again in Khabarovsk. If we were to draw this conclusion, we would be making a big mistake, an error. What has been achieved cannot yet satisfy us in any way. In general, one should never flatter oneself with what has been accomplished. All of us must learn this well. Such are the lessons of the past decades—the last two, at least. And now this is especially dangerous.
>
> No profound qualitative changes that would reinforce the trend toward accelerated growth have taken place as yet. In general, comrades, important and intensive work lies ahead of us. To put it bluntly, the main thing is still to come. Our country's Party, the entire Party, should understand this well. . . .
>
> We should learn as we go along, accomplishing new tasks. And we must not be afraid of advancing boldly, of doing things on the march, in the course of the active accomplishment of economic and social tasks. . . .
>
> Restructuring is a capacious word. I would equate the word restructuring with the word revolution. Our transformations, the reforms mapped out in the decisions of the April plenary session of the Party Central Committee and the 27th CPSU (Communist Party of the Soviet Union) Congress, are a genuine revolution in the entire system of relations in society, in the minds and hearts of people, in the psychology and understanding of the present period and, above all, in the tasks engendered by rapid scientific and technical progress.
>
> There is a common understanding in the CPSU and in the country as a whole—we should look for answers to the questions raised by life not outside of socialism but within the framework of our system, disclosing the potential of a planned economy, socialist democracy and culture and the human factor, and relying on the people's vital creativity.
>
> Some people in the West do not like this. There everyone lies in wait for something that would mean a deviation from socialism, for us to go hat in hand to capitalism, for us to borrow its methods. We are receiving a great deal of "advice" from abroad as to how and where we should proceed. Various kinds of provocative broadcasts are made, and articles are published, aimed at casting aspersions on the changes taking place in our country and at driving a wedge between the Party leadership and the people. Such improper attempts are doomed to failure. The interests of the Party and the people are inseparable, and our choice and political course are firm and unshakable. On this main point, the people and the Party are united.
>
> But we also cannot allow ingrained dogmas to cloud our eyes, to impede our progress and keep us from creatively elaborating theory and applying it in practice, in the given, concrete historical stage through which our society is passing. We cannot allow this, either.
>
> I am saying this also because among us there are still, of course, people who have difficulty in accepting the word "restructuring" [perestroika] and who even sometimes can pronounce it only with difficulty. In this process of renewal, they often see not what it in fact contains but all but a shaking of foundations, all but a renunciation of our principles. Our political line is aimed at fully disclosing the potential and advantages of the socialist system, removing all barriers and all obstructions to our progress, and creating scope for factors of social progress.
>
> I want to say something else. The farther we advance into restructuring, the more the complexity of this task is revealed, and the more fully the enormous scale and volume of the forthcoming work is brought out. It is becoming clearer to what extent many notions

about the economy and management, social questions, statehood and democracy, upbringing and education and moral demands still lag behind today's requirements and tasks, especially the tasks of further development.

We will have to remove layer by layer, the accumulated problems in all spheres of the life of society, freeing ourselves of what has outlived its time and boldly making creative decisions. . . .

Sometimes people ask: Well, just what is this odd business, restructuring? How do you understand it, "what do you eat it with," this restructuring? Yes, we're all for it, some say, but we don't know what to do. Many say this straight out. . . .

Restructuring proposes the creation of an atmosphere in society that will impel people to overcome accumulated inertia and indifference, to rid themselves, in work and in life, of everything that does not correspond to the principles of socialism, to our world views and way of life. Frankly, there is some work to be done here. But in this instance everyone must look first of all at himself, comrades—in the Politburo, in the primary Party organizations—and everyone must make a specific attempt to take himself in hand. In past years, we got used to some things in an atmosphere of insufficient criticism, openness and responsibility, things that do not all correspond to the principles of socialism. I apply this both to rank-and-file personnel and to officials. . . .

In general, comrades, we must change our style of work. It should be permeated with respect for the people and their opinions, with real, unfeigned closeness to them. We must actually go to people, listen to them, meet with them, inform them. And the more difficult things are, the more often we must meet with them and be with them when some task or other is being accomplished. In our country, people are responsive; they are a wonderful people, you can't find another people like them. Our people have the greatest endurance. Our people have the greatest political activeness. And now it is growing. This must be welcomed and encouraged in every way. Let us consider that we have come to an agreement on this in the Khabarovsk Party organization (*Applause.*)

In this connection, some words about public openness [glasnost]. It is sometimes said: Well, why has the Central Committee launched criticism, self-criticism and openness on such a broad scale? I can tell you that so far we have lost nothing, we have only gained. The people have felt an influx of energy; they have become bolder and more active, both at work and in public life. Furthermore, you know that all those who had been trying to circumvent our laws immediately began to quiet down. Because there is nothing stronger than the force of public opinion, when it can be put into effect. And it can be put into effect only in conditions of criticism, self-criticism and broad public openness. . . .

Incidentally, it looks as if many local newspapers in cities and provinces are keeping quiet. The central newspapers are speaking out in full voice, supporting everything good and criticizing blunders and shortcomings. But the local papers are silent. When a group of editors assembled in the Central Committee's offices, they said bluntly: "Well, you tell this to our secretaries in the city and district Party committees." And indeed, why shouldn't people know what is going on in the district or the city? Why shouldn't they make a judgment on it and, if need be, express their opinion? This is what socialism is, comrades. Are there any editors present? (*A voice:* Yes, we're here.)

I hope that the secretaries of the city and district Party committees will take our talk into account. They are the managers. These are their newspapers. We must not be afraid of openness, comrades. We are strong, and the people are in favor of socialism, the Party's policy, changes and restructuring. In general, it is impermissible to approach openness with the yardsticks of traditional short-term campaigns. Public openness is not a one-shot measure but a norm of present-day Soviet life, a continuous, uninterrupted process during which some tasks are accomplished and new tasks—as a rule, still more complicated ones—arise. (*Applause.*)

I could say the same thing about criticism and self-criticism. If we do not criticize and analyze ourselves, what will happen? For us, this is a direct requirement, a vital necessity for purposes of the normal functioning of the Party and of society. . . .

Questions: What did Gorbachev intend by glasnost and perestroika? What problems was he focusing on? What aspects of Soviet politics and society did Gorbachev hope to preserve? Why did the reform movement ultimately prove incompatible with the Soviet state?

Source: From *The Current Digest of the Post Soviet Press* 38, no. 31 (Columbus, OH: 1986), pp. 1–5.

Union—maintained higher birthrates than the majority ethnic group—in this case, ethnic Russians—a differential that caused some concern about maintaining Russian cultural dominance.

Patterns of child rearing showed some similarities to those in the West, as parents, especially in the managerial middle class, devoted great attention to promoting their children's education and ensuring good jobs for the future. At the same time children were more strictly disciplined than in the West, both at home and in school, with an emphasis on authority that had political implications as well. Soviet families never afforded the domestic idealization of women that had prevailed in the West during industrialization. Most married women worked, an essential feature of an economy struggling to industrialize and offering relatively low wages to individual workers. As in the peasant past, women performed many heavy physical tasks. They also dominated some professions, such as medicine, though these professionals were much lower in status than were their male-dominated counterparts in the West. Soviet propagandists took pride in the constructive roles of women and their official equality, but there were signs that many women were suffering burdens from demanding jobs with little help from their husbands at home.

The features that Soviet society shared with the West because of common urban and industrial experience showed in aspects of popular culture. Youth concerns about acquisition, romance, and school success might have a very Western, or more properly modern-industrial, ring. Thus graffiti—a traditional site of wish lists since late tsarist days—on a Leningrad church wall in the late 1970s displayed familiar personal aspirations.

> "Lord, grant me luck, and help me to be accepted into the Art Academy in four years."
>
> "Happiness and health to me and Volodya."
>
> "Lord strangle Tarisyn."
>
> "Lord, help me get rid of Valery."
>
> "Lord, help me in love."
>
> "Lord make Charlotte fall in love with me."
>
> "Lord, I'm hungry."
>
> "Lord, help me pass the exam in political economics."
>
> "Lord, help me pass the exams in: 1) electrical technology; 2) electrical vacuum instruments; 3) Marxism-Leninism."
>
> "Help me pass my driver's license test, Lord."
>
> "Lord, take the arrogance out of my wife."
>
> "Lord, help me win a transistor radio, model AP-2-14, in the lottery." (Added on by another person:) "All we have is P-20-1. Archangel Gabriel."

Overall, Soviet society and culture displayed a distinctive blend of basic features. Several key traditions persisted, like belief in a Russian soul. Revolutionary emphases produced distinctive artistic forms and a large bureaucratic class. Industrialization generated many familiar features of urban life, even in such intimate areas as family behavior and personal aspirations.

The grim-faced collection of leaders reviewing military parades from atop Lenin's tomb in Moscow became a fixture of the cold war decades. Here Khrushchev's central position indicates that he has moved to the apex of the ruling Communist Party pyramid.

De-Stalinization

The rigid government apparatus created by Stalin and sustained after World War II by frequent arrests and exiles to forced labor camps was put to a major test after Stalin's death in 1953. The results gradually loosened, without totally reversing, Stalinist cultural isolation. Focus on one-man rule might have created immense succession problems, and indeed frequent jockeying for power did develop among aspiring candidates. Yet the system held together. Years of bureaucratic experience had given most Soviet leaders a taste for coordination and compromise, along with a reluctance to strike out in radical new directions that might cause controversy or arouse resistance from one of the key power blocs within the state. Stalin's death was followed by a ruling committee that balanced interest groups, notably the army, the police, and the party apparatus. This mechanism encouraged conservatism, as each bureaucratic sector defended its existing prerogatives, but it also ensured fundamental stability.

In 1956, however, Nikita Krushchev emerged from the committee pack to gain primary power, though without seeking to match Stalin's eminence. Indeed, Krushchev attacked Stalinism for its concentration of power and arbitrary dictatorship. In a stirring speech delivered to the Communist Party congress, Krushchev condemned Stalin for his treatment of political opponents, for his narrow interpretations of Marxist doctrine, even for his failure to adequately prepare for World War II. The implications of the de-Stalinization campaign within the Soviet Union suggested a more tolerant political climate and some decentralization of decision making. In fact, however, despite a change in tone, little concrete institutional reform occurred. Political trials became less common, and the most overt police repression eased. A few intellectuals were allowed to raise new issues, dealing, for example, with the purges and other Stalinist excesses. Outright critics of the regime were less likely to be executed and more likely to be sent to psychiatric institutions or, in the case of internationally visible figures, exiled to the West or confined to house arrest. Party control and centralized economic planning remained intact. Indeed, Khrushchev planned a major extension of state-directed initiative by opening new Siberian land to cultivation; his failure in this costly effort, combined with his antagonizing of many Stalinist loyalists, led to his quiet downfall.

ANALYSIS

The Nature of Totalitarianism

At the height of the cold war, in the 1950s, many analysts and many ordinary U.S. citizens worried about the almost superhuman capacities of a totalitarian state. Spy stories reflected the cruel resolve of the Soviet totalitarian system, though plucky Westerners were supposed to win out after incredible difficulties. Sober political science analysis sought to contrast totalitarian systems with 20th-century democracies as decisively modern, but decisively different, forms of government.

Totalitarianism differed from democracy in repressing free expression of opinion and preventing real choice of leadership. Decisions came from above, and voting merely confirmed what had already been decided. Parliaments were rubber stamps, elections presented no alternative parties or candidates; all competing political movements were swept away.

Totalitarianism also, however, differed from more traditional authoritarian regimes, such as the tsarist government of prerevolutionary Russia. Totalitarianism depended on modern, industrial technology to organize an extensive bureaucracy, monitor the population, and reach the people with bombardments of propaganda. It wanted active popular loyalty to the government, and it wanted the state not simply to maintain order but to change the society as well—and this meant extensive controls. Vastly expanded police; mass meetings; radio, film, and poster notices that glorified the leader and blasted the enemies of the state; and elections that provided seeming and sweeping popular endorsement—these were the hallmarks of the totalitarian system. Finally, totalitarian regimes were held to be supremely efficient, badgering and forcing the people into line. With opposition leaders killed or jailed, police forces omnipresent, churches and other institutions attacked, totalitarian regimes pushed the concept of a police state to new heights. Resistance was crushed, and no totalitarian state so far has been dislodged by protest from below.

These judgments of totalitarianism, and its newness and importance in the 20th century, retain great validity. But with the Nazi totalitarian system crushed in war and the Soviet system undermined from within, some questions arise about the totality of totalitarianism. By the later 20th century, historians began to take some second looks.

Totalitarian states could not be oblivious to certain interest groups within the society. They did not grind every element uniformly beneath the state, and they did sometimes listen, informally, to pressures from below. Hitler thus attacked Protestant churches, forcing revisions in their presentations to include a more Germanic image of Christ, more thoroughly than he did the internationally powerful Catholic Church, though he forced some concessions from it as well. The Stalinist regime listened for complaints from factory worker groups in the later 1930s, even though it banned independent unions and crushed outright dissidence.

Totalitarian states also did not win uniform compliance from ordinary citizens, though they made protest very difficult. They did create widespread fear. But they were much less successful in generating new beliefs than was often imagined. Seventy years of Communist rule in the Soviet Union thus did not eliminate religion, though it did manage to limit religious practice. When Communist rule eased in the later 1980s, religious interest turned out to be significant among many groups. Minority nationalisms obviously had not been crushed. Indeed, even under Stalin, Soviet leaders themselves realized that Marxism was not enough to cement mass loyalty, and turned to an emphasis on Russian nationalism as a supplement.

Communist China offers yet a final example of some of the qualities but also the limits of totalitarianism; by 1991 it was increasingly clear that massive state campaigns to persuade peasants to adopt a low birthrate were not succeeding as planned, for peasants either evaded restriction or expressed traditional values by getting rid of daughters in order to try to ensure a male heir. Here, too, the capacity of a totalitarian state to restructure deep-seated habits was far from infinite.

The totalitarian state was a very real phenomenon, and it expresses important features of 20th-century world history. It is, however, more complex than the simplest textbook definitions can convey.

One other impact of totalitarianism does command attention concerning the 1990s: Experience with a totalitarian state, although not forcing a robot-like conformity, may tend to freeze opinions in certain respects. Although East Germans, for example, did not accept Communist ideology fully or uniformly, they did retain more remnants of Nazi thinking than did their counterparts in the West; there was less opportunity for them to discuss and reconsider. Bulgarians who used newfound freedom to belabor their Turkish minority in the 1990s, expressing ethnic nationalism of an early 20th-century variety, may have similarly reflected a tendency to rely on older beliefs as a fallback against the pressures of a totalitarian state. This impact of totalitarianism, in constraining the evolution of beliefs, raised some obvious issues for areas emerging into new, less rigid political forms in the 1990s.

Questions: How is a totalitarian state different from a more conventional authoritarian regime? Why is it difficult to dislodge an established totalitarian state? Did Nazi Germany and Soviet Russia develop the same kinds of totalitarianism, despite their different ideologies?

A Challenge: Pick one of the main cases of 20th-century totalitarianism—Nazi Germany, Stalinist Russia, Communist China—and discuss what kinds of resistance were attempted and why they failed. What balance of repression and positive satisfaction with the regime was involved?

After the de-Stalinization furor and Khrushchev's fall from power, patterns in the Soviet Union remained stable into the 1980s, verging at times on stagnant. Economic growth continued but with no dramatic breakthroughs and with recurrent worries over sluggish productivity and especially over periodically inadequate harvests, which compelled expensive grain deals with Western nations, including the United States. A number of subsequent leadership changes occurred, but the transitions were handled smoothly.

Global Relationships

Political change in the Soviet Union inevitably had important implications for the rest of the world. Larger cold war tensions eased somewhat after Stalin's death. Khrushchev vaunted the Soviet ability to outdo the West at its own industrial game, bragging on a visit to the United States that "we will bury you." The Khrushchev regime also produced one of the most intense moments of the cold war with the United States, as he probed for vulnerabilities. Exploiting the new alliance with Cuba, the Soviets installed missiles in Cuba, yielding only to a firm U.S. response in 1962 by removing the missiles but not their support of Communist regime on the island. Khrushchev had no desire for war, and overall he promoted a new policy of peaceful coexistence. He hoped to beat the West economically and actively expanded the Soviet space program; Sputnik, the first space satellite, was sent up in 1957, well in advance of its U.S. counterpart. Khrushchev maintained a competitive tone, but he shifted away from an exclusive military emphasis. Lowered cold war tensions with the West permitted a small influx of Western tourists by the 1960s as well as greater access to the Western media and a variety of cultural exchanges, which gave some Soviets a renewed sense of contact with a wider world and restored some of the earlier ambiguities about the nation's relationship to Western standards.

At the same time, the Soviet leadership continued a steady military buildup, adding increasingly sophisticated rocketry and bolstered by its unusually successful space program. The Soviets maintained a lead in manned space flights into the late 1980s. Both in space and in the arms race, the Soviet Union demonstrated great technical ability combined with a willingness to settle for somewhat simpler systems than those the United States attempted, which helped explain how it could maintain superpower parity even with a less prosperous overall economy. The active sports program, resulting in a growing array of victories in Olympic Games competition, also showed the Soviet Union's new ability to compete on an international scale and its growing pride in international achievements.

The nation faced a number of new foreign policy problems, although maintaining superpower status. From the mid-1950s onward the Soviet Union experienced a growing rift with China, a Communist nation with which it shared a long border. Successful courtship of many other nations—such as Egypt, a close diplomatic friend during the 1960s—often turned sour, though these developments were often balanced by new alignments elsewhere. The rise of Muslim awareness in the 1970s was deeply troubling to the Soviet Union, with its own large Muslim minority. This prompted a 1979 invasion of Afghanistan, to promote a friendly puppet regime, which bogged down amid guerilla warfare into the late 1980s.

Soviet advances in science and technology both surprised and threatened the United States and western Europe. Manned space flights were but one area in which the Soviets challenged the material supremacy of the West.

On balance, the Soviet Union played a normally cautious diplomatic game, almost never engaging directly in warfare but maintaining a high level of preparedness.

Domestic Problems: Toward the Collapse of Soviet Communism

Problems of work motivation and discipline loomed larger in the Soviet Union than in the West by the 1980s, after the heroic period of building an industrial society under Stalinist exhortation and threat. With highly bureaucratized and centralized work plans and the absence of abundant consumer goods, many workers found little reason for great diligence. High rates of alcoholism, so severe as to cause an increase in death rates, particularly among adult males, also burdened work performance, and caused great concern to Soviet leaders. More familiar were problems of youth agitation. Although Soviet statistics tended to conceal outright crime rates, it is clear that many youths became impatient with the disciplined life and eager to have greater access to Western culture, including rock music and blue jeans.

Soviet output continued to grow, though the economy by the 1980s was lagging behind the West and Japan in adopting new technologies, such as computers (aside from military applications). Military and space technologies still kept pace with Western levels, as both sides fed the arms race. But a higher percentage of Soviet output had to go to military uses than in the West, because of the continued differential in per capita wealth. Despite the consumer shortages that resulted, most Soviet citizens seemed to accept the necessity, given what they were told about the West's aggressive intentions and their own memory of invasion in World War II. Some skepticism about the existing system, however, showed in the minority of beleaguered intellectuals who occasionally ventured criticism of domestic and foreign policies, including armaments policies. Cynicism cropped up also in humor magazines and popular jokes, which poked fun at the luxurious living of Communist officials and the inefficiencies of the bureaucracy. Humor may at the same time have provided some outlet for grievances that might otherwise have festered.

CONCLUSION: BEFORE THE FALL

Most observers thought the Soviet Union remained firmly established in the early 1980s, thanks to careful police control, vigorous propaganda, and real, popular pride in Russian achievements. Even though the U.S. Central Intelligence Agency failed to identify major problems, economic conditions were in fact deteriorating rapidly, and the whole Soviet system would soon come unglued. Yet its collapse was all the more unsettling because of communism's huge success for many decades. At great cost to many people, the Soviet Union had attained world power. Many rejoiced in its fall, but many were also disoriented by it. What could and should replace a system that had dominated huge stretches of Europe and Asia for so long?

The issues involved were most intense, of course, in the Soviet Union itself and in east-central Europe, but there were global implications as well. In terms of power politics, the Soviet Union had balanced the military might of the United States for four decades. What would happen when, because of Soviet collapse, the United States became the world's only superpower? Many people had long looked to the Soviet system for domestic inspiration, seeing it as an alternative way to build an industrial society or simply as a more equitable option than Western-style capitalism. While large Marxist parties did not exist in Africa, a number of leaders had been inspired by the Marxist vision. The same was true in Latin America and several parts of Asia. Further, even as the Soviet system unraveled, strong commitments to a communist state continued in China, North Korea, Vietnam, and Cuba. Would communism indeed die out? And what would replace it in rallying efforts at social justice for those who found Western patterns unacceptable?

In the larger scheme of world history, the cold war did not last very long. It was a transition between a European-dominated world and some other international system that has yet to be fully defined. At the same time, though brief, it was an intense engagement, often a frightening one even though leaders on both sides ultimately showed enough restraint to avoid the devastating conflict that many people anticipated when the rivalry began. For over a generation, Soviet energy and ambition had affected governments and individuals on every continent, bringing many local tensions under the larger umbrella of cold war competition. Inevitably, as the Soviet system finally declined, there were huge questions about what would come next. Leaders in many areas decided it was now safe to revive older regional conflicts. Africans worried that their continent would experience greater global neglect, now that cold war competition for allies had ended. Many people cast about for new ways to oppose the West and capitalism, now that the communist alternative had faded. Most obviously, many Russians themselves wondered what their new role in the world should be.

FURTHER READING

On themes in Eastern European history since 1945, see H. Setson Watson's *Eastern Europe Between the Wars, 1918–1941* (1962), F. Fetjéo's *A History of the People's Democracies: Eastern Europe Since Stalin* (1971), J. Tampke's *The People's Republics of Eastern Europe* (1983), Timothy Ash's *The Polish Revolution: Solidarity* (1984), H. G. Skilling's *Czechoslovakia's Interrupted Revolution* (1976) (on the 1968 uprising), and B. Kovrig's *Communism in Hungary: From Kun to KAdAr* (1979).

On the early signs of explosion in Eastern Europe, see K. Dawisha's *Eastern Europe, Gorbachev and Reform: The Great Challenge* (1988). Joseph Rothschild's *Return to Diversity: A Political History of East Central Europe Since World War II* (2000) stands as the authoritative political history. Sabrina Ramet, ed., *Eastern Europe: Politics, Culture and Society Since 1939* (1998), presents a cultural and social history survey through each country and includes a relevant bibliography.

On Soviet culture, Jeffrey Brooks' *Thank You, Comrade Stalin! Soviet Public Culture from Revolution to Cold War* (2000) is a cultural history of the Communist press. James von Geldern and Richard Stites, eds., *Mass Culture in Soviet Russia: Tales, Poems, Songs, Movies, Plays, and Folklore, 1917–1953* (1995), is a valuable repository of primary cultural texts and documents.

ON THE WEB

Nikita Krushchev and his role in the de-Stalinization of the Soviet Union, as well as his own rise and fall, are addressed at

http://encarta.msn.com/encyclopedia_761574624/ Nikita _Khrushchev.html

http://mars.acnet.wnec.edu/~grempel/courses/russia/ lectures/44fallkhrush.html

http://en.wikipedia.org/wiki/History_of_the_Soviet_ Union_(1953-1985)

The space race between the Soviets and Western democracies is explored at

http://www.nasm.si.edu/exhibitions/gal114/SpaceRace/ sec100/sec100.htm

http://www.centennialofflight.gov/essay/ SPACEFLIGHT/soviet_lunar/SP21.htm

A roundtable discussion of the Soviet and American space programs by leading Soviet officials and others, including Neil Armstrong, the first man to walk on the moon, is presented at

http://www.pbs.org/newshour/bb/science/july-dec97/ sputnik_10-2a.html

The 1956 uprising in Hungary is explored at

http://www.rev.hu/archivum/tanulforr.html

http://en.wikipedia.org/wiki/Hungarian_Revolution, _1956

A participant's son offers an interesting survey of the uprising and its place in world history at

http://www.cserkeszek.org/scouts/webpages/zoltan/1956 .html

Czechoslovakia's failed effort to throw off the Stalinist yoke in 1968 is presented at

http://rferl.org/nca/special/invasion1968/

An overview of the later revolutions in Eastern Europe that heralded the end of the Soviet empire can be found at

http://mars.acnet.wnec.edu/~grempel/courses/wc2/ lectures/rev89.html

Several sites examine those Eastern European leaders who sought a different socialist path in close proximity to the Soviet state, including Alexander Dubcek

http://rferl.org/nca/special/invasion1968

and Polish labor leader Lech Walesa

http://www.nobel.se/peace/laureates/1983

An overview of the ill-fated Soviet invasion of Afghanistan is provided at

http://www.afghanland.com/history/ussr.html

Posters made by the Afghan resistance can be viewed at

http://chronicle.uchicago.edu/020124/posters.shtml

The Polish experience of communism can be traced in an exhibit entitled "Some Like it Red: Polish Political Posters, 1944–1989," at

http://www.theartofposter.com/RED/Red.htm

The building of the Berlin Wall is traced in text, video, and photographs at

http://207.25.71.25/resources/video.almanac/1989/ index3.html

http://members.aol.com/johball/berlinw2.htm

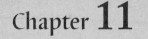
The Postcolonial Era
in Africa, the Middle East,
and Asia

Women played a vital role in the mass demonstrations that toppled the shah of Iran and brought Ayatollah Khomeini to power. In many ways women's support for political movements in the postcolonial period was a continuation of their active participation in earlier struggles against European colonial domination. But increasingly in the postcolonial era, women organized not only to promote political change but to force social and economic reforms that would improve the quality of their own lives.

Chronology

1944	Bretton Woods Conference—World Bank and IMF established
1948	First Arab-Israeli War; Afrikaner Nationalist Party to power in South Africa; beginnings of apartheid legislation
1951	India's first Five-Year Plan for economic development launched
1952	Farouk and khedival regime overthrown in Egypt; Nasser and Free Officers to power
1955	Bandung Conference; beginning of Non-Aligned movement
1956	Abortive British-French intervention in Suez
1958	South Africa completely independent of Great Britain
1960	Sharpeville masacre in South Africa
1966–1970	Biafran secessionist war in Nigeria
1966	Nkrumah overthrown by a military coup in Ghana
1967	Six-Day War between Israel and the Arabs
1970s	Peak period for the OPEC cartel
1972	Bangladesh becomes an independent nation
1973	Third Arab-Israeli War
1979	Shah of Iran overthrown; Khomeini-led Islamic republic declared
1980s	AIDS world epidemic
1980–1988	Iran-Iraq or the First Gulf War
1989	De Klerk charts a path of peaceful reform in South Africa
1990	Nelson Mandela released from prison; Iraqi invasion of Kuwait
1991	Second Gulf War
1994	First democratic elections in South Africa

INTRODUCTION

In *The Battle of Algiers*, Gillo Pontecorvo's moving film on the struggle for independence in Algeria, one member of the high command of the National Liberation Front (FLN) reflects on the nature of the revolutionary struggle in a conversation with a young guerrilla fighter, the protagonist of the film. When the young man expresses his anxieties about the outcome of the general strike then taking place in the city of Algiers, the thoughtful leader of the FLN seeks to put the immediate crisis in a larger perspective. Revolutions, he observes, are difficult to get going and even harder to sustain. But the real tests, he concludes, will come when the revolutionary struggle has been successfully concluded. Once independence has been won, the leaders of the liberation struggle must assume power and face the greatest challenges of all—building viable nations and prosperous societies for peo-ples disoriented and deprived by decades or, in many cases, centuries of colonial rule.

These reflections on the process of decolonization anticipated the actual experience of the peoples in the new nations across Africa, the Middle East, and Asia that were carved out of the ruins of the European colonial empires. Once the European colonizers had withdrawn and the initial euphoria of freedom had begun to wear off, Western-educated nationalist leaders were forced to confront the sobering realities of the fragile state structures and underdeveloped economies they had inherited. With the common European enemy gone, the deep divisions between the different ethnic and religious groups that had been thrown uneasily together in the postcolonial states became more and more apparent and disruptive. These related challenges, which were faced by all of the newly independent peoples of Africa, the Middle East, and Asia are explored in the opening sections of this chapter.

The leaders of the new nations found their efforts to spur economic growth constricted by concessions made to the departing colonizers and by the very nature of the international economy, in which the terms of investment and trade heavily favored the industrialized nations. They saw their ambitious schemes to improve living standards of formerly colonized peoples frustrated by a shortage of expertise and resources, and by population growth rates that quickly ate up whatever modest advances could be made. Population increase and efforts to spur economic development often had highly detrimental effects on the already ravaged environments of the newly independent nations. Loggers and land-hungry farmers cut and burned vast swaths of the rainforests throughout much of Africa and Asia. Unable to afford the expensive antipollution devices that reduced environmental degradation in wealthier industrialized countries, many developing nations experienced an alarming fouling of their air, water, and land in the decades since independence.

Increasing poverty, official corruption, and a growing concern for the breakdown of traditional culture and social values produced widespread social unrest. Dissent and civil disturbances called into question the leadership abilities of the nationalist politicians who had won independence but floundered as heads of new nations. Challenges to the existing order came both from Communist and Socialist parties on the left of the political spectrum and religious revivalist movements, whose positions were often a complex blend of radicalism and conservatism. Dissident movements espousing Socialist upheavals have frequently clashed with those intent on religious revivalism over a wide range of issues from the place of religion in the newly independent nations to the proper roles and rights of women.

To remain in power and to ensure that they would be able to realize their visions of economic and social development in the postcolonial era, Western-educated nationalist leaders adopted various strategies to beat back these threats. As we shall see in the latter sections of this chapter, these strategies met with widely varying degrees of success. The price for failure was often a fall from power and at times the execution of former nationalist heroes. In many instances, their places were taken by military commanders who assumed dictatorial powers, forcibly silenced dissent, and suppressed interethnic and religious rivalries. In a few cases, the champions of religious revival and resistance to Western influences, most notably those in Iran, swept moderate reformers and dictators from power.

THE CHALLENGES OF INDEPENDENCE

The nationalist movements that won independence for most of the peoples of Africa, the Middle East, and Asia usually involved some degree of mass mobilization. Peasants and working-class townspeople, who hitherto had little voice in politics beyond their village boundaries or local labor associations, were drawn into political contests that toppled empires and established new nations. To win the support of these groups, nationalist leaders promised them jobs, civil rights, and equality once independence was won. The leaders of many nationalist movements nurtured visions of postindependence utopias in the minds of their followers. They were told that once the Europeans, who monopolized the best jobs, were driven away and their exploitive hold on the economies of colonized peoples was brought to an end, there would be enough to give everyone a good life.

Unfortunately, the realities of the postcolonial situation in virtually all new African, Middle Eastern, and Asian nations made it impossible for nationalist leaders to fulfill the expectations they had aroused among their followers and, to varying degrees, among the colonized populace at large. Even with the Europeans gone and the terms of economic exchange with more developed countries somewhat improved, there was simply not enough to go around. Thus, the socialist-inspired ideologies that nationalist leaders had often embraced and then propagated among their followers proved misleading. The problem was not just that goods and services were unequally distributed, leaving some people rich and the great majority poor. The problem was that there were not sufficient resources to take care of everybody, even if it had been possible to distribute them equitably.

When utopia failed to materialize, personal rivalries and long-standing divisions between different classes and ethnic groups, which had been more or less successfully muted by the common struggle against the alien colonizers, resurfaced or intensified. In almost all the new states these rivalries and differences became dominant features of political life. They produced political instability and often threatened the viability of the nations themselves. They consumed resources that might have been devoted to economic development. They also blocked—in the name of the defense of subnational interests—measures designed to build more viable and prosperous states. Absorbed by the task of just holding their new nations together, African and Asian politicians neglected problems—such as soaring population in-

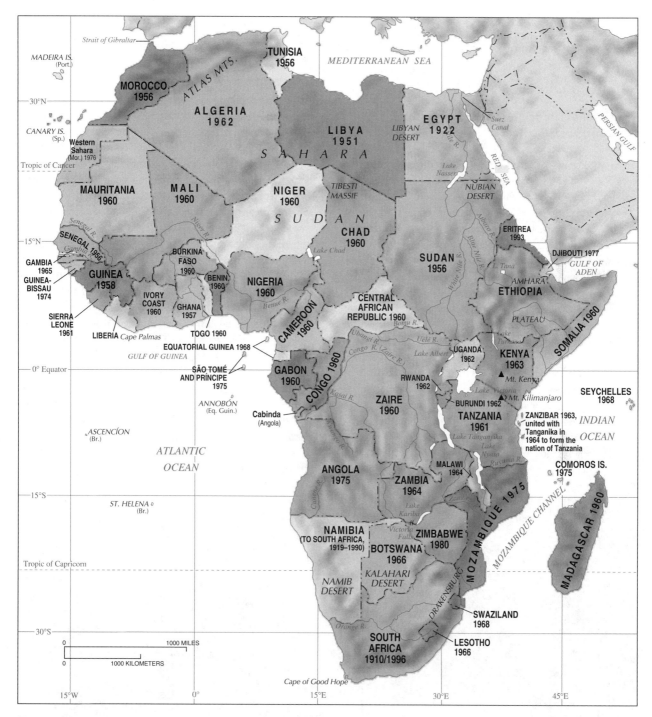

The Postcolonial Nations of Africa

creases, uncontrolled urban growth, rural landlessness, and environmental deterioration—that soon loomed just as large a threat as political instability to their young nations.

ANALYSIS

Artificial Nations and the Rising Tide of Communal Strife

Again and again in the postcolonial era, the new states of Africa, the Middle East, and Asia have been torn by internal strife. Often much of what people in the industrialized West know of these areas is connected to the breakdown of their political systems and the massive human suffering that has resulted. In just the last few years, for example, international news reports have often featured descriptions of massive famines generated by civil wars in Somalia, the Sudan, and Mozambique; by harrowing images of refugees fleeing for their lives from Rwanda, Angola, and Cambodia; by religious riots in India and mass slaughter in Timor. Western observers are often tempted to take this instability and suffering as proof that peoples in the emerging nations are unfit to rule themselves, that they are incapable of building viable political systems. Some commentators have even begun to ask whether many of these areas were not better off under colonial rule and to call for more active intervention by Japan and the West.

Although these responses are understandable given the crisis-focused coverage of African, Middle Eastern, and Asian affairs by international news agencies, they fail to take into account the daunting obstacles that have confronted nation-builders in these areas. They ignore the important ways in which Western colonialism contributed to the internal divisions and political weaknesses of newly independent states. They also overlook the deep, and often highly disruptive, social divisions within Western societies—the long history of racial conflict in the United States, for example, or the vicious civil war in the former European nation of Yugoslavia. Clearly, a longer-term and comparative perspective is required if we are to understand the persistent difficulties that African and Asian peoples have had building viable nations and functioning pluralistic societies.

Any analysis of the recurring political crises of postcolonial nations ought to begin with the realization that virtually all the nations that emerged from the process of decolonization were artificial creations. The way the empires had been built and their boundaries demarcated ensured that this would be the case. European generals conquered and European explorers staked out claims to territories in ways that rarely, if ever, took into account the interests or history of the peoples who occupied these lands. As Lord Salisbury, one of the more prominent late 19th-century champions of imperialist expansion, confessed in the 1890s,

One of the earliest states to be carved out of the former colonies, Pakistan, contained extreme contrasts of lush tropical and arid semidesert environments. The cultures of East and West Pakistan were equally diverse, generating the violent secession of what became the nation of Bangladesh in 1972. From the Sudan to Nigeria, similar differences have threatened the viability of the new nations of Africa.

the conquerors knew next to nothing about the lands they divided up around the green felt tables at conferences in Berlin, Paris, and other European capitals:

> We have been engaged in drawing lines upon maps where no white man's foot ever trod; we have been giving away mountains and rivers and lakes to each other [Europeans] only hindered by the small impediment that we never knew exactly where the mountains and rivers and lakes were. . . .

If they could not locate the mountains and rivers, European diplomats could hardly have been expected to know much about the peoples who lived on or along them. As a consequence, the division of Africa, the Middle East, and Asia was completely arbitrary. Colonial boundaries divided peoples: the Shans of Southeast Asia, the Kurds of the Middle East, the Somalis of the horn of East Africa. They also tossed together tens, sometimes hundreds, of very different and often hostile ethnic or religious groups. The roads and railways built by the colonizers, the marketing systems they established, and the educational policies they pursued all hardened the unnatural boundaries and divisions established in the decades of the late 19th century. It was these artificial units, these motley combinations of peoples that defied the logic of history and cultural affinity, that nationalist leaders had to try to meld into nations in the decades after World War II.

The point is not that there was perfect harmony or unity among the peoples of Asia, the Middle East, and Africa before the coming of colonial rule. As we have seen, there was a great diversity of ethnicity, languages, and religions among the peoples who built civilizations in these areas in the precolonial era. Intense competition, communal conflict, and innumerable wars occurred between different ethnic and religious groups. European colonization exacerbated these divisions while tending to suppress violent confrontations between different communities. In fact, European colonial regimes were built and maintained by divide-and-rule tactics.

Very often the colonizers selectively recruited minority ethnic or religious groups into their armies, bureaucracies, and police forces. The Tutsi minority, for example, in strife-torn Rwanda and Burundi, was much favored by first the Belgians and later the French. The Europeans widely admired the taller, fine-featured Tutsis. Their admiration was enhanced by the fact that Tutsi kingdoms had dominated the Hutu majority before the colonizers arrived. In the colonial period, the Tutsis had greater access to missionary education, military training, and government positions than

the Hutu majority. These advantages gained a disproportionate share of political power and social standing for the Tutsis after independence. But they also made them the obvious target for persecution by disgruntled Hutus. Rivalry and violent conflict between the two groups has frequently made a shambles of nation-building initiatives in both Rwanda and Burundi over the past several decades and reached catastrophic proportions in the mid-1990s. It has continued to simmer in the years since, at times spilling over into political struggles in neighboring states such as the Congo.

The inequities of the colonial order were compounded by the increasingly frequent resort to divide-and-rule policies by European officials in the last years of their rule. In addition, the colonizers' desire to scuttle and run from their colonial responsibilities when it was clear that days of colonial rule were numbered opened the way for the ethnic and religious strife. Communal violence, in turn, prompted the mass exodus of refugees that accompanied the winning of independence in many colonies, most notably in South Asia, Nigeria, the Belgian Congo, and Palestine. The Western-educated leaders who came to power in these and other newly independent states soon realized that only a small portion of the population was genuinely committed to an overarching nationalist identity. Even among the Westernized elite classes, which had led the decolonization struggle, national loyalties were often shallow and were overridden by older, subnational ethnic and religious identities. As a result, many of the new nations of Africa and Southeast Asia have been threatened by secessionist movements.

The most spectacular collapse of a new state came in Pakistan, the unwieldy patchwork of a nation the British had thrown together at the last minute in 1947 to satisfy Jinnah's demands for majority rule in Muslim areas of the Indian subcontinent. A glance at the map on page 276 reveals the vulnerability of Pakistan, split into two parts: West and East Pakistan, separated by over 1000 miles of hostile Indian territory. East and West Pakistan also differed greatly in their natural environments, and in the ethnic makeup of their peoples and the languages they used. They even diverged significantly in their approaches to the Islamic faith that had justified including them in the same country in the first place.

Fragile national ties were rapidly eroded by the East Pakistanis' perception that they had been in effect recolonized by West Pakistan. West Pakistanis held highly disproportionate shares of government jobs and military positions, and West Pakistan received the lion's share of state revenues despite the fact that the East generated most of

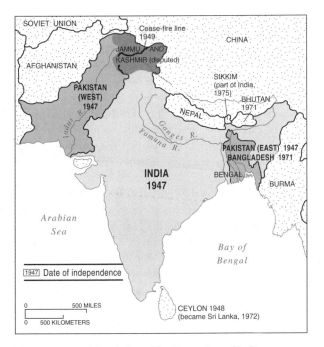

The Partition of South Asia: The Formation of India, Pakistan, Bangladesh, and Sri Lanka

Pakistan's foreign earnings. By the early 1970s, East and West Pakistan were locked in a bloody civil war, which ended with the creation of the nation of Bangladesh from East Pakistan in 1971.

India, which relished the chance to contribute to the breakup of Pakistan, has itself been repeatedly threatened by civil strife between different linguistic, religious, and ethnic groups. Sikh guerrillas carried on a violent campaign for separation in the north, and the Indian government has been forced to intervene militarily in the violent struggle between different ethnic and religious groups in Sri Lanka (Ceylon), its neighbor to the south. In 1997, an avowedly Hindu communalist party came to power in New Delhi, in defiance of the staunch adherence to the principle of a secular state by leading Indian nationalist figures in the colonial era and all of the earlier postindependence governments. The victory of the Bharatya Janata Party (BJP) understandably intensified the anxieties of the large Muslim minority and other non-Hindu religious groups regarding the possibility of discrimination and even open persecution. With the return to power in 2004 of the secularist Congress Party in alliance with a complex coalition of national and regional parties, communal tensions have abated a good deal. But the forces of Hindu zealotry that carried the BJP to national prominence remain and wait for the current govern-ment to falter, thus enabling them to regain control of India's vast democracy.

In Africa, where there was often even less of a common historical and cultural basis on which to build nationalism than in South or Southeast Asia, separatist movements have been a prominent feature of the political life of new states. Secessionist movements currently rage from Morocco in the northwest to Ethiopia in the east and Angola in the south. Civil wars, such as the decades-long struggle of the non-Muslim peoples of the southern Sudan against the Muslim rulers from the northern parts of that country—that spilled over into the eastern Dafur region in the early 2000s—have also abounded.

Although the leaders of the emerging nations have been acutely aware of the injustices and persecutions of minority groups that have often precipitated these conflicts, none has seriously suggested altering the unnatural boundaries established in the colonial era. The reverse in fact is the case. These divisions have become sacrosanct. African national leaders, for example, fear that a successful secession movement in a neighboring country might provide precedents for dissident minorities in their own nation.

In all cases the artificial nature of the new nations of Africa, the Middle East, and Asia has proved costly. In addition to internal divisions, boundary disputes between newly independent nations have often led to border clashes and often to open warfare. India and Pakistan have fought three such wars since 1947. Iraq's Saddam Hussein justified his 1990 annexation of Kuwait with the argument that the tiny, oil-rich Arab "sheikhdom" was an artificial creation of the British colonizers, who had carved Kuwait out of land that had historically been part of Iraq. And the attempts of the American-led coalition that invaded Iraq in 2003 and toppled Saddam Hussein to establish a stable regime have been bedeviled by historic divisions between its three major religious and ethnic groups: the Sunnis, the Shi'as and the Kurds.

Democracy has often been one of the main victims of the tensions between rival ethnic groups within African, Middle Eastern, and Asian nations and threats from neighbors. Politicians in virtually all the new states have been quick to play on communal fears as well as on ethnic and religious loyalties to win votes. As a result, freely elected legislatures have often been dominated by parties representing these special interests. Suspicions that those in power were favoring their own or allied groups have led to endless bickering and stalemated national legislatures, which have become tempting targets for the attempted coups of military strongmen. One of the more predictable reasons these usurpers have given for dictatorial rule has been the need to contain the communal tensions aroused by democratic election campaigns.

The threats from rival ethnic and religious groups felt by those in power have also contributed to exorbitant military spending by Asian and African leaders—spending that their impoverished societies can rarely afford. In countries where civil wars have actually occurred, such as Ethiopia, Mozambique, and Angola, economic development has ground to a virtual standstill. At the same time, military clashes have resulted in widespread death, destruction, epidemic disease, and famines that have persisted in some areas for decades. These conflicts have often proved impervious to international peacekeeping efforts, and the misery and despair they have inflicted on the peoples caught up in them have frequently overwhelmed even the best-organized of humanitarian agencies.

Questions: How might colonial policies have been altered to reduce the tensions between different ethnic and religious communities? Why were these sorts of measures not taken? What can be done now to alleviate these divisions? Should the United Nations or industrialized nations like the United States or Japan intervene directly to contain communal clashes or civil wars in Africa and Asia? What is to be done with the rapidly growing refugee populations that are created by these conflicts?

The Perils of the Population "Explosion"

The nationalist leaders who led the colonized peoples of Africa, the Middle East, and Asia to independence had firmly committed themselves to promoting rapid economic development once colonial restraints were removed. In keeping with their Western-educated backgrounds, most of these leaders envisioned their nations following the path of industrialization that had brought national prosperity and international power to much of western Europe and the United States. This course of development was also fostered by representatives of the Soviet bloc, who had emphasized heavy industry in their state-directed drives to "modernize" their backward economies and societies. Of the many barriers to the rapid economic breakthroughs postcolonial leaders hoped for, the most formidable and persistent were the spiraling increases of population that often overwhelmed whatever economic advances the peoples of the new nations managed to make.

The factors implemented to sustain population increases in already quite densely populated areas of the emerging nations had begun to take effect even before the era of high colonialism. Food crops, mostly from the New World, had contributed to dramatic population growth in China and India as early as the 17th century. They also helped sustain high levels of population in areas such as the Niger delta in West Africa, despite heavy losses of both males and females as a result of the slave trade. The coming of colonial rule reinforced these upward trends in a number of ways. It ended local warfare that had caused population losses and, perhaps more significantly, had indirectly promoted the spread of epidemic diseases and famine. The new railroad and steamship links established by the colonizers to foster the spread of the market economy also cut down on the regional famines that had been a major check against sustained population increase since ancient times. Large amounts of food could now be shipped from areas where harvests were good to those where drought or floods threatened the local inhabitants with starvation.

With war and famine—two of the main checks that Malthus and others had identified as major barriers to population increase—much reduced, growth began to speed up. This was particularly true in areas such as India and Java that had been under European control for decades. Death rates declined, but birthrates remained much the same, leaving more and more sizable net increases. Improved hygiene and medical treatment played little part in this rise until the first decades of the 20th century. From that time efforts to eradicate tropical diseases, as well as global scourges such as smallpox, and to improve sewage systems and purify drinking water have given further impetus to sharp upswings in population.

Virtually all the leaders of the emerging nations headed states in which population was increasing at unprecedented levels. This increase continued in the early years of independence. In much of Asia it has begun to level off in recent decades. But in most of Africa, and some Middle Eastern nations such as Egypt, population growth continues at very high rates. In some cases, most notably South Asia, rather moderate growth rates have produced prodigious total populations because they were adding to an already large base. As a result, in the 1970s population experts predicted that at the then-current rates South Asia's population of over 600 million would more than double by the year 2000. Though this prophecy was not fulfilled by the early years of the 21st century, the region's population had risen to over a billion and threatened to overtake China as the world's most populous area.

In Africa, by contrast, which began with relatively low population levels, given its large land area, very high birthrates and diminished mortality rates have resulted in very steep population increases in recent decades. The magnitude of this increase can be envisioned if one considers the predictions of some population experts that, if present growth rates continue, by the middle of the 21st century Nigeria will have a population equal to that of present-day China. In view of the AIDS epidemic that has spread through much of central and eastern Africa in the 1980s and 1990s, some of the estimates for population increases in Africa as a whole may have to be revised downward. But recent measures of African productivity and per capita incomes suggest that even more moderate increases in population may be difficult to support at reasonable living standards. This sobering prospect is dramatically underscored by estimates that the 400 million people of Africa are currently supported by a continental economy with a productive capacity equal to just 6 percent of that of the United States, or roughly equal to that of the state of Illinois.

On the face of it, the conquest of the Malthusian checks to sustained population growth throughout much of human history—war, disease, and famine—was one of the great achievements of European colonial regimes. It was certainly an accomplishment that colonial officials never tired of citing in defense of the perpetuation of European dominance. But another side of the colonial legacy rendered this increase a quandary in which most of the emerging nations were soon to find themselves. The European policy of limiting industrialization in their colonial dependencies meant that one of the key ways by which Europe had met its own population boom in the 19th and early 20th centuries was not available to the new nations of Asia, the Middle East, and Africa. They lacked the factories to employ the exploding population that moved to the cities from the rural areas, as well as the technology to produce the necessities of life for more and more people. Unlike the Europeans and the Americans, the emerging nations found it difficult to draw food and mineral resources from the rest of the world to feed this ever-proliferating population. In fact, these were the very things the colonized peoples had been set up to sell to the industrialized countries. Even in countries such as India, where impressive advances in industrialization were made in the postcolonial era, gains

in productivity were rapidly swallowed up by the population explosion.

In most postcolonial societies there has been considerable resistance to birth control efforts aimed at bringing runaway population growth in check. Some of this resistance is linked to deeply entrenched social patterns and religious beliefs. In many of these societies, procreation is seen as a key marker of male virility. In addition, the capacity to bear children, preferably male children, continues to be critical to the social standing of adult women. In some cases, resistance to birth control is linked to specific cultural norms. Hindus, for example, believe that a deceased man's soul cannot begin the cycle of rebirth until his eldest son has performed special ceremonies over his funeral pyre. This belief increases the already considerable pressure on Indian women to have children, and it encourages families to have several sons in order to ensure that at least one survives the father.

In Africa children are seen as indispensable additions to the lineage—the extended network of relatives (and deceased ancestors) that, much more than the nuclear family, makes up the core social group over much of the subcontinent. As in India or the Middle East, sons are essential for the continuation of the patrilineal family line and the performance of burial and ancestral rites. The key roles played by women in agricultural production and marketing make female offspring highly valued in Africa societies. This is not true in many Asian societies, where high dowries and occupational restrictions limit their contribution to family welfare.

Before the 20th century, the high incidence of stillbirths and high rates of infant mortality more generally meant that mothers could expect to lose many of the children to whom they gave birth—10 to 12 deaths among 15 or 16 children conceived was not unheard of. Beyond the obvious psychological scars left by these high death rates, they also fostered the conviction that it was necessary to have many children to ensure that some would outlive the parents. In societies where welfare systems and old-age pensions were meager or unknown, survival of children took on special urgency because they were the only ones who would care for their parents once they could no longer work for themselves. The persistence of these attitudes in recent decades, when medical advances have greatly reduced infant mortality, has been a major factor contributing to soaring population growth.

In the early decades after independence, many leaders in the developing nations were deeply opposed to state measures to promote family planning and birth control. Some saw these as Western attempts to meddle in their

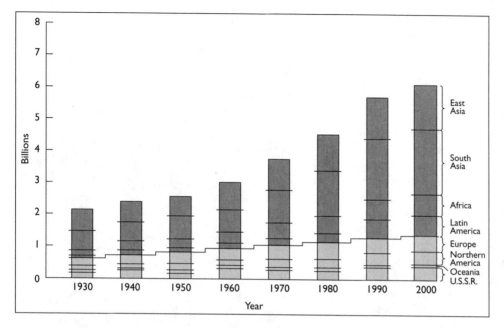

This graph shows the growth of the world population by major global geographic areas between 1930 and 2000. It illustrates the near stabilization of the upswing in populations of the West and much of the former Soviet Union that began with industrialization in the 18th century. An explosion is seen to occur in recent decades in the areas of the globe that were colonized, both formally and informally, by the industrial powers in the 19th and early 20th centuries. These increases surpass those of any other epoch in human history.

internal affairs; others proudly declared that the socialist societies they were building would be able to take care of the additional population. As it has become increasingly clear that excessive population increase renders significant economic advances impossible, many of these leaders have begun to reassess their earlier attitudes toward birth control. A particular cause for alarm is the fact that in many developing countries a high percentage of the population is under the age of 15 (as high as 40 percent in some areas) and thus dependent on others for support. But even for those who now wish to actively promote family planning, the obstacles are staggering. In addition to the cultural and social factors just discussed, African, Middle Eastern and Asian leaders often find they lack sufficient resources and the educated personnel required to make these programs effective. High rates of illiteracy, particularly among women, need to be overcome, but education is expensive. Perhaps no form of financial and technical assistance from the industrialized to the developing world will be as critical in the coming decades as that devoted to family planning.

Parasitic Cities and Endangered Ecosystems

As population increase in the rural areas of emerging nations outstripped the land and employment opportunities available to the peasantry, mass migrations to urban areas ensued. The massive movement of population from overcrowded villages to the cities was one of the most dramatic developments in the postcolonial history of most African, Middle Eastern and Asian countries. Ambitious youths and the rural poor crowded into port centers and capital cities in search of jobs and a chance to win the "good life" that the big hotels and restaurants and the neon lights of the city center appeared to offer to all comers. But because most cities in the developing world lacked the rapidly expanding industrial sectors that had made possible the absorption (with considerable difficulty) of a similar migrant influx earlier in the West, they were often dead ends for migrants from the rural areas. There were few jobs, and heavy competition for them ensured that wages would remain low for most workers. The growing numbers of underemployed or unemployed turned to street vending, scavenging, huckstering, begging, or petty crime to survive.

In the independence era the urban poor have become a volatile factor in the political struggles of the elite. They have formed the crowds willing for a price to cheer on one contender or jeer down another, and ready to riot and loot in times of government crisis. In deeply divided societies the poor, working-class, or idle youths of the urban areas have often formed the shock troops in communal clashes between rival ethnic and religious groups. Fear of outbursts by urban "mobs" also forced regimes in the emerging nations to expend considerable portions of their scarce resources to subsidize and thus keep low the price of staple foods, such as bread, kerosene, and other necessities.

The great and sudden influx of population from the rural areas to cities without the jobs or infrastructure to support them has greatly skewed urban growth in the emerging nations. Within decades Asian and Latin American cities have become some of the largest in the world, while African urban areas have sprawled far beyond their modest limits in colonial times. The wealth of the enclaves of the upper- and middle-class minorities, dominated by glitzy hotels and high-rises, contrasts disturbingly with the poverty of the vast slums that stretch in all directions from the city centers. Little or no planning was possible for the slum quarters that expanded as squatters erected makeshift shelters wherever open land or derelict buildings could be found. Originally, most of the slum areas lacked electricity, running water, or even the most elementary sewage facilities. As shanties were gradually converted into ramshackle dwellings, many governments scrapped plans to level slum settlements and instead attempted to provide them with some semblance of electrical and sanitary systems. As an increasing number of development specialists have reluctantly concluded, slums often provide the only housing urban dwellers are likely to find for some time to come.

These conditions have burdened most developing nations with parasitic rather than productive cities. This means that they are heavily dependent for survival on food and resources drawn from their own countryside or from abroad. In contrast to the cities of western Europe and North America—even during the decades of rapid urban expansion in the 19th century—few African, Middle Eastern or Asian cities have had the manufacturing base required to generate growth in their surrounding regions or the nation as a whole. They take from the already impoverished countryside, but they are able to give little in return. Urban dependence on the countryside further stretches the already overextended resources of the rural areas.

Rural overpopulation in the decades after independence has led to the depletion of the soil in many areas that have been worked for centuries or millennia. It has also resulted in an alarming rate of deforestation throughout the developing world. Peasant villagers cut trees for fuel or they clear land for farming and their flocks. Deforestation and overgrazing not only pose major threats to wild animal life but also upset the balance in fragile tropical ecosystems, producing further soil depletion and erosion and encouraging desertification. This environmental degradation is intensified by industrial pollution from both the developed countries and the emerging nations

In the urban areas of undeveloped nations, the contrast between the wealth of the few and the poverty of the majority is revealed by the juxtaposition of the high-rise apartments of the affluent middle classes and the shantytowns of the urban poor. The city centers of Africa and Asia are much like those of the industrial West or Japan. But the cities as a whole in the emerging nations often are more like collections of large villages than integrated urban units. Many of these villages are vast shantytowns with varying levels of basic services such as running water, sewer systems, and transportation networks to the city center.

themselves. Though the industrial sectors in the latter are generally small, pollution tends to be proportionally greater than in the developed world because African and Asian nations rarely have the means to afford the antipollution technology introduced over the last few decades in western Europe, Japan, and North America.

Women's Subordination and the Nature of Feminist Struggles in the Postcolonial Era

The example of both the Western democracies and the Communist republics of Eastern Europe, where women had won the right to vote in the early and middle decades of the 20th century, encouraged the founders of the emerging nations to write female suffrage into their constitutions. The very active part women played in many nationalist struggles was perhaps even more critical to their gaining the right to vote and run for political office. Female activism also produced some semblance of equality in terms of legal rights, education, and occupational opportunities under the laws of many new nations.

The equality that was proclaimed on paper, however, often bore little resemblance to the actual rights that the great majority of African, Middle Eastern, and Asian women could exercise. It often also had little bearing on the conditions under which they lived their daily lives. Despite the media attention given to women like Indira Gandhi, Corazon Aquino, and Benazir Bhutto, who have emerged in the decades since independence as national leaders, political life in most developing countries continues to be dominated by men. The overwhelming majority of elected officials and government administrators, particularly at the upper levels of state bureaucracies, are men. Because they are usually less well educated than their husbands, women in societies where genuine elections are held often do not exercise their right to vote, or they simply vote for the party and candidates favored by their spouses.

Even the rise to power of individual women like Indira Gandhi, who proved to be one of the most resolute and powerful of all African or Asian leaders, is deceptive. In almost every case, female heads of state in Africa or Asia entered politics and initially won political support because they were connected to powerful men. Indira Gandhi was the daughter of Jawaharlal Nehru, India's first prime minister; Corazon Aquino's husband was the martyred leader of the Filipino opposition to Ferdinand Marcos; and Benazir Bhutto's father was a domineering Pakistani prime minister who had been toppled by a military coup and was executed in the late 1970s. Lacking these sorts of connections, the vast majority of African, Middle Eastern and Asian women have been at best relegated to peripheral political positions and at worst are allowed no participation in the political process.

The limited real gains made by women in postcolonial nations in the political sphere are paralleled by the second-class position to which most are consigned in many societies. In some respects their handicaps are comparable to those that constrict women in the industrialized democracies and Communist nations. But the obstacles to female self-fulfillment, and in many cases mere survival, in emerging nations are usually much more blatant

and fundamental than the child-rearing patterns, education and job discrimination, and other restrictions women have to contend with in developed societies. To begin with, early marriage ages for women and large families are still the norm in most African, Middle Eastern or Asian societies. This means that women spend their youthful and middle-age years having children, a period during which there is little time to think of higher education or a career.

Because of the low level of sanitation in many developing societies and the scarcity of food in many, all but elite and upper-middle-class women experience chronic anxiety regarding such basic issues as adequate nutrition for their hungry children and their susceptibility to disease. The persistence of male-centric customs directly affects the health and life expectancy of women themselves. The Indian tradition, for example, which dictates that women first serve their husbands' and sons' meals and then eat what is left, has obvious disadvantages. The quantity and nutritional content of the leftovers are likely to be lower than those of the original meals, and in tropical environments flies and other disease-bearing insects are more likely to have fouled the food.

The consequences of these social patterns can be quite injurious for women. In the 1970s, for example, it was estimated that as much as 20 percent of the female population of India was malnourished and that another 30 percent had a diet that was well below acceptable UN levels. In sharp contrast to the industrial societies of Japan, the United States, and Europe, where women outnumber (because on the average they outlive) men, in India there are only 930 females for every 1000 males.

Although the highly secular property and divorce laws many new states promulgated after independence have given women much greater legal protection, many of these measures have been ignored in practice. Very often, women in the developing world have neither the education nor the resources to exercise their legal rights. The spread of religious revivalism has in many cases further eroded these rights, even though advocates of a return to tradition often argue that practices such as veiling and stoning for women (but not men) caught in adultery actually enhance their dignity and status. No matter what position is taken on these questions, there is little doubt that most African, Middle Eastern, and Asian women continue to be dominated by male family members, are much more constricted than males in terms of career opportunities, and are less likely to be well fed, educated, and healthy than males at comparable social levels.

Neocolonialism, Cold War Rivalries, and Stunted Development

The schemes of nationalist leaders aimed at building an industrial base that would provide adequate support for the rapidly increasing populations of their new nations soon floundered amid the economic realities of the postcolonial world. Not only did most of the nations that emerged from colonialism have little in the way of an industrial base, but their means of obtaining one were depressingly meager. In order to buy the machines and hire or train the technical experts they needed to get industrialization going, developing countries needed to earn capital they could invest for these ends. Some funds could be accumulated by saving a portion of the state revenues collected from the peasantry. In most cases, however, there was precious little left once the bureaucrats had been given their salaries, essential public works and the extension of education had been funded, and other state expenses had been met. Thus, most emerging nations have relied on the sale of cash crops and minerals to earn the foreign exchange they need to finance industrialization. As their leaders soon discovered, the structure of the world market was heavily loaded against them.

The pattern of exchange promoted in the colonial era left most newly independent countries dependent on the export production of two or three crops or industrial raw materials. The former included cocoa, palm oil, coffee, or jute and hemp. Key among the latter were minerals, such as copper, bauxite, and oil, for which there was a high demand in the industrialized economies of Europe, North America, and increasingly Japan. Since World War II, the prices of this sort of export—which economists call primary products—have not only fluctuated widely but have steadily declined when compared to the prices of most of the manufactured goods that emerging nations usually buy from the industrialized world. Price fluctuations have created nightmares for planners in developing nations. Revenue estimates from the sale of coffee or copper in years when the price is high are used to plan government projects for the construction of roads, factories, and dams. Market slumps can wipe out these critical funds, thereby retarding economic growth, and throw developing countries deeply into debt. These setbacks are doubly frustrating because in order to get industrialization going, emerging countries are often forced to export precious and finite mineral resources that they themselves will require if they succeed in industrializing.

The leaders and planners of African, Middle Eastern, and Asian countries have had little success in improving the terms under which they participate in the global market economy. Even the gains made by the oil cartel in the early 1970s proved to be confined to a few select nations and to be temporary. They were soon rolled back to a large degree by divisions among the oil-producing states. After falling through most of the 1980s and 1990s, oil prices have been rising sharply in recent years due to heightened global demand—fed to a significant degree by China's rapidly expanding economy. By 2005, gasoline prices in the United States had far exceeded those of even the years after the OPEC embargo that followed the 1973 war in the Middle East.

Most leaders of the emerging nations have been quite ready to blame the legacy of colonialism and what they have termed the "neocolonial" structure of the global economy for the limited returns yielded thus far by their development schemes. Though there is much truth to these accusations, they do not tell the whole story. These leaders themselves must also share the responsibility for the slow pace of economic growth in much of the developing world. The members of the educated classes that came to dominate the political and business life of newly independent nations often used their positions to enrich themselves and their relatives at the expense of their societies as a whole. Corruption has been notoriously widespread in most of the new nations. Government controls on the import of goods such as automobiles, television sets, and stereos, which are luxury items beyond the reach of most of the people, have often been lax. As a result, tax revenues and export earnings that could have fueled development have often gone to provide "the good life" for small minorities within emerging nations. The inability or refusal of many African and Asian regimes to carry out key social reforms, such as land redistribution, which would spread the limited resources available more equitably over the population, has contributed vitally to the persistence of these patterns.

Badly strapped for investment funds and essential technology, developing nations have often turned to international organizations, such as the World Bank and the International Monetary Fund, or to rival industrial nations for assistance. Though considerable resources for development have been generated in this way, the price for international assistance has often been high. Both the United States and the Soviet Union, as well as their allies, have normally extracted major concessions in return for their aid. These have ranged from commitments to buy the products of, and favor investors from, the lending countries to entering into alliances and permitting military bases on the territory of the client state. Loans from international lending agencies have almost invariably been granted only after the needy nation agreed to "structural adjustments." These are regulations that determine how the money is to be invested and repaid, and they usually involve promises to undertake major "reforms" in the economy of the borrowing nation.

In recent years, these promises have often included a commitment to remove or reduce state subsidies on food and other essential consumer items. State subsidies were designed to keep prices for staple goods at a level that the urban and rural poor–the great majority of the people in virtually all emerging nations–could afford. When carried through, subsidy reductions have frequently led to widespread social unrest, violent riots, and the collapse or near collapse of postcolonial regimes. These violent outbursts have served as dramatic reminders of just how precarious social stability is in much of the developing world, and of how limited and perilous are the solutions devised thus far for the problems confronting the new nations that won their independence from the European colonial empires.

PATHS TO ECONOMIC GROWTH AND SOCIAL JUSTICE

However much the leaders of the new nations of Africa, the Middle East, and Asia might have blamed their societies' woes on the recently departed colonizers, they soon felt the need to deliver on the promises of social reform and economic well-being that had done so much to rally support to the nationalist cause. Different leaders adopted different approaches, and some tried one strategy after another. Though it is obviously impossible to deal with all of these efforts at nation-building and economic development in depth, the basic elements of several distinctive strategies will be considered in the concluding portions of this chapter. The discussion of each strategy will focus on a single, prominent case example.

Depending on their own skills, the talents of their advisors and lieutenants, and the resources at their disposal, the leaders of the emerging nations have tackled the difficult tasks of development with varying degrees of success. Ways have been found to raise the living standards of a significant percentage of the population of some of the emerging nations. But these strategies have rarely benefited the majority. Solutions to specific problems have often given rise to new dilemmas. For example, the Green Revolution in agriculture that many development

experts credit with averting global famine in the last three decades has rendered staple crops over much of the developing world more dependent on irrigation and oil-based fertilizers and more vulnerable to plant diseases. A growing dependence on the world market has also left developing nations vulnerable to downward fluctuations of their key export crops or minerals. These shifts have frequently made sustained government planning for development difficult, and caused widespread deprivation among the rural and urban poor in many of the new nations.

Postcolonial regimes that have pursued strategies aimed at a genuine redistribution of wealth that will benefit all levels of society have floundered under bureaucratic paralysis, planning errors, and insufficient resources. In many cases, the emerging nations have needed to borrow extensively from the World Bank and the International Monetary Fund, which were established by the Western allies at the Bretton Woods Conference in 1944 to provide development assistance for national reconstruction after the end of World War II. The heavy indebtedness that has often resulted from the inability of hard-pressed new nations to repay these loans has led to the imposition of "structural adjustments" by international lending agencies on debtor nations. These demands have usually forced cutbacks in government subsidies to education, health care, and programs designed to keep down the costs of subsistence foods and fuel for the poor.

It may be too early to judge the outcomes of many development schemes. But, thus far, none has proved to be the path to the social justice and general economic development that nationalist leaders envisioned as the ultimate outcome of struggles for decolonization. Though some countries have done a good deal better than others, successful overall strategies to deal with the challenges facing the nations of Africa, the Middle East, and Asia have yet to be devised.

Charismatic Populists and One-Party Rule

One of the least successful responses on the part of leaders of emerging nations who found their dreams for reform and renewal frustrated has been a retreat into authoritarian rule. This approach has often been disguised by calculated, charismatic appeals for support from the disenfranchised masses. Perhaps the career of Kwame Nkrumah, the leader of Ghana's independence movement, illustrates this pattern as well as that of any Asian

DOCUMENT

Between Africa and the West—the Emerging Elites of the Developing World

The many novels of the Nigerian writer Chinua Achebe explore some of the most fundamental challenges faced by the peoples of Africa and Asia undergoing the process of decolonization and struggles to build new nations. The setting for the excerpts included here, from his novel *No Longer at Ease,* is an Ibo village in southeastern Nigeria. A young man, Obi Okonkwo, has recently returned from attending university in Great Britain to take up a positon in the British colonial bureaucracy in the last days of colonial rule. He travels to his home village, which has turned out for a celebration of his educational triumphs that, as it turns out, have been supported by his kinsmen in the expectation that they and his village will benefit from his rise in the emerging nation's bureaucracy. One of the village leaders of Umuofia's Progressive Union opens the scene with praise for Obi's "unprecedented academic brilliance."

He spoke of the great honour Obi had brought to the ancient town of Umuofia which could now join the comity of other towns in their march towards political irredentism, social equality and economic emancipation.

"The importance of having one of our sons in the vanguard of this march of progress is nothing short of axiomatic. Our people have a saying 'Ours is ours, but mine is mine.' Every town and village struggles at this momentous epoch in our political evolution to possess that of which it can say: 'This is mine.' We are happy that today we have such an invaluable possession in the person of our illustrious son and guest of honour."

He traced the history of the Umuofia Scholarship Scheme which had made it possible for Obi to study overseas, and called it an investment which must yield heavy dividends. He then referred (quite obliquely, of course) to the arrangement whereby the beneficiary from this scheme was expected to repay his debt over four years so that "an endless stream of students will be enabled to drink deep at the Pierian Spring of knowledge."

Needless to say, this address was repeatedly interrupted by cheers and the clapping of hands. What a sharp young man their secretary was, all said. He deserved to go to England himself. He wrote the kind of

or African politician. There can be little question that Nkrumah was genuinely committed to social reform and economic uplift for the Ghanaian people during the years of his rise to the position of the first prime minister of Ghana in 1957. After assuming power, he moved vigorously to initiate programs that would translate his high aspirations for his people into reality. But his ambitious schemes for everything from universal education to industrial development soon ran into trouble. Rival political parties, some representing regional interests and ethnic groups long hostile to Nkrumah, repeatedly challenged his initiatives and tried to block the efforts to carry out his plans. His leftist leanings won support from the Soviet bloc but frightened away Western investors, who had a good deal more capital to plow into Ghana's economy. They also led to growing hostility on the part of the United States, Great Britain, and other influential non-Communist countries. Most devastatingly, soon after independence, the price of cocoa—by far Ghana's largest export crop—began to fall sharply. Tens of thousands of Ghanaian cocoa farmers were hard hit and the

resources for Nkrumah's development plans suddenly dried up.

Nkrumah's response to these growing problems was increasingly dictatorial. He refused to give up or cut back on his development plans. As a result most failed miserably, owing to lack of key supplies and to official mismanagement. In the early 1960s, he forcibly crushed all political opposition by banning rival parties and jailing other political leaders. He assumed dictatorial powers and ruled through functionaries in his own Convention Peoples' Party.

Nkrumah also sought to hold on to the loyalty of the masses and mobilize their energies by highly stage-managed "events" and the manipulation of largely invented symbols and traditions that were said to be derived from Ghana's past history. Thus, he tried to justify his policies and leadership style with references to a uniquely African brand of socialism and the need to revive African traditions and African civilization. Even before independence, he had taken to wearing the traditional garb of the Ghanaian elite. The very name of Ghana, which

English they admired if not understood: the kind that filled the mouth, like the proverbial dry meat.

Obi's English on the other hand, was most unimpressive. He spoke "is" and "was." He told them about the value of education. "Education for service, not for white-collar jobs and comfortable salaries. With our great country on the threshold of independence, we need men who are prepared to serve her well and truly."

When he sat down the audience clapped from politeness. Mistake Number Two.

Cold beer, minerals, palm-wine and biscuits were then served, and the women began to sing about Umuofia and about Obi Okonkwo *nwa jelu oyibo*—Obi who had been in the land of the whites. The refrain said over and over again that the power of the leopard resided in its claws.

"Have they given you a job yet?" the chairman asked Obi over the music. In Nigeria the governmet was "they." It had nothing to do with you or me. It was an alien institution and people's business was to get as much from it as they could without getting into trouble.

"Not yet. I'm attending an interview on Monday."

"Of course those of you who know book will not have any difficulty," said the Vice-President on Obi's left.

"Otherwise I would have suggested *seeing* some of the men beforehand."

"It would not be necessary," said the President, "since they would be mostly white men."

"You think white men don't eat bribe? Come to our department. They eat more than black men nowadays."

Questions: Why do Obi's kinsmen and fellow villagers have such high regard for so young a man? What does their esteem say about the prestige of connections to the British colonizers and their feelings about their own knowledge and educational system? How do they expect him to repay the financial support he has received for his education in England? How does Obi feel about these obligations? Assuming that Obi is about to take his place among the elite of postindependence Nigeria, why are his obligations to his kinsmen and villagers so troubling? And in the face of these divided loyalties and the pervasive cynicism about the corruption of civil servants, how effective is the governance of the nationalist elite likely to be? Would it be better for the British to stay and continue to rule, given these conditions?

Source: Excerpt from Chinua Achebe, *No Longer at Ease* (Harcourt Education), pp. 37–38.

Nkrumah himself had proposed for the new nation that emerged from the former Gold Coast colony, had been taken from an ancient African kingdom. The original Ghanaian kingdom had actually been centered much farther to the north and had little to do with the peoples of the Gold Coast.

Nkrumah went about the country giving fiery speeches, dedicating monuments to the "revolution," which often consisted of giant statues of himself, and taking a prominent role in the nonaligned movement that was then sweeping the newly independent nations. As the French journalist Jean Lacouture reported in the mid-1960s, Nkrumah's posturing had become a substitute for his failed development schemes. His followers' adulation knew no bounds. Members of his captive parliament compared him to Confucius, Muhammad, Shakespeare, and Napoleon and predicted that his birthplace would serve as a "Mecca" for all of Africa's statesmen. But his suppression of all opposition and his growing ties to the Communist Party, coupled with the rapid deterioration of the Ghanaian economy, increased his

enemies, who laid low and waited for a chance to strike. That chance came early in 1966 when Nkrumah went off on one of his many trips, this time a peace mission to Vietnam. In his absence, he was deposed by a military coup. Nkrumah died in exile in 1972, and Ghana moved in a very different direction under its new military rulers.

Military Responses: Dictatorships and Revolutions

Nkrumah was just one of many civilian leaders in the postcolonial world who have been victims of military coups. In fact, until the 1990s it was far more difficult to find African, Middle Eastern, and Asian (or, as we have seen in Chapter 7, Latin American) countries that have remained under civilian regimes since independence than those that have experienced military takeovers of varying durations. India, the Ivory Coast, Malaysia, Tunisia, and Kenya are some of the more notable of the former; much of the rest of Southeast Asia and Africa have been or are now governed by military regimes. Given the difficulties

Many monumental statues of Kwame Nkrumah, such as this one, rose in the towns and villages of Ghana as he tried to cover the failure of his socialist-inspired development programs with dictatorial rule and self-glorification. Although Nkrumah's efforts to deflect his regime's failures through self-hyperbolic displays and pageantry were extreme, they were not unique. The many photos of the "great leader" of the moment that one finds in developing nations are a variation on Nkrumah's tactics. Such campaigns to glorify dictatorial figures are reminiscent of those mounted by the leaders of the Communist revolutions in Russia, China, and Cuba.

that leaders like Nkrumah had to face after independence, and the advantages the military have in crisis situations, the proliferation of coups in the emerging nations is not all that surprising.

The armed forces in developing countries have at times been divided by the religious and ethnic rivalries that have proved such a disruptive force in new nations. But the regimentation and emphasis on discipline and in-group solidarity in military training have often rendered soldiers more resistant than other social groups to these forces. In conditions of political breakdown and social conflict, the military possesses the monopoly—or

near monopoly—of force that is often essential for restoring order. Their occupational conditioning makes soldiers not only more ready than civilian leaders to use the force at their disposal but less concerned with its destructive consequences. Military personnel also tend to possess some degree of technical training, which was usually lacking in the humanities-oriented education of civilian nationalist leaders. Because most military leaders have been staunchly anti-Communist, they have often attracted covert technical and financial assistance from Western governments.

Once in control, military leaders have banned civilian political parties and imposed military regimes of varying degrees of repression and authoritarian control. Yet the ends to which these regimes have put their dictatorial powers have differed considerably. At their worst, military regimes—such as those in Uganda (especially under Idi Amin), Burma (now Myanmar), and Zaire—have quashed civil liberties while making little attempt to reduce social inequities or improve living standards. These regimes have existed mainly to enrich military strongmen, as well as their cronies and lackeys. Military governments of this sort have been notorious for official corruption and for the imprisonment and brutal torture or outright elimination of political dissidents. Understandably uneasy about being overthrown, these regimes have diverted a high proportion of their nations' meager resources, which might have gone for economic development, into expenditures on expensive military hardware. Neither the Western democracies nor the countries of the Soviet bloc have displayed any inhibitions about supplying arms to these military despots. Military leaders of this type have also been ready to use quarrels and sometimes military conflicts with neighboring regimes to divert attention from the bankruptcy of their domestic policies.

In a few cases, military leaders have proved to be quite radical in their approaches to economic and social reform. Perhaps none was more so than Gamal Abdul Nasser, who took power in Egypt following a military coup in 1952. As we have seen in Chapter 5, the Egyptians had won their independence in the mid-1930s, except for the lingering British presence in the Suez Canal zone. But self-centered civilian politicians and the corrupt khedival regime had done little to improve the standard of living of the mass of the Egyptian people. As conditions worsened and Egypt's governing parties did little but rake in wealth for their limited, largely elitist memberships, revolutionary forces emerged in Egyptian society.

The radical movement that actually succeeded in gaining power, the Free Officers movement, had evolved from a secret organization established in the Egyptian army in the 1930s. Founded by idealistic young officers of Egyptian, rather than Turco-Egyptian, descent, the secret Revolutionary Command Council studied conditions in the country and prepared to seize power in the name of a genuine revolution. For many decades, it was loosely allied to the Muslim Brotherhood, another revolutionary alternative to the khedival regime.

The Brotherhood had been founded by Hasan al-Banna in 1928. Al-Banna was a schoolteacher, who had studied in his youth with the famed Muslim reformer Muhammad Abduh. While at Al-Azhar University in Cairo in the years after World War I, al-Banna had combined a deep interest in scientific subjects with active involvement in student demonstrations in support of Wafd demands for Egyptian independence. During this period, al-Banna, like many other Egyptian students, developed an abiding contempt for the wealthy minority of Egyptians and Europeans who flourished in the midst of the appalling poverty of most of his people.

To remedy these injustices and rid Egypt of its foreign oppressors, al-Banna founded the Muslim Brotherhood in 1928. Though members of the organization were committed to a revivalist approach to Islam, the Brotherhood's main focus, particularly in the early years, was on a program of social uplift and sweeping reforms. The organization became involved in a wide range of activities, from promoting trade unions and building medical clinics to educating women and pushing for land reform. By the late 1930s, the Brotherhood's social service had become highly politicized. Al-Banna's followers fomented strikes and urban riots, and they established militant youth organizations and paramilitary assassination squads. Despite the murder of al-Banna by the khedive Farouk's hit men in 1949, the members of the Brotherhood continued to expand its influence in the early 1950s among both middle-class youths and the impoverished masses.

Following Egypt's humiliating defeats in the first Arab-Israeli War of 1948 and in a clash with the British over the latter's continuing occupation of the Suez Canal zone in 1952, mass anger with a discredited khedival and parliamentary regime gave the officers their chance. In July 1952 an almost bloodless military coup toppled the corrupt khedive Farouk from his jewel-encrusted throne.

The revolution had begun. The monarchy was ended, and with the installation of Nasser and the Free Officers, Egyptians ruled themselves for the first time since the 6th century B.C.E. By 1954 all political parties had been disbanded—including the Muslim Brotherhood, which had clashed with its former allies in the military—and

had been suppressed after an attempt on the life of Nasser. Nasser was only one of several officers at the head of the Free Officers movement, and by no means was he initially the most charismatic. But after months of internal power struggles in the officer corps, he emerged as the head of a military government that was deeply committed to revolution.

Nasser and his fellow officers used the dictatorial powers they had won in the coup to force through programs that they believed would result in the uplift of the long-oppressed Egyptian masses. They were convinced that only the state possessed the power to carry out essential social and economic reforms, and thus they began to intervene in all aspects of Egyptian life. Land reform measures were enacted; limits were placed on how much land an individual could own, and excess lands were seized and redistributed to landless peasants. State-financed education through the college level was made available to Egyptians. The government became Egypt's main employer—by 1980, over 30 percent of Egypt's workforce was on the state payroll. State subsidies were used to lower the price of basic food staples, such as wheat and cooking oil. State-controlled development schemes were introduced that emphasized industrial growth, modeled after the Five-Year Plans of the Soviet Union.

In order to establish Egypt's economic independence, stiff restrictions were placed on foreign investment. In some cases foreign properties were seized and redistributed to Egyptian investors. Nasser also embarked on an interventionist foreign policy that stressed the struggle to destroy the newly established Israeli state, forge Arab unity, and foment socialist revolutions in neighboring lands. His greatest foreign policy coup came in 1956, when he rallied international opinion to finally oust the British and their French allies from the Suez Canal zone. Despite the setbacks suffered by Egyptian military forces, Nasser made good use of the rare combined backing of the United States and the Soviet Union to achieve his aims in the crisis.

However well intentioned, many of Nasser's initiatives misfired. Land reform efforts were frustrated by bureaucratic corruption and the clever stratagems devised by the landlord class to hold on to their estates. State development schemes often lacked proper funding and failed because of mismanagement and miscalculations. Even the Aswân Dam project, which was the cornerstone of Nasser's development drive, was something of a fiasco. Egypt's continuing high rates of population increase quickly canceled out the additional cultivable lands the dam produced. The dam's interference with the flow of

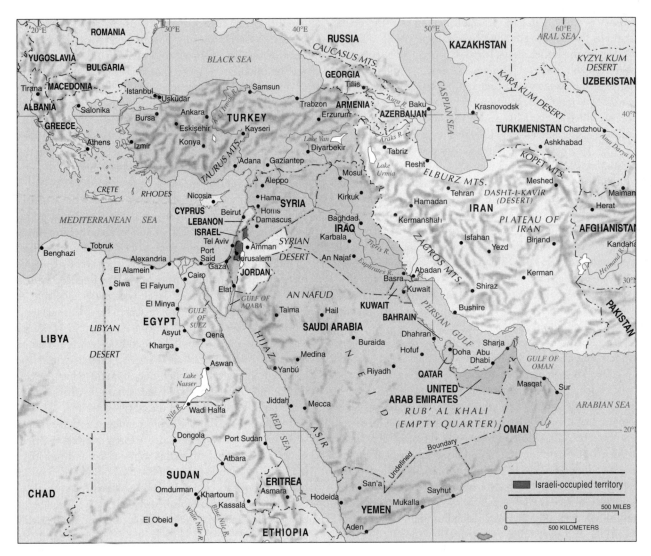

The Middle East in the Cold War Era

the Nile resulted in an increase in the parasites that spread blindness. It also led to a decline in the fertility of farmlands in the Lower Nile delta, which were deprived of the rich silt that had been annually washed down by the river. Foreign investment funds from the West, which Egypt desperately needed, soon dried up. Aid from the much poorer Soviet bloc could not begin to match what was lost, and much of this assistance was military.

In the absence of sufficient foreign investment and with Egypt's uncontrolled population rising at an alarming rate, the state simply could not afford all the ambitious schemes to which Nasser and the revolutionary officers had committed it. The gap between aspirations and means was increased in the later years of Nasser's reign (in the 1960s) by the heavy costs of his mostly failed foreign adventures, including the disastrous Six-Day War with Israel that Egypt was drawn into in 1967.

Although he had to move slowly at first, Nasser's successor, Anwar Sadat, had little choice but to dismantle the massive state apparatus that had been created. He favored private rather than state initiatives. During Sadat's tenure in office, the middle class, which had been greatly restricted by Nasser, emerged again as a powerful force. Sadat also moved, after fighting the Israelis to a stalemate in 1973, to end the costly confrontation with Israel as well as Egypt's support for revolutionary movements in the Arab world. He expelled the Russians and opened Egypt to aid and investment from the United States and western Europe.

Sadat's shift in direction has been continued by his successor and the present leader of Egypt, Hosni Mubarak. But neither the attempt at genuine revolution led by Nasser nor the move to capitalism and more pro-West positions under his successors has done much to check Egypt's rapid population increase or the corruption of its bloated bureaucracy. Neither path to development has had much effect on the glaring gap between the living conditions of Egypt's rich minority and its impoverished masses. No better gauge of the discontent that is bred by these inequities can be found than the proliferation of Muslim fundamentalist movements in the country. One of these succeeded in assassinating Sadat; others have sustained terrorist campaigns aimed at overthrowing the Mubarak regime and become influential leaders in terrorist organizations such as al-Qaeda.

The Indian Alternative: Development for Some of the People

Although the approach to nation building and economic development followed by the leaders of independent India has shared the Nasserite emphasis on socialism and state intervention, India's experience has diverged from Egypt's in several very significant respects. To begin with, the Indians have managed to preserve civilian rule throughout the nearly five decades since they won their independence from Great Britain. In fact, in India the military has consistently defended secular democracy against religious extremism and other would-be authoritarian trends. In addition, though India, like Egypt, has been saddled with a crushing burden of overpopulation, it came to independence with a larger industrial and scientific sector, a better communication system and bureaucratic grid, and a larger and more skilled middle class in proportion to its total population than any other African or Asian country.

During the first decades of its freedom, India had the good fortune to be governed by leaders such as Jawaharlal Nehru and his allies in the Congress Party, who were deeply committed to social reform and economic development as well as the preservation of civil rights and democracy. India's success at the latter has been nothing short of remarkable. Despite continuous threats of secession by religious and linguistic minorities, as well as massive poverty, unemployment, and recurring natural disasters, India remains the world's largest functioning democracy. Except for brief periods of rule by coalitions

of opposition parties, the Congress Party has ruled at the center for most of the independence era. But opposition parties have controlled many state and local governments, and they remain vocal and active in the national Parliament. Civil liberties, exemplified by a very outspoken press and free elections have been upheld to an extent that sets India apart from much of the rest of the emerging nations. Their staying power was perhaps most emphatically demonstrated by the heavy political price that Nehru's daughter and more dictatorially prone successor, Indira Gandhi, paid for attempting to curtail press and political freedoms in the mid-1970s. That attempt led to one of the rare election defeats the Congress Party has suffered until well into the 1990s.

Nehru's approach to government and development also differed from Nasser's in his more moderate mix of state and private initiatives. Nehru and his successors pushed state intervention in some sectors but also encouraged foreign investment from countries in both of the rival blocs in the cold war. As a consequence, India has been able to build on its initial advantages in industrial infrastructure and its skilled managerial and labor endowment. Its significant capitalist sector has encouraged ambitious farmers, such as those in the Punjab in the northwest, to invest heavily in the improved seed strains, fertilizers, and irrigation that are at the heart of the Green Revolution. Considerable industrial and agrarian growth has generated the revenue for the Indian government to promote literacy and village development schemes, as well as family planning, village electrification, and other improvement projects in recent decades.

Despite its very considerable successes, India has suffered from the same gap between needs and resources that all developing nations have had to face. Whatever the government's intentions—and India has been hit by corruption and self-serving like most polities—there have simply not been the resources to raise the living standards of even a majority of its huge population. The middle class has grown, perhaps as rapidly as that of any postcolonial nation. Its presence is striking in the affluent neighborhoods of cities like Bombay and Delhi and is proclaimed by the Indian film industry, the world's largest, and in innumerable sitcoms and dramas about the woes in the lives of Indian-style yuppies. But as much as half of India's people have gained little or nothing from the development plans and economic growth that have occurred since independence.

In part this has been because population growth has wiped out economic gains. But also social reform has been slow in most areas, both rural and urban. Groups like the wealthy landlords, who supported the nationalist drive for independence, have continued to dominate the great mass of tenants and landless laborers, just as they did in the precolonial and colonial eras. Some development measures, most notably those associated with the Green Revolution, have greatly favored those cultivators with the resources to invest in new seeds and fertilizer. They have increased the gap between well-off and poor people over much of rural India. India's literacy rate remains well below that of China (the only rival with which it can be reasonably compared, given the size of each and the magnitude of the problems they face), and a far larger proportion of India's population remains malnourished. Thus, the poor have paid and will continue to pay the price for Indian gradualism. Consequently, those favoring more revolutionary solutions to India's social inequities and mass poverty have plenty of ammunition with which to attack the ruling parties.

Iran: Religious Revivalism and the Rejection of the West

No path of development adopted by a postcolonial society has provided more fundamental challenges to the existing world order than revolutionary Iran under the direction of Ayatollah Khomeini. In many respects, the Khomeini revolution of 1979 represents a throwback to the religious fervor of such anticolonial resistance movements as that led by the Mahdi of the Sudan in the 1880s. Core motivations for the followers of both movements were provided by the emphasis on religious purification and the rejoining of religion and politics, which leaders such as the Mahdi and Khomeini have seen as central to the Islamic tradition. The call for a return to the kind of society believed to have existed in the past "golden age" of the prophet Muhammad was central to the policies pursued by both the Mahdist and Iranian regimes once they had gained power. Both movements were aimed at toppling Western-backed governments: the Mahdists' the Anglo-Egyptian presence in the Sudan; Khomeini's the autocratic Iranian shah and the Pahlavi dynasty.

Although they came from the Sunni and Shi'ite religious traditions, respectively, both the Mahdi and Khomeini claimed to be divinely inspired deliverers. Each promised to rescue the Islamic faithful from imperialist Westerners and from corrupt and heretical leaders within the Muslim world. Both leaders promised their followers magical protection and instant paradise should they fall while waging the holy war against the heretics and infidels. Each leader sought to build a lasting state and social order on the basis of what were believed to be Islamic

precedents. Thus, each revivalist movement aimed at the defense and restoration of what its leaders believed to be the true beliefs, traditions, and institutions of Islamic civilization. The leaders of both movements sought to spread their revolutions to surrounding areas, both Muslim and infidel, and each believed he was setting in motion forces that would eventually sweep the entire globe.

Khomeini's followers proclaimed the revolution that he spearheaded was an alternative path for development that could be followed by the rest of the emerging nations. But its initial success in seizing power was due to a combination of circumstances that was more or less unique to Iran. Like China, Iran had not been formally colonized by the European powers but rather had been reduced to a sphere of informal influence, divided between Great Britain and Russia. As a result, neither the bureaucratic nor the communication infrastructures that accompanied colonial takeovers were highly developed there. Nor did a substantial Western-educated middle class emerge. Thus, the impetus for "modernization" came suddenly and was imposed from above by the Pahlavi shahs. The initiatives taken by the second shah in particular, which were supported by Iran's considerable oil wealth, wrenched Iran out of the isolation and backwardness in which most of the nation lived until the mid-20th century. The shah tried to impose economic development and social change by government directives. Though advances occurred, the regime managed to alienate the great mass of the Iranian people in the process.

The shah's dictatorial and repressive regime deeply offended the emerging middle class, whom he considered his strongest potential supporters. His flaunting of Islamic conventions and his neglect of Islamic worship and religious institutions enraged the ayatollahs, or religious experts. They also alienated the mullahs or local prayer leaders and mosque attendants, who guided the religious and personal lives of the great majority of the Iranian population. The favoritism the shahs showed foreign investors and a handful of big Iranian entrepreneurs with personal connections to highly placed officials angered the smaller bazaar merchants, who had long maintained close links with the mullahs and other religious leaders. The shah's halfhearted land reform schemes alienated the landowning classes without really doing much to improve the condition of the rural poor. Even the urban workers, who benefited most from the boom in construction and light industrialization that the shah's development efforts had stimulated, were disaffected. In the years before the 1979 revolution, a fall in oil prices, had resulted in an economic slump and widespread unemployment in urban areas like the capital, Tehran.

The shah had treated his officers well, but the military rank and file, especially in the army, had been badly neglected. So when the crisis came in 1978, the shah found that few Iranians were prepared to defend his regime. His armies refused to fire on the growing crowds that demonstrated for his removal and the return of Khomeini, then in exile in Paris. Dying of cancer and disheartened by what he viewed as betrayal by his people and by allies such as the United States, the shah fled without much of a fight. Khomeini's revolution triumphed over a regime that looked powerful but in fact proved to be exceptionally vulnerable.

After coming to power, Khomeini, defying the predictions of most Western "experts" on Iranian affairs, followed through on his promises of radical change. Constitutional and leftist parties allied to the revolutionary movement were brutally repressed. Moderate leaders were quickly replaced by radical religious figures, who were eager to obey Khomeini's every command. The "satanic" influences of the United States and western Europe were purged; at the same time, Iran also distanced itself from the atheistic Communist world. Secular influences in law and government were supplanted by strict Islamic legal codes, which included such punishments as the amputation of limbs for theft and stoning for women caught in adultery. Veiling became obligatory for all females, and the career prospects for women of the educated middle classes, who had been among the most favored by the shah's reforms, were suddenly limited drastically.

Khomeini's planners also drew up grand schemes for land reform, religious education, and economic development that accorded with the dictates of Islam. Most of these measures came to little because soon after the revolution, Saddam Hussein, the military leader of neighboring Iraq, sought to take advantage of the turmoil in Iran by annexing its western, oil-rich provinces. The First Gulf War that resulted swallowed up Iranian energies and resources for virtually the entire decade after Khomeini came to power. Though the struggle clearly was initially the fault of the invading Iraqis, it became a highly personal vendetta for Khomeini, who was determined to destroy Saddam Hussein and punish the Iraqis. His refusal to negotiate peace caused heavy losses and untold suffering to the Iranian people. This suffering continued long after it was clear that the Iranians' aging military equipment and handful of allies were no match for Hussein's more advanced military hardware and an Iraqi war machine bankrolled by its oil-rich Arab neighbors, who were fearful that Khomeini's revolution might spread to their own countries.

As the support of the Western powers, including the United States (despite protestations of neutrality), for the Iraqis increased, the position of the isolated Iranians became increasingly intolerable. Hundreds of thousands of poorly armed and half-trained Iranian conscripts, including tens of thousands of untrained and virtually weaponless boys, died before Khomeini finally agreed to a humiliating armistice in 1988. Peace found revolutionary Iran in shambles. Few of its development initiatives had been pursued, and shortages in food, fuel, and the other necessities of life were widespread.

Iran's decade-long absorption in the war and its continuing isolation make it impossible to assess the potential of the religious revivalist, anti-Western option for other postcolonial nations. What had seemed at first to be a viable path to genuinely independent development for African and Asian peoples became mired in brutal internal repression and misguided and failed development schemes. In the years after the Ayatollah Khomeini's death in 1989, the factional divisions that had been pronounced in Iran's revolutionary government from the outset intensified. Reformist leaders, most notably Muhammad Khatami who was elected president in 1997, have sought to curb the power of the more doctrinaire ayatollahs, expand the nation's free market economy at the expense of entrenched government bureaucrats, and enhance the civil rights of the citizenry, especially Iranian women. Khatami and other moderates have also sought to improve Iran's international standing and improve relations with the democracies of western Europe and the United States. Thus far these efforts have been held in check by the conservative clerics and militant Islamic groups, including shopkeepers and urban workers, who provide the main support for the revolutionary regime. The efforts of hardliners among the ruling factions to make Iran into a nuclear power has estranged potential European supporters of reformist elements within the country and greatly increased tensions with the United States in the opening years of the 21st century.

South Africa: The Apartheid State and Its Demise

South Africa was by no means the only area still under some form of colonial dominance decades after India became the first of the former European colonies to gain its independence in 1947. Portugal, the oldest and long considered the weakest of the European colonizers, held onto Angola, Mozambique, and its other African possessions until the mid-1970s. Until 1980, Zimbabwe (formerly Southern Rhodesia) was run by white settlers, who had unilaterally declared their independence from Great Britain. Southwest Africa became fully free of South African control only in 1989, and some of the smaller islands in the West Indies and the Pacific remain under European or American rule to the present day.

By the 1970s, however, South Africa was by far the largest, most populous, richest, and most strategic area where the great majority of the population had yet to be liberated from colonial domination. Since the 1940s, the white settlers, particularly the Dutch-descended Afrikaners, had solidified their internal control of the country under the leadership of the Nationalist Party. In stages and through a series of elections in which the blacks, who made up the great majority of South Africans, were not allowed to vote, the Nationalists won complete independence from Great Britain in 1960. From 1948, when the Nationalist Party first came to power, the Afrikaners moved to institutionalize white supremacy and white minority rule by the passage of thousands of laws that, taken together, made up the system of apartheid that dominated all aspects of South African life until very recently.

Apartheid was designed not only to ensure a monopoly of political power and economic dominance for the white minority, both British and Dutch-descended, but also to impose a system of extreme segregation on all races of South Africa in all aspects of their lives. Separate and patently unequal facilities were established for different racial groups for recreation, education, housing, work, and medical care. Dating and sexual intercourse across racial lines were strictly prohibited; skilled and high-paying jobs were reserved for white workers; and nonwhites were required to carry passes that listed the parts of South Africa where they were allowed to work and reside. If caught by the police without their passes or in areas where they were not permitted to travel, nonwhite South Africans were routinely given stiff jail sentences.

Spatial separation was also organized on a grander scale by the creation of numerous homelands within South Africa, each designated for the main ethnolinguistic or "tribal" groups within the black African population. Though touted by the Afrikaners as the ultimate solution to the racial "problem," the homelands scheme would have left the black African majority with a small percent of some of the poorest land in South Africa. Because the homelands were overpopulated and poverty stricken, the white minority was guaranteed a ready supply of cheap black labor to work in their factories and mines and on their farms. Denied citizenship in South Africa proper, these laborers were forced eventually to return to the homelands, where they had left their wives and children while emigrating in search of work.

To maintain the blatantly racist and inequitable system of apartheid, the white minority had to build a police state and expend a large portion of the federal budget on a sophisticated and well-trained military establishment. Because of the land's great mineral wealth, the Afrikaner nationalists were able to find the resources to fund their garrison state for decades. Until the late 1980s, the government prohibited all forms of black protest and brutally repressed even nonviolent resistance. Black organizations such as the African National Congress were declared illegal, and African leaders such as Walter Sisulu and Nelson Mandela, were shipped off to maximum-security prisons. Other leaders, such as Steve Biko, one of the young organizers of the Black Consciousness movement, died under very suspicious circumstances while in police custody.

Through spies and police informers, the regime attempted to capitalize on personal and ethnic divisions within the black majority community. Favoritism was shown to some leaders and groups to keep them from uniting with others in all-out opposition to apartheid. With all avenues of constitutional negotiation and peaceful protest closed, many advocates of black majority rule in a multiracial society turned to guerrilla resistance from the 1960s onward. The South African government responded in the 1980s by declaring a state of emergency, which simply intensified the restrictions already in place in the garrison state. The government repeatedly justified its draconian repression by labeling virtually all black protest as Communist-inspired and playing on the racial fears of the white minority.

Through most of the 1970s and early 1980s, it appeared that the hardening hostility between the unyielding white minority and the frustrated black majority was building to a major and very violent upheaval. But from the late 1980s, countervailing forces were taking hold in South African society. An international boycott greatly weakened the South African economy. In addition, the South African army's costly and futile involvement in wars in neighboring Namibia and Angola seemed to presage never-ending struggles against black liberation movements within the country. Led by the courageous F. W. de Klerk, moderate Afrikaner leaders pushed for reforms that began the process of dismantling the system of apartheid. The release of key black political prisoners, such as the dramatic freeing of Nelson Mandela in 1990, signaled that at long last the leaders of the white minority were ready to negotiate the future of South African politics and society. Permission for peaceful mass demonstrations and ultimately the enfranchisement of all adult South Africans for the 1994 elections provided a

This photograph of a long line of newly enfranchised citizens waiting to vote in the 1994 elections in South Africa provides a striking contrast with the decreasing participation in elections in the United States and other older democracies in the West. For the first time, the Bantu-speaking peoples, coloreds, and Indians, who made up the vast majority of South Africa's population, were allowed to vote in free elections. Their determination to exercise their hard-won right to vote was demonstrated by the peoples' willingness to wait, often in stifling heat, for many hours in the long lines that stretched from polling stations throughout the country.

way out of the dead end in which the nation appeared to be trapped under apartheid.

The well-run and remarkably participatory 1994 elections brought to power the African National Congress party, led by Nelson Mandela. He has proved to be one of the most skillful and respected political leaders on the world scene as well as a moderating force in the potentially volatile South African arena. The peaceful surrender of power by F. W. de Klerk's losing party, which was supported by most of the white minority, suggested that a pluralist democracy might well succeed in South Africa. But major obstacles remain. Bitter interethnic rivalries within the black majority community, which periodically flared into bloody battles between Zulus and Xhosas in the 1990s, have yet to be fully resolved. Hardline white supremacist organizations among the Afrikaners continue to defy the new regime. And the tasks of reforming the institutions and redistributing the wealth of

South Africa in ways that will make for a just and equitable social order are indeed formidable. Well into the 21st century, South Africa is likely to remain one of the most interesting and promising social experiments of an age in which communalism and ethnic hostility threaten to engulf much of the globe.

CONCLUSION: THE POSTCOLONIAL EXPERIENCE IN HISTORICAL PERSPECTIVE

Although the years of independence for the nations that have emerged from the colonial empires have been filled with political and economic crises and social turmoil, it is important to put the recent history of Africa, the Middle East, and Asia in a larger perspective. Most of the new nations that emerged from colonialism have been in existence for only a few decades. They came to independence with severe handicaps, many of which were a direct legacy of their colonial experiences. It is also important to remember that developed countries, such as the United States, took decades and numerous boundary disputes and outright wars to reach their current size and contours. Nearly a century after the original 13 colonies broke away from Great Britain and formed the United States, a civil war, the most costly conflict in the nation's history, was required to preserve the union. If one takes into account the artificial nature of the emerging nations, most have held together rather well.

What is true in politics is true of all other aspects of the postcolonial experience of the African and Asian peoples. With much lower populations and far fewer industrial competitors, as well as the capacity to draw on the resources of much of the rest of the world, European and North American nations had to struggle to industrialize and thereby achieve a reasonable standard of living for most of their people. Even with these advantages, the human cost in terms of horrific working conditions and urban squalor was enormous, and we are still paying the high ecological price. African, Middle Eastern, and Asian countries (and this includes Japan) have had few or none of the West's advantages. They have begun the "great ascent" to development burdened by excessive and rapidly increasing populations that overwhelm the limited resources that developing nations must often export to earn the capital to buy food and machines. The emerging nations struggle to establish a place in the world market system that is heavily loaded in favor of the established industrial powers in terms of pricing and investment.

Despite the cultural dominance of the West, which was one of the great legacies or burdens of the colonial era, Asian, Middle Eastern, and African thinkers and artists have achieved a great deal. If much of this achievement has been heavily dependent on Western models, one should not be surprised, given the educational backgrounds and personal experiences of the first generations of African and Asian leaders. The challenge for the coming generations will be to find African, Middle Eastern, and Asian solutions to the problems that have stunted political and economic development in the postcolonial nations. The solutions arrived at are likely to vary a great deal, given the diversity of the nations and societies involved. They are also likely to be forged from a combination of Western influences and the ancient and distinguished traditions of civilized life that have been nurtured by African, Middle Eastern, and Asian peoples for millennia.

FURTHER READING

Much of the prolific literature on political and economic development in the emerging nations is focused on individual countries, and it is more helpful to know several cases in some depth than to try to master them all. Robert Heilbroner's writings, starting with *The Great Ascent* (1961), still provide the most sensible introduction to challenges to the new states in the early decades of independence. Peter Worsley's *The Third World* (1964) provides a provocative, if somewhat disjointed, supplement to Heilbroner's many works. Though focused mainly on South and Southeast Asia, Gunnar Myrdal's *Asian Drama* (3 vols., 1968), is the best exploration in a single cultural area of the complexities of the challenges to development. A good overview of the history of postindependence South Asia can be found in W. N. Brown's *The United States and India, Pakistan, and Bangladesh* (1984), despite its misleadingly Western-centric title. Perhaps the best account of Indian politics is contained in Paul Brass's *The Politics of India Since Independence* (1990) in the *New Cambridge History of India* series. On development policy in India, see Francine R. Frankel's *India's Political Economy, 1947–1977* (1978).

Ali Mazrui and Michael Tidy's *Nationalism and New States in Africa* (1984) is a good survey of developments throughout Africa. Also useful are S. A. Akintoye's *Emergent African States* (1976) and J. D. Hargreaves's *Decolonization in Africa* (1988). For the Middle East, John Waterbury's *The Egypt of Nasser and Sadat* (1983) and Timothy Mitchell's *Rule of Experts* (2002) provide detailed accounts of the politics of nation-building and development in the most populous Arab nation.

On military coups, see Ruth First's *The Barrel of a Gun* (1971) and S. Decalo's *Coups and Army Rule in Africa* (1976). Shaul Bakhash's *The Reign of the Ayatollahs* (1984) is perhaps the most insightful of several books that have appeared about Iran since the revolution. Brian Bunting's *The Rise of the South African Reich* (1964) traces the rise of the apartheid regime in great (and polemical) detail, while Gail Gerhart's *Black Power in South Africa* (1978) is one of the better studies devoted to efforts to tear that system down. Nelson Mandela's autobiographical *Long Walk to Freedom* (1994) is not only one of the best works on resistance to apartheid, it is one of the best accounts available on the last phase of colonial domination and the struggles for national liberation. Among the many fine African and Asian authors whose works are available in English, some of the best include (for Africa)

Chinua Achebe, Wole Soyinka, and Ousmene Sembene; (for India) R. K. Narayan and V. S. Naipaul; (for Egypt) Nawal el Saadawi and Naguib Mahfouz; and (for Indonesia) Mochtar Lubis and P. A. Toer. For white perspectives on the South African situation, the fictional works of Nadine Gordimer and J. M. Coetzee are superb.

ON THE WEB

A timeline for decolonization is provided at

http://smccd.net/accounts/helton/decoloni.htm
http://campus.northpark.edu/history/WebChron/World/
   Decolonization.html

Studies of the life and work of famed African novelist Chinua Achebe's writing on imperialism and decolonization can be found at

http://www.scholars.nus.edu.sg/landow/post/achebe/
   achebebio.html
http://www.scholars.nus.edu.sg/landow/post/achebe/
   achebeov.html
http://www.wsu.edu:8000/~brians/anglophone/achebe
   .html

A history of apartheid is offered at

http://www-cs-students.stanford.edu/~cale/cs201/
   apartheid.hist.html
http://www.africanaencyclopedia.com/apartheid/
   apartheid.html

The arguments of pro-apartheid Afrikaners are presented at

http://www.fordham.edu/halsall/mod/1953geyer.html

Reflections on the anti-apartheid struggle are offered at

http://www.pbs.org/pov/tvraceinitiative/facingthetruth/

Kwame Nkrumah's classic indictment of neocolonialism can be found at

http://www.fhsu.edu/history/virtual/nkrumah.htm

while a classically neoconservative view condemning neocolonialism, but not modernization, is offered at

http://www.afbis.com/analysis/neo-colonialism.html

Other postcolonial ideological issues addressed by African leaders are examined at

http://web.uflib.ufl.edu/cm/africana/senghor.htm
http://www.hartford-hwp.com/archives/30/index-fd.html

Gamal Abdul Nasser's cold war era experiments with Arab socialism as the best means of negotiating modernization are discussed at

http://www.arab.net/egypt/et_nasser.htm
http://www.1upinfo.com/country-guide-study/egypt/
   egypt44.html

The debate over the role of religion as a solution to the moral malaise, as well as the disparity of wealth that has come to characterize the postmodern era, is illuminated by the life and works of Eygpt's Hasan al-Banna of the Muslim Brotherhood at

http://www.glue.umd.edu/~kareem/rasayil/
http://www.nmhschool.org/tthornton/hasan_al.htm
http://www.ummah.org.uk/ikhwan/

For further information regarding Iran's Ayattollah Ruhollah Khomeini's role as the supreme leader of the Islamic revolution in Iran see

http://www.iranchamber.com/history/rkhomeini/
   ayatollah_khomeini.php
http://www.asiasource.org/society/khomeini.cfm
http://www.bbc.co.uk/persian/revolution/rev_01
   .shtml
http://www.fordham.edu/halsall/mod/1979khom1
   .html

Current moderating trends in this seedbed of the Islamic movement are analyzed at

http://www.brown.edu/Departments/Anthropology/
   publications/IranisChanging.htm
http://www.brown.edu/Departments/Anthropology/
   Beeman.html

A useful review of India's first 50 years of independence may be found at

http://www.itihaas.com/independent/contrib7.html

Jawaharlal Nehru's views on Marxism, capitalism, and nonalignment are available at

http://www.fordham.edu/halsall/mod/1941/nehru.html

His failure to move the world through his commitment to world disarmament is discussed at

http://www.indianembassy.org/policy/Disarmament/
   India_Disarmament.htm

As a result, India later went down the path to nuclear confrontation with Pakistan. The growing place of religion in Indian political life, which Nehru would have also opposed, is embodied in the platform of the Bharatiya Janata Party, disussed at

http://www.bjp.com

Indira Gandhi's role in postcolonial India is explored at

http://www.sscnet.ucla.edu/southasia/History/
   Independent/Indira.html

Chapter 12

Cold War Confrontations and the Resurgence of Revolution

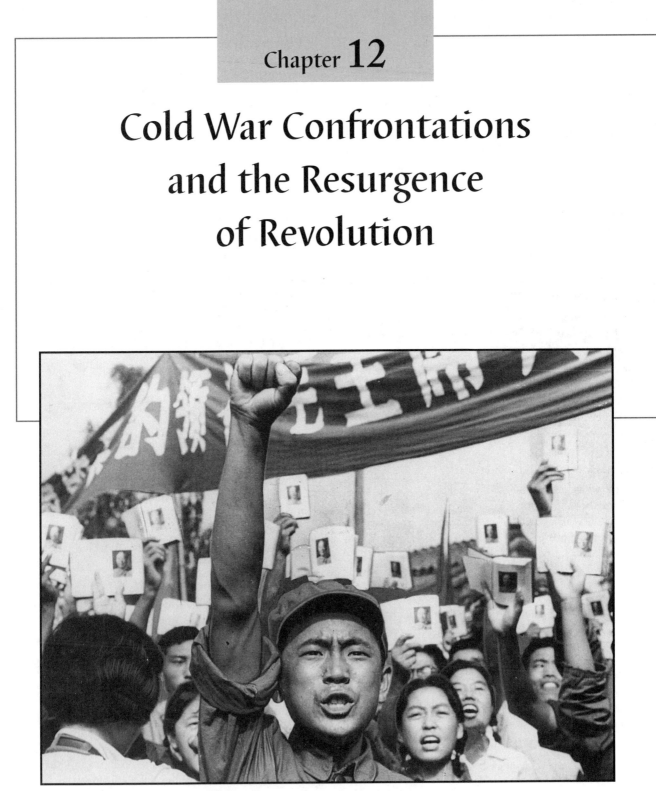

In launching the Cultural Revolution in the mid-1960s, Mao Zedong sought to restore the revolutionary fervor of the 1930s and 1940s. Here members of the Red Guards brandish Mao's "little red book," which served as a "bible" for his followers.

Chronology

1945	Ho Chi Minh proclaims the Republic of Vietnam
1949	People's Republic of China established
1950–1953	Korean War
1953	Beginning of China's first Five-Year Plan
1954	French defeated at Dien Bien Phu; Geneva accords, French withdrawal from Vietnam
1957	"Let a thousand flowers bloom" campaign in China
1958–1960	Great Leap Forward in China; massive famine
1959	Castro to power in Cuba
1961	Failed Bay of Pigs invasion in Cuba
1963	Beginning of state family planning in China
1965–1973	Direct U.S. military intervention in Vietnam
1966–1969	Era of the Cultural Revolution in China
1968	Tet offensive in Vietnam
1975	Communist victory in Vietnam; collapse of the Republic of South Vietnam
1976	Deaths of Zhou Enlai and Mao Zedong; purge of the Gang of Four
1980s	Era of economic liberalization in China
1989	Tiananmen Square massacre in Beijing; pro-democracy movement is crushed

INTRODUCTION

The revolutionary surge that had erupted in the years on either side of World War I was stifled or thrown back throughout much of the world by the rise of powerful Fascist and military regimes in the 1930s. But the dislocations of a second and even more devastating round of global war in the 1940s gave new life to continuing revolutionary struggles in China and Vietnam and elsewhere in the postcolonial world. These peasant-based upheavals were paralleled by revolutionary movements throughout much of Latin America. Although grounded in resistance to enduring mass poverty and political oppression, most of these movements were also an expression of longstanding U.S. informal domination of the economies and international relations of East Asian and Latin American societies. And all of these themes were epitomized by the Cuban revolution led by Fidel Castro that turned that island nation into one of the flashpoints of the cold war.

The Soviet Union's emergence from World War II as one of the two global superpowers gave new impetus to these widespread revolutionary movements. Soviet history served as a model for both insurgency and state-building, and very often Russia provided direct military support to revolutionary organizations. The Soviet Union and its Communist allies also provided encouragement and material support for anticolonial movements throughout Asia and Africa. The Western-educated, largely middle-class elites who led these movements were often quite willing to accept Soviet backing. But, as we have seen in Chapter 11, they usually worked toward nonviolent and basically nonrevolutionary transfers of power. They also favored, at least initially, more democratic political institutions and a larger role for market forces than was possible under Soviet-style, Communist economies.

The assistance that the Soviet Union and other nations in the Communist bloc provided for leftist revolutionaries in both the developing world and western Europe was almost invariably counterbalanced by the often formidable aid provided by the United States and its industrial allies for middle-class elites that favored gradualist, reformist rather than revolutionary transformations. During the decades of the cold war, much of the Third World—which included most of the nations of Africa, Asia, and Latin America—became contested terrain in the global contests between the hostile capitalist and Communist camps—or what contemporaries thought of as the "First" and "Second" worlds, respectively. The struggle was in part ideological, with the proponents of Communism and capitalism vying to convince the peoples of the Third World that they, not their rivals, could provide the best path to rapid economic development and social stability. But it was also a contest for control of the considerable natural resources, market outlets, and strategic locales of Latin America and the formerly colonized areas of Africa and Asia. Ironically, both the Communist and capitalist blocs offered the peoples of the Third World similar models for development. Both emphasized large-scale projects and heavy fossil-fuel consumption that had their origins in the process of industrialization as it had occurred in western Europe and the United States. The communists stressed state control, in contrast to the capitalists who touted the advantages of market mechanisms. But both gave priority to high tech, science, and industrialization—and both approaches to development have had devastating effects on the fragile tropical environments of much of the Third World, and very often the more temperate ecologies of the superpowers' homelands themselves.

At times the developing nations were little more than pawns in these ongoing contests. But often the larger and more advanced of the new nations, such as India and Egypt, could take advantage of superpower conflicts by playing off one camp against the other to win economic aid and military hardware. In the long term, these stratagems often backfired against the peoples of Third World countries. Aid usually proved to have strings attached that stunted overall growth or, by favoring established groups, further skewed social and economic imbalances in African, Asian, and Latin American countries. The armaments that the superpowers funneled—often at great profit to themselves—into developing countries both drained resources from productive investment and took a heavy toll in the wars and civil strife that have been so pervasive in postcolonial and Latin American societies since 1945. In areas where revolutionary movements (which were usually labeled "communist" whatever the predilections of those waging them) were an important force, military interventions by the United States or its surrogates became a familiar occurrence in the last decades of the 20th century.

Although cold war confrontations between the Soviet bloc and the capitalist West influenced the outcomes of civil wars and revolutionary insurgencies throughout the developing world, the forces that created social conflict and revolutionary movements were overwhelmingly indigenous to the societies where these struggles occurred. As we shall see in the examples of both successful and failed revolutions in China, Vietnam, and Latin America, perceived (and very often real) exploitation by

foreign powers contributed to the conditions that produced social unrest and dissident movements. But internal dislocations—natural calamities, the breakdown of bureaucratic systems, rampant social injustice, and economic inequities—were the central factors behind the risings of the peasantry and the working poor of postcolonial and Latin American societies convulsed by revolutionary movements. With the exception of small and excessively vulnerable nations, such as those of Central America, interventions by one or the other of the superpowers or their proxies could prolong the life of repressive regimes and thus delay the seizure of power by revolutionary forces. But as the cases of China, Cuba, and especially Vietnam illustrate so strikingly, even the military might of the U.S. colossus could not turn back the revolutionary tide if insurgent movements had won the support of large numbers of the indigenous population and, conversely, the regimes in power were corrupt and inept.

As we shall see in this chapter, the victory of the revolutionaries did not guarantee utopia for the societies in which leftist parties came to power. In fact, China, Vietnam, and Cuba were often isolated from all but a few sympathetic, but themselves impoverished, Communist nations. As a consequence, they were deprived of critical economic assistance from the outside that might have given impetus to development schemes that often fell far short of their ambitious targets. In addition, once in power successful revolutionaries have often refused to tolerate opposition parties and have been quite willing to sacrifice some human rights—free speech and elections, for example—for others, such as universal employment, education, and health care. Leftist leaders have tended to direct state resources toward centrally controlled, large-scale industrial development and mechanized, communal farming, both of which have proved much less productive and usually much more damaging to the environment than their capitalist counterpoints. As a result, the same malaise and society-wide crises that overtook Communist societies in the Soviet Union and Eastern Europe in the late 1980s diminished faith in the possibility of Communist utopia in Vietnam, Cuba, and China over the last decade of the 20th century.

In order to understand the long-term effects of revolutionary upheaval in the 20th century, it is necessary to examine these recent developments. They are discussed in each of the three main sections of this chapter that cover the rise and course of revolutionary movements and the states and societies they produced in three key areas during the cold war era. The first section surveys the final stages of the civil war in China that ended in

1949 with the victory of the Communists over the Guomindang. After tracing the very troubling history of the Communist regime in power through the 1990s, we analyze the post-1945 struggles of the Vietnamese Communists to seize and hold power in the face of foreign interventions, most notably by the French and the Americans, and the resistance of the puppet regimes backed by the hostile Western powers. The final sections of the chapter explore revolutionary and repressive impulses in Latin America from World War II to the present with an emphasis on Cuba, where the most dynamic and influential Communist regime in the Western Hemisphere has held power, in defiance of persisting American efforts to undermine it, since the late 1950s.

MAO'S CHINA AND BEYOND

The guerrilla warfare that the Communists waged against the Japanese armies in the 1930s proved far more effective than Chiang Kai-shek's conventional approach. With the Nationalist extermination campaigns suspended, the Communists used their anti-Japanese resistance efforts to extend their control over large areas of north China. By the end of World War II, the Nationalists controlled mainly the cities in the north; they had become (as Mao prescribed in his political writings) islands surrounded by a sea of revolutionary peasants. The Communists' successes and their determination to fight the Japanese, while Chiang and his advisors vacillated, won them the support of most of China's intellectuals and many of the students who had earlier looked to the Nationalists for China's salvation. By 1945 the balance of power within China was clearly shifting in the Communists' favor. In the four-year civil war that followed, Communist soldiers, who were well treated and fought for a cause, consistently routed the much-abused soldiers of the Nationalists, who went over in droves to the Communist side.

The Japanese invasion proved critical in the Communist drive to victory. But equally important were the Communists' social and economic reform programs, which eventually won the great majority of the peasantry, the students and intellectuals, and even many of the bureaucrats to their side. While Chiang, whatever his intentions, was able to do little to improve the condition of the great mass of the people, Mao made the peasants' uplift the central element in his drive for power. Land reforms, access to education, and improved health care gave the peasantry a real stake in Mao's revolutionary movement and good reason to defend their soviets

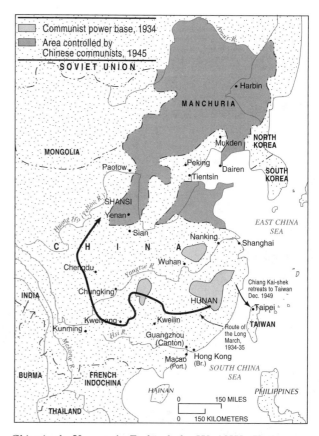

China in the Years at the End and after World War II, the Final Phase of the Civil War

against both the Nationalists and the Japanese. In contrast to Chiang's armies, whose arrival meant theft, rape, and wanton murder to China's villagers, Mao's soldiers were indoctrinated with the need to protect the peasantry and win their support. Lest they forget, harsh penalties were levied, such as execution for so much as stealing an egg.

As guerrilla fighters, Mao's soldiers had a much better chance to survive and advance in the ranks than did the forcibly conscripted, brutally treated rank and file of the Nationalists. Mao and the commanders around him, such as Lin Biao, who had been trained at Chiang's Whampoa Academy in the 1920s, proved far more gifted—even in conventional warfare—than the often corrupt and inept Nationalist generals. Thus, though the importance of the Japanese invasion cannot be discounted, the Communists won the mandate to govern China because they offered solutions to China's fundamental social and economic problems. Even more critically, they actually put their programs into action in the areas that came under their control. In a situation where revolutionary changes appeared to be essential, the Communists alone convinced the Chinese people that they had the leaders and program that could implement them.

Massive arms shipments to the Nationalists from the United States, whose postwar leaders were anxious to prevent the "loss" of China to the Communist camp, delayed but could not prevent the rout of Chiang and his allies. By 1949, it was over. Chiang and what was left of his Nationalist supporters fled to the island of Formosa (renamed Taiwan) off the China coast, and Mao proclaimed the establishment of the People's Republic of China in Beijing.

Challenges Facing the Maoists in Power

In assuming power in 1949, the Communists faced the formidable task of governing a vast nation in ruins. But in contrast to the Bolsheviks, who seized power in 1917 in Russia quite easily but then had to face years of civil war and foreign aggression, the Communists in China claimed a unified nation from which foreign aggressors had been expelled. Unlike the Bolsheviks, the Communist leadership in China could move directly to the tasks of social reform and economic development that China so desperately needed. In so doing, they could build on the base they had established in the "liberated" zones during their long struggle for power. In these areas, land reforms had already been tested, mass literacy campaigns had been mounted, and young people, both male and female, had enjoyed opportunities to rise in the party ranks on the basis of hard work.

Although deep social divisions remained, the Chinese faced far less serious splits between different religious and ethnic groups than most other new nations of Africa and Asia. Millennia of common history and common cultural development had given the peoples of China a sense of identity and a tradition of political unity. The decades of resistance to foreign aggressors had strengthened these bonds and impressed upon the Chinese the importance of maintaining a united front against outsiders if they were to avoid future humiliations and exploitation. The Communists' long struggle for control had left the party with a strong political and military organization that was rooted in the party cadres and the People's Liberation Army. The continuing importance of the army was indicated by the fact that most of China was administered by military officials for five years after the Communists came to power. But the army remained clearly subordinate to the party. Cadre advisors were attached to military contingents at all levels and the central committees of the party were dominated by nonmilitary personnel.

With this strong political framework in place, the Communists moved quickly to assert China's traditional preeminence in East and much of Southeast Asia. Potential secessionist movements were forcibly repressed in Inner Mongolia and Tibet, though resistance in the latter has erupted periodically and continues to the present day. In the early 1950s, the Chinese intervened militarily in the conflict between North and South Korea—an intervention that was critical in forcing the United States to settle for a stalemate and a lasting division of the peninsula. Refusing to accept a similar, but far more lopsided, two-nation outcome of the struggle in China itself, the Communist leadership has periodically threatened to invade the Nationalists' refuge on Taiwan, in several cases touching off international incidents in the process. China also played an increasingly important role in the liberation struggle of the Vietnamese to the south, though that would not peak until the height of American involvement in the conflict in the 1960s.

By the late 1950s, the close collaboration between the Soviet Union and China that marked the early years of Mao's rule had broken down. Border disputes, focusing on territories the Russians had seized during the period of Manchu decline, and the Chinese refusal to play second fiddle to Russia, especially after Stalin was succeeded by the less imposing Khrushchev, were key causes of the split. These causes of the breakdown in collaboration greatly exacerbated the differences resulting from the disappointingly meager economic assistance provided by the Soviet "comrades." They also fed Mao's sense that with the passing of Stalin, he was the number-one theoretician and leader of the Communist world. In the early 1960s, the Chinese flexed their very considerable military and technological muscle by thrashing India in a brief war that resulted from a border dispute. More startling, however, was the Chinese success in exploding the first nuclear device developed by a nonindustrial nation.

Planning for Economic Growth and Social Justice

On the domestic front the new leaders of China moved with equal vigor, though with a good deal less success. Their first priority was to complete the social revolution in the rural areas that had been, to some extent, carried through in Communist-controlled areas during the wars against the Japanese and Guomindang. Between 1950 and 1952, the landlord class and the large landholders, most of whom had been spared in the earlier stages of the revolution, were dispossessed and purged. Village tribunals, overseen by Party cadre members, gave tenants and laborers a chance to get even for decades of oppression. Perhaps as many as 3 million people who were denounced as members of the exploitative landlord class were executed. At the same time, the land taken from the landowning classes was distributed to peasants who had none or little. For a brief time, at least, one of the central pledges of the Communist revolutionaries was fulfilled: China became a land of peasant smallholders.

Communist planners, however, saw rapid industrialization, not peasant farmers, as the key to successful development. With the introduction of the first Stalinist-style Five-Year Plan in 1953, the Communist leadership turned away from the peasantry, which had brought them to power, to the urban workers as the hope for a new China. With little foreign assistance from either the West or the Soviet bloc, the state resorted to stringent measures to draw resources from the countryside to finance industrial growth. Some advances were made in industrialization, particularly in heavy industries such as steel. But the shift in direction had consequences that were increasingly unacceptable to Mao and his more radical supporters in the party. State planning and centralization were stressed, party bureaucrats greatly increased their power and influence, and an urban-based privileged class of technocrats began to develop. These changes, and the external threat to China posed by the American intervention in Korea and the continuing friction between the United States and China, led Mao and his followers to force a change of strategies in the mid-1950s.

Mao had long nurtured a deep hostility toward elitism, which he associated with the discredited Confucian system. He had little use for Lenin's vision of revolution from above, led by a disciplined cadre of professional political activists. He distrusted intellectuals, disliked specialization, and clung to his faith in the peasants rather than the workers as the repository of basic virtue and the driving force of the revolution. Acting to stem the trend toward an elitist, urban-industrial focus, Mao and his supporters introduced the Mass Line approach, beginning with the formation of agricultural cooperatives in 1955. In the following year, cooperatives became farming collectives that soon accounted for over 90 percent of China's peasant population. The peasants had enjoyed their own holdings for less than three years. As had occurred earlier in the Soviet Union, the leaders of the revolution who had originally given the land over to the mass of the peasants later took it away from them through collectivization.

In 1957 Mao struck at the intellectuals through what may have been a miscalculation or perhaps a clever ruse. Announcing that he wished to "let a hundred flowers bloom," Mao encouraged professors, artists, and other intellectuals to speak out on the course of development under Communist rule. His request stirred up a storm of angry protest and criticism of Communist schemes. Having flushed the critics into the open (if the campaign was indeed a ruse) or having been shocked by the vehemence of the response, the party struck with demotions, prison sentences, and banishment to hard labor on the collectives. The flowers rapidly wilted in the face of this betrayal.

The Great Leap Backward

With political opposition within the party and army apparently in check (or in prison), Mao and his supporters launched the Great Leap Forward in 1958. The programs of the Great Leap represented a further effort to revitalize the flagging revolution by restoring its mass, rural base. Rather than huge plants located in the cities, industrialization would be pushed through small-scale projects integrated into the peasant communes. Instead of the communes' surplus being siphoned off to build steel mills, industrial development would be aimed at producing tractors, cement for irrigation projects, and other manufactures needed by the peasantry. Enormous publicity was given to efforts to produce steel in "backyard" furnaces that relied on labor rather than machine-intensive techniques. Mao preached the benefits of backwardness and the joys of mass involvement, and he looked forward to the withering away of the meddling bureaucracy. Emphasis was placed on self-reliance within the peasant communes. All aspects of the lives of their members were regulated and regimented by the commune leaders and the heads of the local labor brigades.

Within months after it was launched, all indicators suggested that the Great Leap Forward and rapid collectivization were leading to economic disaster. Peasant resistance to collectivization, the abuses of commune leaders, and the dismal output of the backyard factories combined with the failure of the rains to turn the Great Leap into a giant step backward. The worst famine of the Communist era spread across China. For the first time since 1949 China had to import large amounts of grain to feed its people—and the numbers of Chinese to feed continued to grow at an alarming rate. Defiantly rejecting Western and UN proposals for family planning, Mao and like-thinking radicals charged that socialist China could care for its people, no matter how many they were. Birth control was viewed as a symptom of capitalist selfishness and inability to provide a decent living for all of the people.

Like those of India, China's birthrates were actually a good deal lower than those of many emerging nations. Also like India, however, the Chinese were adding people to a massive population base. At the time of the Communist rise to power, China had approximately 550 million people. By 1965 this had risen to approximately 750 million. If that rate of growth had continued, some experts at the time predicted that China would have 1.8 billion people by the year 2000.

In the face of the environmental degradation and overcrowding that this leap in population inevitably produced, even the party ideologues came around to the view that something must be done to curb the birthrate. Beginning in the mid-1960s, the government launched a nationwide family planning campaign designed to limit urban couples to two children and those in rural areas to one. By the early 1970s, these targets had been revised to two children for either urban or rural couples. But by the 1980s, just one child per family was allowed. Though there is considerable evidence of official excesses—undue pressure for women to have abortions, for example—these programs have greatly reduced the birthrate and have begun to slow China's overall population increase. But again, the base to which new births are added is already so large that China's population will not stabilize until well into the 21st century. By that time there will be far more people than now to educate, feed, house, and provide with productive work.

Advances made in the first decade of the new regime were lost through amateurish blunders, excesses of overzealous cadre leaders, and students' meddling. China's national productivity fell by as much as 25 percent. The population increase soon overwhelmed the stagnating productivity of both the agricultural and industrial sectors. By 1960 it was clear that the Great Leap must be ended and a new course of development adopted. Mao lost his position as State Chairman (though he remained the head of the Party's Central Committee). The "pragmatists," including Mao's old ally Zhou Enlai, along with Liu Shaoqui and Deng Xiaoping, came to power determined to restore state direction and market incentives at the local level.

"Women Hold up Half of the Heavens"

In Mao's struggles to renew the revolutionary fervor of the Chinese people, his wife, Jiang Qing, played an increasingly prominent role. Mao's reliance on her was quite consistent with the commitment to the liberation of Chinese women he had acted upon throughout his political career. As a young man he had been deeply moved by a newspaper story about a young girl who had committed suicide rather than be forced by her family to submit to the marriage they had arranged for her with a rich but very elderly man. From that point onward, women's issues and the support of women for the Communist movement became important parts of Mao's revolutionary strategy. Here he was drawing on a well-established revolutionary tradition, for women had been very active in the Taiping Rebellion of the mid-19th century, as well as the Boxer revolt in 1900 and the 1911 revolution that had toppled the Manchu regime. One of the key causes taken up by the May Fourth intellectuals, who had a great impact on the youthful Mao Zedong, was women's rights. Their efforts put an end to footbinding. They also did much to advance campaigns to end female seclusion, win legal rights for women, and open educational and career opportunities to them.

The attempts by the Nationalists in the late 1920s and 1930s to reverse many of the gains made by women in the early revolution brought many women into the Communist camp. Led by Chiang's wife, Madam Chiang Kai-shek, the Nationalist counteroffensive (like comparable movements in the Fascist countries of Europe at the time) attempted to return Chinese women to the home and hearth. Madam Chiang proclaimed a special Good Mother's Day and declared that "virtue was more important [for women] than learning." She taught that it was immoral for a wife to criticize her husband (an ethical precept she herself regularly ignored).

The Nationalist campaign to restore Chinese women to their traditional domestic roles and dependence on men contrasted sharply with the Communists' extensive employment of women to advance the revolutionary cause. Women served as teachers, nurses, spies, truck drivers, and laborers on projects ranging from growing food to building machine-gun bunkers. Though the Party preferred to use them in these support roles, in moments of extreme crisis women became soldiers on the front lines. Many won distinction for their bravery under fire. Some rose to become cadre leaders, and many were prominent in the anti-landlord campaigns and agrarian reform. Their contribution to the victory of the revolutionary cause truly bore out Mao's early dictum that the energies and talents of women had to be harnessed to the national cause because, after all, "women hold up half of the heavens."

As was the case in many other African and Asian countries, the victory of the revolution brought women legal equality with men—in itself a revolutionary development in a society like China's. For example, women were given the right to choose their marriage partners without familial interference. But arranged marriages persist today, especially in rural areas, and the need to have party approval for all marriages represents a new form of control. In the post-1949 period, women have also been expected to work outside the home. Their opportunities for education and professional careers have greatly improved. As in other socialist states, however, openings for employment outside the home have proved something of a burden for Chinese women. Until the late 1970s, traditional attitudes toward child rearing and home care prevailed. As a result, women were required not only to hold down a regular job but also to raise a family, cook meals, clean, and shop—all without the benefit of the modern appliances available in Western societies. Though considerable numbers of women held cadre posts at the middle and lower levels of the party and bureaucracy, the upper echelons of both were overwhelmingly controlled by men.

As in other developing societies, the rather short-lived but very considerable power amassed by Mao's wife, Jiang Qing, in the early 1970s ran counter to the overall dominance of men in politics and the military. Like her counterparts elsewhere in Africa and Asia, Jiang Qing got to the top because she was married to Mao. She exercised power mainly in his name and was toppled soon after his death when she tried to rule in her own right. Women have come far in China, but—as is the case in most other societies in both the developed and developing worlds—they have by no means attained full equality with men in terms of career opportunities, social status, or political power.

Mao's Last Campaign and the Fall of the Gang of Four

Having lost his position as head of state but still the most powerful and popular leader in the Communist party, Mao worked throughout the early 1960s to establish grass roots support for yet another renewal of the revolutionary struggle. He fiercely opposed the efforts of Deng Xiaoping and his pragmatist allies to scale back the communes, promote peasant production on what were in effect private plots, and push economic growth over political orthodoxy. By late 1965, Mao was convinced that his support among the students, peasants, and military was strong enough to launch what would turn out to be his last campaign, the Cultural Revolution. With mass student demonstrations paving the way, he launched an all-out assault on the "capitalist-roaders" in the Party.

Waving little red books of Mao's pronouncements on all manner of issues, the infamous Red Guard student brigades, who are shown in the photograph that opens this chapter, publicly ridiculed and abused Mao's political rivals. Liu Shaoqui was killed, Deng Xiaoping was imprisoned, and Zhou Enlai was driven into seclusion. The aroused students and the rank and file of the People's Liberation Army were used to pull down the bureaucrats from their positions of power and privilege. College professors, plant managers, and the children of the bureaucratic elite were berated and forced to confess publicly their many crimes against the people. Those who were not imprisoned or, more rarely, killed were forced to do manual labor on rural communes to enable them to understand the hardships endured by China's peasantry. In cities such as Shanghai, workers seized control of the factories and local bureaucracy. As Mao had hoped, the centralized state and technocratic elites that had grown steadily since the first revolution won power in 1949 were being torn apart by the rage of the people.

However satisfying for advocates of continuing revolution like Mao, it was soon clear that the Cultural Revolution threatened to return China to the chaos and vulnerability of the prerevolutionary era. The rank-and-file threat to the leaders of the People's Liberation Army eventually proved decisive in prompting countermeasures that forced Mao to call off the campaign by late 1968. The heads of the armed forces moved to bring the rank and file back into line; the student and worker movements were disbanded and in some cases forcibly repressed. By the early 1970s Mao's old rivals had begun to surface again. For the next half decade, a hard-fought struggle was waged at the upper levels of the party and the army for control of the government. The reconciliation between China and the United States that was negotiated in the early 1970s suggested that, at least in foreign policy, the pragmatists were gaining the upper hand over the ideologues. Deng's growing role in policy formation from 1973 onward also represented a major setback for Jiang Qing, who led the notorious Gang of Four that increasingly contested power on behalf of the aging Mao.

The death in early 1976 of Zhou Enlai, who was second only to Mao in stature as a revolutionary hero and who had consistently backed the pragmatists, appeared to be a major blow to those whom the Gang of Four had marked out as "capitalist-roaders" and betrayers of the revolution. But Mao's death later in the same year cleared the way for an open clash between the rival factions. While the Gang of Four plotted to seize control of the government, the pragmatists acted in alliance with some of the more influential military leaders. The Gang of Four were arrested, and their supporters' attempts to foment popular insurrections were easily foiled. Later tried for their crimes against the people, Jiang Qing and the members of her clique were purged from the Party and imprisoned for life after having death sentences commuted.

In the past decade the pragmatists have been ascendant, and leaders such as Deng Xiaoping have opened China to Western influences and considerable capitalist development, if not yet democratic reform. Under Deng and his allies the farming communes have been discontinued and private peasant production for the market has been encouraged. Private enterprise has also been promoted in the industrial sector, and experiments have been made with such archcapitalist institutions as a stock exchange and foreign hotel chains.

Unfortunately, economic reforms have not been reinforced by political liberalization. This fact was brutally demonstrated by the government's violent repression of students and workers participating in pro-democracy demonstrations in Tiananmen Square in Beijing and other Chinese cities in June 1989. The harsh prison sentences and summary executions meted out to prodemocracy advocates since the Tiananmen massacres suggest the continuing refusal of China's aging leadership to allow for greater freedom of expression or for fuller participation by the people of China in the political process. The feebleness of the international response to the persecution of dissidents in the People's Republic abets an increasingly dangerous disjuncture between economic change and political repression. The new climate of free enterprise and market competition clashes strongly with the state's ossified Marxist-Leninist ideologies and the corrupt and bloated bureaucracy of an overcentralized political system. As the generation of leaders who made the Maoist revolution and have ruled China for over 40 years die off, the deep contradictions that have developed in Chinese society could well lead to renewed social unrest and perhaps widespread civil strife in the coming decades.

Although it has become fashionable to dismiss the development schemes of the Communist states as misguided failures, the achievements of the Communist regime in China over the past four decades have been considerable. Despite severe economic setbacks, political turmoil, and a low level of foreign assistance, the Communists have managed a truly revolutionary redistribution of the wealth of the country. China's very large population remains poor, but in education, health care, housing, working conditions, and the availability of food, most of it is far better off than it was in the prerevolutionary era. The Chinese have managed to provide a de-

Crack regiments and heavy tanks crush bicycle-wielding student demonstrators in Tiananmen Square, Beijing, in early June 1989.

cent standard of living for a higher proportion of their people than perhaps any other large developing country. They have also achieved higher rates of industrial and agricultural growth than neighboring India, with its mixed state-capitalist economy and its democratic polity. And the Chinese have done all of this without leaving up to half their people in misery, and with much less foreign assistance than most developing nations. If the pragmatists remain in power and the champions of the market economy are right, China's growth in the coming decades should be even more impressive. But the central challenge for China's leaders will be how to nurture that growth as well as the improved living standards without a recurrence of the economic inequities and social injustice that brought about the revolution in the first place.

THE VIETNAM WARS FOR NATIONAL LIBERATION

During World War II, operating out of bases in south China, the Communist-dominated nationalist movement, known as the Viet Minh, established liberated areas throughout the northern Red River delta. The abrupt end of Japanese rule left a vacuum in Vietnam, which only the Viet Minh was prepared to fill. Its programs for land reform and mass education had wide appeal among the hard-pressed peasants of the north, where they had been propagated during the 1930s and especially during the war years. The fact that the Viet Minh actually put their reform and community building programs into effect in the areas they controlled won them very solid support among much of the rural population. The Viet Minh's efforts to provide assistance to the peasants during the terrible famine of 1944 and 1945 also convinced the much-abused Vietnamese people that here at last was a political organization genuinely committed to improving their lot.

Under the leadership of General Vo Nguyen Giap, the Viet Minh skillfully employed guerrilla tactics similar to those devised by Mao in China. These offset the advantages that first the French and then the Japanese enjoyed in conventional firepower. With a strong base of support in much of the rural north and the hill regions, where they had won the support of key non-Vietnamese "tribal" peoples, the Viet Minh forces advanced triumphantly into the Red River delta as the Japanese withdrew. By August 1945, the Viet Minh were in control of Hanoi, where Ho Chi Minh proclaimed the establishment of the independent nation of Vietnam.

Vietnam after It Was Divided at the 1954 Geneva Conference into North and South

Though the Viet Minh had liberated much of the north, they had very little control in the south. In that part of Vietnam a variety of Communist and bourgeois nationalist parties jostled for power. The French, eager to reclaim their colonial empire and put behind them their humiliations at the hands of the Nazis, were quick to exploit this turmoil. With British assistance, the French reoccupied Saigon and much of south and central Vietnam. In March 1946 they denounced the August declaration of Vietnamese independence and moved to reassert their colonial control over the whole of Vietnam and the rest of Indochina. An unsteady truce between the French and the Viet Minh quickly broke down. Soon Vietnam was consumed by a renewal of the Viet Minh's guerrilla war for liberation, as well as bloody in-fighting between the different factions of the Vietnamese. After nearly a decade of indecisive struggle, the Viet Minh had gained control of much of the Vietnamese countryside, while the French, with increasing U.S. financial and military aid, clung to the fortified towns. In 1954 the Viet Minh decisively defeated the French at Dien Bien Phu in the mountain highlands hear the Laotian border. The victory won the Viet Minh control of the northern portions of Vietnam as a result of an international conference at Geneva in the same year. At Geneva elections throughout Vietnam were promised within two years to decide who should govern a reunited north and the still politically fragmented south.

The War of Liberation Against the United States

The promise at Geneva that free elections would be held to determine who should govern a united Vietnam was never kept. Like the rest of East Asia, Vietnam had become entangled in the cold war maneuvers of the United States and the Soviet Union. Despite very amicable cooperation between the Viet Minh and U.S. armed forces during the war against Japan, U.S. support for the French in the First Indochina War and the growing fame of Ho Chi Minh as a Communist leader drove the two farther and farther into opposition. The anti-Communist hysteria in the United States in the early 1950s fed the perception of influential U.S. leaders that South Vietnam, like South Korea, must be protected from Communist takeover.

The search for a leader to build a government in the south that the United States could prop up with economic and military assistance led to Ngo Dinh Diem. Diem appeared to have impeccable nationalist credentials. In fact, he had gone into exile rather than give up the struggle against the French. His sojourn in the United States in the 1940s and the fact that he was a Catholic also recommended him to U.S. politicians and church leaders. Unfortunately, these same attributes would alienate him from the great majority of the population.

With U.S. backing, Diem was installed as the president of Vietnam. He tried to legitimize his status in the late 1950s by holding rigged elections in the south, in which the Communists were not permitted to run. Diem also mounted a series of campaigns to eliminate by force all possible political rivals. Because the Communists posed the biggest threat (and were of the greatest concern to Diem's U.S. backers), the suppression campaign increasingly focused on the Communist cadres that remained in the south after Vietnam had been divided at Geneva. By the mid-1950s the Viet Cong (as the Diem regime dubbed the Communist resistance) were threatened with extermination. In response to this threat the Communist regime in the north began to pump

weapons, advisors, and other resources into the southern cadres, which were reorganized as the National Liberation Front in 1958.

As guerrilla warfare spread and Diem's military responses expanded, both the United States and the North Vietnamese escalated their support for the warring parties. When Diem proved unable to stem the Communist tide in the countryside, the United States gave the go-ahead for the military to overthrow him and take direct charge of the war. When the Vietnamese military could make little headway, the United States stepped up its military intervention.

From thousands of special advisors in the early 1950s, the U.S. commitment rose to nearly 500,000 men and women, who made up a massive force of occupation by 1968. But despite the loss of nearly 60,000 U.S. lives and millions of Vietnamese casualties, the Americans could not defeat the Communist movement. In part their failure resulted from their very presence, which made it possible for the Communists to convince the great majority of the Vietnamese people that they were fighting for their independence from yet another imperialist aggressor.

Though more explosives were dropped on tiny Vietnam, North and South, than in all of the theaters of World War II, and the United States resorted to chemical warfare against the very environment of the South Vietnamese they claimed to be trying to save, the Communists would not yield. The indomitable Vietnamese emerged as the victors of the Second Indochina War. In the early 1970s, U.S. diplomats negotiated an end to direct U.S. involvement in the conflict. Without that support the unpopular military regime in the South fell apart by 1975.

The Communists united Vietnam under a single government for the first time since the late 1850s. But the nation they governed was shattered and impoverished by decades of civil war, revolution, and armed conflict with two major colonial powers and the most powerful nation of the second half of the 20th century.

After Victory: The Struggle to Rebuild Vietnam

In the years since 1975 and the end of what was, for the Vietnamese, decades of wars for liberation, Communist efforts to complete the revolution by rebuilding Vietnamese society have floundered. In part this failure can be linked to Vietnam's isolation from much of the rest of the international community. This isolation resulted in part from pressures applied by a vengeful United States against

By the mid-1990s, the failed efforts of the United States to isolate Vietnam gave way to increasing economic and diplomatic contacts. One example of American corporate penetration is depicted in this street scene from Hanoi in 1993. The opening of Vietnam to foreign investment, assistance, and tourism accelerated through the 1990s and into the 21st century. In this atmosphere it has been possible to begin to heal the deep wounds and animosities generated by decades of warfare waged by the Vietnamese people against advanced industrial nations such as Japan, France, and the United States.

relief from international agencies. It was also exacerbated by border clashes with China that were linked to ancient rivalries between the two countries. Deprived of substantial assistance from abroad and faced with a shattered economy and a devastated environment at home, Vietnam's aging revolutionary leaders pushed hard-line Marxist-Leninist (and even Stalinist) political and economic agendas. Like their Chinese counterparts, they devoted considerable energies to persecuting old enemies (thus setting off widespread migration overseas from what had been South Vietnam), and imposed a dictatorial regime that left little room for popular responses to government initiatives. In contrast to the Chinese in the past decade, however, the Vietnamese leadership also attempted to maintain a highly centralized economy. The rigid system that resulted stifled growth and, if anything, left the Vietnamese people almost as impoverished as they had been after a century of colonialism and decades of civil war.

By the late 1980s the obvious failure of these approaches and the collapse of Communist regimes throughout Eastern Europe prompted measures aimed at liberalizing and expanding the market sector within the Vietnamese economy. The encouraging responses of Japanese and European corporations, eager to open up Vietnamese markets, have done much to begin the revival of the Vietnamese economy. Growing investments by their industrial rivals have placed increasing pressure on U.S. firms to move into the Vietnamese market. Combined with a genuine willingness shown by the Vietnamese leadership in the past few years to work with U.S. officials to resolve questions concerning POWs and MIAs from the Vietnam War, these economic incentives provide some hope for a new and much more constructive era in Vietnamese–United States relations in the 21st century.

REVOLUTIONS AND SUPERPOWER INTERVENTIONS IN LATIN AMERICA

By the 1940s frustration had built up considerable pressure for change in Latin America. Across the political spectrum there was a desire to improve the social and economic conditions of the region and a general agreement that development and economic strength were keys to a better future. How to achieve these goals, however, remained in question. One-party rule continued in Mexico and the "Revolution" became increasingly conservative, more interested in economic success than social justice. In

Venezuela and Costa Rica reform-minded democratic parties were able to win elections in an open political system. Elsewhere, such a solution was less likely or less attractive to those who hoped for reform. Unlike the Mexican revolutionaries of 1910 through 1920, those seeking change in the post–World War II period could turn toward Marxian socialism as a guide. Such models, however, were fraught with dangers because of the context of the cold war and the ideological struggle between western Europe and the Soviet bloc.

Throughout Latin America the failures of political democratization, economic development, and social reforms led to the consideration of radical revolutionary solutions to national problems. During the 1950s three major attempts at radical change were made in Latin America with very different results.

Guatemala: Reform and U.S. Intervention

The first place where more radical solutions were tried was Guatemala. This predominantly Indian nation had some of the worst of the region's problems. Its population was mostly illiterate and suffered poor health conditions and high mortality rates. Land and wealth were distributed very unequally, and the whole economy depended on the highly volatile prices for its main exports of coffee and bananas. In 1944 a coalition of middle-class and labor elected a reformer, Juan José Arevalo, as president. Under a new constitution, he began a series of programs within the context of "spiritual socialism" that included land reform and an improvement in the rights and conditions of rural and industrial workers. An income tax, the first in the nation's history, was projected and educational reforms were planned. These programs and Arevalo's sponsorship of an intense nationalism brought the Arevalo government into direct conflict with foreign interests operating in Guatemala, especially the United Fruit Company, the largest and most important foreign concern there. That company had operated in Guatemala from the turn of the century and had acquired extensive properties. It also controlled transportation and shipping facilities. Its workers were often better paid than the average, and their health and other benefits were more extensive, but because it was a foreign company with such a powerful role in Guatemala, United Fruit was the target of nationalistic anger.

In 1951, after a free election, the presidency passed to Colonel Jacobo Arbenz, whose nationalist program was more radical and whose public statements against foreign economic interests and the landholding oligarchy were more extreme than under Arevalo. Arbenz announced several programs to improve or nationalize the transportation network, the hydroelectric system, and other areas of the economy. A move to expropriate unused lands on large estates in 1953 provoked opposition from the landed oligarchy and from United Fruit, which eventually was threatened with the loss of almost half a million acres of reserve land. The U.S. government, fearing Communist penetration of the Arbenz government and under considerable pressure from the United Fruit Company, denounced the changes and began to impose economic and diplomatic restrictions on Guatemala. At the same time, the level of nationalist rhetoric intensified, and the government increasingly received the support of the political left in Latin America and in the socialist bloc.

In 1954, with the help of the U.S. Central Intelligence Agency, a dissident military force was organized and invaded Guatemala. The Arbenz government fell, and the pro-U.S. regime that replaced it turned back the land reform and negotiated a settlement favorable to United Fruit. The reform experiment was thus brought to a halt. By the standards of the 1960s and later, the programs of Arevalo and Arbenz seem rather mild, although Arbenz's statements and his acceptance of arms from Eastern Europe undoubtedly contributed to U.S. intervention. The reforms promised by the U.S.-supported governments were minimal. Guatemala continued to have a low standard of living, especially for its Indian population. The series of military governments after the coup failed to address the nation's social and economic problems. That failure led to continual violence and political instability. A coalition of coffee planters, foreign companies, and the military controlled political life. A guerrilla movement grew and provoked brutal military repression, which fell particularly hard on the rural Indian population. Guatemala's attempt at radical change, an attempt that began with an eye toward improving the conditions of the people, failed because of external intervention. The failure was a warning that change would not come without internal and foreign opposition.

The Bolivian Revolution: A Loss of Direction

Another predominantly Indian nation, Bolivia, was the scene of a similar revolutionary movement, but its outcome differed. Long characterized by political instability and weakened by its loss of territory and access to the sea after a war with Chile (the War of the Pacific, 1879–1883), Bolivia experienced rapid expansion in the 1920s as demands for its major products, silver and tin, increased. Foreign companies, such as Standard Oil of New Jersey, secured rights to exploit its major resources, and the government took large loans from U.S. banks to finance various projects. With the world financial crisis of 1929 and a drop in the price of tin, the Bolivian economy was thrown into crisis. To make matters worse, a war broke out with neighboring Paraguay over the disputed region of the Chaco, which blocked Bolivia's access to rivers leading to the Atlantic and which was thought to contain rich petroleum deposits. The Chaco War (1932–1935) led to high casualties on both sides and more political instability in Bolivia, as defeat by Paraguay led to disillusionment.

Despite rhetoric to the contrary, little had been done to lessen the great social gap between the mass of the Indian population and the urban elites or to improve the conditions of the miners, the backbone of the nation's workforce. As late as 1950, more than 90 percent of the land was in the hands of 6 percent of the population, and Indians were often treated like serfs. Conditions in the mines were abysmal, and to a large extent three foreign-owned or controlled companies regulated that sector of the economy. Little could be done to change this situation. Because of literacy requirements and gender exclusion for voting, less than 7 percent of the population was entitled to cast ballots.

After an army coup to forestall the electoral victory of a reformist and nationalist political coalition called the National Revolutionary Movement (MNR), a revolt erupted in 1952. Although initially an urban political movement, it soon became a real revolution as Indian peasants and mining workers joined in, taking up arms and seizing lands and mines. This was a violent social movement in which armed peasants and miners joined with students and radical middle-class interest groups against the army, mine owners, and landed elite. Winning the government, the MNR initiated a series of reforms, including universal suffrage, nationalization of the mines, land expropriation and redistribution, and the movement of population from the Andes to the unused lands in the nation's eastern lowlands. The mines, long controlled by three great companies, were nationalized, and the government raised wages and benefits. Land redistribution was extensive. With militant and armed worker and peasant organizations, the government cut back on support for the military, whose power was greatly reduced for a while. The United States, faced with these revolutionary changes, acted cautiously, but since the level of socialist rhetoric was relatively muted and there seemed to be no direct "external" involvement, the United States recognized the revolutionary government and offered financial assistance, sometimes in large amounts.

The momentum of revolutionary change could not be sustained, however. Mining and agriculture were disrupted by the changes and by poor world prices in the 1960s for tin and other Bolivian products. Fearing the radical unions, the government allowed the military to regain some of its power and then the MNR began to maneuver to insure its continuity in power. By 1964 the military stepped in again. Since then a series of military governments has ruled for most of the time. Although a few governments promised reforms and a continuation of the principles of the 1952 revolution, most have been more interested in keeping order. By the 1980s little was left of the revolutionary program, and new cartels of cocaine producers linked to politicians and the military emerged. The Bolivian Revolution failed not because of outside intervention as much as from mistakes of its leadership, the weight of the nation's past, and its problems that continue to the present day.

The Cuban Revolution: Socialism in the Caribbean

The differences between Cuba and Guatemala underline the diversity of Latin America and the dangers of partial revolutions. The island nation had a population of about 6 million, most of whom were the descendants of Spaniards and the African slaves who had been imported to produce the sugar, tobacco, and hides that were the colony's mainstays. Cuba had a large middle class, and its literacy and health care levels were better than in most of the rest of the region. Rural areas lagged behind in these matters, however, and there the working and living conditions were poor, especially for the workers on the large sugar estates. Always in the shadow of the United States, Cuban politics and economy were rarely free of U.S. interests. U.S. investments in the island were heavy during the 1940s and 1950s and by the 1950s about three-fourths of what Cuba imported came from the United States. Although the island experienced periods of prosperity, fluctuations in the world market for Cuba's main product, sugar, revealed the tenuous basis of the economy. Moreover, the disparity between the countryside

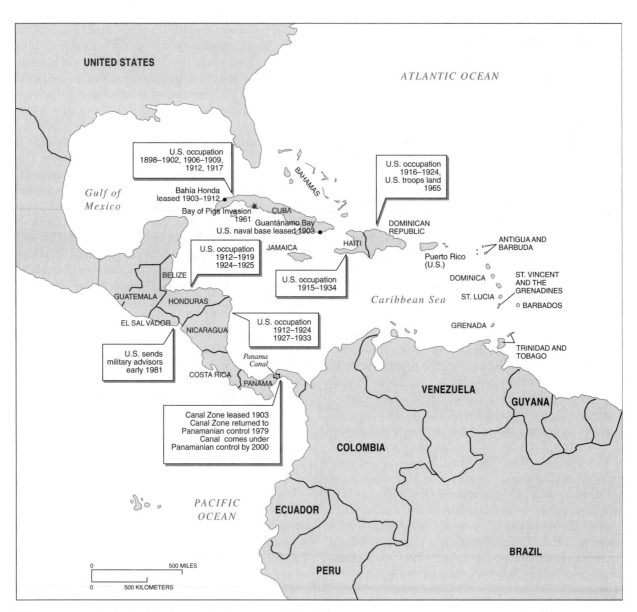

U.S. Interventions in Latin America and the Caribbean, 1898–1981

and the growing middle class in Havana underlined the nation's continuing problems.

From 1934 to 1944, Cuba had been ruled by Fulgencio Batista, a strong-willed, authoritarian reformer who had risen from the lower ranks of the army. Among his reforms were a democratic constitution of 1940 that promised major changes, nationalization of natural resources, full employment, and land reform. However, Batista's programs of reform were marred by corruption,

and when in 1952 he returned to the presidency, there was little left of the reformer but a great deal of the dictator. Opposition developed in various sectors of society. Among the regime's opponents was Fidel Castro, a young lawyer experienced in leftist university politics and an ardent critic of the Batista government and the ills of Cuban society. On July 26, 1953, Castro and a few followers launched an unsuccessful attack on some military barracks. Captured, Castro faced a trial, an occasion he

Fidel Castro and his guerrilla army brought down the Batista government in January 1959, to the wild acclaim of many Cubans. Castro initiated sweeping reforms in Cuba that eventually led to the creation of a socialist regime and hostility toward the United States.

used to expound his revolutionary ideals, aimed mostly at a return to democracy, social justice, and the establishment of a less dependent economy.

Released from prison, Castro fled to exile in Mexico where, with the aid of Ernesto "Che" Guevara, a militant Argentine revolutionary, he gathered a small military force. They landed in Cuba in 1956 and slowly began to gather strength in the mountains. By 1958, the "26th of July Movement" had found support from students, some labor organizations, and rural workers and was able to conduct operations against Batista's army. The bearded rebels, or *barbudos*, won a series of victories. The dictator, under siege and isolated by the United States (which because of his excesses refused to support him any longer), was driven from power, and the rebels took Havana amid wild scenes of joy and relief.

What happened next is highly debatable, and Castro himself has offered alternative interpretations at different times. Whether Castro was already a Marxist-Leninist and had always intended to introduce a socialist regime (as he now claims) or whether the development of this program was the result of a series of pragmatic decisions

is in question. Rather than simply returning to the constitution of 1940 and enacting moderate reforms, Castro launched a program of sweeping change. Foreign properties were expropriated, farms were collectivized, and a centralized socialist economy was put in place. Most of these changes were accompanied by a nationalist and anti-imperialist foreign policy. Relations with the United States were broken off in 1961, and Cuba increasingly depended on the financial support and arms of the Soviet Union to maintain its revolution. With that support in place, Castro was able to survive the increasingly hostile reaction of the United States. That reaction included a failed U.S.-sponsored invasion by Cuban exiles at the Bay of Pigs in 1961 and an embargo on trade with Cuba. Dependence on the Soviet Union led to a crisis in 1962, when Soviet nuclear missiles, perhaps placed in Cuba to thwart another U.S. invasion, were discovered and a confrontation between the superpowers ensued. To a large extent the Cuban Revolution survived because the politics of the cold war provided Cuba with a protector and a benefactor.

The results of the revolution have been mixed. The social programs were extensive. Education, health, and housing have improved greatly and rank Cuba among the world's leaders—quite unlike most other nations of the region. This is especially true in the long-neglected rural areas. A wide variety of social and educational programs have mobilized all sectors of the population. The achievements have been accompanied by severe restrictions of basic freedoms.

Attempts to diversify and strengthen the economy have been less successful. An effort to industrialize in the 1960s failed, and Cuba turned again to its ability to produce sugar. The world's falling sugar and rising petroleum prices led to disaster. Only by subsidizing Cuban sugar and supplying petroleum below the world price could the Soviet Union maintain the Cuban economy. Since the breakup of the Soviet Union in the 1990s, the Cuban situation has deteriorated; along with China, the island has become one of the last socialist bastions. Despite these problems, the Cuban Revolution offered an example that has proved attractive to those seeking to transform Latin American societies. Early direct attempts to spread the model of the Cuban Revolution, such as Che Guevara's guerrilla operation in Bolivia, where he lost his life in 1967, were failures, but the Cuban model and the island's ability to resist the pressure of a hostile United States has proved attractive to other nations in the Caribbean and Central America, such as Grenada and Nicaragua, which have also exercised the revolutionary option. U.S. reaction to such movements has been containment or intervention.

The Search for Reform and the Military Option

Programs based in Catholic, Marxist, and capitalist doctrines continued to seek solutions to Latin America's problems. Military governments in the 1960s and 1970s based on nationalism and advocating economic development created new "bureaucratic authoritarian" regimes, which for a while served the cold war interests of the United States. By the 1980s a new wave of democratic regimes was emerging.

The revolutionary attempts of the 1950s, the durability of the Cuban Revolution, and the general appeal of Marxist doctrines in the Third World underlined Latin America's tendency to undertake revolutionary change that left its economic and social structures unchanged. How could the traditional patterns of inequality and international dependency be overcome? What was the best path to the future?

For some, the answer was political stability, imposed if necessary, to promote capitalist economic growth. The one-party system of Mexico demonstrated its capacity for repression when student dissidents were brutally killed during disturbances in 1968. Mexico enjoyed some prosperity from its petroleum resources in the 1970s, but poor financial planning, corruption, and foreign debt again caused problems by the 1980s, and the PRI seemed to be losing its ability to maintain control of Mexican politics.

For others the Catholic Church, long a power in Latin America, provided a guide. Christian Democratic parties formed in Chile and Venezuela in the 1950s, hoping to bring reforms through popularly based mass parties that would preempt the radical left. The Church often was divided politically, but the clergy took an increasingly engaged position and argued for social justice and human rights, often in support of government opponents. A few, such as Father Camilo Torres in Colombia, actually joined armed revolutionary groups in the 1960s.

More common was the emergence within the Church hierarchy of an increased concern for social justice. By the 1970s, a "liberation theology" combined Catholic theology and socialist principles in an effort to improve conditions for the poor. When criticized for promoting communism in his native Brazil, Dom Helder da Camara, archbishop of Pernambuco, remarked, "The trouble with Brazil is not an excess of Communist doctrine but a lack of Christian justice." The position of the

Church in Latin American societies was changing, but there was no single program for this new stance or even agreement among the clergy about its validity. Still, this activist position provoked attacks against clergy such as the courageous Archbishop Oscar Romero of El Salvador, who was assassinated in 1980. The Church also played an important role in the fall of the Paraguayan dictatorship in 1988.

Out of the Barracks: Soldiers Take Power

The success of the Cuban Revolution also impressed and worried those who feared revolutionary change within a Communist political system. The military forces in Latin America had been involved in politics since the days of the caudillos in the 19th century, and in several nations, military interventions had been common. As the Latin American military became more professionalized, however, a new philosophy underlay the military's involvement in politics. The soldiers began to see themselves as above the selfish interests of political parties and as the true representatives of the nation. With technical training and organizational skills, military officers by the 1920s and 1930s believed that they were best equipped to solve their nations' problems, even if that meant sacrificing the democratic process and imposing martial law.

In the 1960s, the Latin American military establishments, made nervous by the Cuban success and the swing to leftist or populist regimes, began to intervene directly in the political process, not simply to clean out a disliked president or party, as they had done in the past, but to take over government itself. In 1964 the Brazilian military (with the support of the United States and the Brazilian middle class) overthrew the elected president after he threatened to make sweeping social reforms. In Argentina, growing polarization between the Peronists and the middle class led to a military intervention in 1966. In Chile, the socialist government of president Salvador Allende was overthrown in 1973 by the Chilean military, which until then had remained for the most part out of politics. Allende had nationalized industries and banks and had sponsored peasant and worker expropriations of lands and factories. His government was caught in an increasing polarization between groups trying to halt these changes and those pushing for faster and more radical reforms. By 1973 the economy was in serious difficulty, undermined by resistance in Chile and by U.S. policies designed to isolate the country. Allende was killed during the military coup against him, and throughout Latin America there were demonstrations against the military and U.S. involvement. But Chile was not alone. Similar coups took place in Peru in 1968 and in Uruguay in 1973.

The soldiers in power imposed a new type of "bureaucratic authoritarian regime." Their governments were supposed to stand above the competing demands of various sectors and establish economic stability. Now, as arbiters of politics, the soldiers would place the national interest above "selfish interests" by imposing dictatorships. Government was essentially a presidency, controlled by the military, in which policies were formulated and applied by a bureaucracy organized like a military chain of command. Political repression and torture were used to silence critics, and stringent measures were imposed to control inflation and strengthen the economies. Laws limited political freedoms, and repression often was brutal and illegal. In Argentina violent opposition to military rule led to a counteroffensive and a "dirty war" in which thousands of people "disappeared," (were kidnapped) and tortured or killed by government security forces.

Government economic policies fell heaviest on the working class. The goal of the military in Brazil and Argentina was development. To some extent, in Brazil at least, economic improvements were achieved, although income distribution became even more unequal than it had been. Inflation was reduced, industrialization increased, and gains were made in literacy and health, but basic structural problems such as land ownership and social conditions for the poorest people remained unchanged.

There were variations within these military regimes. All were nationalistic. The Peruvian military tried to create a popular base for its programs and to mobilize support among the peasantry. It had a real social program, including extensive land reform, and was not simply a surrogate for the conservatives in Peruvian society. In Chile and Uruguay the military was fiercely anti-Communist. In Argentina nationalism and a desire to gain popular support in the face of a worsening economy led to a confrontation with Great Britain over the Falkland Islands (Islas Malvinas), which both nations claimed. A short war in 1982 resulted in an Argentine defeat and a loss of the military's credibility that contributed to its loss of authority.

The New Democratic Trend

In Argentina and elsewhere in South America, the military had begun to return government to civilian politicians by the mid-1980s. Continuing economic problems and the pressures of containing opponents wore heavily on the military leaders, who began to realize that their solutions were no more destined to success than those of civilian governments. Moreover, the populist parties, such as the Peronists and Apristas, seemed less of a threat, and the fear of Cuban-style communism had diminished. Also, the end of the cold war meant that the United States was less interested in sponsoring regimes that, though "safe," were also repressive. In Argentina elections were held in 1983. Brazil began to restore democratic government after 1985 and in 1989 chose its first popularly elected president since the military takeover. The South American military bureaucrats and modernizers were returning to their barracks.

The process of redemocratization was not easy, nor was it universal. In Peru "Sendero Luminoso" (Shining Path), a long-sustained leftist guerilla movement, controlled areas of the countryside and tried to disrupt national elections in 1990. In Central America the military cast a long shadow over the government in El Salvador. After the elections of 1990, which removed the Sandinista party from control in Nicaragua, an uneasy truce continued between them and the centralist government of Violeta Chamorro, the newly elected president. By the late 1990s civilian government had returned to Guatemala as the country struggled to overcome the history of repression and rebellion and the animosities they had created. In 1999, a furor resulted when it was discovered that the "eyewitness" account of the military repression in that country, written by Rigoberta Menchú, an Indian who had won the Nobel Peace Prize, was not entirely accurate, although her defenders claimed it was still essentially true. The United States demonstrated its continuing power in the region in its invasion of Panama and the arrest of its strongman leader, Manuel Noriega. Symbolic of the difficulty of the return to democracy was the furor caused when the elderly Augusto Pinochet, the general who had overthrown the socialist Allende regime in Chile in 1973, was arrested and charged with crimes associated with his government by a Spanish court.

Latin American governments in the last decades of the century faced tremendous problems. Large foreign loans taken in the 1970s for the purpose of development, sometimes for unnecessary projects, had created a tremendous level of debt that threatened the economic stability of countries such as Brazil, Peru, and Mexico. High rates of inflation provoked social instability as real wages fell. Pressure from the international banking community to curb inflation by cutting government spending and reducing wages often ignored the social and political consequences of such actions. An international commerce in drugs, which produced tremendous profits,

DOCUMENT

The People Speak

Scholarly analysis of general trends often cannot convey the way in which historical events and patterns affect the lives of people or the fact that history is made up of the collective experience of individuals. It is often very difficult to know about the lives of common people in the past or to learn about their perceptions of their lives. In recent years in Latin America, however, a growing literature of autobiographies, interpreted autobiographies (in which another writer puts the story down and edits it), and collections of interviews have provided a vision of the lives of common people. These statements, like any historical document, must be used carefully because their authors or editors sometimes have political purposes, because they reflect individual opinions, or because the events they report may be atypical. Nevertheless, these personal statements do put flesh and blood on the bones of history and provide an important perspective from those whose voice in history is often lost.

A Bolivian Woman Describes Her Life

Domitilia Barrios de Chungara was a miner's wife who became politically active in the mine workers' political movement. Her presence at the United Nations–sponsored International Woman's Year Tribunal in 1975 moved a Brazilian journalist to organize her statements into a book about her life. This excerpt provides a picture of her everyday struggle for life.

> My day begins at four in the morning, especially when my *compañero* [husband] is on the first shift. I prepare his breakfast. Then I have to prepare *salteñas* [small meat pastries] because I make about one hundred *salteñas* every day and I sell them on the street. I do this in order to make up for what my husband's wage doesn't cover in terms of our necessities. The night before, we prepare the dough and at four in the morning I make the *salteñas* while I feed the kids. The kids help me.
>
> Then the ones that go to school in the morning have to get ready, while I wash the clothes left soaking over night.
>
> At eight I go out to sell. The kids that go to school in the afternoon help me. We have to go to the company store and bring home the staples. And in the store there are immensely long lines and you have to wait there until eleven in order to stock up. You have to line up for meat, for vegetables, for oil. So it's just one line after another. Since everything is in a different place, that's how it has to be.
>
> From what we earn between my husband and me, we can eat and dress. Food is very expensive: 28 pesos for a kilo of meat, 4 pesos for carrots, 6 pesos for onions. . . . Considering that my *compañero* earns 28 pesos a day, that's hardly enough is it?
>
> We don't ever buy ready made clothes. We buy wool and knit. At the beginning of each year, I also spend about 2,000 pesos on cloth and a pair of shoes for each of us. And the company discounts some of that each month from my husband's wage. On the pay slips that's referred to as the "bundle." And what happens is that before we finish paying the "bundle" our shoes are worn out. That's how it is.
>
> Well, from eight to eleven in the morning I sell the *salteñas*. I do the shopping in the grocery store, and I also work at the Housewives Committee talking with the sisters who go there for advice.
>
> At noon, lunch has to be ready because the rest of the kids have to go to school.
>
> In the afternoon I have to wash clothes. There are

---

stimulated criminal activity and created powerful international cartels that could even threaten national sovereignty, as they did in Colombia. In countries as diverse as Cuba, Panama, and Bolivia, the narcotics trade penetrated the highest government circles.

Despite the problems, the 1990s had seemed to demonstrate that the democratic trends were well established. In Venezuela and Brazil, corruption in government led to the fall of presidents. In 2000 Mexico elected Vicente Fox and by doing so broke the hold of the PRI on the political system. Fox had to confront the continu-

ing agitation of an active guerrilla movement which had erupted in 1994 in the heavily Indian southern state of Chiapas. Calling themselves *Zapatistas* in honor of Emiliano Zapata, a hero of the Mexican Revolution, young men and women defied the government and demanded work, housing, education, and health care for the long-neglected Indian population. The government was forced to negotiate and a truce established, but the Zapatistas became enormously popular as Mexicans sought to reestablish the social goals and principles of the Mexican Revolution. President Fox had to meet this challenge at

no laundries. We use troughs and have to get the water from a pump.

I've got to correct the kids' homework and prepare everything I'll need to make the next day's *salteñas*.

From Peasant to Revolutionary

Rigoberta Menchú, a Quiché Indian from the Guatemalan highlands, came from a peasant family that had been drawn into politics during the repression of Indian communities and human rights in the 1970s. In these excerpts, she reveals her disillusionment with the government and her realization of the ethnic division between Indians and *ladinos*, or mestizos, that complicates political action in Guatemala.

The CUC [Peasant Union] started growing; it spread like wildfire among the peasants in Guatemala. We began to understand that the root of all our problems was exploitation. That there were rich and poor and that the rich exploited the poor—our sweat, our labor. That's how the rich got richer and richer. The fact that we were always waiting in offices, always bowing to the authorities was part of the discrimination that we Indians suffered.

The situation got worse when the murderous generals came to power although I did not actually know who was the president at the time. I began to know them from 1974 when General Kjell Langerud came to power. He came to our region and said: "We're going to solve the land problem. The land belongs to you. You cultivate the land and I will share it out among you." We trusted him. I was at the meeting when [he] spoke. And what did he give us? My father tortured and imprisoned.

Later I had the opportunity of meeting other Indians. Achi Indians, the group that lives closest to us. And I got to know some Mam Indians too. They all told me: "The rich are bad. But not all *ladinos* are bad." And I started wondering: Could it be that not all *ladinos* are

Achi Indians, the group that lives closest to us? And I know some Mam Indians too. They all told me: "The rich are bad? . . ." There were poor *ladinos* as well as rich *ladinos*, and they were exploited as well. That's when I began recognizing exploitation. I kept on going to the finca [large farm] but now I really wanted to find out, to prove if that was true and learn the details. There were poor *ladinos* on the *finca*. They worked the same, and their children's bellies were swollen like my little brother's. . . . I was just beginning to speak a little Spanish in those days and I began to talk to them. I said to one poor *ladino*: "You are a poor *ladino*, aren't you?" And he nearly hit me. He said: "What do you know about it, Indian?" I wondered: "Why is that when I say poor *ladinos* are like us, I'm spurned?" I didn't know then that the same system which tries to isolate us Indians also puts barriers between Indians and *ladinos*. . . . Soon afterwards, I was with the nuns and we went to a village in Uspantán where mostly *ladinos* live. The nun asked a little boy if they were poor and he said: "Yes, we're poor but we're not Indians." That stayed with me. The nun didn't notice, she went on talking. She was foreign, she wasn't Guatemalan. She asked someone else the same question and he said: "Yes, we're poor but we're not Indians." It was very painful for me to accept that an Indian was inferior to a *ladino*. I kept on worrying about it. It's a big barrier they've sown between us, between Indian and *ladino*. I didn't understand it.

Questions: What was distinctive about lower-class life and outlook in late 20th-century Latin America? How had lower-class life changed since the 19th century?

Source: Domitilia Barrios de Chungara, *Let me Speak: Testimony of Domitilia, A Woman of the Bolivian Mines* (New York: Monthly Review Press 1978); Rigoberta Menchú, *I, Rigoberta Menchú: An Indian Woman in Guatemala*, Elisabeth Burgus-Debray, ed. (London: Verso, 1984).

---

the same time that he was forced to lead Mexico through the complexities of the NAFTA trade agreement with the United States, which sought to integrate the economies of the region in the age of globalization.

In Brazil a leftist working-class presidential candidate, Lula (Luiz Inacio Lula da Silva), who had lost in 2000 when Brazilians voted for a moderate, former college professor, was the front runner as the nation began to prepare for new elections in 2004. Even more radical, options were still possible. In Colombia an insurgency continued to threaten that nation's stability, in Venezuela

a populist president articulated a set of independent policies framed in nationalist rhetoric, and in other countries the military was sometimes troublesome, but a commitment to a more open political system in most of the region seemed firm.

The United States and Latin America: Continuing Presence

As a backdrop to the political and economic story we have traced thus far stands the continuing presence of the

United States. After World War I, the United States emerged as the predominant power in the hemisphere, a position it had already begun to assume at the end of the 19th century with the Cuban-Spanish-American War and the building of the Panama Canal. European nations were displaced as the leading investors in Latin America by the United States. In South America private investments by U.S. companies and entrepreneurs, as well as loans from the U.S. government, were the chief means of U.S. influence. By 1929, U.S. investments rose to more than $5 billion, or more than one-third of all U.S. investments abroad.

Cuba and Puerto Rico experienced direct U.S. involvement and almost a protectorate status. But in the Caribbean and Central America, the face of U.S. power, economic interest, and disregard for the sovereignty of weaker neighbors was most apparent. Military interventions to protect U.S.-owned properties and investments became so common that there were more than 30 before 1933. Haiti, Nicaragua, the Dominican Republic, Mexico, and Cuba all experienced direct interventions by U.S. troops. Central America was a peculiar case because the level of private investments by U.S. companies such as United Fruit was very high and the economies of these countries were so closely tied to the United States. Those who resisted the U.S. presence were treated as "bandits" by expeditionary forces. In Nicaragua, Augusto Sandino led a resistance movement against occupying troops until his assassination by the U.S.-trained Nicaraguan National Guard in 1934. His struggle against U.S. intervention made him a hero and the figurehead of the Sandinista party, which carried out a socialist revolution in Nicaragua in the 1980s.

The grounds for these interventions were economic, political, strategic, and ideological. The direct interventions were usually followed by the creation or support of conservative governments, often dictatorships that would be friendly to the United States. These became "banana republics," a reference not only to their dependence on the export of tropical products but also to their often subservient and corrupt governments.

Foreign interventions contributed to a growing nationalist reaction. Central America with its continuing political problems became a symbol of Latin America's weakness in the face of foreign influence and interference, especially by the United States. The Nobel Prize–winning Chilean communist poet Pablo Neruda, in his poem "The United Fruit Co." (1950), spoke of the dictators of Central America as "circus flies, wise flies, learned in tyranny" who buzzed over the graves of the people. He wrote the following eight lines with passion:

*When the trumpet sounded, all was prepared in the
    land,
and Jehovah divided the world between Coca Cola
    Inc.,
Anaconda, Ford Motors, and other companies:
United Fruit Co. reserved for itself the juiciest part,
the central coast of my land,
the sweet waist of America
and baptized again its lands
as Banana Republics. . . .*

The actions of the United States changed after 1933. In that year, president Franklin Delano Roosevelt introduced the Good Neighbor Policy, which promised to deal more fairly with Latin America and to stop direct interventions. After World War II, however, the U.S. preoccupation with containment of the Soviet Union and communism as an ideology led to new strategies in Latin America. They included participation in regional organizations, the support of governments that at least expressed democratic or anti-Communist principles, the covert undermining of governments considered unfriendly to U.S. interests, and, when necessary, direct intervention. Underlying much of this policy was also a firm belief that economic development would eliminate the conditions that contributed to radical political solutions. Thus U.S. programs such as the Alliance for Progress, begun in 1961, aimed to develop the region as an alternative to those solutions. The alliance had limited success despite good intentions and more than $10 billion in aid. Because of its record, Latin Americans and North Americans both began to question the assumption that development was basically a problem of capital and resources and that appropriate strategies would lead to social and economic improvement, which in turn would forestall revolution.

During the 1970s and 1980s, U.S. policy often was "pragmatic," accepting Latin American "as it was," which meant dealing on friendly terms with the military dictatorships. President Jimmy Carter (1976–1980) made a new initiative to deal with Latin America and to influence governments there to observe civil liberties. Most significantly, a treaty was signed with Panama that ceded to that nation eventual control of the Panama Canal.

Increasing violence in Central America in the 1980s and the more conservative presidencies of Ronald Reagan and George Bush led the United States back to policies based on strategic, economic, and defense considerations in which direct intervention or support of counterrevolutionary forces played a part. Thus in 1989 and 1990 the United States toppled a government in Panama that was authoritarian, defied U.S. policies, and controlled drug smuggling, replacing it with a cooperative regime backed by American troops.

Human Rights in the 20th Century

In Latin America, the question of human rights became a burning issue in the 1960s and continued thereafter. The use of torture by repressive governments, the mobilization of death squads and other vigilante groups with government acquiescence, and the use of terrorism against political opponents by the state and by groups opposed to the state became all too common in the region. Latin America's record on the violation of human rights was no worse than that of some other areas of the world. However, the demonstrations by the Argentine "Mothers of the Plaza del Mayo" to focus attention on their disappeared children; the publication of prison memoirs recounting human rights violations in Brazil, Cuba, and Argentina; and films dramatizing events such as the assassination of Archbishop Oscar Romero in El Salvador have all focused attention on the problem in Latin America. Moreover, because Latin America shares in the cultural heritage of Western societies, it is difficult to make an argument that human rights there have a different meaning or importance than in Europe or North America.

The concept of human rights—that is, certain universal rights enjoyed by all people because they are justified by a moral standard that stands above the laws of any individual nation—may go back to ancient Greece. The concept of "natural law" and the protection of religious or ethnic minorities also moved nations in the 19th century toward a defense of human rights. To some extent, the international movement to abolish the slave trade was an early human rights movement. In modern times, however, the concept of human rights has been strongly attached to the foundation of the United Nations. In 1948, that body, with the experience of World War II in mind, issued a Universal Declaration of Human Rights and created a commission to oversee the human rights situation. The Universal Declaration, which guaranteed basic liberties and freedoms regardless of color, sex, or religion, proclaimed that it should be the "common standard for all peoples and nations." However, one critic has stated that of the 160 nations in the United Nations, only about 30 have a consistently good record on human rights.

A major problem for the international community has been enforcing the Universal Declaration. The UN commission did not have any specific powers of enforcement, and much debate has taken place on the power of the United Nations to intervene in the internal affairs of any nation. More recently, various regional organizations have tried to establish the norms that should govern human rights and to create institutions to enforce these norms.

One specialist has claimed that "human rights is the world's first universal ideology." The defense of human rights seems to be a cause that most people and governments can accept without hesitation, but the question is complex. Although the rights to life, liberty, security, and freedom from torture or degrading punishment are generally accepted in principle by all nations, other "rights" remain open to question. What is a right, and to what extent are definitions of rights determined by culture?

The question of universality versus relativism emerged quickly in the debate over human rights. What seemed to be obvious human rights in Western societies were less obvious in other parts of the world, where other priorities were held. For example, laws prohibiting child labor were enforced by most Western societies, but throughout the world perhaps 150 million children worked, often in unhealthy and exploitive conditions. They worked because of economic necessity in many cases, but in some societies such labor was considered moral and proper. Such cultural differences have led to a position of relativism, which recognizes that there are profound cultural variations in what is considered moral and just. Critics of the original Universal Declaration contend that its advocacy of the right to own property and the right to vote imposed Western political and economic values as universals. Cultural relativism had the advantage of recognizing the variety of cultures and standards in the world, but it has also been used as a shield to deflect criticism and to excuse the continued violation of human rights.

The definition of human rights is also political. The West emphasizes the civil and political rights of the individual. The socialist nations place social and economic justice above individual rights, although by the 1990s movements in Eastern Europe and China indicated that there was pressure to modify this approach. In developing nations, an argument for peoples' rights has emerged in which the "right to development," which calls for a major structural redistribution of the world's resources and economic opportunities, is a central concept. As Leopold Senghor of

The abuse of human rights by military regimes in Latin America during the 1970s and 1980s including the sequestering, torture, and killing of suspected opponents without charges or trials mobilized broad resistance movements often led by family members of the "disappeared" victims as illustrated here. With the return to democracy and civilian rule, countries like Chile, Guatemala, and Peru were faced with the question of whether to grant amnesty or to set up courts to investigate those abuses and thus open up the political division once again.

Senegal put it, "Human rights begin with breakfast"; or as a report on Ghana stated, "'One man, one vote' is meaningless unless accompanied by the principle of 'one man, one bread.'" Whereas the right to development is seen as a human right in developing nations, it is viewed as a political and economic demand in wealthier nations of the West.

Another dimension of human rights is the extent to which it influences national foreign policies. Governments may make statements pledging respect for human rights in their foreign policies, but considerations of national defense, sovereignty, or other goals often move human rights concerns into a secondary position. Disputes over the role of human rights in foreign policy sometimes are posed as a conflict between "moralistic utopians" who see the world as it should be and "pragmatists" who see the world as it is. Neither approach necessarily denies the importance of human rights, but there are differences in priority and strategy. Pragmatists might argue that it is better to maintain relations with a nation violating human rights in order to be able to exercise some influence over it in the future, or that other policy considerations must be weighed along with those of human rights in establishing foreign policy. Moralists would prefer to bring pressure by isolating and condemning a nation that violates international standards.

These different approaches have been reflected in the U.S. policy shifts toward Latin America. In the 1950s human rights considerations were secondary to opposing the spread of communism in the hemisphere, and the United States was willing to support governments that violated human rights as long as they were anti-Communist allies. During the 1960s this policy continued, but increasing and systematic abuses by military regimes in Brazil, Uruguay, Chile, Nicaragua, and elsewhere in Latin America began to elicit some changes. In 1977 President Carter initiated a new policy in which human rights considerations would be given high priority in U.S. foreign policy. The U.S. refusal to support or aid governments that violated human rights contributed to the weakening of some regimes and stimulated resistance to human rights violations in Latin America, but by the 1980s a more pragmatic approach had returned to U.S. policy. Criticism of human rights violations sometimes was made selectively, and abuses in "friendly" governments were dismissed. The extent to which human rights concerns must be balanced against issues such as security, the maintenance of peace, and nonintervention continues to preoccupy policymakers.

Attention to human rights will continue to play an important role in international affairs. Problems of definition still remain, and there is no universal agreement on the exact nature of human rights. Controversy on the weight of political and civil rights and social, cultural, and economic rights continues to divide richer and poorer nations. Still, the United Nations Declaration of Human Rights, to which 160 nations are signatories, provides a basic guide and an outline for the future.

Questions: Why might various regimes oppose human rights, and on what basis? Is the human rights movement a Western replacement for imperialism as a way to exert international political influence? Have international human rights movements produced political change?

Societies in Search of Change

Despite the structural, political, and international conditions that have frustrated Latin American attempts at profound reform, there have been great changes during the 20th century. Problems of ethnicity, gender, and class continue to influence many of these societies. The movement of populations and their settlement have also been a major feature of the century. These aspects of social life are just two of the continuing historical processes of Latin America.

Social and gender relations have changed during the century. We have already seen how countries such as Mexico, Peru, and Bolivia sought to enfranchise their Indian populations during this century in different ways and with differing degrees of success. National ideologies and actual practice often are not the same, and discrimination on the basis of ethnicity continues in many places. To be called "Indian" is still an insult in many places in Latin America. Although ethnic and cultural mixture characterizes many Latin American populations and makes Indian and African elements important features of national identity, relations with Indian populations continue to be marked by exploitation and discrimination in diverse nations as Brazil, Nicaragua, and Guatemala.

Slow Change in Women's Roles

The role of women has changed slowly. After World War I, women in Latin America continued to live under inequalities in the workplace and in politics. Women were denied the right to vote anywhere in Latin America until Ecuador enfranchised women in 1929 and Brazil and Cuba did the same in 1932. Throughout most of the region, those examples were not followed until the 1940s and 1950s. In some nations, the traditional associations of women with religion and the Catholic church in Hispanic life made reformers and revolutionaries fear that women would become a conservative force in national politics. This attitude, combined with traditional male attitudes that women should be concerned only with home and family, led to a continued exclusion of women from political life. In response, women formed various associations and clubs and began to push for the vote and other issues of interest to them.

Feminist organizations, suffrage movements, and international pressures eventually combined to bring about change. In Argentina, 15 bills for female suffrage were introduced in the senate before the vote was won in 1945. Sometimes the victory was a matter of political expediency for those in power. In the Dominican Republic and some other countries, the enfranchisement of women was a strategy used by conservative groups to add more conservative voters to the electorate in an effort to hold off political change. In Argentina, recently enfranchised women became a major pillar of the Peronist regime, although that regime suppressed female political opponents such as Victoria Ocampo, editor of the important literary magazine *Sur*.

Women eventually discovered that the ability to vote did not in itself guarantee political rights or the ability to have their specific issues heard. After achieving the vote, women tended to join the national political parties, where traditional prejudices against women in public life limited their ability to influence political programs. In Argentina, Brazil, Colombia, and Chile, for example, the integration of women into national political programs has been slow, and women have not participated in

As this photograph of a cement works spewing toxic smoke into a working class neighborhood in Cairo illustrates, industrial pollution has become an increasing problem in much of the developing world, including rapidly growing countries like Mexico and Brazil.

proportion to their numbers. In a few cases, such as in the election of Perón in Argentina in 1946 and Eduardo Frei in Chile in 1964, or in the popular opposition to Salvador Allende in 1973, women played a crucial role.

Some of the earliest examples of mobilization of women and their integration into the national labor force of various Latin American nations came in the period just before World War I and continued thereafter. The classic roles of women as homemakers, mothers, and agricultural workers were expanded as women entered the industrial labor force in growing numbers. By 1911 in Argentina, for example, women made up almost 80 percent of the textile and clothing industry's workers. But women found that their salaries often were below those of comparable male workers and that their jobs, regardless of the skill levels demanded, were considered "unskilled" and thus less well paid. Under these conditions, women, like other workers, joined the anarchist, socialist, and other labor unions and organizations.

Labor organizations are only a small part of the story of women in the labor force. In countries such as Peru, Bolivia, and Ecuador, women working in the markets control much small-scale commerce and have become increasingly active politically. In the growing service sectors, women have also become an important part of the labor force. Shifts in attitudes about women's roles have come more slowly than political and economic changes. Even in revolutionary Cuba, where the Law of the Family guaranteed equal rights and responsibilities within the home, enforcement has been difficult.

By the mid-1990s, the position of women in Latin America was closer to that in western Europe and North America than to the other areas of the world. Women made up 9 percent of the legislators in Latin America, a percentage higher than in any other region of the world. They also held 9 percent of the cabinet posts, standing second only to North America's 12 percent. In terms of demographic patterns, health, education, and place in the workforce, the comparative position of women reinforced Latin America's intermediate position between the developed and developing nations.

The Movement of People

Although in 1950, the populations of North America (United States and Canada) and Latin America were about 165 million each, by 1985 Latin America's population had grown to more than 400 million, compared with 265 million for North America. Declining mortality and continuing high fertility were responsible.

At the beginning of the 20th century the major trend of population movement was immigration to Latin America, but the region has long experienced internal migration and the movement of people within the hemisphere. By the 1980s, this movement had reached significant levels, fed by the flow of workers seeking jobs, the demands of capital for cheap labor, and the flight of political refugees seeking basic freedoms. In the 1920s Mexican workers crossed the border to the United States in large numbers at the same time Guatemalans were crossing the border to Mexico to work on coffee estates. During World War II, government programs to supply laborers were set up between the United States and Mexico, but these were always accompanied by extralegal migration, which fluctuated with the economy. Conditions for migrant laborers often were deplorable, although the extension of social welfare to them in the 1960s began to address some of the problems. By the 1970s, more than 750,000 illegal Mexican migrants a year were crossing the border—some more than once—as the United States continued to attract migrants.

This internationalization of the labor market was comparable in many ways with the movement of workers from poorer countries such as Turkey, Morocco, Portugal, and Spain to the stronger economies of West Germany and France. In Latin America it also reflected the fact that industrialization in the 20th century depended on highly mechanized industry that did not create enough new jobs to meet the needs of the growing population. Much of the migration has been to the United States, but there has also been movement across Latin American frontiers: Haitians migrate to work in the Dominican Republic and Colombians illegally migrate to Venezuela. By the 1970s, about 5 million people per year were migrating in Latin America and the Caribbean.

Politics has also been a major impulse for migration. Haitians fleeing political repression and abysmal conditions have risked great dangers in small open boats to reach the United States. One of the great political migrations of the century has been caused by the Cuban Revolution. Beginning in 1959 when the Cuban middle class fled socialism, and continuing into the 1980s with the flight of Cuban workers, almost 1 million Cubans left the island. The revolutionary upheaval in Nicaragua and political violence in Central America have contributed to the flight of refugees. Often it is difficult to separate political and economic factors in the movement of people from their homelands.

International migration is only part of the story. During the 20th century there has been a marked movement in Latin America from rural to urban areas. Whereas in the 19th century Latin America was an agrarian region, by the 1980s about one-half of the population lived in cities of more than 20,000, and more than 25 of these cities had populations of more than one million. Some of these cities had reached enormous size. In 2004 Mexico City and its suburbs had more than 21 million inhabitants, São Paulo had 19 million, and Buenos Aires had 12 million. Latin America was by far the most urbanized area of the developing world and only slightly less urbanized than western Europe. By 2000 this pattern had intensified.

The problem is not simply of size but rate of growth. The urban populations have grown at a rate about three times that of the population as a whole, which itself has grown rapidly. Urban economies have not been able to create enough jobs for the rapidly increasing population. Often recent migrants lived in marginal neighborhoods or in shantytowns, which have become characteristic of the rapidly growing cities of Latin America. These *favelas*, to use the Brazilian term, have created awful living conditions, but over time some have become poorer neighborhoods within the cities, and community cooperation and action within them have secured basic urban services.

In socialist Cuba, a concerted effort to deemphasize Havana and other large cities and reverse the rural-urban migration pattern was made, but in most of the region urbanization has continued as growing populations seek better opportunities. In part, this movement is explained by a general population growth rate of more than 2.5 percent per year since the 1960s.

Although Latin American urbanization has increased rapidly since 1940, the percentage of its people living in cities is still less than in western Europe but more than in Asia and Africa. Unlike the 19th-century European experience, the lack of employment in Latin American cities has kept rural migrants from becoming part of a laboring class with a strong identification with fellow workers. Those who do succeed in securing industrial jobs often join paternalistic labor organizations that are linked to the government. Thus there is a separation between the chronically underemployed urban lower class and the industrial labor force. Whereas industrialization and urbanization promoted a strong class solidarity in 19th-century Europe that led to the gains of organized labor, in contemporary Latin America nationalist and populist politics have weakened the ability of the working class to operate effectively in politics.

Cultural Reflections of Despair and Hope

Latin America remains an amalgamation of cultures and peoples trying to adjust to changing world realities. Protestant denominations have made significant inroads, but the vast majority of Latin Americans are still Catholic. Hispanic traditions of family, gender relations, business, and social interaction influence everyday life and help to determine responses to the modern world.

Latin American popular culture remains vibrant. It draws on African and Indian traditional crafts, images, and techniques but arranges them in new ways. Also part of popular culture are various forms of Latin American music. The Argentine tango of the turn of the century began in the music halls of lower-class working districts of Buenos Aires and became an international craze. The African-influenced Brazilian *samba* and the Caribbean *salsa* have spread widely, a Latin American contribution to world civilization.

The struggle for social justice, economic security, and political formulas in keeping with the cultural and social realities of their nations has provided a dynamic tension that has produced tremendous artistic achievements. Latin American poets and novelists have gained worldwide recognition. We have already noted the artistic accomplishments of the Mexican Revolution. In 1922 Brazilian artists, composers, and authors staged a Modern Art Week in São Paulo, which emphasized a search for a national artistic expression that reflected Brazilian realities.

That theme also preoccupied authors elsewhere in Latin America. The social criticism of the 1930s produced powerful realist novels that revealed the exploitation of the poor, the peasantry, and the Indians. Whether in the heights of the Andes or in the dark streets of the growing urban slums, the plight of the common folk provided a generation of authors with themes worthy of their effort. Social and political criticism has remained a central feature of Latin American literature and art and has played an important role in the development of newer art forms such as film.

The inability to bring about social justice or to influence politics has also sometimes led Latin American artists and intellectuals to follow other paths. In the 1960s a wave of literature that became known as magical realism evolved, in which novels that mixed the political, the historical, the erotic, and the fantastic were produced by a generation of authors who found the reality of Latin America too absurd to be described by the traditional forms or logic. Writers such as the Argentine Jorge Luis Borges (1899–1980) and the Colombian Gabriel García Márquez (b. 1928) won acclaim throughout the world. García Márquez's *One Hundred Years of Solitude* (1967) used the history of a family in a mythical town called Macondo as an allegory of Latin America and traced the evils that befell the family and the community as they moved from naive isolation to a maturity that included oppression, exploitation, war, revolution, and natural disaster but never subdued the spirit of its people. In that way, his book outlined the trajectory of Latin America in the 20th century.

Struggling Toward the Future

By 2005, Latin America had continued to search for economic growth, social justice, and political stability. No easy solutions were available. In many ways, Latin American societies remained "unrevolutionary," unable to bring about needed changes because of deeply entrenched class interests, international conditions, or power politics. However, the struggle for change had produced some important results. The Mexican and Cuban revolutions brought profound changes in those countries and had a broad impact on the rest of the hemisphere, either as models to copy or as dangers to be avoided. Other nations, such as Bolivia, Peru, and Nicaragua, attempted their own versions of radical change with greater or lesser success. New forms of politics, sometimes populist and sometimes militarist, were tried. New political and social ideas, such as those of liberation theology, grew out of the struggle to find a just and effective formula for change. Latin American authors and artists served as a conscience for their societies and received worldwide recognition for their depiction of the sometimes bizarre reality they observed. Although tremendous problems continued to face the region, Latin America remained in some ways the most advanced part of the developing world.

CONCLUSION: MIXED RETURNS FROM REVOLUTION IN A TURBULENT CENTURY

Many more revolutions have occurred in the 20th century than in any comparable time span in human history. Between the Mexican peasant risings in the first decade of the century and the Iranian upheavals of the late 1970s, tens of revolutionary movements have threatened or toppled seemingly powerful regimes in virtually all regions of the globe. Without question revolutions have been one of the most powerful forces shaping global history in the 20th century. But as the tide of revolution has apparently receded in the past decade or so and the revolutionary regimes of Eastern Europe and elsewhere have collapsed or fallen on hard times, there has been a tendency to disparage the accomplishments and stress the high costs of violent revolutionary upheavals. Gradualist reforms and the peaceful workings of the globalized market are currently widely seen as the best antidotes to pervasive poverty, corrupt governments, and state oppression.

It would be absurd to ignore the appalling costs in human lives and material destruction caused by revolutionary struggles and the civil wars and external aggressions often associated with them. But it is equally distorting to ignore or minimize the quite considerable accomplishments of victorious revolutions. As the histories of the many revolutions we have considered reveal, the returns from these upheavals in the 20th century have been mixed and have varied widely. Though revolutionary regimes have not managed to create the utopian societies that radical 18th- and 19th-century political theorists, such as Saint-Simon and Marx imagined, each has brought some clear improvements in the lives of many of the ordinary citizens for whom they ostensibly seized power in the first place.

On the political side the revolutionary balance sheet has shown only meager gains and at times substantial losses. Inept despotisms, such as that of Qing China or tsarist Russia, and corrupt dictatorships, like Batista's in Cuba or Díaz's in Mexico, were toppled. But very often they were replaced by even more highly centralized bureaucratic machines, with a greatly increased capacity to intervene in the everyday lives of those whom they govern. In some instances, such as in the Soviet Union under Stalin or in China during the Cultural Revolution, state repression has vastly exceeded anything that prerevolutionary despots could imagine. Revolutions have also often brought about the substitution of a class of rapacious and self-serving state functionaries for the extravagant and aloof aristocrats or self-styled patricians who dominated prerevolutionary societies. These new elites of revolutionary functionaries, whom Milovan Djilas dubbed the "new class" in the 1950s, have often stunted reform and innovation by monopolizing political power, stifling all criticism, and siphoning off for their own purposes resources that might have been invested in broader social improvements. Often in response to perceived external threats, revolutionary elites have militarized their societies to an extent far exceeding that achieved by prerevolutionary regimes. They have also expended scarce resources in foreign wars and efforts to spread their revolutions to other countries.

Revolutionary regimes have rarely tolerated meaningful political opposition or championed those human rights so prized in Western democracies—the freedoms of speech, the press, and genuine elections. But some of their greatest accomplishments have involved developing social programs aimed at providing all of their citizen-subjects with other sorts of human amenities that have been denied to large and increasing minorities in the industrial West and to the majority of the populations of most nonrevolutionary developing nations. Communist regimes in particular, like those in the Soviet Union, the People's Republic of China, and Cuba, have transformed the lives of once poverty- and disease-ridden workers and peasants through the provision of universal health care, schooling and recreation facilities, and state-built housing. In Communist societies, women at all income levels have enjoyed opportunities for advanced education and work outside the home that are made possible by state-financed child care services. In most Communist societies, they have played major roles in professions like medicine and education, though these pursuits often do

not earn them the prestige or salaries attained by doctors or university professors in the West. A lower level of consumer production, especially in household appliances, has meant that working women in postrevolutionary societies, Communist as well as Islamic, have had to perform traditional chores in the home after long hours on the job. Persisting macho notions of appropriate male activities have done much to discourage their husbands from reducing the burden of the women's dual roles.

In the economic sphere the gains under postrevolutionary regimes were once thought to be impressive. Within decades, the Soviet Union joined the ranks of the industrial giants, while the countries of Eastern Europe greatly expanded their industrial sectors. Cuba's drive for industrialization in the 1960s failed, and Iranian aspirations to build on the start made under the Shah were frustrated by the long war with Iraq in the 1980s. But China has built an impressive industrial sector with very little foreign assistance, and as Vietnam breaks out of the isolation largely imposed by American hostility, it shows considerable potential for healthy growth. Industrialization has brought impressive military power to many postrevolutionary nations—power that, for example, allowed the Soviet people to withstand the fierce Nazi onslaught and China to support successfully small neighbors like North Korea and Vietnam in their wars with the U.S. colossus.

Nonetheless, the collapse of the Soviet Union and its satellites has revealed the waste and inefficiency that has stunted growth in the highly centralized, command economies of the Communist bloc. In trying to catch up with the industrialized West and Japan, Communist regimes sacrificed sophistication to sheer scale and volume, and ravaged the rich environments of a substantial portion of the globe. Most critically, the burden of the prolonged arms race between the Soviet and U.S. superpowers had much to do with the collapse of the Soviet economy, just as it helps to account for the erosion of the U.S. stature as the leading industrial nation.

State controls over intellectual expression and artistic creativity, which have been characteristic of postrevolutionary regimes, have greatly constricted cultural productivity. When contrasted with prerevolutionary painting, music, and architecture, the massive and pedestrian buildings, murals, and statues of the Social Realist and functionalist schools underscore the heavy cultural costs of revolutionary dogmatism. These have been somewhat offset by considerable achievements in the sciences and engineering of communist regimes, particularly in the Soviet Union and China. At another level, from China to Cuba, communist regimes have developed athletic programs that, despite their grueling training routines, were the envy of the West for decades. In addition, despite state controls, writers and artists in postrevolutionary societies have produced a surprisingly large corpus of significant work, from Boris Pasternak's poetry to the plays of Vaclav Havel.

As the foregoing suggests, evaluating the impact of 20th-century revolutions is not a simple matter. They have not produced utopian societies, but they have made for real improvements in the conditions under which once oppressed groups, such as peasants and workers, live their lives and raise their children. In any case, in most of the societies where successful revolutions have occurred, prerevolutionary conditions for the great majority of the people were so desperate that there was little inclination to speculate about revolutionary outcomes. Meaningful reforms were blocked by the regimes struggling to hold power, and they were in any case seen by revolutionary leaders and those who supported them as inappropriate for societies where human misery was too acute and pervasive to allow for gradualist solutions. Though Communist solutions are presently in disrepute, the persisting poverty and state oppression of a sizable portion of the world's population provide ample grounds for further revolutionary upheavals. The spreading appeal of Islamic revivalism and liberation theology suggest that new revolutionary alternatives may prove a major force in shaping global history in the 21st century.

FURTHER READING

A good summary of the final stages of the civil war in China is provided in Lucien Bianco's *Origins of the Chinese Revolution, 1915–1949* (1971). Perhaps the best overview of modern Chinese history from the Qing dynasty era through the Tiananmen Square massacre can be found in Jonathan D. Spence, *The Search for Modern China* (1990). Other useful accounts of the post–1949 era include Maurice Meisner's *Mao's China and After 1984* (1984); Michael Gasster's *China's Struggle to Modernize* (1987); and Immanuel C. Y. Hsu, *China Without Mao* (1983). On the pivotal period of the Cultural Revolution, see Roderick MacFarquhar's two-volume study on *The Origins of the Cultural Revolution* (1974, 1983), and Lowell Dittmer's *Liu Shao-ch'i and the Chinese Cultural Revolution* (1974). For a highly critical assessment of the Maoist era, it is difficult to surpass Simon Leys's

Chinese Shadows (1977). On cultural life in the postrevolutionary era, see the essays in R. MacFarquhar, ed., *The Hundred Flowers Campaign and the Chinese Intellectuals,* and Lois Wheeler Snow, *China on Stage* (1972). Elisabeth Croll's *Feminism and Socialism in China* (1978) remains by far the best single work on the position of women in revolutionary and Maoist China.

The first war of liberation in Vietnam is covered in Ellen J. Hammer's, *The Struggle for Indochina, 1940–1955* (1966). The best of many surveys of the second is Marilyn Young's *The Vietnam Wars, 1945–1990* (1989). Of a number of fine studies on the origins of American intervention in the area, two of the best are Archimedes Patti's, *Why Vietnam?* (1980), and Lloyd Gardner's, *Approaching Vietnam* (1988). A fine assessment of the roots of the failure of American intervention and the course of the second war of liberation is provided by Jeffrey Race, *The War Comes to Long An* (1972). Powerful firsthand accounts of the guerrilla war and U.S. combat include Mark Baker's *Nam* (1981); Philip Caputo's *A Rumor of War* (1977); and Troung Nhu Tang's *A Viet Cong Memoir* (1985).

The post-1945 period in Latin American history is ably covered in Thomas Skidmore and Peter Smith's *Modern Latin America* (1989) and in John Charles Chasteen's *Born in Fire and Blood* (2001). On Cuba, there is Louis Pérez, *Cuba: Between Reform and Revolution* (1995), which gives a reliable account. Tad Szulc's *Fidel* (1986) reviews the life of the revolution's architect. Alejandro de la Fuente's *Race, Inequality and Politics in Twentieth Century Cuba* (2001) covers the continuing importance of race in Cuban life. Thomas Skidmore's *The Politics of Military Rule in Brazil, 1964–85* (1988) deals with the militarist period in Latin America in that country. Greg Grandin's *Blood of Guatemala* (2000) discusses the condition in Guatemala that led to the pressure for reform. Gilbert Joseph et al., eds., *Close Encounters of Empire* (1998), deals with the various forms of impact of the United States on Latin America while John Coatsworth's, *Central America and the United States* (1998) examines the political and economic dimensions of that relationship.

ON THE WEB

The Cultural Revolution in China is examined at http://library.thinkquest.org/26469/cultural-revolution/ A virtual tour of the Cultural Revolution, including files of documents and personal reminiscences, is located at http://www.cnd.org/CR/english/

Art played a major role in the Cultural Revolution, as is borne out by two exhibitions, entitled "Rethinking Cultural Revolution Culture" and "Picturing Power: Art and Propaganda in the Great Proletarian Cultural Revolution." The first is found at

http://www.sino.uni-heidelberg.de/conf/propaganda/

and the second at

http://kaladarshan.arts.ohio-state.edu/exhib/poster/
    exhibintro.html

The story of the Red Guards as viewed through their songs can be explored at

http://www.indiana.edu/~easc/resources/working_paper/
    noframe_10b_song.htm

Attacks by the Red Guards on teachers is discussed at

http://www.cnd.org/CR/english/articles/violence.htm

The nature of the Chinese Peoples' Liberation Army is described at

http://en.wikipedia.org/wiki/People's_Liberation_Army

The limits of the recent movement toward liberalization in China, and by extension in the remaining communist nations, were tested during the student occupation of Tiananmen Square in 1989. This event is explored at

http://www.tsquare.tv/

The site offers film and music clips, a photo gallery, and a transcript of Deng Xiaoping's June 9, 1989, speech declaring martial law.

A transcript of the Public Broadcasting Company's superb documentary on the Tiananmen Square protests in China in 1989 can be found at

http://www.pbs.org/wgbh/pages/frontline/gate/

See also

http://www.historywiz.com/demonstration.htm

The National Security Archives' briefing book and a wealth of documents on the Tiananmen Square protests is found at

http://www.gwu.edu/~nsarchiv/NSAEBB/NSAEBB16/

Still photography of the protests, their repression, and ongoing efforts at democratization in China is offered at

http://www.christusrex.org/www1/sdc/tiananmen.html

A 360 degree moving image view of the square can be viewed at

http://www.roundtiananmensquare.com/

http://www.thebeijingguide.com/tiananmen_square/
    index.html

A balanced survey of Vietnamese history encompassing the Vietnamese revolution and its aftermath can be found at

http://www.viettouch.com/history/

The Web is particularly rich in sites documenting Vietnam's wars of national liberation, including the Emperor Bao Dai's letter of abdication of August 25, 1945, and Vietnam's Declaration of Independence of September 2, 1945

http://www.fordham.edu/halsall/mod/1945vietnam.html
http://www.vwip.org/doc-top.html
http://www.vwip.org/vwiphome.html

The Viet Cong's Program of 1962 as found at

http://www.fordham.edu/halsall/mod/1962vietcong1
    .html

There are excerpts from a host of American documents on the war at

http://depts.vassar.edu/~vietnam/

A site devoted to reflecting the service of American women in Vietnam can be found at

http://www.vietvet.org/women.htm

To learn about Vietnamese women who followed their female ancestors into battle, see

http://womenshistory.about.com/od/trung1/
http://www.gendergap.com/military/Warriors-2.htm
http://www.onlinewomeninpolitics.org/vietnam/
    vietleads.htm
http://www.library.wisc.edu/guides/SEAsia/vnimage/
    women.htm
http://www.library.wisc.edu/guides/SEAsia/vnimage/
    rsponsib.htm

View American and Vietnamese propaganda (on both sides) at

http://www.library.wisc.edu/guides/SEAsia/vnimage/
    vnintro.htm#links
http://www.i-kirk.info/2nd14th/propag1.html
http://members.aol.com/_ht_a/firstbn6thin/
    VCpropaganda.html
http://currahee.hispeed.com/his1stbnvnmemo04.html
http://www.parascope.com/articles/0497/phoenix.htm
http://www.landscaper.net/propgand.htm

Audio feed and visual images of U.S. Secretary of Defense Robert McNamara's speech on the instability of the Republic of Vietnam, President Johnson's announcement of his decision not to run for reelection and focus on a negotiated settlement of the war, the screams of students reacting to a National Guard unit's shooting of passersby as well as antiwar demonstrators at Kent State University in May 1970, and President Nixon's announcement that he had achieved peace with honor in Vietnam can be found at

http://www.historychannel.com/speeches/index.html

A great deal on Latin American politics and social conditions can be gathered from the Internet. From a well-researched critical stance, see the North American Congress on Latin America (NACLA) reports at

http://www.nacla.org

The revolutions in Chile are discussed at

http://www.hartford-hwp.com/archives/42a/130.html
http://www.soc.ucsb.edu/projects/casemethod/foran
   .html

Cuba is discussed at

http://www.worldsocialist-cwi.org/publications/Cuba/
   index2.html?/publications/Cuba/cuapp1.html

Guatemala is discussed at

http://www2.truman.edu/~marc/webpages/revsfall98/
   guatemala/guatemala.html
http://www.hartford-hwp.com/archives/47/index-ce
   .html
http://www.gwu.edu/~nsarchiv/NSAEBB/NSAEBB4/

and Mexico at

http://nt2.ec.man.ac.uk/multimedia/
   Mexican%20Revolution.htm

The leaders of these movements often seem larger than life. See Cuba's Castro at

http://www.cnn.com/SPECIALS/cold.war/kbank/
   profiles/castro/
http://www.marxists.org/history/cuba/archive/castro/

and the women of the Mexican revolution at

http://www.u.arizona.edu/ic/mcbride/ws200/mex-jand
   .htm

An iconic image of Argentine doctor and Cuban revolutionary Che Guevara can be found at

http://www.pbs.org/newshour/forum/november97/che
   .html.

Additional information is available at

http://www-sul.stanford.edu/depts/hasrg/german/
   exhibit/GDRposters/che.html/
http://www.pbs.org/newshour/forum/november97/che
   .html
http://www.fmch.ucla.edu/Exhibits/guevara.htm

The hopes of many Latin Americans for a more egalitarian society were celebrated in the works of artists such as Diego Rivera and Jose Orozco, discussed at

http://www.diegorivera.com/
http://www.dartmouth.edu/~hood/collections/
   orozco-murals.html

These hopes, ultimately broken during the Cold War, are discussed at

http://www.coldwar.org
http://turnerlearning.com/cnn/coldwar/backyard/
   byrd_ttl.html

They now largely rest with those who see the free market as the solution to poverty and inequality. There are doubts, however, that the free market is the panacea for the region's long-standing economic and social ills, particularly regarding the Mayan farmers of Chiapas, discussed at

http://nativenet.uthscsa.edu/archive/nl/9407/0164.html
http://lanic.utexas.edu/project/Zapatistas/
http://www.american.edu/ted/chiapas.htm
http://www.zapatistas.org
http://www.providence.edu/polisci/projects/zapatistas/
   nafta.html

For the official U. S. government position on NAFTA, see

http://www.fas.usda.gov/itp/Policy/NAFTA/nafta.html
http://www.ustr.gov/Trade_Agreements/Regional/
   NAFTA/Section_Index.html

For other views, see

http://www.citizen.org/trade/nafta/
http://www.epinet.org/content.cfm/
   briefingpapers_nafta01_index
http://www.fair.org/extra/9709/nafta.htm

Chapter 13

Up from the Ashes:
Japan and the Pacific Rim
in New Global Roles

*Tokyo at night at the beginning of the 21st century epitomizes
the resurgence of Asian economies following World War II.*

Chronology

1945	Japan defeated; American occupation
1948	Korea divided
1950–1953	Korean War
1951	American occupation ends in Japan
1954	U.S.-Taiwan defense treaty
1955	Japanese production reaches prewar levels
1955	Liberal Democratic Party formed in Japan
1959	Singapore declares independence from Malaysian Federation
1965	Growing Hong Kong autonomy
1980	End of U.S.-Taiwan treaty alliance
1984	British-Chinese agreement to return Hong Kong to China in 1997
1988–1989	Growing student agitation for liberal political reform in South Korea; elected civilian government installed
1989	Violent suppression of a democratic rally in Beijing's Tianament Square and end of widespread democratic agitation in China
1992–1993	Stock market decline and economic slowdown in Japan
1993	Liberal Democratic party defeated in Japanese elections; coalition government takes power
1997	Hong Kong rejoined with China

INTRODUCTION

The rise of coastal areas in eastern Asia to world importance forms one of the major facets of the rebalancing of major societies in the last phase of the 20th century. Unmarked by formal revolution—in contrast to Russia—the Pacific Rim gained momentum as an economic rather than as a military superpower following the upheaval of World War II. The dynamism of Asia's Pacific coast centered in several societies long in China's shadow, as Eastern Asian civilization was redivided and redefined, and the same societies began to influence international patterns in unprecedented ways. Societies that had been shaped by Confucian influence began to take very different paths. After 1978, however, rapid manufacturing growth in China suggested a decisive expansion of the economic impact of East Asia overall.

The rise of the Pacific Rim contributed greatly to the framework of contemporary world history, particularly from the 1970s onward. Its impact was more subtle than that of the cold war or decolonization, but it was considerable. Economic growth in Japan and neighboring countries, and later in China, added to the demand for raw materials, including oil, and other products. Japan became Australia's principal customer, for example, for foods and metals, as it became the second largest economy in the world. The spillover of Japanese demand helped galvanize economies in places like Thailand and Malaysia. In 2003, half of all the concrete produced anywhere went to China. Economic consequences flowed the other way as well. Japan became a leading exporter of electronic goods. Japan and South Korea, along with the West, generated some of the great multinational companies, with production branches from Arkansas to Africa. Cultural influence developed: Japan and South Korea played growing roles in world opinion, often in opposition to the arms race and militarism. Japan became a major center both for science and popular consumer culture.

In its global influence and in its internal development, the Pacific Rim combined successful industrialization—joining the West as an advanced industrial society—with distinctive cultural and organizational traditions. The region's economic vigor showed that it was possible to become successfully "modern" without becoming fully Western. This, too, contributed to the changing global context of the late 20th century, providing new competition for Western economies but also some challenging alternative models.

The key actor was Japan, but changes in the rest of the Pacific Rim were striking as well. Levels of prosperity and influence in South Korea and Taiwan gained ground rapidly, challenging the Japanese lead in certain export

The Pacific Rim Region by 1960

in fashions and electronic gadgetry, as predictors for trends that would spread to consumers worldwide. The Pacific Rim had varied faces as it balanced changes and traditions, and its role in world affairs was accordingly complex.

THE AFTERMATH OF WORLD WAR II IN EAST ASIA

The victors in World War II had some reasonably clear ideas about how East Asia was to be restructured as part of the dismantling of the short-lived Japanese empire. Korea, freed from Japanese control, was divided between a Soviet zone of occupation in the north and a U.S. zone in the south. Taiwan was restored to China, which was in principle and to some extent in fact ruled by a Guomindang government headed by Chiang Kai-shek. The United States regained the Philippines but pledged to grant independence quickly—save for retaining some key military bases. European powers restored colonial controls over their former holdings in Vietnam, Malaya, and Indonesia. Japan was occupied by U.S. forces bent on introducing major changes that would prevent a recurrence of military aggression.

sectors and making a profound impact on international markets. Many observers predicted that coastal eastern Asia, perhaps joined by parts of China and other areas, would replace the West in world leadership. This had not yet occurred by 2004, but a profound rebalancing of global attention was undeniable. At the same time, East Asia had never been so heavily engaged in interactions with broader global institutions and styles.

The emergence of the Pacific Rim also commands interest because it has formed such a challenging exception to the general difficulty faced by 20th-century societies that were still struggling to enter into a genuine industrial revolution. Here, South Korea and other areas that successfully industrialized after 1960 were even more interesting than Japan, where the Pacific Rim process of change had been launched so much earlier.

In 1994 an American teenager, living in the prosperous Singapore city-state with his family, was arrested for spray painting some cars and sentenced to a caning. The American government, judging the punishment too severe, protested, but Singapore stuck to its guns, arguing that its traditional emphases on discipline and the primacy of social order over individual expression were in fact superior to Western values. In 2003, *Wired* magazine began to feature the purchases of Japanese teenage girls,

New Divisions and the End of Empires

Not surprisingly, given the complex impact of the war and the complication of the new cold war struggle between the United States and the Soviet Union, the Pacific regions of Asia did not quickly settle into agreed-on patterns. A decade after the war's end, the Philippines, Indonesia, and Malaya were independent—part of the postwar tide of decolonization. Taiwan was still ruled by Chiang Kai-shek, but the Chinese mainland was in the hands of the new and powerful Communist regime. Chiang's Nationalist regime claimed a mission to recover China, but in fact Taiwan was now a separate republic. Korea remained divided but had undergone a brutal north-south conflict in which only U.S. intervention preserved South Korea's independence. Japan, rather ironically, was one of the few Pacific regions where matters had proceeded somewhat according to plan, as the nation began to recover while also adjusting to a considerably altered political structure.

Eastern Asia's postwar turmoil forms a complex story, only part of which is directly relevant to the emergence of the Pacific Rim economy. The Communist phase of China's revolution maintained a separation between

China and the parts of its traditional regional hinterland that showed little interest in communism; Vietnam's decolonization struggles also demand special attention. What came to be called the Pacific Rim turned out to be composed of areas traditionally influenced by Chinese culture but not brought under Communist control. This somewhat complex definition was forged in part by the actual experience of key Pacific regions during the period of postwar confusion.

Japanese Recovery

Japan in 1945 was in shambles. Its cities were burned, its factories destroyed or idle, its people impoverished and shocked by the fact of surrender and by the trauma of bombing, including the atomic devastations of Hiroshima and Nagasaki. However, like the industrial nations of the West, Japan was capable of reestablishing a vigorous economy with surprising speed. And its occupation by U.S. forces, eager to reform Japan but to avoid punitive measures, provided an opportunity for a new period of selective Westernization. Japan resumed its work as a center of growth and reform that had characterized it during the Meiji period and the 1920s.

The U.S. occupation government, headed by General Douglas MacArthur, worked quickly to tear down Japan's wartime political structure. The military forces were disbanded, the police decentralized, some officials removed, and political prisoners released. For the long run U.S. authorities pressed for a democratization of Japanese society by giving women the vote, encouraging labor unions, and abolishing Shintoism as a state religion. The emperor was retained, but as a figurehead, not a divine leader. Several economic reforms were also introduced, breaking up landed estates for the benefit of small farmers, who quickly became politically conservative, and dissolving the holdings of the *zaibatsu* combines, a measure that had little lasting effect, as Japanese big business quickly regrouped.

A new constitution tried to cut through older limitations by making Parliament the supreme government body from which the cabinet was appointed; various civil liberties were guaranteed, along with gender equality in marriage and collective bargaining rights; military forces with "war potential" were abolished forever, making Japan a unique major nation in its limited military strength. Even as Japan accepted many political and legal concepts, it inserted its own values into the new constitution. Thus a 1963 law defined special social obligations to the elderly, in obvious contrast to Western approaches to this subject,

The signing on the battleship *Missouri* of the terms of surrender by the Japanese foreign minister, Namoru Shigemitsu, brought the official end to a long and bloody global conflict. General Douglas MacArthur, who accepted the Japanese surrender, strove to establish democratic institutions and to rebuild the Japanese economy in the years of U.S. military occupation following the war.

at the statutory level: "The elders shall be loved and respected as those who have for many years contributed toward the development of society, and a wholesome and peaceful life shall be guaranteed to them. . . ."

These new constitutional measures were in the main embraced by the Japanese people, many of whom became avid opponents of any hint of military revival. Japan did ultimately create a self-defense force, and military capacity quietly grew well beyond what the constitution intended, but military expenditures remained a minuscule part of the overall budget. The United States retained military power and responsibility in the region long after the occupation period, keeping important bases in Japan. Many of the political features of the new constitution worked smoothly, in large part, of course, because the Japanese had experienced parliamentary and political party activity for extended periods in previous decades. Two moderate parties, both with substantial prewar traditions, vied for power during the late 1940s, with the Liberal Party holding sway; in 1947 a minority Socialist Party gained ground by winning 26 percent of the vote in the first postwar elections. The Socialist threat indeed spurred a 1955 merger of the moderate parties into the new Liberal Democratic Party, which monopolized Japan's government into the 1990s.

Amid political reconstruction, Japan's economy gradually recovered, a process that required about ten years. By 1955 production in the major industrial branches regained prewar levels. At that point many experts anticipated a moderation of growth, but in fact a huge surge ensued—the surge that propelled Japan into the first rank of world industrial powers. By this point, of course, the postwar adjustment period was clearly past, a fact expressed by the signing in 1951 of a peace treaty between Japan and 48 of its former wartime opponents; U.S. occupation ended in the following year, with an agreement on postwar bases. The Soviet Union, now locked in the cold war (which had in fact spurred the United States to convert Japan from defeated enemy to dependent ally) did not officially make peace, and its continued occupation of former Japanese islands in the north was a source of serious friction. Nevertheless the Soviets acquiesced in the new arrangements, leaving Japan free from major diplomatic distractions.

Korea: Intervention and War

Korea's postwar adjustment period was far more troubled than Japan's. Leaders of the Allied powers during World War II had agreed in principle that Korea should be restored as an independent state. But U.S. eagerness to obtain Soviet help against Japan, combined with long-standing Soviet interest in the area, determined that the northern part of the peninsula was occupied by the Soviet Union after the war. As the cold war intensified, U.S. and Soviet authorities could not agree on unification of the zones, and in 1948 the United States sponsored the Republic of Korea in the south, matched by the Soviet-dominated People's Democratic Republic of Korea in the north. North Korea's regime drew on an earlier Korean Communist Party founded in exile in the 1920s. North Korea quickly became a Communist state with Stalinist-type emphasis on the power of the leader, Kim Il-Sung. The South Korean regime, bolstered by ongoing U.S. military presence, was headed by the nationalist Syngman Rhee, another politician who had earlier worked in exile against Japanese occupation. Rhee's South Korea developed parliamentary institutions in form but maintained a strongly authoritarian tone.

In June 1950 North Korean forces attacked the South, hoping to impose unification on Communist terms. The United States, eager to maintain South Korea as protection for its deeper interests in Japan, reacted quickly (after some confusing signals about whether or not South Korea was inside the U.S. "defense perimeter"). President Truman insisted on drawing another line against Communist aggression and orchestrated U.N. sponsorship of a largely U.S. "police action" in support of South Korean troops. Under General Douglas MacArthur's leadership, Allied forces pushed North Korea back, driving on toward the Chinese border; this in turn roused concern on the part of China's Communist regime, whose "volunteers" drove U.S. troops back toward the south. The front stabilized in 1952 near the original North-South border. The stalemate dragged on until 1953, when a new U.S. administration was able to agree to an armistice. Korea then continued its dual pattern of development. North Korea produced an unusually isolated version of one-man rule, as Kim concentrated powers over the only legal political party, the military, and the government. Even Soviet liberalization in the late 1980s brought little change. South Korea and the United States concluded a mutual defense treaty in 1954; U.S. troops levels were reduced, but the South Korean army gained more sophisticated military equipment and the United States poured considerable economic aid into the country, initially to prevent starvation in a war-ravaged land.

The political tenor of South Korea continued to be authoritarian but with sporadic protests on behalf of a more genuine democracy. In 1961 army officers took over effective rule of the country, though sometimes a civilian government served as a facade. Economic change, however, began to gain ground in the south, ushering in a new phase of activity and international impact. Tensions between the two Koreas continued to run high, with many border clashes and sabotage, but outright warfare was avoided. By the 1990s South Korea developed new contacts with the North, while North Korea, which had by this point developed nuclear weaponry, periodically menaced its neighbors in a situation that remained complex and unresolved.

Taiwan, Hong Kong, and Singapore

Postwar adjustments in Taiwan involved yet another set of issues. As the Communist revolutionary armies gained the upper hand in mainland China, between 1946 and 1948 the Guomindang (Nationalist) regime prepared to fall back on its newly reacquired island, which the Communists could not threaten because they had no navy. The result was imposition over the Taiwanese majority of a new leadership, bureaucracy, and massive military force drawn from the mainland and, particularly in its

Korean War. American soldiers prepare to dispose of the bodies of Chinese soldiers, killed during an attack on an American outpost in 1953. Three nights of assault cost the Chinese 3,500 casualties. Ultimately, however, Chinese efforts pushed U.S. forces back, leading to renewed division of the Korean peninsula.

early years but in principle for several decades, devoted to regaining mainland authority from the Communists.

The authoritarian political patterns the Nationalists had developed in China, centered on Chiang Kai-shek's personal control of the government, were amplified by the need to keep disaffected Taiwanese in check. Tensions with the communist regime across the Taiwan Strait ran high. In 1950 the United States sent its Seventh Fleet to protect the island, and in 1954 a mutual defense treaty was signed (ended only in 1980, in the aftermath of U.S. diplomatic recognition of the Communist regime). In 1955 and 1958 the Communists bombarded two small islands controlled by the Nationalists, Quemoy and Matsu, and wider conflict threatened as the United States backed up its ally. Tensions were defused when China agreed to fire on the islands only on alternate days; U.S. ships supplied them on the off-days, thus salvaging national honor on both sides. Finally, the United States induced Chiang to renounce any intentions of attacking the mainland, and conflict eased into mutual bombardments of propaganda leaflets. During this period, as in South Korea, the U.S. devoted considerable economic aid to its Taiwanese ally, ending assistance only

in the 1960s, when growing prosperity (and increasing competition with U.S. firms in the manufacture of inexpensive consumer items) seemed assured. The Chinese communist regime continued to assert its claims over Taiwan, and the two occasionally traded threats, but outright conflict was avoided into the early 21st century.

Two other ultimate participants in Pacific Rim economic advance were distinguished by special ties to Britain. Hong Kong, leased from China under British pressure in 1898, remained a British colony after World War II; only in the 1980s was an agreement reached between Britain and China for its 1997 return to the Chinese fold. Hong Kong gained increasing autonomy from direct British rule. Its Chinese population, already considerable, swelled at various points after 1946 as a result of flights from Communist rule. Singapore, a city founded by British imperialists in the 19th century, retained a large British naval base until 1971, when Britain abandoned all pretense of significant power in eastern Asia. An even earlier merger with independent Malaya (granted self-government in 1957) collapsed on racial grounds in tensions between multiethnic Malaysia and Chinese-dominated Singapore. Because Singapore's presence made the Chinese in Malaysia a plurality (44 percent to the Malays 41 percent), Malay nationalists rejected the association with Singapore, which gained independence as a vigorous free port in 1959.

Overall, by the end of the 1950s a certain stability had emerged in the political situation of the smaller eastern Asian nations, with the vital exception of Vietnam and its neighbors in Indochina. Despite unresolved problems, such as a divided Korea or Taiwanese-Chinese relations, a number of nations had acquired de facto independence or, like Japan, had accepted important alterations in previous political and military structures. Several of these nations in turn had received special Western attention and economic support during this same adjustment period. It was from the 1960s onward that some of these same areas, combining Western contacts with important earlier traditions of group activity and vigorous group loyalty, moved from impressive economic recovery to new international influence on the basis of manufacturing and trade.

JAPAN, INCORPORATED

As Japanese politics developed under its postwar constitution, its chief emphasis lay in a rather conservative stability. The Liberal Democratic Party, formed by the merger of two conservative units in response to Socialist challenge, held the reins of government from 1955 onward. This meant that Japan, uniquely among the democratic nations of the postwar world, had no experience with shifts in party administration. Changes in leadership, which at times were frequent, were handled through negotiations among the Liberal Democratic elite, not directly as a result of shifts in voter preference.

The Distinctive Political Style

Clearly, this system revived many of the oligarchic features of Meiji Japan and the Japan of the 1920s, in which parliamentary rule was mediated through the close ties among the members of the elite. The system also encouraged cooperation between government bureaucracy and big-business combines, based on shared participation in the leadership group. The Liberal Democrats also revived some other features of Japan's previous political tradition. In the late 1950s, for example, it recentralized the police force. Socialist opponents of these programs reacted bitterly, protesting what they termed a revival of authoritarianism; Japan's political atmosphere for a time turned venomous, and there were many strikes and street demonstrations to protest government policies. During the 1960s, however, the Liberal Democrats shifted to avoid needless confrontations, and they strongly emphasized policies of economic development. During the prosperous 1970s and 1980s, economic progress and the Liberal Democrats' willingness to consult opposition leaders about major legislation reinforced Japan's effective political unity. Only at the end of the 1980s, when a number of Liberal Democratic leaders were branded by corruption of various sorts and Socialist strength revived somewhat, were new political questions raised. In 1993, the ruling party split, losing its majority for the first time in the general elections. The Liberal Democrats returned to government by the late 1990s, but political competition in the early 21st century remained higher than it had been a few decades earlier.

Japan's distinctive political atmosphere, even under a Western-influenced constitution, showed clearly in the array of functions the government undertook in cooperation with business leaders. Economic planning was extensive, and the state set production and investment goals in many sectors while actively lending public resources to encourage investment and limit imports. There was a scant sense of division between public and private spheres, another reminder of older Japanese traditions, in this case encouraged by Confucian principles. The government-business coordination to promote economic

growth and export expansion prompted the half-admiring, half-derisory Western label of "Japan, Incorporated."

Close business and political interactions resulted in part from the needs of postwar reconstruction and from Japan's precarious resource position, as the nation needed to import petroleum and most other vital raw materials and so depended on success in the export sector to an unusual degree. Government initiative extended also to the demographic sphere, as postwar leaders realized that when Japanese imperial expansion ended it was vital to control population size. The government actively campaigned to promote birth control and abortion, and demographic growth, though still somewhat higher than Western levels until the 1970s, slowed notably. Here again was a product of the strong national tradition of group cohesion; although it did not prevent strong political party differences, this tradition united many Japanese in a sense of common purpose with the government. Later, however, Japan's aging population prompted the government to try to limit birth control by making a number of common methods illegal; here Japan's people proved more recalcitrant, as high costs of living kept families small.

Expansion of the educational system was another practical contact between state and citizens. The extensive school system developed from the Meiji era was further expanded, giving many more Japanese an opportunity to attend secondary schools and universities, which in turn were strongly oriented toward technical subjects. Japanese children were encouraged to achieve academic success, with demanding examinations for entry into universities defining much of the youth of ambitious men and women. The scientific and technical focus encouraged further secularization in Japanese culture, with strong emphasis on rational inquiry and practical knowledge. The deep impact of this cultural focus was evident in not only growing creativity in science and technology, as Japan began to generate innovative discoveries instead of specializing in clever imitation of ideas developed elsewhere, but also the unusually high test scores of Japanese children. Again, traditional elements entered the picture, as education stressed somewhat mechanical group learning, based on disciplined memorization, over more eccentric individual achievements. Government policy oscillated somewhat between encouraging educational reform toward more emphasis on individual creativity, and a desire to use the schools to promote group loyalty and distinctive Japanese virtues.

Japanese culture more generally preserved other important traditional elements that provided aesthetic and spiritual satisfactions amid rapid economic change and an ongoing interest in Western forms. Customary styles in poetry, painting, tea ceremonies, and flower arrangements continued; each New Year's Day, for example, the emperor presided at a poetry contest, and masters of traditional arts were honored by being designated "Living National Treasures." Kabuki and No theater also flourished. Japanese films and novels often recalled earlier history, including the age of the samurai warriors; they also stressed group loyalties, as opposed to individuality or strong assertions of will. Japanese painters and architects participated actively in the "international style" pioneered in the West, but they often infused it with earlier Japanese motifs, such as stylized nature painting. City orchestras played the works of Western composers, both classical and contemporary, and also native compositions with passages played on the Japanese flute and zither. Both Buddhism and Shintoism remained significant forces in Japanese life as well, despite the strong secular emphasis. Overall, Japan in the later 20th century blended new cultural interests, which allowed the Japanese to incorporate many Western forms with distinctive recollections of strictly national ways.

At the same time, however, Japanese consumer culture steadily gained greater vitality. Japanese animation blended traditional interests in design with modern computer graphics, and had wide international influence. Japanese toys and rock music helped shape youth culture particularly in other parts of East Asia, but to some extent worldwide.

The Economic Surge

Particularly after the mid-1950s rapid economic growth produced Japan's clearest mark internationally and commanded the most intense energies at home. By 1983 the gross national product was equal to the combined totals of China, both Koreas, Taiwan, India, Pakistan, Australia, and Brazil. Per capita income, though still slightly behind such leading Western nations as West Germany, had passed that of many centers, including Britain. Annual economic growth reached at least 10 percent regularly from the mid-1950s onward, surpassing the regular levels of every other nation during the 1960s and 1970s, as Japan became one of the top economic powers in the world. Leading Japanese corporations, such as the great automobile manufacturers and electronic equipment producers, became known for both their volume of international exports and the high quality of their goods. On the basis of its export surge, Japan became a major factor in international markets of all sorts—in banking, foreign investment (both in raw-materials areas and in the United States), and foreign economic aid—as the relatively small, resource-poor island nation reached toward control of almost one fifth of total world trade. Japanese competition challenged the United States and western Europe, and its demand for raw materials figured prominently in Canada, Latin America, Australia, and the Middle East as well as Asia.

A host of factors fed this astounding economic performance. Active government encouragement was a vital ingredient, as the government made economic growth its top priority. Cheap loans for technological innovations and direct technical research in government laboratories, as well as carefully calculated international trade policies, translated this priority directly. The educational expansion played a vital role, as Japan began to turn out far more engineers than did more populous competitors, such as the United States. Foreign policy also figured prominently. Japan was able to devote virtually its entire capital to investment in productive technology, for its military expenses were negligible given reliance on U.S. protection. Labor was a central feature. Japan had a growing available labor force based on continued if slower population growth and a rapid reduction of the agricultural population (from 47 percent in 1945 to the standard advanced-industrial rate of about 10 percent by the mid-1980s).

Workers were abundant and highly organized, mainly in company unions that engaged in important social activities and some serious bargaining for improved benefits; the unions, however, remained careful not to impair their companies' productivity. Leading corporations solidified this cooperation, which spurred zealous work from most employees. Few days were lost to strikes, because paternalistic policies provided important benefits to workers despite wages that remained somewhat low by Western standards. Social activities promoted and expressed group loyalty (including group exercise sessions before the start of the working day), and managers displayed active interest in suggestions by employees. The Japanese system also ensured lifetime employment for an important part of the labor force, a policy aided by economic growth, low average unemployment rates, and a relatively early retirement age. This network of policies and attitudes made Japanese labor seem both less class-conscious and less individualistic than labor forces in the advanced industrial nations of the West; it reflected older traditions of group solidarity in Japan, going back to feudal patterns. Other popular habits encouraged economic

DOCUMENT

Wariness of the West and Defense of Japanese Traditions

Since the tumultuous 1850s, when Japanese society was forced by the United States and the European powers to open itself to the outside world, leading Japanese thinkers and writers have expressed the ambivalent, often anxious responses of their people to the increasing influences from the West. In the present day, best-selling Japanese novelists and social commentators deplore the erosion of traditional Japanese values and sensibilities as a result of U.S.-induced corporate commercialism, consumerism, and democratization following Japan's defeat in World War II. Wide media coverage is given to gatherings in which Japanese intellectuals lament the demise of Japan's ancient culture in the face of the Western onslaught. Japan-bashing ads and books in the United States are countered in Japan by politicians and writers who are highly critical of U.S. society, which many regard as violence-ridden, lazy, and clearly in decline.

Each of the following selections was written by a prominent post–World War II novelist. The first passages, taken from the novel *Runaway Horses* (first published in 1969) by Yukio Mishima, reflect Japanese uneasiness or open hostility to Western influences in the 1920s and 1930s, when Japan emerged as a global power for the first time in history. Mishima's novel focuses on the training of the paramilitary forces of an ultrapatriotic secret society whose young adherents seek to overthrow Japan's democratically elected civilian government and turn all power over to the emperor and his advisors. The incidents in the novel are often loosely based on historical events. In the following excerpt from *Runaway Horses*, an officer in the Japanese army lectures several of the paramilitary youths about the threats from abroad and Japan's dismal domestic situation during the depths of the Great Depression.

> Once he had abandoned his subtle questions, Lieutenant Hori's conversation became both interesting and profitable, quite capable of arousing their zeal. The shameful state of foreign affairs, the government's economic program which was doing nothing to relieve rural poverty, the corruption of politicians, the rise of communism, and then the political parties' halving the number of Army divisions and, by championing the cause of arms cutbacks, bringing constant pressure to bear upon the military. In the course of this conversation, the Shinkawa *zaibatsu's* [big industrialists'] exertions in purchasing American dollars came up, something of which Isao [the novel's protagonist] had already heard from his father. According to the Lieutenant, Shinkawa's groups had been making a great show of restraint ever since the May Fifteenth Incident [in May 1932 extremist plotters assassinated the Japanese Prime Minister, Inukai Tsuyoshi, as part of a broader assault on the parliamen-

growth, including a high (20 percent) savings rate born of a cautious attitude toward materialist acquisitiveness and the need to set aside money for old age. The result was considerable capital for investment in further innovation.

Japanese management displayed a distinctive spirit, again the result of adapting older traditions of leadership. There was more group consciousness, including a willingness to abide by collective decisions once made and less concern for quick personal profits than was characteristic of the West and particularly the United States. Few corporate bureaucrats changed firms, which meant that their own efforts concentrated on their company's success.

Japan, in other words, produced a distinctive economic culture that was clearly compatible with impressive results, that responded to particular Japanese needs and traditions, and that differed in important ways from Western norms. It had costs, however. Workers faced intense pressure to produce and were deprived of much

protest outlet. Personal consumer standards did not rise as rapidly as national output did, because of the concentration on savings and group benefits and the government-sponsored push to promote exports rather than drain output toward internal use. For several decades, leisure life remained meager by Western standards, and many Japanese even proved reluctant to take regular vacations. Here, however, an evolution did occur, with growing emphasis on nightlife and international tourism providing more leisure time, by the early 21st century, than Americans enjoyed.

Not surprisingly, the society that developed under the rapid industrial spurt showed features similar to the West's slightly earlier experience. Japanese women, though increasingly well educated and experiencing an important decline in birthrates, did not follow Western patterns precisely. A feminist movement was confined to a small number of intellectuals. Women's work outside

tary government]. However, the Lieutenant went on to say, there were not grounds at all for placing any trust in the self-control of people of that sort.

Japan was sorely beset. Storm clouds were piling up in an ever-growing mass, and the situation was enough to make a man despair. Even the august person of His Sacred Majesty was affronted. The boy's knowledge of current evils to be deplored was greatly expanded.

The fears and targets of the young extremists in Mishima's novel can be contrasted with the very different critique of outside influences expressed in Kenzaburo Oë's novel *A Personal Matter* (first published in 1964). Reflecting major post–World War II social concerns in Japanese society, the novel focuses on the personal struggles of a student named Bird. Once a member of a gang of juvenile delinquents, Bird, now in his late twenties, unwillingly confronts the responsibilities of adulthood, including an unhappy marriage and the birth of a deformed child. Bird's sense of isolation and alienation are sharpened throughout the story by the ugly, Westernized cityscapes that form the backdrop for his attempts to cope with urban life in modern Japan.

> Bird was looking for a drugstore when an outlandish establishment on a corner stopped him short. On a giant billboard suspended above the door, a cowboy crouched with a pistol flaming. Bird read the legend that flowered on the head of the Indian pinned beneath the cowboy's spurs: Gun Corner. Inside, beneath paper flags of the United Nations and strips of spiraling green and yellow crepe paper, a crowd much younger than Bird was milling around the many-colored, box-shaped games that filled the store from front to back. Bird, ascertaining through the glass doors rimmed with red and indigo tape that a public telephone was installed in a corner at the rear, stepped into the Gun Corner, passed a Coke machine and a juke box howling rock-n-roll already out of vogue, and started across the muddy wooden floor. It was instantly as if skyrockets were bursting in his ears. Bird toiled across the room as though he were walking in a maze, past pinball machines, dart games, and a miniature forest alive with deer and rabbits and monstrous green toads that moved on a conveyor belt; as Bird passed, a high-school boy bagged a frog under the admiring eyes of his girlfriends and five points clicked into the window on the side of the game.

Questions: What foreign threats does the lieutenant in Mishima's *Runaway Horses* directly and indirectly seek to impress on his youthful listeners? What within Japan is threatened? What sorts of Japanese collaborate with the foreigners? What solutions does the lieutenant advocate? How has the foreign threat changed in Oë's novel about postwar Japan? What sort of view of U.S. society do the artifacts in the game parlor convey to the reader? Who does Oë suggest is being corrupted by these cultural imports? What items in Oë's description suggest that the setting is the 1950s or perhaps the early 1960s?

the home was slightly less common and considerably more segregated than in the postwar West. Within the family, women shared fewer leisure activities with their husbands, concentrating more heavily on domestic duties and intensive child rearing than was prevalent in the West by the 1970s. Divorce rates were lower (merely one-third of U.S. levels), a sign of Japanese family stability after the disruptions of earlier stages of modernization, but this stability was predicated on the acceptance of considerable differences in gender roles and power.

Japanese methods of child rearing reflected distinctive family values. Conformity to group standards was emphasized far more than in the West or in Communist China. A comparative study of nursery schools thus showed Japanese teachers bent on effacing their own authority in the interests of developing strong bonds among the children themselves. Shame was directed toward nonconformist behaviors—a disciplinary approach the West had largely abandoned in the early 19th century. Japanese television game shows, superficially copied from the West, accordingly imposed elaborate, dishonoring punishment on losing contestants.

The same group-oriented culture shone through in diverse facets of Japanese life. The nation had few lawyers, for it was assumed that people could make and abide by firm arrangements through mutual agreement. Japanese psychiatrists reported far fewer problems of loneliness and individual alienation than in the West, as the Japanese remained devoted to group activities. Conversely, situations that promoted competition among individuals, such as the university entrance tests, produced far higher stress levels than did analogous Western experiences. The Japanese had particular ways to relieve tension; bouts of heavy drinking were more readily tolerated than in the West, as a time when normal codes of conduct could be suspended under the helpful eyes of friends. Businessmen and some politicians had recourse to traditional geisha houses for female-supplied pampering, as a normal and publicly accepted activity. Japanese teenagers participated in higher rates of sexual activity than was common in the West, another sign, perhaps, of a distinctive Japanese combination of hard work with recreational release.

Japanese popular culture was not static, because of both ongoing attraction to Western standards and rapid urbanization and economic growth. The U.S. presence after World War II brought a growing fascination with baseball, and a number of professional teams were set up. Individual Japanese athletes began also to excel in such sports as tennis and golf. In popular as well as more formal culture, change and Westernization continued to cause concern among conservatives, who worried that vital traditions might be lost for good. In the mid-1980s the government, appalled to discover that a majority of Japanese children preferred knives and forks in order to eat more rapidly, invested considerable money to promote chopstick training in the schools—a minor development but indicative of the ongoing tension between change, with its Western connotations, and a commitment to Japanese identity. At the end of the 1980s a new assertion of women's political power against some Japanese politicians who kept mistresses suggested the possibility that a more Western-style feminist consciousness might gain ground as part of Japan's ongoing evolution and its growing tourism abroad, as women gained more awareness of the standards of other societies. Veneration of old age was challenged by some youthful assertiveness and also by the sheer cost of the rapidly growing percentage of older people—for Japan relied heavily on family support for elders. Questions abounded about how Japan would combine distinctiveness with its industrial achievement in the future, but to Western eyes the Japanese ability to adapt traditions to change and imitation remained the most striking characteristic of the nation by the end of the 20th century.

Japan's continued success in international competition remained the dominant theme. Many nations in the West and in Asia resented Japanese competition and the Japanese reluctance to open their own markets to outside goods. Calls for retaliation by erecting tariff barriers against Japan were a recurrent threat, and the Japanese tried to respond—for example, by increasing their economic aid to developing nations and by investing directly in the United States and Europe—without changing their policies entirely. By the 1960s pollution became a serious problem as cities and industry expanded rapidly;

Traditional settings are found in modern Japan. Here students visit the *yomei-mon* gateway, at the mausoleum of Ieyasu in Nikko.

traffic police, for example, sometimes wore protective masks, though the government (eager to preempt a potential opposition issue) paid increasing attention to environmental issues after 1970. Some Japanese experts, worried that the nation's economic vigor would prove fragile amid such problems as growing fuel costs, foreign hostility, and internal problems, wrote articles with such titles as "The Short, Happy Life of Japan as a Superpower." Western observers continued at times to expect that Japan would soon become like the West, that is, would experience the same levels of crime, strikes, individualism, family instability, youth unrest, and feminist assertiveness as the West had come to know. This expectation combined a certain amount of wishful thinking—that a wider array of problems would impede Japan—with an implicit belief that industrialization must in the long run produce the same kinds of society regardless of the starting point. In the 1990s, in fact, the Japanese economy did slow, producing growing unemployment and a sense that Japan might be losing ground to growing Chinese vitality, though there were signs of recovery by the early 21st century.

Even amid fluctuations, increasing recognition developed that Japan must be understood in its combination of change with distinctiveness. Some observers even advocated that the West copy key Japanese values, particularly in the areas of diligence and group loyalty. Quite possibly, now that advanced industrialization had ceased being a Western monopoly, Japanese models would gain an increasing audience, though how much the West could or would imitate remained unclear. What was obvious, though confusing to many in the West, was Japan's achievement in reaching full economic equality—in becoming a genuine economic superpower—without adopting all Western forms of politics, family life, or personal values.

THE PACIFIC RIM: NEW JAPANS?

Economic and to some extent political developments in several other middle-sized nations and city-states on Asia's Pacific coast mirrored important elements of Japan's 20th-century history, though at a slightly later date. Political authoritarianism was characteristic, though usually with periodic bows to parliamentary forms and with recurrent protest from dissident elements that wanted greater freedom. Government functions extended to careful economic planning and promotion and to rapid expansions of the educational system, with the emphasis on technical training. Group loyalties promoted diligent labor and a willingness to work hard for relatively low wages. Economic growth burgeoned.

The Korean Miracle

South Korea was the most obvious exemplar of the spread of new economic dynamism to other parts of the Pacific Rim. The Korean government rested normally in the hands of a political strongman, usually from army ranks. Syngman Rhee was forced out of office by massive student demonstrations in 1960, but a year later a military general, Chung-hee, seized power. He retained his authority until his assassination in 1979 by his director of intelligence. Then another general seized power. Intense student protest, backed by wider popular support, pressed the military from power at the end of the 1980s, but a conservative politician won the ensuing general

election, and it was not clear how much the political situation had changed. Opposition activity was possible in South Korea, though usually heavily circumscribed, with many leaders jailed. There was some freedom of the press except for publications from Communist countries.

As in postwar Japan, the South Korean government from the mid-1950s onward placed its primary emphasis on economic growth, which in this case started from a much lower base after the Korean War and previous Japanese exploitation. Huge industrial firms were created by a combination of government aid and active entrepreneurship. Exports were actively encouraged; by the 1970s, when Korean growth rates began to match those of Japan, Korea was competing successfully in the area of cheap consumer goods, steel, and automobiles in a variety of international markets. In steel Korea's surge—based on the most up-to-date technology, a skilled engineering sector, and low wages—indeed pushed past Japan. The same held true in textiles, where Korean growth (along with that of Taiwan) erased almost one-third of the jobs held in the industry in Japan.

Huge industrial groups, such as Daewoo and Hyundai, resembled the great Japanese holding companies before and after World War II and wielded great political influence. Hyundai, for example, was the creation of the entrepreneur Chung Ju Yung, a modern folk hero who walked 150 miles to Seoul, South Korea's capital, from his native village to take his first job as a day laborer at the age of 16. By the 1980s, when Chung was in his sixties, his firm had 135,000 employees and embraced 42 overseas offices throughout the world. Hyundai virtually governed Korea's southeastern coast. It built ships, including petroleum supertankers; it constructed thousands of housing units given to relatively low-paid workers at below-market rates; it built schools, a technical college, and an arena for the practice of the traditional Korean martial art, Tae Kwon Do. With their lives carefully provided for, Hyundai workers responded in kind, putting in six-day weeks with three vacation days a year and participating in almost worshipful ceremonies when a fleet of cars was shipped abroad or a new tanker launched.

South Korea's rapid entry into the ranks of newly industrialized countries generated a host of more general changes. Population growth soared, as by the 1980s over 40 million people lived in a nation about the size of the state of Indiana, producing the highest population density on earth, about 1000 people per square mile. Here was one reason that even amid growing prosperity, many Koreans emigrated, and the government gradually began to encourage couples to limit their birthrates. Seoul expanded to embrace nine million people, with intense air pollution and a hothouse atmosphere of deals and business maneuvers. Per capita income advanced despite demography, rising almost ten times from the early 1950s to the early 1980s—but to a level still only one-ninth of that of Japan. Huge fortunes coexisted with considerable poverty in this setting, though the poverty itself had risen well above levels characteristic of less developed nations.

Advances in Taiwan and the City-States

The Republic of China, as the government on Taiwan came to call itself, experienced a rate of economic development similar to that in Korea, though slightly less impressive in terms of outright industrialization. Productivity in both agriculture and industry increased rapidly, the former spurred by substantial land reform that benefited small commercial farmers. The government concentrated increasingly on economic gains, as its involvement in plans for military action against the mainland Communist regime declined. As in Japan and Korea, formal economic planning reached high levels, though not at the expense of considerable latitude for private business. Massive investments were also poured into education, with basic literacy rates and levels of technical training rising rapidly. The result was important cultural and economic change for the Taiwanese people. Traditional medical practices and ritualistic popular religion remained lively but expanded to allow simultaneous use of modern, Western-derived medicine and some of the urban entertainment forms popular elsewhere.

The assimilation of rapid change gave the Taiwanese government considerable stability despite a host of new concerns. With the U.S. recognition of the People's Republic of China came a steadily decreasing official commitment to Taiwan. In 1978 the United States severed diplomatic ties with the Taiwanese regime, though unofficial contacts—through the American Institute in Taiwan and the Coordination Council for North American Affairs established by the republic in Washington—remained strong. The Taiwanese also built important regional contacts with other governments in eastern and southeastern Asia that facilitated trade; Japan, for example, served as the nation's most important single trading partner, purchasing foodstuffs, manufactured textiles, chemicals, and other industrial goods. Japanese prosperity was helping to propel economic growth elsewhere in the region.

Taiwan also developed some informal links with the Communist regime in Beijing, even as the latter continued to claim the island as part of its territory. The republic survived the death of Chiang Kai-shek and the accession of his son, Chiang Ching-kuo, to power in 1978. The young Chiang emphasized personal authority less than his father had and reduced somewhat the gap between mainland-born military personnel and native Taiwanese in government ranks. A strong authoritarian strain, however, continued, and political diversity was not encouraged.

Conditions in the city-state of Singapore, though less enveloped in echoes of Great Power politics, resembled those in Taiwan in many ways. The prime minister, Lee Kuan Yew, took office in 1959, when the area first gained independence, and held power for the next three decades. The government established tight controls over its citizens—here going beyond anything attempted elsewhere in the Pacific Rim. Sexual behavior and potential economic corruption, as well as more standard aspects of municipal regulation and economic planning, were carefully scrutinized, as the government proclaimed the necessity of unusual discipline and restraint given a large population crowded into limited space. Among the results were unusually low reported crime rates, limited tensions between the Chinese majority and other ethnic groups, and the virtual impossibility of serious political protest. The authoritarian strain in politics developed increasingly, after an initially democratic constitution; the dominant People's Action Party suppressed opposition movements, though there was some easing in the late 1980s. Authoritarian politics were rendered somewhat more palatable by extraordinarily successful economic development, based on a combination of government controls and initiatives and free enterprise. Already the world's fourth largest port, Singapore saw manufacturing and banking surpass shipping as sources of revenue. Electronics, textiles, and oil refining joined shipbuilding as major sectors. By the 1980s Singapore's population enjoyed the second highest per capita income in Asia, though well after Japan. Educational levels and health conditions improved commensurately. Government regulation and propaganda combined to reduce population growth, which leveled off notably.

Finally, Hong Kong retained its status as a major world port and branched out increasingly as a center of international banking, serving as a bridge between the Communist regime in China and the wider world. Export production, particularly in textiles, combined high-speed technology with low wages and long hours for the labor force, yielding highly competitive results. Although textiles and clothing formed 39 percent of total exports by the 1980s, other sectors, including heavy industry, had

Hyundais on a loading dock, awaiting export to the United States.

developed impressively as well. As in other Pacific Rim nations, a large and prosperous middle class had developed, with cosmopolitan links to many other parts of the world, Western and Asian alike.

COMMON THEMES IN THE PACIFIC RIM

Overall, the Pacific Rim states, including Japan as a special case of advanced industrial success, had more in common than their rapid growth rates and expanding exports. They all stressed group loyalties against excessive individualism and in support of hard work and somewhat limited consumer demands. Confucian morality was often used, implicitly or explicitly, as part of this effort, for all the Pacific Rim states were either ethnically Chinese or had been strongly influenced by Chinese values. Pacific Rim areas thus sought to merge rapid change and considerable imitation of Western ways with preservation of core standards that were distinctly eastern Asian. Pacific Rim states also shared, despite diverse specific political systems, considerable reliance on government planning and direction, amid limitations on dissent and instability. Greater democratization did occur in South Korea and Taiwan from the 1990s onward, with less police repression and more open political competition. In Hong Kong, however, the return to China (despite promises of tolerance for a different political system) raised questions about continuing a more open political system; popular protest recurrently clashed with the communist-appointed governor in the early 21st century.

The Regional Impact of the Pacific Rim

By the 1980s the steady economic growth of the Pacific Rim states, headed of course by Japan, drew in other parts of eastern and southeastern Asia. Economic growth rates accelerated in Malaysia, for example. During the early 1960s the Malaysian government launched a program of diversification of its export crops, to improve foreign earnings. The manufacturing sector, in 1960 only responsible for about 15 percent of total national income, began to expand as well. Malaysia began to develop a consistent export surplus, as it targeted raw materials (including newly discovered petroleum reserves) and inexpensive manufactured products to Japan. Tourist facilities expanded as well, again directed toward Japanese and Western resort goers. Malaysia was not yet experiencing an industrial revolution; its economic status lagged behind that of South Korea or Taiwan. But there was no question that significant change was occurring, as the region benefited from Japan's expanding market. Some observers believed that full industrialization was imminent and that equal participation in an expanding Pacific Rim was assured.

Thailand was another entrant to the region's rapid-growth sector. A significant stream of Thai workers labored in Japan (joining workers from the Philippines and Korea, as Japan's labor force no longer sufficed for all the nation's needs). Exports from Thailand rose, and again the manufacturing segment expanded. Thailand also served as a major tourist center for Japan and other societies, including considerable involvement in sex tourism. Though it grew at a slightly slower pace, Indonesia was also drawn into the expanding trade zone of the Pacific Rim.

The rise of the Pacific Rim inevitably had an impact on regional economic policy. Communist China, turning to a more open trade policy after 1978, called extensively on Japanese expertise. The same held true for Vietnam, where economic reforms were introduced to spur growth in 1987. In 1990 Mongolia, China, and North and South Korea signed a trade and development agreement, another sign of the growing openness of the Communist regimes to a commitment to market reforms and economic growth. This also reflected the power of the Pacific Rim example—in this case, that of South Korea—in prompting new, if limited, regional alignments. Mongolia, for example, had been a virtual protectorate of the Soviet Union for decades, but now it turned to a Pacific Rim state for cooperation. A 1991 pacification plan in Cambodia, long a troubled state in southeast Asia, called for a massive Japanese role in financing and economic

The Pacific Rim as a U.S. Policy Issue

Whenever power balances change among nations or larger civilizations, policy issues arise for all parties involved. The rise of the Pacific Rim economies posed some important dilemmas for the West, particularly for the United States, because of its military role in the Pacific and its world economic position. The United States had actively promoted economic growth in Japan, Korea, and Taiwan as part of its desire to sponsor solid regional development that would discourage the spread of communism. Although U.S. aid was not singly responsible for Pacific Rim advance and although it tapered off by the 1960s, the United States took some satisfaction in the fruits of its efforts and in the demonstration of the vitality of non-Communist economies. The United States was also not eager to relinquish its military superiority in the region, which gave it a stake in continued conciliation of Asian opinion; it did not want to see tensions translated into outright hostility that might threaten U.S. bases (as in South Korea) or lead to independent military efforts (a potential in the case of Japan).

Yet the threats posed by growing Pacific Rim economic competition, if more subtle than the military challenges characteristic of changing power balances, were real and growing. Japan seemed to wield a permanent superiority in balance of payment; exports to the United States regularly exceeded imports by the 1970s and 1980s, which contributed greatly to the U.S. unfavorable overall trade balance between the United States and Japan. Japanese investment in U.S. companies and real estate, although helping to bridge the international payments deficit by bringing yen for dollars, increased the growing indebtedness of the United States to foreign nations. Symbolic problems existed as well. Japanese observers pointed out with some justice that the United States seemed more worried about Japanese investments than about larger British holdings in the United States, an imbalance that smacked of racism. Certainly the United States found it more difficult to accept Asian competition than European, if only because it was less familiar. Thus a Korean advertisement for a major firm, placed in a 1984 copy of *Fortune* magazine, featured tales of technological prowess and also pictures of three leading executives wearing the sweatshirt of their U.S. alma maters (MIT, Wisconsin, and Cal Tech)—a combination that rankled many in the United States both because of the boasts and because of the partially justified sense that U.S. know-how was being used against it. More concretely, Japanese ability to

gain near monopolies in key industries, such as electronic recording systems—in some of which initial inventions still came from the United States, but their successful implementation shifted to Asia—and the growing Korean challenge in steel and automobiles meant or seemed to mean loss of jobs and perhaps a threat of more fundamental economic decline in years to come.

These problems intensified with the rise of Chinese industry. Exports of Chinese manufactured goods to the United States, in a whole range of consumer items, expanded steadily by the 1990s. Many American firms set up production outlets in China (and Vietnam) to take advantage of cheap labor. The result was a $40 billion trade gap.

Several general lines of response were suggested to deal with the new competitive balance between the United States and the Pacific Rim. Some observers downplayed any sense of crisis. They argued that some readjustment was acceptable—the United States did not have to maintain its brief economic superiority worldwide and could not indeed do so. They urged that acceptance of East Asian economic vigor in tandem with U.S. military strength in eastern Asia was a viable combination—each society specialized in areas it had talent for, to the benefit of both.

Other observers, far more concerned about a worsening economic imbalance, urged that the United States imitate the bases of Pacific Rim success by opening more partnerships between government and private industry and doing more economic planning; it should teach managers to commit themselves to group harmony rather than to individual profit seeking and it should build a new concord between management and labor based on mutual respect, greater job security, and cooperative social programs. Some U.S. firms did introduce certain Japanese management methods, including more consultation with workers, with some success.

A final set of observers, also concerned about long-term erosion of U.S. power on the Pacific Rim, urged a more antagonistic stance. A few wanted the United States to pull out of costly Japanese and Korean bases so that the Pacific Rim would be forced to shoulder more of its own defense costs. Others wanted to mount tariffs against Asian goods, at least until Pacific Rim nations made it easier for U.S. firms to compete in Asian markets. Some limits on Asian competition were introduced by law during the 1980s, and Japan occasionally agreed to stabilize exports lest more hostile restrictions ensue. Aggrieved U.S. workers sometimes smashed imported cars and threatened Asian immigrants, though many U.S. consumers continued to prefer Pacific Rim products and many U.S. firms continued to expand their East Asian connections. Clearly, the options were complex, and U.S. policy continued to veer among them.

Pacific Rim nations also faced choices about orientation toward the West, particularly the United States. Questions that had arisen earlier about what Western patterns to copy and what to avoid continued to be important, as the Japanese concern about forks and chopsticks suggests. Added now were issues about how to express pride and confidence in modern achievements against what was seen as Western tendencies to belittle and patronize. In 1988 the summer Olympic Games were held in South Korea, a sign of Korea's international advance and a source of great national satisfaction. During the games a great deal of Korean nationalism flared against U.S. athletes and television commentators, based on real or imagined tendencies to seek out faults in Korean society. South Korea, like Japan, continued to look heavily toward Western markets and U.S. military assistance, but there was clearly a desire to put the relationship on a new and more fully equal footing. This desire reflected widespread public opinion, and it could also have policy implications.

Finally, continued economic growth virtually ensured pressures for further change in the policy arena. In 1991 a new prime minister of Japan vowed to reconsider Japan's diplomatic and military policies, to bring them more in line with the nation's international economic surge. This shift reflected, among other things, Japanese annoyance with Western complaints that the nation had not done enough during the war against Iraq earlier in the year, when a U.S.-led alliance had attacked Iraqi efforts to gain greater control over Middle Eastern oil. Japan contributed $13 billion to the war effort, somewhat grudgingly, but encountered criticism for inactivity as other shouldered the burden of ensuring the flow of Middle Eastern oil—oil on which Japan depended. Here was a dramatic illustration of the tensions between massive economic power and a rather limited diplomatic role. Constitutional limitations prohibiting Japan from sending troops abroad now passed under new review. A total restructuring of Japanese policy seemed unlikely, but a more activist, assertive stance, more in line with international economic realities, seemed likely. Indeed, in the 2003 war against Iraq Japan did send some supporting military forces—which actually frightened some neighboring states, worried about a revival of the military. Although the United States professed to favor a less passive Japan, there was no assurance it would be pleased with the results of change.

Questions: How great were the challenges posed by the Pacific Rim to the U.S. world position and well-being? What are the most likely changes in American–Pacific Rim relations over the next two decades?

A Challenge: Research one of the debates where, during the past two decades, observers (both American and Asian) have suggested that the United States should copy Asian example: in economic policies; in corporate and labor organization; or in education and school success. How well do you think the arguments stand up at this point?

---

reconstruction. Clearly, the regional spillover of the Pacific Rim, throughout eastern Asia, grew steadily greater.

Finally, Pacific Rim dynamism prompted new trade discussions among eastern Asian states, Canada, the United States, Australia, New Zealand, and some of the Pacific coastal nations of Latin America, including Mexico. A new association was established to sponsor these discussions. With the Asian market growing steadily because of not only Pacific Rim prosperity but also the new expansion of such states as Malaysia, and with new regional economic blocs forming in Europe and, possibly, the Americas, discussions of trade policies on both sides of the Pacific seemed increasingly vital. Some Asian and U.S. experts urged a new orientation toward Pacific trade partnerships, along with, and possibly instead of, the historical orientation of nations such as Canada, the United States, and Australia to trade with Europe. Future prospects were by no means clear, but the importance of Pacific Rim trade connections promised further impact on policy.

The Rise of China

Until the 1980s, the successful Pacific Rim states stood in marked contrast to the communist nations of East Asia. Vietnam, of course, was long mired in conflict and then struggled to recover after the war with the United States and the unification of the nation. North Korea was unusually isolated, investing heavily in military forces including a nuclear weapons program but suffering from widespread famine and slow economic growth—a pattern that continued into the early 21st century. China, preoccupied with building a communist society, also lagged economically. But in 1978, the Chinese regime made the historic decision to convert to a more market-based, rather than state-directed economy. It opened widely to foreign investment and technical advice, while launching an aggressive export program. It also adopted a striking new population policy, forbidding marriage before age 25 and seeking to restrict each couple to no more than one child, hoping obviously not just to slow but to reverse population growth that was draining resources away from economic development.

The results were dramatic, and linked China in many ways to the wider Pacific Rim. Technical advice and investment funds came from many sources, including the United States and Europe. Many Chinese students began to be sent abroad to study. But investments from Japan, South Korea and even Taiwan were particularly important, even when formal diplomatic relations with the Chinese state were strained. Many multinational corporations based in Japan or the United States began to locate production branches in China, taking advantage of low labor costs and lax environmental regulations. Even countries like Mexico began to lose jobs to China because of the cost advantage. Chinese production of home appliances, toys (including Christmas gifts), clothing and other items soared. This was the surge that propelled China to a 10 percent annual growth rate, even as the rate of population growth slowed dramatically. While not yet at the level of the Pacific Rim leaders in terms of technical sophistication and certainly standards of living, China's new focus on advances in the global economy, given its huge size, propelled it to a powerful position, in the East Asian economy and in the world at large.

The regime made no secret of its new focus. While tight political controls continued to inhibit internal dissent, the embrace of the market economy was clearly the main point. After 2000 the Communist Party even opened its membership to wealthy entrepreneurs. A major tension did develop with a new, Buddhist-derived religious movement, the Falun Gong, which the regime attacked as an enemy of the state—in line with earlier Chinese traditions of state oversight of religion. Many religious leaders were imprisoned. This aside, the concentration on economic advance was relatively single-minded. The nation pursued fairly cautious diplomatic policies, in contrast to earlier aggressive assertions during the Mao era. Tremendous investments were poured into infrastructure, including highway building. Higher education expanded rapidly, and in 2003 the regime made a commitment to educate 15 percent of the relevant age group at the university level—a percentage below Western and Japanese levels, to be sure, but a massive undertaking in terms of the numbers of students. Huge new campuses sprang up almost literally overnight, and the regime also pursued a wide range of linkages with universities in the Pacific Rim and the West.

Problems remained, and with them some questions about whether this push would carry China fully into the ranks of the leading industrial states. Pollution problems expanded with industry, and Chinese cities filled with industrial gases known as the "yellow dragon." By 2004, China ranked second to the United States in its contributions to overall environmental pollution, as not only factories but growing use of automobiles steadily increased emission levels. Huge gaps opened between countryside and city. Urban prosperity visibly advanced, with a vigorous consumer culture to match. Even childhood obesity began to be a problem in the growing middle classes, as food availability combined with a sedentary lifestyle in the familiar pattern. But rural conditions stagnated. To be sure, peasant entrepreneurs were able to take advantage of the new market policies. Wang Xin, for example, was a peasant who had been frustrated during the commune period, with its arbitrary regulation of agriculture; by the 1980s he was able to set up a poultry business that was soon earning him more in a single year than he had made in a decade previously. He was able among other things to buy a radio cassette for his daughter, to help her study for college examinations, and he encouraged some of his neighbors to join in the poultry business. Far more peasants, however, continued to rely on fairly traditional methods, in isolated villages. Many of them, unable to make ends meet, had to enter the factory labor force (sometimes in similarly isolated factories), where long hours, unsafe conditions and low wages were the norm. Would China's overall economic advance ultimately pull up its rural majority? Finally, in the economic problem category, some state-run enterprises, particularly in heavy industry, remained inefficient, yet the government hesitated to shut them down and contribute to unemployment.

There were also some unintended consequences of the new population policy. Confined to a single child, many parents lavished affection and worked hard to ensure success in school. But traditions, again particularly in the countryside, almost certainly induced some parents to practice female infanticide, so that their "one" child would turn out to be a boy; and girls outnumbered boys 9 to 1 in Chinese orphanages. The result, by the early 21st century, was a surplus of some 3 million young men over young women, with interesting, possibly troubling implications for sexuality and even the political order.

And questions certainly surrounded the political order itself. Could China pull off the combination of a vibrant, internationally open economy and a closed political system? What would the consequences be of any increase in political dissent—based, for example, on growing use of the Internet?

With an array of issues for the future, it is important not to lose sight of China's huge changes during the final decades of the 20th century and the initial years of the 21st. The nation continued to advance economically even during the mid-1990s, when Pacific Rim economies elsewhere faltered. Its impact on the world economy was immense, not only in its supply of manufactured products but in its purchases of key raw materials from other areas. By 2003 the nation was even beginning to generate international tourists—taking package trips to Australia or elsewhere—a sure sign of contemporary global impact. There seemed little doubt that the nation would play a growing role in world affairs in the 21st century, adding to the impact—indeed, potentially dominating the impact—of East Asia more generally.

CONCLUSION: THE PACIFIC RIM AS EXCEPTION OR AS MODEL

The rise of the Pacific Rim nations was based on a combination of factors. First, the nations shared aspects of the Chinese cultural and political heritage, mediated, as in Japan, by many prior adaptations and additions. A roughly common culture helped account for similar tendencies to emphasize cooperation, to build tight links between state and society, and to seek to maintain distinctive identity even amid change and imitation of aspects of Western technical and social forms. Second, the Pacific Rim nations shared some special contacts with the West through unusually intense interaction with the British or through postwar dealings with the United States. These contacts provided a certain amount of economic or military support at key junctures and also some unusual opportunities to grasp aspects of the West's technology, politics, and even popular culture. Finally, the principal Pacific Rim centers, including Japan, had been rocked by 20th-century events, which virtually forced considerable rethinking and innovation.

The shared features of the Pacific Rim were very general. The region was not unified geographically or in any

other way, though growing mutual trade provided an important bond in some instances. Japan was far more advanced industrially than the rest of the Pacific Rim. Political structures and diplomatic and military contexts varied considerably. Japan's record in World War II generated fears and hostilities that persisted in East Asia, in China and the Koreas alike. The apparent similarities of Pacific Rim nations might therefore prove temporary. Certainly, even in the short run, there was substantial mutual rivalry, most obviously in the economic competition between Japan and Korea, exacerbated by mutual memories of Japanese occupation.

At least for an important moment in the later 20th century, however, the emergence of the Pacific Rim nations involved important innovations both in the cultural and political maps of eastern Asia, newly divided between Communist and capitalist, and in the economic map of the world as a whole. The Pacific Rim, headed by Japan but joined by the self-sustaining industrializations achieved elsewhere, provided the clearest challenge to the West's long international economic leadership. Though not wedded to commensurate military power, the Pacific Rim's economic surge might foreshadow wider international influence later on, as cultural forms and values, for example, begin spreading both ways instead of primarily mainly west to east. And what of China, and possibly Vietnam, where different issues dominated much of the 20th century but where many features were shared or could be resurrected that would mesh with the factors responsible for Pacific Rim dynamism? As China experimented with new economic forms in the late 1970s and early 1980s, many observers wondered if this Asian giant, or at least its coastal cities, would soon join in the Pacific Rim ascendancy. What will happen, for example, as Hong Kong is further integrated with China? The city rejoined China in 1997, and the Communist regime pledged to give the city-state considerable latitude. Would the Hong Kong–China combination encourage more general Chinese adaptation to a more mixed economic structure that, in turn, could propel more rapid economic growth?

Certainly the success of the Pacific Rim states after World War II raised substantial questions about the contrast to China, questions that linked history to present patterns. Confucian tradition was not only clearly compatible with rapid industrial advance but also could contribute to it. Chinese zest for commerce showed directly in Hong Kong, Taiwan, and Singapore. Huge population pressure and a long period of foreign exploitation did not hold South Korea back. Was eastern Asia durably divided between industrial states and societies that, although changing, remained largely agricultural, or between non-Communist and Communist? Here was a key question for Hong Kong as it prepared to accept Chinese rule in 1997. And here was a larger question for the future, where recent experience and long-term tradition suggest different answers.

Ongoing evolution within the Pacific Rim states and the expansion of the Pacific Rim dynamism to include such nations as Malaysia raises a final set of questions. Both Japan and South Korea continue to express tension between change and considerable imitation of Western forms on the one hand and periodic traditionalist-nationalist reactions on the other. Usually, to be sure, a compromise prevailed that maintained distinctive social forms without preventing rapid change. Japan's interwar experience, as well as some of the political frustrations visible in South Korea late in the 1980s, remind us that adaptive compromise might not always be successful.

Even without these speculations for the future, the entry of the Pacific Rim into the mainstream of international trade represented a vital new development both for the region and for the world economy. Unsupported by military might after World War II and not joined as yet by any missionary culture of the sort that helped propel the Arabs or western Europeans in the past, the rise of the Pacific Rim was an unusual development in world history, quite apart from its contrast with the region's substantial isolation in earlier eras. It is not surprising that this rise provokes questions about a wider ultimate international role. If a choice has to be made for the next internationally dominant region—and it is not clear that it is sensible to project a choice in the early 21st century—eastern Asia seems the most obvious single candidate.

The Pacific Rim story is a continuing one. As we will see in Chapter 14, many Pacific Rim nations participated in greater political democracy during the 1990s. Taiwan, for example, experienced more contested elections as the hold of the Chinese Nationalist Party diminished, South Korea elected presidents amid considerable competition, and one successful presidential candidate had in fact been jailed earlier for political dissidence. By the mid-1990s, Pacific Rim economic growth slowed. South Korea experienced a brief crisis but then returned to greater vigor. Japan's economy slowed over a longer term, and the process was not over by 2001. Some Western observers believe that the Pacific Rim pattern of close government-industry cooperation is part of the problem, and that more competition has to be allowed. In 2001 a reformist government in Japan, though drawn from the Liberal Democratic Party, vowed to address some of these issues. It is clear that the importance of the Pacific Rim economy is an international issue, and not just important within the region itself.

FURTHER READING

The best account of contemporary Japanese society and politics is E. O. Reischauer's *The Japanese* (1988). For a recent history, see M. Hane's *Modern Japan: A Historical Survey* (1992). On the economy, consult E. F. Vogel, *Japan as Number One: Lessons for America* (1979); William G. Beasley, *The Rise of Modern Japan* (1995); and Edward R. Beauchamp, ed., *Women and Women's Issues in Post World War II Japan* (1998).

Several novels and literary collections are accessible and useful. J. Tanizaki's *The Makioka Sisters* (1957) deals with a merchant family in the 1930s; see also H. Hibbett, ed., *Contemporary Japanese Literature: An Anthology of Fiction, Film, and Other Writing Since 1945* (1992). An important study of change, focusing on postwar rural society, is G. Bernstein, *Haruko's World: A Japanese Farm Woman and Her Community* (1983). Another complex 20th century topic is assessed in R. Storry's *The Double Patriots: A Story of Japanese Nationalism* (1973).

On the Pacific Rim concept and its implications in terms of the world economy, see David Aikman, *Pacific Rim: Area of Change, Area of Opportunity* (1986); Philip West et al., eds., *The Pacific Rim and the Western World: Strategic, Economic, and Cultural Perspectives* (1987); Stephen Haggard and Chung-In Moon, *Pacific Dynamics: The International Politics of Industrial Change* (1988); Roland A. Morse et al., *Pacific Basin: Concept and Challenge* (1986). Vera Simmons' *The Asian Pacific: Political and Economic Development in a Global Context* (1995) is a comparative survey of postcolonial state building and international cultural connections. S. Ichimura, The *Political Economy of Japanese and Asian Development* (1998).

Excellent introductions to recent Korean history are provided in Bruce Cumings's *The Two Koreas* (1984) and David Rees's *A Short History of Modern Korea* (1988). A variety of special topics are addressed in Marshal R. Pihl, ed., *Listening to Korea: Economic Transformation and Social Change* (1989). See also Paul Kuznets' *Economic Growth and Structure in the Republic of Korea* (1977) and Dennis McNamara's *The Colonial Origins of Korean Enterprise, 1910–1945* (1990).

For a fascinating exploration of cultural change and continuity in Taiwan regarding issues in health and medicine, see Arthur Kleinman's *Patients and Healers in the Context of Culture* (1979). On Singapore, Janet W. Salaff's *State and Family in Singapore* (1988) is an excellent study; see also R. N. Kearney, ed., *Politics and Modernization in South and Southeast Asia* (1975).

Recent work includes Duncan McCargo, *Contemporary Japan* (2004); John Dower, *Embracing Defeat: Japan in the Wake of World War II* (1999); Edward Beauchamp, *Women and Women's Issues in Post–World War II Japan* (1998); Gary Allinson, *Japan's Postwar History* (2004); Bong Lee, *The Unfinished War: Korea* (2003);

On the rise of China, see I. Hsu, *China Without Mao: The search for a New Order* (1983); Ian Cook, *China's Third Revolution: Tensions in the Transition Towards a Post-Communist China* (2001); and Merle Goldman, *Historical Perspectives on Contemporary East Asia* (2000).

ON THE WEB

The life of General Douglas MacArthur and the art and society of the post–World War II occupation or "Confusion" era in Japan is discussed at

http://educate.si.edu/spotlight/korean.html

Japan's difficulty in accepting responsibility for its wartime atrocities, particularly the abuse of Korean and other Asian women by Japanese occupation troops, is discussed at

http://online.sfsu.edu/~soh/comfortwomen.html
http://online.sfsu.edu/~soh/cw-links.htm
http://csf.colorado.edu/bcas/sample/comfdoc.htm

Korekiyo Takahashi's role in the building of the modern Japanese economy and his conflict with the war party led by Tojo Hideki is examined at

http://netec.mcc.ac.uk/WoPEc/data/Papers/
  hithitueca395.html
http://www.historynet.com/ (search name for many
  links).

The place of Takahashi's policies in today's Japan is examined at

http://www.atimes.com/Japan-econ/AB12Dh01.html

Much of the history of postwar Japan was shaped by the Korean War, which can be studied at

http://mcel.pacificu.edu/as/students/stanley/home.html

Oral histories of the Korean War are available at

http://mcel.pacificu.edu/as/students/stanley/home.html

The Korean War also helped shape the career arc of leading personalities in the rise of modern Korea, such as Syngman Rhee

http://www.kimsoft.com/2000/rhee.htm
http://us.cnn.com/ SPECIALS/cold.war/kbank/
  profiles/rhee/

The nature of the Korean economy and the dominant role of *chaebol*, large corporate entities in postwar Korea, are explored and compared with Japanese *zaibatsu* and *keiretsu* at

http://www.megastories.com/seasia/skorea/chaebol/
  chaebol.htm
http://1upinfo.com/country-guide-study/south-korea/
  south-korea92.html

The rapid postwar industrialization of East Asia owed much to Japan's participation in the postwar revolution in technology

http://www.iss.u-tokyo.ac.jp/Newsletter/SSJ1/gluck.html

However, much of the postwar recovery of East Asian economies was due to close cooperation between business and government, a relationship traced at

http://www.kimsoft.com/1997/sk-econ.htm
http://www.let.leidenuniv.nl/history/econgs/japan.html

This relationship has been criticized even in Japan, where politicians were caught with trunks full of cash provided by leading Japanese companies. The manner in which the Liberal Democratic Party in Japan pursued this relationship and its results are explored at

http://countrystudies.us/japan/122.htm

This pattern, which was followed by the eastern Pacific Rim's economic tigers as part of an authoritarian development strategy, is most clearly expressed by Singapore's Lee Kwan Yew, who has made comparisons between himself and Machiavelli:

http://www.sfdonline.org/Link%20Pages/Link%20
  Folders/Political%20Freedom/Machiavelli.html

However, a recent economic recession in the region is discussed at

http://www.ifg.org/khor.html
http://www.facts.com/icof/i00063.htm
http://www.rice.edu/rtv/speeches/19981023lee.html

This has forced some to question whether the East Asian model of economic growth is worthy of emulation elsewhere.

PART IV

AFTER THE FALL: TOWARD A NEW MILLENNIUM

A burnt-out, Soviet-supplied, Iraqi tank and burning oil wells reflect both the triumph and perils of the American-led war in 1991 to drive Saddam Hussein's forces from occupied Kuwait. The high-tech coalition victory catapulted the U.S. to "hyper-power" status, but wasted oil and environmental damage presaged the instability to come in the Persian Gulf region.

Chronology

1979–1989	First Gulf War between Iran and Iraq
1985–1989	Gorbachev leads reform *(perestroika)* movement in the Soviet Union
1988	Soviet withdrawal from Afghanistan
1989–1990	Collapse of Communist regimes in the Soviet Union and Eastern Europe
1989	Move to reform apartheid regime in South Africa
1990	Reunification of Germany
1990	Mainland China's shift to a market economy accelerates
1990–1991	Iraqi invasion of Kuwait; U.S.-led alliance wins the Second Gulf War
1990–2001	Ethnic Chechnyans revolt against the Soviet Union
1991–1992	Ethnic conflicts result in the dismemberment of Yugoslavia
1992	First Global Environmental Conference in Rio de Janeiro
1994	Genocidal Hutu assault on Tutsis in Rwanda
1995	UN–U.S. interventions in Bosnia
1998–1999	Broad agreement in global scientific community that global warming is underway
1999	U.S.–NATO war against Yugoslavia
2000	First non-PRI Mexican president elected
2000–2002	Second Intifada in Palestine-Israel
2001	Terrorist attacks against the World Trade Center, New York, and the Pentagon
2001–2002	U.S. war on al-Qaeda militants and Taliban regime in Afghanistan
2002	Nations in the European Economic Union adopt a common currency (the Euro)
2002	Israeli armies reoccupy Palestine
2003	U.S. and allies invade Iraq

In the 1990s, the last chronological decade of the 20th century, global history took another, rather abrupt turn. With the remarkably sudden collapse of the Soviet Union and the Communist regimes of Eastern Europe, the long and tense cold war came to an end. By this time, the parallel process of decolonization had been completed, symbolized by the admission of well over a hundred new states into the United Nations between the 1960s and 1980s. The end of colonialism, which had been a dominant force throughout the 20th century, and of the cold war, which had been such a major force in the last decades of the 1900s, opened up new possibilities for global historical development. Some of these gave promise of human improvement, especially the spread of new technologies and medicines. Others, which were often revivals of earlier patterns, threatened to become new sources of social conflict and international confrontations. Whether constructive or menacing, all the seemingly novel themes and directions that emerged globally in the post–cold war years were grounded in the history of the troubled century that had given rise to them. And by the turn of the third millennium C.E., it was clear that they would shape world history for decades, perhaps centuries, to come.

By the 1990s, the map of the world that the final burst of colonial expansion had set in place for the first two phases of the 20th century had been utterly redrawn. Not only had the European, American, and Japanese empires been replaced by a patchwork of emerging nation-states, but, as we shall see in Chapter 14, the Soviet

ARCTIC

GREENLAND

ICELAND

See inset

ATLANTIC
OCEAN

Alaska
(U.S.)

CANADA

UNITED STATES

MEXICO

Hawaii
(U.S.)

PACIFIC
OCEAN

Puerto
Rico
(U.S.)

HAITI
DOM.
REP.

CUBA

JAMAICA

BELIZE
HONDURAS
GUATEMALA
EL SALVADOR

NICARAGUA

COSTA RICA

PANAMA

BARBADOS

GRENADA ★

TRINIDAD & TOBAGO

VENEZUELA

GUYANA

French Guiana
(France)

SURINAME

COLOMBIA

ECUADOR

PERU

BRAZIL

BOLIVIA

PARAGUAY

URUGUAY

ARGENTINA

CHILE

FALKLAND
ISLANDS

MOROCCO

ALGERIA

LIBYA ★

Western Sahara
(Mor.)

MAURITANIA

MALI

NIGER

CHAD

GAMBIA

SENEGAL

GUINEA-BISSAU

GUINEA

BURKINA
FASO

NIGERIA

BENIN

SIERRA LEONE

CÔTE
D'IVOIRE

CENTR.
AFRICAN

CAMEROON

LIBERIA

GHANA

TOGO

EQ. GUINEA

GABON

DEMO.
REPL.
OF THE

CONGO

SÃO TOMÉ & PRÍNCIPE

Cabinda
(Ang.)

ANGOLA

NAMIBIA

BO

SC
AF

TUNISIA

0   2,000 MILES

0   2,000 KILOMETERS

NATO countries
■   Communist countries
▼   SEATO (est. 1954)
●   ASEAN (est. 1967)
◆   ANZUS
★   U.S. military intervention since 1945
☭   Soviet intervention since 1945

The World in 2000

empire had also disintegrated. It too was replaced by numerous successor states, from the reborn Baltic republics to the new states of the Muslim steppe regions that now flanked the Russian core of the old empire across the south. The new political alignment of the globe remained volatile and the source of ongoing civil wars and interstate clashes. But in stark contrast to the political division of the world at the onset of the 20th century, there was far greater local and regional sovereignty, however much different ethnic and religious groups might contest who had the right to exercise it.

TOWARD GLOBALIZATION: PROMISE AND PERILS

The collapse of the Communist bloc of Eastern Europe and the end of the cold war standoff of the superpowers also opened up the possibility of a truly globalized economy, which is one of the themes emphasized in Chapter 15. The smaller nations of the former Warsaw Pact allies, such as Poland and Hungary, quickly moved to throw off the state regulations that had stifled economic growth and to integrate their economies into the market-oriented network dominated by their European neighbors, the United States, and Japan. With greater difficulty, Russia itself also struggled to make the transition from communism to capitalism. And, with surprisingly little time lag and greater ease, the People's Republic of China, Vietnam, and, to a lesser extent, Cuba, soon followed suit. Communist regimes that resisted these trends, such as North Korea and Albania, were soon isolated, impoverished, and under siege, if not toppled. The demise of the Communist option also gave added impetus to international trade agreements, such as NAFTA and GATT, which were designed to break down barriers to the exchange of goods, and especially the movement of capital investment. It also brought even greater power to international lending agencies, such as the World Bank and the IMF, which had played such a major role in shoring up the economies and stabilizing the polities of the capitalist bloc in the cold war era.

Although many, especially in the West, greeted these globalizing trends as forces that would liberate humanity and make possible decent standards of living globally, their impact thus far has been much more varied, and in important respects a cause for concern. New wealth was generated on an unprecedented scale in the 1990s, but this increase tended to favor the social groups, both in developing and industrialized areas, that were already well-to-do. These groups controlled the capital, educational advantages, and contacts that made it possible for them to take best advantage of the potential for innovation and profit that globalization opened up. New—and in the case of countries like India, Japan, and Korea, very sizable—middle classes emerged worldwide. But in most cases, the absolute numbers of the poor and malnourished grew even more rapidly, especially in postcolonial societies, many of which actually fell further behind Japan and the West in scientific and technological advancement.

The poor and unskilled working classes participated to some extent in the vastly expanded consumer culture that was spreading globally. And in many areas, jobs in assembly or processing plants provided sources of income that would not have been available without global linkages. But for the most part workers were drawn into the globalizing economy at the very lowest levels. Working class and rural men and women alike were integrated into the global network mainly as poorly paid sweatshop workers, who labored in regimented, unhealthy, and often dangerous assembly-line environments. The designer clothes and electronic devices they produce are shipped mainly to markets in more affluent countries or sold to the wealthy elites in their own societies. And the profits of their labors are overwhelmingly reaped by international corporations and the mercantile networks associated with them.

As we shall see in Chapter 15, these imbalances have prompted considerable criticism and grass-roots protest movements against globalizing tendencies throughout the world. A major focus of this resistance has been the World Trade Organization, whose meetings in Seattle and Genoa became the focus of mass demonstrations mounted by union, environmental, peasant, and minority organizations from both industrialized and developing nations. At times these confrontations have turned violent, underscoring the need to be attentive to the diverse effects, both good and ill, of the globalizing process. The disparities in living standards and opportunities that globalization has thus far intensified have also been linked in many societies with interethnic tensions and civil strife. They have also proved an impetus for youthful slum dwellers in countries like Egypt and India, where the contrast between minority wealth and the poverty of the majority is so apparent, to join religious revivalist movements, which promise them education, food, and shelter at the very least.

Interestingly, these divisions have been both muted and exacerbated by the spread of a common world consumer culture that is one of the core elements of the larger process of globalization. GAP sweatshirts, Sony cassette players, Yankee baseball caps, Mento mints, Pokémon trading cards, and McDonald's eateries have become pervasive material artifacts and cultural symbols of a new age in world history. Even groups explicitly hostile to globalization find it difficult to resist these consumer attractions; the repressive Taliban regime in Afghanistan after all made something of a fetish of driving Toyota trucks. But highly variable degrees of access to the globalized market and its much advertised promise of a better life, has increased social divisions and in many cases conflict in many locales and globally. At the same time, market imperatives have very often undermined the support systems and mutual assistance that the peasants, workers, uprooted immigrants, and like groups who still make up the majority of humanity have depended on for millennia.

TROUBLING CONTOURS OF A NEW WORLD ORDER

Like the globalizing process, other key themes that have emerged in the global history of the post–cold war era have been a mix of promise and peril. As we shall see in Chapter 15, the collapse of the Soviet Union and its Communist satellites unleashed a host of bitter ethnic and religious animosities and rivalries that have often led to violent clashes and prolonged civil wars. This trend has compounded the growing ethnic conflicts that were often the result of the artificial, counterhistorical, political units that were a legacy of the colonial era. In some areas, particularly sub-Saharan Africa where the states created by the colonizers had the weakest grounding in precolonial ethnic and political patterns, the number and brutality of civil wars have increased alarmingly. A parallel trend has been the growing incidence of genocides or intended genocides; with Rwanda, Bosnia, and Cambodia key instances of the former, and Kosovo a major example of the latter.

Ethnic divisions have very often been charged by religious differences, which have often been the ideological focus of revivalist groups. At times, religious zealotry has become a major factor in disputes over land. As we shall see in Chapter 15, some of these disputes have become major causes for international concern in the transition period between the 20th and 21st centuries. These include, for example, clashes between Orthodox Jewish settlers and such militant Palestinian organizations as Hamas in the occupied territories and the continuing warfare between the Armenians and the Azerbaijanis in the former Soviet Union. Religious fervor has also fueled major internal conflicts, such as the genocidal warfare between the Orthodox Serbs, Catholic Croats, and Muslims who battled for control of Bosnia in the mid-1990s, and the persisting and brutal struggles between Muslims and Christian-animists in the Sudan. As was readily apparent by the late-1990s, religious zealotry had also become a major source of a global epidemic of terrorism that was very often directed against the forces of globalization.

Underlying these trends in social interaction and human enterprises were a number of themes that are very likely to become increasingly prominent as the 21st century unfolds. In different ways in Chapters 15 and 16, we will explore both the possibilities for higher living standards and better health that new technologies and ongoing scientific discoveries offer, and the fundamental threats posed by the growth of human populations and the global advance of consumer cultures. Sophisticated computer technologies, for example, and the World Wide Web have made possible a frequency and immediacy of cross-cultural exchanges beyond anything that could have been imagined even a half century ago. They have also created the potential to develop systems of extraction and production that are far more conserving of natural resources and environmentally sustainable than the industrial systems that have dominated the last two centuries. But these advances, many of which are still potential rather than realized, have been more than offset thus far by environmental deterioration and growing shortages of critical resources—perhaps most alarmingly water—over much of the earth. These trends have been accompanied by the emergence of new strains of epidemic disease and the decimation of the nonhuman animal and plant species of the earth. The capacity of humans to curb their material desires, balance the distribution of the earth's bounty, and stem the environmental degradation that is accelerating over much of the planet will go far to determine the course of global history in the 21st century. Given the control humankind now exerts over the planet and its physical resources, this capacity is also likely to shape global history in the centuries beyond.

Chapter 14

The End of the Cold War and the Shape of a New Era

*Early in his first administration, President Ronald Reagan
referred to the Soviet Union as the "Evil Empire" and showed
little interest in cooperating in any way with Moscow. After the
accession of Mikhail Gorbachev, Reagan changed his attitude,
and the two men worked closely to ease tensions between
the two great powers.*

INTRODUCTION

During the second half of the 1980s, the cold war began to wind down, and it ended definitively with the collapse of the Soviet empire. A number of factors contributed to this great change, including shifts in both Chinese and American policy. But intensifying weaknesses within the Soviet system played the greatest role.

The end of the cold war was also part of a larger process in which democratic political systems spread more widely in the world than ever before. During much of the 20th century, democracy had competed with both fascist and communist totalitarianism and also with authoritarian regimes, particularly common in the many new nations. Now, without winning through entirely, democracy gained ground.

By 2004, the framework that had replaced the cold war was not fully defined. The United States stood as the world's only remaining superpower, the only country capable of military intervention literally anywhere in the world. But U.S. policies were not always clear and consistent. And while the nation had unrivaled military technology, it could not in fact intervene everywhere because the regional power even of medium-sized states, like Iran, could make actual invasion too costly to contemplate. China gained new global influence in the wake of the cold war, as did India. At the same time, the place of certain regions in a post–cold war world raised new questions; now that Africa was not wooed by two great rivals, for example, there was a concern that the conti-

nent would be neglected, aside from continued exploitation of resources.

Though the dangers of all-out nuclear war receded, the sense of safety did not increase as much as some optimists had hoped when the cold war ended. Democratic systems gained ground, but in many places their solidity was suspect. There were observers who hailed the "new world order" or the "end of history," as if the cold war's demise ushered in a dramatic new chapter in human existence; but reality, a decade and a half later, seemed messier. Some people came to miss the cold war, partly because they longed for clear-cut rivalries.

This chapter focuses on three themes that defined a new period as the 20th century merged into the 21st: (1) the spread of democracy, which sets part of the new context, (2) the end of the cold war, which provided the most striking events of this new transition, and (3) the resultant emergence of the United States as the world's only superpower, along with reactions to this. All three themes contributed greatly to a changing global experience. Democracy became a global trend in itself, and the end of the cold war, while focused on the Soviet Union and its empire, had wide impact, generating the new position of the United States and bringing American power to bear on many areas.

THE SPREAD OF DEMOCRACY

Democracy, as practiced in western Europe, the United States, Japan, and India, involves fairly open competition

355

among two or more political parties, which can gain or lose power depending on the votes received. The process also involves the existence of enough press freedom to allow this competition to occur. From the late 1970s onward, the tide seemed to turn toward democracy, thus defined, in many regions that had long been inhospitable.

Economic and political success in western Europe, including the drawing power of the Common Market, helped propel Spain, Portugal, and Greece to democratic systems in the mid-1970s, after long periods of authoritarian control. The democratic wave then hit Latin America, backed by U.S. and western European support. Beginning with new regimes in Argentina and Brazil, authoritarian controls were replaced by free elections. The process continued through the 1990s, when literally all Latin American countries except Cuba were in the democratic camp. Revolutionaries and right-wing militarists accepted democracy in the late 1980s; Paraguay was the final authoritarian regime to yield a decade later. In 2000, Mexico elected its first president from a party other than the Party of the Institutionalized Revolution that had monopolized control since the revolution.

Democratic systems gained ground in South Korea and Taiwan in the 1980s. In the Philippines, an authoritarian ruler was cast aside, amid considerable popular pressure, in favor of an elected government. It was at this point that the democratic current had penetrated the Soviet bloc, with democratic systems winning out in most of east-central Europe and Russia itself.

Although most of Africa remained authoritarian, democratic change spread to this region by the 1990s, headed of course by the triumph of democracy over apartheid in South Africa. After new assertions of military control, Nigeria, the continent's most populous country, turned to democracy in 1999. At this point also a near-revolution toppled another authoritarian system, in Indonesia, and replaced it with competitive elections.

Never before had democracy spread so widely, among so many otherwise different societies. Only China, Vietnam, and North Korea held out in East Asia, though China of course constituted a huge exception. Democracy made only halting inroads in the Middle East, aside from Turkey and Israel, and the new post-Soviet states of Central Asia also largely reverted to authoritarian, one-man or one-party rule.

Elsewhere, the relative political stability and economic prosperity of democracies in the West and Japan seemed to win the day. The collapse of European communism removed one of the great global rivals to democ-

racy; communist regimes survived, but they were no longer seeking to convert other parts of the world. The end of the cold war also reduced the Western need to ally with authoritarian regimes as part of a resistance to Soviet power. The United States became more consistent in its encouragement of democratic reforms, under Jimmy Carter and again in the 1990s.

For many societies, the spread of democracy was accompanied also by a growing conversion to free-market economies. It was widely assumed—and urged by the United States—that this combination was more likely to promote economic growth. Even India, though already democratic, reduced its state intervention in the economy. China and Vietnam encouraged market economics, even while resisting democracy in politics. The tide seemed irresistible, but huge questions remained about the future. The new democracies were not always solid. The assumption that democracy would bring economic prosperity made the system vulnerable to disappointed expectations.

THE END OF THE COLD WAR

Advancing democracy set part of the context for the collapse of communism in Russia and east-central Europe, regions with historic ties to the West in any event. Other factors added in, however, in one of the great—and most unexpected—developments of the whole 20th century.

Changing Circumstances

The cold war had lasted for 30 years when its overall context began to shift. The Russian empire had been expanding, off and on, for literally 500 years, interrupted only briefly by World War I and the initial phases of the Russian Revolution before it resumed its growth, to unprecedented levels. What could cause these two firmly established patterns, the cold war and the Russian empire, to change course dramatically?

A final verdict, of course is not in, for the developments are very recent, making perspective difficult. As historians assemble an analysis of causes, a number of factors must inevitably be considered, for great change almost invariably responds to a combination of developments.

Leadership is surely one component. After Stalin and then Khrushchev, Soviet leadership had turned conservative. Party bureaucrats, eager to protect the status quo, often advanced only mediocre people to top posts, men whose major leadership characteristic was their unwillingness to rock the boat. Many of these leaders then continued to hold power when their own aptitude declined with illness and age.

Of more general significance was the reassertion of initiative from some parts of the world surrounding the Soviet Union, despite continued pressures from the superpowers. The rise of Islamic fervor, evident in the Iranian Revolution of 1979, inevitably created anxiety in the Soviet Union with its large Muslim minority. To reduce this new threat, the Soviets invaded neighboring Afghanistan late in 1979, hoping to set up a puppet regime that would protect Russian interests. The war proved difficult, as Afghan guerrillas, with some backing from the United States, held their ground fiercely. Costs and casualties mounted, and the war—the first formal action the Soviets had indulged in since World War II—quickly proved unpopular at home.

At the same time, the success of western Europe's economy pushed communism into a defensive and retreating posture throughout Eastern Europe. The attraction of Western institutions and consumer standards gained ground. Within the Soviet empire itself, a new free trade union movement resumed in Poland, which was linked to the Catholic Church. Although this movement was repressed through Soviet-mandated martial law in 1981, the stress of keeping the lid on would continue to increase.

Changes in Chinese policy entered in. China of course had separated itself from Soviet direction in the 1960s. But in 1978 the regime made its choice to participate in the world economy and to admit more market forces and competitive free enterprise in the internal economy as well. There was no relaxation of political controls, and a democratic movement was vigorously quashed in 1989. But the Chinese economy now differed dramatically from that of the Soviet Union, and change was quickly rewarded, both with international investment and with rapid growth. The Soviets now had to contend not only with China's massive population, but with its superior economic performance.

Finally, U.S. diplomatic policy tightened. While President Jimmy Carter hoped to reduce tensions in the late 1970s, he was a vigorous human rights advocate, particularly eager to point out Soviet deficiencies. American conservatives heightened their own opposition to the Soviet Union. A new strategic arms limitation agreement (SALT II) was negotiated in 1979, but quickly encountered resistance in the U.S. Senate. After the Soviets moved into Afghanistan, President Carter reacted vigorously, claiming that the incursion was a "stepping stone to their possible control over much of the world's oil supplies" and, even more dramatically, the "gravest threat to world peace since World War II." American participation in the 1980 Moscow Olympics was cancelled.

Then, in 1980, the new, conservative president, Ronald Reagan, who had denounced the Soviet Union as an "evil empire," announced a massive increase in U.S. defense spending. Domestic programs were cut (promoting, among other things, a surge in homelessness), but conservatives accepted a growing budget deficit in favor of the new military outlays. The president also announced a "Reagan doctrine" of assisting anticommunism anywhere, and followed up with an invasion of a small, Marxist controlled Caribbean island, Grenada, and support for anti-Marxist military action in Central America.

These moves put new pressure on the Soviets, already stretched to the limit to maintain military and global competition with the United States, and beset with an unpopular war and new regional pressures as well. The stage was set for the events that, initially promoted for quite different reasons, undid the cold war.

The Explosion of the 1980s and 1990s

From 1985 onward the Soviet Union entered a period of intensive reform, soon matched by new political movements in Eastern Europe that effectively dismantled the Soviet empire. The initial trigger for this extraordinary and unanticipated upheaval lay in the deteriorating Soviet economic performance, intensified by the costs of military rivalry with the United States. There were reasons for pride in the Soviet system as well, and many observers believed that public attitudes by the 1980s were shaped much less by terror than by satisfaction with the Soviet Union's world prestige and the improvements the Communist regime had fostered in education and welfare. But, to a degree unperceived outside the Soviet Union, the economy was grinding to a standstill. Forced industrialization had produced extensive environmental deterioration throughout Eastern Europe. According to Soviet estimates, half of all agricultural land was endangered by the late 1980s; more than 20 percent of Soviet citizens lived in regions of ecological disaster. Rates and severity of respiratory and other diseases rose, impairing both morale and economic performance. Infant mortality rates also rose in several regions, sometimes to among the highest levels in the world.

More directly, industrial production began to stagnate and even drop as a result of rigid central planning, health problems, and poor worker morale. Alcoholism increased, with direct impacts on productivity and on mortality rates. Growing inadequacy of housing and common goods resulted, further lowering motivation. As economic growth stopped, the percentage of resources allocated to military production escalated, toward a third of all national income. This reduced funds available for other investments or for consumer needs. At first only privately, younger leaders began to recognize that the system was near collapse.

The Age of Reform

Yet the Soviet system was not changeless, despite its heavy bureaucratization. Problems and dissatisfactions, though controlled, could provoke response beyond renewed repression. After a succession of leaders whose age or health precluded major initiatives, the Soviet Union in 1985 brought a new, younger official to the fore. Mikhail Gorbachev quickly renewed some of the earlier attacks on Stalinist rigidity and replaced some of the old-line party bureaucrats. He conveyed a new, more Western style, dressing in fashionable clothes (and accompanied by his stylish wife), holding relatively open press conferences, and even allowing the Soviet media to engage in active debate and report on problems as well as successes. Gorbachev also further altered the Soviet Union's modified cold war stance. He urged a reduction in nuclear armament, and in 1987 he negotiated a new agreement with the United States that limited medium-range missiles in Europe. He ended the war in Afghanistan, bringing Soviet troops home.

Internally, Gorbachev proclaimed a policy of *glasnost,* or openness, which implied new freedom to comment and criticize. He pressed particularly for a reduction in bureaucratic inefficiency and unproductive labor in the Soviet economy, encouraging more decentralized decision making and the use of some market incentives to stimulate greater output. The sweep of Gorbachev's reforms, as opposed to an undeniable new tone in Soviet public relations, remained difficult to assess. Strong limits on political freedom persisted, and it was unclear whether Gorbachev could cut through the centralized planning apparatus that controlled the main lines of the Soviet economy. There was also uncertainty about how well the new leader could balance reform and stability.

Indeed, questions about Gorbachev's prospects recalled many basic issues in Soviet history. In many ways Gorbachev's policies constituted a return to a characteristic ambivalence about the West as he reduced Soviet isolation while continuing to criticize aspects of Western political and social structure. Gorbachev clearly hoped to use some Western management techniques and was open to certain Western cultural styles without, however, intending to abandon basic control of the Communist state. Western analysts wondered if the Soviet economy could improve worker motivation without embracing a Western-style consumerism or whether computers could be more widely introduced without allowing freedom for information exchange.

Gorbachev also sought to open the Soviet Union to fuller participation in the world economy, recognizing that isolation in a separate empire had restricted access to new technology and limited motivation to change. Although the new leadership did not rush to make foreign trade or investment too easy—considerable suspicion persisted—the economic initiatives brought symbolic changes, such as the opening of a McDonald's restaurant in Moscow and a whole array of new contacts between Soviet citizens and foreigners.

Gorbachev's initial policies did not quickly stir the Soviet economy, but they had immediate political effects, some of which the reform leader had almost certainly not anticipated. The keynote of the reform program was *perestroika,* or economic restructuring, which Gorbachev translated into more leeway for private ownership and decentralized control in industry and agriculture. Farmers, for example, could now lease land for 50 years, with rights of inheritance, and industrial concerns were authorized to buy from either private or state operations. Foreign investment was encouraged. Gorbachev pressed for reductions in Soviet military commitments, particularly through agreements with the United States on troop reductions and limitations on nuclear weaponry, in order to free resources for consumer goods industries. He urged more self-help among the Soviets, including a reduction in drinking, arguing that he wanted to "rid public opinion of . . . faith in a 'good Tsar,' the all powerful center, the notion that someone can bring about order and organize perestroika from on high." Politically, he encouraged a new constitution in 1988, giving considerable power to a new parliament, the Congress of People's Deputies, and abolishing the Communist monopoly on elections.

More than any other leader, Mikhail Gorbachev effected the changes that brought an end to the cold war. Here he works to convince independence-minded Lithuanians of the advantages of staying in the Soviet Union.

Important opposition groups developed both inside and outside the party, pressing Gorbachev between radicals who wanted a faster pace of reform and conservative hard-liners. Gorbachev himself was elected to a new, powerful presidency of the Soviet Union in 1990.

Reform amid continued economic stagnation provoked agitation among minority nationalities in the Soviet Union, from 1988 onward. Muslims and Armenian Christians rioted in the south, both against each other and against the central state. Baltic nationalist and other European minorities also stirred, some insisting on independence (notably in Lithuania), some pressing for greater autonomy.

Even social issues were given uncertain new twists. Gorbachev noted that Soviet efforts to establish equality between the sexes had burdened women with a combination of work and household duties. His solution—to allow women to "return to their purely womanly missions" of housework, child rearing, and "the creation of a good family atmosphere"—had a somewhat old-fashioned ring to it.

Dismantling the Soviet Empire

Gorbachev's new approach, including his desire for better relations with Western powers, prompted more definitive results outside the Soviet Union than within, as the smaller states of Eastern Europe uniformly moved for greater independence and internal reforms. Bulgaria moved for economic liberalization in 1987 but was held back by the Soviets; pressure resumed in 1989 as the party leader was ousted and free elections were arranged. Hungary changed leadership in 1988 and installed a non-Communist president. A new constitution and free elections were planned, as the Communist Party renamed itself Socialist. Hungary also reviewed its great 1956 rising, formally declaring it "a popular uprising . . . against an oligarchic system . . . which had humiliated the nation." Hungary moved rapidly toward a free-market economy. Poland installed a non-Communist government in 1988 and again moved quickly to dismantle the state-run economy; prices rose rapidly as government subsidies were withdrawn. The Solidarity movement, born a decade before through a merger of non-Communist labor leaders and Catholic intellectuals, became the dominant political force. East Germany displaced its Communist government in 1989, expelling key leaders and moving rapidly toward unification with West Germany. The Berlin Wall was dismantled, and in 1990 non-Communists won a free election. German unification occurred in 1991, a dramatic sign of the collapse of postwar Soviet foreign policy. Czechoslovakia installed a new government in 1989, headed by a playwright, and sought to introduce free elections and a more market-driven economy.

Although mass demonstrations played a key role in several of these political upheavals, only in Romania was there outright violence, as an exceptionally authoritarian Communist leader was swept out by force. As in Bulgaria, the Communist Party retained considerable power, though under new leadership, and reforms moved less rapidly than in Hungary and Czechoslovakia. The same held true for Albania, where the unreconstructed Stalinist regime was dislodged and a more flexible Communist leadership installed.

New divergences in the nature and extent of reform in Eastern Europe were exacerbated by clashes among nationalities, as in the Soviet Union. Change and uncertainty

Post–1989 East-Central Europe and Central Asia

brought older attachments to the fore. Romanians and ethnic Hungarians clashed; Bulgarians attacked a Turkish minority left over from the Ottoman period. In 1991 the Yugoslavian Communist regime, though not Soviet-dominated, also came under attack, and a civil war boiled up from disputes among nationalities. Minority nationality areas, notably Slovenia, Croatia, and Bosnia-Herzogovina, proclaimed independence, but the national, Serbian-dominated army applied massive force to preserve the Yugoslav nation.

Amid this rapid and unexpected change, prospects for the future became unpredictable. Few of the new governments fully defined their constitutional structure, and amid innovation the range of new political parties almost compelled later consolidations. Like the Soviet Union it-

self, all the Eastern European states suffered from sluggish production and massive pollution—economic problems with the potential to lead to new political discontent.

With state controls and protection abruptly withdrawn by 1991, tensions over the first results of the introduction of the market economy in Poland brought rising unemployment and further price increases. These in turn produced growing disaffection from the Solidarity leadership. Diplomatic linkages among small states—a critical problem area between the two world wars—also had yet to be resolved.

The massive change in Soviet policy was clear. Gorbachev reversed postwar imperialism completely, stating that "any nation has the right to decide its fate by itself." In several cases, notably Hungary, Soviet troops were rapidly withdrawn, and generally it seemed unlikely that a repressive attempt to reestablish an empire would be possible. New contacts with Western nations, particularly in the European Economic Community, seemed to promise further realignment in the future.

Renewed Turmoil in 1991 and 1992

The uncertainties of the situation within the Soviet Union were confirmed in the summer of 1991, when an attempted coup was mounted by military and police elements. Gorbachev's presidency and democratic decentralization were both threatened. Massive popular demonstrations, however, asserted the strong democratic current that had developed in the Soviet Union since 1986. The contrast with earlier Soviet history and the suppression of democracy in China two years before were striking.

In the aftermath of the attempted coup, Gorbachev's authority weakened. Leadership of the key republics, including the massive Russian Republic, became relatively stronger. The three Baltic states used the occasion to gain full independence, though economic links with the Soviet Union remained. Other minority republics proclaimed independence as well, but Gorbachev struggled to win agreement on continued economic union and some other coordination. By the end of 1991 leaders of the major republics, including Russia's Boris Yeltsin, proclaimed the end of the Soviet Union, projecting a commonwealth of the leading republics, including the economically crucial Ukraine, in its stead.

Amid the disputes Gorbachev fell from power, doomed by his attempts to salvage a presidency that depended on some survival of a greater Soviet Union. His leadership role was taken over by Boris Yeltsin, who as president of Russia and an early renouncer of communism now emerged as the leading, though quickly beleaguered, political figure.

The resulting Commonwealth of Independent States won tentative agreement from most of the now independent republics. But tensions immediately surfaced about economic coordination amid rapid dismantling of state controls; about control of the military, where Russia—still by far the largest unit—sought predominance, including nuclear control amid challenges from the Ukraine and from Kazakhstan (two of the other republics with nuclear weaponry on their soil); and about relationships between the European-dominated republics, including Russia, and the cluster of Central Asian states. How much unity might survive in the former Soviet Union was unclear.

The fate of economic reform was also uncertain, as Russian leaders hesitated to convert to a full market system lest transitional disruption further antagonize the population. Here again, more radical plans emerged at the end of 1991, calling for removal of most government price controls.

Nor, finally, was it clear what role remained for the once proud Communist Party or what political movements would replace it. Russian leaders sought to outlaw the party for its leadership of the failed coup, but an alternative party system emerged only slowly. Citizens took new delight in tearing down the old emblems of the revolution, including massive socialist realist statues of Lenin. Even old tsarist flags and uniforms were trotted out for display. But effective new emblems had yet to be generated. Furthermore, in some republics, including Central Asia, party leadership retained considerable vigor.

Russia itself faced internal unrest even after the basic dissolution of its empire. A Muslim region, Chechnya, rebelled against Moscow in 1994, bringing massive military retaliation. But the Chechen rebels could not be entirely repressed, as they generated periodic terrorism in other parts of the Soviet Union, on into the 21st century.

Democracy After the Cold War

It is clear the end of the cold war reflected and contributed to the global spread of democracy. But setbacks and qualifications emerged as well, including the fact that not all of the former Soviet republics accepted this political form. In Russia, Vladimir Putin, a former secret police official, won the presidency in 2000. By this point the Soviet economy was improving, partly on the basis of oil exports, though the conversion to private enterprise remained incomplete. Putin paid lip service to democracy, but steadily reduced the effective freedom of the press and arrested some political opponents. The majority of the Russian people approved this turn toward greater authoritarianism; polls suggested only modest support for democracy, as opposed to an emphasis on order.

In some other countries economic difficulties raised new questions about the acceptance of democracy. In Venezuela a new president claimed a popular mandate and seemed impatient with a normal democratic political process. His support came largely from promises to aid ordinary people, in a style reminiscent of earlier Latin American authoritarians. Another set of questions developed as

DOCUMENT

Democratic Protest and Repression in China

On June 4, 1989, Chinese troops marched on political protesters, many of them students, camped in Beijing's central Tiananmen Square. The protesters had been agitating for weeks for a more open, democratic system and against communist one-party control. The military move caused hundreds of deaths and additional political imprisonments and exiles. It crushed the protest movement, differentiating China from the many other societies that were establishing new democracies at that time. (The imminent visit of Russia's democratizing president, Mikhail Gorbachev, was one spur to the protesters.) China continued, instead, its interesting experiment with authoritarian politics amid rapid economic change.

The following document is excerpted from a speech given on Chinese television in mid-May by Li Peng, a leading Communist Party official. It establishes the kind of reasoning that, to the government, justified its later repression. The speech mixes some standard government claims about the nature of protest with some specific Chinese as well as communist traditions concerning politics and order.

> Comrades, in accordance with a decision made by the Standing Committee of the CPC Central Committee, the party Central Committee and the State Council have convened a meeting here of cadres from party, government, and army organs at the central and Beijing municipal levels, calling on everyone to mobilize in this emergency and to adopt resolute and effective measures to curb turmoil in a clear-cut manner, to restore normal order in society, and to maintain stability and unity in order to ensure the triumphant implementation of our reform and open policy and the program of socialist modernization [applause].
>
> The current situation in the capital is quite grim. The anarchic state is going from bad to worse. Law and discipline have been undermined. Prior to the beginning of

May, the situation had begun to cool down as a result of great efforts. However, the situation has become more turbulent since the beginning of May. More and more students and other people have been involved in demonstrations. Many institutions of higher learning have come to a standstill. Traffic jams have taken place everywhere. The party and government leading organs have been affected, and public security has been rapidly deteriorating. All this has seriously disturbed and undermined the normal order of production, work, study, and everyday life of the people in the whole municipality. Some activities on the agenda for state affairs of the Sino-Soviet summit that attracted worldwide attention had to be canceled, greatly damaging China's international image and prestige. The activities of some of the students on hunger strike at Tiananmen Square have not yet been stopped completely. Their health is seriously deteriorating and some of their lives are still in imminent danger. In fact, a handful of persons are using the hunger strikes as hostages to coerce and force the party and the government to yield to their political demands. In this regard, they have not one iota of humanity [applause].

> The party and the government have, on one hand, taken every possible measure, to treat and rescue the fasting students. On the other hand, they have held several dialogues with representatives of the fasting students and have earnestly promised to continue to listen to their opinions in the future, in the hope that the students would stop their hunger strike immediately. But, the dialogues did not yield results as expected. The square is packed with extremely excited crowds who keep shouting demagogic slogans. Right now, representatives of the hunger striking students say that they can no longer control the situation. If we fail to promptly put an end to such a state of affairs and let it go unchecked, it will likely lead to serious consequences which none of us want to see.
>
> The situation in Beijing is still developing, and has already affected many other cities in the country. In many places, the number of demonstrators and protestors is increasing. In some places, there have been many inci-

the United States, newly concerned about Islamic terrorism, began supporting authoritarian regimes in central Asia and in Pakistan in return for assistance against this new threat.

It remained true that, in 2004, the democratic tide was confirmed in most areas where the system had taken hold. In 2003 the United States invaded Iraq and overthrew the dictatorial regime of Saddam Hussein. Though America promised to create a democratic system in the occupied country, an ill-prepared postconquest administration, the wartime devastation of Iraq's quite developed infrastructure, and a combination of resistance on the part of internal dissidents and Islamic militant groups from abroad has so far stymied recon-

dents of people breaking into local party and government organs, along with beating, smashing, looting, burning, and other undermining activities that seriously violated the law. Some trains running on major railway lines have even been intercepted, causing communications to stop. Something has happened to our trunk line, the Beijing-Guangzhou line. Today, a train from Fuzhou was intercepted. The train was unable to move out for several hours. All these incidents demonstrate that we will have nationwide major turmoil if no quick action is taken to turn and stabilize the situation. Our nation's reforms and opening to the outside world, the cause of the modernization [program], and even the fate and future of the People's Republic of China, built by many revolutionary martyrs with their blood, are facing a serious threat [applause].

Our party and government have pointed out time and time again that the vast numbers of young students are kindhearted, that subjectively they do not want turmoil, and that they have fervent patriotic spirit, wishing to push forward reform, develop democracy, and overcome corruption. This is also in line with the goals which the party and government have striven to accomplish. It should be said that many of the questions and views they raise have already exerted and will continue to exert positive influence on improving the work of the party and government. However, willfully using various forms of demonstrations, boycotts of class, and even hunger strikes to make petitions have damaged social stability and will not be beneficial to solving the problems. . . .

One important reason for us to take a clear-cut stand in opposing the turmoil and exposing the political conspiracy of a handful of people is to distinguish the masses of young students from the handful of people who incited the turmoil. For almost a month, we adopted an extremely tolerant and restrained attitude in handling the student unrest. No government in the world would be so tolerant. The reason that we were so tolerant was out of our loving care for the masses of youths and students. We regard them as our own children and the future of China. We do not want to hurt good people, particularly not the young students. However, the handful of behind-the-scenes people, who were plotting and inciting the turmoil, miscalculated and took the tolerance as weakness on the part of the party and government. They continued to cook up stories to confuse and poison the masses, in an attempt to worsen the situation. This has caused the situation in the capital and many localities across the country to become increasingly acute. Under such circumstances, the CPC, as a ruling party and a government responsible to the people, is forced to take resolute and decisive measures to put an end to the turmoil [applause].

Comrades, our party is a party in power and our government is a people's government. To be responsible to our sacred motherland and to all people, we must adopt firm and resolute measures to end the turmoil swiftly, to maintain the leadership of the party as well as the socialist system. We believe that our actions will surely have the support of all members of the Communist Party and the Communist Youth League, as well as workers, peasants, intellectuals, democratic parties, people in various circles, and the broad masses [applause].

We believe that we will certainly have the backing of the People's Liberation Army [PLA], which is entrusted by the Constitution with guarding the country and the peaceful work of the people [applause]. At the same time, we also hope that the broad masses will fully support the PLA, the public security cadres, and the police in their efforts to maintain order in the capital [applause].

Questions: Why does Li Peng object to the protest movement? How does he try to persuade ordinary Chinese that the protest should cease? What arguments resemble those many governments use against protest? What arguments reflect more distinctively Chinese traditions or communist values? Why did the Chinese decide to repress political democracy?

Source: From http://www.tsquare.tv/chronology/MartialLaw.html.

---

struction and the installation of a democratic system. The resistance has also forced an ongoing and costly commitment of mostly American and British forces in the region, and it has generated widespread hostility to the United States worldwide. The deep divisions between Iraq's three main ethnic-religious groups—the Sunnis, Shi'as and Kurds also threaten to destroy whatever is left of the artificial state put together by the British after World War I.

THE GREAT POWERS

The end of the cold war and the spread of democracy raised important issues for the world's leading powers.

Most obviously, the United States became the lone superpower, the only country with the capability of military intervention around the globe—at least through its dominance in air power; operations on land were far less uniformly feasible. Russian power declined dramatically. The nation faced severe economic problems, as economic growth was limited. Military forces were cut back, a portion of the fleet simply left to rust in harbors. By 2001 military spending, at $4 billion a year, was only one-thirtieth of that of the United States (where levels remained high). The splitting off of Ukraine and Kazakhstan, where some former Soviet missiles had been mounted, further reduced Russian capacity. The United States contributed a bit of funding to help pay for the retirement of some missiles and nuclear weapons. Russian weaponry remained considerable, though its state of readiness was questionable. Russian leaders alternated between playing up to the United States and Western powers and attempting to assert a more independent role. They enjoyed some success in influencing some of the former Soviet republics, notably Belarus and Moldova, through political alliances, economic influence, and even continued troop placement. But there was no question that the Russian counterweight to the United States was a thing of the past.

Other countries worried visibly about unchallenged American strength. China in particular alternated between seeking favorable economic arrangements with the U.S. government (China enjoyed a great balance of trade advantage with the United States) and seeking to increase military rivalry. China's claims to control Taiwan, combined with U.S. involvement in defense of the island, were a particularly fruitful source of tension. China's military buildup, however, did not threaten the United States directly. Efforts to forge alliances against U.S. power, by greater cooperation with Russia or with other countries like Iran, roused United States concern but they did not emerge as full-fledged partnerships.

By 2001, even western European countries expressed some misgivings about U.S. strength, particularly when the United States seemed to ignore international collaboration in areas such as the environment. After 2000, in fact, the United States rejected a growing number of proposed international agreements, not only on the environment but also on such measures as banning land mines. In 2001, in an interesting gesture of anti-Americanism, the United Nations excluded the United States from membership on its Human Rights Commission, the first time this had happened since the commission was formed.

The expansion of the European Union, to include former communist states like Poland and Hungary as well as other nations like Cyprus, was not motivated by anti-Americanism directly. But there was an awareness that an expanded Europe might provide more economic counterweight to the United States. The EU itself introduced further moves toward economic integration, notably a new single currency, the euro (not accepted by all members) which was introduced with surprising success in 2002. A more explicit wedge between much of Europe and the United States occurred in 2003, when the United States ignored strong majorities in many European countries opposed to intervention in Iraq. Growing questions also arose about the old NATO alliance. It survived, and even expanded to include the Baltic States, Poland and other east-central European nations still somewhat fearful of Russia. But efforts to use NATO for a wider world role, mainly at the urging of the United States, had little effect, and it became increasingly unclear what the alliance was for.

Still, no systematic counterpoise to U.S. power emerged in the 15 years after the cold war's end. U.S. power was indeed enhanced, through most of the 1990s, by unusually rapid economic growth and by U.S. leadership in burgeoning new fields of information technology and bioengineering. Even Japan did not keep pace with U.S. innovations in technology and business organization, as the Pacific Rim encountered new economic difficulties at the very end of the 20th century. The United States also continued to maintain high levels of military spending, including investments in ever-more-sophisticated military technology. Hopes that the end of the cold war might significantly reduce the military burden in the United States were not widely realized. The Iraq war of 2003, with American air and land units rapidly defeating the conventional forces arrayed against them, revealed the great advances in American military might in the post–cold-war years, despite the problems of the ensuing occupation where technological sophistication counted for much less. The United States opened a growing gap with the military levels even of its west European allies.

What was the United States to do with its world power? U.S. leaders clearly felt emboldened to tell other parts of the world how to organize their societies. Both business and political experts argued that the U.S. model of a free market economy should be adopted everywhere—for example, as a cure-all against the economic doldrums of the more state-directed Pacific Rim. The United States also sought to use its leadership to resolve some longstanding world tensions. President Bill Clinton did contribute to the reduction of Catholic–Protestant tensions in Northern Ireland, and he worked tirelessly,

In the last decade of the 20th century in both the Balkans and, as this photo of Tutsi victims attests, in Rwanda in east-central Africa, the specter of genocide returned yet again to a century that had seen more episodes of this most extreme form of human violence against other humans than any other period in global history.

though without success, to reach a settlement between Israelis and Palestinians. U.S. leaders also worried about new kinds of threats that would replace the old great-power confrontations. Thus they identified small nations that sponsored terrorism or that might manage to send isolated but deadly nuclear weapons against the United States, such as Iran, Iraq, or North Korea. These threats were used to justify considerable military expenditure in the United States and focused new efforts to assemble allies willing to pressure or isolate what the United States sometimes termed "rogue states" or an "axis of evil."

We will see in the following chapter that the United States also took a direct role in a number of regional conflicts during the 1990s, but it also stayed out of other situations, worrying about the risks and costs of being the world's policeman. Most obviously, major clashes in Africa, at times involving massive slaughter, as in the Rwanda genocide, characteristically found the United States urging peace but providing little direct support.

Two sources of the complexity of the post–cold-war world thus emerged: the lack of a clear definition of the uses of U.S. power and an edginess about this power in many countries that could not, however, come up with a clear alternative.

The massive terrorist attack on the United States in 2001 raised another set of issues. Clearly, U.S. power was drawing hostility from groups concerned both about specific policies in the Middle East and about wider U.S. power or, as they termed it, arrogance. To the Middle Eastern terrorists, the United States interfered with Middle Eastern countries, defiling "sacred ground" by stationing troops in Saudi Arabia and offending further by strongly supporting Israel. U.S. bombing raids on places like Iraq were taken as a sign of military might run out of control. There was also resentment of U.S. cultural influence and its promotion of more open sexuality and materialism. The terrorist response—hijacking airliners to crash into buildings symbolic of U.S. financial and military might—killed approximately 3,000 people, but the terrorists regarded this as justifiable retaliation against a nation they could not hope to fight by conventional means. Initially backed by most of the world's nations, the United States vowed to end terrorism. Its 2001 invasion of Afghanistan toppled an extremist regime that had harbored the leading terrorist network. But the 2003 attack on Iraq, which U.S. leaders claimed was part of the same war on terror, had less conclusive results and consumed extensive American military resources while also infuriating Muslim and wider world opinion. Clearly, a new dynamic was underway, with unclear prospects for the future. Was this conflict, between terrorists and their enemies headed by the United States, the new framework for 21st century world history?

ANALYSIS

How Much Historical Change?

As the cold war drew to a close, a number of analysts, primarily in the United States, looked forward to dramatic shifts in human affairs. There were two related lines of argument. The first, summed up in the "end of history" concept, emphasized the new dominance of the democratic form of government. The contest among political and economic systems, particularly between democracy and communism, was over; democracy would now sweep over the world. With this, the need for basic questioning about political institutions would also end: Democracy worked best, and it was here to stay. Further, the change in political structure also had implications for power rivalries. Some analysts contended that democracies never war on each other. Once the people control affairs of state through their votes, the selfishness and power trips that lead to war would end. Ordinary people understand the horror of war. They appreciate the common humanity they share with other democratic peoples. Just as democracy resolves internal conflicts through votes, democracies resolve external conflicts through bargaining and compromise. People do not vote for wars of aggression, at most sanctioning defense against attack.

Another argument, that might be combined with the democracy approach, focused on the spread of consumer capitalism around the world. Put forward in a popular book *The Lexus and the Olive Tree,* by a U.S. journalist, Thomas Friedman, the consumer capitalism approach emphasized the benefits of a global economy. In this, everyone would gain access to greater material abundance and the wonders of consumerism, and they would not wish to jeopardize this prosperity through war. Shared interests, rather than traditional disputes over limited resources, would carry the day.

These kinds of arguments assumed that the world was poised to depart substantially from prior history, based on new political systems or new economic systems or both. This is a challenging kind of forecasting because it cannot be easily disproved, until the future does or does not correspond to the dramatic projections. The consumerism argument, particularly, had no precedent in the past. At the same time, the predictions also could not be proved, for example by pointing to some prior historical analogy. How, then, should they be assessed?

Questions: Was the world changing so rapidly and fundamentally as these predictions implied? Were new systems spreading as uniformly and consistently as the democracy and global consumerism arguments implied? Were past rivalries and cultural and institutional commitments to war and dispute so easily wiped away?

A Challenge: Read one of the optimistic predictions in the wake of the cold war, like Francis Fukuyama's *End of History* or Thomas Friedman's *The Lexus and the Olive Tree.* Why do they think things are headed in such a clearly good direction? How do their predictions look in light of developments over the past five years? Have they been disproved or merely complicated? How much should American policy be based on predictions of this sort?

CONCLUSION: NEW TRENDS IN THE POST-COLD WAR ERA

The spread of democracy and the end of the cold war helped promote two other changes in world affairs, that were frankly contradictory. The first change evolved as a set of processes many people called globalization. This involved increasingly intense interactions among the world's societies — economic, cultural, political, and environmental. With Russia and China now participating actively in connections with the rest of the world, and with major technological changes that accelerated contacts, a new chapter opened in the level of global integration. The power of the United States promoted these trends as well, though many other societies were active in promoting and shaping the globalization process.

At the same time, new divisions and tensions surfaced as well. Some of these, as we have seen, resulted directly from the end of the cold war. The collapse of the Soviet system revived more local nationalisms in parts of east-central Europe and Central Asia. But the end of the cold war also reduced some earlier barriers to regional clashes: Russia no longer had the power to intervene against developments that might weaken its world position, and the United States was not willing or able to regulate every conflict. Old rivalries flared up in this new context, while a host of new ethnic and religious tensions surfaced in some regions, particularly Africa. Many conflicts were also shaped by a larger resurgence of religious fervor. The revival of religion had deeper roots than the end of the cold war, but the end of cold war rivalries gave it new scope. Religious resurgence bore a complex relationship to the spread of democracy, for it often gained ground where people did not have opportunities for democratic expression but it was not necessarily committed to democratic principles in return.

Both globalization and the rise of regional clashes affected the position of the United States as superpower. The nation backed many aspects of globalization, particularly in economic and cultural domains, though it resisted global intrusions on national sovereignty. Regional clashes prompted U.S. efforts to restore the peace and occasionally led to direct intervention. For some regional leaders, the United States emerged as a direct enemy because of its power position and its promotion of globalization. American policymakers struggled in turn to define the situations and ways in which national power would be used in the post–cold war world.

The passing of the cold war, the spread of democracy and the new position of the United States represented huge changes in world society on the eve of a new century. The reduction of the threat of all-out nuclear conflict was a major development in itself. But the results also facilitated other trends and other tensions. The 1990s and the first years of the 21st century saw some spectacular achievements in global integration. They also witnessed a troubling amount of death and destruction. We turn in the next chapter to the twin processes of globalization and regional and religious rivalry.

FURTHER READING

On the future of NATO, see Martin A. Smith, *NATO in the First Decade After the Cold War* (2000).

On the struggle to build the European Community, see G. W. White, *Nationalism and Territory: Constructing Group Identity in Southeastern Europe* (2000); T. L. Friedman, *The Lexus and the Olive Tree: Understanding Globalization* (2000); and Andrew Valls, ed., *Ethics in International Affairs: Themes and Cases* (2000).

The internal dissolution of the Soviet leadership in the 1980s and 1990s is explored by David Kotz and Fred Weir in *Revolution from Above: The Demise of the Soviet System* (1997). Mikhail Gorbachev's *Memoirs* (1995) is the central participant's reflections on the end of the Soviet Union. Raymond L. Garthoff's *The Great Transition: American-Soviet Relations at the End of the Cold War* (1994) provides the foreign policy context. Karen Dawisha and Bruce Parrott, eds., *The Consolidation of Democracy in East-Central Europe* (1997), discusses recent experience toward democratization and includes a country-by-country survey. Nanette Funk and Magda Mueller's *Gender Politics and Post-Communism: Reflections from Eastern Europe and the Former Soviet Union* (1993) deals with women's role in the transition. Tina Rosenberg's *The Haunted Land: Facing Europe's Ghosts After Communism* (1995) is an engaging narrative that explores the legacies of repression in Germany, Poland, and the Czech Republic. For problems in part of the region, see Paul Hockenos, *Free to Hate: The Rise of the Right in Post-Communist Eastern Europe* (1994).

ON THE WEB

A beginning study of the final breakup of the Soviet Union and the changes in its former republics since 1991 can be found at

http://www.learner.org/exhibits/russia

The role of Mikhail Gorbachev in the endgame of the Soviet Empire is explored at

http://www.cs.indiana.edu/~dmiguse/Russian/mgbio .html

http://www.mikhailgorbachev.org/

Boris Yeltsin's parallel role in that event is discussed at

http://www.cs.indiana.edu/~dmiguse/Russian/bybio .html

http://en.wikipedia.org/wiki/Boris_Yeltsin

The social, political, and economic "perestroika" or restructuring of the Soviet state they favored is described at

http://www.ibiblio.org/expo/soviet.exhibit/perest.html

The demise of the Berlin Wall is traced in text, video, and photographs at

http://207.25.71.25/resources/video.almanac/1989/ index3.html

http://members.aol.com/johball/berlinw2.htm

http://userpage.chemie.fu-berlin.de/BIW/wall.html

http://nhs.needham.k12.ma.us/cur/Baker_00/2001_p4/
Baker_dr_bd_mh_p4/berlin_wall.htm

For the subsequent breakup of Yugoslavia and the continuing crisis in the Balkans, see

http://www.truthinmedia.org

or the "beginner's guide to the Balkans" at

http://abcnews.go.com/sections/world/balkans_content/

The collapse of the communist regime in Romania was unique in its level of violence due to the unpopularity of its egomaniacal Communist ruler, Nicolae Ceaucescu. His bloody fall is described at

http://www.globalsecurity.org/military/world/war/
romania.htm

The Web also offers resources for the study of Vaclav Havel at

http://www.hrad.cz/president/Havel/ cvp_uk.html

His Velvet Revolution is discussed at

http://www.radio.cz/ history/history15.html

As NATO and the Warsaw Pact seem to be merging, it is appropriate to examine their parallel histories and the impact of their past antagonisms on world history, an effort attempted at

http://www.isn.ethz.ch/php/

An examination of the nature and future of NATO, and analyses of recent events and significant speeches in Europe, as well as analyses of NATO actions, can be found at

http://www.nato.int/

The European quest for union is explored at

http://www.eurunion.org
http://europa.eu.int/index_en.htm

Globalization and Its Enemies: The Challenges of Fashioning a 21st-Century World Order

The mixtures of peoples and cultures that had become such a predominant feature of world history by the end of the 20th century is wonderfully illustrated by this group of Muslim schoolchildren in a French school.

Chronology

1988	Soviet withdrawal from Afghanistan
1989–1990	Collapse of the Soviet Union and Warsaw Pact regimes
1990	Iraqi invasion of Kuwait
1991	Gulf War, U.S.-led coalition defeats Iraq
1991	Slovenia and Croatia secede from Yugoslavia
1992	North American Free Trade Agreement (NAFTA) inaugurated
1992	Bosnia withdraws from Yugoslavia
1992–1993	UN–U.S. interventions in Somalia
1992	First World Environmental Conference in Brazil
1994	Mass genocide in Rwanda
1994	U.S. intervention in Haiti
1995	U.S.–NATO interventions in Bosnia
1997	Second World Environmental Conference, Kyoto, Japan
1998	Serbian assault on Albanians in Kosovo
1999	U.S.–NATO war against Yugoslavia
2000	International Human Rights Conference, South Africa
2000–2002	Second Intifada in Palestine and Israel
2001	Mass demonstrations against the World Trade Organization in Genoa
2001	Terrorist attacks on the World Trade Center and the Pentagon
2001	U.S.–Northern Alliance coalition topples the Taliban regime in Afghanistan
2002	India and Pakistan mobilize armies over Kashmir dispute
2003	Outbreak of Severe Acute Respiratory Syndrome (SARS) in China, Canada, and elsewhere.
2003	U.S.-led invasion of Iraq; end of Saddam Hussein regime.

INTRODUCTION

Two dramatically different visions of the post–cold war world emerged in the 1990s, and both continue to be debated in the early 21st century. One vision involved an optimistic view of spreading globalization. The other saw the world mired in new conflicts among major civilizations.

Globalization pundits correctly identified the increasingly intense network of contacts that embraced most of the world's societies. This network was forged by new technologies but also enhanced by the new participation of the former Soviet Union and China. Optimists imagined that globalization would bring increasing prosperity and the fruits of democracy to all the world's peoples, and that causes for major conflict would progressively shrink. In one arresting image, a globalization partisan argued that no two societies that both had McDonald's

outlets could war with each other—in other words, that consumer pleasures would trump traditional motives for aggression.

The alternative viewpoint might be termed the "clash of civilizations" model, in which the world would be increasingly divided along the fault lines between three major civilizations that had developed historically—especially Western or European (including the U.S.), Islamic, and Chinese or "Confucian." These differing systems of values would lead to increasing competition, hostility, and violent conflict. As decolonization progressed, the shared Western value systems that had been imposed on much of the world in the nineteenth century would be rejected by peoples nurtured in non-Western value systems.

Freed from the yoke of Euro-American domination, the peoples of Asia, Africa, and the Middle East were again free to reorganize their political systems, social orders, and modes of cultural expression according to long-held practices and both religious and secular belief systems. And the end of the cold war removed another set of constraints that had been imposed by the rivalry between the capitalist and communist systems championed by the Soviet and American superpowers. Those who were convinced that this clash of cultures was the wave of the future admitted that not all parts of the world were embraced by any of the main civilizational options, and predicted there would be competition for the allegiance of swing societies, such as Russia and India. And some thinkers focused on what they saw as an inevitable conflict between the West and Islam, which they believed would prove stronger than the cross-cultural connecting forces of globalization.

Each of these approaches—globalization and clash of civilizations—could tend toward oversimplification. Each also risked some self-fulfilling qualities: there was real worry, for example, that people in the West who took clash of civilization too seriously might pursue policies that would make conflict far more likely. Most important, however, was the fact that developments in the 1990s and early 2000s generated some support for both approaches. Globalization did accelerate, bringing gains and problems in its wake. One symptom was a growing attempt to protest globalization itself—on a global basis. But a variety of narrower clashes also broke out—far more widely than many had predicted in the optimism of the cold war's end. Some of these clashes were regional, but others threw broader value systems into conflict.

This chapter covers both developments. Globalization comes first, including the increasing challenges of global impacts on the environment. We then turn to various kinds of conflicts, ultimately dealing with some of the major confrontations that have among other things introduced increasing levels of terrorism to contemporary world history. Consideration of new or renewed kinds of conflicts must also include new types of interventions, including those by great powers such as the United States, in a world that did not seem to be heading toward lessened complexity.

THE RESURGENCE OF GLOBALIZATION

The collapse of the Soviet Union and the Warsaw Pact alliance, which effectively ended the long cold war stalemate, rather abruptly opened up manifold possibilities for new transglobal connections that had been limited after 1914 by successive wars and international crises. In many instances the new linkages between states and re-

gions that were created or greatly expanded after 1989 represented revivals of processes that had begun to flourish in the decades before World War I. But major, late-20th-century innovations in communications, banking, and computing—all of which came together in quite remarkable ways on the Internet—made possible transmissions of information, economic exchanges, and cultural collaborations at a speed and intensity beyond anything imaginable in earlier epochs. Particularly noteworthy was the rapidity with which the republics that emerged from the former Soviet Union, including Russia, and the former Communist states of Eastern Europe, were incorporated into expanding global networks. Mainland China, which remained Communist politically, also moved to adopt market capitalism and increase its trade with the United States, Japan, and the other industrial nations of the European Union.

As the cold war faded in relevance, many experts saw what they called globalization as the dominant theme of present and future world history. Globalization meant the increasing interconnectedness of all parts of the world, particularly in communication and commerce but in culture and politics as well. It meant accelerating speed for global connections of various sorts. It meant openness to exchanges around the world.

Globalization did not, of course, begin in the 1990s. Increasing connections had been forming for many centuries, particularly since the advent of industrial technology with the telegraph, steam ships, and railways. Already in the late 19th century international conventions, like the Postal Union, showed that global arrangements must accompany new technology. Companies were busily setting up branch offices literally around the world by the late 19th and early 20th century. American movie companies, for example, had branch offices and distributing operations in Latin America, the Middle East, Australia, and Japan, as well as Europe, by 1920.

Developments through the 20th century intensified globalization in many ways. Air travel and radio links, for example, speeded communication and transportation. International agencies, like those associated with the League of Nations and then the United Nations, worked on issues of health or labor standards across national boundaries. Globalization must be seen as a gradual process, extending over considerable stretches of time.

But the new focus on globalization in the 1990s did reflect two or three really novel developments. First, the end of the cold war and the absence of systematic patterns of international conflict meant new opportunities for, and new attention to, global connections. China, even more than the former Soviet Union, became much more fully open to international trade and many if not all the other facets of globalization. More broadly, the growing commitment around the world to more free market arrangements, and less state intervention, opened up opportunities for foreign investment and the extension of manufacturing operations to additional areas. Latin America, India, and other places participated in this movement, along with the Communist and former Communist world. By the 1990s only a handful of spots— Myanmar, North Korea, parts of the former Yugoslavia— were largely outside the network of globalization.

Second, the late 20th century saw a new round of technological developments, associated particularly with the computer, that greatly accelerated the speed and amount of global communication. The new technology particularly facilitated international commerce, but there were global cultural and political implications as well.

Finally, though more tentatively, more people around the world became accustomed to global connections. New patterns of migration, including the use of airplanes to return home for periodic visits, and new patterns of international tourism both reflected this development. At least in some areas, intensive nationalism declined in favor of a more cosmopolitan interest in wider influences and contacts. A poll taken in the early 21st century, for example, showed young people both in the West and in East Asia increasingly eager for international styles, compared to their elders: here was a basis for what some scholars called an emerging global youth culture. The spread of English as a world language, though incomplete and often resented, was part of this connection. English served airline travel, many sports, and the early Internet as a common language. This encouraged and reflected other facets of global change.

The New Technology

A globalization guru tells the following story. In 1988 a U.S. government official was traveling to Chicago and was assigned a limousine with a cellular phone. He was so delighted to have this novelty that he called his wife just to brag. Nine years later, in 1997, the same official was visiting the Ivory Coast in West Africa, and went to a remote village, reachable only by dugout canoe, to inaugurate a new health facility. As he prepared to leave, climbing in the canoe, a government official handed him a cellular phone and said he had a call from Washington. Cellular phones became increasingly common, one of the key new communication devices that, by the 1990s, made almost constant contact with other parts of the world feasible, and for some people unavoidable. Western Eu-

rope and East Asia led in the cellular phone revolution, but leading groups in all parts of the world participated.

During the 1980s, steady improvements in miniaturization made computers increasingly efficient. By the 1990s, the amount of information that could be stored on microchips increased by over 60 percent annually. Linkages among computers improved as well, starting with halting efforts in the 1960s mainly for defense purposes. E-mail was introduced in 1972. In 1990 a British software engineer working in Switzerland, Tim Berners, developed the World Wide Web, and the true age of the Internet was born. Almost instantaneous contact by computer became possible around the world, and with it the capacity to send vast amounts of text, imagery, and even music (both legally and illegally). While the Internet was not available to everyone—by 2001 only 25 percent of the world's population had any access to it—it did provide global contacts for some regions otherwise fairly remote. In eastern Russia, for example, international mail service was agonizingly slow and telephone access often interrupted—but a student could sit at an Internet café in Vladivostok and communicate easily with counterparts in the United States or Brazil.

Satellite linkages for television formed a final communications revolution, making simultaneous broadcasts possible around the world. A full quarter of the world's population now could, and sometimes did, watch the same sporting event, usually World Cup soccer or the Olympics, a phenomenon never before possible or even approachable in world history. Global technology gained new meaning.

Business Organization and Investment

Thanks in part to new technology, in part to more open political boundaries, international investment accelerated rapidly at the end of the 20th century. Stock exchanges featured holdings in Chinese utilities or Brazilian steel companies as well as the great corporations of the West and Japan. U.S. investments abroad multiplied rapidly, almost doubling in the first half of the 1970s. By the 1980s foreign operations were generating between 25 and 40 percent of all corporate profits in the United States. Japan's foreign investment rose fifteenfold during the 1970s. During the 1980s Japanese car manufacturers set up factories in the United States, Europe, and other areas. German cars, French tires, German chemicals and pharmaceuticals, and Dutch petroleum all had substantial U.S. operations. At the end of the 1990s the German Volkswagen firm introduced an imaginative new car design, the bug, with production facilities entirely based in

Mexico, but marketing in the United States and around the world.

Globalization in business involved rapid increases in exports and imports, the extension of business organization across political boundaries—the so-called multinational corporations—and division of labor on a worldwide basis. Cars in the United States were manufactured by assembling parts made in Japan, Korea, Mexico, and elsewhere. Japanese cars often had more American-made parts in them than Detroit products had. Such was the new structure of global production. Firms set up operations not simply to produce closer to markets in order to save transportation costs; they also looked for centers of cheap labor and relaxed environmental regulations. Computer boards were made by women in the West Indies and Africa. India developed a huge software industry, subcontracting for firms in the United States and western Europe. The linkages were dazzling.

International firms continued a longstanding interest in finding cheap raw materials. Companies in the West and Japan thus competed for access to oil and minerals in the newly independent nations of Central Asia, after the collapse of the Soviet Union. International investments also followed interest rates. During the 1990s relatively high U.S. interest rates drew extensive investment from Europe, Japan, and the oil-rich regions in the Middle East.

Multinational companies often had more power, and far more resources, than the governments of most of the countries within which they operated. They could thus determine most aspects of labor and environmental policy. They could and did pull up stakes in one region if more attractive opportunities opened elsewhere, regardless of the impact in terms of unemployment and empty facilities. Yet the spread of multinationals also promoted industrial skills in many previously agricultural regions, and they depended on improvements in communications and transportation that could bring wider changes.

American factories located in northern Mexico, designed to produce goods largely for sale back in the United States, showed the complexity of the new international economy. The factories unquestionably sought low-paying labor and lax regulations. Factories often leaked chemical waste. Wages were barely 10 percent of U.S. levels. But the foreign factories often paid better, nevertheless, than their Mexican counterparts. Many workers, including large numbers of women, found the labor policies more enlightened and the supervisors better behaved in the foreign firms as well. Evaluation was tricky. A key question, not yet answerable, involved what

would happen next: Would wages improve, and would the industrial skills of the new factory workers allow a widening range of opportunities? Or would the dependence on poverty-level wages persist?

One part of the answer involved the continued willingness of multinational companies to change locales, always seeking the best deal. The rise of production in China, Vietnam, Indonesia, and some parts of Africa, sometimes at the expense of places like Mexico, showed a persistent interest in seeking lowest wages. By the early 21st century even some service and clerical jobs, not just manufacturing jobs, could be sent to countries like India, where English was spoken and where phone lines permitted communication with households in the United States or Great Britain.

Efforts to tally the overall economic effects of globalization were both difficult and contested. Some parts of Africa lost traditional manufacturing jobs to the new global competition; unemployment rates could rise to 30 percent or beyond. Trade in young women for sex was another sign of economic dislocation and poverty. In South and Southeast Asia, the rates of child labor actually rose, in contrast to overall global trends. Societies like India or Brazil that converted to a more market-based economy reduced social payments to poor families, which helped account for some newly desperate measures like heightened child labor. On the other hand, new global economic opportunities saw an increase in per capita income in the two giants, China and India, by the early 21st century. Inequality was not systematically increasing, though there were some clear losers in the economic globalization process.

Migration

Broad international patterns of migration had developed by the 1950s and 1960s, with the use of "guest workers" from Turkey and North Africa in Europe, for example. Here, patterns in the 1990s built clearly on previous trends. But the fact was that easier travel back and forth plus the continued gap between slowly growing populations in the industrial countries, and rapidly growing populations in Latin America, Africa, and parts of Asia, maintained high levels of exchange. A few countries, like Italy, Greece, and Japan, had almost ceased internal population growth by the 1990s, which meant that new labor needs, particularly at the lower skill levels, had to be supplied by immigration.

Japan hoped to avoid too much influx by relying on high-technology solutions, but even here worker groups were brought in from the Philippines and Southeast Asia. Migration into Europe and the United States was far more extensive, producing truly multinational populations in key urban and commercial centers. By 2000 at least 25 percent of all Americans, mostly people of color, came from households where English was not the first language. Here was an important source of tension, with local populations often fearing foreigners and worried about job competition. Here also was a new opportunity, not just for new laborers but for new cultural inspiration as well.

Cultural Globalization

Thanks in part to global technologies and business organization, plus reduced political barriers, the pace of cultural exchange and contact around the world accelerated at the end of the 1990s. Much of this involved mass consumer goods, spread from the United States, western Europe, and Japan. But art shows, symphony exchanges, scientific conferences, and Internet contact increased as well. Music conductors and artists held posts literally around the world, sometimes juggling commitments among cities like Tokyo, Berlin, and Chicago within a single season.

The spread of fast-food restaurants from the United States, headed by McDonald's, formed one of the most striking international cultural influences from the 1970s onward. The company began in Illinois in 1955, and started its international career in 1967 with outlets in Canada and Puerto Rico. From then on, the company entered an average of two new nations per year, and accelerated the pace in the 1990s. By 1998 it was operating in 109 countries overall. The company won quick success in Japan, where it gained its largest foreign audience; "makadonaldo" first opened in Tokyo's world famous Ginza, already known for cosmopolitan department stores, in 1971. McDonald's entry into the Soviet Union in 1990 was a major sign of the ending of cold war rivalries and the growing Russian passion for international consumer goods. The restaurants won massive patronage despite (by Russian standards) very high prices.

Even in gourmet-conscious France, McDonald's and other fast-food outlets were winning 26 percent of all restaurant dining by the 1990s. Not everyone who patronized McDonald's really liked the food. Many patrons in Hong Kong, for example, said they went mainly to see and be seen, and to feel part of the global world. And Japan became a major source of cultural globalization as well, with influential exports of fashions, youth music, and animation, as well as the latest technological gadgets. By 2003, exports of "cool" products became Japan's largest category.

Cultural globalization obviously involved increasing exposure to American movies and television shows. Series like *Baywatch* won massive foreign audiences. Movie and amusement park icons like Mickey Mouse, and products and dolls derived from them, had international currency. Western beauty standards, based on models and film stars, won wide exposure, expressed among other things in widely sought international beauty pageants. MTV spread Western images and sounds to youth audiences almost everywhere.

Holidays took on an international air. American-style Christmas trappings, including gift giving, lights, and Santa Claus, spread not only to countries of Christian background, like France, but also to places like Muslim Istanbul. Northern Mexico picked up American Halloween trick-or-treating, as it displaced the more traditional Catholic observance of All Saints' Day.

Consumer internationalization was not just American. Japanese rock groups gained a wide audience. The Pokémon toy series, derived from Japanese cultural traditions, won a frenzied audience among American children in the 1990s, who for several years could not get enough. A Japanese soap opera heroine became the most admired woman in Muslim Iran. South Korea, historically hostile to Japan, proved open to popular Japanese music groups and cartoon animation. And of course European popular culture, including fashion and music groups, gained large followings around the world as well.

Dress was internationalized to an unprecedented extent. American-style blue jeans showed up almost everywhere. A major export item for Chinese manufacturing involved Western clothing pirated from famous brand names. A "Chinese market" in the cities of eastern Russia contained entirely Western-style items, mainly clothing and shoes.

Cultural internationalization obviously involved styles from industrial countries, wherever the products were actually made, spreading to other areas, as well as within the industrial world itself. Degrees of penetration varied—in part by wealth and urbanization, in part according to degrees of cultural tolerance. Foreign models were often adapted to local customs. Thus foods in McDonald's in India (where the chain was not very popular in any event) included vegetarian items not found elsewhere. Comic books in Mexico, originally derived from U.S. models, took on Mexican cultural images including frequent triumphs over "gringo" supermen. At the same

DOCUMENT

Protests Against Globalization

In December 1999, a series of protests rocked Seattle on the occasion of a World Trade Organization (WTO) meeting designed to discuss further international tariff cuts in the interests of promoting global trade. The following passage was written by Jeffrey St. Clair, a radical journalist who is co-editor of the political newsletter *CounterPunch*. St. Clair describes the atmosphere of the Seattle protests and some of the groups involved. These events foreshadowed a regular sequence of popular demonstrations at the meetings of such groups as the World Bank, which continued into 2001, involving many of the same groups and issues.

Monday

And the revolution will be started by: sea turtles. At noon about 2,000 people massed at the United Methodist Church, the HQ of the grassroots [organizations], for a march to the convention center. It was Environment Day and the Earth Island Institute had prepared more than 500 sea turtle costumes for marchers to wear. The sea turtle became the prime symbol of the WTO's threats to environmental laws when a WTO tribunal ruled that the U.S. Endangered Species Act, which requires shrimp to be caught with turtle excluder devices, was an unfair trade barrier.

But the environmentalists weren't the only ones on the street Monday morning. In the first showing of a new solidarity, labor union members from the Steelworkers and the Longshoremen showed up to join the march. In fact, Steelworker Don Kegley led the march, alongside environmentalist Ben White. (White was later clubbed in the back of the head by a young man who was apparently angry that he couldn't do his Christmas shopping. The police pulled the youth away from White, but the man wasn't arrested. White played down the incident.) The throng of sea turtles and blue-jacketed union folk took off to the rhythm of a familiar chant that would echo down the streets of Seattle for days: "The people will never be divided!"

I walked next to Brad Spann, a Longshoreman from Tacoma, who hoisted up one of my favorite signs of the entire week: "Teamsters and Turtles Together at Last!" Brad winked at me and said, "What the hell do you think old Hoffa [former Teamster leader] thinks of that?"

The march, which was too fast and courteous for my taste, was escorted by motorcycle police and ended essentially in a cage, a protest pen next to a construction site near the convention center. A large stage had been erected there hours earlier and Carl Pope, the director of the Sierra Club, was called forth to give the opening speech. The Club is the nation's most venerable environmental group. . . .

Standing near the stage I saw Brent Blackwelder, the head of Friends of the Earth. Behind his glasses and somewhat shambling manner, Blackwelder looks ever so professional. And he is by far the smartest of the environmental CEOs. But he is also the most radical politically, the most willing to challenge the tired complacency of his fellow green executives. . . .

Blackwelder's speech was a good one, strong and defiant. He excoriated the WTO as a kind of global security force for transnational corporations whose mission is "to stuff unwanted products, like genetically engineered foods, down our throats." . . .

After the speechifying most of the marchers headed back to the church. But a contingent of about 200 ended up in front of McDonald's where a group of French farmers had mustered to denounce U.S. policy on biotech foods. Their leader was José Bove, a sheep farmer from Millau in southwest France and a leader of Confederation Paysanne, a French environmental group. In August, Bove had been jailed in France for leading a raid on a McDonald's restaurant under construction in Larzac. At the time, he was already awaiting charges that he destroyed a cache of Novartis' genetically engineered corn. Bove said his raid on the Larzac McDonald's was promoted by the U.S. decision to impose a heavy tariff on Roquefort cheese in retaliation for the European Union's refusal to import American hormone-treated beef. Bove's act of defiance earned him the praise of Jacques Chirac and Friends of the Earth. Bove said he was prepared to start a militant worldwide campaign against "Frankenstein" foods. "These actions will only stop when this mad logic comes to a halt," Bove said. "I don't demand clemency but justice."

Bove showed up at the Seattle McDonald's with rounds of Roquefort cheese, which he handed out to the crowd. After listening to a rousing speech against the evils of Monsanto, and its bovine growth hormone and Roundup Ready soybeans, the crowd stormed the McDonald's breaking its windows and urging customers and workers to join the marchers on the streets. This was the first shot in the battle for Seattle.

Who were these direct action warriors on the front lines? Earth First, the Alliance for Sustainable Jobs and the Environment (the new enviro-steelworker alliance), the Ruckus Society (a direct action training center), Jobs with Justice, Rainforest Action Network, Food Not Bombs, Global Exchange, and a small contingent of Anarchists, the dreaded Black Bloc.

There was also a robust international contingent on the streets Tuesday morning: French farmers, Korean greens [environmentalists], Canadian wheat growers, Mexican environmentalists, Chinese dissidents, Ecuadorian anti-dam organizers, U'wa tribespeople from the Columbian rainforest, and British campaigners against genetically modified foods. Indeed earlier, a group of Brits had cornered two Monsanto lobbyists behind an abandoned truck carrying an ad for the *Financial Times*. They detained the corporate flacks long enough to deliver a stern warning about the threat of frankencrops to wildlife, such as the Monarch butterfly. Then a wave of tear gas wafted over them and the Monsanto men fled, covering their eyes with their neckties.

Around 12:30 someone smashed the first storefront window. It could have been an anarchist. It could have been an agent provocateur or a stray bullet or concussion grenade. What's clear, though, is that the vandalism—what there was of it—started more than two hours after the cops had attacked nonviolent protesters amassed at 6th and Union; protesters who had offered themselves up for arrest. At most, the dreaded Black Bloc, which was to become demonized by the press and some of the more staid leaders of labor and green groups, amounted to 50 people, many of them young women. Much of the so-called looting that took place was done not by Anarchists, but by Seattle street gangs.

As the march turned up toward the Sheraton and was beaten back by cops on horses, I teamed up with Etienne Vernet and Ronnie Cumming. Cumming is the head of one of the feistiest groups in the U.S., the Pure-Food Campaign, Monsanto's chief pain in the ass. Cumming hails from the oil town of Port Arthur, Texas. He went to Cambridge with another great foe of industrial agriculture, Prince Charles. Cumming was a civil rights organizer in Houston during the mid-sixties. "The energy here is incredible," Cumming said. "Black and white, labor and green, Americans, Europeans, Africans, and Asians arm in arm. It's the most hopeful I've felt since the height of the civil rights movement."

Vernet lives in Paris, where he is the leader of the radical green group EcoRopa. At that very moment the European delegates inside the convention were capitulating on a key issue: The EU, which had banned import of genetically engineered crops and hormone-treated beef, had agreed to a U.S. proposal to establish a scientific committee to evaluate the health and environmental risks of biotech foods, a sure first step toward undermining the moratorium. Still Vernet was in a jolly mood, lively and invigorated, if a little bemused by the decorous nature of the crowd. "Americans seem to have been out of practice in these things," he told me. "Everyone's so polite. The only things on fire are dump-

sters filled with refuse." He pointed to a shiny black Lexus parked on Pine Street, which throngs of protesters had scrupulously avoided. In the windshield was a placard identifying it as belonging to a WTO delegate. "In Paris that car would be burning."

[David] Brower [environmental leader] was joined by David Foster, Director for District 11 of the United Steelworkers of America, one of the most articulate and unflinching labor leaders in America. Earlier this year, Brower and Foster formed an unlikely union, a coalition of radical environmentalists and Steelworkers called the Alliance for Sustainable Jobs and the Environment, which had just run an amusing ad in the *New York Times* asking, "Have You Heard the One about the Environmentalist and the Steelworker?" The groups had found they had a common enemy: Charles Hurwitz, the corporate raider. Hurwitz owned the Pacific Lumber company, the northern California timber firm that is slaughtering some of the last stands of ancient redwoods on the planet. At the same time, Hurwitz, who also controlled Kaiser Aluminum, had locked out 3,000 Steelworkers at Kaiser's factories in Washington, Ohio, and Louisiana. "The companies that attack the environment most mercilessly are often also the ones that are the most anti-union," Foster told me. "More unites us than divides us."

I came away thinking that for all its promise this tenuous marriage might end badly. Brower, the master of ceremonies, isn't going to be around forever to heal the wounds and cover up the divisions. There are deep, inescapable issues that will, inevitably, pit Steelworkers, fighting for their jobs in an ever-tightening economy, against greens, defending dwindling species like sockeye salmon that are being killed off by hydrodams that power the aluminum plants that offer employment to steel workers. When asked about this potential both Brower and Foster danced around it skillfully. But it was a dance of denial. The tensions won't go away simply because the parties agree not to mention them in public. Indeed, they might even build, like a pressure cooker left unwatched. I shook the thought from my head. For this moment, the new, powerful solidarity was too seductive to let such broodings intrude for long.

Questions: What were the principal groups involved in the globalization protests? Why did they feel such passion? Was this a global protest, or did different parts of the world have different issues? Was the movement likely to be able to hold together? Can you think of other reasons to oppose globalization?

Source: From Alexander Cockburn, Jeffrey St. Clair, Allan Sekula, *Five Days That Shook the World* (London: Verso, 2000), pp. 16–17, 18–19, 20–21, 28, 29, 36–37.

time, global cultures also penetrated some surprising corners. Muslim observance of Ramadan, for example, the month of self-denial, began to include greeting cards and presents for the kids, a clear echo of global consumerism. And the American jingle "happy birthday," with its implications about children's individualism and rights to entertainment, was translated into virtually every language. Cultural internationalization, though complex and incomplete, was a development of real significance.

Institutions of Globalization

On the whole, political institutions globalized less rapidly than technology or business, or even consumer culture. Many people worried about the gap between political supervision and control, and the larger globalization process. UN activity accelerated a bit in the 1990s. With the end of the cold war, more diplomatic hotspots invited intervention by multinational military forces. UN forces tried to calm or prevent disputes in a number of parts of Africa, the Balkans, and the Middle East. Growing refugee populations called for UN humanitarian intervention, often aided by other international groups. UN conferences broadened their scope, dealing for example with gender and population control issues. Major conferences on women, for example, occurred once a decade from 1975 onward. While the results of the conferences were not always clear, a number of countries did incorporate international standards into domestic law. Women in many African countries, for example, were able to appeal to UN proclamations on gender equality as a basis for seeking new property rights in the courts. By 2001, the United Nations became increasingly active as well in encouraging assistance to stem the AIDS epidemic. Actions by the World Health Organization, as well as by individual Asian nations and Canada, helped contain a potentially dangerous international epidemic of severe acute respiratory syndrome (SARS) in 2003.

Supplementing international institutions and proclamations was a growing role for world opinion. Beginning as early as the antislavery campaigns of the 19th century, certain issues called forth expressions of moral outrage on the part of people in many different countries. This kind of world opinion helped prompt an end to nuclear testing in the atmosphere during the cold war; it had significant impact in the struggle against South African apartheid in the 1980s, backed by boycotts of the South African economy. Headed by Amnesty International (founded in 1961) a variety of nongovernmental organizations rallied world opinion on behalf of human rights abuses, labor exploitation, and environmental concerns. World opinion was not always consistent or effective, but it played a significant role in diplomatic calculations by the end of the 20th century.

As more nations participated actively in international trade, the importance of organizations in this arena grew. The International Monetary Fund (IMF) and the World Bank had been founded after World War II to promote trade. Guided by the major industrial powers, these organizations offered loans and guidance to developing areas and also to regions that encountered temporary economic setbacks. Loans to Mexico and to southeast Asia during the 1990s were intended to promote recovery from recessions that threatened to affect other areas. Loans were usually accompanied by requirements for economic reform, usually in the form of reduced government spending and the promotion of more open competition; these guidelines were not always welcomed by the regions involved. The IMF and the World Bank were widely viewed as primary promoters of the capitalist global economy.

Annual meetings of the leaders of the seven leading industrial powers (four from Europe, two from North America, plus Japan) also promoted global trade and policies toward developing regions.

Finally, the regional economic arrangements that had blossomed from the 1950s onward gained growing importance as globalization accelerated. The European Union headed the list, but the North American Free Trade Agreement and other regional consortiums in Latin America and East Asia also pushed for lower tariffs and greater economic coordination.

Protest

Accelerating globalization attracted a vigorous new protest movement by the end of the 1990s. Meetings of the World Bank or the industrial leaders were increasingly marked by huge demonstrations and some violence. The current began with massive protests in Seattle in 1999, and they continued at key gatherings thereafter. Protesters came from various parts of the world and they featured a number of issues. Many people believed that rapid global economic development was threatening the environment. Others blasted the use of cheap labor by international corporations, which was seen as damaging labor conditions even in industrial nations. Rampant consumerism was another target. Most generally, many critics claimed that globalization was working to the

In recent years, the periodic meetings of the World Trade Organization have become the focus for protest against the inequities of globalization. As this 1999 confrontation between a policeman and protester in Seattle illustrates, at times these demonstrations have turned violent, even though most of the participating groups have stressed nonviolent tactics.

benefit of rich nations, and to the wealthy in general, rather than the bulk of the world's population. They pointed to figures that suggested growing inequalities of wealth, with the top quarter of the world's population growing richer during the 1990s while the rest of the people increasingly suffered. This division operated between regions, widening the gap between affluent nations and the more populous developing areas. It also operated within regions, including the United States and parts of western Europe, where income gaps were on the rise. Bitter disagreements increasingly divided the supporters and opponents of globalization.

GLOBALIZATION AND THE ENVIRONMENT: GLOBAL WARMING AND A PLANET IN PERIL

Globalization had obvious implications for the environment, as developments in one area—more manufacturing, more deforestation for the sake of agricultural exports—had increasing consequences beyond single regions. Many basic problems, however, were not new. Indeed, one of the most sobering revelations after the communist collapse were those associated with the environment. Increased access for travelers and reporters to once restricted areas of the Soviet Union and Eastern Europe made it clear that the drive for industrial development in the Communist nations had been even more environmentally devastating than the capitalist variant of that process, even in its colonial manifestations. Perhaps most sobering was the realization that if communism had not failed economically, it would have eventually rendered utterly unsustainable the environmental underpinnings of the societies that it had captured, and to which it would have continued to spread.

The impact of these revelations was intensified by the prospect of communist China's new "market-Leninist" path to industrialization, which stressed grafting free market capitalism onto an authoritarian, highly bureaucratized political systems like those long associated with communism. China's rapid industrial growth did produce increasing environmental pollution. Equally alarming have been reports on the ecological fallout of rapid development in southeast Asia, where multinationals based in Japan and in the newly industrialized countries of East Asia are extracting resources with abandon and the rain forest is disappearing even more rapidly than in Brazil. Similar trends have been documented in sub-Saharan Africa.

An additional repercussion of the environmental and economic breakdown of societies in Eastern Europe and the former Soviet Union has been the virtual elimination of these major sources of financial assistance, technology, and technical expertise for postcolonial societies in Asia and Africa. It has also occasioned a significant and growing shift of Western investment aid and technology transfer to formerly Communist areas at the expense of other developing regions, particularly sub-Saharan Africa. The available options for ecologically sound, sustained growth in many parts of the postcolonial world and Latin America are questionable at best.

By the early 1990s, even the ever-optimistic experts at the World Bank and the IMF conceded that 40 years of development strategy have been largely a failure both in terms of raising living standards and the devastation they have wrought in the fragile African environment. Throughout the cold war, both capitalist planners and their communist rivals have promoted large-scale, high-tech development schemes that rarely took into account local needs or the environmental costs of "development." These projects have favored industry over agriculture and ignored grass-roots resistance and counterproposals. They have also very often been forced on postcolonial regimes that have lacked the organizational and managerial skills

Fire destroys a large swath of the Brazilian rainforest. Such conflagrations, often started by humans, have both reduced the forest cover of the globe, thereby destroying the CO_2 "sinks" that absorb carbon emissions, and producing CO_2 gases that are the major source of global warming.

and that have been too riddled with cronyism and corruption to implement them effectively.

By century's end, the wealthy one-fifth of humanity living in the industrialized nations consumed four-fifths of all marketed goods and resources. And they also produced over 70 percent of the earth's pollution. In 1998, tiny Belgium, with nine million people, had a gross domestic product equal to that of the 40 countries of sub-Saharan Africa whose combined population was 450 million. It has been estimated that at present rates of economic growth it would take most "developing" nations 150 years to reach the average levels of productivity achieved in 1980 by wealthy nations like the United States, Japan, and those of western Europe. And many of these societies may not have even a fraction of this time to find sustainable solutions to dilemmas of mass poverty, overpopulation, and environmental degradation. In apocalyptic idioms the journalist, Marc Cooper, recently chronicled the outcome of political inertia and failed development strategies for the citizenry of the world's largest conurbation, Mexico City, where oxygen is now widely sold by peddlers in the streets:

> . . . the city's poised on the abyss of a world-class bio/technic disaster . . . its infrastructure is crumbling, . . . the drinking water mixes with sewer effluent, . . .

many of the scars of the 1985 killer quake won't be healed before the next tumbler strikes. [And even then] Mexico City still beats the eternally depressed, sun-baked countryside.[1]

At the turn of the 21st century, environmental issues had emerged as focal points of public debate and government policy in most human societies. They have also been hotly debated at growing numbers of critical global forums, most notably successive international conferences on the global environment and world population. After a century of unprecedented levels of mechanized warfare, scientific experimentation, and the spread of industrialization a wide variety of complex and often interrelated environmental disruptions threaten not only humanity but all other life forms on our planet.

Most scientists now agree that the greenhouse effect caused by the buildup in the atmosphere of excessive amounts of carbon dioxide and other heat-trapping gases has led to a substantial warming of the earth in recent decades. Some of the chief sources of the pollutants responsible for the atmospheric buildup are industrial

---

1. Marc Cooper, "Free to Open Landfills," *The Village Voice*, September 10, 1991.

wastes—including those resulting from energy production through the burning of fossil fuels like coal—and exhaust from millions of cars, trucks, and other machines run by internal combustion engines that burn petroleum. But other major sources of the greenhouse effect are both surprising and at present essential to the survival of large portions of humanity. Methane, another greenhouse gas, is introduced into the atmosphere in massive quantities as a by-product of the stew of fertilized soil and water in irrigated rice paddies, which feed a majority of the peoples of Asia, the world's most populous continent. Methane is also released by flatulent cattle, which produce milk and meat for human populations over much of the globe. Other gases have had equally alarming effects. Chlorofluorocarbons (CFCs), for example, which were once widely used in refrigeration, air conditioning, and spray cans, deplete the ozone layer, thereby removing atmospheric protection from the ultraviolet rays emanating from the sun.

If scientific predictions are correct, global warming has already and will increasingly cause major shifts in temperatures and rainfall throughout much of the globe. Fertile and well-watered areas now highly productive in foods for humans and animals may well be overwhelmed by droughts and famine. If widely accepted computer simulations are correct, coastal areas at sea level—which from Bangladesh and the Netherlands to New Jersey are among the most densely populated in the world—are likely to be inundated. And they are threatened not just by rising water levels in the world's oceans but by hurricanes and tropical storms that may in the coming decades generate winds up to 200 miles an hour. As climates are drastically altered, vegetation and wildlife in many areas will be radically altered. Temperate forests, for example, may die off in many regions and be replaced by scrub, tropical vegetation or desert flora. Some animal species may migrate or adapt and survive, but many, unable to adjust to such rapid climatic changes, will become extinct.

Not all of the sources of global warming are the product of the industrial revolution and its rapid spread and intensification, which have been major themes in world history in the 20th century. Most human societies have raised cattle and sheep for millennia and methane has been flowing from rice paddies into the atmosphere since the Neolithic revolution which began in some areas as early as the middle of the ninth millennium B.C.E. But the 20th century has seen the intensification of other nonindustrial processes that have accelerated the greenhouse effect and global warming. The cutting and burning of the world's forests is one of the more notable. Not only does the smoke produced contribute massively to CO_2 buildup in the atmosphere, but the destruction of the rain forests in particular, deprives the earth of the natural "sinks" of plant life that suck up carbon dioxide and turn it into oxygen.

The destruction of the rain forests is especially troublesome since, unlike the temperate woodlands, they cannot regenerate themselves. And the rain forests have in terms of evolution been the source of most of the species of plant and animal life that now inhabit the earth. In this and so many ways, human interventions now affect global climate and weather in the short term and will determine the fate of the planetary environment in the centuries, perhaps millennia, to come. Levels and kinds of pollution and environmental degradation that human activities produce and humans have the power to regulate will go far to determine whether or not a century from now great mountains are snow-capped or bare, and whether whales and dolphins swim in the oceans and tigers roam the forests of northeast India or pandas those of south China.

Models of industrial growth spread around the world have obviously spurred an increase in environmental degradation: many societies, pressed also by population growth, believe that expansion of output is far more important than environmental caution—just as the industrial societies themselves believed when they were launching their process. More specifically, pressures to produce for the global export market—to raise more beef in Brazil, for example—have encouraged rapid deforestation, in turn a key factor in global warming. Cross-regional pollution results from oil spills from giant tankers supplying the global economy; tall smokestacks, designed to reduce local pollution in the American Midwest or the German Ruhr, damage forests in distant parts of North America or Scandinavia. Multinationals often seek locations with loose environmental controls, leading to chemical runoffs and other systemic problems. Small wonder that environmental concerns fuel many of the protests against globalization.

Global political institutions have tried to respond. Greenpeace and other nongovernmental organizations formed since the 1970s often rouse world opinion against environmental damage. A variety of conferences, including a 1997 summit in Kyoto (Japan), sought agreement on lowering gas emission standards, and some protocols have been signed by many industrial countries headed by the European Union and Japan. So far, global politics have lagged behind pollution levels, but the surge of international concern is an important development in its own right.

REGIONAL, ETHNIC, AND RELIGIOUS CONFLICTS

Even as globalization was spreading, a variety of conflicts broke out or resumed in many parts of the world. Although a variety of concrete issues were involved, including control over key territories, the conflicts generally expressed a desire for separate identities. In this sense, they ran counter to globalization and, in some cases, explicitly asserted a desire to find new means for local expressions in an increasingly globalized world. Some of the most fervent identities, particularly those associated with religious resurgence, might attack globalization directly.

The revival of regional conflicts came in a wide variety of shapes and sizes, and they should not be put into a single category. There were three main currents. First was the continuation of longstanding disputes, as with the Israeli-Palestinian clash or the dispute between India and Pakistan over the territory of Kashmir. Second was the emergence of newly sharp ethnic disputes in several of the nations that emerged from the collapse of the Soviet system or in other regions with weak formal governments. Finally, religious revival, surging since the 1970s, brought another set of issues into sharp relief, triggering internal conflicts in countries like China or Egypt, and pushing onto the international stage as well. All of the new conflicts, but particularly the last, sometimes generated terrorist tactics.

Although the end of the cold war standoff opened up diverse possibilities for transglobal linkages, it also unleashed old ethnic and religious enmities or exacerbated hostilities that had proved major forces for the disruption of postcolonial societies. Even within Western Europe, new local assertions surged forward. The British government granted limited autonomy to Scottish and Welsh governments at the end of the 20th century, for example. France and Spain became more tolerant toward linguistic minorities such as the Catalans and Bretons. But separatist demands from the Basque ethnic group triggered periodic acts of terrorism, particularly in Spain. And anti-immigrant sentiment triggered clashes against ethnic groups in many parts of Europe, including violence against Turks in Germany and desecration of Jewish temples and monuments.

Far more systematic problems arose in several parts of the former Soviet empire. One of the more notable achievements of communist regimes wherever they developed was to submerge ethnic and religious rivalries in an overarching class war. The global struggle of the working classes against the capitalist middle classes and remnants of precapitalist or "feudal" social groups became the focus of Communist regimes in power and revolutionary movements aspiring to do so. Highly centralized regimes, such as those of Soviet Russia and Maoist China, sought to impose single languages, Russian and Mandarin Chinese respectively, on the polyglot minority groups that inhabited what in effect were empires that they had inherited from the Romanov and Qing dynasties that had preceded them.

Soviets and Maoists also systematically proscribed the religions of majority and minority peoples in the name of Marxist secularism and atheism. They sought to replace ancient customs and cultural norms with their brand of modernity, which exalted the cult of the leader and allegiance to no other god than the state. Throughout the cold war decades, these highly bureaucratized, and very often quite violent, campaigns of repression appeared to have smothered ethnic and religious identities. But in the wake of the fall of the Soviet empire and its Warsaw Pact allies, it was soon clear that pre-Communist faiths and sociocultural bonds were far from erased and very able to reemerge as major forces in world history.

The Soviet Union itself was replaced by a patchwork of new nations, from the reborn Baltic republics and the independent Ukraine in the west to the huge belt of states from Georgia to Kyrgyzstan and Kazakhstan across the south. Very often the relations between these new countries, which more often than not were formed to correspond with the areas where particular ethnic groups were concentrated, were extremely tense. In some cases they quarreled over borders or resource-rich areas; in others ancient enmities drove state policies. Both factors, and religious differences, figured in the low-level war that ran through the 1990s between Armenia and Azerbaijan. A number of ethnic clashes also occurred in the newly independent nation of Georgia.

The Russian state that remained when these areas broke away from the Soviet Union was itself a powerful expression of nationalism, based on language, history, and culture, and for substantial numbers of the citizenry, a revived Orthodox church. Some peoples who remained within Russia, most notably the Chechens who lived far to the south along the western shore of the Caspian Sea, rose in a violent revolt against continuing Russian domination. In a war that has raged for much of the past decade, the Chechens initially expelled Russian military forces only to succumb later to a massive and brutal

Russian military campaign of reconquest. The Russian reoccupation continues to be resisted, but at a much reduced level, by both Chechens from within and Islamic resistance fighters trained in Afghanistan and other Muslim states from without. Recurrent acts of terrorism, including explosions in Moscow apartment buildings, plane crashes, and seizures of theaters or schools resulting in massive loss of life, involved Russia as a whole in this bitter regional dispute.

Eastern Europe and the Yugoslav Implosion

Although there were border quarrels and other disagreements between the new non-Communist regimes that took power in the former Soviet allies of the Warsaw Pact, they rarely led to violent confrontations. Immediately after the fall of communism, clashes occurred against the Turkish minority in Bulgaria. Disputes between Czechs and Slovaks led to the dismantling of Czechoslovakia in favor of two separate states, though the process was peacefully negotiated.

Yugoslavia, however, was another matter, involving longstanding tensions among different Slavic groups (Orthodox Serbs and Catholic Croats, or Serbs and Muslim Bosnians) and between Slavs and minority nationalities like Albanians. The communist regime of Marshall Tito had long held these diverse groups together, but after Tito's death, and particularly after the

The Implosion of Yugoslavia, 1991–1999

collapse of the Soviet system, animosities surged forward with frightening intensity.

The sources of Yugoslavia's implosion can be traced to the very creation of the nation as part of the failed settlements of World War I. The victorious allied powers pressured a motley mix of peoples of different ethnic extractions and religious creeds to join with Serbia to form a highly artificial nation that had virtually no historical precedents to justify their combination. For several decades after World War II, the centuries-old quarrels and animosities of these peoples had been papered over by the strong leadership of Marshall Tito (Josip Broz). Having led the successful partisan resistance to the Nazi occupiers during World War II, Tito established a Communist regime independent of Moscow in the years after 1945. The heroic aura he had acquired in the struggle with the Nazis and the quite successful efforts of his regime to promote economic development and the incorporation of various ethnic groups into the government and bureaucracy appeared to be melding the polyglot Yugoslav peoples into a genuine nation. Tito's Croatian origins also served to mollify longstanding fears that the Serbs, who were numerically the largest ethnic group, would attempt to assert their dominance over the Croats and other minority peoples.

The long peace and prosperity—at least relative to virtually all other Communist nations—that Tito's rule brought to Yugoslavia began to break down soon after his death in May 1980. All through the decades of Tito's leadership, the peoples of the two northernmost and most prosperous of the Yugoslav republics, Slovenia and especially Croatia, had resented what they saw as the drag on their economies due to the need to funnel resources and funds to the more impoverished areas in the south of the country. Once Tito's mediating genius and strong leadership was removed, the feuding and resentments of the various ethnic and religious groups intensified steadily. A growing national crisis turned violent with the secession of Slovenia and Croatia in June 1991. These moves, and the international recognition of Bosnian independence in April 1992, touched off a bloody civil war that centered on Serbian-led military offensives against both Croatia and the Muslim-led coalition of groups seeking to establish an independent Bosnia. The Serbs, who still retained the adherence of Montenegro and Macedonia as well as substantial Serb minorities in Croatia and especially Bosnia, claimed to act to preserve the Yugoslav Republic.

Because the Serbs controlled the bulk of the former Yugoslavia's military hardware and most of the armed

Half-starved Bosnian Muslims at Srebrenica in the former Yugoslavia epitomized the return of ethnic cleansing to Europe in the 1990s. Tens of thousands were murdered before the United Nations and the United States intervened with force in the mid-1990s.

forces, the war that followed was loaded in their favor. Angered by persisting resistance, both regular Serb armies and allied, irregular Serbian forces in Bosnia in particular soon resorted to brutal assaults on civilians in seceding areas, and widespread genocidal campaigns against Croats and especially Muslims in contested areas. An epidemic of mostly Serbian-initiated mass rapes, concentration camp atrocities, attacks on innocent civilians, and widespread property destruction soon elevated what had begun as local conflicts into matters of international concern. It required military intervention by NATO to end the unrest and create a fragile new state of Bosnia-Herzogovina under outside military protection.

Another set of conflicts arose at the end of the 1990s, when Albanians in the province of Kosovo began to press for independence and were greeted by massive Serbian repression. Again, massive violence against civilians occurred from both sides, and again only outside intervention, including bombing raids on Serbia and ultimately the ouster of the ultra nationalist Serbian president, Milosevic, brought at least temporary peace. Yugoslavia was effectively dismantled, with only Serbia-Montenegro surviving what had been a far more ambitious ethnic

unification, and Milošević was brought to the International Court for trial as a war criminal.

Communist Remnants and Colonial Legacies

In global perspective, the fragmentation of the Communist states of Eastern Europe and the breakup of the Soviet Union were part of a larger surge of subnationalism over much of the world in years of transition between the 20th and 21st centuries. In China, the ongoing struggles of the Tibetans and a number of the Muslim minority peoples of western China quite often prompted forcible, at times brutal, responses on the part of the Maoist regime and its allegedly less repressive Communist successors. In important ways these confrontations represented the continuation of the historic Chinese domination of neighboring non-Chinese peoples and minority ethnic groups after the establishment of the Communist People's Republic. Similar neocolonial policies were pursued by the Communist regime in unified Vietnam. There the lives of the so-called tribal or hill peoples and ethnic minorities, such as the Khmers (Cambodians) and Chams, were subjected to ever more stringent state regulation and campaigns by the majority Vietnamese to undermine the cultures and weaken the separate identities of minority peoples. The Vietnamese also asserted their dominance over neighboring peoples, such as the Laoatians and especially the Cambodians, whose genocidal, Khmer Rouge leadership was driven from power by a Vietnamese invasion.

Although failed Communist regimes were a major factor in the post–cold-war resurgence in ethnic and religious rivalries and confrontations, the continuing aftershocks of colonialism were equally critical over much of the globe. In some postcolonial countries, such as Angola and Mozambique, colonial divisions were complicated by power struggles between Communist and non-Communist political movements. The very costly, decades-long civil wars that resulted were very often further muddied by superpower interventions on behalf of various contenders for national leadership. In other areas, particularly in west and central Africa, ethnic competition for political and economic dominance led in the 1980s and 1990s to the complete breakdown of newly independent states.

In areas like Sierre Leone and Liberia political power devolved to local warlords and their often vicious gangs who warred with each other, remnants of postcolonial governments, and UN forces sent in to restore order. In the anarchic zones of conflict that resulted, the civilian population was caught in the middle and subject to horrific atrocities carried out by roving mercenary forces. These included summary executions and the widespread practice in some areas of hacking off the hands and arms of suspected enemies or simply innocents in the wrong place at the wrong time. The ranks of these "armies" were often filled by juvenile fighters, called boy soldiers, who themselves had been orphaned by the civil wars and were concerned with little more than their own survival. Some observers in the 1990s viewed these seemingly never-ending conflicts in apocalyptic terms, as portents of the coming collapse of much of the new global order.

As we have seen, very often religious differences played a major role in the emergence of conflicting, militant subnationalisms, such as those in the former Yugoslavia among Croats (Roman Catholic), Serbs (Greek Orthodox), and Muslim Bosnians and Kosovars of Albanian extraction, who were also Muslim. Very often violent clashes in areas as widely separated in time, history, and culture as Nigeria, the Sudan, and Indonesia have been driven by religious zealots and fundamentalist beliefs. In longstanding subnational disputes, from Ireland (Protestant and Catholic) and India and Pakistan (Hindu

and Muslim) to Sri Lanka (Hindu and Buddhist) and Israel and Palestine (Jewish settlers and Muslim and Christian Arabs), these unyielding true believers have very often been seedbeds for extremist politics. They have insisted on violent solutions to the admittedly difficult and manifold problems faced by multiethnic and multireligious states.

In all instances where ethnic supremacists or religious fundamentalists have become a major political force, the civilian population on all sides has suffered from violent assaults and reprisals and lives distorted by constant fear. Horrifying evidence of the outrages they have had to endure are omnipresent in newspaper photos and in video clips on the network news. But already decades ago, Maurice Collis, a British administrator in colonial Burma, poignantly captured the human costs of communal outrages in the following description of the aftermath of an assault by Burmese rioters on the camps of impoverished, immigrant Indian workers who were said to threaten the locals' jobs:

> The condition of the tenements proved there had been savage play. The corpses had been removed, but everything reeked of blood; boxes had been broken open, their contents looted or slashed; the very walls dripped blood; little pictures of the gods had not escaped destruction.[2]

Turmoil in Africa

The surge of ethnic conflicts, often conjoined to religious difference and rivalries among independent nations, had particularly devastating consequences in Africa in the 15 years after 1990. During the 1990s, even as South Africa celebrated the end of apartheid and the achievement of democracy, conflict between tribal groups, the Hutus and the Tutsis, broke out in Rwanda. Here as elsewhere, old rivalries blended with disputes over current power; the Tutsis had long ruled, but they were outnumbered by resentful Hutus. Intervention from neighboring states like Uganda contributed to the confusion. Tremendous slaughter resulted, with hundreds of thousands killed and many more—over two million—driven from their homes. And while outside power, the Organization of African States and the United Nations, urged peace, there was no decisive outside intervention. Bloodshed

---

2. Maurice Collis, *Trials in Burma* (London, 1938).

finally ran its course, but ethnic disputes continued in central Africa, contributing to simmering civil war in countries like the Congo (formerly Zaire), where millions were killed, maimed, or displaced in a conflict that continued in the early 2000s.

Ethnic and religious disputes were also involved in a number of other African trouble spots. Battles between Muslims and Christians in southern Sudan led to two million casualties, though the United States helped broker an uneasy peace by 2004. Another set of conflicts between Arabs and black Africans in the western province of Darfur in Sudan, led to tens of thousands of deaths and massive displacement in 2004; in this case, both of the contesting groups were Muslim.

Clearly, ethnic tensions were leading to acts of warfare and genocide against civilians, including women and children, and the creation of massive refugee populations. Reactions from the world at large varied. In some instances, violence provoked great power intervention, though always with great hesitation. No policies emerged that offered great promise for pushing back the new potential for ethnic conflict.

ANALYSIS

Terrorism, Then and Now

In the last years of the 20th century, terrorism became a major issue for the international media, the world's political and military leaders, and increasingly for civilians across the globe who became both targets and mass victims of increasingly indiscriminate violent assaults. For Americans terrorism on home soil arrived gradually as the initial, and largely failed, attempt to bomb the World Trade Center in New York City in 1993 faded from memory. By contrast, for much of the rest of the world, fear of and precautions against terrorist violence had become ongoing and a major concern as early as the late 1960s. From Basque separatists in Spain and Protestant and Catholic paramilitary units in Northern Ireland to Tamil suicide bombers in Sri Lanka and cult plotters in Japan, terrorism has become an ever-present menace in the lives of leaders and ordinary citizens alike over much of the globe. This is particularly true in the growing conurbations where much of humanity has come to be concentrated. The well-coordinated and appallingly destructive attacks of September 11, 2001, on both the World Trade Center in New York and the Pentagon in Washington brought these concerns and their vulnerability to terrorism home to Americans with mind-numbing force.

Although current commentators often treat the late-20th-century global epidemic of terrorism as a phenomenon without historical precedent, in fact, in the decades before World War I, terrorist attacks were also a major concern and carried out by dissident groups in many areas of the globe. From the capitols and metropolitan centers of Europe (especially those of tsarist Russia) and the United States to the port cities and imperial centers of the far-flung colonial empires of the great industrial powers, assassinations and bombs killed and maimed, disoriented societies, and challenged political regimes. But in critical ways—including the nature and causes espoused by terrorist groups, the targets they favored, and the amount of damage or numbers of casualties their attacks caused—terrorism in the 1880s or the early 1900s differed significantly from its counterpart in the 1970s or 1990s. An exploration of some of these key differences can tell us a great deal not only about the transformation of terrorists' motivations and operations, but also about key contrasts in terms of the global and local contexts in which each wave of terrorism occurred.

In both time periods, the main source of terrorist assaults were small, secret, and highly politically motivated organizations. In both the early 20th century and in the decades at its end, the main objectives of the members of these organizations was to discredit, weaken, and ultimately overthrow political regimes that they believed were oppressive and supportive of exploitation at both the national and international levels. Their operations were also designed to advertise the causes these extremist groups espoused and draw attention to injustices they believed could not be effectively addressed through less violent or less confrontational modes of protest. But in the pre–World War I era, most terrorists were driven either by (1) anarchist aspirations to destroy increasingly centralized states, (2) radical Marxist programs for workers to overthrow the capitalist world order, or (3) struggles for the liberation of colonized peoples from Ireland to India. The most spectacular terrorist assault of the era was of the latter type—Bosnian Serb Gavril Princip's assassination of the Archduke Ferdinand and his wife, Sophie, which precipitated the crisis that led to World War I.

At the turn of the 21st century, by contrast, terrorist assaults have come mainly from sectarian extremists claiming affiliation with one of the world's great religious traditions—including Christianity, Hinduism, Judaism, and Islam—or from subnationalist groups, such as the Basques in Spain or Protestant and Catholic militias in Northern

New Yorkers flee across the Brooklyn Bridge after the terrorist assaults on the World Trade Center on September 11, 2001. The terrorist attack was one of the most ambitious and horrific in history and arguably ushered in a new era in international relations.

Ireland. Interethnic civil wars, such as those that have raged in Lebanon, Cyprus, Bosnia, and Sri Lanka in recent decades, have also proved to be major sources of terrorist activities. Periodically, radical environmentalists and groups opposing international institutions, such as the International Monetary Fund and World Trade Organization, that promote economic globalization have also resorted to terrorist tactics.

The targets terrorists selected in each time period very often tell us a good deal about the differing causes they espoused. Many of the regimes that anarchists struck at in the pre–World War I period—for example, the tsarist empire or the British Raj in India—were in fact autocratic, often indifferent to the oppressive living conditions of the great majority of their subjects, and prone to respond to even peaceful protest with violent repression, including torture. Scholarly investigations of these and current causes of terrorist activities have made us aware of the frequent resort to terrorist tactics by bureaucrats, the military, and state officials who so vehemently condemn dissident violence. In fact, terrorist activities have often proved far less lethal and destructive than the violence employed by regimes in power. Though these discoveries do not justify violence, particularly that directed against innocent civil-

ians, they help us to understand in part why terrorist groups resort to it rather than trusting the state they are dealing with to carry through the reforms they demand or to negotiate with them peacefully and in good faith.

In both time periods terrorist acts were carried out mainly by young men. But in the decades at the turn of the 20th century, many of the operatives were middle aged, and separatist activists in both eras have included young women. Targets differed significantly in each phase of the 20th century. In the decades before World War I, individuals—monarchs (and their spouses), government officials (including President McKinley of the United States), business tycoons, and colonial officials—were most often chosen, in part because of the propaganda value of striking at the powerful and wealthy. At times, bombs placed in public areas were used to instill mass panic and disrupt normal social life. In the case of anarchist and Marxist extremists, indiscriminate mass killings and widespread destruction in fashionable quarters of urban areas were seen as symbolic assaults on the bourgeois, capitalist global order.

At the turn of the 21st century, indiscriminate assaults on defenseless civilians have become the preferred tactic of terrorists from Ireland and Spain to Israel and Palestine and Sri Lanka and Japan. Technological advances that allowed terrorist operatives to miniaturize bombs and automatic firearms contributed to this preference. But perhaps more critical were great advances in surveillance devices and the elaborate security measures taken to defend national and world leaders. Quite simply it became more and more dangerous to target soldiers, policemen, and political leaders, and increasingly even economic magnates or religious figures. Technological change also affected the nature of terrorist operations in other important ways. The spread of communications technologies, such as the telephone and television, complex networks for delivering electric power and fuels like natural gas, and nuclear reactors and centers of scientific experimentation created a whole new range of what have often proved to be very vulnerable targets. Trains, buses, and airplanes have also become tempting objects for capture or destruction at the hands of hijackers and bombers. Finally, invention and scientific experimentation have made a whole new generation of terrorist weapons feasible, including gases like Sarin that wreaked havoc on Tokyo's subways, toxic bacterial agents like anthrax, and miniaturized nuclear devices that, theoretically at least, can be packed in the proverbial suitcase and carried into the heart of major urban centers.

Between the 1970s and the 1990s, these shifts in science and technology greatly reduced the odds of success in operations aimed at well-defended leaders, government institutions, or military organizations themselves. This situation turned unarmed civilians going about their daily lives into ever more tempting targets for terrorist gunmen or bombers. The emergence of suicide bombers or attackers, particularly in the 1990s, made this pattern even more disturbing. Terrorist organizations were confident that these *kamakazi* tactics would serve several purposes. To begin with, they dramatically publicized the grievances that inspired armed resistance. Highly lethal attacks on civilians were also seen to destabilize target societies and deprive citizens of the sense of security required to live productive and fulfilled lives. Both outcomes, in turn, were believed to discredit targeted political regimes. The dissident groups who launched the assaults hoped they would weaken governments in power to the point where they would either make major concessions or prove vulnerable to even more ambitious attempts to overthrow them.

These expected outcomes have very rarely come to pass. In fact, indiscriminate terrorist acts have usually outraged public and world opinion, and obscured or distorted the causes that dissident groups were attempting to publicize. They have also greatly enhanced the latitude of retaliatory responses open to national governments and international agencies as well as public support for these measures.

This has been true even in situations where large numbers of new civilian casualties occurred as a result. Equally critical, the terrorists' willingness to launch mass assaults on innocent civilians has tended to be equated with religious fanaticism or political radicalism that are so extreme that they preclude negotiation and even rational explanation. As a consequence, violent repression has very often been deemed the only viable response to the death and suffering visited upon innocent civilians by terrorist true believers.

These shifts in the nature and targets of terrorist assaults between the pre-World War I era and the last decades of the 20th century have in most instances greatly increased the cost in human lives and property due to their assaults. The magnitude of these losses has also been linked to the growing globalization of terrorist networks. This has meant a proliferation of complex linkages between dissident groups in different nations and regions, who are very often espousing radically different causes. Perhaps most sobering in this regard was the way in which the attacks on New York City and Washington on September 11, 2001, demonstrated the possibilities for well-funded and organized terrorist groups to turn highly advanced civilian technologies, embodied in modern passenger planes, into appallingly lethal weapons that could be aimed at innocent and unsuspecting civilian victims. The collapse of the towers after each had been struck by hijacked airliners also revealed the vulnerability of even the most imposing modern buildings to this sort of assault. At literally the same time, the crash of another airliner into the Pentagon demonstrated that even the headquarters of the most powerful military organization the world has ever known was not immune to terrorist attack. These events may mark a fundamental shift in the nature of violent protest and warfare that will be played out in the century to come.

Questions: What are some of the specific technologies that have shaped changes in terrorist operations over the 20th century? What sorts of systems and devices have been used by states and military organizations to counter these shifts? Are there instances in which terrorist organizations have been successful politically? And, if so, what does success mean in these situations? Is terrorism likely to become the dominant mode of warfare in the 21st century?

A Challenge: What kinds of measures might to be taken to bring the terrorist epidemic of the late 20th century under control in the coming decades? Pick one 20th century case where a cause that generated terrorism was ultimately resolved. Are there any lessons here for current terrorist campaigns?

The Revival of Religious Sectarianism

A global religious revival took shape in the final decades of the 20th century. New religious movements were not necessarily opposed to globalization, and many of them made use of new technologies such as the Internet. They did add to the new insistence on separate identities, however, and they were often opposed to specific features of global cultures such as excessive materialism, more open sexuality, and changes in the status of women. Indeed, dissatisfaction with the results of globalization, including widespread poverty and unemployment in many cities, helped fuel the turn to religion. The decline of communism also contributed, by largely canceling one of the main secular faiths of the 20th century.

Signs of religious fervor cropped up in many places. As communism receded, Christianity revived in many parts of eastern Europe, including Orthodox practices in Russia; and a new wave of evangelical Protestant missionaries, mainly from the United States, flooded the region as well. Protestant fundamentalism also spread rapidly in parts of Latin America, particularly Guatemala and Brazil. In China, the rise of the Falun Gong religious movement, a derivate from Buddhism, caused great concern to the communist regime; but arrests of many leaders did not prevent millions from being attracted to the movement. Hindu fundamentalism surged in India, and Hindu nationalists gained control of the government for several years. Clashes between Hindu faithful and Muslims in India became more severe, with Hindu fundamentalists insisting on state support and decrying excessive tolerance. Fundamentalism also gained ground in Islam, particularly in the Middle East and nearby parts of Africa and southern Asia. Whether Christian, Hindu, Muslim, or Buddhist, fundamentalists tended to urge a return to the primacy of religion and religious laws, often opposing greater freedoms for women and criticizing Western-style consumerism. They usually sought government support for religious values and they often displayed growing levels of intolerance. In a few cases, as with the Taliban regime in Afghanistan, religious fundamentalists gained control of the state.

In many places the rise of religious fundamentalism provoked new debates and conflicts, both with more moderate religious groups and with secular value systems. Many Middle Eastern countries, including Turkey and Egypt, saw fierce attacks by fundamentalists on the more moderate or secular state; in Turkey the conflict included periodic acts of terrorism. In India, elections in 2004 dislodged the Hindu Nationalist regime, which had been fairly moderate in practice in any event; but tensions remained. The role of fervent Christianity in politics became an ongoing issue in the United States.

Islamic fundamentalists developed the widest range of action, though many of their concerns remained focused on regional contests with established, more secular governments. Fundamentalists played a leading role in Afghanistan in opposing Soviet occupation (with support from the United States during the final phase of the cold war) and then in taking over the regime. They supported the Chechen uprising in Russia. They focused heavily on support for the Palestinian struggle against Israel, which revived in 2000. And they deeply criticized the United States and its allies, particularly for what they claimed was excessive support for Israel and for military presence near some of the religion's holiest sites, particularly in Saudi Arabia. Here was a final, crucial ingredient of the new patterns of conflict that defined much of world history during the 1990s and early 2000s.

Religious fundamentalism was not, however, monolithic. Islamic fundamentalists, for example, vigorously debated the use of violence, with many leaders opposing attacks on civilians as contrary to the principles of Islam as well as damaging to the religion's image internationally. Many fundamentalists were far more opposed to repressive regimes within the Middle East than to more remote Western policies. And of course many faithful in all the major religions did not adopt the fundamentalist approach. The religious revival and its political repercussions were important developments, but they did not point in a single direction.

THE UNITED STATES AND THE NEW PATTERN OF CONFLICT

As representatives of the world's only superpower, U.S. leaders were forced to grapple with the uncertainties of a profoundly altered world order. For most of the 1990s, they responded with a wide range of initiatives designed to shape a U.S.-dominated new world order that predictably privileged international investment, free trade, democratization, and a high level of interventionism in regional disputes or domestic disruptions in areas deemed of strategic importance. They largely supported globalization, in other words, while working selectively against the new surge of conflicts. The terrorist attacks of 2001 altered this pattern somewhat, as the nation turned to a more single-minded war on terrorism at some cost both to globalization and to the management of several other conflicts.

The Second Gulf War, 1990–1991

The crisis in the Persian Gulf region, brought on by an Iraqi invasion of Kuwait in early August 1990, provided an almost immediate and major opportunity to gauge the nature of the post–cold-war world order. The underlying origins of what became a conflict with global dimensions can be traced to many key developments in the 20th century. The artificial boundaries that the European powers had imposed on much of the colonized world were critical. The aggressor state, Iraq, had been carved out of the defunct Ottoman empire, chiefly by British and French diplomats, when the Mandates were set up in the Middle East after World War I (see Chapter 5). Like most postcolonial political creations, Iraq was a nation deeply divided. There were three main regions: (1) a northern area inhabited mainly by Kurds, (2) the central core of the artificial state around Baghdad and dominated by Sunni Muslims, and (3) the southern districts, heavily populated by Shi'ite Muslims, that extended to the northern end of the Persian Gulf.

Kuwait was the very epitome of a state created by European colonial imperatives. At the end of the 19th century, the British declared the region around Kuwait a protectorate as part of a broader scheme to firm up their dominance in the Persian Gulf. In so doing, they recognized the al-Sabah family as the overlords of the area, a position the family had established well over a century before.

As was the case over much of postcolonial Africa and Asia, the border between Iraq and Kuwait had been drawn up by outsiders and was consequently highly contested by local leaders. Saddam Hussein, who had fought his way to become Iraq's dictatorial leader in the 1960s and early 1970s, had repeatedly invoked Iraq's historic claims to control over the Kuwait region. He had long coveted the Kuwait area for its access to the Persian Gulf, which a nearly landlocked Iraq sorely lacked. On their side, Kuwait's rulers insisted on ownership of large portions of the oil reserves that were officially located on the Iraqi side of the border. Their slant drilling, which was secretly drawing off oil from the Iraqi side through underground pipelines, was in fact a major pretext for the Iraqi invasion.

The Iraqi invasion was also directly linked to the decade-long First Gulf War between Iraq and neighboring Iran, which had in the late 1970s undergone revolutionary upheavals that brought the Ayatollah Khomeini to power. For most of the 1980s, a World War I–style, trench war raged between the two states, with the extremely high casualties associated with that sort of conflict. With the financial backing of the oil-rich Arab states of the Gulf region, and the sophisticated weaponry that Saddam Hussein could purchase in the West or cajole the Soviets and even the United States into providing, the Iraqis finally prevailed. But in so doing, they ran up huge debts to, among other backers the Kuwaitis, and the al-Sabahs were pressing hard for repayment in the months before the Iraqi invasion.

Mistakenly believing that neither the United States nor its allies in Europe and Japan, all of whom were actually more dependent on oil from the Gulf than the U.S., would do little to retaliate, Saddam Hussein launched a massive invasion of Kuwait, whose tiny defense forces could do little to resist. With the Iraqis' longtime Soviet bloc supporters in disarray, the United States could move massively and decisively against Iraq's aggression, which some believed might continue on to the capture of Saudi Arabia and leave Saddam Hussein in control of the bulk of the Middle East's oil reserves. After gaining UN backing in November 1990, President George H. Bush and his advisors skillfully put together a large coalition force of U.S., European, and Arab troops. In the air assaults that opened the Second Gulf War in mid-January 1991, and then the land-based operations that followed at the end of February, the vastly superior weaponry of the coalition first destroyed Iraq's air force and the country's communication and command structure, then routed its armies. In effect Saddam Hussein prepared his forces to fight another World War I–style war, which rendered them highly vulnerable to the advanced aircraft, guided missiles, and armored divisions that could be deployed with great effect in the vast and open Iraqi terrain.

Superb generalship on the coalition side made it possible to fight the war the way the U.S. military had decided that conflicts in the developing world must be handled after the debacle in Vietnam. The key imperatives of this new style of war were clearly defined and limited objectives, rapid but carefully calculated responses, the massive application of firepower, and quick withdrawal once the initial objectives were deemed to have been obtained. Though these principles proved an impressive combination during the war, they became something of a handicap at the end. Having driven the Iraqis from Kuwait and badly battered Saddam Hussein's war machine, the coalition armies stopped short of toppling his defeated and highly dictatorial regime. This hesitation

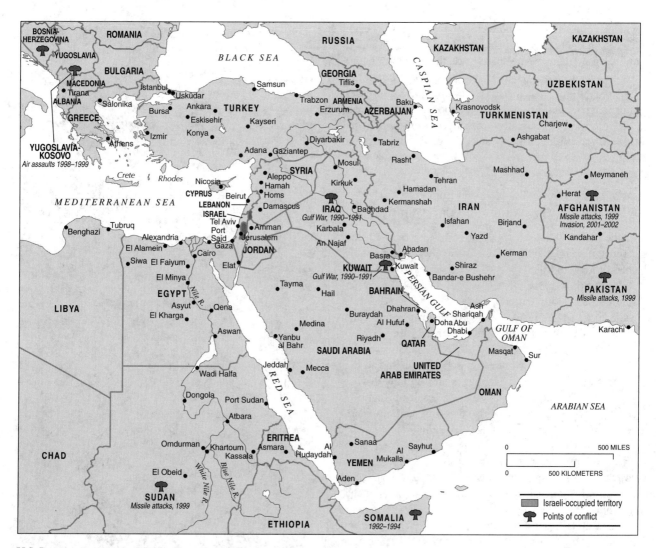

U.S. Interventions in the Middle East, East Africa, and Central Asia in the 1990s

resulted in part from the conviction of many analysts that the defeated Saddam Hussein would soon be toppled from within or by revolts on the part of the long hostile Kurds in the north and Shi'ites (with Iranian support) in the south. But when the United States and its allies refused to do more than encourage these groups to rise up against the regime, their resistance was eventually brutally crushed by a dictator whose staying power was greater than anyone at the time imagined.

Despite a continued embargo and periodic air strikes by British and U.S. forces, Saddam Hussein managed to rebuild his terror state, even though his capacity for foreign aggression remained much reduced. The embargo, which was maintained all through the 1990s and early

2000s, was devastating mainly for the Iraqi people, who were denied even staple foods and medicine. As a result, they died—according to moderate estimates—in the hundreds of thousands. The embargo, on the other hand, appeared to have only a limited effect on the Iraqi regime, which continued to seek ways to restore its military power and regional influence. Saddam Hussein's persisting threats against neighboring states and members of the allied coalition had also forced the United States and some of its original allies to spend billions of dollars annually to police the Gulf region on an ongoing basis.

The persisting U.S. presence in the region, and especially the stationing of U.S. troops in Saudi Arabia, which is the site of the holy cities of the Islamic world, Mecca and Medina, has been deeply offensive to purist, and even moderate, Muslims. It was the most consistent reason advanced by Islamic zealots, especially Osama bin Laden in the 1990s, for strikes against U.S. embassies and military installations in Africa and the Middle East. And it figured prominently in the motives proclaimed afterward for terrorist assaults on the United States itself in September 2001.

A Decade of Interventions and Uncertainties

In the early 1990s, the apparent success of the U.S.-led campaign against Iraqi aggression in the Gulf emboldened those who called for the United States to become in effect the policeman of the world. Without a Soviet counterforce, interventionists argued, the United States could move aggressively in almost any area to bring conflicts under control before they proved disruptive to rapidly expanding global market linkages and investment opportunities. Most of these conflicts were linked to the resurgence of ethnic and religious confrontations that, as we have seen, multiplied rapidly as a result of lingering colonial divisions and the breakdown of Communism. Although the United States usually exerted its now considerable leverage to win UN or NATO backing, very often America acted on its own or escalated multilateral commitments through unilateral measures. But a series of reverses soon called these assumptions and policies into question.

As we have seen, in the summer of 1991, within months of the end of the Second Gulf War, the Socialist Federal Republic of Yugoslavia fell apart. Because it was clear that there were no easy or quick solutions to the complex civil strife that rapidly spread through the region, the United States first prodded its NATO allies to deal with what the Americans argued, with some justification, was a European problem. But the Europeans countered, and also with justification, that the U.S.-centric nature of the NATO alliance left them without the power to act effectively without major support from the U.S. military. The UN condemned the mass killings and related abuses, and imposed arms embargoes and sent peacekeeping forces to the region, beginning in early 1992. But the understaffed and woefully outgunned UN forces could do little to stop the conflict or even prevent genocidal atrocities on the part of the Serbs. In fact, so-called UN "safe areas," simply concentrated Bosnian refugees and left them vulnerable to Serb slaughters,

The seemingly invincible power of American technology is captured in this photo of a helicopter operating near Mogadishu in Somalia. But in clashes that were soon to occur in the city itself, these massive fighting machines proved highly vulnerable to the hand-held grenade launchers wielded by the militia troops of local warlords.

such as the mass killings carried out at Srebrenica in the summer of 1994.

Neither the George H. W. Bush nor the Clinton administrations acted militarily to put an end to these horrors. In both cases, their reluctance was in large part due to fears that the United States would be drawn into another Vietnam quagmire—a situation that offered few opportunities for the application of the rapid, massive, and decisive force that had worked so well in the Gulf. Perversely, in the same years the Bosnia slaughters were occurring, the United States intervened in Somalia, initially to support UN famine-relief efforts in the war-torn country, but gradually and misguidedly becoming involved in local political struggles. In early October 1993, this shift resulted in widespread resistance to a U.S. special operations attempt to capture one of the more prominent warlords in the capital at Mogadishu. The U.S.–UN efforts to influence the formation of a national government for the factionalized region ended in a nightmare battle that took the lives of hundreds of Somalis and 18 Americans. Soon afterward, the U.S. forces withdrew, to be followed a year later by what remained of the UN contingent.

After the October disaster in Somalia, the can-do mentality with regard to policing the world, which had prevailed after the Second Gulf War, evaporated. Despite multiplying evidence of genocidal campaigns on the part of the Serbs in Bosnia, resistance to intervention among U.S. policy makers stiffened. The Mogadishu fiasco also made Clinton and other policymakers very skittish about military force as an antidote to political breakdown and civil strife in nearby Haiti. Even more dramatic, however, and controversial in terms of international responses, was the Clinton administration's refusal to act to stop the massive government-sponsored campaign of genocide that pitted the Hutu majority against the Tutsi minority in Rwanda between March and July of 1994. Somalia was clearly a factor, but the utter lack of a strategic stake in the area and the difficulties of projecting American power into the landlocked, central African state were probably more critical. The paucity of U.S. information on Rwanda, and the patchy and belated reporting of the genocide more generally also had a great deal to do with the slow and feeble U.S. and UN responses. By midsummer between 500,000 and a million Tutsi had been slaughtered, making Rwanda the worst genocidal outburst since the nightmare reign of the Khmer Rouge in Cambodia in the 1970s.

By late 1994 both the UN and the Clinton administration had come under heavy international criticism for their belated and indecisive responses to genocidal campaigns against ethnic and religious minorities in Rwanda and Bosnia respectively. By early summer of 1995, U.S. armed forces were engaged in military actions against Serbian forces. By the end of that year, the former U.S. President Jimmy Carter had brokered a peace agreement, and U.S. and NATO armed forces had been sent

Students and ordinary citizens spearheaded the mass protests that drove the Serbian dictator, Slobodan Milośević, from power in 2001.

to Bosnia to enforce it. Three years later, civil war erupted in one of the remaining regions of Yugoslavia, Kosovo, where the Serbs sought to crush a growing Albanian secessionist movement. With another round of genocidal Serbian assaults building under the thuggish dictatorship of Slobodan Milośević, NATO, with the United States in the lead, launched an extensive air war against Serb forces in Kosovo and the nation of Serbia itself.

The Serbs were forced to retreat from Kosovo, which like Bosnia was then occupied by NATO peacekeeping forces. Many U.S. and European military observers loudly proclaimed that Kosovo had vindicated air power at last, because the Serbs had been forced to capitulate without a land invasion. But the record of the many UN and U.S. interventions of the 1990s suggested that Kosovo may well have been an atypical case. From the

Second Gulf War to the U.S. campaign to destroy the Taliban regime in Afghanistan after the September 2001 terrorist attacks on the United States, a combination of air power and land invasions had been required to thwart or bring down aggressor or oppressive regimes. And the mounting costs of the self-appointed U.S. role as policeman of yet another new world order had impressed on many observers the need to exercise caution, to rely more heavily on multilateral organizations, such as NATO and the UN, and to realize that the United States could not solve all of the world's problems.

There were, among other things, conflicts that the United States did not seem able to resolve. The United States consistently pressed India and Pakistan to pull back from outright warfare over the disputed territory of Kashmir—both countries had nuclear weapons by 2002, so tensions were particularly dangerous. But despite some return to negotiation, the conflict remained unresolved. President Clinton had brokered promising peace talks between Israeli and Palestinian leaders during the 1990s, but the effort collapsed. Bitter violence between the two groups revived in 2000, and in 2002 and 2003 a wave of suicide bombings by Palestinians targeted Israeli civilians, while the Israeli government attacked Palestinian cities and refugee camps in turn. American efforts to promote negotiations faltered, as the United States seemed to side more fully with the Israeli regime as an ally against terrorism.

Afghanistan and Iraq

The terrorist attack on the United States in 2001 unleashed a series of new policy measures. Border controls tightened, and the United States tightened visa requirements for many foreigners in ways that affected international business and student activities. The United States, with wide international support, quickly struck back at the centers of the al-Qaeda terrorist group in Afghanistan, where a combination of air strikes and ground activities quickly toppled the Taliban regime. Efforts to establish a democratic government followed, though regional warlords continued to wield considerable power and al-Qaeda was far from broken.

In 2003 American attention turned to Iraq. American leaders, backed by several allies including Great Britain, displayed concern that Saddam Hussein was amassing dangerous weaponry and aiding terrorists. The evidence for these claims was far from clear, and many wondered about other motives for the threatened military action. Most world opinion profoundly opposed the imminent American attack, and in February 2003, probably as

many as 25 million people demonstrated against the war in cities almost literally all over the world, including the United States. But the United States and its coalition did attack, winning a fairly quick formal victory and toppling the Saddam regime (and later capturing the leader). The ensuing occupation, however, has been extremely troubled, as major violence continues even as the United States continues with attempts to construct a democratic political system. The results of this war, both in Iraq and in terms of broader global reactions to American interests and power, are not yet clear.

CONCLUSION: BACK TO THE FUTURE?

In many ways world history at the beginning of the 21st century appears to have mirrored or renewed major themes of the decades that preceded World War I. The collapse of communism and the end of the cold war led to an intensification of national identity and nationalist sentiment that, as we saw in Chapter 5, was a critical factor in the coming of World War I. In both eras, globalization led to levels of political, economic, and cultural interaction across national boundaries and world regions that were unprecedented when each occurred. In each time period, the process of globalization was challenged by politically inspired terrorist movements, which launched violent assaults on the institutions, networks and citizen-participants of the globalization process. And in both the first and last phase of the 20th century, ecological movements arose to address problems of pollution, resource waste, and environmental degradation.

Although impressive, the parallels and apparent continuities between the opening and closing decades of the 20th century, can also be deceptive. Closer examination reveals important differences between the ways in which each of these defining processes played out historically. Nationalist sentiment at the end of the century, for example, was very often pitched at levels that fragmented and threatened established nation-states. Subnational ethnic and religious identities predominated, and elites who tried to preserve the national units established during the process of decolonization or by the peace settlements of the century's major wars found themselves under siege. Civil wars within existing states were far more prominent than the rivalries between nations that had been such a major factor in the outbreak of World War I.

At another level, the process of globalization occurred at the end of the century in a very different international setting than at the beginning. Many of the financial and communications links that were established in the 1880s or early 1900s were among the metropoles of the great imperial powers of Europe, North America, and Japan and between these centers and their colonial possessions in Africa and Asia and informally dominated dependencies in the Middle East and Latin America. The globalization of the 1990s occurred in a decolonized world, though similar economic, technological, and institutional inequalities persisted between wealthier, industrialized societies and those of the "developing" world. In addition, globalization in the 1990s stressed technological and scientific transfers, multinational corporate expansion, and the free circulation of investment. In the decades before World War I, communication networks, national cartels, and free trade were the focus of globalizing initiatives. The speed and intensity of the process in the two eras was also markedly different, with the Internet and other innovative technologies providing a decisive edge in the more recent.

Not surprisingly, the nature of terrorist and environmentalist challenges in the two eras that framed the 20th century was also noteworthy. Religious and ethnic rivalries were more important sources of terrorist violence at the turn of the 21st century than a century earlier, when anarchist and Marxist ideologies inspired the bulk of terrorist attacks. A century of scientific and technological change had also considerably enhanced the sophistication of the weapons available to terrorist dissidents. But the same waves of innovation had made for far greater advances in state surveillance and means of repression. This combination of factors made for much higher levels of human casualties and physical destruction in more urban and interlinked, and thus more vulnerable societies at the end of the century compared with those at the beginning.

Environmental movements in the early decades of the 20th century stressed conservation of resources and the preservation of wilderness areas. Though these remained concerns at the turn of the 21st century, the very survival of the planet was now clearly at issue. A long century of steadily increasing pollution linked to a wide variety of factors—prolonged global wars; the spread of industrialization, deforestation, and mechanized farming; and a staggering increase in human population—all culminated in ever more obvious and widespread environmental degradation and unprecedented rates of species extinction. Above all, clear evidence of global warming suggested potentially catastrophic climatic change in the short term and an imperiled planet in the not too distant future. Though downplayed by political elites and media establishments infatuated with wars, economic trends, and ephemeral celebrities, environmental issues had by the 1980s and 1990s clearly become the most pervasive

and fundamental challenges that human societies would need to tackle in the 21st century.

FURTHER READING

For very different takes on the resurgence of globalization since 1989, see Thomas Friedman's cautious celebration in *The Lexus and the Olive Tree* (1999), John Gray's more sober appraisal in *False Dawn* (1998), and Thomas Frank's lively critique in *One Market Under God* (2000). Differing perspectives on the cultural ramifications of the new global economic order are provided by Peter Stearns, *Consumerism in World History* (2001); Walter LaFeber, *Michael Jordan and the New Global Capitalism* (2000); and the contributions to James Watson, ed., *Golden Arches East: McDonald's in East Asia* (1998). See also Lewis Solomon, *Multinational Corporations and the Emerging World Order* (1978); Stephen Rees, *American Films Abroad* (1997); Theodore von Laue, *The World Revolution of Westernization* (1997); and Bruce Mazlish and Ralph Buultjens, eds., *Conceptualizing Global History* (1993). For a particular aspect of globalization, see Peter N. Stearns, *Global Outrage: The Origins, Evolution and Impact of World Opinion* (2005).

For a detailed, long-term historical perspective on the successive conflicts in the Balkans, see Misha Glenny, *The Balkans: Nationalism, War and the Great Powers, 1804–1999* (2000), and on the religious dimensions of the Yugoslavia wars, see the essays in Paul Mojzes, ed., *Religion and War in Yugoslavia* (1998). On the successive conflicts of the mid-1990s more specifically, see Misha Glenny, *The Fall of Yugoslavia* (1992); Laura Silber and Allan Little, *Yugoslavia: Death of a Nation* (1995); Tim Judah, *Kosovo: War and Revenge* (2000); and Noel Malcolm, *Kosovo* (1998). From the very substantial literature that has developed on the Rwanda crisis, Gérard Prunier's *The Rwanda Crisis: History of a Genocide* is one of the most detailed accounts, and Mahmood Mamdani's *When Victims Become Killers* (2001) is an interesting analysis of the conflict's larger political and philosophical implications. Levon Chorbajian and George Shirinian's *Studies in Comparative Genocide* (1999) is a good place to begin an exploration of the darker side of 20th-century history.

Of the numerous and highly contentious writings on Islamic revivalism, Dilip Hiro's *Holy Wars: The Rise of Islamic Fundamentalism* (1989) is insightful and more balanced than most. A counterpart on Judaism is Arthur

Hertzberg's *Jewish Fundamentalism* (1991). For Hinduism, see Gurdas Ahuja, *BJP and Indian Politics* (1994). For a comparative view covering Christian movements, see Richard Antoun's, *Understanding Fundamentalism* (2001).

September 11th and persisting communal struggles, such as those in Northern Ireland and Israel and Palestine, have produced a proliferation of books and articles on terrorism in recent decades. A manageable place to begin an investigation of this highly contested and fluid category of social movement is Alexander Yonan et al., eds., *Terrorism: Theory and Practice* (1979). A historical overview with a global range for the modern period can be found in Albert Parry's *Terrorism*. George Woodcock's *Anarchism* remains the classic account of movements that were often connected to terrorism in the late 19th century.

A very substantial literature has developed on the Second Gulf War. The essays in Ibrahim Ibrahim, ed., *The Gulf Crisis* (1992), provide a good historical introduction to the conflict. Two of the better general accounts of the war itself are Lawrence Freedman and Efraim Karsh's *The Gulf Conflict, 1990–1991* (1993) and Michael Gordon and Bernard Trainor's, *The General's War* (1995). An Arab viewpoint of the conflict is provided in Mohamed Heikal, *Illusions of Triumph* (1992), and a strong critique of the media coverage and technowar aspects of the conflict is the focus of *The Persian Gulf TV War* (1992) by Douglas Kellner.

For a provocative and detailed account of U.S. interventionism since the end of the cold war, a good place to begin is David Halberstam's *War in a Time of Peace* (2001). Less compellingly written, but useful for differing perspectives is Lester Brune's *The United States and Post–Cold War Interventions* (1998). Mahood Mamdani's *Good Muslim, Bad Muslim* (2004) develops a provocative argument that stresses the role of U.S. cold war interventions as contributors to religious fundamentalism and terrorism. On specific flashpoints that provoked extensive international involvement and policy debate in the United States and elsewhere, some of the best work is on Somalia, including Mark Bowden's superb recounting of the mission in crisis in *Black Hawk Down* (1990) and Jonathan Stevenson's more policy-oriented *Losing Mogadishu* (1995).

For genuinely global perspectives on environmental issues, see Bill McKibben's *The End of Nature* (1999); Mark Hertsgaard's *Earth Odyssey* (1998); and Ramachandra Guha's *Environmentalism: A Global History* (2000). The best accounts of environmental degradation in key regions of the world include: (1) Brazil—Susanna Hecht and Alexander Cockburn, *The Fate of the Forest* (1990); (2) China—Judith Shapiro, *Mao's War against Nature* (2001), and Vaclav Smil, *The Bad Earth* (1984) and *China's Environmental Crisis* (1993); (3) the Soviet Union—Murray Feshbach and Alfred Friendly Jr., *Ecocide in the USSR* (1992); (4) the United States—Marc Reisner, *Cadillac Desert* (1993); and (5) India—Madhav Gadgil and Ramachandra Guha, *Ecology and Equity* (1995).

Recent work includes *Congressional Quarterly, World at Risk: A Global Issues Sourcebook* (2002); Ronnie Lipshutz, *After Authority: War, Peace, and Global Politics in the 21st Century* (2000); Stanley Brunn, *11 September and Its Aftermath: The Geopolitics of Terror* (2004); Lee Harris, *Civilization and Its Enemies: The Next Stage of History* (2004); Ronald Glossop, *Confronting War: An Examination of Humanity's Most Pressing Problem* (2001); Barbara Walter and Jack Snyder, eds., *Civil Wars, Insecurity, and Intervention* (1999); and Immanuel Wallerstein, *The Decline of American Power: The U.S. in a Chaotic World* (2003).

ON THE WEB

Of the many, often transitory, general sites on globalization, some of the more interesting and historically grounded include:

http://www.stephweb.com/capstone/index.htm
http://www.epinet.org/subjectpages/trade.html

with the latter reporting on international trade.

Analyses and links to both sides of the globalization debate are offered at

http://globalization.about.com/library/weekly/aa080701a
.htm
http://www.emory.edu/SOC/globalization/

A highly critical discussion of economic globalization is found at

http://www.ifg.org/analysis.htm

This site also offers a dark analysis of the role of the World Trade Organization, the World Bank, and the United Nations in this process. The World Bank and the International Monetary Fund offer their own more roseate view of globalization at

http://www1.worldbank.org/economicpolicy/
globalization/
http://www.imf.org/external/np/exr/ib/2000/041200.htm

The impact of globalization on human rights is discussed at

http://www.pbs.org/globalization/

The UN–U.S. intervention in Somalia and its troubling outcomes are considered from different vantage points at

http://www.netnomad.com/
http://www.unsomalia.org/

The terrorist attacks on September 11, 2001 on New York City and Washington, D.C. are recounted from many perspectives at

http://www.freepint.com/gary/91101.html

The management of the global war against terrorism is addressed at

http://www.carlise.army.mil/ssi/pubs/2003/bounding/bounding.htm

For the breakup of Yugoslavia and the continuing crisis in the Balkans, see

http://www.truthinmedia.org

A "beginner's guide to the Balkans" is offered at

http://abcnews.go.com/sections/world/balkans_content/

For general coverage of the wars in the Persian Gulf, see

http://www.pbs.org/wgbh/pages/frontline/gulf/index.html

The debate over the inconclusive end of the war and continuing conflict in the region is discussed at

http://www.pbs.org/wgbh/pages/frontline/shows/syndrome/

For other overviews, see

http://www.pbs.org/wgbh/pages/frontline/gulf/index.html

http://www.globalsecurity.org/military/ops/iraqi_freedom.htm

A good page on the 2003 U.S.–Iraqi war, with abundant links, can be found at

http://www.disinfopedia.org/wiki.phtml?title=Operation_Iraqi_Freedom

Chapter **16**

Epilogue: Global History Yet to Come

Midnight, December 31, 1999:
Millenium celebration in Sydney, Australia.

guiding history, moving it in a steady direction and toward a purpose, runs deep in the thought of several cultures, including our own. Whatever the approach, the human impulse to know what we cannot definitely know seems inescapable.

Yet all the evidence suggests that our vision of the future remains cloudy at best. It has been calculated that well over 60 percent of all predictions or forecasts offered by serious social scientists in the United States since 1945—called on to sketch future business cycles, family trends, or political currents, for instance—have been wrong. How many observers just 60 years ago could have predicted such basic recent transformations as decolonization; the rise of new kinds of authoritarianism; fundamental revolutions in China, Iran, and Cuba; the challenge to Communist rule in the Soviet Union; the invention of computer and genetic engineering technologies; or the industrial breakthroughs of many Pacific coast regions of Asia? A few of these events could be discerned in advance, to be sure, but many were great surprises. And other developments that were confidently predicted have not come to pass: People are not normally riding about in helicopters rather than automobiles (a U.S. image of the 1940s), and families have not been replaced by promiscuous communes (a forecast of the 1960s).

Even though we cannot know the future, we can use history to develop a framework for evaluating it and partially anticipating it as it unfolds. We can know what factors to monitor. Recent patterns and their relationship to older themes in world history allow an orientation toward what is to come. This final chapter suggests several vantage points from which to relate past to present to future. We deal with issues of progress and deterioration, with the ongoing tensions between separate civilizations and forces that impact throughout the world, and with trends in the basic political, cultural, economic, and social functions of human society.

INTRODUCTION

Since the formation of civilizations, the history of the world has involved relatively rapid change—sometimes in directions already set, sometimes in new trajectories. This pattern obviously continues in the 21st century. Indeed, some people would argue that the pace of change has accelerated as new discoveries and new technologies press against older ideas and habits. World history, in other words, offers no convenient stopping point at which one can lean back and say, "This is what it all means." Contemporary world history provides no magic vantage point, either, on what is to come. The only thing we know for sure about the future is that we do not know what it will bring.

People in various civilizations have attempted to devise schemes to look beyond their present. From the time of the ancient river-valley civilizations to the 21st century, some people have used astrology or other divinations to predict the future. More systematically, some scholars have assumed that time moves in cycles, so that one could count on repetition of basic patterns. This was a common assumption in Chinese historical thought and also among Muslim historians in the postclassical period. Others, including Christian thinkers and advocates of more secular faiths such as Marxism, have looked toward some great change in the future: the Last Judgment, for example, or the classless society to which history is steadily working. The idea of some master plan

TRENDS

Many social scientists believe they know several things about what the world will be like in 2050. The four biggest economies, for example, will be the United States, China, India, and the European Union—possibly in that order. The rate of population increase will have slowed dramatically, and many societies—headed by western Europe and Japan—will be rapidly aging, except for the immigration of younger people from other parts of the world. Business- and consumer-minded middle classes will continue to grow in many societies, becoming the most important social group (though not the largest) as the aristocracy seems gone for good.

These are important changes from the world of today, but we think we know them because they are already taking shape, as in the case of the rapid economic growth of China and India combined with their great size. Predictions of this sort extrapolate from recent trends—like the fact that birth rates are dropping everywhere which will ultimately lead to global aging.

There are two problems with extrapolating from trends, of course. One is that some other factors may come in and divert the trend. Possibly, for example, China's environmental problems will derail its economic growth. Back in the 1930s experts were confident that Americans would continue to have small families, but then the baby boom occurred, quite unexpectedly, and derailed predictions for about 20 years.

The second limitation of extrapolating from trends is that we do not always know what current trend will predominate. Will we see continued globalization, for example, or will regional disputes, perhaps even a clash of civilization, grind it to a halt? (After all, globalization around 1900 was halted for several decades by wars and revolutions; it could happen again.) Will democracy continue to gain, a clear recent trend that some believe is also supported by new technologies that make it easier to spread diverse opinions? Or will recent efforts to limit democracy, for example in Russia, introduce new complexity? Will women's rights and educational levels continue to gain, or will movements opposed to these trends win out, at least in some crucial cases? What about the nation-state and nationalism? Have they outlived their usefulness, in an age of European unions and multinational corporations and, indeed, sweeping religious loyalties? Or will they hang on as the modern world's characteristic political unit—so eagerly sought by anticolonial resisters just 30 years ago. Will global rates of obesity continue to advance (a definite current trend), or will health campaigns or possibly some new limitation of food supply reverse them? Will global prosperity advance, as it recently has in India and China, or will the gap between rich and poor (within nations and among nations) prove to be the more permanent pattern? How long will the current conflict with terrorists last? We can ask diverse questions about the future, but when the current trend is disputed the answers are just speculation.

Even some once-certain trends can be called into doubt. It long seemed quite clear that explicit Western imperialism was a thing of the past—one of the developments that made the 20th century a really new period in world history. But to some observers, the 2003 American invasion of Iraq was essentially an imperialistic exercise, and some Americans themselves began to talk of a new American empire, perhaps necessary as a counter to terrorism. So is modern imperialism over or not?

The 20th century ushered in a new period in world history—from the relative decline of western Europe to dramatic new global technologies. This fact makes it inherently more difficult to predict the future. We know that some long-familiar patterns are over—for example, imperialism, at least from Europe, or monarchy, which seems unlikely to revive even though it was a dominant form a hundred years back—but it is much harder to discern what comes next.

NEW DIRECTIONS

Instead of interpreting current trends in a narrow way, some pundits find it more important to seize on a recent development and argue that it will change the whole shape of the human experience.

Just as some historians have long sought a basic factor to explain historical change—through technology, trade levels, or cultural values—so the most dramatic breed of forecasters points to the single emerging revolutionary factor that will make almost everything different. The resultant dramatic forecast differs from general extrapolation from trends by seizing on one decisive ingredient and by anticipating massive contrasts between future and present.

Overcrowding and Environmental Scenarios

In the 1960s and early 1970s gloomy "population bomb" predictions received a considerable audience. Experts correctly noted the unprecedented size and growth rates of world population and argued that, unchecked, the sheer number of people would outstrip available resources, produce unmanageable environmental degradation, and create rivalries for space that could usher in a series of bitter wars. Concern about world population trends had lessened somewhat by 1990, in part because growth rates had slowed in critical areas, such as China and Latin America. The fact that the food supply had kept up with growth in most places, thanks to developments like the "green revolution," threw some cold water on the population bomb idea. Some experts claimed that resources could continue to expand with population growth and noted that, historically, population expansion had often been a major source of innovation and creativity. Some also claimed a racist element in population-bomb forecasts, insofar as these involved Western pundits urging people of color to have fewer babies. Such forecasts have not been discounted entirely, and environmentalists have picked up some of their concerns. As a tool for gauging the future, however, the "bomb" approach is yesterday's fad, though in 1990 it remained true that world population continued to grow at a rate of 250,000 new people every day.

A variant on the population-bomb approach, though less widely publicized, played up the exhaustion of frontiers. Only by the later 20th century, some world historians argued, had human societies fully run out of room to expand—pending as yet unrealized space travel. Each previous period of world history had featured expansions into relatively empty spaces; thus the postclassical period saw movements into Eastern Europe and western China and Bantu migrations southward in Africa, whereas the 19th century had climaxed the history of human frontiers with the fuller peopling of the Americas and Australia as well as Russian settlement in Siberia. With frontiers gone by the late 20th century, organized societies bumped against one another far more than ever before. Thus immigration inevitably now meant movement not into relatively unsettled terrain but rather into highly populous, often suspicious host societies. The implications for potential conflict, environmental exhaustion, and efforts to impede human movement were considerable, if this major factor is viewed as a basic distinction between society future and society past.

Environmental concerns themselves can trigger yet another kind of catastrophic forecast. If global warming continues, many argue that the results, in terms of rising sea levels and coastal flooding, more unpredictable and violent weather, and possibly heightened disease could dominate the future of humankind, making speculations about lesser developments like democracy quickly outmoded.

A final set of forecasts involved predictions of a return of contagious diseases, as overused medicines would prove ineffective against mutated germs and viruses. The AIDs epidemic might prove a foretaste of larger disease pressures still to come. Here was another way that the future could prove far different from the present, with current trends overwhelmed by new or renewed problems.

A Postindustrial World

Another effort to identify dramatic causation highlights a revolutionary wave of technological change associated with computers, genetic engineering, robotics, and new devices for transmitting energy. According to some popular forecasters, late 20th-century society entered a postindustrial revolution fully as dramatic as the Industrial Revolution two centuries ago—with exactly the same potential for altering the whole framework of

Change and continuity in rural India. New irrigation and electrification combine with traditional methods of tilling the soil as agricultural production rises.

human existence. As technology continues to take over production, postindustrial society will feature service occupations dealing with people and information exchange, as not only agriculture but also industrial production are handled largely by machines. Social status will depend on technical knowledge, not money or landed property. Cities will change, becoming centers for meetings and recreation, not basic points of exchange and production. This picture is striking, and some observers have claimed to find ample evidence of its accuracy in existing trends. The postindustrial vision is also usually optimistic in assuming that key industrial problems will be resolved in the new order. Routine, repetitive work, for example, will be eliminated by automation, and computers will allow labor to become more varied and individualized. In some cases, postindustrial optimism joins with assumptions about globalization to predict a prosperous, peaceful future for humankind.

Critics of the postindustrial vision raise several objections. They are not certain that the transformation discernible in the United States or western Europe, for example, is as fundamental as the analogies to the Industrial Revolution suggest. Change is occurring, to be sure, but it preserves management and labor structures similar to the patterns of industrial society. There is no relocation of people as massive as industrial-based urbanization had involved and no need for such fundamental shifts in habits of thought. Computers can make work more routine, not less, as rigorous supervision becomes automated. Corporate and government bureaucracies continue to expand. New technology, in other words, does not necessarily change most basic trends, and technological determinism should not be pressed too far. Further, if distinctive postindustrial societies are developing, they concentrate in the West and Japan; postindustrialization may exacerbate the economic inequalities among major areas that had already arisen as part of the world economy. How useful, then, is the concept for forecasting overall world history?

Dramatic forecasting of this sort, whether imbued with postindustrial optimism or population-bomb gloom, relies heavily on a single basic causal factor—technology or population determines all, and everything falls into place once this factor is established. Yet most historians reject this kind of determinism. The analysis of the past shows the power of continuity rather than a single-minded transformation. Major changes do occur, but they result from the confluence of several factors, not a single cause. Though some cataclysm is always possible, most historians assume that complexity will continue. Eye-catching forecasts can help organize thinking about what makes history tick and how present relates to past, but there are other orientations toward the future as well.

OPTIMISTS AND PESSIMISTS

A key question about the future involves discussion of whether it is likely to bring progress or deterioration. This leads back to an assessment of recent trends, but now with evaluation attached.

Here, too, the 20th century proves immensely complicated. It has witnessed some of the greatest triumphs of the human experience. Never has science revealed so much about how nature works; the increases in basic knowledge have been unrivaled. Never, even in poor societies, have so few children died before reaching maturity, thanks to public health advances. Never have so many people, and particularly so many women, been literate.

But the 20th century has been a terrible century as well. Never before have so many people killed other people—the Holocaust and more recent, even ongoing cases of genocide make this starkly clear. Never have people done so much damage to the environment. This list is long as well. And some would add more subtle deteriorations, like a global trend toward higher divorce rates and other signs of family instability.

How we look at the future depends partly on what criteria we emphasize—technology or personal life, science or destruction—in trying to judge the recent past.

REGIONS, CIVILIZATIONS, AND WORLD FORCES

A final set of issues for the future returns us to more complex prospects, different from the stark drama of all-or-nothing forecasts and their reliance on one primary source of causation and different also from the progress/deterioration debate, though it can be applied.

For many centuries, world history has involved a tension between the operations of individual civilizations and wider international forces that shape the way people think and behave across civilizational boundaries and sometimes almost through the entire world. Launching a new period in world history, the 20th and 21st centuries raise important new questions about this tension. As usual when large but inherently uncertain interpretive problems are at stake, some polar positions are available. It is possible to predict a new splintering among civilizations—like the clash of civilizations model, with each area emphasizing its own flavor now that the hothouse period of Western dominance is cooling down. There are also new centripetal forces, however, that may reduce the scope for individual cultures in favor of more literally international trends.

The Quest for Separate Identities

Events in the 1980s raised the prospect of new fragmentations to a surprising level. Peoples in relatively small regions showed the fierce persistence of old loyalties. Thus Slavic groups in Eastern Europe, even in a single small nation such as Yugoslavia, turned on one another with demands for separation or at least autonomy. French descendants in Quebec, seeking greater independence, encountered hostility from their English-descended neighbors elsewhere in Canada. A host of established units, including the successor states of the former Soviet Union, were newly vulnerable to regional ethnic, linguistic, and religious loyalties.

The magazine of the destroyer U.S.S. Shaw explodes during the Japanese attack on Pearl Harbor, Hawaii, on December 7, 1941

On a larger, civilizational scale, many recent developments continued to reflect civilization boundaries. Thus both China and India newly struggled against high birthrates. The Indian government, however, proved relatively ineffective, given traditional resistance to state involvement, whereas Chinese efforts, though far from completely successful against older family habits, could build on earlier patterns of state intervention.

Regions and civilizations have not remained changeless, but they have combined distinctive traditions, distinctive recent experiences, and a distinctive filter by which even common experiences are modified. This pattern survives in the early 21st century. A basic theme of 20th-century history, almost certain to extend well into the 21st century, thus involves an understanding of how each major civilization will interpret the forces of modern politics and industrialization to create its own amalgam—as Japan has already done, in creating a successful industrial society that is however different from the West.

The quest for cultural autonomy in several major societies is particularly marked in contrast to the homogenizing impulses of modern mass culture. Indian films reproduce the themes and spirit of the great Hindu sagas in the world's largest movie industry. Islamic societies, quite like other Third World areas in many respects, maintain particularly vigorous religious strains, expressed also in distinctive birthrates and family patterns. Latin American intellectuals deal with problems of identity and loneliness that derive from this civilization's particular past. Japan uses habits of group loyalty to generate modes of industrial governance different from those of the West, within an equally successful economic framework.

The Forces of International Integration

Previous crosscutting forces in world history, from agricultural technologies to the great world religions to new foodstuffs or inventions, such as the printing press, all promoted transformation *within* the separate civilizations. Even the rise of Western-dominated world trade and imperialism did not fuse the civilizations into a single basic pattern.

This balance, between separate regional and civilizational identities and international pressure, may now be changing decisively. Many of the arguments about globalization—including those that attack globalization for overriding treasured local cultures—point precisely to an unprecedented level of contact and even homogenization around the world. The crosscutting forces of the past century or so have unquestionably stepped up the impact of international forces. International movements of women, computer hackers, or soccer fans clearly override civilization boundaries, and they may gradually make those boundaries less distinct.

The fact of growing world contacts and a spreading array of global forces produced the understandable but erroneous attempt a generation ago to simplify recent world history into a study of how rapidly each society yielded to the inevitable impulse to become essentially Western. Thus serious scholars assumed that the Western version of modernization—including industrialization, mass education, democratic parliamentary politics, low birthrate, a consumer society, and greater equality for women—would take hold around the world. Each civilization could thus be measured by the speed at which it generated the standard modern (meaning Western) features. This analytical approach confused some undeniably common impulses, including the desire to alter traditional patterns in the name of nationalism and economic development, with homogeneity. And it did not, moreover, allow for the revived force of traditional values in societies such as Islam.

Still, if the simplest modernization model has proved clearly inaccurate, as the world's civilizations continue to handle certain common impulses distinctively, the sense that a new simplifying framework may be right around the corner persists. Will one of the new technologies taking hold, for example, do the trick? This is a crucial aspect of any postindustrial argument applied at a world level. The spread of computer networks is sometimes held to foreshadow new, common patterns of organization, research, and thinking, bringing far greater similarities to the societies involved than the rhythms of the factory or the farm ever did. Some advocates even believe that agricultural societies can shift to a computer system for production and communication without going through a classic industrial phase.

Common cultures generate other forces through which specific international communities are obliterating civilizational distinctions. Scientists and social scientists from almost every society can now meet and discuss common methods and common basic assumptions. Political or other divisions may complicate this harmony, but a fundamental international community exists with a shared frame of reference. At another level, soccer and a few other sports elicit very similar enthusiasms around much of the world, even though they also express competition among the societies fielding the teams. Some scholars argue that a global youth culture has sprung up, uniting urban youth in virtually all societies around common fashions and music styles.

International business constitutes another integrating force. As Japanese and Korean firms join with North American and European businesses in setting up branches of production in almost every regional market,

The arrival of the euro in 1999 as the currency uniting 11 European countries was hailed as a first step toward creating a single economy capable of rivaling that of the United States in the 21st century.

and as business leaders strive to imitate each other's organizational forms and labor policies, civilizational boundaries retreat considerably.

On several different fronts, then, the intensification of international networks, itself part of a long and varied process in world history, has proceeded to the point that various scholars could seriously see in the late 20th century the beginning of the end for the civilizational form. World diversities and inequalities will obviously persist amid new international communities, but coherent regional civilizations may gradually pull apart at the seams.

For the moment, separate civilizations are still very much alive, often highlighted by religious revival. An equilibrium between distinct civilizations and unifying developments provides the most obvious interpretive basis for asking questions about the future. Increasingly rapid and intense contacts around the world have not created a single framework for world history. The pull of regional as well as civilizational loyalties remains strong.

The surge of divisive allegiances in many parts of the world from the early 1990s onward surely reflects a human need to find a way to counterbalance the large, impersonal forces stemming from international developments. The world, in some ways growing smaller, is becoming no less complex. Distinctive traditions continue to modify, sometimes to reverse, seemingly powerful unifying forces, though these forces persist as well.

CONCLUSION: ASKING QUESTIONS

Whatever the vantage point, questions easily outweigh answers in contemplating the future. The relevance of particular models—such as Western democracy or mass culture—and the international power of industrial business and technology pose new challenges to particular civilizations. This is not a mere replay of earlier tensions between world currents and separate civilizational traditions. Yet continuities or revivals from the past—the surge of religious sentiment in Eastern Europe, for example—and possibly new needs for smaller-scale identities make predictions of an imminent triumph of a single world framework sheer folly. We know that the interplay between the regional and the global will be an important part of the future, along with new technologies and crucial environmental issues—for such interplay between contacts and divisiveness has shaped world history for many centuries. We do not know, however, what the precise results will be.

History contributes more than an understanding of the traditions and patterns that will continue to play some role in the future. Through analogies to past situations—such as earlier interactions between individual societies and a world economy—and through an understanding of changing trends, history improves our ability to ask good questions about the future and to evaluate the major types of forecasting available. We can count on the emerging world future to challenge our understanding, but we can also learn to use a grasp of the world past as a partial guide.

FURTHER READING

Several serious books (as well as many more simplistic, popularized efforts) attempt to sketch the future of the world or the West. On the concept of the postindustrial society, see Daniel Bell's *The Coming of Post-Industrial Society* (1974). For other projections, consult R. L. Heil-broner's *An Inquiry into the Human Prospect* (1974) and L. Stavrianos's *The Promise of the Coming Dark Age* (1976).

On environment and resource issues, D. H. Meadows and D. L. Meadows's *The Limits to Growth* (1974), Al Gore's *Earth in the Balance* (1992), and L. Herbert's *Our Synthetic Environment* (1962) are worthwhile. M. ul Haq's *The Poverty Curtain: Choices for the Third World* (1976) and L. Solomon's *Multinational Corporations and the Emerging World Order* (1978) cover economic issues, in part from a non-Western perspective.

On military and diplomatic issues, A. Sakharov's *Progress, Coexistence, and Intellectual Freedom* (1970) is an important statement by a Russian dissident; other useful texts include S. Hoffman's *Primacy or World Order: American Foreign Policy Since the Cold War* (1978), S. Melman's *The Peace Race* (1961), and W. Epstein's *The Last Chance: Nuclear Proliferation and Arms Control* (1976).

On a leading social issue, see P. Huston's *Third World Women Speak Out* (1979). A major interpretation of the 20th-century world is Theodore von Laue's *The World Revolution of Westernization* (1989).

ON THE WEB

The threat of HIV/AIDS to world civilizations is discussed at

http://www.msnbc.msn.com/id/4779877/

http://usinfo.state.gov/journals/itgic/0700/ijge/ijge0700.htm

http://www.globalhealth.org/news/article/2606

This threat is also explored in regions as diverse as Afghanistan

http://www.hivandhepatitis.com/recent/developing/061202g.html

Africa

http://news.bbc.co.uk/1/hi/world/africa/3128973.stm

Europe

http://www.who.int/mediacentre/news/releases/2004/pr14/en/

India

http://lnweb18.worldbank.org/sar/sa.nsf/0/9ef0514dfcb6154385256839006979ef?OpenDocument
http://archives.cnn.com/2000/ASIANOW/south/09/05/india.health.challenge.ap/

Laos

http://www.aegis.com/news/re/2003/RE030628.html

and Pakistan

http://lnweb18.worldbank.org/SAR/sa.nsf/Countries/
Pakistan/A1BFFF1F91AAB5B385256C4D00693C
7E?OpenDocument

The transcript (as well as streaming video) of a round-table discussion on global over population can be accessed at

http://www.uncommonknowledge.org/700/726.html

This discussion can be supplemented by other interviews and discussions, such as at

http://www.findarticles.com/p/articles/mi_m1279/
is_n163/ai_19645105

For religious and libertarian groups that see the idea of a growing world population as a myth or believe that controlling it is not worth the price, go to

http://www.libertyhaven.com/noneoftheabove/
population/exploding.shtml
http://www.libertyhaven.com/noneoftheabove/
population/bomb.shtml

This debate is explored by Robert McNamara at

http://www.foreignaffairs.org/19840601faessay8386/
robert-s-mcnamara/time-bomb-or-myth-the-
population-problem.html

The belief that technological advance is the solution to humanities ills has been tested by the mixed results of the Green Revolution. A variety of sites that engage in the debate over its success or failure in larger terms can be accessed at

http://www.foodfirst.org/media/opeds/2000/
4-greenrev.html
http://www.arches.uga.edu/~wparks/ppt/green/
http://www.actionbioscience.org/biotech/borlaug.html

India's experience of the Green Revolution is analyzed at

http://www.indiaonestop.com/Greenrevolution.htm

Industrial agriculture is called into question at

http://www.ssu.missouri.edu/faculty/jikerd/papers/
brsm1-95.htm

The nature of postindustrial society is defined at

http://www.searchspaniel.com/index.php/
Post-industrial_society
http://www.columbia.edu/itc/english/f2007/jameson/
concepts/postindus.html
http://www.sociology.org.uk/p1ne4.htm

The place of women in postindustrial society is addressed at

http://www.findarticles.com/p/articles/mi_m1310/
is_1992_Nov/ai_13615016

Patterns of postindustrialization are examined at

http://www.macalester.edu/courses/geog61/afdavis/
post.htm
http://ideas.repec.org/p/cdl/issres/issr-1066.html
http://www.randburg.com/fi/general/general_8.html

A possible trend toward authoritarianism in some postindustrial societies is traced at

http://www.esiweb.org/docs/showdocument
.php?document_ID=63
http://globalization.icaap.org/content/v3.1/04_beliaev
.html
http://www.theglobalist.com/DBWeb/StoryId
.aspx?StoryId=2987

The future of democracy in the Middle East is explored at

http://www.ceip.org/files/Publications/wp35
.asp?from=pubdate
http://www.islamreview.com/articles/democracy.shtml
http://www.cato.org/dailys/11-30-03.html
http://news.bbc.co.uk/2/hi/americas/3789631.stm

The opportunities and challenges to democracy inherent in the instability of the contemporary world are studied at

http://www.secularhumanism.org/library/fi/kurtz_25_1
.htm
http://globalization.icaap.org/content/v3.1/04_beliaev
.html
http://www.theglobalist.com/DBWeb/StoryId
.aspx?StoryId=2987

The text of, and debate over the accuracy of, Samuel Huntington's argument that the world is heading toward a "clash of civilizations" can be found at

http://www.alamut.com/subj/economics/misc/clash.html
http://www.lander.edu/atannenbaum/Tannenbaum
%20courses%20folder/POLS%20103%20World
%20Politics/103_huntington_clash_of_civilizations
_full_text.htm
http://www.shunya.net/Text/Articles/EdwardSaid.htm
http://csf.colorado.edu/wsystems/jwsr/archive/vol4/
v4n2r2.htm
http://www.ndsu.nodak.edu/ndsu/ambrosio/civ.html

Credits

TEXT CREDITS

Page 125: "Snow Upon Paris" by Leopold Sedar Senghor from *Collected Poetry of Leopold Sedar Senghor* by Melvin Dixon, ed. Copyright © 1991. Reprinted with permission of the University Press of Virginia. **125:** 5 lines from "Return to My Native Land" from *Aime Cesaire: Collected Poetry,* translated and edited by Eshleman, Clayton, & Annette Smith. Copyright © 1983 The Regents of the University of California. Reprinted by permission of The University of California Press. **154:** *Socialist Realism* by Andrey Zhdanov, Soviet Writer's Congress of 1934. All rights reserved. **186:** *New Economic Crisis in the Capitalist Countries, Intensification of the Struggle for Markets and Sources of Raw Materials, and for a New Redivision of the World,* by Joseph Stalin to the 18th Communist Party Congress, March 1939. All rights reserved. **206-207:** Hisako Yoshizawa, *Showa sensoo bungaku zenshuu; shimin no nikki (War Literature of Showa; Diaries of Citizens).* All rights reserved. **238:** Steven M. Tipton, *Getting Saved from the Sixties: Moral Meaning in Conversation and Cultural Change.* Copyright © 1981 The Regents of the University of California. Reprinted by permission of the University of California Press. **239:** Table from "What They Believe: A Fortune Yankelovich Survey," *Fortune,* January 1969. Copyright © 1969 Time, Inc. Reprinted by permission. All Rights Reserved. **239:** Table from Melvin Zelnik, John Kantner, and Kathleen Ford, *Sex and Pregnancy in Adolescence,* p. 65. Copyright © 1981. Reprinted by permission of Sage Publications, Inc. **262-263:** "Mikhail Gorbachev's Speech at the Conference of the Aktiv of the Khabarovsk Territory Party Organization, July 31, 1986," published in English by *The Current Digest of the Post Soviet Press* 38, no. 31 (1986), pp. 1-5. Translation copyright © 1986 by *The Current Digest of the Post Soviet Press,* published weekly at Columbus, Ohio. Reprinted by permission of the *Digest.* **284:** From *No Longer at Ease* by Chinua Achebe. Reprinted by permission of Harcourt Education. **315:** Excerpt from *Let Me Speak: Testimony of Domitilia, a Woman of the Bolivian Mines* by Domitilia Barrios de Chungara with Moema Viezzer, translated by Victoria Ortiz. Copyright © 1978 by Monthly Review Press. Reprinted by permission of Monthly Review Press. **315:** Excerpt from *Rigoberta Menchu: An Indian Woman in Guatemala* by Rigoberta Menchu. Introduction by Elisabeth Burgas-Debray. Translated by Anne Wright. Reprinted by permission of Verso, London, New York. All rights reserved. **316:** "The United Fruit Company" from *Selected Poems of Pablo Neruda,* translated by Ben Belitt. Copyright © 1961 by Ben Belitt. Used by permission of Grove/Atlantic, Inc. **336:** From *Runaway Horses* by Yukio Mishima, translated by M. Gallagher, copyright © 1973 by Alfred A. Knopf, a division of Random House, Inc. Used by permission of Alfred A. Knopf, a division of Random House, Inc. **337:** Excerpt from *A Personal Matter* by Kenzaburo Oe, translated by John Nathan. Copyright © 1969 by Grove Press, Inc. Used by permission of Grove/Atlantic, Inc. **363:** Speech by Li Peng in Mid-May, 1989. Online at http://www.tsquare.tv/chronology/MartialLaw.html Reprinted by permission of Long Bow Group. **377:** Excerpt from *Five Days That Shook the World* by Alexander Cockburn, Jeffrey St. Clair, and Allan Sekula. Copyright © 2000. Reprinted by permission of Verso, London, New York. All rights reserved.

PHOTO CREDITS

Page 6, Ted Russell/Polaris; **14,** Library of Congress; **17,** Bettmann/Corbis; **24,** V & A Picture Library; **25,** Bettmann/Corbis; **27,** Culver Pictures; **34,** Metropolitan Museum of Art, Gift of Lincoln Kirstein, 1959 (JP3346); **42,** Sovfoto; **43,** Bettmann/Corbis; **52,** National Army Museum, London; **58,** Mary Evans Picture Library; **60,** Hulton/Deutsch/Liaison/Getty Images; **62,** Hulton Archive/Getty Images; **65,** Samuel Thomas Gill/Bridgeman Art Library; **72,** Peabody Essex Museum; **82,** Robert Frerck/Woodfin Camp & Associates; **86,** Bettmann/Corbis; **89,** Mary Evans Picture Library; **95,** Photos12.com/Polaris; **102,** Wadsworth Atheneum Museum of Art, Hartford, CT. The Ella Gallup Sumner and Mary Catlin Sumner Collection Fund; **108,** Imperial War Museum; **116,** Imperial War Museum; **119,** Bettmann/Corbis; **127,** The Granger Collection; **130,** Bettmann/Corbis; **136,** Schalkwijk/AMI/Art Resource; **139,** Culver Pictures; **142,** Bettmann/Corbis; **147,** Culver Pictures; **153,** © bpk, Berlin; **162,** Bettmann/Corbis; **168,** Sovfoto; **171,** Library of Congress; **175,** National Archives; **182,** Library of Congress; **183,** Bettmann/Corbis; **188,** Sovfoto; **194,** AP/Wide World Photos; **198,** National Archives; **203,** National Archives; **205,** AP/Wide World Photos; **212,** AP/Wide World Photos; **215,** AP/Wide World Photos; **222,** Tom Stoddart/Woodfin Camp & Associates; **228,** Jean Pierre Laffont/Sygma/Corbis; **234,** AP/Wide World Photos; **236,** Jonathan Blair/Corbis; **240,** The Granger Collection; **245,** Hedrich Blessing/Chicago Historical Society; **246,** Dana Smillie/Polaris; **254,** Reuters/Corbis; **258,** Bettmann/Corbis; **264,** Sovfoto; **267,** Sovfoto; **270,** Bettmann/Corbis; **274 (L),** Bettmann/Corbis; **(R),** Abbas/Magnum Photos; **280,** Stock Boston LLC; **286,** Bettmann/Corbis; **293,** Mark Peters/Liaison/Getty Images; **296,** AP/Wide World Photos; **304,** Jacques Langevin/Sygma/Corbis; **311,** Bettmann/Corbis; **318,** Enrique Shore/Woodfin Camp & Associates; **320,** Mohamed-El Dakhakhny/AP/Wide World Photos; **328,** Kevin R. Morris/Corbis; **331,** Official U.S. Navy Photograph; **333,** AP/Wide World Photos; **338,** Palmer Pictures; **341,** Anthony Suau/Liaison/Getty Images; **348,** David Longstreath/AP/Wide World Photos; **354,** Bettmann/Corbis; **359,** Alain Nogues/Corbis; **365,** Peter Turnley/Corbis; **370,** Jacques Pavlovsky/Sygma/Corbis; **379,** Don Krauss/AP/Wide World Photos; **380,** Dado Galdieri/AP/Wide World Photos; **384,** I.T.N./Rex Features/Sipa; **387,** Patrick Andrade/Polaris; **392,** Greg English/Sygma/Corbis; **393,** Yannis Kontos/Polaris; **398,** Reuters/Corbis; **401,** Corbis; **403,** Corbis; **404,** AFP/Getty Images.

Index

NOTE: Page numbers in *italics* refer to illustrations. Entries for place names are not duplicated under individual nations and larger geographic areas; therefore, use general terms (Africa; Middle East) in addition to country names.